Agrarian Reform in Russia

The Road from Serfdom

This book examines the history of reforms and major state interventions affecting Russian agriculture: the abolition of serfdom in 1861, the Stolypin reforms, the New Economic Policy (NEP), the collectivization, the Khrushchev reforms, and finally the farm enterprise privatization in the early 1990s. It shows a pattern emerging from a political imperative in imperial, Soviet, and post-Soviet regimes, and it describes how these reforms were justified in the name of the national interest during severe crises – rapid inflation, military defeat, mass strikes, rural unrest, and/or political turmoil. It looks at the consequences of adversity in the economic environment for rural behavior after reform and at long-run trends. It has chapters on property rights, rural organization, and technological change. It provides a new database for measuring agricultural productivity from 1861 to 1913 and updates these estimates to the present. This book is a study of the policies aimed at reorganizing rural production and of their effectiveness in transforming institutions.

Dr. Carol S. Leonard is a Fellow of St. Antony's College, Oxford, and university lecturer, University of Oxford. She is the author of *Reform and Regicide: The Reign of Peter III* (1993) and numerous scholarly articles. She is also the editor of *Microeconomic Change in Central and Eastern Europe* (2002) and the co-editor of *Agrarian Organization during Industrialization: Europe, Russia and America in the Nineteenth Century* (1989) (with George Grantham). She has also served as the U.S. Treasury economic and budget advisor for agriculture to the Russian Ministry of Finance and as a consultant for the Harvard Institute for International Development Macroeconomic Unit in Kiev, Ukraine, and the National Bank of Kazakhstan. She has taught public-sector economics at the St. Petersburg School of Management and the economics of science and technology for the graduate program in management and innovation at the Eurasian National University in Astana.

Agrarian Reform in Russia

The Road from Serfdom

CAROL S. LEONARD
University of Oxford

CAMBRIDGE
UNIVERSITY PRESS

CAMBRIDGE UNIVERSITY PRESS
Cambridge, New York, Melbourne, Madrid, Cape Town, Singapore,
São Paulo, Delhi, Dubai, Tokyo, Mexico City

Cambridge University Press
32 Avenue of the Americas, New York, NY 10013-2473, USA

www.cambridge.org
Information on this title: www.cambridge.org/9780521858496

First published 2011

Printed in the United States of America

A catalog record for this publication is available from the British Library.

Library of Congress Cataloging in Publication data

Leonard, Carol Scott, 1945–
Agrarian reform in Russia : the road from serfdom / Carol Leonard.
p. cm.
Includes bibliographical references and index.
ISBN 978-0-521-85849-6 (hbk. : alk. paper)
1. Land reform – Russia – History. 2. Land reform – Soviet Union – History. 3. Land reform – Russia (Federation) – History. 4. Agriculture and state – Russia – History. 5. Agriculture and state – Soviet Union – History. 6. Agriculture and state – Russia (Federation) – History. 7. Russia – Economic conditions – 1861–1917. 8. Soviet Union – Economic conditions. 9. Russia (Federation) – Economic conditions – 1991– I. Title.
HD1333.R9L46 2009
333.3′147–dc22 2009009366

ISBN 978-0-521-85849-6 Hardback

For Nancy, Larry, and Claire

Contents

Tables and Figures

TABLES

FIGURES

Preface

The idea for this book originated in a project that I began as Visiting Fellow at All Souls College in Oxford in 1996. The warmth of that fellowship and, particularly, the encouragement of Charles Feinstein and Paul David were invaluable in the early stages of my work.

My understanding of contemporary agrarian reform emerged in the course of my work in Moscow from 1993 to 1995 as U.S. Treasury economic advisor to the Russian Ministry of Finance. A colleague whose kindness and knowledge particularly assisted my work was Eugenia Serova. Among those to whom I am also deeply endebted are Brian Foster, Christian Foster, Tatiana Gusarova, Renata Ianbykh, William Liefert, Vic Miller, Allan Mustard, Aleksandr Nikonov, and David Sedick.

My study of Russian agrarian history over the past twenty-five years gained especially from the works and encouragement of Paul Gregory, and from discussions with Leonid Borodkin, Harold Carter, Knick Harley, Ivan Koval'chenko, William Liefert, Leonid Milov, Boris Mironov, Alan Olmstead, and Judith Pallot. I am thankful for the opportunities I was given for this study by the Davis Center (formerly Russian Research Center) at Harvard University; the International Research and Exchanges Board; the National Council for Eurasian and East European Research; the National Science Foundation; the State University of New York, College at Plattsburgh; and Moscow State University. For assistance and training in economics as a Visiting Scholar at the California Institute of Technology, I am grateful for the generosity of the economists and political scientists of the Social Science and Humanities Division, and particularly Kim Border, Rodney Kiewet, John Ledyard, Peter Ordeshook, and Charles Plott. I am deeply appreciative of the encouragement of Lance Davis at the California Institute of Technology and Alan Olmstead at the University of California at Davis for making possible my two-year stay at Caltech as a Visiting Scholar.

In the preparation of this book, I acknowledge invaluable advice from those who kindly read chapters, including Roger Bartlett, Paul Chaisty,

Daniel Field, Brigitte Granville, Paul Gregory, Mark Harrison, David Moon, Benjamin Noble, Bill Tompkins, and Gavin Wright, who bear no responsibility for content. Dilyara Ibragimova provided invaluable assistance in the preparation of a database on nineteenth-century agriculture for this study.

I warmly thank my colleagues and the staff at St. Antony's College, particularly Robert Service, Paul Chaisty, and Alex Pravda, for their remarkable good cheer and assistance. I am especially grateful for the affection and support of my sister Nancy Leonard, Nancy Condee, Donald Bogle, Margaret Bent, John Landers, and Judy Pallot.

Finally, I express deep gratitude for the patience and kindness of my editor at Cambridge University Press, Eric Craham, and the producers of the volume, Manish Sharma and Pushpender Rathee.

Carol S. Leonard
The University of Oxford

Introduction

On October 28, 1991, just months before the dissolution of the Soviet Union, at a time when the Communist Party was weakened by internal divisions, inflationary pressure was rising and the deficit stood at 20 percent of gross domestic product (GDP), Boris Yeltsin addressed the Congress of Peoples' Deputies of the Russian Federation, calling for major reform. It was too late for "small steps." "Resorting to deeds, not words, Russians had to begin extricating themselves from the swamp that was pulling them in deeper and deeper. Only a 'large-scale reformist breakthrough' could save Russia's economy from disintegration, its people from poverty, and its state from collapse."[1]

Crisis opens a window of opportunity for long overdue reforms, including the reorganization of agricultural production. That crisis facilitates macroeconomic reform is a well-understood concept.[2] Interests blocking inflation control in democratic countries of Latin America, for example, where there are recurring bouts of hyperinflation, yield to reform pressures when the national interest is paramount.[3] Lobbies can also block liberalizing reform in authoritarian regimes, where conflict will arise in the supply of public

[1] Boris Yeltsin, speech to the Congress of Deputies of the Russian Federation, October 28, 1991, *Sovetskaya Rossiia*, October 29, 1991, p. 2, cited in Aron (2001), p. 489.

[2] Drazen and Easterly (2001), p. 129: "The hypothesis that an economic crisis often induces policy change (or, even stronger, that crisis is not only sufficient to induce reform but also necessary; that is, that significant reform takes place only in the wake of a crisis) has become, in the eyes of many, the new orthodoxy." Drazen and Easterly provide an empirical test, and they distinguish in effects between kinds of crises. Cross-country evidence suggests the importance of political crises for reform, Campos, Hsaio, Nugent (2006). On induced reform, see Olson (1982); Nelson (1990); Rodrik (1996); Drazen (1998, 2000); Tommasi and Velasco (1996); Williamson (1994).

[3] Olson (1971, second edition), p. 13: "Patriotism is probably the strongest non-economic motive for organizational allegiance in modern times." These emotional resources are used to compel the financing of "basic and vital activities" of the state. See also McCargo (2005) with reference to Thai monarchy, 1973–2001.

goods.[4] In Russia, which has experienced authoritarian rule over much of the past two centuries, to produce a major reform or change in the laws has nearly always required a serious crisis. The following agrarian measures, including some of the most ambitious reforms in Russian history, are illustrative:

1. **The emancipation of the serfs** (1861) followed Russia's defeat in the Crimean War (1853–1856). On March 19, 1856, in a manifesto, Alexander II (1855–1881) promised "laws equally just for all."[5] Sharply elevated levels of debt and a banking scare put pressure on the budget,[6] and on March 5, 1861, the tsar ended private ownership of settled lands and landlords' power over the personal lives of the peasants. A military defeat played a powerful role in discrediting the rigid social and political system and the elite interests that upheld it.[7]
2. **The Stolypin reforms** (1906–1910) followed urban revolt and rural unrest in its aftermath, which were among the outcomes of Russia's defeat in the Russo-Japanese War (1904–1905). The tsar and his entourage, wrote statesman Pavel Miliukov, granted concessions "in a moment of fever."[8] Nicholas II issued a Manifesto of Fundamental Rights (1906),[9] created a parliament (the Russian Duma, 1906–1917), swept away most civil distinctions based on *sosloviia* (estates), and founded a new system of justice, with expanded rights of property ownership and new *zemstvo curiae* (provincial courts). Prime Minister Peter Stolypin then produced an agrarian reform. His laws granted titles to producers' allotment land and allowed their removal from communal holdings.
3. **Nationalization of the land after the October revolution** (1917) followed irreparable losses in Russia's effort in World War I.[10] Peasants, returning from the front, found local land and food supply committees set up to procure grain for the army and the cities. Their resistance to requisitions met with further government intervention and land

[4] The paper on roving vs. stationary bandits by McGuire and Olson (1996) shows that the incentives to supply public goods are present in authoritarian regimes, and when revenues decline at the margin, to cease taxation. The formal argument they make brings democratic and autocratic regimes into same reform framework.

[5] Cited in Lincoln (1990), p. 57 [S. S. Tatishchev, *Imperator Aleksandr II: ego zhizn' i tsarstvovanie* (St. Petersburg 1911), I:189].

[6] Hoch (1991).

[7] Rieber (1971), p. 47.

[8] P. Miliukov describes the circumstances of Nicholas II's manifesto of October 17, 1905, in P. E. Shchegolev, ed. *Padenie tsarskogo rezhima* (Leningrad, 1925–1927), 6:294–95, cited in Florinsky (1961), p. 96, n. 2.

[9] Ceded by Tsar Nicholas II (1893–1917).

[10] See particularly Wade (2003), Chamberlin (1987), vol. I, Rabinowitch (1976), among numerous works on the Russian Revolutions of 1917.

seizures both by the government and the peasants.[11] The Provisional Government, created after the abdication of Nicholas II, was increasingly influenced by socialists and unwilling to turn to market forces to resolve the threat of social revolution. Prince Lvov, head of the Provisional Government, wrote, that the government was"tossed about like debris on a stormy sea."[12] November 7 (New Style), 1917, the Bolsheviks came to power in a coup d'état, and they responded to the crisis by nationalizing the land (February 19, 1918).

4. **Forced requisitions of war communism** (**1918–1920**) followed the end of Russia's participation in World War I and accompanied the outbreak of the civil war (1918–1921), by which the Bolsheviks, fighting domestic opposition and foreign powers, secured the food supply as they nationalized industry, banned private trade, and partially substituted barter for a money economy.[13]
5. **The New Economic Policy (NEP)** (**1921–1928**) began a course toward economic liberalization after the civil war ended. The Bolsheviks relaxed direct control over distribution to revive production and voluntary marketing.[14] They replaced requisitions with a tax in kind and later in money.
6. **Forced collectivization** (**1929–late 1930s**) ended the NEP, as the government deplored the continued low level of marketed grain, which was considered insufficient for rapid industrialization. Confronting severe conditions, in 1927 and 1928, Stalin and his allies, wrote Lynne Viola, "continually warned not only of the dangers of war, but of the threat of hunger and urban instability if the grain procurement crisis was not forcefully addressed."[15] Stalin ended the NEP to drive rural dwellers into collective (*kolkhoz*) and state (*sovkhoz*) farms. The regime imposed targets for production and supplied improved equipment and capital investment, and released rural labor for urban industrialization.
7. **Khrushchev's reforms** (**1953–early 1960s**) followed the death of Stalin in 1953, a time of political turmoil. Nikita Khrushchev, on becoming First Secretary of the Communist Party, arguing that yields had remained practically identical to those in the NEP,[16] and cereals output was only slightly higher,[17] used the explosive September plenum of

[11] Lih (1990); Patenaude (1995); Wade (2003).

[12] *Iz Dnevnika A. N. Kuropatkina* in *Krasnoi arkhiv*, 20, 66. Entry under the date of April 25, 1917, cited in Florinsky (1961), 9. 229.

[13] Borrero (2003); Lih (1994); Patenaude (1995); Figes (1989).

[14] Viola (2005); Harrison (1990), and others.

[15] Viola (2005), p. 19.

[16] 8 and 8.6 centners per hectare.

[17] From 1928–1930 to 1952–1953, they had advanced by 101.5 percent. Nimitz (1967), p. 200, using 1928 prices; Narkhoz 1959 (1960), p. 308, using 1913 prices, places production in 1952–1953, 13.5 percent higher.

the Central Committee in 1953 to to gain political advantage over his rivals, Molotov, Malenkov, Voroshilov, Kaganovich, and Bulganin, and argue for agrarian reform.[18] He hiked processing and procurement prices to raise incentives.[19] In 1954, he expanded agricultural cultivation into marginal and virgin lands in Kazakhstan, western and eastern Siberia, the Urals, and the Volga regions.[20] In 1958, attempting to make collective farms more efficient, he gave them control over the purchase and repair of machinery and abolished Machine Tractor Stations (MTS).

8. **Gorbachev's agrarian reforms** (1985–1991) were carried out as the country plunged into hyperinflation. His perestroika included agricultural measures intended to revitalize the farm regime. Its main design for agriculture allowed collective farm workers to contract services and acquire inheritable family farms.
9. **Farm enterprise privatization** (1991–1993) was bundled with the liberalization of prices and trade under Boris Yeltsin, first president of the Russian Federation (1991–1999), under continuing severe inflation. He privatized most collective and state farms as producer cooperatives and joint stock associations with almost no aid for restructuring or management training. Agriculture like industry entered a severe downturn.[21] Individual property rights in land, upheld in the Federal Constitution of 1993, were brought closer to realization under Vladimir Putin (2000–2008), who provided practical adjustments to the new Land Code and funded government programs for rural development.

The outcomes of macroeconomic reforms imposed during a crisis show that inflation tends to survive. After the urgency of the threat passes, governments tend to loosen fiscal constraints, mitigating the effects of redistribution. For similar reasons, agrarian reforms can have an equally disappointing denouement. In Latin America, liberal agrarian reform frequently gives way to counter-reform.[22] Once the intensity of crisis dissipates, opponents of reform press for its modification or reversal.[23] In Russia, reversal occurred two times – after the Stolypin reforms during the revolution, and after the

[18] Nikonov (1995), p. 327.

[19] Increasing state procurement prices for vegetables, for example, by 25–40 percent, Nikonov (1995), p. 302.

[20] From 1954 to 1955, the figure for ploughed hectares went from 166.1 to 185. Diamond (1966), p. 373. Nikonov (1995), p. 308.

[21] On the transformational recession see Kornai (1993).

[22] Judging by persistent high and variable inflation rates, Latin American comparisons also show that such reform is readily abandoned if support erodes. Hirschman (1985); Drazen and Crilli (1998); Labán and Sturzenegger (1994).

[23] As in the example of Chile: after the coup of 1973, ceilings on land tenure were removed for the new landowning elite; see also Guatamala. Janvry (1981), p. 388.

NEP. Indeed, considerable modification de-radicalized the course toward secure disposable rights of land ownership in the 1990s, despite that they had been enshrined in the Federal Constitution of 1993.

Most often, the poor prospects for agrarian reform in a crisis stem from the weakening of the real economy. Industry stagnates, and rural by-employment declines, thereby reducing household income in village communities at a time when reform aims to create opportunities for entrepreneurship. Given budgetary stringencies in a crisis, implementation slows down, and beneficiaries are forced to pay some of the costs of restructuring. In the instances when agrarian reform is bundled with trade liberalization, as it was in the 1990s, the terms of trade will turn against the agricultural sector, and agriculture will experience a deep and lingering recession. Crises leave their marks for decades. In advanced economies GDP can be permanently reduced when plants and equipment are scrapped prematurely. In developing economies, although the effects of crises such as a banking run, rapid inflation, military defeat or social revolt are mainly urban, even indirect effects through foregone remittances can long be felt in the impoverished rural sector.

In the decades immediately following most of the agrarian reforms listed above, rural transformation was exceedingly slow. The sense that these reforms had failed, at least in the short run, is captured in contemporary commentaries and amply attested to in statistical assessments reviewed here. Following the 1861 serf emancipation, for example, more than a decade passed before output made even moderate advancement. After the introduction of the NEP in the 1921, in another example, the recovery of grain marketings from their suppression under War Communism was so uncertain by 1929 as to spell the end of the liberal reform period. In a final example, farm enterprise privatization in the 1990s was followed by a deep recession, holding back farm restructuring.

To be sure, frustration with agrarian reform grew in measure with the critique by observers who had favored more radical reform. The conservative orientation of most reforms was visible in the generous terms by which landed elites were compensated in the imperial period, and the large former collective and state farms were privileged in the post-Soviet period. The terms of reform were indeed hard on small producers in both reform eras. The allocation of land and other assets resulted in the fragmentation of small holdings, while the large farms retained their market power. It was also important, however, that even large farms were strongly affected by adverse economic conditions of the reform era, which resulted in labor hoarding and slowing of implementation of measures to improve efficiency.

One factor considered to be of primary importance in the disappointing outcomes of Russian agrarian reforms and mass interventions such as collectivization, was resistance by the rural populace. As this book shows in later chapters, historians have held the rigidity of peasants' own traditions responsible for the continuing backwardness of Russian agriculture. Some rural traditions did persist over several centuries. This book weighs the role Russia's agrarian institutions are held to have played with factors emerging in development literature about why the status quo tends to persist after reforms, or why poverty endures. In Russia, a factor rarely cited in the literature but powerfully important, was the policy of discouraging rural mobility during reforms, which slowed the critical ingredients of successful institutional change, information flows and rural emigration.

The resistance of rural dwellers to outsiders is legendary in Russian history, but was it the reason that rural Russia remained backward, at least in the imperial period? This book asks that question in different ways, emphasizing the nature of reforms, the protection that local institutions gave rural dwellers, and the conditions at the time. It also stresses the importance of an industrial upturn for agricultural growth and for the integration of the sectors in the growth process. Despite protectionism, for example, the industrial policies of Finance Minister Sergei Witte boosted the output of the agricultural sector, showing the importance of demand in providing incentives for market-oriented transformation in the critical era of the 1890s.

To some extent, collectivization does not fit well in this study. It was not market-oriented. Indeed, it created a factory style regime in agriculture, eliminating household autonomy. Although it imparted some benefits, including mass tractorization, its drawbacks were equally apparent in the use of force and monitoring required on collective and state farms, and in the loss of the generational build-up of local knowledge that usually has a priority place in farm decision-making. Critical problems related to the absence of markets set the agrarian economy back and required extensive investment to maintain production targets.

In regard to the nature of the decision-making process, however, collectivization does fit the pattern explored in this book. Decisions ending the NEP were taken during – and because of – a crisis, and crisis had something to do with the lag in output recovery for up to a decade. Adjustment costs were steep, and, on the whole, rural dwellers paid the price.

This introduction continues, below, with some definitions of the role of agrarian reform in economic development. Research on the theories and practice of reform with citations to the literature is discussed below to explain why most governments undertake this large project in the course of modernization. To a conceptual understanding provided by that literature, the introduction adds a note describing the critical place of reform in social policy, which has something to do with why agrarian reforms end up in a bundle of emancipatory measures in times of crisis. The introduction goes on to address another central concern of the book: reform as a bureaucratic enterprise. To understand why crisis was necessary for the Russian government to produce innovative policy, a problem observed across regimes, it is important to set this book in an innovation management context. Some space is given to the dynamic efficiency for the bureaucracy of managing policy this way, gains over time that help explain the repetition of an essentially failed strategy for sectoral reform over several centuries. The final section of the introduction is a brief survey of the modernization of the Russian economy over the entire period.

1 AGRARIAN REFORM

The Concepts

According to G. Feder, A. Sen, and K. Hoff, agrarian reform is a grant of "the substantive freedoms" – enabling or expanding choice.[24] Agrarian reform is a process by which individuals gain rights, or powers, to consume, obtain income from, and transfer landed assets. The main element of what is called land reform is land titling.

Yet land titling alone does not amount to agrarian reform because it can fail to resolve contradictions between customary land tenure and the demands for development. Land reform must close the distance between the law and informal practice, which is the root of social cleavage.[25] It must separate the ownership rights enjoyed by elites and the state from producers' customary rights, which govern actual norms of land tenure. It must as a priority replace tax exemptions and credit distortions favoring large farms. Otherwise, farms of large scale may remain relatively unaffected by reform and redistribution, and they may continue to enjoy exclusive access to imported technology. In a resulting bimodal distribution, small family farms will largely be limited to biological and chemical technologies that evolve in labor-intensive systems.[26]

Agrarian reform is the larger package of land reform, tax reform, and other measures in support of markets. In modern terms, it consists of a multi-instrument design for rural development.[27] Multiple instruments emphasize financial and technological assistance to promote change through new production techniques and mechanization. They aim at consistency across sectors and policies to diminish a variety of supply-side obstructions where markets are weak. They ease barriers to the exit of households and individuals from a community or region. Multi-instrument reforms make rural organization sufficiently flexible to release labor and other resources for use in more productive sectors.[28] By definition, a reform that promotes

[24] Sen (1999), p. 74; Feder (1988).

[25] Hoff (1993), Ch. 11, and others.

[26] In other words, reform in the developing world aims to break down the bimodal system, characterized by a mass of small relatively inefficient peasant farms and a small number of large-scale farms capable of using imported technology. See Ruttan (1984).

[27] Hoff (1993); Burg (1977).

[28] Prosterman and Riedinger (1987).

departures from the village, along with productivity improvement, draws on a vision of the future of the entire economy.[29] Departures from the village, permitted by improved technologies, reduce costs along the food chain, making industry more competitive and reducing poverty. The agricultural sector is expected to shrink during the modernization process, although its productivity will grow, and exports will provide revenues for the state.[30] This is the underlying objective of multi-instrument packages.

While agrarian reform is generally associated in the literature with policy strategies, it is important to orient this discussion of conceptual definitions taking into account their roots in economic understandings.

Agrarian Reform and Industrial Policy

It is a commonplace that agrarian reform is treated in the frame of industrial policy. This is because agriculture is modeled as a declining sector in GDP, by contrast with the leading industrial sector. As agriculture becomes more productive, it releases labor and fosters industrial development. The path by which agriculture releases labor begins with urban financial institutions making farm credit more widely available, which increases demand for the purchase or lease of new technologies in agriculture. Once its credit supply constraint is relaxed, agriculture improves in yields and therefore rural incomes improve. At this point, rural dwellers begin to leave the land.

To summarize, industrial policy is designed to accelerate the process of change in agriculture. This model of industrial policy goes back to notions of a dualistic economy in the writings of Frederick List (1789-1846), who reasoned that protectionist policies would promote "national economies" and the welfare of future generations After him the concept of a modern and traditional sector – the latter seen as sociologically and technologically backward – became widespread in development theory.[31] In the developing world, industrial policy shifts the terms of trade against agriculture, squeezing the agricultural sector to encourage industrialization without causing inflation. This is done by overvalued exchange rates, tariffs on manufactured commodities, and export duties on agricultural commodities to force out a

29 See reform and a multisector vision in Balcerowicz, Blaszczyk, and Dabrowski (1997), pp. 135.

30 In their analysis of applications to U.S. agricultural development of standard growth models, Olmstead and Rhode describe "Mellor's law" (2007), p. 2: "In 1966 Mellor posited that 'the faster agriculture grows, the faster its relative size declines' [Mellor (1995)]. Mellor's observation stems from the possibility that technological changes can overcome the effects of a growing population, and following Engel's Law, as per capita income increases, the percentage of income spent on food will decline leading to a relative decline in the size of the agricultural sector."

31 Kaufman and Hodson (1982) review the literature on the dualistic economy.

labor contribution from the agricultural sector and to adjust the components of the net surplus flow between sectors. Rural emigration and technological improvement are the instruments of change.[32]

Among the most enduring models of development is that of the transfer of surplus labor between sectors, a leading sector approach developed by R. Lewis and revised by J. Fei and G. Ranis.[33] Surplus labor is a concept from disequilibrium theory, which models the savings constraint on industrialization. The reasoning is that landlords' consumption is taxed by rural emigration and by other means, which mobilizes savings and enhances revenues. Policy that encourages the extraction of labor resources will encourage rural savings and economic surplus from the agricultural sector.[34] Such policy, as noted above, will contribute to industrialization by lowering food costs and adding to foreign exchange by commodity exports.

In recent years, there has been a move away from this model or any model applied to all countries. The post-"Washington consensus" policy understanding is that constraints on growth differ among countries and regions.[35] Whether more urban workers promote growth, for example, depends on sectoral differences in rates of return, giving importance to the kind of industry where jobs are being created, and on whether peasant migrants have the skills for those jobs. Industrial policy can easily be used to shift the price advantage to industry, but the market rate of return may not justify that investment.[36] To assess this and other country constraints requires highly complex models, including rates of return on investment across the economy, income and price elasticities of demand for food, and the impact of appropriately advanced technologies. Data are required about taxpayers, land boundaries, and future administrative costs. In view of data fragility for developing countries, as K. Sah and J. Stiglitz (1992) show, such complicated models can fail to reflect reality.

Even if a model could theoretically be designed to reflect completely the constraints in a given country, many policies that might be essential for effective reform are out of reach in the developing world. This is because the set of feasible taxes is extremely limited.[37] Also, the size of the agricultural

[32] Rosenstein-Rodan (1943); Johnston and Mellor (1961); Lewis (1955); Fei and Ranis (1964, 1966).

[33] For a recent review of the theory and an expansion of the theory to account for the diversity of experience in the developing world, see Fei and Ranis (1997). The classic works are Lewis (1955); Fei and Ranis (1964, 1966). A more extensive introduction to the theory as applied to Russian growth policy is in Gatrell (1986).

[34] Oman and Wignaraja (1991), p. 44.

[35] See, for the Spence Report, http://www.growthcommission.org/index.php?option=com_content&task=view&id=96&Itemid=169F, and for a review of models, see Olmstead and Rhode (2007).

[36] This analysis follows Oman and Wignaraja (1991).

[37] Sah and Stiglitz (1992), pp. 30–3.

economy and the extent of poverty may be such that savings across the economy will fail to finance industrial growth. Continued taxation of the agricultural sector in this circumstance will not help because it will prevent the rise in demand for industrial goods. Moreover, since the demand for industrial goods in modern times comes mostly from government investment and services in urban areas, input price support, the standard tool of industrial policy, will not address effectively the causes of economy-wide backwardness. Taxing the agricultural sector will have mixed results.[38]

Agrarian Reform and Social Policy

Among its political appeals, land reform has populist support. In Latin America in the 1960s, for example, many governments introduced agrarian reform to break up latifundia and to create small farms. They targeted large farms as a source of injustice although they also underscored the efficiency of smaller-scale farming, that is, the importance of factor proportionality in agricultural productivity.[39] Governments anticipated that an equitable distribution of land could result in an increase of between 10 and 30 percent in food production.[40] The Punta del Este Charter of the Organization of American States adopted for its platform in 1967 that all organization members should pass land reform laws.[41] Governments sought to induce development and reduce poverty while fostering trade and creating a common market.

The experience of land titling, in most instances, has a poor record of results. Farm fragmentation undermined the success of land titling and other reforms in Brazil, Chile, Mexico, Peru, Venezuela, Nicaragua, Guatemala, Zimbabwe, and South Africa. There have been examples of successful mixed-benefit land-titling reforms, but only where fragmentation was avoided.[42] One example, in Japan, where major land reform from 1945 to 1950 was widely touted to have been one of the most successful occupation reforms,

[38] Gerschenkron (1962); Sah and Stiglitz (1992); Oman (1991).

[39] Barry and Cline (1979).

[40] Dasgupta (1993), p. 525; Berry and Cline (1979).

[41] *Declaration of the Presidents of America, Punta del Este, Uruguay, April 14, 1967*, Chapter 4. "The living conditions of the rural workers and farmers of Latin America will be transformed, to guarantee their full participation in economic and social progress. For that purpose, integrated programs of modernization, land settlement, and agrarian reform will be carried out as the countries so require."

[42] Examples of mixed success include Taiwan, South Korea, and Egypt. The Zamindari Abolition Act for Eastern India, postwar land reforms in Iran, Japan, and China (China's transformation of collectives into family farms under the household responsibility system in 1978), the Philippines' tenancy reform, Kenya's Land Settlement program in the 1960s were also examples where there were beneficial outcomes, at least in the medium term. Examples of reforms that failed to improve incomes of the poorest and where small farming did not achieve the productivity levels of large farms include Algeria's nationalization of French estates in 1964. See Binswanger (1984); Oman and Wignaraja (1991), p. 47.

eliminating problems of tenancy by sweeping redistribution, the reform was so focused on tenancy that it failed to deal with farm fragmentation.[43] Such reforms have also not resolved problems produced by concentration, the coexistence of large farms with fragmented small ones, and this is particularly evident in transition economies, for example, in the Baltic and southeastern Europe, where land was redistributed among agriculturalists by spontaneous mass privatization.

Agrarian Reform and Technology Policy

Modern agrarian reform has a substantial technological component. In the 1950s and 1960s, technological development in agriculture was promoted by the World Bank as the "green revolution," oriented to new seeds, better farm management, measured amounts of fertilizers, pesticides, and water. These programs constituted what V. Ruttan calls the "High-Payoff Input Model" – based on the insights of T. Schultz.[44] Technological improvements were labor intensive, land saving, scale neutral, and efficient in the use of costly capital resources to meet the needs of developing countries.[45] For many reasons, these efforts tended to be insufficient, although there certainly were some countries and regions in which the green revolution produced striking results. The primary drawback was that the new technologies required appropriate institutional settings. Agrarian communities sometimes did not absorb technological innovation. For example, where plots were small and scale-neutral technologies had been imposed, the technologies were ill-adapted to local custom.[46] In the High-Payoff Input Model, too, problems of poverty were generally unaddressed.[47]

That said, a technological focus is important in agrarian reform: technology's vital role in agricultural advancement is attested by world experience. However, a focus on labor skills and market infrastructure is equally critical. Effective aid, which is tailored to country needs and directed at education, training and infrastructure, will help mobilize savings for investment in new and/or improved technology. The risk in high-payoff models is that they can leave large farms dominant, with technological innovation held back on small subsistence farms. The model also deprives the economy of the benefits of competitiveness that is assured on small as well as large farms, once

43 "Absentee landlords were compelled to sell their entire holdings of arable land to the state at 1945 prices; resident landlords were allowed to retain no more than about 7 acres of arable land on average.... by 1950, some 90 percent of all arable land... was owned by those who cultivated it." Waswo (1996), p. 136.

44 Ruttan (2001), p. 186; Schultz (1964).

45 Kaneda (1969); Hayami and Ruttan (1971); Ruttan (1984); Oman and Wignaraja (1991).

46 In some regions of India, for example, outcomes were positive, but in others not. Griffin (1989); Broehl (1978).

47 Sen (1957); Kaldor (1967); Kalecki (1976).

property rights secure the autonomy of producers. Finally, models too focused on technology can have an undesired ecological impact.[48]

Concepts of Agrarian Reform: A Summary

Currently the best agrarian reforms are thought to be those that least distort markets, rely on multiple instruments and aim at rural development. Such measures will include support for learning, property rights, business plans, and training both for agriculturalists and farmers who choose to leave agriculture. Along with the critically important provision of financial infrastructure, effective reforms also tend to promote aid for self-sustaining improvement in marketing and technologies by means of marketing boards and research and extension.

It is still not well understood, however, that successful reforms require one further condition, that they be timed pro-cyclically. Evidence for India, Taiwan, Iran, Japan, and China shows that reform has maximum impact in an industrial growth cycle. The increased capacity of the agricultural sector is matched by the increased capacity of other sectors.[49] By contrast, if a government continues to inject resources into agriculture despite urban employment reaching a maximum, then self-sustaining complementarities end, and support for the agricultural sector is dead weight on industry, choking off growth through taxation, as occurred in the Soviet Union after the 1970s. Growth, by definition, is the only means in the long run of reducing rural poverty.[50]

There are two country experiences that illustrate highly successful agrarian reforms, that is, positive outcomes for gradualist technology-led multi-instrument reforms carried out during a period of growth. The first is South Korea, where in the late 1940s and early 1950s, about 80 percent of all land farmed under tenancy conditions and land owned by absentee landlords was redistributed, and land titling was completed. In the 1970s, new technologies were fostered in the New Community Movement, which promoted diversification of production and construction of new roads and bridges and installation of electricity and water supplies. The whole economy grew by about 10 percent per year between 1965 and 1981, and the rising gini coefficient for rural household income during this period showed the penetration of entrepreneurship.[51] "Dramatic improvements in land productivity based on technological advancements," wrote S. Kwack, "account for most of the growth of agricultural production."[52]

48 Griffin (1979).
49 Karshenas (1995).
50 Mellor (1984); Ruttan and Hayami (1984); Ruttan (1984); Tracy (1992); OECD (1998).
51 In 1965 it was 0.2852, and in 1976, 0.3273. Kwack (1990), p. 122.
52 Kwack (1990), p. 77.

The other is China. Reform began with decollectivization. Incentives were provided for individual farming through the Household Responsibility System (HRS), which made the household the residual claimant on the land. Between 1978 and 1989 agricultural output (in constant prices) nearly doubled in gross value of output.[53] In China, as in Korea, technological change and nonconventional inputs were promoted: research and extension for improved seed and fertilizers, services, including credit and marketing agencies and cooperatives, and rural governmental resources for building feeder roads and market information infrastructure. Reform has not been a success in all regions, but in some, farm incomes rose. Food became cheaper, more diverse, and better in quality. In both countries, incentive reform was not led by liberalization, which occurred afterward. A. de Brauw, J. Huang, and S. Rozelle observe: "Had China led reforms with market liberalization rather than incentive reform, it is unclear that market liberalization would have led to the same gains in agriculture."[54] Timing and historical circumstance are important for reforming the rural sector effectively.

2 THE STATE AND AGRARIAN REFORM

Dynamic Efficiency

Political theory – concerned with the contribution of interests, ideas, and routines to policy – helps explain the costly politics of crisis-induced reform. A theory explaining why the state repeatedly uses this policy instrument must be based on positive feedback from reform, that is, some source of dynamic efficiency to make up for other losses. The crucial benefit, as pointed out in the examples above, was consolidation of support around the state's position, the winning over of elites without coercion. Direct confiscatory appropriations, are politically far less palatable to governments.[55] The struggle over redistribution between fiscal authorities and economic elites is essentially a war of attrition.[56] There is considerable savings in ending the conflict, with the state enhancing its authority.

Among the several means of compensating elites in a crisis is bundling. One reform is bundled with another difficult measure; several can be justified by the same rationale. For example, Alexander II, "Tsar Liberator" and "champion of justice and humanitarian ideals," bundled the emancipation of the serfs with measures, including press liberalization, reform of

[53] After 1985, the success of agrarian reform considerably weakened in crop production. Sicular (1993), pp. 127–28.

[54] de Brauw et al. (2002), p. 26.

[55] Binswanger and Elgin (1984), p. 353; Drazen (2000), p. 403.

[56] Delayed reform is seen by Axelrod (1984) as a cooperative game in which rival elites must co-exist, a war of attrition.

the universities, the judiciary, taxation and the military, that together are referred to as "The Great Reforms."[57] In another example, Stalin linked collectivization with the First Five Year Plan (1928–1932). The rhetoric used during collectivization drew it into the rhetoric of revolutionary social and economic transformation of the entire country.[58]

Bundling compensates elites and benefits the state by diluting reform or undercutting the benefits to producers. The Khrushchev price incentive reforms in 1956 are an example. The government's initial decree (March 6) guaranteed monthly advance payments to collective farm workers. On the same day the government then issued a decree, the Charter of the Collective Farm, which qualified the guaranteed remuneration by reducing the permitted number of household cattle and amount of labor time that the farm worker could spend on the private plot.[59] A government has no monopoly over this tactic.[60] Bundling was used strategically by the opposition in the Yeltsin era to undermine his success in privatizing farm enterprises and grant of individual landownership rights in the Constitution of 1993. The opposition-led parliament held back implementation of landownership rights in the 1990s by attaching to the Land Code clauses excluding arable land in its provisions.

Bundling has the advantage of compensating the state for loss of revenues. Again an illustration from the Great Reforms is useful. The government's agenda included both the abolition of serfdom and the introduction of universal military conscription, complementary reforms that transferred the expenses of recruitment to the state, since the nobles could no longer be responsible for this service. The advantage for the state lay in the supply of men and the ease of recruiting them. Another example is from the Stolypin era. The simultaneous guarantee of private property in land and universal citizenship reduced costs for the state in tax administration.

Thus there were fiscal benefits to agrarian reform in a crisis. Producers were induced to pay heftier long-term net costs than they might otherwise have had to pay, and the state was the beneficiary of any difference. There is always tax benefit by redistribution.[61] An improvement in taxation, even in small amounts, is difficult to achieve, however, although it can have substantial rewards. Even a marginal improvement in tax revenues with effects realized over a number of years would be dynamically efficient. Where the budget deficit tends to be large, minor upward adjustment of budgetary

57 Wortman (2000), pp. 59, 61.

58 Viola et al. (2005).

59 McCauley (1976), p. 111.

60 Mark Harrison contributed important insights to this analysis.

61 Sanchez (2005); Tommasi and Velasco (1996); Nelson (1990); Williamson (1994); Rodrik (1996); Drazen (2000), p. 444; see also Acemoglu, Johnson, and Robinson, "Why Did the West Extend the Franchise?" *Quarterly Journal of Economics* 115 (2003), 1167–99.

revenues will considerably lower the debt/GDP levels.[62] Even small fiscal gains in times of budgetary deficit are quite sufficient to justify agrarian reform.

In summary, the political economy of reform promises that producing it in a crisis will be dynamically efficient. Elites can be compensated effectively; fiscal capacity can be stretched; and more than one overdue reform can be bundled together in a larger agenda.[63] Of course, there is some coercive element in this strategy. Using a crisis to push forward reform is not without reputational damage to the government, and it has costs, including monitoring of the implementation.[64]

The Bureaucracy and Reform

The pattern of governance reflected in these reforms, long eras of policy stagnation, broken up by brief eras of intensive reform activity, can be understood conceptually through organization theory. The process of change in huge complex organizations has been closely examined because of the large firm's generally conservative culture. How does innovation occur? In a large, closely networked organization such as a firm, corporate culture is fairly inertial and focused on its core competence. Innovation much of the time tends to be incremental and not disruptive of the core. Major disruptive innovations tend to occur, therefore, with break-through new technologies brought to the market by small firms, frequently founded by disgruntled designers and engineers who have left the larger firms to pursue their innovative designs. At larger firms, only a crisis or opportunity of major proportions, for example, a serious threat to market share, or the opening of a new source of demand, will result in the adjustment or abandonment of the core competence and its clientele. Radical change, if it occurs, will also be associated with a change the firm's management.[65] The theory of how firms innovate has a parallel in the notion of scientific revolutions, which finds scientists avoiding radical new courses in their experimental work. That is, they adhere to a research paradigm, even one thought to be weakly explanatory, up until the point when it is entirely discredited.[66] A further parallel, returning to the problem of governance, lies in the retention by governments of policies that are functional, even though seriously flawed or even unethical, until a major discrediting event occurs. Then change will be sudden. Moreover, it can be sweeping. A breakthrough in one part of

[62] Bayer and de Boer (2002), pp. 42–3.
[63] Harberger (1993).
[64] Kreps (1992), p. 116.
[65] Utterback (1994), Hargadon (2003).
[66] Kuhn (1962).

a technological or social system can lead to transformation throughout it, before system stability is restored.[67]

The pattern of major breakthroughs –inertia to innovation, and then back to an inertial state – is called in conceptual terms a punctuated equilibrium.[68] To summarize in regard to systems of governance: deeply nested bureaucratic hierarchies sustain an equilibrium until an external shock or cultural shift occurs.[69] The disturbance makes way for new couplings, new ideas, and modified structures of decision making authority. The new adaptive ideas or changes are used to rearrange and/or expand the functions of governance, and then also to restore stability in the system by new mechanisms with greater potential for control.[70] Examples of punctuated equilibria in government include unpredictable consequences of social revolutions, financial crises and political upheaval.[71]

The bureaucratic nature of Russian governance tradition, well known in the literature, allows Russian policy formation to be set in this context.[72] Indeed, as a bastion of conservative culture, the Russian state is arguably ideal example of an organization with inertial tendencies. *Sui generis*, D. Orlovsky writes, the Russian bureaucracy did not undergo at any point in the nineteenth century a genuine transformation into a western (Weberian) structure, in contrast to the modernization of the state in western European countries.[73] It remained a rigidly hierarchical structure with elites of all kinds forming interrelated and ranked cumuli of central and regional authorities. In imperial Russia, most of the servitors at the highest rank were landowners,

[67] A technological trajectory can thus be "locked in," or in an inertial state. Arthur (1989); Cowan (1990); David (1985); Malerba (1992, 1999); Mokyr (1990); Ruttan (2001).

[68] The term derives from evolutionary biological theory in Eldredge and Gould (1972). Its best known application is by Kuhn (1970) to scientific paradigm shifts.

[69] Gersick (1991); Aoki (2000); Wollin (1999); Sabaherwal (2001); Somit and Peterson (1992). See also empirical work in the social sciences, Romanelli and Tushman (1994); Gaudy (1994).

[70] Wollin (1999), p. 36.

[71] This point was observed in regard to the Gorbachev and Yeltsin reforms by White (2000), p. 10.

[72] Bucher, G. (2006); Field (1976); Gleason (1981); Herrera (2006); Lincoln (1990); Macey (1976); McAuley (1984); Orlovsky (1981, 1996); Pintner (1980); Raeff (1983); Ryavek (2003); Sakwa (2007); Strauss (1961); Törke (1974); Weissman (1981); Whelan (1982); Wortman (1969); Yaney (1973); Zaionchkovskii (1958).

[73] Orlovsky (1976) finds unconvincing the idea of major turning points, such as that observed by the Soviet-era scholar Troitskii (1974), who posited a more western absolutist bureaucracy in the eighteenth century, or others who saw reforms of Alexander I and Speranskii or Nicholas I as turning points. Orlovsky (1976), p. 454: There was "a continuum of institutional development-a long process beneath the surface of formal change expressed in legislative acts and decrees. From this point of view the Muscovite *prikazy,* highly organized offices staffed by careerists that were at times devastatingly efficient, were direct antecedents of the institutions and practices that evolved during the eighteenth and nineteenth centuries."

but many at lower ranks were as well.[74] In the Soviet era the government remained highly bureaucratic; the privileged higher levels of state authority were elites with linkages through ministerial positions to sectoral interests.[75]

According to this understanding, which emphasizes the importance of overcoming bureaucratic inertia as well as compensating elites, we find that what is known about decision making in the imperial, Soviet and post-Soviet periods fits uncommonly well in the model. Agrarian interests were deeply embedded across ministries and at the highest levels of government. One example serves to illustrate that in the bureaucracy even the most powerful reformers in the government were easily outnumbered and defeated. Looking back in an essay on the peasantry on his own limited contribution to social reform in the 1880s and 1890s, then Minister of Finance Sergei Witte recalled pressing other ministers to support individual peasant landownership, a concept at the core of Stolypin's legislation two decades later.[76] In the 1890s, Witte wrote, he had urged the resettlement of large numbers of landless peasants and their families by railroad to eastern Siberia. In regard to both proposals, Witte describes his colleagues' disinterested response, and sometimes opposition.[77] In this period, bureaucratized autocracy in its Byzantine opacity stifled the voice of reformers. The period about which Witte talks followed a reign of considerable achievements, that of Alexander II, whose era was known for its Great Reforms, including the serf emancipation. But after the ruler's death in 1881 his successor, Alexander III (1881-1894), restored the rigid, hierarchical lines of authority, indeed, strengthened the system to secure the autocrat against disloyalty.[78] Witte's experience proved remarkably similar to that of reformers in the Soviet era, from the 1960s through the early 1980s.

3 RUSSIAN ECONOMIC GROWTH

In the eighteenth century, Russia was no crossroads of trade; serfdom deepened the isolation of rural communities, and its legacies slowed advancement in manufacturing and agriculture through the early twentieth century, when the capital cities, Moscow and St. Petersburg, experienced strong growth and benefits of foreign trade. Meanwhile, the economic history of

[74] Although most of those serving in the top ranks, which included all the significant posts, were of the hereditary nobility in 1850, most had no property or less than 100 serfs. Pintner (1980), cited in Orlovsky (1976), p. 458.

[75] Axelrod (1984), see also analysis of the Soviet bureaucracy in McGuire and Olson (1996), Gregory (2003).

[76] Macey (1987), p. 219.

[77] Witte, "Krestianskii i dvorianskii voprosy" in *Vospominaniia* (2003), 2:531.

[78] Orlovsky (1976).

England and Holland in the seventeenth and eighteenth centuries shows rapid economic advances associated with export expansion, industrial development, and the political evolution of individual property rights in land, still not entirely defined in Russia in 1914. In parts of the Russian empire, Estland, Livonia and Kurland (now Estonia and Latvia), and, after 1795, the Congress Kingdom of Poland, serfdom ended after the Napoleonic invasion, but in the interior of Russia, it lasted to 1861. To be sure, within a few decades after the serf emancipation there was accelerated economic development, showing it to have been a landmark measure. Even so, legacies of serfdom, including bottlenecks in the labor supply to industry and technological and cultural barriers to change, made the course of growth in Russia exceptionally uneven and unpredictable.[79]

The modern economic growth stream in Russia, as O. Crisp (1976) and others have written, began with the stimulus to mining and manufacturing and export promotion under Peter I in the the eighteenth century. Trends in industry had some impact on agriculture and the standard of living into the 1860s.[80] However before the mid-1880s, overall economic achievement in Russia on a per capita basis was meager in comparison to that of western Europe.[81] Russian economic growth did not exceed population growth by much in the period between 1795 and 1857, when the population grew by somewhat less than 1 percent per annum.[82] In the next period, between 1867 and 1913, the population grew much faster, on average, 1.5 percent per annum, accelerating further in the years before World War I.[83] The rate of growth of agricultural output tended to exceed the rate of growth for most decades, but until the 1890s, not by much. There was a significant improvement in the supply of low-cost food and progress in the acceleration of agricultural indicators in the era before the Russian revolution. Between 1887 and 1913, industry probably grew annually by as much as 6.65 percent.[84] By 1913, Russia was the fourth- or fifth-largest industrial

79 See Gregory (1994); Leonard (2004).

80 For long-run trends in the economy going back to that era, see Crisp (1976); Gatrell (1986); Vainshtein (1960); Kahan (1985, 1989); Mironov (1991).

81 See eh.net "What is its Relative Value"; Vainshtein (1969), pp. 33–4.

82 Kabuzan (1963), pp. 162–63; Mironov (1991), p. 145.

83 Hoch (1994), p. 58.

84 Establishing the exact rate of this high period's industrial growth, 1887–1913, is difficult. L. Borodkin points to the limitations of estimates by western scholars emerging mainly from indices provided by N. D. Kondratieff's Institute of Conjuncture in the 1920s. Another set of indices by L. V. Kafengauz, compiled when he was in prison in 1930 but published only in 1994, uses a larger number of goods and prices, making these western estimates by A. Gerschenkron (1952), R. Goldsmith (1955), and W. Nutter (1962) based on Kondratieff misleading. Indices published by N. D. Kondratieff in *Ekonomicheskii biuleten'* (1926) and by L. V. Kafengauz (1994). See L. I. Borodkin, "O promyshlennom rosti dorevoliutsionnoi Rossii," *Ekonomicheskaia istoriia, Obozrenie, Vypusk 12, Trudy istoricheskogo fakul'teta MGU*, 35 (2006), p. 193.

power in the world, along with the United States, the United Kingdom, France, Germany, and possibly Austria-Hungary.[85] The agricultural record was not as significant.

In the first decades of the Soviet era, the government vigorously narrowed the gap with the West in regard to GDP, building on trends since the 1880s; per capita GDP more than doubled between the end of 1880s and 1950.[86] Russian growth then kept up with that of the West. For the period 1950 to 1973 Russia's growth was almost 1 percent per annum faster than that of the United States (4.84 and 3.83).[87] Soviet annual productivity growth, beginning with the First Five Year Plan through the Khrushchev era, was 2 percent (1928 to 1966). This compares relatively well with the long-run productivity growth rates of other countries (United States for the years 1929 to 1969 at 2.2 percent, France for 1913 to 1966 at 2.2 percent).[88] Growth rates give a picture of how considerably the Russian economy was changing during the early and middle years of the Soviet era.

Difficulties began in the 1970s, a period that Gorbachev and his successors have called the *zastoi* (stagnation). More decentralized and less coercive, the economy could no longer take advantage of extensive growth, having no untapped labor resources for industry.[89] On the basis of exhaustive research and new models of development Robert Allen attributes declining growth thereafter primarily to the weak investment strategy of the late Soviet era.[90] Total factor productivity (TFP) in three industrial branches declined by more than 10 percent between 1975 and 1985.[91] Yet, the economy was also institutionally weakened by widespread bribes and payoffs, a supply diversion that caused an increasingly unreliable performance.[92] Central Intelligence Agency (CIA) estimates find that the annual growth rate of TFP between 1960 and 1989 was less than 1 percent.[93] Technological gains were slowing.

The deceleration of growth was such that by 1991 the economy was in a severe state of crisis. In that year GDP fell by 12 percent, and system-wide

[85] Gregory (1982), p. 154, especially, n. 3.
[86] Maddison (1995), Allen (2003), p. 5. Probably the gap was larger. Estimates for per capita national income in Russia are scarce for the late eighteenth–early nineteenth century, but a look at estimates for the late eighteenth century would suggest that Maddison's figure is for households rather than individuals. See Vainshtein (1969), pp. 33–4.
[87] Maddison (2001), p. 187.
[88] Gregory (1998), p. 230.
[89] On Soviet growth, see Gregory and Stuart (1998).
[90] Allen (2001).
[91] Coal, oil, and ferrous metals, see Allen (2003), p. 203.
[92] Ickes (2001), pp. 86–8; Murphy, Shleifer, and Vishny (1992).
[93] With 1982 as the base year. With 1960 as the base year, growth rates for the 1960s would have been .5 percent higher but still less than one for the entire period. Pitzer and Baukol (1991), p. 74, who use an elasticity of substitution of 0.5, in line with calculations of Weitzman (1970, 1983) and Ofer (1987).

collapse resulted in a new government.[94] Price and trade liberalization in 1992 led Russia into a transformational recession, affecting first industry, then agriculture. Poverty spread, and by 1999 four out of ten people lived in poverty.[95] Some signs of recovery and macroeconomic stability were achieved by 1995, but in 1998 another financial crisis spread from Asia and affected Russia's exposed banking sector.

The transformational recession finally bottomed out in 2000. Subsequent recovery was rapid. The rise in the growth rate paralleled a rise in government revenues, which was buoyed by high global prices for Russia's abundant mineral resources. By 2002, the poverty rate was cut in half, with an annual average GDP growth rate between 1999 and 2002 of 6.4 percent, and in 2005, 5.6 percent.[96]

To summarize, in the Soviet era and afterwards, during the transition from Communism, agricultural trends paralleled those in industry. The investment policies of the Brezhnev regime helped shrink the yield gap in cereals with western Europe and North America, but output targets in regard to agriculture were costly to maintain. The sustainability of high performance was in question. After Brezhnev, during the 1980s and 1990s, when the heavy financing of agriculture came to an end, agriculture collapsed and made only a slow recovery. Meanwhile equipment deteriorated and the creation of a state leasing program filled the gap only for a small number of the largest farms. The laws for agricultural producers had never been more promising: the enterprise privatization and the new Land Code, improved by amendments in Putin's first term, had created an enormous opportunity for farming. A considerable gap still remains, between the promise and its realization.

4 SUMMARY AND ORGANIZATION OF THE BOOK

When successful in the developing world, by redistributing the land and granting autonomy to producers, reform relieves producer debt and improves production. Historically, agrarian reform has failed more often than it has succeeded.[97] Successful reforms are inherently coercive, but the degree of coercion varies historically. For example, in England and France, parliaments relied on a multitude of new laws and their universal enforcement to establish new property rights. In Korea and China, the state was a powerful force behind the initiation of change in rural areas. The use of force or significant levels of aid, however, does not guarantee an outcome.

94 Economist Intelligence Review, Country Profile (2002), p. 26.
95 Kornai (1993).
96 World Bank (2003), p. i; World Bank (2005), pp. ii–iii; EBRD *Transition Report 2005* (2006), p. 171.
97 de Janvry (1981).

Even high payoff models have proved insufficient in the long run for lasting rural change.

To say there is no universal template for successful agrarian reform echoes the understanding of Gerschenkron, who held country differences in the impact of framework reforms, as he called them, to be paramount.[98] The country-by-country orientation is shared by Sah and Stiglitz (1992), who observe that complex models and estimates of how supply will respond prove too weakly predictive to be useful in a practical sense in the developing world. For example, it is difficult to predict the impact on agriculture of a country's entry into the World Trade Organization (WTO).[99] The effectiveness of agrarian reform will depend greatly on local traditions and historical factors. Such factors include, but are not limited to, the way a government approaches the reform process; the adequacy of budgetary resources and their expenditure on reconstruction; the flexibility of available tax instruments; and the macroeconomic conditions in which reforms are begun. Russia's relatively weak historical record in the sphere of agrarian reform shows the potential weight of these and other constraints.

Discussing these Russian reforms together is not meant to diminish their differences. No two agrarian reforms in Russia dealt with exactly the same concerns. The mid-nineteenth-century tsarist government sought to create a new social order in which newly emancipated peasants enjoyed some freedom and rights, while society retained its rigid castelike order. Social stability and tax benefits were far more immediate concerns for the government than producers' landholding rights. By contrast, the Stolypin reforms after 1906 focused on land rights and titling, along with improved efficiency of farming. Social stability was a powerful concern, to be achieved by the long term goal of the emergence of a new class of peasant landowners, *zazhitochnye* (well off) producers. In an even greater contrast, Stalin and his successors from 1929 through the 1980s were concerned mainly with technological advancement and the productivity of labor. They sought to stimulate change by investment to "put the *muzhik* on a tractor."[100] There was no support for household autonomy. Then, finally, after the end of Communism in Russia, in reforms of the Russian Federation government we revisit key priorities from the early twentieth century. One was to promote rural markets. Another was to preserving social stability amidst the disorganizing effects of change.

Critically, the way in which these reforms showed integration with each other was in the persistence of a single motive force. The impetus to reform in each case showed a similar perception of the unreliability of rural producers and the disappointing performance of the sector. The perception

98 Gerschenkron (1962), p. 19.
99 Leonard (2007).
100 Quoted in Lewin (1975), p. 456.

of backwardness was a driving force among voices for change, including Stalin's, whose reference to "... our age-old backward 'Russian' past" had particularly harsh implications for the agricultural sector.[101]

This introduction has been concerned with definitions, concepts, policy choices and the historical background, which help explain the widespread use of agrarian reform as an instrument of agrarian policy. The chapters of the book approach the study of the government's use of laws and structural reforms to manage agricultural sector problems essentially as a set of case studies. Both the reform process and the short- and long-run change in the sector form the units of study. The book is not, therefore, an agrarian history of Russia; its coverage is selective. As in other kinds of case studies, this series will not provide unambiguous answers for policy analysts. It will, however, assess the value of some components of the reforms as a response to rural backwardness. In this sense, it furnishes the conceptual understanding of the political economy of reform with some empirical evidence. It emphasizes the importance in economic history of examining long-run developments and follows the contribution of sociologists and geographers, who attempt to capture the complexity of long-run adaptive processes.[102]

The book is organized as follows. It begins in Part I with narratives detailing the deliberations prior to reforms and the crises that moved the government to act on the advice of commissions. It describes the intentions of reformers, the shape of their enactments, and the reforms' implementation and impact. Important to the assessment of their impact is their public reception and its weight in later histories of Russia.

Thematic chapters follow in Parts II and III. They explore in greater depth the evolution of rural economic institutions and technological advancement. Chapter 7 compares the effectiveness of individual reforms and weighs their cumulative impact on the productivity of Russian agriculture. The conclusion brings together the issues raised by the short-run productivity effects and long-run organizational continuities in Russian agriculture. It asks, again, from the perspective of a close look at the evidence, about the role of Russia's rural collectivist institutions in determining long-run growth patterns in agriculture.

101 Ibid.

102 Shanin (1972), Wegren (2002), Pallot (1998), Pallot and Nefedova (2007) and others.

PART I

DILEMMAS OF AGRARIAN REFORM IN RUSSIA

1

Imperial Reforms, 1861–1913

INTRODUCTION

There were two major property rights reforms in late imperial Russia, the emancipation of the serfs from personal bondage (1861–1863), and the Stolypin reforms, introduced by edict on November 9, 1906, and completed by legislative acts (1906–1910).[1] Critically important for the evolution of secure property rights in Russia, the first reform replaced usufruct with peasant ownership of allotment land, thus severing landlords' sovereignty over the village and strengthening its governance unit, the Land Commune. Showing its conservative design, it made the nobles' implementation of land redemption voluntary. It also placed restrictions on peasant movement by empowering the Land Commune to approve resettlement, frustrating observers who had hoped for more rapid change.[2] Forty-five years later, the Stolypin reforms finally allowed individual households to claim ownership and titles to allocated strips of land (*nadel*), to gather these strips into independent farms, and to dispense with the authority of the commune. These measures proved an effective model of land reform, taking agricultural development much further by the outbreak of World War I.

[1] Recent works on the politics of the serf emancipation include Bartlett (2003), Dolbilov (2002), and Lituev (1997); classical Western treatments also include Emmons (1963); Field (1976); Moon (2001a); Pintner (1967); Rieber (1966); among Russian scholarly works, see especially Semevskii (1888); Zaionchkovskii (1954); and Zakharova (1984). On politics of the Stolypin era reforms see Afanas'ev and Ivnitskii (1995); Ascher (2001); Avrekh (1968); Conroy (1998); Dubrovskii, 1963); Korelin (2002); Karpov (1925); Macey (1987, 1990); Pallot (1998); Sidel'nikov (1973); Simonova (1953); Teliak (1995); Tiukavkin (2001); Vronskii (1999); Waldron (1998); Williams (2006); Yaney (1961); Zenkovskii (1986); Zyrianov (2002).

[2] Druzhinin (1987), pp. 287–288, describes the failed efforts of two "liberals" in particular, K. Kavelin and A. Unkovskii. For example, they sought to make redemption contracts obligatory.

The social upheaval that resulted from Russia's entry into World War I increased social control over agricultural change. The spontaneous seizure of nobles' lands by the peasants in the summer of 1917 showed how fragile were the market institutions emerging from the grant of property rights in land. Agricultural development achieved before World War I, however, proved sustainable, giving both reforms profound economic significance. Without the abolition of serfdom and its realization in a thriving land market, particularly after the founding of a Peasants' Land Bank in 1883, the pace of industrialization in the late nineteenth and early twentieth century would have been considerably slower. Serfdom imposed too powerful a constraint on growth. The two measures also adequately served political and fiscal objectives. The repeated use of this policy instrument, large-scale agrarian reform in extreme crisis, speaks to clearly positive feedback in both political and fiscal terms.

This chapter lays the foundation of the larger concern in this book for long-run political patterns, especially those that emerge from the constraining effects of crisis. First, the government's excessive concern for order and stability was counter-productive at a time when change was desirable. Controls impeded, for example, the necessary movement of labor out of agriculture after the serf emancipation. Second, applicable to the serf emancipation, the government was unable to provide an adequate budget for restructuring. The Stolypin reforms were superior to the serf emancipation in this regard; the number of land surveyors went from zero in 1906 to nearly 7,000 by the time World War I began, for example.[3] Third, crisis conditions heightened risk in agriculture and slowed the progress of implementation. Fourth, the government permitted exaggerated expectations. When hopes of change were dashed by the use of coercion or the resistance of the peasantry, or frustrated by weak generally results, opinion turned against the reforms and the regime.

I THE ABOLITION OF SERFDOM, 1861

Extended Deliberations

The idea of ending Russian serfdom[4] was on the agenda of the Russian autocracy in the eighteenth century. In the 1750s, Grand Princess Catherine, later the ruler of Russia as Catherine the Great (1762–1796), wrote in her memoirs that serfdom was unjust and inefficient.[5] Beginning in the

[3] Fedorov (2002), 1: 371, cited in Williams (2006), p. 158.

[4] The word for serf, *krepostnoi*, designated, as evolved from the time of the origin of the regime, a peasant tied to a servitor for reasons of state interest, similar to the bondage of nobles to service to the tsar for reasons of state interest. See note 23 in Bartlett (2003), p. 58.

[5] Catherine (1859, 1957).

1760s, from the start of her rule, she pressed forward with plans to free the serfs. However, her legislative assembly, convened for the purpose of discussing this and other issues in 1767, showed its opposition and thwarted the ambitious Catherine. Her key advisor, J. J. Sievers, continued to urge her toward reform.[6] However, in her reign, serfdom deepened and even spread across Ukraine, where it had not previously existed. Meaningful agrarian reform was delayed in Russia until the next century. Elsewhere in Europe, the Napoleonic campaigns led to the liberation of the serfs, as in Prussia, for example, where serfdom was formally abolished following the humiliating Peace of Tilsit (1807).[7] Napoleon's campaign was defeated in Russia, however, which helped strengthen the centralized autocratic authority, the powers of the bureaucracy and the landowning privileges of the corporative elite.[8] Serfdom persisted through the Crimean War (1853–1856).

Policy Trials

In a continuity of stable landholding rights from the era of Catherine II, due to the priority of short-run policy goals, the autocracy in the first half of the nineteenth century did not risk liberalizing the conditions of serfdom.[9] Some kind of reform of serfdom, however, seemed on the agenda under Alexander I. In 1803, Alexander I established procedures for voluntary emancipation, should nobles wish to free their serfs with land. He also created a committee to examine "the improvement of the condition of the Baltic peasants," and he allowed that process to move to completion: the emancipation of the serfs in the Baltic area – Estland (Estonia), Kurland, and Lifland (Livonia, present-day Latvia, and southern Estonia) – carried out from 1816 to 1819. Under Alexander I, nobles therefore accommodated themselves to the idea of reform, and they read up on the use of hired labor, one of the few uncensored topics related to serf emancipation that filled the elegant published almanacs and leisure time journals.[10]

Alexander's first two small-scale efforts failed. The Baltic model of serf emancipation, a landless settlement, depressed the condition of the peasantry, decreased the size of rented lands, and increased the incidence of

6 An observation made by R. Bartlett.

7 Il'in et al. (1996), p. 44, draw a comparison between Prussia and Russia in regard to the importance of military defeat.

8 On Russian absolutism, see Troitskii (1974); Mironov (1999); Raeff (1983). On fiscal policy and absolutism in Europe, see Collins (1988).

9 This is controversial. See Walter Pintner: "In the realm of economic policy the most striking characteristic of economic administration was the predominance of a short-range, essentially hand-to-mouth view of the economic problems that was based on the belief that significant economic progress could only be achieved at such a very slow pace that it was virtually irrelevant to current policy" (Pintner [1967]), p. 253. See for another view, Barlett (2003).

10 Zakharova (1994), pp. 20–3.

peasant violence.[11] The decree on voluntary emancipation in 1803 encouraged few nobles to do so.[12] Moreover, in Russia peasant unrest was spreading.[13] As pressures for reform mounted, a third initiative followed. In 1818 the Emperor instructed his cabinet to make proposals for peasant reform, with the caveat that landlords must not be subjected to oppressive or compulsory conditions.

Before taking up this last initiative, however, Alexander died. His successor, Nicholas I (1825–1855), appointed a high-level administrative committee to study "the status of the peasantry," but the only concrete initiative that resulted was focused on Ukraine. In 1847-1848 in the non-Russian Ukraine, Nicholas carried out his so-called inventory reform. The decree instructed landowners in right-bank Ukraine to take written inventories of Ukrainian (largely Orthodox) peasants to set a ceiling on seigniorial obligations.[14] It also fixed the allotment size at a minimum, below which landlords could not reduce serf allotment land, and to which they did reduce it. This measure represented another failed effort by the autocracy. Far from being perceived by the peasants as a step toward freedom, it provoked over 300 peasants disturbances and was considered a failure.[15] In 1837, Nicholas I then took another step.

He transformed the status of peasants who resided on public, or treasury lands, to that of free agriculturalists,[16] a reform that was the most important step in the two reigns. It was a project lasting from 1837 to 1856 headed by the Minister of State Domains, Pavel Kiselev, affecting the status of a large class of Russian peasants (including peasants on crown as well as treasury lands, and those residing on land belonging to monasteries and other

[11] The 1858 "war at Makhtra" in Estonia. See Kakhk (1980).

[12] By the reign of his successor, Nicholas I, Alexander's law had led to the freeing of 33,782 male peasants, or less than one-half per cent of all serfs. Zaoinchkovskii (1954), p. 67.

[13] Bartlett (2003) observes that peasant revolt did not actually threaten the regime itself. The significance of the peasant unrest "... lay more in the realm of social psychology: ruling elites were always fearful of what rampant peasants might do, and in times of social tension, this could become a factor in elite behaviour and state policy" (p. 51). See Zaionchkovskii (1954), Ch. 1.

[14] See Moon (1999), pp. 96–7.

[15] Moon (2001b), p. 653.

[16] To this category belonged the collection of peasants not previously enserfed. The creation of Peter I, the state domains were under the Treasury control. The category embraced former *odnodvortsy* (single householders), descendants of military servitors who had settled on the southern frontiers and Siberia after serving there, and the Tatar and other non-Slavic ethnicities who resided in the Volga basin and elsewhere, including tax-paying state peasants (*chernososhnie*), Siberian plowmen (*pashennie liudi*), and peasants from the Volga and Ural regions who paid tax in furs (*iasachnie*). The number of state peasants continually increased, and, like privately owned serfs, they were subject to the poll tax, state *obrok* (oklad), and military conscription. See Zaionchkovskii (1978), p. 17; Moon (1999), p. 98; Anisimov (1989), pp. 33–58; on slavery, its demise, and the complex outcomes, see Hellie (1982); Druzhinin (1946–1958), Vols. I–II.

church institutions (secularized in 1762–1764). State villages dominated in the borderlands, the Northeast, the Southwest, and Siberia, and in some provinces, they formed nearly the entire population. Between the late eighteenth century and the time of abolition, their relative numbers rose from 39 to 52 percent of the rural population, and the lands on which they resided embraced almost half of the surface area of European Russia (940,000 of 1.9 million square miles).

Under the Kiselev reforms, "free agriculturalists" were not entirely autonomous, in that they remained under the control of the state apparatus in an essentially fiscal experiment.[17] They were charged a tax on the land instead of on the household, a provision that showed the reform's fiscal reasoning. As former state peasants, they already possessed substantially greater mobility and more choice of occupation than peasants on privately owned estates, and they already enjoyed the right to retain earnings from seasonal outwork and avoid dues in kind. In addition to these special conditions, they received new local services: land surveys, famine relief, health care, education, and assistance with technological innovation.[18]

The law on free agriculturalists served as the model in most respects for the later reform of the appanage (*udel)* lands in 1861–1863 and of the state domains in 1866 and 1886. It had the advantage of simplifying revenue collection, enforced by a system of guardianship, which provided welfare in the instance of harvest failure. The Kiselev reforms did not, however, serve as a model for the abolition of serfdom except in regard to the incidence of the main tax.[19]

Like Sievers in the eighteenth century, Kiselev aimed to improve the lives of the peasants without emancipating them. To this end, with regard for privately owned lands, he drafted a decree, issued on April 2, 1842, on obligated peasants, by which landlords voluntarily could draw up contracts with serfs to use land on a contractual basis, with the rental agreement signed by both parties. By contrast with his reform of the public sector, however, this measure had few advantages for either the producers or the nobles. The allocation of the land entirely to nobles was unattractive to the serfs, and the nobles did not wish to relinquish their rights to free labor without additional incentives.[20] The lesson learned, in short, was no less discouraging than those learned from earlier experiments. The Kiselev reforms were no no model for the private sector, where resolving conflicting claims to the land were a critically important part of the settlement for both nobles and peasants. The long period of deliberation and experimentation

17 Zaionchkovskii (1974).

18 Pintner (1967), pp. 173 ff.; Fuller (1982), pp. 34–5; and Druzhinin (1946), vol. I.

19 See Druzhinin (1946).

20 See Zaionchkovski (1954), p. 69, who notes that 0.25 percent of the peasants in the private sector were put on such contracts.

with Kiselev's reforms had resulted in no readily transferrable project and no resolution of counter claims to the same land.

Conflicting Guarantees in Manorial Law

Tradition was a powerful sanction of nobles' claims to ownership of settled land. Eighteenth-century traditions of imperial law and even older guarantees of boyar estates guarded against the destruction of the servile order. In 1785, a charter of nobles' rights incorporated their privileges while removing most of their previous obligations. Among these privileges was sole proprietorship of populated land (1764–1801). R. Bartlett has shown that for the eighteenth century this guarantee was highly significant for nobles' support of imperial policy.[21] Educated Russians of all strata in the nineteenth century accepted the notion of exclusivity of nobles' rights, much as in western Europe, norms of restricted rights were accepted, although they differed from those in Russia.[22] Without abjuring tradition, how was the state to issue new guarantees of land to the peasants?

Social caste – estates – was a component of Russia's stylized absolutist political regime, a dynamic force under the tsars. The term for social estate, *soslovie*, was used as the source of privilege in the Charter of 1785, and elite status was thus etymologically kin to that of a state institution in its permanence.[23] Thus the estate system evolved and matured in nineteenth-century Russia with full patronage of the state, by contrast with Europe, where estates were dissolving. In Russia, the regime acquired an attribute of caste. This made noble ownership of settled land a formidable principle to overturn.[24]

As in medieval Europe, however, the tsars had also guaranteed serfs' historical rights to usufruct in allotment land, a right accepted in practice if never made clear by laws.[25] Allotment land (*nadel*) belonged to serfs by custom, a community-held right to parcels among the demesne, which were distributed and redistributed to adjust allotment size to work capacity of households. The peasants exercised their rights through the repartitional land commune, whose governing unit was the regular collective gathering of village heads of households (*skhod*). Authority among the peasants was exercised through the elder (*starosta*) of the village or villages. Deprived of their land, the commune itself would appeal to the tsar. In brief, overlapping

21 Bartlett (2003), p. 48; (1994), p. 73.

22 Field (1976), pp. 57–9, see also Pipes (1999), who underscored that property rights were a privilege for the few and not a universal right.

23 Freeze (1986), p. 20.

24 Freeze (1986), p. 20; Raeff (1983).

25 Leonard (1993); Dukes (1965); Omel'chenko (1993); Raeff (1971, 1983); Troitskii (1974); and others.

claims reinforced by custom provided no easy basis for redistributing sown land between the peasants and the lords.

Pressures for Reform

In Europe, enlightenment thought was the foundation for change. In Russia, it generated anti-slavery sentiments among intellectual elites and some pressure in imperial circles for a more socially liberal policy. Liberal economic theory, common in journal publications beginning in the 1820s and 1830s, addressed concerns of landlords over the lack of incentives in the system. The economic literature shows ample concern with obvious inefficiencies of serf labor in grain production, including the high costs of its monitoring. In an address to the Council of State, Nicholas pointed to the regime's concern for the immorality of serfdom in his often quoted remark, that serfdom was "an evil, palpable to all."[26] After the threatening events in the 1848 European revolutions, the regime again began with cautious experiments. Reviving hopes of more radical reform, Nicholas permitted serfs to acquire immovable property in their own name, provided the landlord agreed.[27] The threat of revolt, however, remained significant.[28] Outbreaks were common, and they were used by Alexander in his famous 1857 pronouncement to argue that it was better to emancipate the serfs from above, in his words, than to see them do so from below.[29]

On the whole, serfs were effectively subordinated to the landlords' will in the manorial regime, and the village elder was complicit in their subordination.[30] There was little of the welfare-oriented paternalism that rationalized the slaveowner's presence on plantations and improved the conditions of slavery in the US South at around the same time. Kolchin (1987) compares the absentee mentality of Russian landlords and the paternalism of antebellum Southern planters. Even when landlords resided on their estates in Russia, with a hired German steward to run them, the Russian serfs suffered far worse material conditions than did American

[26] Cited by Field (1976), p. 57.

[27] Zaionchkovskii (1954), p. 25.

[28] Zaionchkovskii (1954), pp. 44 ff. cites the basic work by Ignatovich (1911) on the influence of rising numbers of peasant rebellions on the increasing concern of the government over serfdom, although Field (1976) and Zakharova (1984) agree that the threat probably had more to do with the shaping of reform in the late 1850s than the decision by Alexander to agree to it.

[29] Semevskii (1905); Ignatovich (1902); Okun' (1957).

[30] Hoch's (1986) argument applies to one region, Tambov, and to a large well-organized estate, essentially, both a regional and estate perspective. It is supported by common sense, in that the servile order functioned ordinarily without risk to landlords and the state of the kind of disobedience that they could not handle. Agency problems, however, tend to show up not in the estate records but in surveys, taken by outsiders. See Shcherbina (1900); Leonard (1990).

slaves.[31] There were few sanctions against maltreatment of serfs. The nobles and the government responded harshly to resistance and imposed their will by force. Indeed, part of the legacy of that era is the force used by local authorities and the conviction that serfs were unable to manage their own affairs.

This impression was strengthened by widespread resort to passive resistance, evidence of the classical agency problem and high costs of this regime. The fiscal inefficiency of agriculture under serfdom, for this reason, was probably of greater concern to the government than the threat of massive rebellion, since the poll tax (per capita) could scarcely be raised. That, and the economic inefficiency of a system that required close monitoring, were steep costs of preserving a forced labor regime. Nobles strained for profitability, and few, apart from the wealthiest, could afford to hire stewards.[32]

The total economic impact of serfdom cannot be assessed, furthermore, without regard to opportunity costs: the lack of any strong effects from the natural complementarity of Russia's regions. In the South, large estates offered better conditions for cereals production. The land was more productive – soils were more fertile – and peasants met their servile obligations by intensive labor on the demesne. Further to the North, the soils were far less fertile, and obligations were met mainly by pecuniary or mixed payments; the northern regime also tended to be less costly, however, since the conduct of agriculture was self-monitored. The North/South grain trade thrived under serfdom, but market spillovers were weak.

This is not to say that the threats to the social order were of little concern to the regime. There was some fear that the wholesale abolition of serfdom would undermine the stability of the rural regime. It was no simple matter to design a reform that would ease one kind of threat without causing another.

Timing of Reform

The peasant question came up with greater urgency after Russia's defeat in the Crimean War. Along with a surge of peasant revolt at that time, there was a leadership change brought about by the death of Nicholas I and the accession of Alexander II. The literature is clear about the impact of Russia's military defeat: the autocracy took it as a warning of "being overtaken militarily and technologically by the Western powers."[33] The failure of the tsar's armies and the diplomatic setback in the Peace of Paris (1856), which ended the war, brought home the inadequacy of the political,

[31] Kolchin (1987), p. 148–49. But see V. I. Semevskii and I. Turgenev, who wrote that landlords did have a historical responsibility for serfs' welfare. See Dolbilov (2002), pp. 69–71.

[32] Zaionchkovskii (1954), ch. 1; Leonard (1990); Aleksandrov (1976).

[33] Shanin (1985), p. 55; Rieber (1966, 1982).

military, social, and economic institutions of the country.[34] The government required a larger army and universal conscription, which required that all peasants be on equal legal footing. In the manifesto announcing the Peace of Paris, the tsar spoke of the importance that law be "equally just for all and equally protective of all."

D. Field (1976) emphasizes, however, that the exact outcome of deliberations, even then, was by no means entirely clear. Indeed, in the same passage as the above, the tsar also said that he opposed giving serfs their freedom. During the next few years, proponents of abolition remained cautious. The power of vested interests had created a conservative culture in the state bureaucracy.[35] The government actually reached a decision to adopt the more liberal of two versions of reform only after the start of a banking crisis that followed from the rampant inflation affecting major cities during the war.[36] The crisis began with high inflation following major purchases of grain near battle areas in the South, and although its effects were mainly local, there was some price instability in centers of trade, such as Nizhnii Novgorod.[37] The banking crisis then struck particularly the two capitals, Moscow and St Petersburg, a suitable background to the urgency with which discussions began again (in 1857 a new committee was set up) to examine the issue of the peasantry. On 4 December, 1858, Alexander II announced, that the decision had been taken to abolish the serfdom and prepare for a post-servile order.[38]

The banking crisis gave the resolution of the problem of serfdom a fiscal urgency.[39] The state budget could not function without stability in the banking system. State banks provided essential resources to finance extraordinary government activities, since peasants paid the burden of direct taxes in the budget. Ordinary revenues depended largely on agriculture, and the sector was too weak for Russia to remain competitive militarily in the preindustrial era. It was not technological innovation or industry that won wars in this period in Europe but putting an army into battle, Pintner (1984) observes, that is, the ability of the state to mobilize resources from the economy.[40]

34 Rieber (1966); Zaionchkovskii (1954); Zakharova (1984); Field (1976); Bartlett (2003), n. 61, p. 63, who commented on Kagan (1999), that Russian performance in the war did not discredit the tsarist regime (p. 243), by drawing attention to the author's own inconsistency in observing that the government had systematically concealed its military vulnerability.

35 See also discussion of vested interests in Semevskii (1988); Lituev (1997); Dolbilov (2002); Emmons (1963); Zakharova (1984); Rieber (1966); Moon (2001a); Pintner (1967), and others.

36 Hoch (1991).

37 Pintner (1959); Hoch (1991).

38 Field (1976), p. 61; Zaionchkovskii (1954), Ch. 2.

39 Hoch (1991).

40 Pintner (1984), p. 240.

By the mid-nineteenth century in Russia, as in most European countries, the revenue base grew chiefly by indirect taxation. Indirect taxes amounted to much more than half of all revenues, including from borrowing, yet they were confining and confiscatory. They captured surpluses from the land, from the church, from luxury consumption by elites, including nobles and merchants, from credit rationing, and from extraordinary collections including recruitment. When direct and indirect taxes were too little, then confidence in the system could be maintained only by printing money. For example, the value of assignats (paper money) fell in the 1820s after the enormous emissions of the Napoleonic years; even small copper coins could not be exchanged. In the 1830s, there was a period of stability, owing to Minister of Finance Egor Kankrin's conservative fiscal regime. He gradually withdrew assignats from circulation and generated a budget surplus. In 1841, his monetary system was introduced on exchangeable notes, but expenditures rose again during the Crimean War in the 1850s.[41]

It was not only the expenditures on the war, however, that threatened future budgetary balances. By 1858, war had come to an end. The war had only utilized some 2 percent of the populace in manpower and not nearly as much in total military expenditures as the war against Napoleon. Military expenditures were ordinarily high in the budget, around 45 percent of total expenditures.[42] Although they rose to 61 percent of total expenditures during the Napoleonic war, after falling back, they came to about 41.2 percent during the Crimean War, ignoring the government borrowing at the time.[43] Now the state needed more resources for reconstruction.

Spending projections were for railways and other instruments of the acquisition of power, as S. Hoch (1991) describes in an article on the link between the banking crisis and serf emancipation. Russia's backwardness in military engagement with western European states required new expenditures to make the economy more competitive. Among projects Hoch finds under consideration in 1857 were funds for new companies and for the first railroad network across Russia. The plans for expenditure required more credit, generally obtained by the government by internal loans, the issue of assignats.

Hoch has described the financial problems of 1857–1859 and their effect on the review of peasant status in the late 1850s.[44] The strength of the currency had declined during the war, destabilizing state credit institutions.[45] The state operated a loan bank for the landowners' long-term capital needs, a commercial bank for short-term lending to merchants, and two savings

[41] See Belousov (2000); Pintner (1967).
[42] Pintner (1984), p. 237.
[43] Pintner (1984), p. 248.
[44] Hoch (1991).
[45] Belousov (2000), pp. 44–5.

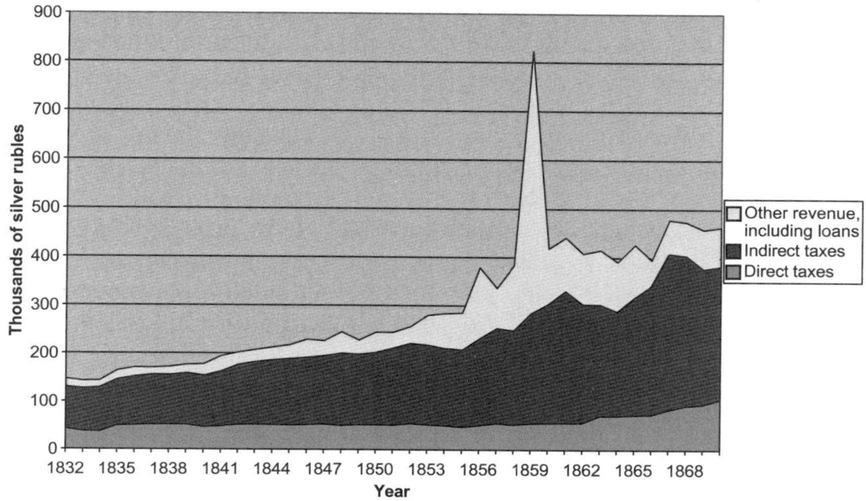

FIGURE 1.1. Composition of Russian State Revenues, 1832–1870.
Source: Compiled from Obruchev (1871); Khromov (1950), pp. 444–451.

banks used to cover state deficits. These banks, as Hoch describes, were required to take demand deposits and pay interest. They also had to provide long-term low-interest loans since private banking was nonexistent. When capital for the new projects could not be raised in St. Petersburg and Warsaw, the state reduced demand deposits by lowering interest rates on deposits in state credit institutions from 4 to 3 percent. The resulting withdrawal of deposits produced widespread insolvency that lasted until 1859, when the banks were restructured.[46] The fragility of the banking system, in turn, forced the government to review the possibility of creating a larger tax base. The government had no resort but to find other sources of revenue and the means to ensure them for the long run.

Figure 1.1 shows the scale and origin of resources used for ordinary and development projects. It also shows indirect taxes and the increasing share of loans.

The spike in the trend in Figure 1.1 for the late 1850s shows elevated levels of debt in the pre-abolition era. This would account for the urgency of an increase in permanent revenues, that is, by expanding or changing the tax base, as occurred in 1861 and in the reforms thereafter.

The tsarist regime might have extended the incidence of taxes to the nobility, and there was a proposal in Russia to institute personal income tax put forward in 1861 by Minister of Internal Affairs P. A. Valuev.

[46] Hoch (1991).

However, it was rejected by the state committee for financial reform. Elsewhere in Europe, non–estate-based tax systems affecting elites had already been introduced, although certainly not everywhere. England was the front-runner, putting in place a personal income tax by mid-century.[47] At the time of abolition, no change was envisioned in financing the deficit, and even though railroad building provided a stimulus to domestic and foreign trade, the deficit grew.[48] Bouts of high spending alternated with fiscal restraint. On average for the period from 1830 to 1870, the deficit amounted to 17 percent of budgeted spending.[49]

The Tax Base under Serfdom

In 1861, at the time of the abolition, there were 59.33 million rural dwellers in the forty-nine provinces (*gubernii*) of European Russia. Enserfed on private lands were 21.16 million peasants according to the tenth population census (*reviziia*), or 37.5 percent of the peasants of European Russia; the remainder lived on lands belonging mostly to the state and the crown.[50] Serfs were spread out unequally across the territory of Russia: 28.5 percent in the twelve non–black earth central regions, 22.5 percent in the central black earth regions, 17.8 percent in the provinces of Ukraine, only 6 percent in provinces along the Volga River, 1.9 percent in the Urals region, and 3.2 percent in New Russia.[51] Nearly 7 percent of privately owned serfs by the tenth *reviziia* (1.3 million) were domestic serfs (*dvorovye*). They performed the same services that slaves had until slavery was outlawed in 1723. Domestic serfs amounted to a particularly large percentage in black earth regions (21 percent in Ekaterinoslav and 24 percent in Kherson, Kursk, and Khar'kov).[52]

The serfs and state peasants had varied obligations as a consequence of subordination to different kinds of landlords. In European Russia, most serfs performed labor dues (*barshchina*); the rest paid dues either entirely in pecuniary form (*obrok*), or in both pecuniary and labor, a mixed form of obligation.[53] The dominance of *obrok* or *barshchina* varied by region. For example, in Ukraine, 98 percent of serfs' obligations were owed by *barshchina*. Across the North, at the time of the abolition, most were on *obrok* or

[47] Bowman (1993).

[48] Chernukha (1978), pp. 199–210.

[49] Calculated from Obruchev (1871), pp. 820–25.

[50] Troinitskii (1982).

[51] For the numbers and a description of the categories of serfs and their obligations, see Zaionchkovskii (1954), Ch. 1.

[52] See Moon (1999), p. 77.

[53] For conditions of serfdom, see Blum (1961); Bohac (1989); Ignatovich (1902); Field (1976); Gromyko (1991); Hoch (1986); Melton (1987); Milov (1998, 2000); Mironov (1999); Moon (1999); Rubinshtein (1957); Sivkov (1951), and others.

mixed forms.[54] In general, in the thirteen central non–black earth provinces, 47 percent of serfs were obligated in the *obrok* regime, 30 percent owed dues in *barshchina*, and 23 percent lived on estates where there was a mixture.[55] Overall, at the time of abolition, 71.9 percent of all privately owned serfs owed *barshchina*.[56] The differences in form of dues meant large differences in the state of the local economy, with serfs on obrok combining agriculture with extended off-season, off-estate labor for supplementary wages. *Corvee* (roughly half *obrok* and half *barshchina*) would allow punitive shifts to *barshchina* and thus increased the effectiveness, if also costs, of serfdom for landlords who sought to sell their grain.

On all estates, some obligations were exchanged for common law easements. The servitudes, or easements, of greatest importance in Russia included the right of pasturage on the lord's demesne, the right to cut wood or peat for fuel, and the right to fish in rivers and streams. Serfs on smaller estates, in principle, could expect emergency provision of food, shelter, seeds, animals, or whatever else was needed in times of harvest failure or other natural disasters. In Russia, the servitudes were held by the household (*dvor*) rather than the individual peasant, and if they were more limited on large manorial bureaucratically managed estates in the mid-nineteenth century, they remained important elsewhere on the smaller estates.[57]

The second main category of peasants in the servile era was the state peasantry, numbering 20.05 million by the tenth population census (*reviziia*). The state peasantry had experienced some reform, as described above. Except in the Baltic, right-bank Ukraine, Lithuania, and Belarus, where they had some labor obligations, they were mainly on *obrok*, and they paid taxes for the upkeep of local infrastructure and government offices. They enjoyed rights, including the possibility of transferring to another estate, acquiring property in their own name, and forming townships (*volosts*) with limited rights of self-governance. However, they could also be transferred by the state to military settlements, and they were subject to conscription.[58]

The final category included peasants resident on land owned by the imperial family, or appanage (*udel*). In more than forty-nine provinces, this embraced 2.07 million people. In addition, 240,000 worked in the

[54] Data for one district in the 1850s, Maloga in Iaroslav province, where natural resources were abundant and the land fairly good, with plentiful black earth soils, show that only 8 percent, 22 serf estates, had officially registered village elders, including eight with fairly substantial agencies headed by stewards hired by landlords to oversee the estate (Leonard [1990]).

[55] Zaoinchkovskii (1954), p. 16.

[56] Data from Ignatovich (1902), p. 47; cited in Zaionchkovskii (1954), p. 16.

[57] Anderson (1980).

[58] Zaionchkovskii (1954), pp. 28–33.

state mines, and roughly the same number belonged to other government agencies.[59]

Reform in Sight

With pressure on resources increasing due to a financial crisis and to the budgetary constraint, although the outcome of planning was not entirely clear in 1857–1858, prospects were stronger than they had ever been.[60] Emancipation had opponents, and they remained active throughout the reform preparation years. If they took defeat calmly in 1858, after the tsar's announcement, it was because they had already succeeded in softening the terms for their compensation. In preparation for the enactment, beginning in 1858, Alexander consulted with the nobility and received reports from forty-six provincial committees and deputies. By comparison with the recommendations of the Editorial Commission and the State Council, however, consultations produced small additions to already prepared documents. The nobility was acquiescent, and in the emancipation statutes the landowners' interests were mostly met.[61]

Reform in a Package of Liberalizing Measures

The statutes published on February 19, 1861, contained, as their main and most historically significant component, the liberation of serfs from bondage. The abolition was actually a series of separate laws regulating this grant of freedom and its implementation. A main provision set forth the right of peasants to permanent use of their allotment land, a right of considerable value to the westernization of tsarist Russia's image.[62]

The serf emancipation was the beginning of a stream of liberalizing measures, the "Great Reforms" (1856–1874).[63] They brought relaxed restrictions on travel, lifted censorship and improved the educational system, updating the content of instruction and granting some autonomy to universities. New judicial statutes declared equality of all before the law (although peasants were judged in separate courts) and created public trial by jury, incorporating the right of the defence to produce witnesses. Reforms improved local

[59] See Khromov (1950), pp. 82–3, who estimates over twice the number for appanage serfs provided in Zaionchkovskii (1954), p. 33. The latter's figures are not used here because he selected a smaller number of provinces for his citations and chose different dates for each category.

[60] Field (1976), p. 142.

[61] Belousov (1999); Dolbilov (2002); Emmons (1970); Field (1976); Hoch (1991); Lincoln (1982); Moon (2001a); Rieber (1966); Zakharova (1984).

[62] I am indebted to Daniel Field and David Moon for comments here.

[63] Eklof (1994); Zakharova (1992); Lincoln (1982, 1990); Bol'shakova (1996); Dzhanshiev (1896).

government by introducing the *Zemztva* organs in provinces (*gubernii*) and district (*uezdy*) to oversee economic activity and support education, medicine, and welfare. They provided for elected officials for district courts. From 1870, town government was transformed by the introduction of new structures, including an elected assembly with power to make laws. This measure was accompanied by new property qualifications for holding office, designed to secure nobles' and townsmen's compliance.[64] Reforms affected military service. The duration of active service was reduced to six or seven years; universal conscription from the age of twenty was introduced to replace recruitment. Corporal punishment in the military was eliminated, and military schools were founded (possibly one of the most significant measures spreading literacy among the male populace).[65]

To summarize their most important components, Alexander's reforms decentralized governance while freeing the labor force. Although well short of fundamentally shifting political authority to a larger governing group, these reforms did enhance the role of local institutions and stimulated social welfare programmes (Nafziger 2008). Their major limitation was that they placed no limitation on the personal powers of the autocrat, nor did they fully or immediately grant land ownership to all individual producers. Peasants' land ownership rights remained conditional on the arrangement for and payment of redemption fees.

Serf Emancipation

Although granting serfs immediate personal freedom, the state permitted the disposal of the land in stages, and terms were set forth with complicated details.[66] The terms of the reform, first, required a choice by peasants. Those who hoped to retain their whole allotment share would wait for two years, continuing in temporary further obligation to their former landlords until "charters" were registered locally. Those who did not wish to be "temporarily obligated" might take a quarter of the minimum allowed allotment and be free of further payments. By 1882, some three percent of peasants had received their one-fourth share. These *darstvenniki* (donation beneficiaries) chose relative poverty and immediate freedom; the rest remained temporarily obligated on privately owned estates and continued to owe

[64] Zakharova (1973) showed the fears of excessive democracy on the part of those who created this measure, including the author of the project, Minister of Internal Affairs P. A. Valuev, who wrote that elected officials and independent agencies should be introduced with great care and in a limited way (p. 122).

[65] For a brief review of these measures see Il'yn et al. (1996), pp. 44–53; Pirumova (1977), pp. 30–1; for more extensive treatment see Bolshakova (1996); Dzhanshiev (1896); Eklof (1994); Lincoln (1990); Mironov (1999); Starr (1972); Zakharova (1992).

[66] See the discussion in Moon (2001a), especially Ch. 8, regarding the statutes and their implementation.

quit-rent or labor dues, while waiting for the land to be theirs.[67] Nobles also had a choice. They might, if they wished, continue to subordinate the former serfs on their estates and collect rent in the form of money or labor, although the latter form of dues was to be phased out, or they might grant a settlement with concurrence of the peasant commune. Where the peasants resisted settlement, the nobles could ask the government to intervene.

State peasants already enjoyed the status of free agriculturalists and, as such, were entitled to acquire or to appropriate unpopulated state lands as property with ownership entitlements given to communities. They might transfer to urban areas or to other rural estates, and they might make contracts (including debts and wills in their own name). Four years later, in 1866, the statutes granting freedom to state peasants gave them broader ownership rights with allotments guaranteed in perpetuity and records distributed to communities. This brought the rights of state peasants and former serfs into conformity. The state peasants were granted land almost on the same condition as former serfs, that is, use was conditional upon the approval of two-thirds of the local community, and households could only acquire the land as full proprietors by paying off the capitalized *obrok* to the treasury. The difference from the terms for former serfs was that former state peasants acquired all the land at current rates of *obrok*; this might include forests, for which they would owe a tax on products used.

The legal status of free agriculturalists was distinguished from that of non-taxpaying citizens. They did not enjoy the right of unrestricted social and geographical mobility, an exclusion that lasted until the military and poll tax reforms of 1874–1887.[68] The statutes subjected peasants for judicial matters to special courts ruling on customary rather than codified law, except in capital cases. The separateness and cultural distinctions dividing peasants from other estates was a powerful force through the end of the imperial era.[69] In granting new their new status, the statutes made provision for former serfs to become full proprietors of the allotment land but only upon payment of the full redemption fee, and until then, the commune itself was the owner of the land and monitor of agreements.

In the first few years of reform, chartered agreements with the commune (*ustavnye gramoty*) were drawn up to allocate an allotment (*nadel*) to each household in the commune. The nadel consisted of a subsistence minimum amount of arable, pasture and hay meadows, and the homestead, including the garden plot, for the household's perpetual use. The size of the *nadel* varied, depending upon the soil zone (black earth, non–black earth, steppe) and regional tradition (e.g., the left-bank Ukraine required a special

67 Druzhinin (1987), p. 303.
68 Freeze (1986), p. 21.
69 Freeze (1986), p. 26.

statute because of the absence of communes). Although two years were granted for nobles, peasant communes, and government officials to draw up the charters, over half were drawn up within the first year.[70] Institutions of peasant governance were set up with local and township (*volost'*) courts. Until local courts were set up, nobles retained policing power over villages.

The second stage of reform was to be carried out within another extended interval, during which time no peasant could reject the settlements agreed upon unless the full amount, capitalized at 6 percent, were paid off. Meanwhile, landlords were encouraged to reach redemption agreements or contracts (*vykupnye sdelki*) with the land communes. For the waiting period, the government set limits to the increase of temporary obligations and ordered the commutation of labor dues. As Moon (2001) points out, however, during this period the commune and the volost' governments could withhold temporary and permanent internal passports for peasants and thus raise wages: landlords were now forced to hire labor in thin markets.

After 49 years, when interest and principle were paid back to the state, after subtracting any mortgage payments landlords owed to the state before compensation, the law transformed peasants into proprietors. Two scholars have recently reviewed the literature on whether the redemption fees reflected a fair price for the land. It was a common claim in the late nineteenth century that the overcharge was serious, but this claim cannot be justified on the basis of statistical analysis.[71] Rather than being determined by demand, the price of allotment land – the rate of redemption charges – was estimated as an accounting sum: the average of monetary dues, or *obrok*, paid per *desiatina* to landlords in the locality, capitalized at six percent.

In general, the terms were imposed by government intervention. The peasants sought as much land as was possible, especially in conditions, as in the North of Russia, where the difficult soils required more arable, than in the South. There were delays by nobles as well as by peasants. Small noble landholders had no funds for restructuring.[72] Eventually, the resources needed for structural adjustment, including education and technical assistance, were funded through new local taxes collected by the commune and the *volost'* administration. As Hoch (1991) explains, strapped local budgets were the main resource for implementing the serf emancipation through the redemption operation. By contrast with precedents in Austria and Prussia and Russia's own experiment on state lands, where the state paid the loan principal and all administrative costs, peasants' payments were to cover all interest and principal and nearly all administrative costs and all contingencies.

70 Moon (2001a).

71 See Domar (1985) and Hoch (2004).

72 Hoch (1991), p. 810.

The Reception of the Serf Emancipation of 1861

Perception of the serf emancipation varied by social group. David Macey commented that the peasants, on the whole, were disillusioned. For the peasants, he wrote,

> ... emancipation was an anti-climax. They had been granted their personal freedom, together with such specific legal rights as the right to marry, conclude civil contracts, own land, and bring suit; but their relationship to their former owners continued much as before. As a consequence, large numbers of disillusioned peasants refused in the first two years to fulfil obligations to their former owners and engaged in other forms of disorder.[73]

Rumors that the real freedom was coming and that the charters were a trap evoked some resistance in the beginning. The election of officials for volost' administration in 1861 and 1863 caused fierce opposition, for example, especially in parts of Ukraine and across black earth Russia, where armed force was used to suppress unrest.[74] Most charters were drawn up by 1862, but by the beginning of 1863, over 50 percent of those charters had not been signed by the peasants.[75] Unrest occurred in forty-two of the forty-three provinces where the reform went into force. The resistance to land charters in many areas took on a violent form.[76] By the summer of 1863, however, the movement died down.

On the frontier, where the redemption fees were relatively low, with the exception of Perm, the redemption process neared completion by 1871. By contrast, in the central black earth and non–black earth central areas, where settlements tended to be clustered near urban areas, by 1871, the redemption process had not been completed on roughly half of the land. Low rates of redemption, associated with high cost of the land, strongly suggest the impact not only of the nobles' resistance but also of the crisis conditions in agriculture in the 1860s. Peasants in these areas could have had little confidence in the new order for over a decade.

Perceived peasant dissatisfaction affected intellectuals' response to the serf emancipation. The imposition of temporary obligation to landlords rather than an immediate bestowal of freedom on former serfs, along with the brutal repression of peasant protest, provoked an article, for example, by Nikolai Ogarev entitled "Analysis of the New Serfdom" in *The Bell,* published in London by Alexander Herzen and Ogarev. Radical intellectuals found their journal, *The Contemporary*, published domestically, banned for eight months in 1862. Leading journalists were arrested. This suppression

[73] Macey (1987), p. 11.
[74] Zaionchkovskii (1954), Ch. 5; Field (1989).
[75] Zaionchkovskii (1954), pp. 177–78.
[76] See the episode in Bezdna, described and analyzed in Chapter 2 of *Rebels in the Name of the Tsar* by Field (1989).

of response to serf emancipation widened the rift between the government and the elites, and when the radical movement next surfaced, it was more united, more skilful in conspiratorial organization, and more tending to violence.[77]

The nobility on the whole responded with passivity to the decree. Some nobles from the provinces of Tula and Smolensk protested the terms of emancipation in hopes of representation in government, but this protest was suppressed. Although less well-off nobles were put at a considerable disadvantage in labor costs after serf emancipation, the decree was received, on the whole, as one that accommodated noble interests, and in 1883, in a populist era, the government ended its tolerance of voluntary compliance and made redemption contracts obligatory.

The most important reflection on the reform's success with the public, however, was the dispute over the claim that the amount expected by nobles for the land was exorbitant, given the small average size of the *nadel* (Ianson 1877). With Ianson, whose findings were not challenged, there was a chorus of considerable publicistic work arguing that the reform had been seriously flawed: redemption payments had worsened conditions for the nobility as well as for the peasantry and had deprived the treasury of budgetary resources.[78] At this time, in the late 1880s and early 1890s, there was forceful support in educated circles behind the abolition of redemption payments and resettlement of poor peasants on state property.

The Medium Term Impact: Regional Divergence

Analysis and formal estimates of the rate of institutional and productivity change follow in later chapters. The concern in the following section on medium term impact is the background of the Stolypin reforms of 1906 to 1911.

The impact of reform was not uniform across regions or across former categories of peasants (serfs and state peasants). Former state peasants in the frontier areas had more generous land allotments, sometimes on very good land. Former serfs generally acquired less land than they held before emancipation. In 1860, taking the two categories together, the average *nadel* per male soul was 4.8 *desiatiny* (1 *desiatina* = 1.092 hectares) of arable. By 1900, the average *nadel* shrank to 2.6 desiatiny, far less than their guaranteed subsistence allotment of six desiatiny. The dramatic decline of allotment size was particularly noted in locales around urban areas, where population clustered.

77 For the intellectual response to emancipation, see a review in Saunders (1992), pp. 239–45, and a general history of radical thought in Malia (1961); Gleason (1983); Bartlett (1984); Venturi (1983); Berlin (1978), and others.

78 Druzhinin (1987), p. 290; Hoch (2004), p. 247.

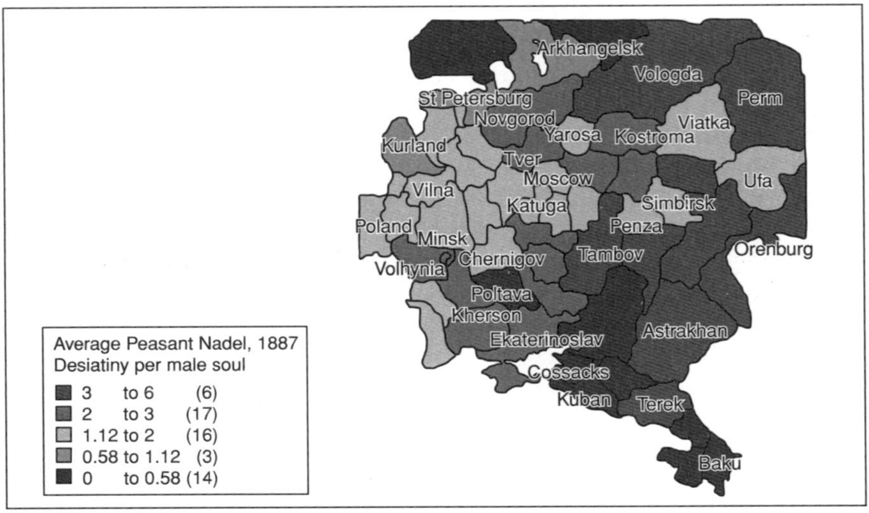

FIGURE 1.2. Average Peasant Allotment Size (allotment land per male soul) by Region, 1887.
Source: "Raspredelenie zemel' po vladeniiam v 1877 i 1887 godakyh," *Materialy vysochaishe uchrezdennoi 16 noiabria 1901 g. Kommissii* (1902), Issue 1, chapter 2, table 3, pp. 29–31.

Figure 1.2 shows for 1887 a map of the nineteenth century imperial Russian provinces to illustrate the range in size of the nadel by region.

The map shows that the *nadel* was larger in frontier areas, and that the most crowded regions were those where the average *nadel* was smallest. Hoch (2004) has criticized the aggregation in these estimates of the size of nadel, but for the purpose of establishing a range in assessing the results of reform, the *nadel* size and its decline are useful. In the populated black earth southern regions, the average allotment size fell by half between 1861 and 1900. To be sure, those with "the beggars' share" included former house serfs, who were particularly numerous in black earth southern regions. Also, increasing flows of seasonal migrant labor must have relieved to some extent the pressure on the land in all areas, since increased seasonal earnings are observed especially in the most crowded areas near urban settlements, where jobs were available.[79] In parts of northern Russia, by contrast, the average nadel was larger at the beginning and grew. The broad disparities among regions in regard to the arable/labor ratio can be seen in columns 3, 4 and 5 in Table 1.1.

[79] From 1860 to 1900, in Kursk, the average allotment declined from 3.1 to 1.7 *desiatiny*, and in Chernigov, from 3.9 to 2.0 *desiatina* per male soul (Zyrianov [2002], p. 163).

TABLE 1.1. *Regional Indicators of Agricultural Change in Russia, 1860–1900*

Region	1871 Meadows, as % of Arable	1877 A/L*	1887 A/L*	1900 A/L*	1860–1900 Sown Land Per Cap, Growth, %	1860–1900 Grain Harvest, Per Cap, Growth, %	1860–1900 Potato Harvest Per Cap Growth, %	1860s Yield**	1881–1900 Yield***
Central Industrial	34	1.88	1.95	2.53	−32.96	−0.21	2.76	3.58	2.93
Central Black Earth	19	2.42	2.48	1.88	−45.78	−37.35	118.35	3.77	5.44
Middle Volga	56	3.05	3.56	3.00	−41.08	−28.03	132.21	4.05	5.29
Ural	64	4.44	5.30	4.50	−20.52	22.66	132.58	3.37	5.91
Southern Volga	300	5.61	6.17	9.23	−38.81	−24.48	209.70	2.62	3.58
New Russia	186	2.10	2.15	3.76	−24.03	29.96	193.27	4.53	3.88
Ukraine	41	2.25	2.50	1.62	−34.23	0.58	95.17	3.53	5.37
West	26	1.40	1.40	2.32	−32.45	−4.58	140.40	3.19	4.69
North and Northwest	53	1.40	2.10	6.53	−24.12	−3.72	169.56	3.27	5.39
Baltic	89	1.13	0.80	...	0.71	4.54	202.43	4.69	6.79

* Allotment Land per Agricultural Laborer.

** Yield, 1864–1866.

*** Yield, Allotment, Rye.

Central Industrial	Vladimir, Moscow, Kaluga, Tver, Iaroslav, Kostroma
Central Black Earth	Kursk, Orel, Tula, Riazan, Tambov, Voronezh
Middle Volga	Saratov, Simbirsk, Penza, Kazan, Nizhegorod, Ufim
Ural	Viatka, Perm
Southern Volga	Samara, Orenburg, Astrahan
New Russia	Bessarabia, Kherson, Tavrida, Ekaterinoslav, Don
Ukraine	Podolsk, Kiev, Volynsk, Khar'kov, Chernigov, Poltava
West	Mogilevsk, Minsk, Vitebsk, Smolensk, Vilensk, Kovensk, Grodnensk
North and Northwest	St. Petersburg, Pskov, Novgorod, Olonetz, Vologda, Arkhangel
Baltic	Lifland, Kurland, Estland

Source: Svod statisticheskikh svedenii po sel'skomu khoziaistvu Rossii k kontsu XIX v. (St Petersburg: Department of Economics and Agricultural Statistics, Ministry of Agriculture and State Domains, 1902), vyp. 1, pp. 20–24; 82–85; 156–171.

Table 1.1 would be more an indictment of the serf emancipation in terms of farm fragmentation if all of the land in use were counted. This is by no means the case. In Chapter 6, the non-*nadel* arable is taken into consideration and the picture comes out differently. The figures in Table 1.1 are presented mainly for an overall impression that could have been formed at the time by the existing statistics on the *nadel*. It gives an impression of poverty and backwardness of the Russian peasants in some regions. One point is indisputable, that some regions remained over time far more densely settled than others, showing the slow introduction of incentives for outmigration from the village.

Until the 1880s, restrictions on outmigration, except where there was obvious overcrowding, were the main barrier to improvement in conditions shown above. Regulations and restrictions on travel and departure from villages were monitored by local registries and communal authorities.[80] The regulatory regime was perhaps more severe in the South, where there were large depressed areas of highly fragmented holdings.[81] Research based on the census of 1897 for Poltava and Kharkov suggests little evidence of marked stratification of wealth among these peasants, but the state of small impoverished holdings contrasts with many other areas of the country, especially in the industrializing North.[82]

By contrast, in the North, legal restrictions on leaving the village seem to have had little impact. There was some movement out of agriculture entirely and some resettlement in more fertile regions. In at least one northern region, St Petersburg surroundings, migration was extensive. Rural wages can be shown empirically to have responded to urban wages, presenting a positive picture of agricultural performance and villages enriched by remittances. This is far different from a picture drawn on villages in the lower Volga.[83] In the increasingly urbanized and commercialized Northwest, to a lesser extent in the interior central non–black earth regions, and certainly in the Baltic and the Southwest of Russia, the figures reporting *nadel* are therefore less informative than might be thought about peasant welfare.[84] Indeed, the northern villages had a strikingly different governance structure, on the whole. The communal authorities allowed a lax regime favoring off-farm seasonal labor and some commerce. In the South, the repartitional commune was dominant, although repartition was probably very rare, and farm workers were more intensively engaged in agricultural production. Household supported themselves mainly by their allotment holdings and marginal lands brought into production. Lands on the frontier, which belonged mainly to the state,

[80] Anderson (1980); Druzhinin (1978).

[81] Korelin (2002), pp. 240–41; on the economy, see Gatrell (1986).

[82] Koval'chenko et al. (1982), Table 11–1, pp. 231 ff. See also Field (1989).

[83] Borodkin, Granville, and Leonard (2007).

[84] See a study of the commercializing region in late tsarist Russia by Economakis (1998).

provided room for considerably more expansion. To be sure, conditions in frontier areas were not entirely attractive, since the state prohibited the transformation of state land into privately owned land.[85]

Some estimate of land peasants came to acquire and their relative position among all landowners can be seen in Table 1.2. Peasant allotment land showed up at a constant ratio of 56 percent of the total taxable arable in use in the whole period, but land purchased by peasants increased from 2 percent of all privately owned land in 1877–1878 to 10 per cent in 1905. Nobles' percentage of the privately owned arable declined from 35 to 24 percent between 1877 and 1905.

While Table 1.2 shows gains made by the peasantry, it does not show the dynamic over time. The pace of peasant land purchases picked up after emancipation. The peaks of land purchases by peasants occurred in the 1870s through the 1890s. A picture of regional purchases of land by peasants, provided below by a bar chart in Figure 1.3, shows that the growth rate of peasant purchases of land especially build in the 1870s.

The estimates in Figure 1.3 of annual growth by period of peasant landholding by region thus show a rise in purchases in many regions once the period of temporary obligation ended. Ukraine was an exception because emancipation itself was delayed until the crisis was over. In three regions, the Southwest, Northwest and Ukraine, the annual average growth of purchases for the whole period (1875–1900) was significantly higher than for the rest of the European provinces. This fits with the impression gained elsewhere that these were areas of considerable attraction for the quality of the land and potential for agriculture, which greatly exceeded that of other regions. The Southeast, Southwest and Ukraine, and to some extent, the Northeast, experienced a boom around the turn of the century, possibly a response to more lax laws regulating migration.[86]

These indicators of the expansion of peasant holdings may also point to pockets of poverty. The slowing of the expansion of peasant holdings for the central and Middle Volga regions in the 1890s are an example. But such a conclusion would require supportive evidence of the rate of population growth and out-migration, including seasonal migration. Moreover, it would require a check of state peasant settlements, not included in the above figure for private landholding. To summarize the significance of the data above, in brief, the Southeast, Southwest, Ukraine and blackearth areas of the North would seem to have had vital land markets by the end of the nineteenth century.

[85] Even after the Stolypin reforms, in 1911, when the Council of Ministers prepared a decree turning the *otruby* and *khutory* into private property, the Duma rejected the idea that state lands might be converted into private holdings, and so in imperial Russia, this did not happen. Safronov (1977), p. 277.

[86] Anfimov (1969, 1980); Kingston-Mann (1990); Field (1989).

TABLE 1.2. *Land Distribution by Ownership, European Russia, 1877–1905*

	Desiatiny (1 desiatina = 2.7 acres)					
		% of Cultivated Land			In % of all Cultivated Land	
Categories of Land	1877–1878 Millions	Including State Lands	Excluding State Lands	1905 Millions	Including State Lands	Excluding State Lands
State and public lands	167.9	45		154.7	39	
Total land excluding state lands	(209.1)	2		(240.5)		
Peasant allotment land	116.7	31	56	133.8	33.9	56
Total owned by private persons:	(92.4)			(108.8)		
Nobles	73.1	19	35	58.2	14.7	24
Peasants	5.0	1	2	24.7	6.3	10
Merchants and industrialists	11.5	3	1	16.7	4.2	7
Others	2.8	1	1	7.2	1.8	3
TOTAL	377.0	100	100	395.2	100	100

Sources: Antsyferov (1930), pp. 20–21; Shanin (1985), vol. 1, p. 137; *Statistika zemlevladeniia 1905* (St. Petersburg, 1907), pp. 188–189.

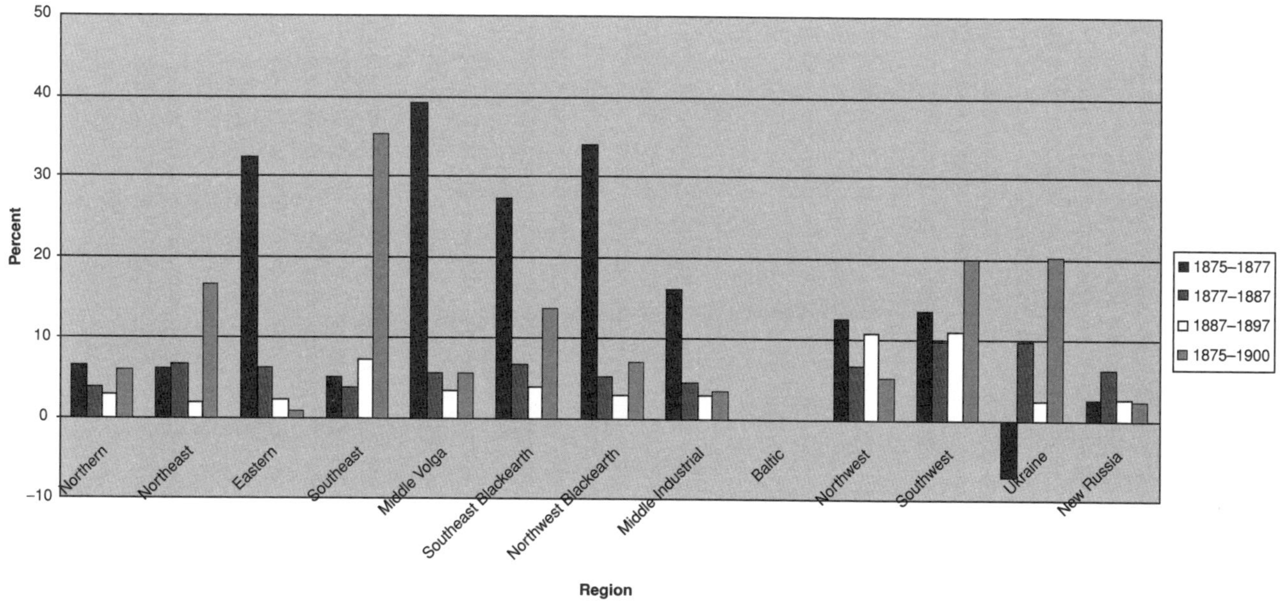

FIGURE 1.3. Average Annual Growth of Peasants' Landed Property (in %, 1875–1900).
Source: "Dopolnenie II k tabl. O razpredelenii oblagaemhykh zemel' mezhdu kategoriami vladel'tsev," *Materialy vysochaishe uchrezdennoi 16 noiabria 1901 g. Kommissii* (1902), Issue 1, ch. 1, pp. 72–73.

This summary in tabular form confirms conclusions by Gregory regarding rising effective demand for farmland and rising farm income. What do these tables display regarding earnings and welfare after reform? To the history of allotment land, its size and scale, one must add, at a minimum, taxation for a truer picture. The government continued to collect taxes mainly from the peasants.[87] Peasant arrears in the redemption fees, constant early on at roughly 20 percent, probably were not excessively onerous, but they were eventually cancelled in 1906, which suggests their political sensitivity.[88] Gregory concludes that on average, some 6 percent of household income was paid in direct taxes, but this figure differed dramatically by region.[89] The burden of indirect taxes may have been far more substantial, especially in cities where there were farm migrants and where land taxes were significant. That the government did not raise direct taxes at this time shows an operative constraint, and the continued rise in indirect taxes would have exceeded the comfortable threshold. Anthropometric data supports Gregory's view, that on the whole, from a regional sampling, peasants were not as impoverished as once was thought, and certainly by 1900, consumption was improving (Mironov 2010), which provides a case for saying that indirect taxes were also tolerable in this era.

There are many views about the depth of rural poverty in late imperial Russia.[90] The demand for land rose, and nobles sold their holdings to peasants, showing a rising purchasing power. Non-*nadel* purchased and rented land were not included in public reports about the size of the *nadel*, which used as a proxy for the land/labor ratio. At this time in imperial Russia, in the 1880s and 1890s, in a period of relative macroeconomic stability, informal arrangements may well have mitigated the poverty that was officially reported.

One historical institution that cannot entirely be written off by those favoring the representation of peasants as market-oriented and advancing rapidly in the late imperial period is the constraint on production imposed by the repartitional commune, which continued to dominate as a form of peasant governance.[91] However, the authority of the commune varied from locale to locale. Even Lenin understood that the commune was a cauldron of views and behaviors, some of which enforced tsarist impositions and

87 In 1899, these amounted to 92.3 million in redemption fees, 9.3 in the tax on land, 45.8 in district taxes, and 46.1 in community taxes. Shvanebakh (1903), p. 139.

88 Although peasants probably had paid off what was due by the early twentieth century. See Hoch (1994).

89 Gregory (1994), p. 53.

90 Hoch (1994).

91 Among works on this issue, see Aleksandrov (1976); Atkinson (1983, 1990); Bartlett (1990); Bideleux (1990); Borodkin and Leonard (1994); Goriushkin et al. (1977); Leonard (1990); Mironov (1990); Male (1971). The repartitional Land Commune is discussed further in Chapter 4 on Property Rights.

others promoting resettlement and individual land use.[92] On aggregate, as observed above, sweeping repartitions of the land were more and more rare after 1861, and a law in 1893 limited them to at most, every twelve years. The continued demographic pressure for small partial repartitions and collective grazing perpetuated the general system of collective protection of peasant welfare. In 1903, the government attempted to remove the fiscal authority exercised by the land commune over redemption payments, but the commune remained powerful in the countryside through the era of the Stolypin reforms. It is to that topic, that this chapter now turns.

2 THE STOLYPIN LAND REFORMS, 1906–1910, AND THE DECLINE OF THE RUSSIAN LAND COMMUNE

The policy background of the Stolypin reforms lies in the 1890s in the ongoing public discussion of the role of the commune. The general impression of Marxist revolutionaries and others was that agricultural backwardness stemmed from Russia's communal traditions, while populists defended the commune as a central feature of Russian culture and an agency of equalization. In both views, institution symbolized enduring features of the Russian economy. Frustration with relative backwardness –an impression reinforced by pockets of deep poverty – was felt in the famous remark by industrialist and finance minister Sergei Witte in his report on the budget of 1899, that no country in Western Europe was so frequently in the grips of famine or had a peasantry so impoverished.[93]

Witte argued to the Tsar that the economy should be driven by an entirely independent peasantry. Although at that time his views were not accepted, he succeeded in getting the promulgation of a decree in 1903, by which he sought to abolish the commune's authority over out-migration. This decree was weakened by contradictory language, but in effect, it took the major step of ending the fiscal authority of the commune over the village. This decree anticipated a key component of the Stolypin reforms.

Background: State Finance and Social Upheaval

An era of macroeconomic stability was introduced in Russia in the 1880s by the minister of finance, Nikolai Bunge (from 1881). It lasted through the era of Sergei Witte, who introduced the gold standard in 1895, boosting Russia's investment potential and budgetary resources by accessibility of

[92] This application of the Hegelian dialectic in Lenin's understanding was also the reason for his support for the commune, freed of "feudal residuals" in the 1920s. Goriushkin (1977), pp. 4–5.

[93] Simonova (1973), p. 243.

foreign loans. His policies also helped railroad building accelerate.[94] The expansion of railroads more than doubled, the infusion of foreign investment capital spread the outcomes to new sectors of industry in central regions of the country.[95] The highest rates of growth came between 1896 and 1899 and 1909 and 1913. From 1870 to 1897 Russia experienced a 25-fold increase in the production of coal and 200-fold increase in the production of oil.[96] Witte led talks at the beginning of Nicholas II's reign (1894–1917) for structural reform to further improve the economy. He initiated measures to increase investment, advance financial institutions, and extend transportation infrastructure, while keeping budgets stable.

In these years, the treasury emerged from deficit. The budget was balanced by increases primarily in the rates of indirect taxes. Meanwhile, outwork was improving rural income.[97] Tax revenues doubled in the 1890s, and other state revenues grew by six times. It was auspicious, to be sure, that the treasury still had difficulty covering extraordinary expenditures. Between 1890 and 1900 and between 1900 and 1913 the ordinary and extraordinary expenditures of the budget doubled. Meanwhile, payment on the state debt rose between 1861 and 1901 from 50 to 275 million rubles and by 1913 to roughly 460 million. Military expenditures, which had fallen to 30 percent of the budget, rose briefly during the Russo-Japanese war to some 6.5 billion rubles, over twice the size of the annual budget. They had to be funded by extraordinary resources.[98]

Defeat in the Russo-Japanese war reminded the government of another era, except that this time, the public criticism of Russia was not led by thoughts of renewal, as after the Crimean War. It was more sharply focused on misallocated resources and the need for more radical change. Military defeat in the Russo-Japanese War led, in other words, to urban and rural unrest at a level far exceeding what it had been after the Crimean War.

1905 was the crucial year. The country was confronted with a massive peasant upheaval that began along the Volga and spread elsewhere after 1905, and the peasant question came again to dominate politics in now unstable financial and fiscal conditions. In May, a congress of peasant representatives established an All-Russian Peasant Union, and radical organizers formulated demands for redistribution of noble landholding to make more land available to peasants. The imperial regime cancelled redemption fees owed by peasants (Nov. 3, 1905). It then had to come up with a way to make up for the loss of some eighty million rubles per year from the category of extraordinary revenues. The minister of finance proposed a personal

94 See Gregory (1994).
95 See Part III.
96 Borodkin (2006).
97 The incidence of indirect taxes may well have affected rural dwellers who worked in urban areas off-season.
98 Bovykin (1989), p. 178; Gregory (1994).

income tax at a low rate of 2 to 5 percent, with compensation to businesses by eliminating the tax on industry. It was rejected,[99] but it would have eased Russia's reliance on indirect taxes, which more than doubled between 1880 and 1901 (393 to 819.6 million rubles), while the relatively fixed direct taxes rose only from 172.9 to 220.9 million rubles. Indirect taxes fell on such basic products as kerosene, matches, tobacco, and spirits, purchases of urban dwellers who had led the revolution of 1905.[100]

In the last months of 1905, a run on bank deposits drained the newly formed commercial sector of vital stability in a difficult period, and financial chaos threatened further instability. R. Gorlin, in his study of tax reform, describes the state of crisis in Russia in 1905:

> The disastrous war with Japan and the revolutionary disturbances of 1904–5 dramatically demonstrated the consequences of inferior industry and technology, as well as the dangers of low cultural levels and living standards. Simultaneously, these shocks made it even more difficult for the government to launch a program of substantial improvements by creating a serious crisis in Russian finances. As a result of dislocations in the country's industry, agriculture, commerce, and transportation due to military mobilization, the strike movement, and loss of authority by government agencies, normal revenue totals in 1904 and 1905 were actually below that of 1903.[101]

Sergei Witte eventually obtained a loan from the French stock exchange for nearly one billion rubles that allowed Russia to stay on the gold standard but added to an already massive state debt, entailing larger interest payments and the complete liquidation of short-term loans.[102]

Looking back at the years 1905 and 1906 in his memoirs, Witte wrote that the crisis represented an opportunity. Referring to the months in the spring of 1906, before he resigned from the government, he recalls advising the tsar even as he was attempting to stave off financial catastrophe, to move immediately forward with a proposal for the Duma to restructure the peasant economy:

> The Council at this meeting [5 March] declared that among important [programs] was a speedy end to the work under preparation on peasant affairs, since the question of restructuring the way of life of the peasants was, without question, the most urgent and substantial of these.[103]

Later, writing to the emperor on April 14, he warned, in particular, that the Duma would hold the government hostage to revenues and press forward with its own reform program if the Cabinet did not act first. In effect, he was still advising the government on budgetary matters. The so-called October

[99] Until midway through World War I, see Bovykin (1989), pp. 188–89; Bowman (1993).
[100] Shvanebakh, pp. 31, 100, 104.
[101] Gorlin (1977), p. 247.
[102] Bovykin (1989), p. 184; Gregory (1994); Gorlin (1977), p. 247.
[103] Witte (1991), p. 601.

Manifesto, granting a semi-constitutional order, and the Fundamental Laws of 1906, showed that far more than the budget was at stake: agrarian reform was only one of a larger design of reforms.

Stolypin's agrarian reform was produced in a way that undercut the voices from below and eased the concerns of the landed nobility over confiscation. By imperial edict of November 9, 1906, the reform was framed under Article 87 of the new Fundamental Laws,[104] which allowed the government, when the Duma was not in session, to act independently. Avoiding confrontation with noble representatives in the Duma, Stolypin was able to equalize rights among members of taxed and untaxed estates and end discriminatory laws against the peasant estate. He accorded peasants direct voting rights in local government elections and allowed peasant smallholders to vote in the landlords' curia. By avoiding confrontation with peasant representatives in the Duma, he was able to secure the privileges attached to nobles in local government and reject the idea of confiscation.[105]

Reform was also accompanied by the announcement that force would be used. In the village, harsh means could be used to exert control over the process of reform. Reform was bundled with repression at a time of instability.[106]

Reform

Prime Minister Peter Stolypin's reforms have been described in detail in a rich scholarly literature.[107] They reflected long deliberations and a crisis-response, but this time, mainly to spreading peasant rebellion. Their aim was to secure a more supportive base among the peasantry by building up individual household proprietorship in place of communal agriculture. Many peasants gained entitlements to parcels of land, especially in non-black earth regions, and they withdrew land from the commune and enclosed it where the commune was supportive of their requests. Communes too, at a later stage, gained assistance in land reorganization.

The main laws of June 14, 1910, and the Land Settlement Act of May 29, 1911, together with the imperial edict, have been called a two-phased reform: the first broke down the authority of the commune and helped individual families set up separate homesteads, taking their allotment land with them, and the next, more conciliatory after 1911, worked with the commune to rearrange holdings at the inter-communal level without changing

104 Granted by the government in concession after the Revolution of 1905.

105 Pallot (1999).

106 Macey (1987), p. 224: "Stolypin spelled out his joint policy of repression *and* reform in two government reports on 15 August and 24 August."

107 On the Stolypin reforms see Afanas'ev and Ivnitskii (1995); Ascher (2001); Avrekh (1968); Dubrovskii (1963, 1975); Macey (1987, 1998); Pallot (1998); Simonova (1953, 1987); Tiukavkin (2001); Vronskii (1999); Williams (2006); Yaney (1982); Zenkovskii (1986); Zyrianov (2002); and a historiographic review in Teliak (1995).

the status of the land.[108] Tenure changes in some communes, where there had been no repartition for many years, were made automatic, and this, at a stroke, eliminated communal structures across black– and non–black earth Russia. Land was made available for purchase through the Peasant Land Bank. The bank provided start-up short-term credit and also long-term mortgage-based investment credit. To obtain this credit, it was not necessary to be a family or household after the 1911 law on land settlement, which met a long-term need and allowed group investment and enclosures so that land was kept in either communal or household hereditary tenure. For enclosure, the reorganization of household land, a simple majority of households had to approve; a two-thirds majority was required if the entire commune was being enclosed. The reform also targeted governance and rights. Care was taken that individual peasants maintained rights to common lands, meadows, forests, and other non-arable common resources.

In areas that underwent reform, farming in strips was eliminated and servitudes to which peasant lands had been subject were removed. Where reform was well advanced, plots were consolidated and enclosed. The restructuring took place by either creating small farms on the edge of the collective's land (*otrub*) or more substantial enclosed farms from the entire of the communes' property (*khutora*). The titles to these holdings were undergirded with new rights for peasants. In 1911, the government granted the partitioning of pastures.[109]

Along with these measures, the government organized assistance and provided funds for technical assistance and infrastructure development. The Ministry of Agriculture was reorganized to oversee the reform. The Chief Administration for Land Settlement and Agriculture and the Committee for Land Settlement Affairs managed the land reform and had oversight over provincial officers and inspectors.[110] Their aim was to increase the area of land at the disposal of the peasants and access to financing through the Peasant Land Bank. New lands, previously belonging to the crown and state in central Russia and Siberia, were added to the fund of land available for purchase.

Immediate Outcomes

No delay inhibited the implementation of the Stolypin reforms by contrast with a decades-long drawn out implementation of serf emancipation. The use of force to separate holdings from communal property was common, but there is also evidence of peasants' demand for consolidation of their

108 Rogalina (2002).
109 Pallot (1999).
110 Pallot (1999), pp. 2–3.

holdings. After 1906, land purchase by peasants spread far faster and wider than immediately after serf emancipation, and peasant landholdings were modernized. Between 1908 and 1913, demand for agricultural machines increased so significantly that the domestic production of agricultural machines approximately doubled.[111]

The pace of implementation was aided by panic selling of noble land in the black earth area. Parcels were transferred by the intermediary of the Peasant Land Bank or sold on the open market. It seems likely that roughly two million desiatiny a year were transferred to the peasants between 1906 and 1917.[112] By 1915, an area of land roughly the size of England had been transformed into an area of small peasant landholding, and roughly nine percent of all allotment land had been consolidated, or removed from communal holding.[113] Between 1906 and 1915 one-fifth of all households had departed from the land commune; 10.7 percent of households, with 9.5 percent of all allotment land, had their holdings consolidated in European Russia.[114] By 1917, there were probably 7.7 million peasant farms in all.[115] To be sure, the spontaneous consolidation of holdings had begun even before the Stolypin reforms, as a consequence of the end of the fiscal authority of the commune in 1903.

Of those who undertook the reconstruction either by purchasing land on their own or through the Peasant Land Bank, 59 percent were individual households and 41 percent were group or inter-communal organizations.[116] From 1906 to 1917, more than ten million *desiatiny* were transferred by the bank to peasants, who used the bank as a financial intermediary and real estate agency. Since there was a ceiling on how much land could be transferred to any individual family (six allotments), this meant that a substantial number of small peasants received land in this fashion. The reform also allowed wealthier peasants to improve their holdings.[117] By contrast with what once was thought, there was no slacking off of the pace of reform from 1910 to 1914, according to V. Tiukavkin.[118] By 1916, according to N. Oganovskii, the peasants' share of actively cultivated land had already climbed from 56 to 89.1 percent. Flax, hemp, and vegetables came almost entirely to be produced on land belonging to peasants, along with 94 or 95 percent of the livestock.[119]

111 Gatrell and Davies (1990), p. 147.
112 Khromov (1967), pp. 495 ff.
113 Williams (2006), p. 114, citation of research results by Davydov (2003), p. 260; Fedorov (2002), 1: 371;
114 Jasny takes this data from Pavlovsky (1930), p. 135; Jasny (1949), p. 142.
115 Oganovskii (1921), p. 82.
116 Rogalina (2002), pp. 546–47.
117 Khromov (1967), pp. 495 ff.
118 Tiukavkin (2001).
119 Jasny (1949), p. 145; from Oganovskii (1922), pp. 78–9.

As before, regional differences remained important in how agriculture changed. Again, peasants in the central areas – around the urban areas of Moscow and St. Petersburg and in the central agricultural and industrial regions – found their per capita cultivated acreage continuing to shrink.[120] In the South, the Lower Volga, and the Southwest, peasants gained significant amounts of farmland. The pressure of population was relieved in the central areas by the government's active support for migration. Between the law encouraging settlement of June 6, 1904, and 1912, on average, 350,000 households per year went to Siberia.[121]

The overall positive impact of reform on the peasantry is emphasized by a number of scholars, including N. Rogalina, V. Tiukavkin, G. Yaney, and D. Macey,[122] who notes the special consideration loans granted to indigent peasants by the Peasant Bank. Pallot has shown, however, that the state had to use force to get peasants to start land reconstruction with the sale of their lands and creation of *otruba* and *khutora*.[123] Even Rogalina, who emphasizes the positive, points out that failure to accommodate poor peasants and ordinary members of the commune was the Achilles heel of the Stolypin reforms and that government intervention alienated massive numbers of peasants.[124]

Also, as a result of wholesale rapid transfers from collectives to individual households, allotment land remained highly fragmented in some regions. This locked the newly reformed farms into subsistence agriculture, with peasants trapped in traditional occupations by titles to the land. S. Dubrovskii (1975) found that landowners could hire winter laborers among impoverished peasants for one-third or one-half the wage of the harvest season.[125] There is ample evidence of continuing regional poverty showing up in aggregrates. Wheatcroft, for example, reestimated per unit (household) livestock ownership, one measure of wealth. The numbers of peasant households possessing no or only one working horse went from 55 percent in the late 1880s to 63.5 percent in 1912. The share with three or more shrank from 23 percent in the late 1880s to 14.3 percent in 1912.[126] The distributional extremes of rich and poor, the inheritance of fifty years of maturation of a postcolonial-type political economy following the flawed serf emancipation left the countryside with a bimodal structure, a few large

[120] Antsyferov (1930), p. 26, provides a list of provinces with increased hectares ploughed, including the South, by 52.6 percent, the Lower Volga, by 51.2 percent, the Southwest (13.3), the Middle Volga (9.9), and others; the central agricultural region experienced decline by 6.2 percent and central industrial by 15.5.

[121] Brutskus (1922), p. 84.

[122] Macey (1987).

[123] Pallot (1998).

[124] Rogalina (2002), p. 554.

[125] Dubrovskii (1975), p. 275.

[126] Wheatcroft (1994), p. 254.

privileged landowners surrounded by small peasant holders. Most important, no substantial and loyal segment of well-off peasants with secure property rights materialized in support of the legitimacy of the tsarist regime in February (March) 1917. When the imperial order collapsed, there was no evident support by the peasants for continued land reform under parliamentary rule, and the more radical peasant demands were realized after the Bolshevik coup, ending parliamentary rule in October (November) 1917.

In summary, under Stolypin the government reinforced the institution of settled farming largely as a consequence of peasant revolt and for the sake of acquiring support for the embattled regime among the peasantry. Funds and initiatives complementing reform encouraged the migration of the rural populace eastward to Siberia to settle new lands, although some 16 percent of those who migrated returned. With its emphasis on land rights, the Stolypin reforms aimed to strengthen civil consciousness in rural European and Siberian lands.[127] Reforms carved out *otruba* and *khurora*, aiming to create an individualist foundation upon which the future semi-parliamentary regime might rest. The actual results show the impact of several decades of change – sweeping new structures in some regions – and in others, impoverished rural dwellers burdened by great uncertainty about the future.

Reception of Reform

Opposition to the Stolypin reforms was not prominent among the causes of the first Russian revolution in February 1917, which had more to do with Russia's entry into and poor performance in World War I.[128] The peasantry did not take part in the overthrow of the tsarist regime. However, the peasantry's support for the new regime eroded during that spring and summer. The peasants on the whole had wanted compulsory expropriation of nobles' lands to be included in the reform, which was rejected. The peasant faction in the First Duma had called in 1906 for:

> the expropriation of all private, state, and institutional lands above the amount that could be cultivated by personal labor and its transfer into a national fund for distribution to anyone who wished to cultivate it with his own labor, with compensation paid by the state, not the peasantry.[129]

From land seizures in the summer of 1917 and afterward, it would seem that this platform echoed widely the sentiments of the peasantry.

127 Wcislo (1990), p. 210.

128 David Macey emphasized this in his remarks at a panel at the AAASS in Washington, DC, November 17, 2006, "Challenging Historical Stereotypes about the Russian Peasantry" (Roundtable).

129 Quoted in Macey (1987), p. 195.

The reform was, on the whole, conciliatory of the interests of the nobility, and it did not evoke their lasting opposition. It was a reform that emerged through the bureaucracy, as the previous tsarist reform had done. Conflict was resolved before the enactment was promulgated, and the landed nobility had been won over.[130]

3 SUMMARY AND CONCLUSION

This chapter concerned the first two of the modern Russian agrarian reforms. Both reforms conformed to a pattern well known in political theory. Reform was justified as dramatic change in the national interest evoked by crisis conditions. The first reform was the abolition of serfdom, which followed the defeat in Crimea in 1855. It coincided with a banking crisis beginning in 1857. The reform was carried out in stages, by the first of which the land commune and landlords reach a negotiated agreement regarding the total amount of allotment land. At stage one, landlords were required to form contracts to provide a per capita income to cover subsistence in village communities. Peasants were liberated as free agriculturalists, and they were entitled to homesteads and plots around them. During stage two, as they took up the tilling of their parcels of land in permanent usufruct, as confirmed by charters with nobles, they remained temporarily obligated to fulfil former obligations until contracts, or *vykupnye sdelki*, would be drawn up for the redemption of the land. By the terms of contract, the land commune guaranteed repayment by peasant households of the full amount, capitalized at 6 percent, over forty-nine years, with the state providing the compensation to landlords and peasants repaying the loan to the state. The guarantor was the repartitional or nonrepartitional land commune, which monitored seasonal labor off the estate and managed other governance issues in the village.

The second reform consisted of measures to end the hold of communal authority over withdrawal of land and resettlement and to help peasants enclose fields within the commune or consolidate larger separate holdings elsewhere. These were carried out by a series of acts initiated in and after 1906 by Stolypin. Lessons had been learned, and the decree focused on development. The laws targeted entitlement, and they included intervention to bring about immediate change. They provided funds for restructuring, migration, and financing the purchase of land.

The environment for producers benefited after both reforms from some accompanying liberalizing measures. The abolition of serfdom was the first of the "Great Reforms" of Alexander II, and the constitutional order established in 1906 was the background for agrarian reform in 1906. The agricultural sector benefited from these and other dramatic developments across

[130] Macey (1987), Ch. 9.

society, which eased regulations allowing peasants to find non-agricultural employment. Implementation in regard to both measures was affected adversely, however, by macroeconomic volatility. Downstream risk faced by producers in the 1860s, after centuries of bondage, and in 1906, in the midst of revolutionary conditions, was unusually severe.

Both reforms embraced a large vision of a new social order and, as such, promised to open up the authoritarian regime from which they emerged. Thus within the bureaucracy were public servants who aimed broadly to represent the popular interest in a country dominated by a landed elite. Reformers in tsarist Russia did not present themselves as innovators, however, but as upholders of ancient values. These moments, as Wortman wrote, were "scenarios of power."[131] The vision was associated with the rescue from crisis. His analysis of the emancipation is illustrative:

> Freeing the serfs was not to be understood as an administrative imposition furthering the interests of the state but rather as an act of general sacrifice in which all gave for the common good. Emancipation was the first step toward a renovation of monarchy, a popular autocracy linked with the estates through bonds of affection and mutual gratitude.[132]

The emancipation enhanced the immense personal authority of the autocrat, who commanded the obedience of the sovereign estates. This tradition was common to Prussian, Byzantine, and even Enlightenment and Bonapartist expression of public law: justification by acclaim. Similarly, the inaugurating edict of the Stolypin reforms bypassed the Parliament: it was an imperial edict.

The lack of a clear and open reform orientation in government is suggestive of an aversion at high levels of the Russian administration to policy innovators.[133] Institutions of power were timeless and unchanging; crisis and shifts in relations with Western powers were met passively. This rigidity, as D. Orlovsky observed, did not discourage discussion; it discouraged action – except for military action to reinforce the established order.[134]

The failure of an "action orientation" to be attractive to reformers had the added disadvantage that follow-up policies and adjustments took a great deal of time. B. Mironov describes this as a fatal flaw in Russian governance: "The inability of Russia's governing institutions to develop and implement policies that could ameliorate specific political and social problems."[135] He explains that it was difficult in non-crisis times for reforming ministers to change or adjust administrative routines of government, where they lacked

[131] Wortman (1995, 2000).
[132] Wortman (2000), p. 60.
[133] Orlovsky (1981), p. 2.
[134] Ibid.
[135] Ibid.

effective and transparent controls over subsidiary units.[136] After a reform era passed, there was little possibility of further policy transformation. Lasting and flexible solutions to social and economic problems were beyond the reach of the imperial tsarist government, which did not revisit its major decisions.[137]

On one hand, the lack of an activist tradition among reform-oriented bureaucrats explains some flaws in the reform procedure. On another, the blocking of change at the ministerial level served an important purpose. It limited arbitrariness of rule, and it allowed tradition to be a ready source of appeal against extreme decisions in the imperial period.[138] Thus rigidity served to maintain a low-cost internal consensus and the status quo.

The next chapter concerns the political transformation under the Bolsheviks. The first major policy shift, nationalization, was followed by harsh conditions of so-called War Communism, and then by the liberalizing New Economic Policy (NEP), and, finally, by forced collectivization. The Bolshevik regime began as a decentralized, horizontal authority, represented by the local soviets. Power was intended to be based on mass support, representing workers and peasants at every level of governance. Over time, however, the increasing powers of executive committees and ministerial departments over their employees returned the more familiar bureaucratic structure. In principle, after the Constitution of 1936, there were direct elections. Local soviets of workers' deputies and representatives to the republican Supreme Soviets were to be democratically selected. However, as Stephen Whitefield shows, the system of soviets, with no legislative base, lapsed in importance, and the government swerved toward its historical path, a centralized system of decision making, which restricted local flexibility in social innovation.[139] The state determined the allocation of resources, the rate of saving, the level and nature of production, the allocation of investment, the rate of interest, relative and absolute prices, imports and exports, and even the location of households.[140] Recentralization then restored rigid resistance to policy adjustments. Even the least effective sector, agriculture, was relatively more vulnerable to real transformation, only in a crisis.

136 Mironov (1999), I, p. 199.
137 Olson (1965); Mironov (1999), I.
138 Katz (1972).
139 Whitefield (1993).
140 Tanzi (1993), pp. 3–5.

2

The NEP, Collectivization, and Post-Stalin Reforms, 1921–1989

INTRODUCTION

Soviet-era policies created a revolution across sectors. In regard to agriculture, in 1917, after the collapse of the parliamentary regime that had governed the country since the February revolution, the Bolshevik successor government eliminated private property rights in land and supported communal farming. The Bolsheviks exchanged market prosperity and savings that might have resulted, had the Stolypin era reforms continued, for the principle of equity in an age of revolution.

From 1921 through the mid-1920s, some better-off peasants tried to hold on to their large farms. After the mid-1920s, this became more difficult. Macroeconomic conditions continued to generate risk, and tax policy, showing the Bolsheviks' preference for communal or collective agriculture, discouraged individual farm growth. By the end of the 1920s, that preference became a dictate in forced collectivization. Stalin's government sought to use savings from agriculture for industry; and to construct a factory-style labor force on huge mechanized agricultural complexes to improve production and overcome resistance of the peasants to state command.

The ideology of communism sought to raise the contribution of the peasantry from the small tax base it had constituted in tsarist Russia to the center of a new growth strategy, even if this required the highly coercive power of its army, which had succeeded in the civil war against the Whites.[1] In this sense and in others, collectivization was a costly experiment. It was an act of hostility against the peasantry, with lasting negative impact on labor incentives. It confined rural entrepreneurship to the garden plot, where vegetables could be grown for a semiprivate market, in which peasants might sell local

[1] The Whites, or White Army, was a loose confederation of forces opposed to the Bolshevik revolution.

produce. Suppressing other forms of entrepreneurship had the chief result of discouraging cost minimization across the farm sector. After five decades, the state was still exhausting scarce resources on the cultivation of crops and livestock production.[2] After a little over two decades, Soviet policies had relaxed some of the harsh measures introduced by Stalin, such as low procurement prices, and shifted to a growth strategy favouring the external sector, which improved conditions in agriculture. But the losses still outweighed the gains. Farm debts rose to significant levels by the mid-1980s. At that time, suppressed inflation and goods rationing provided the crisis that resulted in the reversal of the decision to collectivize agriculture.

This chapter is divided into four parts, organized chronologically. It begins with the nationalization of land during the revolution of 1917 and covers the New Economic Policy (NEP) and collectivization, and then the reforms under Khrushchev, Kosygin, Brezhnev, and Gorbachev. There is no space here to elucidate or to contribute to the literature on the causes of the shifts in policy from 1917 through the NEP and the 1930s, and these are covered in greater detail in a large monographic literature.[3] Detail here is selective, designed to cover the conditions in which state intervention and liberalizing reforms were initiated and some of the consequences of these measures.

1 THE EARLY AND MID-1920S: AGRARIAN REFORMS

The Decree on Land (1917)

The Bolsheviks' land policy endorsed the peasants' spontaneous seizure of lands in the summer of 1917, after the monarchy had ended. Peasants claimed the land previously owned by the nobles and the state and partitioned it among members of existing communes. Once in power, the Bolsheviks issued a decree on land (November 8, 1917) that swept the peasants' platform of August 19, 1917 into law: the 242 peasant instructions to the All-Russian Soviet of Peasant Deputies had sought the socialization of all land – state, crown, church, possessional, urban, private, public, peasant. Lenin's decree of October 26, 1917, confirmed the equalization of all holdings, their socialization, and their use by anyone who was willing to work the land under any form of land use (*khutora, otruby*, repartitional [by labor unit] and nonrepartitional [*podvornyi*, or allotments distributed by consumption needs] communes) *podvornyi* [allotments distributed

[2] Eggertson (1990), p. 335; Winiecki (1986), p. 337.

[3] Allen (1997, 2003); Danilov (2000); Davies (1991); Dmitrenko (1998); Fitzpatrick (1984, 1991, 1994); Gimpel'son (2004); Gregory et al. (2003); Gregory (2005); Harrison (1986); Johnson (1993); Nove (1992); Sedik (1991, 1994); Seniavskii (2006); Sokolov (2001); Telytsin (2002); Viola (1996, 2002); Wheatcroft et al. (1994).

according to consumption], or artel' [guild or craft organization]).[4] There was to be no hired labor, however, and the land was never to be sold, bought, leased, used as collateral, or in any other way alienated.[5]

From 1918, after civil war broke out, anarchy, destruction, and looting breeched attempted government controls and prolonged the already severe agrarian crisis.[6] Excess deaths during the war and afterwards reached sixteen million, with the number of births falling to ten million less than what had been expected by this time before the war.[7] The government's response to the widespread outbreak of peasant resistance and the formation of counter-revolutionary forces was a policy called War Communism, which would not only field an army but initiate Marxian transformation of the state and the economy. The Bolshevik regime banned private manufacture and transferred the system of production to state allocation; it banned private trade and seized peasant surpluses (*prodrasverstka*). The value of money shrank to insignificance in the economy. In December 1920, the government tried to control the planting and harvesting of crops as well as distribution of output.[8] Beginning in 1918 and 1919, it disallowed further repartition, without express justification, and forbade repartition or reduction in size of plots that had been transferred to multi-field crop rotation, that is applied advanced technologies.

War Communism was not well received by the peasants; it destabilized the economy and society, and fostered revolts against forced requisitions. There were strikes, and there was a flare-up of resistance at Kronstadt, the naval base, which was followed by the brutal suppression of the sailors in 1921. War Communism was a policy without a future after the civil war was over. To end it, in 1921 Lenin retreated from its militarism and launched the NEP, a set of measures overturning the harsh regulations of the war era in support of more moderate ways of resolving the continuing crisis in output.[9]

The NEP gave some stimulus to the economy in permitting markets, but the state retained ownership of the commanding heights, or crucial sectors, including banking, foreign trade, mining, and much of industry, including large-scale manufacturing. Small-scale private enterprises were made legal and leasing was encouraged.[10] The reforms also introduced a

4 Kolodezhnyi (2002), p. 353.
5 Cited in Kolodezhnyi (2002), p. 352.
6 Wheatcroft (1994).
7 Wheatcroft and Davies (1994), pp. 57–8.
8 Nove (1992), p. 71.
9 Avrich (1970); Naumov and Kosakovskii (1997).
10 On NEP see Gregory (1994); Allen (1997); Ibragimova (1997); Merl (1981); Harrison (1986); Davies (1991); Barnett (1995); Danilov (1977, 1988, 2000); Johnson (1993); Sedik (1994), and others.

stable currency, the *chervonets*, which promised success for liberalization and macroeconomic stability. At the same time, it restored free movement of retail prices. Although state and cooperative organizations shared wholesale markets, retail trade was dominated by private traders.[11]

The Land Code (1922)

The land policy under the NEP shifted away from the severe pro-communist stance of war communist requisitions, the *prodrazverstka*, which by 1921 could no longer be maintained. The new land policy replaced forced requisitions by a tax in kind, the *prodnalog*, which substantially lowered previous delivery targets. Peasants were allowed, after paying this reduced tax, to use the remainder of their produce as they wanted for sale or consumption. The Bolshevik government also retreated on endorsing socialization of property, that is, allocation of the land to those who work on it, the slogan of the radical peasant-oriented (SR) Social Democratic Party. In a new regulation of March 21, 1921, the government asserted state ownership of the land and allowed the limited use of hired labor. Also, land could now be leased in one-year contracts.

The land policy of the NEP was embodied in the Land Code of 1922, which imposed new regulations for cultivation and distribution. The code prohibited repartitions more frequently than every nine years.[12] The Land Code allowed leasing but reduced the period over which the land could be leased to two crop rotations. It confirmed permission to hire labor, but when families hired labor, they also had to work the land. Peasants could leave the commune, and no one who wanted to work the land could be refused an allotment. However, the code authorized the commune to continue monitoring the use of land while permitting individual consolidation of holdings. In other words, the NEP policies fostered a somewhat more collectivist order while relaxing the previous regulatory decrees. It continued the policy discouraging repartition, and it took improved land out of the repartition cycles to support peasant entrepreneurship. The NEP invested in individuals rather than the household, in a new turn in Russian land law. But collectivist principles were supported by the village. According to a survey in 1922, overwhelmingly communal landholding dominated agriculture in the 1920s.[13]

[11] Gregory (1994), p. 95.

[12] Land Code RSFSR (SU RSFSR, 1922, No. 68).

[13] In the northern, Lower Volga, and eastern *gubernii* communal governance was used on 96–98 percent of the arable; in the center, the Urals, western Siberia, and the Southeast, 90–95 percent. In the central regions, the Lower Volga and eastern Siberia, less than 1 percent of the arable was cultivated in *khutora* and *otruby*, and 4–6 percent in western Siberia and the industrial *gubernii* of the center. Kolodezhnyi (2002), p. 373.

Early Results of the NEP

At first there was little evidence of impact in output growth. Harvests of 1920 and 1921 were 54 and 43 percent of the prewar (1909–1913) average.[14] The severe inflation and monetary chaos, after the initial Bolshevik attempt to abolish money, along with renewed fragmentation of farming by continual repartitions, gave the NEP a slow start.

By the mid-1920s, however, outcomes had improved. The economy was buoyed by a strong currency following the establishment of the state bank in 1921 and the issue of the *chervonets* along with paper rubles in 1922 and 1923. In February 1924, the *chervonetz* became the sole currency and the government was able to generate a balanced budget, stable currency, and sound finance, which assisted in the revival of trade. The budget flourished, benefitting from new excise taxes, taxes on private and state firms and on income and property, a military tax, the commutation of the agricultural tax in kind and in labor into money payments, and voluntary and forced savings, including a 6 percent bond issue. By 1925–1926, there was a budgetary surplus.[15]

Agriculture underwent revitalization. The livestock recovery was complete. The recovery of the 1913 levels of horses, cattle, and pigs was achieved by 1925. A good harvest in 1922 allowed peasants to increase sown areas up to 90 percent of prewar areas. Regarding crops, the outcome of the NEP is less certain. Agriculture was held back by the isolation of villages and slow pace of transportation improvements, which made wholesale and retail distribution inefficient. It was held back by low levels of labor productivity in agriculture and industry. R. Davies argues that by 1928, agricultural production exceeded its prewar level.[16] S. Wheatcroft finds that even in excellent weather conditions of 1925 and 1926, output was still 6 to 12 percent lower than before the war.[17] M. Harrison describes the situation as follows:

> So far as is known, in the 1920s Soviet grain output did not recover to the level of its pre-war maximum, falling below the 1909–1913 average in 1926, the best harvest of the NEP period, by 3–4 per cent. However, in pre-war comparison, even after taking this into account, the net surplus of grain potentially available for direction by the Soviet government into industrial development was reduced far more than the fall in output.[18]

His remarks point to the politically more vital problem of the decline of grain marketings, due to which exports declined and the food supply to the

[14] Nove (1992), p. 81.
[15] Sedik (1994).
[16] Davies (1994), p. 9.
[17] Wheatcroft (1990), p. 95.
[18] Harrison (1990), p. 109.

growing urban population was of concern.[19] Davies summarizes the reasons for the decline in marketings: the deterioration of the terms of trade since 1913; the lower taxation allowing producers to keep more of their output; the low price of grain relative to other agricultural commodities, which discouraged sowings.[20] From October to December 1927, the marketed grain was half what it had been during those months in 1926.[21]

The social variables show evidence of mixed recovery. Per capita income shrank, since most of the one hundred twenty million rural dwellers of Russia now engaged primarily in agriculture. Small producers seemed increasingly worse off. The share of peasant households with no horses or only one working horse increased from 63.5 percent in 1912 to 85.9 percent in 1922 and remained at that share through 1925. Possibly initial land adjustments were insufficient; more and more producers lived separately and seized land to do so. Those without land, the landless agricultural laborers, decreased in number from three million in 1913 to 1.2 million in 1926.[22] The number having three or more shrank from 14.3 percent in 1912 to 3.4 percent in 1926.[23] Households split to create better livelihoods as confiscated land was repartitioned or just to ease conditions in large extended families. The number of households increased from 18.7 million in 1914 to twenty-four million in the spring of 1927[24] as the number of rural residents remained roughly the same.

Better-off rural producers, called *kulaks*, increased in number by the mid-1920s to between 5 and 7 percent of the peasantry, a relative wealth that averaged two horses and two cows and enough land to ensure subsistence year round along with something to trade. The numbers of households hiring labor were also growing, if from a small scale: those employing labor almost doubled, but from 1 percent of the households in 1922 to almost 2 percent in 1925.[25] The NEP was certainly no failure by comparison with war communism.

The Late NEP

Most scholars agree in hindsight that NEP had potential for assisting industrialization, and one recent work argues that this contribution might have

[19] Davies (1994), p. 10.

[20] Davies (1994), p. 11 for the controversy among scholars regarding the elasticity of peasants' response to terms of trade.

[21] Davies (1994), p. 11.

[22] Ibid. p. 84.

[23] Wheatcroft (1994), p. 254, cites Anfimov (1980), pp. 152–53.

[24] Barber and Davies (1994), p. 84.

[25] Nove (1992), p. 104.

been substantial under different price incentives.[26] Agriculture seemed to respond rapidly to incentives in the early NEP; rural producers were taxed no more than urban dwellers.[27] However, by manipulating the rural/urban exchange rate in the mid-1920s, the government began to use stronger means to promote industry, and this made recovery less certain. The opening and closing of a gap between industrial and agricultural prices, the well-known price scissors in the 1920s, moved first against agriculture in October 1923. The ratio of desired exchange by the government was 3:1, with industrial prices three times higher than agricultural based on pre-war prices. After the state intervened to lower the industrial and raise agricultural prices, the scissors seemed to be closing, more to the benefit of agriculture.[28] However, if the terms of trade are measured by retail prices for consumer goods and wholesale prices for agricultural goods, then the adverse terms of trade probably persisted much longer.[29]

The policy environment of late NEP, 1926–1927, was torn between hoped for but uncertain gains from market-based agriculture and necessary support for rapid industrialization. Policies to promote construction and industrial development had been in place throughout the NEP. Price policy, beginning in 1925–1926, showed a greater tendency toward administrative means than before, and ceilings were placed on agricultural prices. This struck at poorer as well as wealthier peasants by lowering prices after the harvest in the fall, and it showed the abandonment of the effort to keep prices high in the fall and lower in the spring, when the wealthier peasants marketed their grain.[30] Since taxes on most of peasant outputs from the garden, on poultry and pigs, and on crafts were powerfully raised beginning in 1926 just as procurement prices were lowered, policy showed a clear shift away from the general interests of the consumer and the peasant.

2 COLLECTIVIZATION

Crisis of Marketings

The failure of grain marketings to meet expectations in 1928 was one of the crises used to criticize the NEP. Marketings were probably at low levels, although statistics for the period are unreliable.[31] The continued low government prices for its overwhelming share of purchases (75 percent)

[26] Allen (1997).
[27] Bergson (1961); Gregory (1994).
[28] Nove (1992); Wheatcroft (1991).
[29] Allen (1997).
[30] Telytsin (2002), p. 222.
[31] See Wheatcroft (1994); articles in Davies (1994); Gregory (2002); Telytsin (2002, 2002b); and others.

of grain output encouraged producers to seek private channels of trade and to shift into livestock production, as observed previously. Economists tend to agree there was no failure in the market mechanism that should bear responsibility for what followed.[32] The consensus of new research, including fresh archival resources, stresses political rationales for collectivization.[33]

The collectivization was, in a sense, a dramatic intensification of a policy already being put in place by the late NEP government to force greater savings from the rural sector for more rapid industrialization. Increasing credits to industry showed the clear turn to an industrial policy. Without a further shift of policy, agricultural marketings would not meet demand. The idea was to develop the state and collective farm enterprises already in existence into the dominant form of farming and use procurement norms and output targets to meet demand.

It was clear that the use of force would be necessary for collectivization across the territory of Russia and other republics. The relative failure of state and collective farms in the 1920s to attract rural dwellers had demonstrated to the government that producers could not be persuaded to join voluntarily: 0.1 percent of peasant households lived on state farms or collectives in 1918, and still less than 1 percent by 1927. Leading agronomists and many in the leadership opposed the use of force.[34] However, it was assumed that marketings of grain could not be significantly increased with rural markets unless prices went up as well.

Collectivization forced the increase in marketings, shifted costs to producers, and imposed an experimental design on farming. In an act utterly lacking the classic focus in reform on producer autonomy and rural welfare, the policy initiative began with emergency requisitions in 1928. Between 1929 and 1937, the government used force to collectivize some 93 percent of agriculture.[35] The reform crushed the *edinolichniki* (individual farmers). Millions of *kulaks*, and others so identified, were exiled or executed. What was left of the private sector after 1937 were households' garden plots averaging less than a half hectare apiece on *kolkhozy*. Along with the forced relocation of millions of households, collectivization resulted in a loss of 58 percent of the value of herds at the beginning of 1928 and 14 percent of the total capital at that date.[36]

[32] Hunter and Szyrmer (1992); Gregory (2003); cf Millar (1990).

[33] See a review and new perspective by Gregory (2003); Hunter and Szyrmer (1992); Davies (1980); Lewin (1965, 1985); Danilov (1973, 1999, 2000, 1996a, 1996b); Viola (1996, 2002), and others.

[34] Davies (1994), n. 38; Tucker (1973); Cohen (1974); Hunter and Szyrmer (1992); Millar (1970, 1990a, 1990b, 1990c).

[35] *Sel'skoe khoziastvo SSSR* (1988), p. 6.

[36] Moorsteen and Powell (1966), p. 144.

New Farm Structures

Two initially distinct types of farms were created, the state farm, or *sovkhoz*, and the collective farm, or *kolkhoz*, far more numerous and not subsidized. The self-financing *kolkhoz* dominated production; procurement targets had to be met and labor supplied.

The principal economic justification for large state or cooperative farms is to capture economies of scale. Faith in the importance of scale, which had roots in Marxism, was not well founded over a certain size.[37] Economies of scale are relatively unimportant in grain farming, at least for non-plantation crops.[38] Among inefficiencies are the compartmentalization of farming (with livestock separated from field production) and specialization without regard to regional endowments. Equally important are administrative costs, which include supervision of the labor force on farms of enormous scale due to spatial dispersion of field crops. Cooperatives can function well, as in Canada, but the collectivization in the 1930s was not an experiment in cooperatives.

Utopianism and impatience with the market, not best practice, inspired the collectivization.[39] The government used both coercion and conciliation to make it work.[40] The trial and error approach was described by R. Davies:

> This was a learning process on a vast scale, and in an extremely brief period of time, in which party leaders and their advisers, local party officials, the peasants and economic regularities all contributed to the outcome.[41]

Losses in the 1930s and the weakness of the incentive system proved that there was little to justify it. The *kolkhoz* regime established in 1929–1930 nevertheless survived the whole of Stalin's rule and for some time after.

Early response was chaotic at local levels. "Gigantomania," a term used retrospectively for the enthusiasm that in 1929 and 1930 drove competing authorities to construct larger and larger *kolkhozy*, some spreading over more than 10,000 hectares and hundreds of villages.[42] Greater realism later

37 That is, unit costs decline as farm size increases, at least up to the size of the reasonably efficient one- or two-man farms; what most analysts call economies of scale is actually variable economies, since it is difficult not to change the mix of inputs and equipment as farms gain in size. See Upchurch (1961).

38 An economic argument used to rationalize socialized farming was economies of scale. However, substantial research has not found, with the exception of a few crops (bananas, sugar, and tea), much evidence in support of that assumption. Deininger (1995), p. 1320; Binswanger, Deininger, and Feder (1995); Jensen and Meckling (1979).

39 Cited in Nove (1992), p. 147.

40 Lewin (1965).

41 Davies (1980), pp. 14–15.

42 Fitzpatrick (1994), pp. 105–06.

on resulted in mostly smaller *kolkhozy*, roughly the size of villages. The chaos of the early years was also due to the forced resettlement of households, confiscation and slaughter of livestock, which brought devastation to villages and forced the immediate supply of tractors. The government sought to encourage the *kolkhozy* to invest in machinery, but they did not do so. Therefore centralized supply through Machine Tractor Stations (MTS) was designed to serve the regional *kolkhozy*.[43] The MTS system proved easily accommodated by centralized supply; horsepower rapidly increased. The loss in such a system was on-farm equipment and, especially, the skills and expertise that come from using it.

Short-Run Outcomes of Collectivization

Since grain output from 1933 onward was measured in biological yields – where the maximum possible output of the standing crop in the field was recorded as harvested – the outcomes of collectivization were greatly exaggerated. The good results were praised and featured as a signal victory for the industrialization of agriculture. The overestimation of harvests in 1930–1932 was by 20 to 30 percent, according to Wheatcroft, reducing actual output in both years to a lower level than in any post-revolutionary year.[44] Therefore, initially agricultural output plummeted. Official harvest estimates, however, were adjusted to meet expectations so that historians can do no more than suggest the range within which harvests probably fell, from between sixty-three and seventy million puds in 1928 to fifty-seven to sixty-five in 1931 and, recovering somewhat, back up to between seventy and seventy-seven by 1933.[45]

Total output in 1940 was 23 percent above that in 1913, but this increase just maintained per capita output at the level it had reached before World War I, and given an increase of 27 percent in the area of land under crops, efficiency was slow to improve.[46]

The evidence of decline, indeed, was obvious and the plan for large future gains was so unrealistic that Stalin accepted a compromise and lowered targets for the second Five-Year Plan.[47] By the mid-1930s, prospects improved, and by the late 1930s, recovery in cereals and livestock seemed more certain. Most villagers now belonged to *kolkhozy* and *sovkhozy*, and by 1940, farming was largely mechanized.[48] Table 2.1 shows the increase in equipment and horsepower.

[43] Davies (1980), vol. 2, ch. 2.
[44] Wheatcroft (1994), p. 116.
[45] Davies and Wheatcroft (2004), p. 446.
[46] Karcz (1968), pp. 126–27.
[47] Davies (1980), p. 12.
[48] *Sel'khoz* (1971), p. 10.

TABLE 2.1. *Mechanization of Agriculture, 1928–1940 (End of Year Figures)*

	1928	1940
Capital stock (including livestock, comparable prices) (blns rubles)	17.7	21.3
Energy resources (mlns hp)	21.3	47.5
Tractors (15-hp units)	18	684
Grain combines (thousands)	2	182
Trucks (thousands)	0.7	228

Source: Selkhoz (1979), p. 12.

By comparison with industry, agricultural response to new investment in machines was less impressive, given the resources involved. Table 2.2, which follows, shows the growth gap with other sectors, especially heavy industry. These postwar figures (1948) compare estimates by the head of Gosplan, N. Voznesenskii, by R. Allen (2003), and from reports to the U.S. Congress Joint Economic Committee (1959).

The decline in livestock inventories and a strong initial effect of collectivization offset increased requirements for grain as industrialization proceeded. Hard hit first by collectivization and then by World War II, livestock inventories, according to D. Whitehouse and J. Havelka (1971), took from twenty to thirty years to be fully restored to 1928 levels: hogs by 1953, sheep by 1956, all cattle by 1958, and cows by 1959.[49] After World War II, some relaxation of government controls on private accumulation encouraged increased inventories.

The initial release of agricultural labor to industry was an important outcome for collectivization, however.[50] The combined effect of collectivization and industrialization led to urbanization, although in 1939 the population of the Russian Soviet Federative Socialist Republic (RSFSR) was still 56.6 percent rural. As agriculture was modernized, the collective and state farms faced a rising price for the supply of labor. In a market economy, the large firm would respond to this potentially high cost by long-term contracts and/or by vertical integration.[51] However, the state could not gain such efficiencies due to the relative immobility of the labor market and the necessity of large farms for delivering local government. The farm provided social

49 Whitehouse and Havelka (1971), p. 350.

50 Movement out of agriculture slowed later on. Stalin introduced a new passport system to guarantee a work force for the farms and secure the privileged social order. Of all of the workers in the state, including *sovkhoz* members, *kolkhoz* members were alone refused the right of having an internal passport. See Fitzpatrick (1994), Ch. 3.

51 Coase (1937); see also the discussion from the 1987 conference on the fiftieth anniversary of "The Nature of the Firm" (Williamson and Winter [1993]).

TABLE 2.2. *Industrial Development of the USSR, 1928–1940*

	Voznesenskii Estimates (%) 1928–1940 (Growth)	Allen Estimates (%) 1928–1940	Reports to U.S. Congress (%) 1928–1940
National income	501	178	
Gross output of industry	605	253	163
Gross output of agriculture	80	10	
Livestock products			2
Food crops			25
Industrial crops			101
Transportation and communication	405	402	

Sources: Nikonov (1995), Table 7.1, p. 244 from Voznesenskii (1979), pp. 484–85; Allen (2003), p. 103; Johnson and Kahan (1959), p. 206; Nutter (1959), p. 97.

services to the local populace and even inputs for use in plots.[52] Retaining substantial labor on farm was directly supporting the private sector within agriculture, for which the farm provided socialized inputs (fertilizer and labor). Thus the state paid the full cost of rising wages without gaining the capacity for monitoring or improving the productivity of labor.

Reception of Collectivization

In its impact on output, collectivization in the short run was not much of a success.[53] A particularly vivid review of its harrowing effect on Russia producers is in M. Lewin's *Russian Peasants and Soviet Power*. Behind the figures, he wrote:

> There lay a record of violence such as the peasants had not experienced since the days of the Civil War. The rush to join the *kolkhozes* was inspired by fear and by despair, and it was accompanied by mass destruction of livestock and equipment . . . the cost of these policies in terms of the losses suffered was enormous; seldom was any government to wreak such havoc in its own country.[54]

3 POSTWAR AGRARIAN REFORM

Recovery from the War and Stalin's Death (1953)

Enormous losses – one-fifth of the country's human assets and one-quarter of its physical assets – from World War II were followed by a relatively

[52] Lerman (2002), p. 44.
[53] Wheatcroft (1994), p. 117.
[54] Lewin (1975), pp. 514–15.

fast recovery of pre-war levels.[55] Dissipating effects of World War II on the Russian economy were a source of confidence to the government.[56] The Soviet Union never recovered its pre-war economic trajectory.[57] However, with a far more powerful economy, the USSR was able to supply twenty-five times the defense industry products for the army and air force than the imperial Russian regime had. Also, the war led to a pooling of resources. The government was able to distribute the burden of war equally across urban and rural dwellers by not letting rural producers set products aside for their own consumption, leaving shelves empty.[58]

In agriculture, population deficit, mostly in rural areas, assisted post-war recovery data, making it seem faster than it was.[59] But with the rapidity of post-war general economic recovery, pre-war agricultural output was attained already by the start of the next seven-year plan in 1950. No further reforms seemed urgently necessary.

Khrushchev

Reforms across the economy were initiated by Stalin's successor, first secretary of the Communist Party from 1953, Nikita Khrushchev, following the death of Stalin in 1953. In a time of political turmoil, Khrushchev used his new leadership post as First Secretary of the Communist Party to gain more leverage for his agrarian reform proposals.[60]

His reforms of the agricultural sector began with large-scale "projects": (1) rapid expansion of cultivated areas, (2) higher prices to improve incentives, (3) some decentralization of management, and (4) increased investment in productive capital.[61] Khrushchev launched campaigns to use marginal lands in the Volga region, and to break in virgin lands in Siberia and Kazakhstan, among other areas. He increased sown area by more than a fifth between 1953 and 1956. He also aimed to improve productivity of the high-valued sectors. Discriminatory pricing depressed growth in cereal production through the 1950s, however, and the lack of fodder and special facilities for livestock production held that sector back through the 1960s. On average, between 1954 and 1963, there was an annual increment of 14.1 million tons of grain in an early reward for his agricultural programs, emphasizing feed-level grain. There was also improvement in the cultivation of forage crops, bringing an end to Stalin's forced production of

55 See estimates by Harrison (1996 [2002 ed.]) in Chapter 7; see especially p. 164.
56 Harrison (1996).
57 Harrison (1996 [2002 ed.], p. 165.
58 Harrison (1994), p. 265.
59 Schoonover (1979), p. 91.
60 Nikonov (1995), p. 327.
61 Karcz (1965); Davies (1998); Bush (1966); McCauley (1995); Tompson (1997); Jasny (1966); Millar (1965, 1971, 1974, 1990); Spulber (2004); and others.

wheat. Acreage under seeded forage crops went from twenty-one million hectares in 1950 to sixty-three million in 1960.[62] Khrushchev increased the total amount of cultivated land by 35.9 million hectares between 1953 and 1956.

Producers benefited from improved prices. Prices for most agricultural products were raised immediately after Stalin's death in 1953 and again in 1956, 1958, and 1962. Khrushchev abandoned a three-decades-long experimentation with heavy taxation of the agricultural sector on the understanding that compulsory sales at low prices retarded the growth of much-needed investment for productivity improvement. Aiming for balanced growth, he raised prices for procurements while increasing investments. Over-the-quota premia were raised for grain, potatoes, and vegetables, meat, dairy, produce, sunflower seed, and some for industrial crops, and procurement quotas were lowered to increase incentives for over-quota production. This was an innovation in that previously state prices governed all sales of farm products except for some vegetables and potatoes sold at market prices by *kolkhoz* members and at cooperative retail outlets for negotiated prices. Average procurement prices rose by 21 percent from 1954 to 1956.

Price increases were accompanied by greater farm autonomy. Khrushchev began issuing passports in a limited way to kolkhoz members.[63] He also granted some freedom in decision making to managers. Before Khrushchev, *kolkhozy* and *sovkhozy* operated under clear directives – areas to be seeded to various crops or left fallow, normative yields, size of herds, volume of output to be sold to the state, and the quantities of inputs to buy. Machinery use was controlled by the MTS, which also handled planning, repairs, and operations. After Khrushchev's reforms, *kolkhozy* could plan their own production and be responsible to the state only for sales quotas. Managers could apply for short-term credit by direct bank loans, and long-term debts were written off. Taxes were reduced by 60 percent and shifted to the estimated value of land rather than inventory and output. The MTS were improved by the addition of many qualified agronomists, administrators, and other specialists. In 1958, he initiated the last of his price reforms, unifying prices paid for produce and eliminating over-the-quota premia, which had proved ineffective. He also eliminated the MTS to give farms full autonomy in the use of machinery.

To summarize the impact of these and other reforms, there were impressive output gains in the early years of reform. Gross agricultural output during 1956–1960 was greater than 40 percent above the level of the previous five years, and net grain output also improved.[64] Between 1950 and 1966, agricultural production in the USSR increased by about 70 percent.

62 Schoonover (1979), p. 94.
63 Zelenin (2002), p. 606.
64 See Diamond (1966), pp. 343 ff.

The combined productivity of the land, labor, capital, and other conventional inputs was about 25 percent greater than in 1950, and there was a significant investment in education and training of the labor force. Annual inputs grew by one-third and had heavy support from industry, although investment policy suffered from unpredictability.[65] Also cash incomes per *kolkhoz* household improved from 1952 and 1961 almost four times.[66]

Khrushchev's victory over agricultural problems was temporary. In a few years, beginning in 1959, he witnessed the critical failure of some of his initiatives.[67] Exaggerated expectations generated by the massive nature of his projects and by initial bounteous harvests, particularly in 1958, were doused by evidence of failure in 1959 and 1960. Much of the virgin territory that was ploughed up, for example, showed poor results on marginal land. Apart from lower yields, there was also some expectation of long-term environmental damage. The virgin soils were too light to withstand the use of heavy tractors and combines. This meant that labor and equipment, removed from more productive regions in the all-out campaign on the virgin lands, were now in surplus on less productive lands. Meanwhile, rural emigration to cities had been slowed by the virgin lands project, and this too showed up in lower overall labor productivity figures. Finally, the virgin lands project required a significant increase in investments over a long period of time. Cereals output did improve, but meat production, the higher valued product, did not.[68] The downward trend was evident in gross agricultural production, which rose in 1959 but began to drop off between 1960 and 1963.

These discouraging economic outcomes resulted in an administrative struggle between the party and the government over *kolkhoz* management. The Ministry of Agriculture was demoted to a research and extension service to streamline controls through the party. Khrushchev increased procurements of grain by 25 to 40 percent, and he centralized procurement to link farm management with a separate state committee. His management reform then tightened party control further in 1962 through the Territorial Production Administrations (TPA) to supervise production and procurement.

Tighter party control did not lead to more developmentally oriented long-term policies, however. Khrushchev grew focused on projects for short-term results, in view of the party criticism, and his push for intensive means of improvement slowed. Grasslands and fallow, essential in land-abundant agriculture, were plowed up for more extensive sowing; villages and towns were relocated to meet his objective of surrounding large cities with vegetable and dairy state farms. He spread the production of maize for the sake of

[65] See Diamond (1966), pp. 343 ff.

[66] *Narkhoz* (1961), p. 438.

[67] See a close study by Zelenin (2002).

[68] Zelenin (2002) observes the ideological impulse discouraged the keeping of livestock (pp. 608–09),

volume of output, even where the climate and land were not suitable. After having allowed households some autonomy, Khrushchev then turned against the private sector, a move that thwarted his goal of increased livestock production while depressing rural incomes. Between 1958 and 1962, livestock holdings in the private sector fell from 117 per 100 *kolkhoz* households to 109.[69]

The Reception of Khrushchev's Reforms. In October 1964, blamed for the failure of reforms in agriculture, Khrushchev was ousted. Confronted with stagnation of agricultural production in the face of rising quantitative and qualitative demand for farm products, Khrushchev's successors attacked his policies much the way he had attacked his predecessor's policies by focusing on evident weak outcomes. Critics pointed to the need for faster improvement. The rapid growth of urban population and consumers' purchasing power, the rising expectations due to a higher standard of living, and the demand for meat in particular meant that results of his reforms lagged behind growing consumption needs. The seven-year plan for agriculture he had developed ended in 1965 with results far short of the promised increase in gross agricultural output (GAO) of 70 percent; he had achieved something like 10 percent.[70] His approach to reform was faulted: his policies were seen as arbitrary, excessively oriented against the private sector, inadequate in supplying improved resources, and insufficiently supportive of local farm managers and agriculturalists.[71] Khrushchev's successors, Alexei Kosygin and Leonid Brezhnev, however, maintained his priority of price reform, showing an understanding of the need for improved incentives. They raised investment levels and focused on improving capital investments and inputs.[72]

Kosygin and Brezhnev

In 1965, Brezhnev declared that his goal was to modernize agriculture by improving inputs, a policy that paid off.[73] The output increase was significant: output of crops and livestock increased by almost 50 percent in fifteen years.[74] In 1966, he then began to pay collective farm workers a regular wage and granted permission for them to have internal passports, a major reform

[69] McCauley (1976), p. 204.

[70] USDA, *Outlook* (1966), p. 4.

[71] USDA, *Outlook* (1966), p. 8.

[72] See Millar (1971, 1990); Clayton (1976); Desai (1992); Diamond (1966, 1979); Bush (1966); and others.

[73] See Clayton (1980), p. 446, for L. I. Brezhnev, "O neotlozhnykh merakh po dal'neishemu razvitiiu sel'skokhoziaistva SSSR," Doklad na Plenume, TsK. KPSS, 24 March 1975, p. 5.

[74] Clayton (1980), p. 446; Carey (1976), p. 599.

of political as well as economic significance. This meant that the collective farm worker was almost identical in status to the state farm worker.

Under Kosygin and Brezhnev, the government adopted some market theory. They encouraged subsidiary private plots and ended compulsory deliveries. They lowered procurement targets and raised prices. They equalized product profitability across regions by zoning differentiation and compensation to farms in financial difficulty.[75] They introduced new kinds of contracts and pecuniary sanctions and numerous other profit incentives.[76] They transferred state farms to *khozrashchet*, or economic accountability.[77] Investment focused on irrigation, drainage, electric power lines, and other types of infrastructure.

Brezhnev's salient achievement was the improved production of livestock. He did this by transforming areas of wheat production into seeded forage crops, expanding the initiative under Khrushchev that had seen seeded forage crops increase from twenty-one million hectares in 1950 to sixty-three million in 1963. This required increased investment in drainage and irrigation. By 25 percent between 1965 and 1975 the extent of drained crops areas expanded. Direct producer bonuses were paid to the livestock sector and tied to farm profits. To encourage the production and consumption of meat and livestock products, they also increased the size of herds, and to get larger feed grain output they more than doubled fertilizer deliveries between 1965 and 1975, chiefly to forage crops.[78]

Agriculture responded to this stimulus in the second half of the 1960s. Grain output increased over five years by almost 30 percent, justifying the regular payment of wages to collective farmers. The government increased the flow to farms of industrially produced materials such as fertilizer, lubricants, and electric power, and improved the general level of production. It was only in the 1970s that progress seemed to slow down. Agriculture suffered a series of low harvests, as in 1973, the worst crop in a decade, and it began to seem that these were not temporary setbacks. Researchers diverge on some data series but agree in hindsight on this conclusion. An exacting examination covering the Soviet and transition periods for the Russian Federation from 1970 to 1996 by A. Manellia (1997) found GAO (excluding Ukraine and other new states formed from the previous Soviet Union) rising at 1.3 percent annually. The government had increased expectations of high consumption of meat and other quality foods, and demand outpaced supply.[79]

[75] Ever since their inception in 1919, the state farms (*sovkhozy*) consistently made an overall loss, even during years of bumper harvests; in 1963, nearly 70 percent of all *sovkhozy* operated at a loss and required state subsidies. Bush (1966), p. 467.

[76] Schroeder (1979), p. 312.

[77] Bush (1966).

[78] Diamond and Krueger (1973).

[79] Diamond and Krueger (1973), p. 317.

The slowdown in the 1970s was partly due, to be sure, to weather, since considerable progress was made in increasing farm output during 1966–1970, when the weather had been more favorable. More often the slowdown is attributed to the investment strategy and inability of the system to deal effectively with supply bottlenecks. For example, livestock herds were expanded rapidly without regard for instability in the supply of feed grains and without additional sources of more nutritious food.

Despite an increasing sense of failure, the government continued investing at high levels.[80] Fodder grain was now imported to feed the overdeveloped livestock sector, and for the first time in its history, Russia was no longer self-sufficient in agricultural commodities. Before 1971, grain imports were limited and exports substantial, except in 1963 and 1965, years of exceptionally low harvests. After 1971 imports of grain tended to exceed exports, and grain imports reached twenty-five million tons in 1975 after a disastrous harvest. The next year, the official abandonment of autarkic trade policy was signalled in a long-term agreement with the United States to import at least six million tons of wheat and corn annually over five years.[81]

The Brezhnev government made an effort to resolve these problems in the May 1982 Food Program. It unified the management of branches of the agro-industrial complex, upgraded the system of food storing, handling, and processing, and provided financial incentives to foster higher output.[82] However, within this old reform strategy, there was little evidence of giving farms freedom to make decisions and effectively linking rewards to performance by instituting a price system. The Brezhnev regime witnessed some gains in per capita food production. Supply of fertilizer and pesticides improved, and success in forage crops led to improvement in consumption of high-valued foods, given growth in the livestock sector. Crop production was on average lower between 1983 and 1985 than it had been between 1976–1980, and per capita imports were 60 percent higher. Production costs were rising.[83]

Reception of the Brezhnev-Era Investment Strategy. Widespread scepticism among Western and Russian observers of the government's commitment to meaningful implementation of agrarian reform was the response to the Brezhnev-era improvements.[84] New approaches, including the *podriad* (contract) system, which paid farm workers by achieved output, were promoted in the 1960s but not put into practice. Genuine farm autonomy, the focus of much concern, could not be implemented without interrupting

80 Carey (1976), p. 576.
81 Serova (1997); Schroeder (1973, 1979); Bush (1966).
82 Doolittle and Hughes (1987), pp. 28–9.
83 Doolittle and Hughes (1987), pp. 28–9.
84 Wädekin (1989), p. 28–9; Schroeder (1979).

the entire planning and procurement system.[85] One-third of all fixed capital (excluding housing and services) was in the food production sector. The food sector absorbed 20 percent of the labor force and investment resources, compared with less than 5 percent in the United States, but provided a diet well below that of other industrialized countries in quality and variety.[86] Under Gorbachev, agriculture was promised fresh concern and new plans.

4 THE GORBACHEV ERA

In 1985, the newly elected reform-minded leader of the party and architect of Brezhnev's Food Program as secretary for agriculture, Mikhail Gorbachev, promised to end the long stagnation and reduce the enormous cost of food production by pushing forward delayed reform that had been compromised by concessions under his predecessor. Like his predecessors, Gorbachev invested in industry and encouraged profit-making within the existing system of fixed prices and state ownership. Unlike them, he made some fundamental improvements in rural organization.[87]

In the large farm sector, existing incentives discouraged profitability. Excessive administrative interference in local farm management encouraged inefficient decision making and irresponsibility. Managers would tend to lower estimates of profit and exaggerate estimates of loss because profits had to be shared with procurement agencies while losses were borne entirely by the producers.[88] Gorbachev gave significant autonomy to the farm, which was included in his enterprise legislation of 1988. He announced stable annual procurement quotas for five years, greater control by regional party officials and farms over the disposal of surplus production, and sale of perishables at collective farm market prices.[89] He empowered employees to elect farm managers, form cooperatives, and leave the collective. He legalized the sale of private assets, including apartments, among individuals and the leasing of firms to employees and farms to families. These steps fell far short of privatization of enterprises, to be sure, and there was no mention of privatizing input supply or the land. However, the stimulus to the farm sector was evident.

He encouraged private labor activity by activating the *podriad*, or contracting system. Contracting by brigades, families, and others would have remunerated in a similar way to the former *kolkhoz* principle. Their size was to vary locally, and after 1988, family, small group, or individual

85 Wädekin (1989), p. 29.
86 Doolittle and Hughes (1987), p. 27.
87 On Gorbachev's agricultural policies, see Breslauer (1991); Brown (1996); Levine (1987); McFaul (2000); Millar (1990); Hough (1988); Brock (1994); Brooks (1990); Sutela (1991); Moskoff (1990); Cook (1990); Desai (1991).
88 Doolittle and Hughes (1987), pp. 26–7; Raup (1972), p. 276.
89 Doolittle and Hughes (1987), p. 38.

contracting was widely recommended.[90] The brigade would lease the equipment and other supplies and be remunerated out of gross income, minus the cost of inputs except labor. The chief benefit would be to avoid interference by the state, which had weakened performance of the farm. It is not clear how widely this new system spread before Gorbachev's fall from power.[91]

He shifted investment away from farms into the development of rural infrastructure, food processing, and industries that support agriculture with chemicals and machinery. Avoiding the controversial reforms of prices and decision-making latitude, he attempted to decentralize price signals within the existing system. Gorbachev responded to the need for trade incentives by allowing farms to negotiate prices, and he gave financial responsibility to farm directors, who were to base decisions on consumption needs. Instead of compulsory targets, there were state orders that covered only fundamental requirements, with the rest of production allocated by negotiated contracts.

Overall productivity in agriculture was not improving before the collapse of the Soviet Union, as is captured in the decline of the marginal product of capital with a constant rate of Total Factor Productivity (TFP) growth.[92] From 1986 to 1990 the share of budgetary subsidies in sales rose from 19.4 to 33.9 percent, as total agricultural output declined by 4 percent.[93] Agriculture seemed to bleach resources from the regime. However, Gorbachev opposed more radical market reform, even when the political transformation of eastern Europe challenged the foundations of Soviet power and socialist planning. The output decline encouraged the regime to further stimulate household entrepreneurship, but this occurred as chaos developed in the financial sector. Farm managers were unable to design market-oriented strategies without financial stability, clear incentives regarding disposability of landed resources, and a market-based supply chain.

Reception of Gorbachev's Reforms

The reforms were thought to be unlikely to affect overall farm productivity, although they might reduce losses and improve local food supplies. The policy of bailing out non–profit-making farms continued to keep costs high and incentives inadequate. The regime sought to channel more food products through the quasi-independent consumer cooperative channel where food was sold at a price somewhere between the low state retail price and much higher prices at collective farm markets.[94] This was expected to have some impact on consumption, and substantial progress was expected toward

90 Wädekin (1989), p. 30.
91 Wädekin (1989), pp. 32–3; Brooks (1990); Desai (1991).
92 Probably since 1950, see Easterly and Fischer (1995).
93 The Ministry of Agriculture and Food Production, 1997 (Serova [1999]).
94 Doolittle and Hughes (1987), pp. 40–1.

achieving meat production goals.[95] Larger gains were expected from yields, due to the larger deliveries of fertilizer and pesticides to agriculture.[96]

5 SUMMARY AND CONCLUSION

The early Soviet government ended the era of market reform in agriculture and began a new era of socialist reform. Its early decrees, including socialization of the land, helped secure the support of the peasantry in 1917, but anarchy was the result, and sustained crisis put peasant support in jeopardy. Shortages led the government to requisition food for its armies when civil war broke out. The Bolsheviks' "war communism" militarized the economy to field its armies, whose victory was won by terror, arbitrariness, expropriations, and requisitions. In their struggle against White Russian armies, the Bolsheviks printed money, causing hyperinflation across the country and driving agricultural production into a natural state based on barter exchange. By 1920 it became necessary to rebuild the economy and the Bolshevik base of support. Industrial production had fallen to 20 percent of its level in 1913 and agriculture to 64 percent.[97] The NEP in 1921 regained lost ground with the peasantry. Growth was achieved but in a highly controlled way. By the Land Code of 1922, the Bolsheviks replaced socialization with nationalization, giving peasants permanent use rights to the land. They replaced the ad hoc requisitions with tax incentives. Signs of deterioration in the peasants' position were heavy taxation of those who were well off and their denial of voting rights. Then firm administrative controls over the economy were put into place.[98]

The new strike at the peasantry and wave of major change began in 1928 with emergency measures, rationalized as a crisis of grain marketings. By 1937, peasant farming had disappeared; collectivization ended the NEP. Rural assets came under direct state control through state procurements from the *kolkhoz* (collective farm), the new large farms that reorganized production and replaced peasant farms. When peasants resisted being forced into *kolkhozy*, their livestock were confiscated and the government ensured that the management of farms represented not the peasantry but the state authorities. The government then invested huge sums in centralized units to provide machines, equipment, and expertise to the formerly peasant producers and made Russian agriculture a showcase of the regime's modernization and political victory.[99] The Soviet industrialization of agriculture gave the

95 Severin (1987), p. 59.
96 Severin (1987), p. 55.
97 See Gregory (1994), pp. 86–9.
98 Sedik (1991, 1994).
99 Allen (1997); Barnett (1995); Danilov (2000); Davies (1991); Fitzpatrick (1991); Gregory (2003); Harrison (1986); Johnson (1993); Nove (1992); Preobrazhenskii (1922); Telytsin (2002).

government command over the agricultural surplus, including underemployed rural labor, by which it could powerfully improve the growth rate of heavy industry.[100]

The third era of major change, liberalizing some of the harsh restrictions of Stalinism, was the post-Stalin effort to make farms more self-sustaining. The reformers, Khrushchev, Kosygin, Brezhnev, and Gorbachev, carried out price adjustments, administrative reform, and reinvestment to improve productivity of labor and land. They were highly successful, but at great cost, and in the 1980s, cost became critical. The regime recognized the weight of agriculture on the economy by carrying out another Soviet agrarian reform in the mid-1980s. The last era covered here, the Gorbachev regime, introduced new cooperative arrangements. Like the Stolypin reforms, however, this experiment ended for external reasons after a few years, when communism collapsed.

Probably the most important of these sharp policy interventions – labeled here in a shorthand as reforms – were the price increases under Khrushchev, who campaigned to end the slow growth of farm output. Raising prices had the desired incentive effect only briefly. Whether production responded to prices, that is, prices were incentives that allocated inputs (particularly labor) and changed outputs, or whether they only redistributed income between the state budget and the producers without changing inputs and outputs has been a source of debate.[101] Vlad Treml provided the consensus view on the failure, over the long term, of price policies for Soviet agriculture in the era of reforms:

> Examination of price, subsidy, and output data for the last 15 years reveals no clear pattern of relationships between agricultural performance and the policy of setting prices and subsidies for individual commodities. It would appear that most of the changes in specific procurement prices and subsidies that the price fixing authorities have introduced in this period have been established on an ad hoc basis and that the only common factor in all of these changes is the existence of persistent financial losses to the producers.[102]

The "treadmill" of costly and futile administrative adjustments included the establishment of new agencies, procedural changes in the administration of prices, and centralized rationing of producer goods, centralized research and extension, amalgamation of farms, increased use of financial variables, contracts, and pecuniary sanctions, and numerous other arrangements. These reforms, stabilizing the level of wages, did not make the community more cooperative and the regime more technically efficient.[103]

[100] Grossman (1968), p. 46.
[101] Clayton (1976).
[102] Treml (1982), p. 176.
[103] See Wädekin (1989); Durgin (1978); Clayton (1980); Schroeder (1979); and many others, cited below.

The results of waves of socialist transformation and investment, in other words, did not provide adequate incentives in agriculture.[104] The rural work force was less well educated than the industrial work force in the Soviet era. Beyond its contribution embodied in technology, industrial education in agriculture could not assist productivity. Since 1975, large expenditures were made to improve the productivity and regional distribution of the farm labor force. The productivity of the farm labor force remained low, however. Some Western estimates placed it at 10 percent of that in the United States.[105]

Bottlenecks in the planning system prevented timely supply of parts, and the poor state of equipment repair limited the capacity of the system for change. Manellia and his co-authors at the Government Center for Economic Conjuncture described a growing sense of helplessness by reformers working with socialized agriculture after the 1970s. Investments did not revolutionize growth, in contrast with trends in the West, and environmental and other damage due to waste in socialized agriculture promised to be difficult to reverse. Yields continued to rise, but the cost of production did not fall.[106] The rigidities of Soviet bureaucratic governance were responsible, as in the tsarist era, for the failure of its capacity to resolve major problems without a crisis.

In the billowing economic storms of the mid-1980s, Gorbachev attempted to introduce incentives on a larger scale than before by increasing enterprise autonomy and by adding flexibility to the system through contract brigades and other forms of contracting. His reforms stopped short of allowing the free disposability of land, however, and his agricultural reforms failed to liberalize wholesale prices. Without actual market incentives, managers and independent farmers could not improve their decision-making because of continued bottlenecks in the supply chain. As the general macroeconomic crisis deepened, the early success of the brigade system and a rise in independent farming were not sufficiently powerful to hold off the collapse of farm finances.

104 Schroeder (1971), p. 31.

105 Goodman, Hughes, and Shroeder (1987), p. 102.

106 Note, however, econometric evidence of yield convergence. See SPR (1997), p. 3; Trueblood (2001).

3

The Transition Reforms, 1991–2010

Simultaneous price and trade liberalization in Russia in 1992 was coordinated with an ambitious agenda of rapid enterprise privatization, embracing the farm sector in 1991. Partly as a consequence of that timing, the transformation of state and collective farms into profit-making corporative entities only gradually got underway as managers confronted a deep and lasting recession. Agriculture gained less than might have been expected by a major devaluation in 1998, which was the impetus for a strong industrial recovery. The transformation in agriculture began slowly in cereals production and then in some livestock sectors.[1] By 2005, on the basis of indicators for 2003, observers found no significant change.[2] By 2010, however, farm indicators from 2007, as represented in Table 3.1, showed finally more powerful structural transformation effects from reform in the early 1990s.

The achievements of Russian agrarian reform as shown in Table 3.1 are not as striking as in the selected EU transition economies, including the Czech Republic, Slovakia, and Estonia. However, agriculture has downsized considerably, relative to industry and services, as shown in the table by the sector's share of gross domestic product (GDP)(less than five percent).[3] In 2008, due in part to good weather conditions, gross output rose by an enormous 10.8 percent, or 3.8 percent per capita.[4] There is a continued gap in yields with the advanced countries of western Europe and North America.

Recession was by no means the only reason for agriculture's weak performance in the 1990s. A performance gap was clearly visible well before

[1] Liefert (2001), pp. 254–63.

[2] Journalists continued to see agriculture on a downward trend as late as 2005. Writing in that year in Russia's *International Agricultural Journal* (No. 1, pp. 9–12), M. Korobeinikov describes the state of Russian agriculture as "critical."

[3] OECD (2007), p. 18; World Bank Development Indicators Online (2010).

[4] "Indeksy proizvodstva produktsii sel'skogo khoziastva (v protsentakh k predydushchemu godu)," 9 December 2009, *Rossiiskii statisticheskii ezhegodnik*.

TABLE 3.1. *Main Agricultural Indicators, Selected Countries, 2007*

	Exports[a]	Yield[b]	% GDP[c]	Employment[d]
Upper Middle Income	1.9	2,533.9	6.1	15.1[06]
High Income: OECD	1.6	4,948.6	1.4	3.1
Australia	3.4	1,178.0	3.3[03]	3.4
Canada	4.2	2,988.1	2.3[00]	2.6
Czech Republic	1.3	4,525.8	2.5	3.8
Estonia	6.3	3,029.1	2.7	4.7
Finland	5.5	3,695.2	2.5	4.7
France	0.9	6,421.7	2.2	3.4[03]
Germany	0.8	6,418.5	0.9	2.3
Lithuania	3.0	3,007.0	4.4	10.4
Poland	1.0	3,255.8	4.3	14.7
Russian Federation	2.9	1,839.4	4.8	9.0
Slovak Republic	1.2	3,996.3	3.6	4.2
United Kingdom	0.6	6,771.2	0.9	1.4
United States	2.5	6,683.4	1.1[06]	1.4

[a] Agricultural raw materials exports, % merchandise exports, 2007.
[b] Cereal yield (kg per hectare), 2007.
[c] Agricultural value added (%GDP), [00] = 2000, [03] = 2003, [06] = 2006.
[d] Employment in agriculture in 2007 (% total employment), [03] = 2003, [06] = 2006.
Source: World Bank Development Online Indicators (2010).

the collapse of the Soviet Union. The deep recession in the early 1990s, which affected the entire economy, brought down total agricultural output far more than could have been predicted, by about 40 percent from before price liberalization in 1992. Livestock production fell by about 50 per cent, in response to adverse terms of trade and consumption shifts, which resulted from the sharp decline in income. The livestock economy that had maintained fairly high levels of meat consumption was particularly hurt, and this affected feed grain production.[5] What Table 3.1 essentially shows is that by 2007, yields were still well behind those in most western advanced countries, except for Australia, even after the recession ended, showing a technological lag from the Soviet era.

This chapter addresses both the Soviet legacy and the crisis in the 1990s, usually viewed as initial conditions affecting the reform process.[6] Rapid price liberalization in 1992, combined with the slashing of subsidies in 1993, made

[5] Liefert (1997), p. 99.

[6] Krueger and Ciolko (1998) and Falcetti, Raiser, and Sanfey (2002) find that initial conditions were more important in growth outcomes than reforms; the latter find a simultaneity bias in the results, however; initial conditions are usually defined, as in de Melo (2001) and Stuart and Panayotopoulos (1999), as macroeconomic distortions, although the latter also look at microeconomic distortion; see also the important work on disorganization as a legacy of central planning in some sectors (Blanchard [1997]).

agricultural commodities relatively expensive for consumers, given their low quality, and led to changes in consumption patterns. Meanwhile capital intensive agriculture suffered as Russia's large budget deficit was financed almost exclusively between 1992 and 1995 by money creation, leading to high rates of inflation. As before in Russian history, political conditions were appropriate for agrarian reform, but economic conditions were not.

Why did the government go ahead despite the production risk? Freeing agricultural prices and privatizing farm enterprises, like transition reforms in general, as is well known, were greatly influenced by political considerations.[7] Their timing in a crisis had the advantage that sectoral lobbies within the ministries were weakened and political power was fragmented. Opposition to agrarian reform at the federal and regional level, led by communists and farm managers and including groups on the extreme right, was strong, but not strong enough to block macroeconomic reform to introduce a market economy. Also, a reform path in agriculture was already introduced by Mikhail Gorbachev, whose influence led to the appearance in his term of office of the first reform legislation. Even in the Supreme Soviet of the Russian Federation, which had tended to be a rubber stamp for the Communist Party decisions, there was little effective opposition to market reforms and to the passage of new laws on property rights in 1990, with the exception of a moratorium imposed on the actual sale of arable land for 20 years.[8]

Thus the reformers created private enterprises and reduced state subsidies as the economy went into recession. As during the nineteenth-century reform era, as during the New Economic Policy (NEP) of 1921, and as during collectivization, the results in the first decade show producers to have been ineffective in resolving crisis dilemmas. Large enterprises retained labor on large farms in the 1990s, rather than downsizing their labor force, and many, as a consequence, turned into shells for household production of vegetables.[9] Farm directors reduced their expenditures, including on wages and equipment; old equipment became useless through disrepair. The rural populace, vulnerable to the fate of large enterprises, found security in income from sales of vegetables grown on their small private plots. Traditional plots, requiring no new equipment or new household gardening routines, flourished in an era of insecure property rights to the arable.[10]

This chapter has two parts. Part 1 reviews the politics of creating property rights in arable beginning with the 1990 Peasant Farms Law of the Supreme

[7] Balcerowitz (1997); Blanchard (1997); Blasi et al. (1997); Brabant (1998); Brada (1996); Brada et al. (1996); Clague (1992); Granville (1995, 2001); Kornai (1993); Roland (2000); Shleifer (2000), and others.

[8] Shagaida (2005).

[9] See Lermon (2001).

[10] Bokusheva and Hockmann (2006); Pallot and Nefedova (2007).

Soviet of the Russian Federation up to the final critical stage of reform, its completion by President Vladimir Putin. It emphasizes the changing rates and nature of budgetary support, which treated large farms preferentially. Part 2 addresses mainly the impact of reform in the 1990s: rising farm indebtedness, a small build-up of new farms, a dramatic increase of household production, the spread of barter, and rural poverty. It traces the degree to which these effects were particularly intense in Russia, by comparison with other transition countries.

1 THE END OF CENTRALLY PLANNED AGRICULTURE

Agriculture in the Late Soviet Period

The financial and fiscal crisis of the late 1980s had roots in a decades-long growth strategy. Although similar in some ways to the extensive growth model adopted in Japan and Korea, the Soviet strategy had a problem not typically found in most market economies, low elasticity of substitution between capital and labor, which led to highly problematic diminishing returns to capital.[11] From the 1950s, mineral resource revenues were increasingly vital to the Soviet planning regime: investment in energy sector technology rose, and the dependence on oil output deepened. The volatility of oil prices in the 1980s, with a steep rise through 1986 and then a plunge and leveling off, affected the entire economy.[12] The weakness of a system so dependent upon external activities was that when revenues declined, foreign debt obligations reached "avalanche-like proportions."[13]

Agriculture's factor intensivity in the Soviet era resulted in the increasing cost of resource requirements for improved performance. The agricultural turnover tax (a form of sales tax applied at each stage of the distribution chain) had to be abolished in the 1960s, signaling the end of its contribution of labor to the expansion of industry. From 1986 to 1990 the share of budgetary subsidies in sales rose from 19.4 to 33.9 percent; meanwhile, agriculture annually consumed about 20 percent of all state investment in the economy.[14] To maintain consumption levels of high-valued meat products, the state heavily invested in agricultural equipment and subsidized both consumers and producers. The growth strategy promised high levels of meat consumption for which it was necessary to import fodder.[15] To meet expected levels of meat consumption Brezhnev reinvested in large herds localized at capital-intensive farms. Between 1970 and 1989, when meat production

[11] Easterly and Fischer (1994, 1995).
[12] Dowling and Hilton (1992).
[13] See Gaidar (2003), pp. 28–30.
[14] Brooks (1990), p. 463; *ERS* March 31, 1997.
[15] Liefert (1997, 2002).

in the twelve EC countries rose by 47 percent, in the USSR it rose by 59 percent. The post-Brezhnev regime continued this policy. Consumer and direct producer subsidies to the sector increased by 1989 to 10.8 percent of GDP.[16] This caused the rise, from 1986 to 1990, of the Producer Support Estimate (PSE) to 78 percent, more than twice that of the average of the Organisation for Economic Co-operation and Development (OECD) countries (PSE 28).[17]

Support in the Soviet era was composed almost entirely of domestic prices, which were substantially above the border reference prices (calculated at official exchange rates) and unaffected by world market prices due to the state monopoly of trade.[18] The agricultural producers received three kinds of subsidies: direct budget subsidies (which maintained the gap between producers and consumer prices), the domestic price regime, which held agricultural input costs down and shielded information about the real costs of production, and the price and trade system, elevating domestic producer prices above world prices.[19] In view of the cost of food production, even though it was subsidized, the net result for consumers – the CSE – was a tax between 1986 and 1991 of roughly 50 percent.[20] Meanwhile, as the shortages and inflationary crisis affected production in the late 1980s, gross agricultural output (GAO) started its decline and fell steadily.[21]

In the mid-1980s the government could not respond more adequately to the farm problem without first addressing the source of the economy-wide difficulties. Gorbachev was not a believer in markets, so he rejected price liberalization but relaxed wage and other constraints on managers with inflationary consequences. The country was led deeper into crisis. Even as his agrarian reform made some headway, the decline of his credibility after a coup attempt ended in his resignation in December 1991.[22]

16 Sedick (1993), pp. 42–3; Serova (1999).

17 The measure is Producer Subsidy Equivalent or Estimate (PSE), the annual monetary value of gross transfers from consumers and taxpayers to support agricultural producers. PSE measures the degree to which producer prices deviate from world producer prices. OECD estimates are for producer prices, which are measured at the farm gate, include support, regardless of its nature or objectives and its impact on both farm production and income. The PSE includes implicit as well as explicit payments, price wedges on output or input, tax exemptions, and, included in budgetary payments, those to remunerate nonmarket goods and services. The percentage of PSE, or the PSE as a ratio to the value of total gross farm receipts measured by the value of total production plus budgetary support, can be used for comparisons between countries; see OECD (1999), pp. 239, 287.

18 The price gap measure (the basis for the Market Price Support, or MPS) includes all policies in the period, including fixed prices and margins along the food chain as well as exchange rates (OECD 1998, p. 144).

19 Liefert (2001), p. 263.

20 OECD (1999), p. 239.

21 Source: the Ministry of Agriculture and Food Production, 1997.

22 On perestroika and its consequences, see Bergson (1985, 1989); Ellman (1993, 2000); Hanson (1992); Ericson (1990, 1991); Schroeder (1988, 1991); Hewett (1991).

The First Major Farm Reform

Gorbachev's farm policy was without a doubt a considerable opening. The enterprise reform of 1987 and experimentation with contract pricing gave greater autonomy to individuals to form cooperatives, lease land, and start farms. These measures gave legal stature to private farming, and local decision making strengthened collective and state farm support for reform.

In 1990–1991, the Supreme Soviet of the Russian Federation's State Committee for Land Reform began the course toward farm restructuring. Collective and state farms, whose distinctions were now officially removed, were separated from land leased for personal plots, the latter given in perpetuity to households.[23] Households gained entitlement to an equal share of the rest of the land (*uslovnaia zemel'naia dolia*) and, by seniority, to nonland assets (*uslovnyi imushchestvennoi pai*) of the collective or state farm. Shares could be exchanged, leased, given away, or left in the founding capital of the farm. Those who wanted to be peasant farmers[24] could purchase and withdraw their shares from the collective. In the laws, "On land reform" and "On social development of the countryside," together constituting the Peasant Farms Law, the Supreme Soviet confirmed the entire legal framework of rights, along with the leasing and inheritance of land (February 28, 1990). The Russian Federation Land Code (April 25) guaranteed enforcement of the Peasant Farms Law.[25] When the moratorium (waiting period) expired, the disposition of arable land would be governed by property rights. The next step, price reform, was taken E. Gaidar under Yeltsin.

Price Reform and Recession

Price and trade liberalization took place simultaneously in January 1992. By the first quarter of 1995, prices generally reflected market conditions, although price controls existed in some regions, especially on basic foods.[26] This had a dampening effect on agriculture in that, while liberalization sent input prices to world levels, producer prices on basic foodstuffs were still

[23] Vegetable growers, those who owned "personal subsidiary plots" [on former collective and state farms], individual home owners, livestock cooperatives, and, in principle, those who held land shares in farm enterprises.

[24] This term is no longer used in official Russian documents, except to denote independent farmers, where it does not imply characteristic features of a peasantry, such as subsistence farming, which would be generally inferred from its usage in Western literature.

[25] The Russian Land Code gave extensive rights to local soviets on land reform; their abolition after the abortive coup attempt transfered that authority to other state agencies. On December 29, 1991, a presidential edict on land reform, "On reorganization of the kolkhozy and sovkhozy," was promulgated, and on January 1, 1992, a further presidential decree, "On urgent measures for realization of land reform in the RSFSR," which guaranteed the purchase and sale of land.

[26] Berkowitz and DeJong (1998).

controlled and strongly affected by reduced demand. Federal-level regulation of a range of consumer food prices remained until March 1992.[27] Local urban price controls on grain interfered with the uniform federal policy through 1995. When, in 1995, bread prices in Moscow were finally allowed to rise, they did so at the rate of about 10 percent per month, more than twice the rate of monthly inflation. Retail prices for basic foods were controlled by the mark-up limits and limits on price increases for wholesalers and retailers, restrictions largely relevant for bread, milk, and other dairy products and meat.[28] Terms of trade were also affected by inefficient downstream and upstream industries, which passed their costs onto producers and consumers. Input prices grew 2.3 times faster than producer prices between 1990 and 1993.[29] Terms of trade improved by 1995 but then dipped again in 1996. Farm finance was affected by tight monetary policy resulting from high real interest rates and from the lack of cooperative or other organizations offering commercial credit willing to lend to agriculture. Due to the growing indebtedness and lack of capital, output fell continuously between 1990 and 1996.

The fall in demand was particularly harsh for producers. Per capita meat and milk consumption dropped between 1990 and 2000 by 45 and 44 percent respectively.[30] This was because of consumers' preference for higher quality imports and also because of the dramatic fall in per capita income. Demand for products with high income elasticities declined as wages fell in uncompetitive sectors.[31] The fall in demand for livestock products in turn had an effect on feed grain production. Although consumption of cereals increased, producers were still in need of direct intervention as late as 2002.[32] Among key factors in the difficult path of restoring Russian demand were cheap and attractive imports from the European Union and the United States. Russian producers began to retake the domestic market after devaluation in 1998, but positive effects lasted only a few years and imports again discouraged production.[33]

Downsizing was inevitable. In eight years, 1990 to 1997, agricultural output dropped by 36 percent.[34] In difficult conditions, Yeltsin's government began his agrarian reform, getting around the moratorium on land sales by enterprise privatization. On December 29, 1991, he announced former

[27] Granville (1997).
[28] OECD (1999), p. 13.
[29] Ibid.
[30] William Liefert, "Food Security in Russia:Economic Growth and Rising Incomes are Reducing Insecurity," *Food Security Assessment / GFA-15 / May 2004*, p. 37, http://www.ers.usda.gov/publications/GFA15/GFA15i.pdf.
[31] Granville and Ferguson (2000).
[32] Liefert (2002).
[33] Serova and Shick (2006 July).
[34] OECD (1998), pp. 12–13.

state and collective farms would be re-registered when they would have to declare themselves open or closed joint stock companies, cooperatives, or other listed types, or they could retain their previous registration as state and collective farms, which about one-third chose to do. Corporatization was intended to stimulate the withdrawal of land and asset shares from the enterprise by restructuring. It endorsed the Peasant Farms Law and created incentives for realizing the household entitlements in a decisive and irreversible ownership transfer. It also provided additional stimulus for an even larger exit of independent farmers.

In 1993, before parliamentary elections, using his temporary powers to govern by executive decree, Yeltsin then overturned the moratorium and confirmed by decree individuals' and farms' right without restriction to dispose of (lease, inherit, mortgage, or sell) arable land. The substance of this decree was secured by inclusion in the Federal Constitution of the Russian Federation of December 2003.[35] Researchers for the Institute of the Transition Economy, E. Ivankina and her co-authors, view the law and its confirmation in the constitution as the core of Russian Federation land reform.[36] Divergent regional laws were legally without force of law and eventually reconciled with federal law.

Post-constitution Reform Drift

The parliamentary defeat suffered by liberals in the elections of 1993 led to resignation of reform-oriented ministers, and new official statements about reform objectives were less about individual rights than cooperative obligations. The government focused clearly on the two key strategies: cooperative development and management reform, as in the official statement of goals of agrarian reform in Russia for 1993–1995:

- Incorporating land and other asset privatization and voluntary pooling of resources in single process, accomplished by diverse means, to redistribute assets into joint or partitioned forms of property;
- Creating a competitive milieu by forming a multisector agrarian economy;
- Privatizing and demonopolizing the industrial and service sectors of the agro-industrial complex;

[35] See note 1, also Presidential Decree No. 1767, October 27, 1993 ("On the Regulation of Land Relations and the Development of Agrarian Reform in Russia"), where real estate was defined and land entitlement holders gained the right to sell, lease, give away, mortgage, and bequeath their land entitlements and where titles were guaranteed to land entitlement holders, along with ownership rights. The substance of this decree was guaranteed in the December 1993 Constitution of the Russian Federation (Articles 9, 36, 72), the Civil Code of the Russian Federation, November 1994, where legal forms of enterprises, and ownership of land and procedures for exercising it, were set forth (OECD 1999, p. 79).

[36] Ivankina et al. (2000), p. 56.

- Creating market infrastructure;
- Improving management of the agro-industrial complex;
- Rationalizing the system of state support for agriculture and decisively reducing subsidies to the agro-industrial complex;
- Developing the social infrastructure of the village.[37]

The government avoided imposing any particular restructuring procedure or making more than an indirect reference to independent farming, one component of a multisector economy.

Nevertheless, the laws allowing private property were in place. The issue became one of regulation and enforcement, given joint distribution of authority on the issue of property rights between regions and the central (federal) government in the Constitution of 1993. Under Yeltsin, regional autonomy grew. Diversity in laws was encouraged to the point that some regions exercised sovereignty. Separate treaties were concluded with the regions that sought specific fiscal arrangements.[38] Some regions and republics failed to permit land sales or to decontrol prices; some refused to privatize large state enterprises. Some regional governments failed to pay wages and met production expenses on state farms by transfers negotiated from the federal budget.[39] Regions exercised discretion in the adoption of market institutions. Regional authorities retained considerable power over policy implementation by their control over the branches of federal agencies in the regions.[40]

Thus, although Yeltsin had overturned the parliamentary moratorium on land sales, it remained de facto in place in some regions through 2010. The unpredictability of law enforcement, in turn, raised risks for those who sought to create a small family farm. The numbers of small farms grew rapidly at first and then slowed by 1997 to a figure of roughly 280,000 farms, which held some 6 percent of agricultural land, each farm averaging forty-four hectares. By 2006, independent farms had almost doubled in size at an average of eighty-five hectares.[41] For comparison, in 2007, average farm size in the US was roughly 1032 hectares (418 acres), and in the European Union, or EU (15), 114 hectares. Of two hundred twenty-one million hectares of agricultural land, 38 percent remained in the possession

37 "A Program for Stabilization of the Agro-Industrial Complex, 1993–1995" (Moscow: Goskomstat, 1993).

38 Almost half of the eighty-nine regions and republics (twenty-one republics, six territories, forty-nine oblasts, two cities of federal importance, one autonomous oblast', ten autonomous areas [okrugi]) concluded treaties. See Treisman (1999).

39 The best case study of agrarian reform in the regions is by Amelina (2002). For federal relations with the regions in the 1990s see Granville and Leonard (2006); Hanson; Popov (2001); Lapidus (1999); Bardeleben (1997); Sutela (1996), and others.

40 OECD (2005).

41 Agricultural census data (2006) in *Rossiiskii statisticheskii ezhegodnik* (2008).

of the state or municipal authorities, and 3 percent was owned in the form of plots by sixteen million households, averaging .4 hectares per plot.[42]

Putin's Consolidation of Reform

To address the glaring rural poverty and farm bankruptcies that were the consequence of the relative stagnation of reform in the 1990s, the government of Vladimir Putin revitalized and completed the reform process. The legal framework of constitutional rights was essentially in place, but procedural complications required important adjustments in Russia's regulatory regime to expedite agrarian reform. In now stable macroeconomic conditions, the required laws were enacted and a powerfully centralizing government removed all legislation in the regions that conflicted with federal law. Coming into force on October 30, 2001, a new Land Code replaced the outdated 1991 version, but it excluded as an exception arable land.[43] An amendment dealing with agricultural land, was finally passed, with considerable difficulty, recognizing and regulating land purchase and sale (May 16, 2002), although with some limitations.[44]

Briefly, the Land Code prohibits foreign firms and individuals, stateless persons, or majority-foreign-owned companies from owning arable land. It leaves in place some zoning restrictions and barriers to exit from cooperatives, roughly the same restrictions as in most countries. It tends to privilege the state over other kinds of owners in that the federal authorities own the agencies conducting transactions, but it contains flexible provisions and allows long leases.[45] The state claims the right to confiscation for various reasons, including environmental damage to property, another provision common in modern economies. Its major gap in 2002 was on the subject of collateral. In 2003, the final critical amendment was passed, published in 2004 after reworking by a conciliatory commission, not prohibiting arable land to be used as collateral, a law essential to the functioning of property rights in market economies.

There was a further snag in the regulations that were passed. The law requires that the land registry complete all of its work before transactions in land are carried out. For the registry to be completed, the government had to expedite the land cadastre: producers of different categories had to be

42 OECD (1998), pp. 16–17.

43 "Federal'nyi zakon "O vvedenie v deistvie zemel'nogo kodeksa Rossiiskoi Federatsii," Oct. 25, 2001 g., N 137-FZ.

44 "Federal'nyi zakon ob oborote zemel' sel'skokhoziastvennogo naznacheniia," July 24, 2002 g., N 101-FZ.

45 This is the subject of special treatment by Skyner (2003); see also analysis of Russian land law by UNECE (United Nations Economic Commission for Europe), "Landownership in the Russian Federation: How good land administration can make a difference" (Feb. 6, 2004), http:/www.*unece.org/press/pr2004/04env_p04e.htm*.

uniform by tax bracket, and land and structural assets had to be combined in accounts so that the single cadastral estimate of tax liability could be finished. That these matters were pushed forward in the Putin presidency had decisive effect on Russia's agrarian development, after a decade of regional defiance of the center. Centralization harmonize the laws and reduce resistance in some regions to the privatization of arable land.

One motive for Putin's intensification of the reform process was the resumption of accession negotiations for Russia's entry into the World Trade Organization (WTO) after a hiatus in the year of Russia's financial crisis. As N. Campos (2004) shows for central and eastern Europe, preparation for entry into the WTO can be an effective tool for governments to block sometimes powerful conservative domestic opposition to liberal legislation. The WTO effect has had little impact on trade openness itself or on flows of Foreign Direct Investment (FDI) in Russia, but it assuredly had an impact on the pace of agrarian reform.

2 FISCAL REFORM

The Early Years

Agricultural subsidies under central planning included unit compensation for inputs used in the bulk production of grain and livestock, which is not a budgetary allocation mechanism that is compatible with market incentives. In the command economy, the objective was to maintain low and stable food prices, with the result that the state provided up to half the price of agricultural machinery and fertilizers. In this way, price distortions affected the entire chain of food production. After 1988, subsidies were especially distorting as differentiated purchase prices and price premia were paid directly to producers. Moreover, the subsidy that was required for electricity was actually a tax on industry to the benefit of agriculture. Two other major sources of distortion that lasted into the transition era were directed credit to farm enterprises and, after 1992, compensation to urban consumers and payments to livestock producers (transferred to the regions from 1993 to 1996).[46]

In 1992, state support for agriculture dramatically declined in real terms due to price liberalization, as estimated below in Table 3.2. In Table 3.2 it is also clear that in 1995 state support was partially restored. The table shows percentage PSE[47] (the ratio of the producer support estimate to total

[46] Information provided by the Ministry of Finance.

[47] The Producer Support Estimate (PSE) is an indicator of the annual monetary value of gross transfers from consumers and taxpayers to support agricultural producers, measured at farm gate level, arising from policy measures, regardless of their nature, objectives, or impacts on farm production or income (OECD).

TABLE 3.2. *Estimates of Support to Russian Agriculture, 1991–2005*

	1991	1992	1993	1994	1995	1996	1997	1998	1999	2000	2001	2003–2005
Percentage PSE	60	−94	−24	−13	17	26	30	19	4	8	10	17
Percentage TSE	n.c.	−14	−2.5	−0.8	2.1	3.0	3.9	2.0	0.6	0.8	0.9	1.38

Source: OECD (2002), Annex TableV.6.a, p. 144; OECD (2007), p. 113.

farm receipts plus budgetary support) and percentage TSE (the total support estimate, including transfers from consumers, taxpayers, and budget revenues as a percentage of GDP).

Thus when the budget deficit soared to 20.9 percent of GDP in 1992, budget subsidies were cut as the government tried to find a bridge to voluntary tax payment after the end of central planning. Until the VAT (Value Added Tax) went into effect, monetary and fiscal policy were joined to attempt to bring inflation under control. In mid-1993, after Yeltsin achieved a mandate through the national referendum of April 25, Finance Minister Boris Fedorov and Prime Minister Yegor Gaidar temporarily imposed fiscal control, and in November and December the refinancing rate finally turned positive.[48] By 1992, the level of subsidies in Russia was far less than those of western European countries, as shown in Table 3.3.

That is, federal subsidies fell from 33 percent of agricultural sales and 10 percent of gross national product (GNP) in 1989 to negative numbers between 1992 and 1994, and when restored in 1995, were no more than the level of the EU, at roughly 2.1 percent of GDP. Some federal-level support was maintained, however, for investment. By 1995, 31 percent of investment in fixed capital in the agro-industrial complex was provided by the federal and regional budgets, with the regional share growing.[49]

The government also decreased procurement to allow new channels of trade to open up. Before 1992, almost 100 percent of marketed production was procured by the state (except for potatoes and vegetables, for which the state share was less). Procurement prices, fixed by product and applied to all mandatory deliveries, were composed of a base price and bonuses related to quality and timely delivery. These centrally fixed prices were differentiated by region to match profitability across zones. Supplementary payments above these prices were the main nontransparent means by which the government had rewarded farms that had difficulty in the late Soviet era, even within higher-priced zones. These payments were also the means of delivery

[48] Shleifer and Treisman (2000), p. 43.
[49] *Sel'khoz* (2000), p. 38.

TABLE 3.3. *Ratio of Agricultural Transfers to GDP, 1992, Selected Countries, %*

Australia	0.6
Austria	2.4
Canada	1.6
EC	2.2
Finland	4.1
Japan	1.9
New Zealand	0.2
Norway	3.9
Sweden	1.4
Switzerland	2.4
U.S.	1.6

Source: Leonard and Serova (2001), p. 374.

of regional development projects – the social sphere, soil improvement, and social programs. Supplementary payments were ended in 1992, along with the system of administered food prices and compulsory deliveries. The new procurement system – technically state control on prices for agricultural products delivered to government reserves – was used for state purchases for federal and regional stocks. The procurement decline is documented in Table 3.4.[50]

Some procurement was continued mainly as a means to subsidize credit. The low contract price, in crisis conditions, however, actually was a net tax on producers. After procurement dropped, food sales shifted even more into the shadow economy.

The budgetary reform process was moving toward completion. However, the austerity, combined with high nominal interest rates in this environment, led to barter, in conditions where parliamentary regulation of the sale of land was disputed and uncertain. The opportunity cost of money rose, encouraging financial innovation and the creation of non-money means of payment.[51] The share of barter in the economy grew in response to the decline in procurement.[52] Grain was retained on farm for internal use for feed by households and in payment of wages.[53] Delayed payments due to

[50] *Russian Economy* (1996), p. 64. Figures for meat and dairy procurement as officially calculated, the output of processing agencies authorized as state purchasers, do not include private trade of those establishments. Procurement is therefore exaggerated. These figures also fail to show the regional situation. In some regions, Nizhnii Novgorod, for example, state procurement of meat and poultry was by then eliminated Serova (1997).

[51] Kemme (2003); Granville (1995).

[52] In 1999, Eugenia Serova estimated barter to comprise 20 percent of GAO.

[53] OECD (1999), p. 115.

TABLE 3.4. *Share of Russian Government Procurement in Farm Sales, 1992–2005, Volume, %*

	1992	1993	1994	1995	1997	1999	2000	2005
Grain	56	63	29	38	25	19	17	6
Beet sugar	81	98	32	21	9	17	11	7
Oil seeds	65	32	48	21	13	11	8	5
Potatoes	57	52	33	37		24	24	12
Vegetables	70	71	54	55	27	32	27	14
Cattle and poultry, in live weight	90	79	79	62	45	42	40	21
Milk and milk products	95	97	93	91	82	76	73	52
Eggs	86	92	85	87	75	87	52	23

Sources: Kratkosrochnye ekonomicheskie pokazateli, Rossiiskaia Federatsiia 1996 (1997), Moscow: Goskomstat, p. 55; data from annual reports of agricultural enterprises; *OECD* 1999, p. 112; *Sel'khoz* (2000, 2002, 2004); *Rossiiskii Statisticheskii Ezhegodnik* (2001, 2002, 2005, 2006); in the instance of inconsistency, the most recent information from the official statistical annual for the Russian Federation is given.

inflation encouraged barter with input suppliers. State orders were placed through quasi-fiscal energy suppliers, an ad hoc form of support. This led to a continuation of production by normatives set by state orders at lower than market prices.[54] In 2001, the Centre for Economic Conjuncture provided results of a survey in which 40 percent of directors of large farms and 43 percent of independent farmers acknowledged that they used barter to supplement low state prices for procured goods.[55]

In sum, inflationary conditions combined with slashed subsidies in early transition meant that direct payments were replaced by a soft-budget constraint that operated at considerably lower levels of support and were funded in part at the regional level.[56]

POST-1995

In 1995, as observed, some subsidies were restored at low levels, but budgetary reform was advancing rapidly. Procurement prices were set at roughly one-quarter to one-half of free market prices, an important fiscal step. In figures from the OECD, PSE reached a high of 28 percent in 1997 and a low of less than 1 percent in 1999. After 2001, market price support came to play a relatively larger proportion than budgetary support. In 2005, the PSE stood at a level of less than 16 percent.[57]

[54] Dolgopiatova and Evseeva-Boeva (1995); Leonard (1996).
[55] Matiukhin and Bezrukov (2001).
[56] Kornai (2003), Amelina (2002).
[57] OECD (2007), p. 112 (statlink).

Nearly three-quarters of PSE was comprised of import protection, mainly livestock products and sugar. Aid to the agricultural sector channeled through import tariffs, however, was low by European averages, some 15 percent for most items, except sugar in the mid-1990s.[58] In 2001, tariff reform reduced these further with a new range of 5, 10, 15, and 20 percent, replacing the previous range of 0 to 30. The low tariff rates were somewhat stiffened by excessive regulation and the arbitrary means of customs valuation, with bureaucratic and costly certification, but progress toward WTO accession after 2005 brought some of these non-tariff barriers down. Total support in 2003–2005 was 1.4 percent, down from 2.8 percent relative to GDP in 1995–1997.[59]

By commodity, OECD estimates provide a picture of the level of protection, as measured by the coefficient, NPC (nominal protection coefficient), measuring the ratio between the average price paid by consumers (at farm gate) and the border price (measured at farm gate level). Sugar and the livestock sector are priority targets, with the latter receiving both import protection and input support.[60] Direct payments to the livestock sector between 1992 and 1996 comprised roughly a quarter of all direct payments. Subsidized credit amounted to one-third of the total subsidization in that period, with social services falling from 18.6 percent in 1992 to 9.5 percent in 1996.[61]

Within these base-level policies, two particular dynamics were characteristic: the increasing share of the regions and the use of ad hoc measures. Particular regions were authorized to subsidize livestock and other goods through the annual negotiated component of the budget. Regions were authorized to practice debt write-off for non–profit-making farms.[62] Debt was written off both for producers, who failed to repay regional authorities, and for regional authorities, who failed to repay debts to the federal government. In 1998, a law on insolvency was put into effect, but it was rarely used.

In May 2002, the Duma approved a debt restructuring plan for overdue budgetary loans to enterprises and cooperatives between 1992 and 2002.[63] Almost half of farm enterprises' bank accounts were blocked due to unpaid

58 "O merakh po stabilizatsii ekonomicheskogo polozheniia PK RF v 1996 g.," No. 135, Feb. 7, 1996.

59 OECD (2007), p. 112.

60 Ibid.

61 OECD 1999, p. 138.

62 The degree of disorder and confusion has seemed to some observers tantamount to an incoherent agricultural policy (OECD 1998, p. 19).

63 "O poriadke obespecheniia vozvrata v 2002 gody zadolshennosti po biudzhetnym kreditam, predostavlennennym sel'skokhoziastvennym tovaroproizvoditeliam, organizatsiam agropromyshlennogo kompleksa i potrebitel'skoi kooperatsii s 1992 po 2000 goda," Postanovlenie Pravitel'stva Rossiiskoi Federatsii, No 353.

commercial loans, and a new plan was devised in July to restructure commercial (i.e., energy sector) as well as budgetary loans. The government signed it into law on January 30, 2003.[64] One drawback was that only debt was restructured: problems of profitability remained.[65] Grigorii Sergienko, the director of the Russian energy union, commented: "The government's decision to restructure commercial debt of the village sounds very Soviet. They give the village loans of all sorts and then write them off.... philanthropy..."[66]

Another drawback was that most farms were not in a position to apply. Although in principle 80 percent of enterprises were eligible for debt restructuring, the terms required payment of all current debt within three months, which meant that only a part of farms, those sturdy enough to comply, would actually have their debt restructured. Then vice Premier, Aleksei Gordeev viewed the accumulation of debt by farms as the consequence of the severe policy failure of early reform.[67] Suppliers saw it as ongoing policy failure. Debt write-off has been costly for taxpayers. Outstanding debt by the beginning of March 2000 was about $6.4 billion, a figure exceeding the value of annual sales. By 2003, the agricultural sector owed a sum of three hundred forty billion rubles, of which one hundred seventy billion consisted of overdue and accumulating fines (of which seventy million rubles were written off).

Obligatory crop insurance was another form of debt write-off in existence since the Soviet era. It worked as disaster relief in the regions of West Siberia, Northern Caucasus, the Urals, and the Volga. In the late 1980s, for example, 85 percent of producers requested compensation for crop loss. Eighty percent of Russian arable was categorized as within a zone of high-risk agriculture.[68] Fuel subsidies were also paid, even as the government raised the price of electricity to farms.[69] During the early years of transition, the agricultural sector was given broad tax exemptions, including from profit taxes on agricultural (and, after 1996, on nonagricultural) production and from the fixed assets tax, and a reduction on the road fund payments and pension fund rates.

By 1997, the Russian subsidy system was more or less in harmony with the European and U.S. system of guaranteed prices for a limited quota of

64 "O realizatsii Federal'nogo zakona 'O finansovom ozdorovlenii sel'skokhoziastvennykh tovaroproizvoditelei," Postanovlenie Pravitel'stva Rossiiskoi Federatsii, No. 52, Jan. 30, 2003.

65 Karlova et al. (2002), p. 256.

66 Ol'ga Papkova, "Otpushenie grekhov po-sovetski," *Novye Izvestiia*, Feb. 5, 2003, p. 2.

67 Vladimir San'ko, "Pravitel'stvo opiat' lechit sel'skoe khoziastvo," *Nezavisimaia Gazeta*, Feb. 4, 2003, p. 3.

68 Information provided by Rosgosstrakh.

69 In 1992, the agricultural sector's share was 19 percent of electricity prices paid by industry; in 1997, 61 percent. OECD (1999), p. 129.

purchases when average market prices were lower than the guaranteed price. The Federal Agency for the Regulation of the Food Market (replacing the Federal Food Commission) was established to carry out price support. There was a new budgetary category of support for rural development. The one area of state support for agriculture that was not well advanced was in regard to education. In the category "General Services" was the entire of support for extension, education, and training. O Shik (2002) surveys the structure of expenditures of the budget (consolidated) on agriculture in the category general services and finds that between 1995 and 2001, research and extension received between 0 and 4 percent, falling to 3 percent in 2001. Education averaged 12 percent, assistance for the land registry, falling off by 2001, averaged roughly 27 percent. Assistance to independent farmers fell from 4 percent of the total in 1995 to 0 percent in 2001.[70]

The vital land registry was in this category, and it witnessed diminishing support from the agricultural budget, and, although it was shifted to a federal-level national product, the latter was focused mainly on rural development. Among the greatest shortfalls in the Russian agrarian reform was the lack of concentrated support for this project. As of 2002, no more than 5 percent of the arable land was inventoried (such that borders and structures are clearly delineated), and government funds for the cadastre continued to decline.[71]

To summarize, the subsidy trends were forced down from 1980s levels by fiscal concerns, immediate priorities and budget reform in preparation for accession to the WTO. By 2007, the amount of subsidies through the consolidated (federal and regional) budget were low and stable, but their actual amount depended, as noted previously, on regional subsidies, which were posing a barrier to interregional trade.[72]

3 OTHER REFORM INSTRUMENTS

Credit

The credit system was not reformed until well into transition. Until 1993, the government continued to charge a negative real interest rate on loans to subsidize credit.[73] The use of authorized banks for transfers turned banks into cashiers, and banks were allowed 3 percent profit margins (paid monthly) for servicing loans. The cashier function gave banks an incentive to use the funds and hold back credit. The first major reform was in October

70 Shik (2002), p. 12.

71 Volkov (2002), p. 8.

72 Gardner (2002), pp. 5–12; Shik (2002), p. 10; Batkibekov et al. (2002), 24: 31.

73 Twenty-eight percent annually for large farm enterprises and 8 percent for independent farmers (at a time when the CBR refinance rate was over 150 percent.

1993, when subsidized directed credit was ended. In principle, this step was to help create new financial conditions in which loans would be available at commercial rates. However, by guaranteeing long-term loans at a new rate at a time when three-month loans were all that was commercially available, credit to the large farms that obtained it continued to be heavily subsidized.

Having in principle ended soft credit, the government nonetheless attempted again in 1995 to ease credit conditions by introducing commodity credit. This was allocated to producers in the form of oil products and other inputs with suppliers reimbursed in the form of tax relief. The budget was reimbursed by procurement at a contract price agreed upon before the harvest (financed by an annualized preferential interest rate of 10 percent) and supplied after the harvest.

Commodity credit was linked to grain procurement and not used to finance seasonal work, a scheme that proved unworkable. After their acceptance on the commodity credit scheme, suppliers raised prices of fuels delivered by 20 to 30 percent. Unfavorable terms of trade for producers and failure by regional governments to collect the procured commodities furthered the growing barter economy in agriculture. By 1997, it became necessary to restore soft credit in other forms. A new agency, the Soft Farm Credit Fund, provided preferential short-term credit for producers, aiming to replace commodity credit. Upper limits of soft credit were fixed for each oblast' by the Ministry of Agriculture and Food, with subsidized rates at one-quarter of the Central Bank refinance rate. A number of commercial banks were authorized to issue these credits.[74]

In 1996, the government restructured the huge monobank, by which credit had been channeled in the Soviet era to agriculture. The Agprombank, which had begun to falter, was first merged with the Stolichnyi savings bank under the new name of SBS-Agro and was essentially nationalized, since the government took the majority share. The initial merger, creating an apex structure for pooling resources of local credit cooperatives and loans based primarily on savings deposits, was intended as a new start in rural finance. Commercialization, however, was undercut by restoring preferential loan rates in the new fund created in 1997 for agricultural producers. In 2000, the Agprombank supplied about 70 percent of all loans to agriculture and was funded by the Central Bank and the budget. Credit to agriculture amounted to about 50 percent of the Agprombank portfolio, with much of these funds being for nonproduction purposes.

A new credit policy subsidizing interest rates for medium-term credit was begun in 2001. For working capital, the provision of loans was given to local banks, but producers or processors paid one-third of the Central Bank interest rates and the banks were reimbursed for the rest from the federal budget. In 2001, bank credits for agriculture increased sixfold, by contrast

[74] Leonard and Serova (2001).

with a twofold increase for the rest of the economy. Some 8,000 agro-food firms took advantage of the scheme, in which 212 banks were involved. This seems to be some evidence that this scheme was at least initially successful.[75]

Commodity Markets

Farmers must have commodity exchanges, but this was a weak area of initial government activity. Exchanges were set up in Saratov in 1991 and Rostov-on-Don in 1992. Contracts for grain were computerized, helping establish market prices in the south of Russia even for government procurements. Exchanges began to appear across the country. However, by temporarily raising procurement prices above market levels, in 1992, as procurement agencies attracted grain, exchanges declined in importance.

Commodity exchanges faced numerous barriers. Procurement prices again fell in 1994, but price controls were still in effect in some regions, so large grain producers generally preferred to sell directly to large wholesalers rather than at commodity exchanges. Some of the larger financial groups, Inkombank, Al'fakapital, and Menatep, which purchased grain and sunflower seeds through their own regional organizations and oil companies, also purchased grain through private channels directly from large producers. In short, the movement of grain was drawn into Russia's improvised barter network rather than clearing markets for cash.

By 1996 many of the restrictive conditions in which producers were operating eased. Commodity markets in grain began to function again. In 1997, an agricultural futures market opened in Nizhnii Novgorod, where thirty-two grain contracts were on offer for 320 tons of third-grade wheat from the 1997 harvest. The laws were then developed to permit warehouse certificate use and other forms of rural credit, including credit cooperatives, needed by small farmers.

Vegetable markets were, from 1992, less constrained by government intervention than grain markets, although grain exchanges became common by the end of the decade. Commodity exchanges for vegetables, supplied mainly by households and small-scale farms, spread rapidly, especially in the south of Russia. Trade on these exchanges tended to be conducted by independent traders, both firms and individuals.

Downstream Development[76]

Profitability margins were restricted to reduce the power of processing monopolies. Monopolies (both federal and local), as defined by the State Anti-Monopoly Committee, were subjected to limits on price increases of,

75 OECD (2002), p. 43.

76 Upstream activities refer to the supply of inputs; downstream to the storage, transportation, distribution, and processing, Liefert (2001), p. 255.

for example, 10 percent for sausages and milk (10 percent), 25 percent for sugar, 50 percent for salt and 50 percent for services. Macroeconomic policies, causing the rise in input prices and the ceiling on producer prices – combined with the reduction of budgetary subsidies, as inflation rose – had an adverse effect on downstream development, i.e. processing and distribution, from the start of agrarian reform.

The reformers understood the essential role of demonopolization and privatization of downstream activities as the motor of institutional transformation in agriculture. "Roskhleboprodukt," the government grain processing and procurement agency, was privatized and broken up into separate regional procurement agencies. By 1997, 92 percent of meat, dairy, flour, and flax processors were privatized. In effect, the state processing system had been gradually phased out.

Restructuring the processing sector proved difficult in view of continued government procurement and vertical integration in the agricultural sector. Processors had difficulty locating new supply outlets, and they found profit margins squeezed by antimonopoly policy. The territorial antimonopoly committees at the regional level fixed rates of profit and wage levels, which weakened incentives for investment. The government aimed to solve the investment problem through greater producer involvement in ownership and in 1994 required that processors emit new shares especially for producers. But producers resisted the offer to buy shares in the financially weak processing sector, and the emission never took place.[77]

FDI was a component of restructuring in processing. Cumulative FDI in agriculture's downstream sectors through 1999 may have been as much as a third of Russian FDI through 1998; in 2000 it was still high at 16 percent of the annual flow of FDI.[78] The five agribusiness sectors receiving most FDI from the United States included beverage and confection, tobacco, farm equipment dealerships, food packaging and bottling, and food catering, with some 90 percent going to downstream and 10 percent to the upstream sectors. Given the lack of profitability, debts, and low productivity facing most farms, little went to actual producers. The regions receiving aid were mostly in the consumer base (central, Northwest, and Volga Viatka) and, among producer regions, theVolga Valley and North Caucasus. Case studies show spillover effects on production from FDI to downstream sectors.[79] However, local privatization was overwhelmingly the route most processing took to profitability; in 1996, only about 3 percent of food processing enterprises had been privatized with the participation of foreign capital.[80]

77 Serova (1997).

78 This figure provided by C. Foster of USDA; cf. Russian data, citing less than 20 percent of total FDI. *Rossiiskii Statisticheskii Ezhegodnik* (2005), p. 670.

79 Foster (1999), pp. 198–99.

80 OECD (1999), p. 97.

The less developed sectors during reforms were infrastructure and input supply. Emphasis on transportation infrastructure was a main achievement of Soviet-era budgeting, as emphasized by Elizabeth Clayton:

> The technical evolution of agriculture links its production and the rural population to the industrial and urban economy. The link between producers and consumer is stretched by new intermediaries in food processing and handling; a link between producer and industry is forged between the farm and its input suppliers. A simple index of the growth in interdependence is increased use of transport services.[81]

Capital investment in road construction dramatically increased in the Soviet era and was five times higher in the 1980s than in the early 1970s.

However, comparing the outlay to that in developed market economies, at the time of reforms Russia had relatively weak infrastructure development. The total extent of general purpose roads was about 1.8 million kilometers. By contrast, in the United States there were more than six million kilometers over a considerably smaller territory. The density of hardtop general purpose motorways in the former Soviet Union was ten times smaller than in Estonia, a much smaller state. The shortage of hardtop motorways led to a number of negative consequences, including a slowdown of the distribution of labor, producer loss in transportation (spilled cargo, delays, accidents, untimely deliveries), and losses in the rural social sphere, which received inadequate health care, education, and transport connections.[82] Despite the national project on rural development, with a planned expenditure between 2003 and 2010 of 10.5 percent from the consolidated budget including 43 percent from regional budgets and 46.5 percent from extra budgetary funds, the data show sluggish actual accomplishment.[83] Table 3.5 reports the dynamic to 2005.

Summary: Policy History

To summarize, agricultural sector reform began in the Gorbachev era. The Russian Supreme Soviet provided a legal framework for property rights, although attaching to it a moratorium on land sales. Under Yeltsin, reformers overcame parliamentary opposition and removed the moratorium. The government privatized farm enterprises and secured individual property rights in the Constitution of 1993. Slow progress on a new land code showed a drift in reform leadership, beginning in the mid-1990s. President Vladmir Putin renewed the effort, completed the new land code and a separate one for the sale of arable and its use as collateral.

81 Clayton (1980), p. 447.

82 WBWP 3 (1992), pp. 8–10.

83 "Federal'naia tselevaia programma 'Sotsial'noe razvitie sela do 2010 goda,'" Postanovlenie Pravitel'stva Rossiiskoi Federatsii ot 3 dekabria 2002 g. N 858.

TABLE 3.5. *Rural Infrastructure Improvements in the Russian Transition, 1990–2005*

	1990	1995	2000	2002	2003	2004	2005
Introduced in rural areas:							
Water pipes, km	5902	1608	636	9548	1009	796	978
Gas lines, ths km	7	17	16	13	15	15	14
Automated telephone connections, ths nos	...	130	148	206	324	573	477
Electric lines, ths km							
.4 kw	11	6	3	4	4	4	4
Asphalted roads, ths km							
Local	12	7	6	4	3	2	2
Regional and National	28.3	1.9	0.3	0.1	0.1	0.08	0.07
Rural settlements without links to public roads (%)	...	35	35	33	33	33	34
Vol. of rural telephone facilities, mlns of nos	4	4	5	2.4	2.8	3.4	2.7

Source: Rossiiskii Statisticheskii Ezhegodnik (2005, 2006).

The drift in leadership and the macroeconomic crisis affected the viability of new privatized structures and the pace of restructuring. Early not entirely successful efforts at demonopolization of processing and the collapse of input supply, except for fertilizer, meant reliance on imports.[84] The challenge of the reform project proved so interconnected with general economic recovery, so vulnerable to import competition, and so dependent upon improved finance and infrastructure, that despite a strong legal framework for new property rights and relatively low levels of subsidies, competitiveness only slowly advanced for the first decade.

4 THE IMPLEMENTATION AND INITIAL EFFECTS OF REFORM

Privileging Corporative Farms

Much of state support was biased to favor the corporative farm sector. The subsidized credit program to lease agricultural machinery addressed the shortage and deterioration of large-scale equipment rather than supply smaller equipment for medium-scale farms. Farm inputs were distributed by their former supplier, the newly privatized Rosagrosnab, and regional authorities had discretion over distribution. Rosagrosnab obtained a monopsony position and charged a 5 percent service fee for coordinating and marketing on behalf of machinery producers. The state used Rosagrosnab also to supply

[84] OECD (2007), pp. 118 ff.

funds for fertilizer, seeds, and pedigree cattle to select farms, crowding out competition in highly profitable upstream activities.[85]

In 1997, the system was reformed to make it more transparent. Rosagrosnab lost its monopoly to private leasing companies selected in open tenders. However, even after the bumper harvests of 2001 and 2002, the government continued to supply soft credit through the leasing company, and in 2003, 4.3 billion rubles were allocated partly from budgetary resources for the new state firm, "Rosagrolising."[86] Added to this, the state provided an interest rate subsidy for medium-term (five year) credit. The aim was to stimulate production while not suppressing demand for farm machinery by a government leasing monopoly.[87] Leasing programs – like emergency payments – took on the quality of preferential soft budget constraints, aiding mainly the larger farms.

Large producers of sugar gained during the reform years from profitable and historically record high sugar production. Meanwhile, the sugar industry was the most protected agrifood subsector. Similarly, when grain was beginning to recover sufficiently for steady export, grain interventions beneficial to large farms began, continuing through 2007, when budget funds for grain interventions were increased from 2006 by nine times.[88] Finally, although the fastest-growing agricultural subsector is meat and poultry production, this sector has continued through 2010 to enjoy quota protection.

The political economy of the Russian agrifood sector, in other words, shows producers and influential groups of interests from the era prior to reform to have been privileged in the early reform process. Little effort was made until the Putin presidency to address the increasing rural poverty. So-called protective measures protected not the weakest links in the food chain but the most successful ones.[89] Most budgetary resources, according to a 2001 survey by the Agrarian Institute, go to a small percentage of the largest farms, including a considerable number that are bankrupt.[90]

Farm Restructuring

The free distribution of farm land and assets to farm members was the essence of Russian farm restructuring.[91] It aimed to accomplish three broad

[85] Serova (1997).

[86] OECD (1999), p. 127; Ksenia Nechaeva, "Sel'skomu khoziastvu spishut dolgi," *Kommersant-Daily* (Feb. 5, 2003), p. 2.

[87] Karlova et al. (2002), pp. 254–55.

[88] "Comment on the draft Federal Law 'On 2007 Federal Budget' as concerns expenditures on agriculture," (October 2006), http://www.iet.ru/afe/english/apk.html.

[89] Serova et al. (2002), p. 257.

[90] In 2001, agricultural expenditures were 21 percent of the federal budget and 16 percent of regional budgets. Of these resources, 1.4 percent of farm entities received 22.5 percent, and 15 percent received 66.2 percent. See Petrikov (2002), p. 3.

[91] Serova (2000), p. 103; Brooks (1994); Tillack (2000); Lerman (1999); Brock (1996).

objectives in early transition: efficiency, ownership, and independence from the state.[92] However, restructuring was made voluntary, and it proceeded slowly. As J. Brada (1996) shows for other transition countries, the voluntary aspect of restructuring in Russia inhibited transformation.

Steep costs also slowed farm transformation. Valuation of enterprises, necessary for withdrawal of significant numbers of shares, proved in particular both costly and complex. Despite central and east European precedents for such essential ingredients of enterprise reform, there were no provisions in the Russian reform for investment funds or guaranteed farm restructuring, or even for restructuring assistance.[93] Farm enterprise management faced these costs with new management rules. At the time of re-registration, most farms adopted a form that allowed equal distribution of shareholders' assets to farm members (workers in services and administration, farm workers, and pensioners), who also gained the right to elect their management and govern the restructuring process. In principle, farm members could break up the farm into smaller more technologically efficient units by selling or exchanging their entitlements. On the whole, without financial assistance or retooling, they chose to retain the farm structure and lease their land. Production was reallocated among households with the supply of inputs used in part, as before, for household operations. Cereals output fell steadily, while the household sector, using registered and unregistered produce and service and other input transfers from large farms, rose to half of GAO by the turn of the century.

The most profitable part of the farm was the high valued livestock sector. Supported by their historical rights and equal shares, households claimed livestock along with other assets in 1991. On aggregate, households claimed from 17 to 44 percent of large cattle and 26 to 51 percent of the cows owned between 1990 and 2004.[94] Meanwhile, imports grew. Between 1990 and 2000, the import of processed meat increased by 35 percent, and between 2000 and 2004 by 97 percent in volume.[95] Imports of live and frozen meat nearly doubled in volume between 2000 and 2004.[96] By 1997, 20 to 25 percent of beef and pork consumed in Russia came from imports. The August 1998 devaluation was a major opportunity to close the gap, but imports first fell then rebounded. The result for the economy is that production of live meat and poultry fell from an average of 9.7 million tons between the years 1986–1990 to 4.9 million tons in 2004.[97]

92 See the review of procedures and property rights, and a case study of farm reorganization by Pisano (2002).

93 On transition land reform, see publications by the EBRD (2003); the World Bank, OECD, Serova (1996, 2000, 2000); Wegren (1998, 2002); Van Atta (1994); Leonard and Serova (2001); Liefert (1993); Meliukhina (1994); Nikonov (1995), and others.

94 *Rossiiskii Statisticheskii Ezhegodnik* (2005), p. 458.

95 Ognivtsev et al. (2002), pp. 98–9.

96 *Rossiiskii Statisticheskii Ezhegodnik* (2005), p. 707.

97 *Rossiiskii Statisticheskii Ezhegodnik* (2005), p. 458.

Share equalization gave farm members on average 12.5 hectares per share. They could withdraw their shares, but they were encouraged to lease them to the enterprise. The objective was to make use of large farms and infrastructure from the Soviet era to build a new corporative sector.[98] Leasing simplified the process and allowed restructuring to be postponed.

By leasing arrangements, farm directors acquired control over distribution. By the 2002 law on land transfers, the authority of the farm directors to oversee withdrawal of land shares reinforced managerial authority in general. Their opposition to real restructuring was then a powerful force in slowing further reform and in protecting the household sector. Traditional Soviet networks of power, making the manager the *khoziain* (boss) of the farm, lasted throughout transition.[99] Slow decollectivization[100] and restructuring, a threat to the system of protection as well as production, showed popular support for elite settlement in modern Russian agrarian reform.

The reasons restructuring stalled are complex, to be sure. Few farm employees had access to the knowledge and experience required to manage entirely independent farms. To take one example, restructuring required inventories and valuations of, say, sphere 4 (storage and other infrastructure) of the agro-industrial complex without aid and guidelines. Proposed models of auctions and valuation of assets were accepted by the government but rejected at the farm level, since they too required expensive expertise and alien procedures.[101]

The government's idea of restructuring, the pilot project adopted in Nizhnyi Novgorod, found international funds in 1993. Auctions for this pilot were designed by Russian agrarian specialists: land and other assets were to be auctioned off after full valuations.[102] This Russian-generated and

[98] See for a fuller treatment Uzun (1999).

[99] Matiukhin and Bezrukov (2001).

[100] Non-Russian agricultural economists emphasize the de-collectivization aspect of the process of the break-up of collective farms and the end of collective land use. Tillack and Schulze (2000) and Schulze (1999) use the term "de-collectivisation" for the liquidation of state-owned or collective farm enterprises and formation, in their place, of large and small, corporative and family farms, land used for part-time farming and household subsidiary plots. Pryor (1992) and Davis (1997) use it for the process of separation of individually owned farms; Swinnen (1996) creates a decollectivization index to show the ratio between land used by individuals since 1989 and total agricultural area under national or collective management and ownership.

[101] Uzun (2000).

[102] The scheme was roughly the same as in industry. Within the boundaries of one firm, an inventory of land and assets was taken, with all workers and pensioners receiving certificates of rights to assets and land shares. Evaluation took place with "points" as units for hectares and ruble shares. The share received by an individual depended upon salary and seniority. Nominal owners became property holders in the course of an auction, where the mode of payment was the certificate of right of ownership. Certificates were good for buying plots, forming cooperatives or partnerships, or selling to a neighbor. The first land auction was November 9, 1993, at the farm Pravdinskii in Balakhninski

foreign-sponsored program commenced by a preparatory intensive year-long information campaign about the rights, opportunities, and complexities of dividing the land and other assets in market-based agricultural systems. Publicly endorsed by Prime Minister Victor Chernomyrdin in 1994, the experiment was adopted by the federal government as its national program.[103] Over the following five years, however, only 622 farms in eighteen regions were restructured along the lines of the Nizhnii Novgorod pilot project.[104] The costs of such a model were large, and the outcome was frequently discouragement and frustration.[105] In 2001, a survey conducted jointly by the Federal Presidential Agency for Government Communications and Information and the Center for Economic Conjuncture under the Government of the Russian Federation (carried out in January 2001) reported 41 percent of farm directors and technical supervisors were against valuations and auctions (with 20 percent undecided and 39 percent positive).[106]

In 2002, despite continued soft-budget constraints, the state moved forward with obligatory debt restructuring of qualifying farms.[107] Earlier action might have been a force for the encouragement of overall restructuring. Over a decade, opposition in the Parliament had slowed the passage of the relevant laws for financial restructuring, and only in 2002, was the legislative deadlock broken. Lack of general and financial restructuring led to the situation

rayon. On an area of 3,600 hectares, twelve farms were set up. By 1995, twenty-nine similar experiments had been carried out using this model. Part of the difficulty in judging the success of this method is that most of the farms petitioning restructuring did so because of financial insolvency. E. Ishkova, "Zemlya stanovitsia predmetov torgov, no eshche ne predmetom kupli-prodazhi," *Finansovye Izvestiia*, March 30, 1995.

103 Decrees of the President RF No 1767 "O regulirovanii zemel'nykh otnoshenii i razvitii zemel'noi reformy" (1993); No. 337 "O realizatsii konstitutsionnykh prav grazhdan na zemliu" (1996); Postanovleniia Pravitel'stva RF No. 874 "O reformirovanii sel'skokhoziastvennykh predpriatii s uchetom praktiki Nizhegorodskoi oblasti" (1994) and No. 96 "O poriadke osushchestvleniia prav sobstvennikov zemel'nykh dolei i imushchestvennykh prav" (1995). See the sweeping review by major academic centers, *Programma "Privatizatsiia zemli i reorganizatsiia sel'skokhoziastvenykh predpriatii": Podvedenie itogov* (Moscow: 1995).

104 Shagaida (1999), p. 30.

105 The World Bank in an unpublished review in 1995–1996 documented some of the achievements and failures of the Nizhnii Novgorod project. It provided a harsh picture of the effects of transition on labor discipline, which was undermined by alcoholism, distrust, and corruption.

106 Matiukin and Bezrukov (2001), p. 7.

107 The report on the sector by the Institute for the Economy in Transition notes that debt restructuring, although a necessary step, will not resolve all of the problems emerging from major policy flaws over the past ten years. More farms paid their overdue debts, but profits fell, which meant that the number of profit-making farm enterprises fell from 52.4 percent in 2002 to 48.2 percent in the first half of 2003. Institute for the Economy in Transition (2003), p. 35. For a detailed description of the state of organizational transformation 2002, see Buzdalov (2002).

that in 2006, the number of loss-making corporative farm entities stood at 40 percent.[108]

The weakness in farm finance and management problems depressed the expansion of banks, cooperatives and services, private seed, and other suppliers and channels required for functioning markets. The state still regulated grain and other markets in 2000 and 2001. Thirteen percent of respondents to the survey by the Center for Economic Conjuncture reported barriers to regional export and import of grain and food. Infrastructure for small- and medium-scale farming was still missing: only 10 percent reported the existence of supply cooperatives. There was no decentralized judicial system to enforce transparency of operations and property rights. Heavily criticized for their template design for Russia, the World Bank nevertheless produced forty-five recommendations for restructuring that, had they been followed, might well have cleared away many of these barriers to effective markets.[109]

Restructuring as envisioned aimed to reduce farm size. By the final stage of restructuring, farms typically decreased in size by about 15 percent, although at 4,000 to 8,000 hectares, farms are still large by Western standards.[110] It was also envisioned that farms would divest themselves of services previously provided to rural communities. By 1994, 59 percent of kindergartens and 39 percent of medical facilities had been transferred to municipal governments.[111] By the end of the decade, the divestment of public sector services by farms was in principle complete.[112] However, municipal governments were poorly funded, and services were either de facto privatized or still supported de facto by farm enterprises.[113] Postponing divestment became, in some regions, a farm survival strategy, a way for farms to document their importance to regional authorities.[114] This too slowed the restructuring process.

In the farm sector, the new and successful entrant in the 1990s was the vertical holding company. Gazprom, for example, leases more than 500,000 hectares and manages seventy-six enterprises with more than 25,000 employees.[115] These holding companies provide needed investment and new technology, and they are not very different from similar vertically integrated structures in other countries. In Russia, however, their presence

108 In 1999, courts were created in Omsk, Kirovsk, Nizhegorod, Orel, Volgograd, Vologda, Ivanovsk, Leningrad, Krasnodar, and the Republics Mari El, Chuvashia, and Kalymkia, bringing the total to 2,000 in eleven regions. See Karamazova (2002). *Rossiiskii Statisticheskii Ezhegodnik* (2006), online.

109 See Gardner (2002) for a review, and World Bank (1992), Vols. 1–4.

110 See Lermon (1999, 2000).

111 Nikonov (1995), p. 456.

112 Conversation with Christian Foster, head, ERS, USDA, July 12, 2000.

113 Shishkin (2000); Dmitriev (1997).

114 Amelina (2002).

115 Uzun (2002), pp. 6–7.

also reflects quasi-state ownership in the agricultural sector, since stockholding in these large firms is majority owned by municipal government.[116] These firms are part of a core consisting more broadly of large farms, and holding companies comprise the most profitable farms, a so-called 300 Club.[117]

Independent Farming. Under Gorbachev, independent farmers initially seemed an emerging force. At first, government support was substantial. However, small farm formation was undermined by the disadvantages of their position. Farm employees lacked expertise, skills, contacts, equipment, and the legal framework for setting up an enterprise in the rural sector.[118] The Land Code of 1991, in operation for the first ten years of transition, restricted land market operations, put up barriers to the purchase and sale of land and nonland assets, and discouraged investment. By 1997, more than 90 percent of entitlement holders to land shares had received their official entitlement papers, and roughly 40 percent of those had signed contracts to lease the land.[119] But the number of independent farmers was no longer growing after 1994.

Initially, the independent farm sector was supported by a five-year tax holiday and preferential credit through the Association of Independent Peasant Farms and Cooperatives (AKKOR, formed in 1990). The seasonal credits of billions of rubles (about £57 million in 1991) to AKKOR, however, fell in subsequent years due to concerns about corruption, and by 1994 the total support in real terms for farmers significantly dropped.[120] In a sampled survey carried out in 1992 by Karen Brooks and Zvi Lerman for the World Bank, in 1992 only 6 to 7 percent of independent farmers indicated that AKKOR supplied their short- or long-term credit.[121] General levels of state support for independent farming were low.

Data reported in Table 3.6 show that in constant prices, between 1991 and 1995, the total amount allocated to independent farmers declined by a factor of eight. In 1999, independent farms received 2 percent of the expenditures of the consolidated budget on agriculture, which fell to less than 0.5 percent in 2001.[122] The survey of independent farms in 1999

[116] Almost 70 percent of agricultural land in Russia is owned by municipal government. Volkov (2002), p. 7; "O regulirovanii oborota zemel' sel'skokhoziastvennogo naznacheniia" (Moscow: Gosudarstvennyi Soviet RF), pp. 61–3.

[117] See regular publication of economic indicators about the 300 Club by the journal, *Agrarnaia Reforma. Ekonomika i Pravo,* a publication of the Fond poderzhki agrarnoi reformy i sel'skogo razvitiia (RosAgroFond) and Vserossiiskii institut agrarnykh problem i informatiki Rossiiskoi academia sel'skokhoziastvenykh nauk (VIAPI imeni A.A. Nikonova).

[118] Leonard (2000).

[119] OECD (1998), p. 15.

[120] Galbi (1995).

[121] Brooks and Lerman (1994), p. 88.

[122] Shik (2002), p. 12.

TABLE 3.6. *Russian State Support for the Independent Farming Sector (Federal and Regional Levels, in Constant 1991 Prices)*

Category	1991	1992	1993	1994	1995
Migrants assistance	52	220	174	5	2
Tax relief	0	22	33	19	11
Construction	459	88	97	130	42
Loan guarantees	418	723	258	84	5
Interest-rate subsidies	0	465	275	235	39
Budgetary loans	631	0	0	16	71
Other	0	0	5	10	24
TOTAL	1560	1519	842	515	194

Source: Leonard and Serova (2002), p. 372.

showed 0.9 percent received budgetary support for cereals production, 1.2 percent for livestock, and 1.5 percent for mortgage-based loans.[123] A particular concern for the small farm sector was services, for which they paid through contracting with corporative farms. Independent farmers contributed labor in return for equipment and services, not uncommon among small farmers in other market economies.[124] Nearly all private farms were involved in contracting or joint activity to share services. Of this cooperative activity, between 30 and 40 percent involved cooperation with other private farmers for production, marketing and input supply, use of machinery, and supply or access to credit.

In 2002 the situation for independent farmers financially worsened when the unified agricultural tax went into effect. The law (2001) stipulated that all agricultural producers, for whom up to 70 percent of revenue is from agricultural production, excluding industrial producers such as poultry factories, are subject to the unified tax, differentiated regionally and assessed by performance in 2001. It replaced all other taxes, except the VAT, excise taxes, and taxes on environmental pollution. The new status of independent farms eliminated their tax-free standing, even for new farms.

The new national project for the agrifood sector, determined at the end of 2005 and designed at that time to last two years, comprised roughly 20 percent of federal spending on agriculture. In this project, government focused primarily on small farming, and in 2007, financing for the project was extended, with aid to small farming in the form of soft credit and resources for small cooperatives, in brief, income support and funds for construction of commercial and storage facilities. Significant for its acknowledgment of the importance of small- and medium-size farmers – possibly encouraging their exit from loss-making large farm enterprises – and of the role of households

[123] *Sel'khoz* (2000), p. 42.
[124] Novikov (1996).

TABLE 3.7. *Agricultural Net Output Indices, 1991–2002, Selected Countries, Base: Average of 1989–1991*

Country	1991	1992	1995	1996	1997	1998	1999	2000	2001	2002
Czech Republic			99	80	79	78	80	87	80	77
Estonia		73	53	47	42	43	42	40	38	41
Hungary	101	79	71	76	78	78	75	72	91	75
Latvia		97	57	46	52	47	45	45	41	45
Poland	96	85	84	88	85	91	88	86	89	84
Russian Federation		*88*	*83*	*64*	*67*	*68*	*59*	*58*	*66*	*68*
Slovakia			76	76	91	90	86	82	67	68

Source: FAOStat (2003).

in livestock production, this project is supplemented by a national project for housing in rural areas. The goals of three projects, improvement in livestock production, aid to small farming, and rural housing, are complementary.[125]

Overall Agricultural Outcomes Compared: Russia and the Central and East European Economies (CEE)

Russia's transformational recession in agriculture was deep and lasting, conditions comparable to those in most transition economies of Central and Eastern Europe. Agriculture in all of these countries experienced difficulty in recovering from the initial policy shocks, primarily the effects of price and trade liberalization: agricultural prices dropped relative to the prices of nonagricultural goods.[126] The combined consequences of the worsening of terms of trade and the removal of subsidies, due largely to fiscal austerity programs, drove production levels down. After prices stabilized – parity was restored by the mid-1990s – conditions improved somewhat. Most countries raised tariffs on selected agricultural and food imports and increased budgetary allocations to agriculture, which helped the sector recover. Reform effects seemed strong. The contribution of the public sector, along with strengthening demand, secured a path to recovery in most countries with bumper harvests in 1996 and 1997. However, the buoyancy of markets proved temporary, and depressed commodity prices, poor weather, and financial crisis in 1998 weakened demand, showing recovery in the mid-1990s to have been fragile, as shown in Table 3.7. The depth of decline, especially in the Baltic States, and continued volatility in net agricultural output through 2002 are evident. The data are indexed with 1989–1991 as the base year.

[125] Serova and Shick (July 2006).

[126] The ratio of prices paid in the agricultural sector to those in the industrial sector in Russia went from 0.26 in 1991 to 0.61 in 1997 (OECD 1999, p. 129).

TABLE 3.8. *Employment in Agriculture (% of Total Employment), Selected Transition Economies, 1989–2003*

	1989	1992	1995	1997	1998	1999	2000	2001	2002	2003
High income	6.3	5.1	4.7	4.4	4.3	4.2	4.1	4.0	3.8	3.8
Estonia	21.2	18.1	10.2	9.2	8.9	8.1	7.2	6.9	7.0	6.2
Latvia		20	17.4	21.5	19.1	16.6	14.5	15.1	15.4	13.8
Lithuania				20.7	21.0	19.3	18.7	17.3	17.8	17.9
Czech Republic	11.9	8.0	6.6	5.8	5.5	5.3	5.1	4.8	4.8	4.5
Hungary			8.0	8.1	7.7	7.2	6.7	6.3	6.2	5.5
Poland	25.3	25	22.6	20.5	19.2	18.1	18.8	19.1	19.3	18.4
Russian Federation		15.4	15.7	12.2	11.5	11.8	12.7	10.9	10.7	10.0
Slovakia			9.2	9.2	8.2	7.4	6.6	6.1	6.2	5.8
Ukraine	19.1	20.8	24.3	25.1	26.1	20.5	20.5	19.7	19.8	18.9

Sources: Sel'khoz (2002), p. 18; World Bank Development Indicators (2006).

In most of the CEE, as in Russia, the process of recovery from recession and restructuring of large farms, to enable the release of labor and improve productivity, was prolonged. A key indicator of follow-on reform, a process that required relocation of farm employees, the establishment of job centers with job training, and farm restructuring, was the pace of labor shedding. In this regard, the Russian path showed a somewhat longer course to more efficient agriculture than most of the CEE, but roughly comparable to countries of the former Soviet Union. The pace of reduction of the labor force in agriculture in the early years of transition can be seen in Table 3.8.

As can be seen in the preceding table, in the Czech Republic, Hungary, and Slovakia, employment in agriculture fell significantly. Elsewhere, there was some labor retention, although agriculture began sharply to decline as a share of GDP. This combination suggests a lag in labor productivity and, despite the shrinking of farm size and the labor force, some surplus labor left on the farm. In some countries, there was hidden unemployment in rural areas, although given labor-intensive production and the important role of the household sector as a buffer in the transition period, the significance of the phenomenon is unclear. The countries where hidden unemployment lingered include Russia and Ukraine, and Latvia, Lithuania and Poland among the EU member countries. The following Table 3.9 shows the downward trend in selected countries of the share of net agricultural output in GDP in the first years of transition. In the countries that were offered accession agreements, reforms were faster and the share of output in GDP moved rapidly to a level roughly approximate that in advanced market economies. In regard to this indicator of change, Russia experienced a only a somewhat slower recovery course in CEE countries.

TABLE 3.9. *Share of Agriculture in GDP (%), Selected Transition Economies, 1990–2005*

Country	1990	1994	1995	1999	2001	2002	2003	2004	2005
Low Middle-Income Countries		16	16	12	12	12	12	12	12
High-Income Countries		2	2	2	2	2	2	2	2
Estonia	14	9	6	7	6	6	4	4	4
Latvia	21	8	9	4	5	5	4	4	4
Lithuania	28	8	9	9	7	7	6	6	6
Czech Republic	6	5	4	4	5	4	3	3	3
Hungary	15	7	7	5	4	4	4	3	4
Poland	8	6	6	4	5	5	4	5	5
Russian Federation	17	6	8	7	7	6	5	5	6
Slovak Republic	7	6	5	4	4	4	4	4	3
Ukraine	26	15	15	14	16	15	12	12	11

Sources: World Development Indicators 2000, 2007; *OECD* 1999.

At the time of the writing of this book, rural markets are functioning reasonably well in the Czech Republic, Slovakia, the Baltic states, Hungary, Slovenia and some countries in southeastern Europe, and rural development programs are in place in all countries. As noted above, countries that were offered accession agreements for membership in the EU had an advantage over CIS countries in EU assistance. The CEE governments received guidelines for policy reforms and a legal framework to implement. EU advice was composed of well worn rules with a minimum of discretion. The framework policy had been developed in the European Commission (EC) in the 1970s. It co-evolved with modernized extensive support policies for the agricultural sector, which went into place in the CEE along with new property rights and registry schemes. The EU had reformed the Common Agricultural Policy (CAP) in 1984, which worked well with states joining the EU in several rounds. EU guidelines encouraged rural development, income support and retraining, and exit from farming as a first priority. By contrast, Russian policy was developed in coordination with a parliamentary consensus, which significantly inhibited the reform process, as outlined above. The lack of clear guidelines and slow institutional reform in Russia led to the persistence of widespread bankruptcy among corporative farms well into the twenty-first century and a leveling off of numbers of former farm employees who sought to create private family farms already in the 1990s.

To take one example, the reform of private property rights differed significantly between most Central and Eastern European countries (CEE) and Russia and other states of the Former Soviet Union. In most of the CEE, governments' chosen course was restitution rather than mass privatization into small fragmented holdings. The Hungarian government allowed claimants to substitute shares in firms for their claims to land. Those countries which did not allow restitution, including Bulgaria, Romania, Latvia, and Lithuania, chose the faster course of redistribution, and they found their recovery path difficult. In the latter states, most often, the resulting highly fragmented small farming sector led to unstable output and stalled entrepreneurship. In Armenia and Georgia, where privatization also resulted in very small farms, however, reforms were a greater success. By contrast with Bulgaria and Romania, in Armenia and Georgia, small farms were mostly viable. They consisted of subsidiary plots, averaging between 0.75 and 1.5 hectares on which producers began growing corn, vegetables, fruits, and grapes, and producing milk, meat, and eggs.[127] Russia chose neither path. The government did not attempt restitution but also helped preserve the larger farms.

Even with EU guidelines, it should be noted, both privatization and restructuring in agriculture proved to be a drawn-out process. In general, restructuring was complicated by the particular complexity of the food industry. Making industry more efficient comes from adjusting labor and management and keeping the existing stock of capital. Making agriculture more productive, in most countries, required not only farm break-up but also the decentralization of linked sectors. Clearly, restructuring across farm sectors was helped among EU accession countries by simple, transparent, and uniform rules and by limitation of the scope of discretionary involvement.[128] The demands of institutional change in agriculture make nondiscretionary authority critical. Such centralized authority in Russia was not achieved until well after the turn of the twenty-first century.

With some exceptions, rural markets function better in the CEE than in Russia. It is also the case that agriculture is no longer a sector of much significance in these countries. The shrinking of agricultural employment is a process still underway, to be sure, where restructuring has been delayed and farm management is inexperienced. In two countries, Armenia and Georgia, restructuring proved to be unnecessary: private farmers came to cultivate 80 and 49 percent of arable, respectively, since collective and state farms essentially ceased production.

A final point is that WTO entry has helped the course of reform everywhere and in some cases, output improvement. Results from Chinese entry into the WTO show that grain production has exceeded expectations. Judging by this, Russia can expect a gain in consumption of 7.8 percent (or 4.3 percent of consumption), assuming a reduction in all tariffs to one-half their original level, improved market access, and complete removal of barriers to FDI in services.[129] Three regions, particularly benefitting from FDI, should gain considerably: the Northwest (11.2 percent), St. Petersburg

[127] Armenia (1995); Leonard (1998).
[128] Hayami (1991).
[129] Rutherford and Tarr (2005, 2006).

(10.6 percent), and the Far East (9.7 percent). Some sectors linked to agriculture will, naturally, lose out. These are the protected sectors prior to tariff reduction, sectors that have a much smaller share of exports. There may be an intial drop, for example, in food, machinery and equipment, and construction materials, which have a small share of exports and are relatively protected.[130]

Reception of Reform

Given the relative weakness of the agricultural sector in the Soviet era, Russian public opinion seems to have anticipated that once privatization occurred, it would succeed in improving welfare and production. When this did not occur within the first decade, observers began to report that reform had failed. In one review of expectations and consequences of land reform in Russia, citing surveys of farm employees, a scholar found that less than 10 percent of respondents in 1995 expected living standards or the use of technology to improve in the sector.[131] In 2000, Bogdanovsky writes:

> By now, it would seem, one might expect to see evidence of the achievement of the strategic objectives of reforming the rural social setup: a real increase in the well-being of the rural population and saturation of the national food market with domestic produce. Neither has happened . . .[132]

Bogdanovsky's analysis blamed "the destructive effect of forcing agricultural production in the private mode, predominantly in the form of individual farms."[133] This was the way Russian farm management saw it – many farm managers did not approve of the restructuring process.[134]

However, in a 1999 survey of 500 federal and local experts – agribusiness and agricultural managers, agronomists, extension experts, and others from diverse regions, there was a different kind of interpretation, that growth was stymied because of too little, not too much land reform (29 percent said reforms had not been implemented; 48 percent said that they probably had not been). Fifty-two percent thought that restructuring certainly (23 percent) or probably (29 percent) had not been carried out.[135] Experts

130 Rutherford and Tarr (2006, p. 3) identify in note 1 the effect as that of "non-tradable intermediate goods (primarily producer services, produced under conditions of increasing returns to scale) as an important source of agglomeration exernalities, which account for the formation of cities and industrial complexes, and explanation of the difference in economic performance across regions."

131 Based on a 1995 survey of farm employees in four provinces, Vladimir, Samara, Tambov, and Moscow, see Bogdanovsky (2000), p. 60.

132 Bogdanovsky (2000), p. 57.

133 Ibid.

134 Only 40 percent supported the idea of restructuring in the 1999 survey, see Serova (2000), p. 71.

135 Serova (2000), p. 69.

had a generally low evaluation of reform and the way it had been carried out, and they were pessimistic in their forecast for Russian agriculture.[136]

5 SUMMARY AND CONCLUSION

The establishment of property rights in land in the 1990s was initiated in a severe macroeconomic crisis. The corporative enterprises created by privatization between 1991 and 1993 were in a weakened state. Procedures for restructuring lacked the infusion of supportive credit, which was unavailable in the environment of tight fiscal policy. The issue was resolved eventually by debt write-off. In the destabilizing electoral contest between Yeltsin and his communist opponent, G. Ziuganov, whose victory threatened to reverse the reforms, Yeltsin gained voters by promising this form of help to the corporative farm sector. Subsidies went into effect at regional levels even without federal approval, and debt write-off, with its perverse incentive effects, depressing profitability in agriculture and bank lending to the sector, is still a main stay of farm support, although successive reforms have been attempted to curtail it.[137] In Russia, as in other transition countries, events and unintended consequences of carrying out agricultural reform during a macroeconomic crisis, which had to be resolved as a priority, not only slowed realization of laws, e.g., property rights, but also the delivery of constructive aid.[138]

The main goal of the reform of the early 1990s was enterprise privatization, accomplished with striking speed. As conditions in agriculture worsened, reform initiative stalled, however. Indeed, support for small farming in particular diminished.[139] "The first stage of the reform of agricultural enterprises was predominantly of a formal nature," wrote V. Novikov, deputy head of the Agrarian Policy Department at the Ministry of Agriculture in 1996.[140] Formal re-registration left some 10 percent identified as state farms by 1996.[141]

From 1995, once the economy stabilized and fiscal reform began, a market price support system was put in place. Inconceivable in crisis conditions, supplementary measures were started for finance, construction, input supply and the downstream sector. Commodity markets in grain steadily strengthened, and market information systems spread. However, since

136 Serova (2000), p. 84.

137 The first major debt write-off was in 1994 of 2.5 trln rubles only partially reimbursed by 1996. Schoors (2003).

138 Shleifer (2000, p. 39) emphasizes the consensus in advice to transition governments to bring inflation down quickly.

139 World Bank (1996).

140 A. Novikov, "Institutional Transformations in Agriculture," *Moskovskii economist* (December 1996), 12: 69.

141 Novikov (1996).

the numbers of independent farmers already was in decline, pressures on the government for restructuring large farm enterprises lessened. Household operations, not independent farms, continued to be the main source of income support during a still difficult time in rural areas. The mid-1990s thus witnessed advancement in support for reform, even as funds diminished until the creation of national projects for the rural sector.

Independent farmers were particularly hurt initially by the inaccessibility of credit and the lack of machinery and storage units appropriate for small farms. Barter incumbered their transactions, and delayed payments, steadily accumulating in Russia, slowed supply. These conditions were in large part the results of policy failure. The government's vision of post reform agriculture, a dominant corporative farm sector, surprisingly made no provision for alternative employment, given that efficiency requirements would lead immediately to downsizing. Parliamentary programs heavily favored large farms without support for exit. Across the economy, policies supporting small enterprise development faded in importance. Land rental income was designed to provide income for pensioners, who could not move off the land. Strict zoning was put in place to prevent the reallocation of land away from agriculture by commercial developers, who might have provided employment opportunities for farm families.[142] Watchwords for farms focused on the effort to preserve the corporation.[143]

The lesson not learned from East Asian agrarian reform was that the opening of the economy to foreign trade and the partial elimination of subsidies would not produce change in behavior unless redistribution was successful, support policies were aimed at small farmers, and poverty reduction programs were in place. At the time, the consensus view was that the economic performance of agriculture would deteriorate initially but eventually improve.[144] Recovery would bring poverty amelioration. In hindsight, a too narrow focus of resources on privatization, along with severe macroeconomic volatility, affected the depth of recovery through the early years of the twenty-first century. After devaluation in 1998, the large farm sector and its supply channels were still too weak for more than a moderately positive response.[145] There is no question that getting economic fundamentals right was critical for agriculture. Macroeconomic stability is the cornerstone of economic growth. "Tight fiscal and monetary policies

142 Sedik, Trueblood, and Arnade (1999).

143 Novikov (p. 71) explains that the intent had been "phased transformation," beginning with profit orientation, accounting reform, contractual relations among members, and then separation into separate units with intrafarm leasing and maintenance but with the preservation of a collectivist orientation. The was a strategy formed in the late 1980s and not abandoned in transition, despite some initial government support for the Nizhnyi Novgorod more individualistic model of reform.

144 Sedik, Trueblood, and Arnade (1999), p. 514.

145 Leonard and Serova (2000).

combined with an opening of the economy provided the necessary conditions for private sector development..."[146] However, achieving macroeconomic stability proved exceptionally difficult in Russia. The soft monetary policy of the Central Bank and preference for high reserves by commercial banks discouraged investment of all kinds and, especially in the vulnerable farm sector, and budgetary resources were not available for management training and restructuring in Russia in that period.[147]

Early success in agrarian reform in the CEE showed the weakening effect of initial conditions by the mid-1990s, when aspirants for EU entry speeded up the reform program. In Russia, that new initiative, associated with a push for WTO membership, came in the presidency of Vladmir Putin, who also imposed greater spatial uniformity in the enforcement of law. In his term of office, federal laws permitting private property in arable land began to be implemented more widely, and amendments were made to the Land Code that permitted the mortgaging of arable land. It was also important that new budget laws transformed the nature of support and monitoring, and that more resources were spent in a more targeted way after 2000.[148]

This chapter has focused on how the failure of political consolidation behind individual property rights in land led to the continuity of overwhelming dominance of agriculture by large corporative farming. Small-scale farming in cereals production has become significant, but individual entrepreneurs, who sought to derive an income from agriculture, more often resorted to household production on the large farms This diverted considerable human resources to a relatively inefficient form of production, especially in livestock production, the critically weak sector in collectivized agriculture. On the national level, individual farming, rural development and commercialization of production played a limited role in the vision of the future and in the recovery process.

[146] OECD (2007), p. 32.
[147] Granville (1995); Åslund (1993); Sachs (1994); Shleifer (2000); Schoors (2003).
[148] OECD (2007), p. 111.

PART II

RUSSIAN LAW AND RURAL ORGANIZATION, 1861–2010

4

Property Rights and Customary Law in Rural Russia

In tsarist Russia, as in medieval western Europe, customary law was an important boundary-setting institution. Formal arrangements of rights, duties, powers, privileges, and forbearance in regard to the land were for the nobility. The core of larger social arrangements among rural producers of rights, duties, powers, privileges, and forbearance in regard to the land, however, could not be identified without reference to both authorities, formal, or codified, and customary rights. The authority of custom in Russian law was reinforced rather than diminished as land markets developed after the abolition of serfdom. As T. Shanin (1985) shows, Russian law formalized its system of dual authority by recognizing customary law in peasant courts.[1] Non-peasant social groups, or "estates," were governed by codified law. This chapter explores the evolution of dual law and its historical impact on land arrangements.

Confidence in property and in the political order was traditionally secured in Russia by overlapping producer use rights and owner rights. Despite this discrepancy, it was not the case that there were no rules of inheritance for producers in late tsarist Russia. By customary law, households and collectives had precedence over individuals, and resources were governed by risk pooling.[2] The collective had a voice over the purchase, rental, and allocation of assets. Boris Mironov summarized the constrictive nature of these customary property rights: "customary law decisively guaranteed the communal order, which limited the accumulation of assets and personal rights of peasants – land dealings, inheritance, contracts, migration, exit from the Commune."[3] Formal rights applied to producers only through the collective. Peasant communities, on behalf of households, were registered owners of arable land, along with members of other estates. However, since neither

[1] Shanin (1985), vol. 1, p. 219.

[2] Shepelev (1998); Mozolin (1992).

[3] Mironov (1999), 2: 70.

individuals nor households could partake in these rights, it was customary law that continued powerfully to shape norms in rural Russia – that is, "social rules, conventions, and other elements of the structural framework of social interaction," which are the basis of actual contractual arrangements and are coordinated with public sector policies.[4]

Confidence in norms is instilled by their effective enforcement, thereby reducing asymmetric information and uncertainty and facilitating financial arrangements.[5] In much of western society, the courts, police, financial institutions, the legal profession, land surveys, recordkeeping systems, and titling agencies are the enforcers. In this framework, there is always a large place for private order institutions, for example, the setting of boundaries and allowing the fragmentation that goes into the accumulation of wealth.[6] One might see Russian customary law in the tsarist era as a very different kind of order from a modern land rights regime. However, customary law did function as a private order institution. It was powerful, and it permitted local diversity within a larger set of norms. For example, partial repartitioning of the land was always an option, even in non-repartitional communes, but its use depended upon circumstances. The flexibility of the communal order in adapting to circumstances was demonstrated by its accommodation to the rapid advancement of the rural economy and purchases of nobles' land in many regions during industrialization in the nineteenth century.

Most countries have experienced long eras when customary law dominates relations among producers, which privileges local over general norms. Almost by definition, customary rights are not well delineated. Boundaries must be adjusted according to local need.[7] As parts of customary law are codified, local diversity tends to be protected, while broader official norms are set. Governments then and now understand that interfering with boundaries created by private-order institutions can undermine existing incentives systems and thus reduce the rural community's productive capacity.[8] Ignoring the place of customary law would undermine the functioning system of social interactions and community survival strategies, particularly in historical times, given the level and frequency of aggregate shocks to production.

The theme here is that legal dualism, separating peasants into a separate category of law, had the unintended effect of insulating their property rights regime from further reform, at least in in the late tsarist era, and arguably much longer. This dual legal order may have been a justification

4 Bardhan (1989), p. 3.

5 Barzel (1989) emphasizes that individuals will have a greater incentive, if rights are moderately clear but not entirely well defined, to adjust them to their needs.

6 Heller (1999).

7 Rosenzweig (1988); Feeney (1988); Solow (1985).

8 For a discussion of the importance of boundaries in private property law, see Heller (1999).

for rejecting reforms later on. It may be an embedded cultural association of a special property rights regime. The impact of the protected and perpetuated Russian property rights regime under customary law meant that arable land was difficult to separate from collective. Russian tradition lacked a concept of primogeniture by which arable ownership might be perpetuated across generations through the oldest son. Allotment land was distributed in an egalitarian way among peasants, whose landholding was perpetuated by rights to a share after partition. In other words, regardless of the consequence, or land fragmentation, by customary law, allotments could not be sold for profit or securely consolidated. That is, households believed population increase or decrease required partition; this was the norm affecting property rights, at least through the 1920s.

In principle, lands of both the peasants and the nobles became prone to overuse. The extensive ownership by the state of agricultural land also led to overuse. The impact on land use of the mix of ownership traditions, therefore, despite some distinction between different rights on state lands and privately owned lands, was probably all the same. It is difficult to be certain, particularly for state lands, because agricultural performance in tsarist Russia has not been closely studied for differences based on property ownership. One conclusion seems warranted for the post-revolutionary years. In the 1920s, after the harsh requisitions of the period of war communism, formal private property rights disappeared. Customary law at that time governed the village, and distinctions faded. The land commune experienced a revival, and it forced some compromises during the period of collectivization. Despite the dispersal of the commune, households retained access to some communal resources, and they kept their right to an inheritable personal plot. These residuals of customary law helped shape the law and were preserved at some level in all subsequent periods. The customary tradition in new form found support within government circles and persisted throughout the new age of modernization, a historically tenacious continuity from the era of serfdom. The small private sector posed no real basis for the restoration of land rights in the arable, and it was therefore ideologically tolerable.

From an economic perspective, the impact of this sector was larger and more complex than might be supposed. After collectivization, it played an essential role in gross agriculture production and rural welfare by producing supplementary food sold at kolkhoz markets. However, the cultivation of private household plots drained resources from the large state and collective farms, including labor and mineral fertilizers from the arable. It made no contribution to biological innovation or to improvements in field crops, which were so vulnerable to the continued impact of natural calamity and unpredictability of harvests. Instead, even after the end of the Communist era, the small private sector has served more as a buffer against vicissitudes of weak markets than a basis for the expansion of small farming.

Part 1 of this chapter reviews customary law in nineteenth-century Russia, with emphasis on its institutionalization in land rights after abolition. Customary law and the household's acceptance of it are the pillar of every peasant economy. In Russia, custom outlasted industrialization, after the peasantry, as such, were no longer a major force in agriculture.[9] Part 2 develops this argument by examining the fortunes of customary law after the revolution, when household rights strengthened. Part 3 is about the introduction in the Russian Federation of modern property rights, which unbundle rights from things. Part 4 gives a general assessment of the long-run legacies of peasants' property rights understandings – under the tsars, the New Economic Policy (NEP), Stalin and, finally, the market economy after 1991.

1 CUSTOMARY LAW

The Servile Order

A land rights regime consists of customary and/or codified rules that govern resource allocation – tenure, leasing, or sharecropping, or some combination of these three. It must govern the allocation of resources in ways sufficient for subsistence during local disasters. Either custom must govern the maintenance of storage, or governments must find ways to protect populations, especially against aggregate shocks. Where local shocks are frequent, as in regions of low-yielding technologies, and governments are not inclined to protect the village, customary law has no place for exclusive, transferable, alienable, and enforceable ownership rights, the mainstays of modern land rights regimes. In a modern economy, clear and enforceable property rights encourage investment and growth.[10] In a peasant society, use rights, determined by custom, protect subsistence.

The core of customary law in Russia was common ownership of assets by the household and household control over them by partition (*razdel*), rather than through lines of inheritance. Partitions occurred when new households were formed, dividing into shares the land, farm equipment, and labor. Under this framework of property management, individual insurance was infeasible.[11] Custom, wrote M. Confino, "remained the basis and the backbone of village life. Within custom, there continued to exist rules, injunctions and prohibitions, subsequently referred to as "*obychnoe pravo*" [customary law].[12]

[9] Feder (1993).
[10] Explained by endowments, technology, and preferences.
[11] See Townsend (1995).
[12] Confino (1985), p. 38; Alexandrov (1984); Field (1976); Kolchin (1987), and others.

Custom, as adapted to the servile order, was given formal attributes in 1649, when separate decrees from a much earlier era were bundled and confirmed, binding peasants to villages in which they resided.[13] The law code of 1649 formally recognized the servile order in Russia. Household production was governed by the gathering of village heads (*skhod*), informally the commune (*mir*), or *obshchina,* by which custom and the tsar's laws were enforced. The "age of serfdom," as E. Wirtschafter (2008) calls it, was one in which the commune, represented by the skhod, became the mediator between the serfs and the landlord or government.

In manorial Europe, the serf household's claim was to use a share of land, not an exact piece of property, while the ownership of that land belonged either to the ruler or the nobles or other elites. In early modern Russia, the attribute of title to the land was possessed by the state and the most distinguished nobles, or boyars, and the attribute of use by service nobles and the peasant household. Through much of the eighteenth century, most nobles owned land conditionally in return for state service. Lesser nobles gained some security of tenure under Peter I (1689–1725), who merged the two forms of private landed property, that of temporarily ennobled servitors (*pomest'e*) and the inheritable estate belonging to families of lineage (*votchina*). By virtue of medieval rights of princes, however, the tsar's patrimony embraced the nobles' and the church's land, that is, all of the territory of Russia, thus the right of ownership and the right of use. This principle was underscored in Petrine law, where even the wealthiest nobles lost their right of inheritance without service.[14]

Property Rights in Land: Seizure and Occupation

Of groups whose rights were particularly insecure under this regime, the Orthodox church proved especially vulnerable during and after wars. The final act transferring church lands to the state, or the secularization of ecclesiastical estates, was carried out between 1762 and 1764, after the end of the Seven Year's War, in which Russia had fought with a coalition of western states against Frederick II of Prussia. Under Catherine II (the Great, 1762–1796), nobles secured their rights more firmly than the Church had been able to do by the grant of a Charter of rights and privileges in 1785, promulgated in a brief period of peace before the outbreak of the Russo-Turkish (1787–1792) and the Russo-Swedish (1788–1790) wars. To be sure, for some offenses nobles' lands could still be confiscated in the eighteenth

[13] For a review of the literature on the origins of serfdom, see Hellie (1971), and for an economic understanding, see Domar (1970).

[14] Blum (1978).

century.[15] Security in the possession of landholdings, therefore, tended also to depend on client/patron relationships, which governed contacts, careers, and riches. G. Hosking (2001) has emphasized in the Russian legal environment the power of patronage over the power of law.[16] Patronage, too, was, of course, not always effective protection.[17]

The patronage system applied to elites; little security governed the vicissitudes of peasant life. Customary law arranged the pooling of resources against famine and ensured payment of manorial dues, where possible negotiating between landlords and peasant households to secure egalitarian distribution of assets. Customary law provided little recourse against ordinary impositions. However, bargaining and resistance become a part of serfs' routines where there was arbitrariness and intervention. Regimentation of production and suppression of household decision making can easily be seen in estate records of the nobility, but so can reluctance and moderate resistance.[18]

By contrast with the patronage system, customary law had a place for conflict. Customary law was self-reinforcing because of the occasional "wins" by villagers against exactions by landlords. Disagreement within the skhod could easily turn against the imposed order.[19] Given the requirements of a stable labor force, resistance to outside intervention strengthened common rights against external forces.[20] It is clear that the estate bureaucracy often encountered agency problems as it attempted to impose discipline.[21] Although peasants may not have rebelled often, the potential for localized resistance was real.

Infractions of the economic order, such as illegal use of forests, were met with stiff punishment. Landlords had in practice unlimited freedom to punish serfs for any transgression despite limits in the law.[22] This was because escape was difficult, and movement off-estate was tightly monitored.[23] Each new generation in a peasant household would be reminded of criminal deeds carried out in the past and warned. In this situation, the commune served a critical function in mediating between the landlord and the serfs.

Of the two village authorities, the landlord and the commune, neither required the assistance of the state to enforce the order. As John Hicks

[15] Leonard (1993); Dukes (1967).
[16] Bartlett (2003); Hosking (2001).
[17] Hosking (2001); Raeff (1971); Pipes (1992).
[18] Sivkov (1951a; 1951b).
[19] Field (1989); Hicks (1969), p. 106.
[20] Barzel (1989).
[21] Field (1989); Hoch (1986); Shanin (1972); Aleksandrov (1976, 1984).
[22] See Kolchin (1987).
[23] Mironov, I (1999), pp. 368–69.

wrote in regard to the servile regime of medieval Europe, custom functioned to keep disputes local and private:

There is, as yet, no landownership. The lord has rights in the land, and the peasant has rights in the land; but that is all. It is of much concern to them what these rights are; but it does not need to be made clear to any outsider. The rights are established by custom; it is to custom that an appeal will be made whenever they are challenged.[24]

Tenure disputes between peasants were resolved by the exchange of use-rights among themselves, dispute in which the landlord was not involved. The opacity of the system was reinforced even in an age of increasingly interventionist local authorities and the strong central authority, whose first sweeping population census in 1897 established a basis for more direct state control of the countryside.

Customary law was perpetuated, also, because it was useful to the state for fiscal purposes. Just as it shifted to localities the responsibility for policing and order, the state could slough the expense of emergency relief by depending upon peasant self-insurance. The village protected itself, above all, against effects of harvest failure, occurring as often as every three years.[25] The government's lack of regular assistance to villages was the norm: communities relied on storages and collections, e.g., on their own resources. A. Kahan (1989) wrote, "While certain measures of famine relief were periodically repeated, the Russian government was quite unable (or unwilling) to institute nationwide programs to mitigate the effects of natural calamities upon the food supply."[26] Kahan implies that the state was under an obligation to assist in times of famine. If so, this would only have been after the serf emancipation. Such aid was not expected before the Great Reforms.

Custom and Control over Peasant Departures

Another way in which customary law was useful to the state in the nineteenth century was in its enforcement of residency. The tsarist regime was dependent for its military resources not only on the poll tax (1718–1724) levied on all male members of the lower orders but on the bulk of its armies coming from the peasantry, including serfs working on nobles lands. In part to prevent tax evasion and in part to assist nobles retain their labor, serfs' movement came to be monitored by a passport system enforced by communal restrictions on travel beyond thirty *versts* (roughly 30.1 kilometers) from the serfs' residence. In the servile order, serfs could be relocated to

24 Hicks (1969), p. 107.
25 Kahan (1989), pp. 134–37.
26 Kahan (1989), p. 137.

other estates, but they could not be transferred to estates belonging to other landlords, that is, they could not be separated from the lord's land, even under the circumstance of land shortage.

Nobles' control and obligations over the local recruitment process came to an end after emancipation, just their oversight over peasant welfare did. With the creation of a class of peasant proprietors (*krest'iane-sobstvenniki*), the military's need to rely on the peasant commune intensified. Universal conscription was imposed by necessity. Under this circumstance, communal authority had to be substituted for that of the manorial regime in provisioning the state with recruits for its armies. To be sure, because of continued restrictions on peasant movement, it was no easier after the emancipation for peasants to evade recruitment than it had been before. Even state peasants were tied to their place of birth and residence. After emancipation, state peasants could relocate if, in the overpopulated central areas, the average allotment per person was less than five desiatina. Even so, the burden was on the community left behind to pay the debts of the household that left, although dues after resettlement would be owed from the new place of residence. Migration of state peasants was fully provisioned but controlled. In new areas, departing households resettled on state lands close to or on the frontier – Voronezh, Voronezh, Tambov, Khar'hov, Saratov, Samara, Orenburg, Astrakhan, and the northern Caucasus.[27]

Post-Servile Order

New Formalization of Customary Law. The dual legal framework instituted by the abolition of serfdom assigned special courts for peasant by district (*volost'*) affairs.[28] Peasant magistrates heard civil cases and those of minor criminal offenses, and judges in general were to uphold local tradition.[29] New courts embraced both peasants and other residents, who were merged into a single estate subject to customary law.[30] Shanin compared this situation with that of western Europe at the time:

> The problem of peasant/non-peasant social differences was solved by their recognition and formalization by the state. For the peasant communities, custom and civil law became one . . . The Russian High Court of Appeal assumed over-all supervision of the application of customary law by the peasant courts.[31]

[27] Vil'son (1879), pp. 35–6.

[28] On serfdom and postemancipation customary law, see Confino (1985); Aleksandrov (1984); Gromyko (1991), pp. 55–65; Mironov (1999), 2: 71–3; Akimov (1913); Shanin (1972), pp. 219–27; Risnes (2001); Aleksandrov (1984); Burbank (2004).

[29] This was because of the fragmentation of systems of justice in eastern and western Europe. Courts had many levels, and low justice was carried out locally by the lord, with restrictions imposed by the crown on the nature and degree of the punishment. Blum (1978), pp. 86–9.

[30] Burbank (2004).

[31] Shanin (1972), p. 219.

The authority of the household through the repartitional and non-repartitional land commune enforced private order arrangements regarding households' arable, or allotment land (*nadel*). Various rules governed the new order. Peasants could not purchase each others' plots. However, they could acquire land of other kinds, including nobles' estates, which began to be sold off in the decades following emancipation. By custom and because they lacked individual financial resources, however, households mainly purchased these lands for use by the Russian land commune.

The Commune. The commune's origins are not entirely clear. Although dating the commune is a topic of some importance in Russian social history,[32] for the present purposes, it is sufficient to describe it as the unit of governance, represented by the *skhod*, whose authority embraced usually several villages. The skhod might consist of heads of between four and eighty peasant households, or from 20 up to 500 individuals. The political autonomy and cohesion of the village under the control of the skhod is described in V. Magagna (1991, p. 195).The *skhod* controlled and monitored the peasants' resources and obligations, which were guaranteed by mutual liability (*krugovaia poruka*).

Among these resources and obligations were the regulated use of collective pastures, the cultivation of the demesne (under serfdom), and of the *nadel*, which was the basis of tax payments owed collectively to the state.[33] *Nadel* land was apportioned among households by quality, which varied by location and size. Serfs revenues from the *nadel* covered their labor, seed, fodder, horses, and implements to meet the planting and harvesting needs. Traditionally, dues to landlords where the demesne was extensive and the soil rich, as in the south of Russia, were in labor – *barshchina* – and they supplemented their income by grain traded after the harvest, although they paid the expense of bringing grain to market.[34] In the north, more often dues were in pecuniary form.

At the time of abolition, the authority of the commune was institutionalized to include civil powers as guarantor of redemption payments and public services and as provider for vulnerable members of the community.[35] It provided public works, such as the maintenance of roads, apportioning and collecting fees and taxes owed to the state and the local government (*zemstvo*). It conducted investigations on matters of civil law and losses and damages to peasant property. It served in place of a court and tried criminal cases subject to local custom (exclusive of such offenses as

32 See Aleksandrov (1976); Atkinson (1983, 1990); Bartlett (1990); Bideleux (1990); Frierson (1990); Mironov (1990); Vronskii (2000), and many others.

33 For a description of serfdom, see Field (1976); Confino (1969); Mironov (1999).

34 See Hoch (1986) for a close study of the frontier Tambov region in the south; for general understandings, see Blum (1961, 1978); Field (1976); for obrok estates, see Koval'chenko (1959) and others.

35 See, for example, rural institutions as seen by A. N. Engel'gardt (1993).

arson and murder); it controlled passport registration of peasants and their transfer; it policed the village and provisioned it in times of famine. The commune maintained religious life, supported education and libraries, and conducted relations with state authorities.[36] Just as there was a rigid distinction between peasants and other estates as defined by law, there was a rigid cultural divide, and the commune was the repository of peasant culture. The word commune, in other words, was not in concept the same as either village or community, in the western sense, meaning people who live together.[37]

Repartition. The constraints on the effectiveness of agrarian reform in the nineteenth century lay in large part in the commune's powers over the distribution of assets. At the time of abolition, two kinds of communal land systems were permitted, nonrepartitional and repartitional. If two-thirds of the commune agreed, the land would be divided into household allotments, and repartition would henceforth be forbidden. Roughly one-third of peasant households in the 1860s were in communes that had nonrepartitional status.[38] There was considerable variation by region beyond this fundamental division. For example, there were no communes in the Baltic provinces (*gubernii)* and none in the western provinces. In Siberia, communal landholding was mainly in the western districts close to central *gubernii*. The distinction between repartitional and nonrepartitional in impact on peasant production should not be exaggerated. Sometimes the nonrepartitional communes could have large numbers of peasants who chose the beggar's share, which meant on average land shares could be much smaller than in repartitional communes.[39] The main economic issue was the size of the allotment, and in this regard the numbers of outworkers determined the pressure on the land.

The commune guaranteed an allotment of a size sufficient for subsistence based on the household's size. Repartitional communes carried out repartition when household divisions multiplied beyond capacity of the commune to guarantee welfare and tax payment.[40] The *skhod* met regularly to decide about partial repartition. One serious consequence was continual social conflict when the land was repartitioned or plots reallocated.[41] Property entitlement of the head of household (*bol'shak*), who represented the

[36] Mironov (1990, 1999).

[37] Bartlett (1990), p. 2. For the economic significance of the commune see Aleksandrov (1976, 1984); Atkinson (1983); Mironov (1990, 1999); Danilov (1976); Bidelieux (1990), and others. For a comparative study with the institution of slavery, see Kolchin (1987), particularly Part II.

[38] Zyrianov (2002), p. 154.

[39] Zyrianov (2002), pp. 154 ff.

[40] Alexandrov (1976); Leonard (1990).

[41] Shcherbina (1900).

household (*dvor*) at the *skhod*, became more contentious as population grew and land was purchased.

Reform and Resettlement. It is difficult to know much about the process by which demographic change was accommodated and new non-allotment land was acquired. One way to examine the process is by looking at the population, that is, at the extent of migration. The statutes of February 19, 1861, made no provision for automatic resettlement from densely settled central areas, although the density of settlement was the main condition upon which an individual or household might request to leave a village. In general, there was high premium on exit both for the individual and the community in mutual responsibility for debts.[42] There was no difference in this regard between former serfs and state peasants (emancipated in 1866), who were similarly subject to constraints. Indeed, state peasants lost their relative freedom to move by being put in the same category with former serfs in 1861. They had to delay departures until 1869, when they were allowed to petition local ministry authorities to leave, and for a while afterwards, they lost the support of the Ministry of State Domains to assist their relocation to areas of greater land abundance. From 1868 to 1876 regulations were issued relaxing requirements to depart, but only for some locations (for example, Orenburg and Samara). State peasants had their loans for land purchase restored in the 1870s.

The only reliable information about actual population movement is from the first population census of 1897, over thirty years after serf emancipation.[43] By that time, the commune was no longer impeding out-migration by very much, although it had the power to deny passports and prevent the withdrawal of land shares. B. Tikhonov, using census materials, shows the sharply rising interregional migration figures for the country as a whole. Using a different data base, passport statistics, he also finds no

[42] Peasants were not allowed to leave the repartitional communes for nine years following abolition unless the allotment was entirely redeemed or the landlord gave permission and transferred its redemption to the commune; in Ukraine, with nonrepartitional communes, the peasant who wished to leave for another village had to be landless or living in a household that would pick up payments on the parcel abandoned. After nine years, a peasant might leave for another village under the following conditions: that the entire family give up a claim to allotment land and that those left behind were, nevertheless, assured an income, that all debts and dues were paid up to January 1 of the next year, that a *priemnyi prigovor* (contractual approval) was presented from the commune to which the peasant was moving and that a land parcel had been purchased not more than 15 versts from the commune of resettlement. Vil'son (1879), pp. 41–2.

[43] Those missing from *zemstva* records are households living elsewhere on passports (and not returning home), those who traveled without official permission, and individuals resident elsewhere (since individual departures were not permitted). Tikhonov (1978), p. 4.

restraints on migration in Moscow guberniia.[44] B. Anderson (1980), using census data, showed the direction of population flows, indicating migration of more educated peasants for urban employment and those without education to settlement in agricultural areas.

Another way of looking at population density is from the perspective of the land, and the evidence in this regard shows a dramatic change over time, as discussed in Chapter 7. In some regions, particularly where state lands dominated, as in Siberia, northern Russia, and the Urals, households could seize land as needed from unsettled areas, providing it was unclaimed by other peasants.[45] Former serfs in other regions had less freedom to expand. A statistical survey on the impact of serf emancipation on landholding, prepared by the Ministry of Internal Affairs in conjunction with the Statistical Council in 1880, shows a considerable range of average landholdings by category of peasant.[46] In the area of greatest population pressure, the central black earth gubernii,[47] state peasants in the late 1870s averaged almost twice the amount of allotment land (4.8 *desiatiny* per "soul") as on privately owned land under redemption agreements (2.7 d.).[48] Moreover, 15.6 percent of the land worked by peasants on state lands was actually the households' property, just over five times greater than the 3.1 percent owned by former serfs. Peasants on state lands were without a doubt better able to take advantage of opportunities after the emancipation edicts, making Siberia and other frontier areas not entirely typical for a study of the impact of reform. Only some of the land in Siberia and other frontier areas was held communally by the late 1870s.[49]

Peasant lands, too, may well have been much larger than the allotment land associated officially with the household. Allotment land was not the only land available for use by communes and individual households. In principle, land not allocated to allotments formed a reserve fund, and it could be sold to peasants or to anyone else. Such holdings were designated

44 "Investigation of archival materials about refusal of passports to peasants shows that the power of the commune and of those household heads who did not want subordinates to separate was enormous, and it extended even to those individuals who had no roots either in the village or the household economy. It is important not to underestimate either the forcible attachment of commune members to their allotment nor the degree of inhibition on free out-migration of peasants. However, in contrast to these narrative materials, the statistical materials gathered by zemstva organs and materials from the census of 1897 show that in fact, the commune was helpless to prevent the flight of peasants from the village. The commune might call back the fugitive, but it could not force him to start up the farming of his allotment." Tikhonov (1978), pp. 123–24.

45 Aleksandrov (1990).

46 *Statistika pozemel'noi sobstvennosti naselennykh mest Evropeiskoi Rossii* (St Petersburg: Central Statistical Committee, 1880).

47 Tambov, Tula, Penza, Kaluga, Voronezh, Orel, Riazan, Kursk.

48 *Statistika* (1880), vyp. 1, p. xxx.

49 *Statistika* (1880), vyp. 1, p. xxxiv.

nonallotment land for an indefinite period of time and considered belonging to the commune as a whole. Households were allowed to request credit for purchase of such land from the Peasant Land Bank(founded in 1883) or they might request credit as a *tovarishchestva* (association) on behalf of the village. Sometimes purchases by households were vested in the women in the household, where they formed part of a dowry that was not subject to household division or to reallocation by the *skhod*.[50] The outcomes of such local arrangements are not recorded in statistics on landholding.

Certainly on former serf estates allotments were highly fragmented, forcing peasants to supplement their income by working for hire on large estates. As B. Litvak's quantitative study of the agreements of 1861–1863 (charters) and other contracts shows, in agricultural regions involuntary labor persisted long after abolition; temporarily obligated peasants had forced contracts for up to thirty years, requiring payment in labor as well as in money.[51] The name for the indentured laborer in Russian was *batrak*, common especially in the grain-producing steppe where planting and harvesting were accompanied by a coercive winter hiring system.[52] The emerging hiring market differed by region.[53] In regions of "*batrachestvo*," the residuals of serfdom were powerfully present, and individual households were ordinarily unable to prevent repartition.[54] Wealthier peasants could even be forced to agree to repartition, although the use of force seems unlikely unless there was strong need because of the exhaustion of the quality of the land.[55] On the whole, full repartition was rare, so partial repartitions might have excluded lands belonging to wealthier peasants.

Full repartition was a tool of necessity when subsistence was at issue for years on end. Partial repartition was a more common solution to demographic change. Under any repartitional system, agriculture would be forced into compulsory crop rotation, communal grazing, and scattered strips of allotment land. In 1906, what was called communal tenure (repartitional tenure) still covered at least five-sixths of allotment land. This would fully explain the continuing divergence of yields on nobles' and peasants' lands through that era.[56]

Late Tsarist Russia

The Contentious Issue: Did the Commune Constrain Growth? It is important to be cautious about focusing on the commune as the locus of

50 Gromyko (1991), p. 156.
51 Litvak (1972).
52 Litvak (1972), pp. 399–405.
53 Mixter (1991), p. 304.
54 Gromyko (1991), pp. 162–63.
55 See Atkinson (1990, 1983).
56 Chelintsev (1924), p. 116; for the problem of bias, a comment by Daniel Field.

backwardness in the nineteenth century. It fostered traditional forms of cultivation but also was, itself, an entrepreneur, buying land, generating a credit reputation, and forging networks in different regions. It accommodated to the demands of industrialization, helping to finance the purchase of agricultural machinery. In Ekaterinoslav, for example, local manufactures supplied machinery to communal lands as well as nobles' land. Even where it served as a constraint, the commune did not prevent commodities trade and agricultural output improvement.[57] Russia's continuing relative backwardness showed up in lower literacy rates and slower decline in marital fertility than in Western countries, and in these trends, it may have played some part.[58] Yet its traditional mores did not prevent in the 1880s women's wage in agriculture from dramatically increasing and family life from changing in response to women's new mobility.[59]

The real locus of backwardness seems to have been the large nobles' estates in the black earth region, where the *batrak*, or hired laborer, accepted terms very like servile arrangements. The initially limited hiring system and lack of employment assistance prevented migration as much as government regulations attempted to slow it down. The backwardness produced by insular villages and restraints on movement became particularly obvious to economists and revolutionaries by the end of the century. Lenin, for example, described as the central policy problem in Russia of the late 1890s, "the complete freedom of movement for peasants, freedom to refuse to work the land, to leave the commune, to resettle anywhere without paying redemption fees."[60] In that sense, the restraint on labor mobility, the commune seems a major constraint on economic development. It is not entirely clear from government records, however, that communes did not press the government for the right to leave overcrowded areas. Moreover, those who exited tended to do so with their entire household or village.

The commune was no restraint on new household formation. After 1861, households tended to split into smaller units. The average size of households declined from more than eight to less than seven. As population dramatically grew after abolition, between 1858 and 1877 by 22 percent, the number of households grew by 42 percent. The size of this adjustment seems to show incentive for accumulation by peripheral members of an extended family. It may also signify an end of the extreme circumstances under serfdom in which households required large numbers in order

57 On the role of the railroad in wheat yields, see Goldsmith (1955, 1961), and confirming econometric evidence based on Gregory (1982) in Goodwin (1998).

58 Gattrell provides a close reexamination of scholarly perspectives and of the evidence in his work on the economic history of tsarist Russia, see Chapter 2 (1986).

59 Engel (1994).

60 Cited in Tikhonov (1978), p. 105.

to produce sufficient crops while sending spare labor to urban areas for by-employment and the benefit of remittances (see chapter 7).[61] To be sure, for the latter reason, families continued to be large after abolition. More generally, population growth without free exit from the village produced surplus rural population as contemporary economists saw it.[62]

These more numerous households released larger amounts of labor. The rise in outwork and the new hiring markets meant that nonagricultural earnings became a substantial part of the household income. In the north, in Iaroslav guberniia, households carefully protected their most valuable land on the nonrepartitioned inheritable plot, which on average in 1901 consisted of hayfields (69 percent), vegetable gardens (11.9 percent), and structures (19.1 percent).[63] In Moscow guberniia, according to passport data, almost one-third of all peasant households registered to rural villages had completely stopped agricultural production on allotment land in 1898–1900 with only their gardens planted to support household consumption.[64]

The Stolypin reforms eased barriers to migration in this already transforming rural economy and stimulated both mobility and household autonomy (Davydov 2003). Half of the peasant households in European Russia, with some pressure from the government, petitioned for separation from the commune, and two million households received land in perpetuity by the provisions of November 9. 1.2 million households, or 10.7 percent of peasant households with 9.5 percent of all allotment land, had their holdings consolidated in European Russia.[65] This turned out to be a large share of actively cultivated land in 1916, 89.1 percent.[66] By the time of the revolution, flax, hemp, and vegetables were almost entirely produced on the land belonging to peasants, and 94 or 95 percent of the livestock. Peasant households' share of cultivated land reached roughly four times that of other owners in 1914.[67]

To summarize, in ways that have not been closely examined in the literature, the commune was adaptive to the changing economic conditions. It was supple enough to allow households to split and labor to leave the village for employment in urban areas, and to assist households

[61] *Statistika* (1880), vyp. 1, p. xxxv.

[62] See Litoshenko (2001), whose second chapter (written in 1922) concerned surplus population; later chapters dealt with agrarian crisis. He saw the 1890s as a period of increased family size and worsening conditions (see Gregory [1994]) for a view opposing the notion of agrarian crisis during industrialization in this era.

[63] *Protokoly komissii obrazovannoi po postanovleniiu iaroslavskago gubernskom zemskom sobraniia sessii 1901 goda 7 dekabria po otsenki nidvizhimykh imushchestv iaroslavskoi gubernii* (Iaroslavl', 1902), p. 2.

[64] Tikhonov (1978), p. 130.

[65] Jasny takes this data from Pavlovsky (1930), p. 135; Davydov (2003); Jasny (1949), p. 142; Macey (1998).

[66] Jasny (1949), p. 145; from Oganovskii (1922), pp. 78–9.

[67] Jasny (1949), p. 145.

in acquiring non-allotment land through the powers of the collective. With these trends as a foundation, it can be argued that the Stolypin reforms built upon changes underway. This argument seems supported by the considerable improvement in agricultural performance after the turn of the century, as discussed in Chapter 7.

Property Rights in Land at the End of the Tsarist Regime. The limited access by individual rural dwellers, as opposed to communes or households, to the ownership of land – enabling them to sell it or leave it in inheritance – was a glaring constraint on growth in the late nineteenth century. The legal incorporation of individual land rights was not entirely clarified in the dualistic legal system of tsarist Russia, even by the Stolypin reforms. Individual rights, along with the Roman individualistic concept of ownership rights, were introduced by Mikhail Speransky into Russian codified law in the *Svod Zakonov Rossiiskoi Imperii* in article 420 of the 10th volume.[68] The effects were widely felt in legal writings in the second half of the nineteenth century, showing especially the influence of the German pandectists. The judicial reform of 1864 permitted the departure from tradition in many spheres of law, creating in the more widespread use of case law an important instrument for legal evolution.

The Supreme Court with extensive new powers also introduced a considerable amount of legislative reform and liberal tendencies in Russian jurisprudence (Engelstein 2009; Wagner 1983; Walicki 1987; Wortman 1976). Previously, landownership rights had been principally governed by the concept of patrimonial property *(rodovoe imushchestvo)* W. Wagner (1983, p. 37), explains,

> ... patrimonial property (rodovoe imushche-stvo) constituted the central institution of Russian property and inheritance law. Most of the problems created by the law as well as the controversies surrounding it derived from this institution. Basically, the law identified most of a person's rural or urban immovable property with his extended kinship group or clan (rod).' Transfer of such property to anyone other than the direct legal heirs except by sale was prohibited in order to preserve the property within the clan.

By the early twentieth century, the Supreme Court had used its power to increase the flexibility of legal practice. Wagner goes on, however, the high court "... obviously could not abolish the institution of patrimonial property. But by narrowly restricting and controlling the law's application the high court tried to eliminate or at least mitigate the problems of excessive fragmentation."

[68] In the 1830s; see Silvestri (1993), p. 3.

Yet the application of patrimonial property rights continued to confound reform in the village. A. Luchinskaia, a contemporary expert on family law, wrote about the confusions and contradictions in the law, posing constraints on individual exercise of property rights even after the Stolypin reforms:

> The question is to whom does the allotment land belong? To the head of household or to the entire family, the household (dvor)? This issue was treated ambiguously, vaguely, temporarily, and therefore it still remains a question. The laws giving the peasants the allotment land – the statute of 19 February [1861] and the acts that followed – did not deal with the juridical sphere of the peasants' ties to the land. One can find expressions that, as it were, entirely confirm possession of the land allotment by the peasants' households, and right next to them an expression referring to the exclusive right to the allotment land of the individual head of household.[69]

Another contemporary jurist, V. Akimov, provided an example of continuing force of household rights in customary law, filling in the gaps in formal law:

> As in early modern France and Germany, by customary law, the peasant's claim to revenues from the land depended entirely upon labor and not on rights to the land. If, by error, for example, one peasant sowed and harvested grain on another household's land, the first had rights to the grain harvested, and matters were taken to local courts in Russia.
>
> As for inheritance, since the land belonged to the spousal pair jointly responsible for labor, if the husband, or head of household (*bolshak*), died, the wife inherited the land on behalf of those who worked it with her.[70]

Thus household practice was fixed in customary law, and distribution remained egalitarian, despite the retreat of the formal attributes of the commune and the liberal thinking of much of the judicial literature. Lack of striking household differentiation in some agricultural regions seems evidence of the continuing application of egalitarian principles of the division of land.[71] The persistence of customary law as a set of real governing principles is confirmed after the Bolshevik revolution in 1917 when peasants' ownership of the land ended.[72] Bolshevik policy permitted the restoration of the full force of customary law in the village by the mid-1920s.

69 Luchinskaia (1913), p. 357.

70 Akimov (1913), p. 511.

71 Jasny (1949), p. 149; Field (1989).

72 "... the order helps to form the individual, just as the acts of the individual help to form the order" (Hodgson [1988], p. 13); Shanin (1972), pp. 219–27, Mukhin (1888), on customary law and successive legal reforms.

2 THE SURVIVAL OF CUSTOM IN SOVIET LAW

Before Collectivization

The Revolutionary Era. The village returned to near economic self-sufficiency after the revolution. Manufacturing and rural/urban networks by which trade had thrived before 1914 sharply declined, causing further collapse.[73] The food crisis resulted in compulsory food procurement. The risk of confiscation was significant.

Two decrees, first, the nationalization of the land (the Land Decree of November 8, 1917) and second, the socialization of land (February 19, 1918), restored the rule of customary law in rural Russia. The second required equalization of land holdings and simplified regulations regarding repartition. The Bolshevik government put in place a Socialist Revolutionary doctrine supporting the idea of "Black Repartition" – i.e., the peasantry, acting as a whole, repartitioning the land either by the labor or the consumer standard (the number of work units/number of "mouths" in the household).[74] The process of repartition and redistribution was to be controlled by a simple majority (rather than two-thirds, which had slowed it in the tsarist regime). The two decrees undermined even the limited authority that the household and the individual peasant head of household had gradually acquired over sixty years of Russian law. Orlando Figes described the reversion to communal distribution systems under peasant rule in 1917–1918:

> The peasant rule of these months did not leave any major aspect of rural life untouched.... Communal land tenure was strengthened and extended to cover new rural groups, such as the landless laborers of the pre-revolutionary period and even some of the gentry.... [The peasants] nearly always broke up the consolidated plots and included them in the general redivision, although sometimes the property of the khutora was auctioned separately in order to raise money for the social needs of the village. One study showed that 90% of the villages in Saratov province broke up and divided the *khutora* during 1918. A survey by the TsSU in 1922 showed that 83% of the village in the middle Volga and 90% of the villages in the lower Volga claimed to have included the *khutora* and *otruba* in the communal reparations since 1917.[75]

Individual farms declined, communes rose in number. In Samara, for example, privately worked land shrank from 19 percent in 1916 to 0.1 percent in 1922, in Saratov, from 16 to 0.001 percent, in Stavropol, from 29 to .4 percent, in Moscow, from 9.3 to 3.3 percent, in Petrograd, from 28.7 to 22.7 percent. The consolidated plots associated with the decline

73 Harrison (1990), p. 108.

74 See Taniuchi (1968), for a review of the laws.

75 Figes (1989), pp. 70, 105.

of communal landholdings before and during the Stolypin reforms were brought back into communal use.[76] Even in southern Russia, where before the revolution, consolidated holdings comprised between 10 and 25 percent of all consolidated holdings in Russia, the figure fell to less than 0.1 percent by 1922.[77]

Although Bolshevik laws permitted households to cultivate land separately from the commune, it was generally the commune that obtained use of the extra land. Formerly, nobles' holdings were placed in reserve in a land fund, from which the communes received what they needed. Collectives had seized assets, including forests, and collective shares of land rose after the revolution.[78] By 1919, in thirty-two gubernii, only 4.6 percent of the land was operated by state farms, 1.7 percent by collective farms, and 93.7 percent by communes. Households of all kinds grew in number, from 16.5 million in January 1918 (1922 boundaries) to twenty-four million in 1920, an increase of roughly 50 percent.[79]

The New Economic Policy. The agrarian policy of the NEP was embodied in the Land Code of 1922. The land society, as the commune was called, gained codified rights to newly distributed lands. The Bolsheviks envisioned that in the evolution toward socialism, eventually the village soviet would replace the commune.[80] However, by confirming customary law, the code led to no such consequence. Retained with slight modification through the Soviet era, the Land Code of 1922 reinforced the rights of the household and thus perpetuated a useful and powerful tradition. The property of the household, including structures, machines, supplies, and cash, was owned in common, and when the household broke up, the procedures for dividing this common property were the same as in nineteenth-century customary law.

In the early 1920s, under chaotic and difficult conditions, with three-field crop rotation and strip farming, agriculture absorbed labor, but by the mid-1920s, producers again engaged in supplementary outwork in urban areas to improve their income. Up to 60 percent of all households supplied labor off the farm for work elsewhere in agriculture or in industry and services.[81] Households gained the right to market products and purchase equipment. They could start independent farms by leasing land and implements from other peasants.[82] Within certain limits, *kulaks*, or wealthy peasants, could

[76] Danilov (1977, 1979), pp. 106–7.
[77] Istoriia SSSR, 3 (1958), p. 100.
[78] Figes (1989), p. 127.
[79] Jasny (1949), p. 156.
[80] Taniuchi (1968), p. 31.
[81] Merl (1990, p. 61, 1981).
[82] Wheatcroft (1994), p. 112.

thrive, although they were subject to taxation and exclusion from the privileges of citizenship.

Agrarian policy in the NEP was designed to supply the demand for labor by critical industries at the "commanding heights" in a new industrialization drive. The aim was to squeeze resources from the sector without devastating it, a policy typical in developing countries.[83] The NEP encouraged the marketing of grain to avoid stimulating resistance among producers. However, this policy was a source of continued controversy among the Bolshevik leadership about the most effective way to get the surplus the agricultural sector transferred to industry for rapid industrialization. E. Preobrazhenskii, a prominent party member and economist, argued that the state should increase its capital accumulation by moving the terms of trade against the peasants, heavily taxing the small producer. His ideas may have been behind the later decision on collectivization, even though Preobrazhenskii himself was expelled from the communist party in 1927. N. Bukharin's views about what might materialize from the NEP were more positive, cautioning against the use of force to gain the surplus. Future policy depended less upon the actual outcomes of the liberal NEP, however, than the views of Stalin and the political control he was beginning to exercise on party decisions.

During the NEP, through 1928, the commune was temporarily revived, but its role in land management was what was left of its previously more sweeping authority in the countryside. It had no administrative responsibilities.[84] It shared a place in power alongside the village soviet, the organ preferred by the Bolsheviks for the establishment in Russia of a dictatorship of the proletariat. As long as the village was financially independent, it had some usefulness in the organization of crop rotation and partitions. On December 15, 1928, the Central Committee of the USSR ended its role in land management as well by establishing as a superior authority the village soviets, which were to give priority to poor peasants in the allocation of allotments. This instruction ended the sway of the Russian commune.[85]

Collectivization

The Rule of the Plan, Tempered by Custom. Collectivization created new forms of land use under a general regime of nationalized land. Numerous collective farms and a smaller number of powerful state farms were created for the production of field crops.[86] For supplementary production of vegetables, a private sector was permitted to exist on a very small scale. This

[83] Sah and Stiglitz (1992), Ch. 7.
[84] Telitsyn (2002), p. 217.
[85] Telitsyn (2002), pp. 218–21.
[86] The most effective and complete narrative of these events is in Davies (1980), vols 1–2.

remnant of the old regime, however, grew in importance as an alternative to the state stores as a source of vegetables and meat. This household sector came to be of substantial weight in the agricultural economy, steadily producing in Soviet times roughly a quarter of gross agricultural output (GAO); its share in animal production was a hefty 31 percent. Entrepreneurial rural households created a private (collective farm) market, which allowed them an outlet for the sale of vegetables and animal products other than procurement, for which they received low prices for their goods. In this way, the household economy could realize some commercial profit. By the end of the Soviet era, on collective farms, household had rights to 0.5 hectares of garden and field, although the average was about 0.25 hectares, and to a small number of livestock. Many state farms extended the same rights to households. As K. Wädekin observes, although the traditional peasant organization, commune, had been crushed in 1928, peasant households collectively retained a vital core of tradition, which was endorsed in Soviet law. In his classic work on the private sector, he attributed the survival of the household sector as follows:

> The principal reason given by Soviet authors for the continued existence of the private sector is economic necessity resulting from the still inadequate level of collective agricultural production. The second reason is the political consideration of the 'centuries old attachment of the peasant to his piece of land' which 'has not yet completely died out and which it would be erroneous to ignore.'[87]

In sum, there were theoretically three kinds of land use: public or socialized land, private subsidiary plots (*lichnye podsobnye khoziaistva*), and plots belonging to workers and employees in farm and nonfarm rural activities. The last were relatively less significant (up to 0.15 hectares), but the household plots that were created out of *kolkhoz* land served simultaneously as an incentive system and a source of consumption goods.

Legally, *kolkhoz* household plots were different from plots belonging to workers and employees because individual *kolkhoz* members were not juridically defined as individuals, by contrast with workers and employees. On the farm, in the tradition of customary law, it was the household that possessed the plot. By the 1970s, to be sure, no sharp distinction existed in law between kolkhoz plots and urban dwellers' plots, but there was a gulf between them in practice.[88] The urban supplementary plots were of far less commercial importance than those of the *kolkhoz* workers, and many workers and employees had no plots at all. While the greater part of the product of plots belonging to workers and employees was largely consumed, that of *kolkhoz* households was marketed.

[87] Wädekin (1973), p. 7, although Wädekin calls the affirmation of the importance of customary law a "psychological factor" of secondary significance.

[88] Wädekin (1973), pp. 6, 21.

The *kolkhoz* private plots had the usual historical legal attributes. Called personal plots, as noted above, they were subject to a complicated juridical procedure set forth by customary law, thus formally observed for the rural community. The household was defined as the family and labor community (within it), and kinship was not a prerequisite of belonging to the household as in the past. This complex treatment of the household was not defined or treated in detail, but it was confirmed in the model statute of the agricultural artel' (1935).[89]

Rights to a personal plot were determined by the list of registered households, who were assigned lots from a general fund of noncommunal arable. Personal plots could not be alienated when a member of the household departed, and they reverted to the collective only if the last member of the household died or left the kolkhoz without leaving it to an appointed heir.[90] Proceeds from the private subsidiary plot were common property of the household. This generally included cash and goods received by members for work in the *kolkhoz*, proceeds from sale of livestock and livestock products and vegetables raised on the private plot, and in some cases outside earnings of members.[91]

By contrast with tsarist law, the collective farm, not the household, had claim to outside earnings. The household also had no claim on personal state grants, pensions, and other funds given to individuals, including the head of the family. As in tsarist Russia, women's earnings for tasks (e.g., school teacher, bookkeeper, veterinary assistant) were, as historically, put in a separate fund that was inheritable through the female line.

The Soviet Constitutions. The 1936 Constitution of the USSR confirmed both the authority of the head of the household over its members and that of the collective assembly over households and their personal use and inheritability of land (Articles 7 and 10).[92] It gave to the collective assembly the right to punish households, resembling the custom of the past, for minor and major infractions. Households faced the loss of the use of equipment or access to *kolkhoz* pasture for privately owned livestock or, in extreme cases, membership in the *kolkhoz*.[93] The rights of the individual were in general severely constrained: "The Foundations of Civil Law of the USSR" of 1961 (Article 5), stipulated that an individual's rights were protected only up to the point that they did not conflict with laws of socialist sharing and "moral principles" of the building of communism.[94]

[89] Wädekin (1973).
[90] *Kol'khoznoe Pravo (1955)*, Ch. 13.4.
[91] Dunn (1971), p. 334.
[92] If a kolkhoz family changed its residence to a *Sovkhoz*, it retained the right of use of a private plot.
[93] Dunn (1971), p. 329.
[94] Mozolin (1992), p. 31.

In other words, no real security could be found in Soviet law for the concept of property, naturally, not even the private plot. Formally, the means of production were divided between the state and the *kolkhoz*-cooperatives, unions, and other social organizations. The revolution had made property secure against confiscation by creditors, who no longer existed, but there was no security against the state. Property could not be used as collateral, and the state could liquidate cooperatives and plots, as it did in the 1950s, along with the land of industrial cooperatives.

In the Constitution of 1977, the government attempted to end ambiguity: the two concepts of state and common property were merged legally, ending the conceptual separation of state and *kolkhoz* farm property.[95] Just as a legal distinction between *sovkhoz* (state) and *kolkhoz* (socialized) land was removed, all property held in common was also now viewed officially as state property. However, by custom, the *kolkhoz* members retained a right to their plots, and although they were allocated from a land fund of the *kolkhoz*, a residual sense of ownership remained. The fact that these plots were confirmed as their legally owned property in transition is a sign that the Brezhnev Constitution did not succeed in claiming these plots for the state against traditions of customary law.

3 TRANSITION

Legal Reform: The Early Years

Constitutional Reform. The Constitution of the Russian Federation (1993) for the first time after the end of communism clearly identified the individual's right to own land. However, in practice, the legal foundation was laid by the Supreme Soviet of the Russian Federation, whose chairman in 1990 and 1991 was Boris Yeltsin, also president of Russia in 1990 and 1991. Article 1 of the law of the Russian Soviet Federative Socialist Republic (RSFSR) about peasant (farmers') activities (November 22, 1990) gave rights to households as entities with rights, including landownership and the use of hired labor. Households were permitted to own land: on December 25, 1990, private landownership was decriminalized in a set of laws dealing with independent farms.

The first modern Land Code (1991), in the early post-socialist era, reflected the traditional Russian controls on land transactions: it allowed property to be bought and sold, but only through local soviets (councils). In 1992, that constraint was removed, but a new one was imposed, a moratorium of ten years on land sales. This was the first to underscore the virtuality of rights: titles to arable land were issued, but the right of disposal was withheld. In December 1992, the moratorium was lifted for private subsidiary

[95] Mozolin (1992), p. 126.

plots, which were permitted as inheritable property. Also, land under houses and dachas could be sold. Arable land used in commercial agricultural production, i.e., by independent farmers, could not. For them, the non-disposal constraint still held in the moratorium with one exception: land they had received from state land reserves could not be sold for ten years, but if purchased from local authorities, they could sell it in five years.

In 1993, when Yeltsin had a temporary window of absolute authority and could govern by executive decree, he confirmed the security and guarantee of the right of disposition of private landed property for all citizens, in essence revoking restrictions imposed by the Supreme Soviet. On October 27, he enacted a decree, "On the regulation of land relations and development of agrarian reform in Russia." This decree expressly ended the moratorium on land sales and permitted agricultural land also to be leased, inherited, mortgaged, or exchanged, that is, used as an investment by corporative farms of all kinds. The enterprises could sell or exchange their land shares to outsiders, with all restrictions removed on the procedures required for such sales and for the leasing of land formerly belonging to state and collective farms.

Further executive decrees aimed to narrow these broad freedoms. By a regulation of December 10, Yeltsin gave sole authority over land transactions to the local government committees on land resources, which were to organize auctions and tenders. Restrictions were placed on buyers of land, including limits on ownership by individuals and the requirement that new owners preserve the existing form of land use. Added to its powers, the Central Committee for Land Resources of the Russian Federation was made responsible for creating a land cadastre and land registry for the purpose of an efficient land tax system and the protection of landowners' rights. On December 16, Yeltsin issued an environmental protection act, which defined conservation principles and permitted land to be confiscated for violations. Criticized for according excessive authority to local executive powers and, specifically, to the Committee for Land Resources and its local branches, he rescinded the first two of these decrees in January 1994.[96]

The Arable Land Market. The land market first emerged in the Russian transition for subsidiary and urban plots. Sales of the arable were stalled, since officially they were subject to technical provisions of the Land Code and the existing code was inconsistent with the constitution. Some fifty articles had been revoked. Alexander Zaveryukha, the Cabinet member for agriculture, commented on February 16, 1997, that the lack of a mechanism covering land sales had set back the land market:

> The country lacks not only a legal base for an agricultural reform but even a mechanism for achieving the main goal of the reform – the redistribution of land in favor of more efficient agricultural producers.[97]

[96] Meliukhina (1994), pp. 10–13.
[97] FBIS-SOV-97-032, Interfax Daily Report, Feb. 17, 1997.

The laws, in other words, were unclear about whether sale of arable was permitted. Although federal law permitted the turnover of arable land, it could not be enforced until the government and a new Parliament drafted the complete new Land Code. The preparations for drafting the code became the locus of sharp and divisive controversy. The reformers sought clear property rights consistent with the constitution's intention; the government sought compromise that would go part way toward heavy restrictions sought by opponents. In one draft (1996), for example, the government recommended restrictions on the transfer of land to exclude the right of physical persons to buy land. Russia's Choice (the reformist party led by Yegor Gaidar) submitted a liberal draft. Neither was accepted by the Parliament, which produced several of its own between 1997 and 1998, in which the term "land ownership" remained, but land transfers were not allowed. Both parliamentary drafts were vetoed by the president.[98]

In March 1996, a presidential decree required local authorities to issue certificates to landowners and users of agricultural land on purchase or lease agreements. Only some 4.3 million of the 10.8 million rural dwellers acquired such contracts. Of these, few were actually using the land. Others signed lease contracts in return for in-kind payments. About 50 percent of all entitlements were owned by pensioners or nonfarm workers, who chose not to set up their own farms or use the land to which they were entitled. The 6.5 million who did not conclude contracts with farm managers were unable to gain rent from the land.

The Later Years

Distributional Results of an Uncertain Early Course. The outcome of the contested legal environment was the emergence of a few somewhat smaller, technologically integrated farms and a multitude of weaker large farms. The purchase, exchange, and/or leasing of entitlements had not led to the break-up of large entitles, although in principle, they were partitioned into farmland and plots. Because so few farms were restructured, there was no widespread division of that farmland into individual farms, and no real land market for the arable. Whereas titles were issued to farm employees, their shares were not withdrawn. Out of 10.5 million workers in agriculture, there were initially 4,400 households who set up farms (1991), embracing some 17,000–20,000 individuals, including family members. Of these, indicative of farm employee initial reluctance, 75 percent were individuals from urban areas returning to the land.[99] Within eight years, by 1999, some 15 percent of

[98] Both parliamentary drafts would have ended rights for private farmers and for agricultural entities to mortgage private plots. They envisioned leasing arrangements rather than ownership for those collective farms not yet fully privatized. Farmers who owned land, according to these drafts, would have been deprived of the right to sell it, being obliged to return it to state or municipal ownership on terms set when it was acquired.

[99] *OECD* (1999); Leonard and Serova (2001).

large farm enterprise employees had withdrawn their shares from the farm. The overwhelming percentage leased their shares to be worked by others (42 percent). Thirty-one percent of land shares were not redistributed or titled, and 7.2 percent of the shares were allocated to vegetable gardens.[100] Those not redistributed were under the control of farm management. This meant that together with other kinds of shares (including those leased to the farm or to others), the overwhelming number of shares were retained by the farm. The small share for garden plots is the allotment to households for their own use.

The leasing of land shares (42 percent) was a contentious issue. Farm managers hoped that from the new Land Code leasing might be transformed into perpetual use without rent.[101] Instead of ruling on this critical issue, however, governing almost half the land, the Parliament waved this too controversial issue aside. In the the Land Code of October 30, 2001, it omitted all reference to the arable. For nonarable land, the code formalized the regulation of land ownership and use rights, including perpetual or indefinite use, free fixed-term use, leasehold, lifelong inheritable possession and easements, spelling out that rights other than these would be re-registered under the specified categories. Land in urban areas was to be sold by public tender, and outside of urban areas the code required investors to present a detailed report when requesting land rights. Only 2 percent of Russian territory was affected, but, to be sure, in this 2 percent much of the population resides and most economic activity takes place.

The Completion of Reform. Property rights in land were finally codified by a special land law, enacted to serve in place of the new code to regulate the purchase and sale of agricultural land (May 16, 2002), in effect from January 27, 2003.[102] It brought Russian land law into conformity with that of most European states.[103] Briefly, the law of 2002 covers 427.7 million hectares of land registered as agricultural and belonging to the state by the Federal Land Register Service.

The law is not free of restrictions. For example, it constrains single ownership to limits set regionally. For example, in Saratov, no more than 30 percent of the arable land in any district can be owned by a single landowner. As in other transition countries, it prohibits foreign firms or individuals,

100 Uzun (1999), p. 38.

101 OECD (1999), p. 87.

102 "Federal'nyi zakon ob oborote zemel' sel'skokhoziaistvennogo naznacheniia," July 24, 2002 g., N 101-FZ.

103 There are some distinctive aspects to the law. The ban on foreign ownership restricts access to mortgages, that is, in case of a default, if a foreign bank takes a mortgage on agricultural land, the bank does not have the right to dispose of it during foreclosure proceedings. Also the law does not apply to land with structures, which is governed, instead, by the Land Code.

stateless persons, or majority-foreign-owned companies from owning arable, but it permits long leases. As in most countries, owners cannot use property to violate health standards and the environment or zoning laws. Zoning laws are covered in Article 4 of the Land Code of the RSFSR, which categorizes land by use: (1) agriculture, (2) settlement, (3) industry, transport, communications, security, energy, defense, (4) nature reserve or historical monuments, (5) forest reserve, (6) the reserve fund, and (7) wasteland.[104] Further breakdown of agricultural land between kinds, or categories, of agricultural land ownership, each with separate rights, has remained in the accounting system and in statistics.

There are some important barriers in this law to ease of disposability. In the 2002 economic report of the Institute for the Economy in Transition (Moscow), these are reviewed.[105] Reversing previous laws, the new law prohibits individual contracts for lease/transfer/sale without joint consent by co-owners of collective property. No less than 20 percent of joint owners are required for a vote approving by at least a two-thirds majority the sale of a share of the jointly owned collective property. Thus barriers to exit continue to exist, although large corporative farms are growing smaller. Barriers to exit have a large welfare effect: individuals can easily be prevented from gaining the promised income stream from long-term individual leases. Many of these individuals are pensioners for whom long-term leasing is a source of income and security.

There are also special rights accorded to the state, for example, the right to remove land belonging to someone whose practices have a harmful effect on the environment. Without further clarification, or precise definition of the "zoning" stipulations the law permits arbitrary confiscation. The government has also reserved the right of first purchase within thirty days of the announced sale, which can only lead to corruption through prices negotiated informally.[106]

The Final Step. In 2003, the Parliament finally passed the key companion law to ownership rights over the arable land – the law on mortgaging arable land. The controversial nature of this right had led to the exclusion of this provision from the Land Code, which deferred to the federal law on mortgages, which prohibits the mortgaging of agricultural land. In 2002, the Duma attempted to have the mortgage law amended to enable mortgages using land as collateral, but the upper chamber, the Federation Council, defeated the amendment. A conciliatory commission was required to remove the prohibition. In the most recent version of the law, there is

104 Wegren (1998, 2002); Leonard and Serova (2001); Van Atta (1993); OECD (1997), and others.
105 Karlova et al. (2002), pp. 252 ff.
106 For the full analysis, see IET (2002).

still a glitch. The prohibition against mortgaging arable has been removed, but no sentence permitting mortgages has been inserted. The assumption by Russian law is that what is not prohibited must be permitted. Naturally, greater security would have been provided to potential borrowers had the law been clearer in including arable land among categories of assets that can be mortgaged.[107]

Problems enacting a mortgage law provide insight into past patterns of policy on property rights guarantees. It is important to examine if restrictions, in practice, have slowed the purchase and sale of arable land. Numbers of petitions to claim land from the regional and federal reserves have been few indeed. Without permission to use land as collateral to obtain deeds to plots or farms and equipment loans, having land may seem no bargain. Both the expansion of independent farmers by the purchase of additional land and the downsizing of large farms have been held back by ongoing problems with enforcing property rights in arable land. The very largest corporative entities, which obtain from government sources, have no such restrictions.[108]

Regional Laws: Some Unfinished Business. The security of land tenure now differs by region. The Constitution of 1993 provides for joint jurisdiction of issues related to the land by the federal and regional authorities. However, diverging regional and federal regulations and arrangements must be harmonized. In Tatarstan and Saratov, for example, among the few areas where a land market has actually been well established, local laws are not in conformity with the federal law of July 27, 2002, and may have to be changed. Although federal law requires the regions to comply with all federal legislation within six months, this injunction excludes those regions that have not yet passed their own enactments on land rights. The constitution gives to these regions, such as Krasnodar, right to postpone the purchase and sale of land. The head of the Agrarian Committee of the Federation Council, Ivan Starikov, underscored in describing the January 27, 2003, law "On the turnover of arable land," that it was seriously weakened by these political compromises with the regions. Of those regions that have their own land laws (30–40), "a few," according to Starikov, have allowed land

107 "Federal'nyi Zakon 'Ob Ipoteke (Zaloge nedvizhimosti),'" July 16, 1998, N 102-FZ and amendments of November 9, 2001, N 143-FZ, Feb. 11, 2002, N 18-FZ.; Vasilii Treskov, "Vstupil v silu, chto dal'she, Korrektirovki ne pomeshaiut," *Parliamentskaia Gazeta*, March 12, 2003; Article 63 reads, "This law stipulates that agricultural land that belongs to the state or municipal authorities and to agricultural organisations and peasant (farms), and fields that are part of the private subsidiary plots cannot be mortgaged."

108 Stephenson (1995).

sales; the others permit land either to be rented or to be held as a lifetime inheritance.[109]

To summarize, many factors contributed to the slow pace of development of an arable land market. There were policy problems and setbacks, due in part to macroeconomic conditions and in part to lobbies, expressing opposition to inclusion of arable land in the new land code. Russia's unclear property rights, from a Coasian perspective, would have been an additional source of the continued uneven performance of the excessively large farms and the very slow formation of independent small farms in Russia. Russia's unique set of problems in the establishment of secure and functional rights to dispose of arable property goes back very far historically. Indeed, in western Siberia, where high protein wheat can be grown, there is no history of land market at all, since much of Siberia was allocated as state lands. It is possible that the relatively sparce settlement of this territory throughout the imperial period may have been attributable to weak incentives for farming, despite the quality of the soils. Plans to make these lands available for purchase and sale were rejected by the tsarist government, locking in for many decades a historically important trend.

Barzel (1989) views land rights as effective even when at an intermediate state between totally absent and perfectly well defined. In this situation, individual choice plays a part in rights formation. Such a situation is very much the actual practice in advanced economies. In Russia, the role of individual choice, however, was too buried in customary rights to fit Barzel's adjusted model of effective property rights. Russia's situation was not an intermediate state. Historically, in Russia, individual producers did not have rights to own expanses of arable land although they did have rights they could exercise to plots. By contrast with the slow uptake of arable land, subsidiary plots, which were inheritable by households with rights that are steeped in tradition – experienced rapid turnover. The parcels sold for subsidiary plots jumped after sales were permitted in 1992, increasing by ten times in 1993 to 100,133, amounting to some 10,959 hectares in expanse.[110]

In regard to the arable market, in regions where local laws permitted landownership from the mid-1990s, as in Saratov and Vladimir, a land market did appear. In Saratov oblast' a regional law was passed allowing land sales in 1997. From 1998 it was permitted to sell arable land by auction. In 2001, there were forty-three auctions and almost 11,000 hectares sold by auction in Saratov oblast'. The beneficiaries have been independent farmers, whose average size farm in Saratov went from 75 to 156 hectares in one

[109] Irina Granik, "Zemel'naia reforma, Regiony obvinili v sabotazhe," *Kommersant Daily*, No. 13, Jan. 28, 2003, p. 15.

[110] *Doklad* 1995, p. 86.

year.[111] In both Saratov and Vladimir, the prices exceeded the fixed values determined in 1992 by the first valuation project.[112]

By 2001, the land market spread to a few other regions. Almost 75 percent of farm managers reported in a survey that there was a functioning land market in their region.[113] Saratov and Tatarstan have laws protecting property rights in land, and in these two reform regions, the pace of growth in the land market is steady. By contrast, in the rich agricultural area of Krasnodar krai, land is not yet for sale. Soviet-style land management persists, and leasing rather than ownership is the common form of tenure.[114]

Land Registry: More Unfinished Business. The Russian cadastral survey serves an important legal and fiscal function: it is a registry of boundaries as well as a valuation for tax purposes. The place of land registry in contracting is clear. Land cannot be valued as collateral, nor can exchanges be contractually completed, unless boundaries and soil quality are determined and recorded. The place of the cadastre in fiscal well-being is also clear. Tax rates cannot be set with any accuracy, until the cadastre is complete.[115]

Numerous difficulties – both technical and financial – have plagued the cadastral survey, started in 1992. Among them, surveys are costly, and budgetary resources for this objective were limited, especially since controversies over the sale of the arable led to policy focus on nonagricultural land, where demand and land values were high. By 1996, 4.5 million hectares of arable land had been inventoried, including roughly one-third of the land occupied by independent farms.[116] Technically, the survey of the arable also encountered difficulties. It cannot be carried out efficiently by aerial photography, because land records cover only one-third of Russia's territory. According to the head of the Land Cadastre Service, Sergei Sai, by 2003 only settled and forested land had been surveyed, and the rest could be completed only after the system was automated and holdings were

111 Andriushina (2002), p. 136.

112 The average price per hectare determined by the registry project is 11,040, rubbs. The range is 400 in Nenetz autonomous okrug and 46,000 in Krasnoyarsk krai. Veronika Sivkova, "Zemlia uzhe prodiutsia, v nature," Feb. 12, 2003, *Argumenty i Fakty*, pp. 851–56; Mikhail Sadovnikov, "I nikto ne znaet, skol'ko stoit gektar," *Rossiiskaia Gazeta,* Jan. 28, 2003, p. III.

113 Matiukhin and Bezrukov (2001).

114 Ivankina et al. (2000), p. 57.

115 The federal program, "Development of Land Reform in the Russian Federation, 1999–2000," created by round table discussions, according to the protocol of the meeting of December 26, 1997, No. 2212, and instructions of the Government of the Russian Federation, December 27, 1997, No V, Ch-III-41711.

116 Information provided on the Web page of the Russian State Committee for Land Resources and Land Management, http://www.goscomzem.ru/geninfo.htm.

registered.[117] By 2006, only 7 percent of potentially marketable holdings had been registered.[118] This technical issue led back to the financing problem. Except for new national programs, inclusion of spending regarding the arable has been meager. Budgetary sums for the land cadastre project fell from $62.1 million in 1991–1993 to $10 million in 2001 and $1.7 million in 2002.[119] A report to the Audit Chamber for August 2006 describes a major shortfall of budgetary funds for the cadastre between 2002–2004; during this period, 28 percent of budgetary allocations in constant (2002) prices had actually been allocated by 2005.[120] Parliamentary debates show heightened concern about cutting corners, which threatened to deprive the project of appropriate expertise.[121]

A new approach to the land cadastre was initiated in 2007 for a beginning in 2008 to simplify procedures required to claim land and register it with the structures included in the estimates. That is, after not assessing structures together with the land, Russian land law now does so, in conformity with procedures in western market economies. There is no distinction between structures, privatized and in the possession of new owners, and land beneath the property, which previously belonged to the state (federal, regional, or municipal authorities). From 2008, private owners are able to register the land as well as buildings in their name.[122]

It is well known that technical matters, including the lack of an archived land registry, had an effect on land sales not only in Russia but also across central and eastern European transition countries (CEE), where restitution required expertise and research.[123] Historical value is now only one

117 Konstantin Frumkin, "Zemliu zpriatat' nevozmozhno. Zemel'nyi kadastr tsivilizuet rynok nedvizhimosti i sistemu nalogooblozheniia," *Nezavisimaia Gazeta*, April 7, 2003, No. 60, p. 4.

118 "Otchet o rezul'tatakh proverki effektivnosti ispol'zovaniia sredstv federal'nogo biudzheta, period 2005 goda na vysozdanie avtomatizirovannoi sistemy vedeniia gosudarstvennogo zemel'nogo kadastra..." *Biulleten' Schetnoi palaty Rossiiskoi Federatsii*, No. 8 (August 2006), pp. 18–19. In 2006, the procedure was simplified so that the cadastre would be facilitated. Aleksandra Petrachkova, "Uprostit' zemleustroistva," *Vedomosti*, No. 114, June 26, 2006).

119 Volkov (2002), p. 9.

120 "Otchet o rezul'tatakh proverki effektivnosti ispol'zovaniia sredstv federal'nogo biudzheta, period 2005 goda na vySozdanie avtomatizirovannoi sistemy vedeniia gosudarstvennogo zemel'nogo kadastra..." *Biulleten' Schetnoi palaty Rossiiskoi Federatsii*, No. 8 (August 2006), pp. 18–19. In 2006, the procedure was simplified so that the cadastre would be facilitated. Aleksandra Petrachkova, "Uprostit' zemleustroistva," *Vedomosti*, No. 114, June 26, 2006).

121 "Obrashchenie Gosudarstvennoi Dumy k Predsedateliu Pravitel'stva Rossiiskoi Federatsii M. M. Kas'ianovu o gosudarstvennykh organakh upravleniia zemel'nymi resursami," *Parliamentskaia Gazeta*, April 12, 2003, No. 68.

122 The law "O gosudarstvennom kadastre" was approved at third reading by the Duma. Irina Skliarova, "Kolkoz konchilsia," *Vremia novosti*, No. 116 (July 5, 2007).

123 See Swinnen (1997).

component of market value, since land use changed under the long period of communist rule, sometimes substantially by the addition of new drainage or irrigation facilities or by the construction of roads and the spread of villages. The experience in market valuation in western economies is of little use, moreover, since tax records and previous sale prices, the standard resources, are unavailable in the CEE and the Former Soviet Union (FSU). The difficulty in restitution for the Russian Federation is so great that no attempt was made to encourage or to honor claims for restitution, except in the Baltic countries, where restitution on the basis of pre-World War II conditions was possible.

Restitution there proved important for the reestablishment of property rights but a mixed good for the economy. By virtue of restitution, a mass of small farms was restored especially in Latvia and Lithuania. The resulting inefficiencies from small scale farming have yet to be overcome. Agriculture has shrunk dramatically (in Latvia, agriculture is only 2.5 percent of gross domestic product [GDP], the lowest in the CEE), but employment in the sector is far more. The surplus labor is relatively less skilled and less well educated than in other sectors.[124] In Latvia, farms averaged twenty-four hectares in 2001, a scale associated with high unit costs, outdated technologies, and low investment.[125] Average plot size in Lithuania is even smaller, around seventeen hectares in 2000, too small for commercial viability.[126] Estonia's land registry project has moved more slowly, such that 40 percent was still not registered by 2000, but agriculture stabilized at 3.2 percent of GDP, with 6 percent of employment.[127]

Summary of Contemporary Land Rights Policy. Putin's government has rapidly pushed through to completion the project of modernizing land rights. The trial-and-error policies show lessons learned in decision making. For example, the state at first categorized privately held arable plots as non-disposable. "Individual, supplementary plots of *kolkhoz* and other workers and servitors in rural areas" were not categorized as inheritable but as supplementary income, while urban plots were inheritable. Then rural household subsidiary plots were re-categorized as inheritable property, and, like other kinds of small plots, could be sold to anyone, including foreigners.

Putin's decisiveness echoed that of the early Yeltsin regime, with its decrees confirming constitutional rights to own arable land, a milestone in Russian history. But by contrast with those of Yeltsin, Putin's policies

124 OECD (2002), p. 16.
125 OECD (2001), p. 181.
126 OECD (2001), pp. 187–88.
127 OECD (2001), p. 174.

have been sustained. The Putin era has brought additional security at least in regard to the arable land, as common shares continue to be transformed into parts of larger farms or separated shares. Customary rights to that land, the egalitarian distribution of shares so important at the outset of this reform, are receding as large farms claim firmer entitlements. In other words, distributional issues are still unresolved, but in the key supply-side issue, interregional and rural/urban migration, western principles of law are firmly in place.

In Russia, as elsewhere, the state retains the right to confiscate property for a variety of reasons, but it is expected that constitutional guarantees will eventually make state rights little more than zoning and environmental restrictions, common to all market economies. The course is clear, although there are still large hurdles in practice. These challenges are the long-run problems of rural unemployment and poverty, including customary barriers to out-migration.

4 CHANGE AND CONTINUITY

Radically different in form and content, pre-Soviet, Soviet, and post-Soviet approaches to property rights reforms were similar in their effect on households. After the serf emancipation, households acquired some right of disposal over allotment land, and they retained full rights over subsidiary plots, although large landholders retained the right to determine scale and terms of peasant holding.

With the continual expansion of peasant holdings through purchase of nobles' land, and following the stimulus of the Stolypin land reform, the need for strong attachment to the private plot mayhave receded by 1913. However, in the insecure circumstances of revolution and civil war, and subsequent collectivization, the traditional household sector survived. Customary law upheld a private regime of very small plots within the large farm. How did customary law survive even the highly ideological period of war communism and rapid industrialization of the 1930s? V. Danilov's answer lies in "the great internal vitality of the land Commune and its central role in the economy and society before 1861 and policy afterwards." One should seek linkages, he wrote, looking at the preservation of the commune after 1917.[128]

For the purposes of discussion of property rights, the household, not the individual, was the agent in the Russian rural incentive system. The household's customary place in the commune was, as V. Danilov remarked, a source of internal vitality throughout history. In Russia, the uniqueness and longevity of community and household welfare functions is due in part to

[128] Danilov (1990), p. 288.

the dualistic formalization of law in 1861. Customary law, not extinguished by the Stolypin reforms, was present in "*kolkhoz* law," almost in defiance of the sweeping ambit of collectivization. *kolkhoz* law granted customary claims by households to the subsidiary plot and a share ownership of the *kolkhoz*. Household practices continue to be important in their contribution to output.

Conceptually, the continuous hold of customary law shows the powerful shaping force of private-order institutions. In the 1990s, a more modern system of landholding rights has emerged, as D. Rylko put it, a state of virtual property rights.[129] What he means is that things are clearly separated from rights. Property rights are now a bundle of rights and not things rights, in Heller's distinction.[130] However, this is also a holdover of Soviet law, where subjective rights to assets and the actual property were separated. The owner has a right to own, use, and dispose of assets without specifically having the right to give the actual thing to another individual; the owner can give only the right to own that property to someone else without the right to dispose of the particular asset.[131]

The modern way of looking at property rights as bundles of rights certainly functions in practice to the benefit of an economy. In the Russian village environment, however, transaction costs are high in changing virtual rights into control of actual property. Virtual rights may not give market actors as much of a feel for value, and this may have led to the slow pace of restructuring and arable sales. Significant transaction costs reduce the benefits of the bundle of rights.[132] The new laws will also leave the door open to state interference in contracts.

State interference in contracts has been discussed elsewhere in this book in terms of labor movement restrictions. As observed in Chapter 6, in land-abundant countries, governments will be more concerned to restrict the movement of labor than to establish clear boundaries on the land. Because of the indifferent revenue consequences, before 1861, on public domains, there was active resettlement of peasants into frontier areas Samara, Orenburg, and Siberia, also on public domains. However, between the abolition of the serfs in 1861 and the Stolypin reforms of 1906, the state attempted to stem the flow of migration more broadly. By 1913, landownership rights in Siberia still had not yet been clarified.[133] In the twenty-first century, the kind of full support for small landownership that would be required to

129 See Rylko's use of the term for grant of rights to a share but not the share itself (Rylko 2002).

130 Heller (1999).

131 Mozolin (1992), p. 33.

132 Heller (1999), p. 1222.

133 The Council of Ministers proposed a law (March 10, 1911) "about the transfer of otruby and khutory to settlers as private property," but it was not confirmed by the Duma and was set aside. Safronov (1977), p. 277.

encourage it, including full funding for completion of the land registry and rural development assistance, is not evident.

5 SUMMARY AND CONCLUSION

Property rights to land in Russia characteristically had a strong customary component alongside or within codified law. Most often, a residual from feudalism, legal characteristics were regional: custom led to the consolidation of households in strong local communities. Thus, Russian migration to the frontiers was by households and sometimes by whole communities. Some fragmentation of holdings in terms of allotments or private plots was permitted, and some control over rural entrepreneurship has lasted through the present.

The chapter traced the development and impact of formalization of powers of the household and ambiguous application of more liberal law, embodied in Roman individualistic concepts of land ownership. From 1861, the numbers in households constituted the accounting unit for the repartitional land commune, fostering partial partitions, seasonal migration, repatriation of earnings, and the viability of the community. The household custom held sway in tsarist peasant courts. The land commune had both public- and private-order functions in its active role in the land market – its authority in resettlement of peasants, in provision of credit reputations for members to obtain loans and join cooperatives, and in relieving population pressure by helping peasants gain access to new land and jobs. In Moscow guberniia, one in three peasants was registered in the village but not engaged in agricultural labor.

In the NEP era, communal land organization was fostered and fully restored to the dominant form of land use. The land was nationalized, and procurements grew. Customary law still served a function in chaotic and difficult times of pooling resources and securing the fortunes of vulnerable members against famine, social goals that coincided with those of the new regime. Although much of this course was halted by collectivization, since the small but hardy small plots belonging to households were useful to the state, they survived.

In the 1990s and early twenty-first century, when universal property rights in arable were introduced, individuals finally gained access to arable landownership. In the way that these rights were introduced, however, the state aimed to prevent excessive fragmentation by encouraging the transfer of most rights through the large corporative farms. In this and numerous other ways, individual farm consolidation has been discouraged and labor has been retained on large farms in some areas.

Schumpeter believed entrepreneurship emerged only within a social force: a significant number of individual agents will engage in risky activities, or set an entrepreneurial orientation, only if such norms develop on a substantial scale in an entire community.[134] In Russia, customary law supported entrepreneurship, but it also served to preserve rights of whole communities over individuals in difficult times. Two kinds of law co-existed. In every era, a mix of far more customary law than would be predicted and codified law governed the drawing of boundaries and the use of land. In the tsarist and socialist eras, discouragement of individual rural entrepreneurship was overt in official prohibitions and discriminatory policies. The degree to which current policies are free of that discrimination and are building entrepreneurial norms is the concern of the next chapter.

134 Vecchi (1995).

5

Rural Organization and Entrepreneurship

In 1906, the Stolypin reforms granted universal property rights in land, furthering farm formation, which was already occurring in parts of rural Russia. A large number of new farms were created, as M. Davydov (2002) shows, in response to petitions by individual peasant households and collectives. To be sure, many were consolidated by force.[1] It seems clear that family farming was spreading rapidly by the time of the revolution of 1917. Why, then, did this form of farming not last through the 1920s? In accord with the peasant party's own platform in the parliament of 1917, the Bolshevik regime swept away these fragile new property rights in land.

With foresight, Sergei Witte, who was responsible for an earlier reform (1903) abolishing mutual communal responsibility for peasants' infractions (*krugovaia poruka*), predicted a violent outcome of Stolypin's reforms, which he called a policeman's project. Anger and violence among the peasants, he wrote on January 14, 1912, will not go away. If only compliance had been entirely voluntary and attention had been paid to the conditions of the poorest and ordinary peasants, he rued.[2] Land hunger had driven unrest in 1905, he wrote, when peasants, radicalized by anarchist and Marxist revolutionaries, burned the manor houses and seized the land.[3] The peasants sought access to the fertile land, forests and streams owned by the wealthiest nobles. Stolypin was aware of the need for land, but he gave the Peasant Land Bank for resale only the property of the Crown, too limited in extent and value, especially by comparison with the properties of the wealthiest nobles. State land in Siberia, moreover, was not for sale. There was no equivalent in Russia to the Homestead Act of 1862, which extended

[1] Davydov (2002), pp. 240–300.

[2] S. Witte, "O zakonakh o krest'ianskom zemlevladenii 9 Noiabria 1906 g. i 17 iunia 1910 g. v ministerstvo Stolypina," January 14, 1912, in *Vospominaniia* (2003), 1 (2), 551–52.

[3] S. Witte, "Krest'ianskii vopros posle 17 oktiabria 1905 g., Agrarnye besporiadki posle 17 okriabria 1905 g," Ibid., pp. 549, 551–52.

small farming across the US. The available land for leasing on the frontiers proved an insufficient incentive for mass voluntary resettlement of peasants from the crowded central provinces.

In the post-Soviet era, family farming after agrarian reform was similarly stymied for more than a decade. Numerous agrarian reformers and agricultural experts[4] had been wholly committed to the family farm in the 1990s. The objective of privatization was to introduce universal property rights in land to foster alternatives to the large former collective and state farms. R. Prosterman, R. Mitchell and B. Rorem write in 1997 (p. 1383) that the legal foundations for small farming were in place. By the end of the first decade of reform, however, only 6 percent of all arable was owned by peasant farmers and roughly the same percent of cereals output produced by small farms. What went wrong?

Explaining the continued dominance of large-scale farms throughout reform eras focuses attention on the power of local large farm directors and their lobbies in government in post-reform periods. Rural authorities and elites were able in both eras to slow down the pace of enabling legislation and its implementation. Instances of collusion between local landowners and state officials are well established for the post-serf-emancipation period as a barrier to peasant farming. For example, the approval of nobles' petitions to raise their former serfs' money rent and to avoid having their loans subtracted from the state's compensation plan are among the archival records of the time.[5] During the New Economic Policy (NEP), farmers who wished to expand their holdings in land faced opposition from the local and central government, which created a hostile tax environment in the 1920s. Much diminished by 1929, the "kulak"operations, or well-off farms, did not survive the government's hounding during the collectivization campaign. For the post-Soviet period, the difficultly that small farmers and their organizers had with powerful local representatives of the large farming sector is also well known.[6] Small farmers encountered considerable bias, which raised the costs of entry. They were also stymied by the necessity of retooling.

4 Including the RSFSR Committee on Land Reform, Vladimir Bashmachnikov, President of the Association of Peasant Farms and Agricultural Cooperatives of Russia (AKKOR), and academic authorities such as Aleksandr Nikonov and Evgeniia Serova.

5 Druzhinin (1987), pp. 294–95.

6 Don Van Atta ("Profile of Coup Leader Vasilii Starodubtsev," Radio Liberty, August 19, 1991) describes the communist opposition to "... younger specialists who wish to break out of the old structures. These workers tend to favor either the privatization of agriculture or the establishment of so-called associations of peasants' farms. These last are represented by the Association of Peasant Farms and Agricultural Cooperatives of Russia (AKKOR). The association claims local organizations throughout the RSFSR and is built into the structure of the RSFSR State Committee on Land Reform, the agency charged with recreating peasant farms in the USSR. The president of AKKOR, Vladimir Bashmachnikov, is a deputy chairman of the RSFSR Committee on Land Reform. AKKOR is far from united – many but by no means all of its members support the policies of Yurii Chernichenko's Peasant Party of

There were contrasts between the two eras. In the nineteenth century, there was a paucity of land and other high valued resources available to former serfs; in the post-Soviet era, the situation was entirely different. The small farmers immediately gained access to considerable land resources through the State Land Reserves, which made land abundantly available at zero cost. But in both eras, the real difficulty was in the expectation of reliable and enforceable property rights in land. In the 1990s, farmers had no access to mortgage credit until 2004, for example, which constrained much needed investment. To be sure, even if credit had been available in early transition in the 1990s, agricultural machinery suitable for small family farms was not. Equipment was tailored to the needs of enterprises, and since these had largely not been broken up, even though they were bankrupt, the market for small farm machinery was not promising. Without the possibility of lease or purchase of equipment, there was little chance of creating meaningful incentives to replace hierarchical authority in the cultivation of the land.

The shortage of equipment for small farms highlights the final fundamental reason that, in both reform eras, it was difficult for small farming to spread. There were sunk costs from the previous regime. Backward and forward linkages had developed over many years giving the large-scale exporters in imperial Russia and producers in Soviet and post-Soviet Russia, advantages in rural markets. The old infrastructure outlasted the reform periods, imparting the advantages to the post-reform elites. Vulnerable budgets could not afford new outlays on market infrastructure for more competitive production.

Sunk costs are so much a factor in farm organization in Russia, that a listing of the particular conditions in the cereals sector, favoring established routines, is worth a review here:

- Trade patterns critically depend upon continuity;
- Disrupting production by reorganization creates intense anxieties in the populace and in government about food security;
- Formal financial systems for agriculture are rare, and informal systems create dependencies;
- A competitive farming regime requires competitive and affordable storage and processing, or a new kind of infrastructure, replacing existing structures favoring large entities.[7]

This chapter, in short, concerns the concentration of farming at the producer level and its persistence after reform. It emphasizes, however, that small-scale entrepreneurship in both eras slowly gains momentum as markets improve. It traces this process regionally. It acknowledges that evidence

Russia – but it does seem to be the only organization that has any hope of challenging the alliance of the CPSU and the Peasants' Union in the countryside."

[7] Adapted from Kydd and Bird (1997), pp. 26–27.

for evolutionary advancement of small farmers is fragile, since small-scale rural entrepreneurship is difficult to document.[8] However, it observes the importance for the evolution of the accumulation of human capital and investment resources in rural communities, which can generally be documented. This chapter explains how, in the 2000s, as in Russia in the 1870s and 1890s, small and medium-scale farming strengthens after a lag, despite immediate disadvantages after reform for small farms.

1 CONCENTRATION OF PRODUCTION

In agriculture, market power is typically concentrated high up in the food chain, although there may be concentration of resources on farm.

> Millers have more market power than wheat growers; coffee roasters command greater profits than coffee farmers; and, so on. Market power in agriculture looks like an hourglass: a large number of farmers at the base sell to a small number of processors and distributors and supermarkets in the middle, who sell to a very large number of consumers at the top. In this pattern, agri-business firms often have dependent suppliers (suppliers with nowhere else to sell their production) and dependent buyers (if you need corn, soybeans or wheat, four firms sell the overwhelming majority of production globally). That hourglass creates a series of challenges for policy-makers in agriculture; it has to be worked with and understood.[9]

In other words, while agribusiness is nearly always concentrated in advanced countries, agricultural production is not. Successful farms tend to be moderate in size, and the market is fairly competitive.

In Russian history, in addition to providing government with servitors, large landholdings also provided government with export revenues from the lucrative commodities trade: cereals and industrial crops such as hemp and flax, lumber and mineral resources. Elite estates were linked with trade monopolies in the downstream sector. In imperial Russia, they also served as a powerful political resource in times of war and unrest, for example, during peasant uprisings, and in the socialist era, they were a top down instrument both for social stability and mechanization with benefits not only in agriculture but also in industry, as labor was released from the sector. In both eras, aid to agriculture in times of famine or recession – including debt write-off and equipment supply – had to be delivered by traditional channels through large farms. As the transition has come to an end, even where local subsidies for the large farms have ceased, the rural economy continues in some regions to draw on large production entities.[10] This is not the case, however, where market share of small producers builds up.

[8] Leff (1979), p. 47; Baumol (2002).
[9] Murphy (2006), p. 12.
[10] Amelina (2002), p. 264; see also Czaki (1997); Wegren (1998, 2001).

2 SMALL-SCALE ENTREPRENEURSHIP

Entrepreneurs forge markets. They do not require formal credit arrangements, but they do require access to high-valued investment resources, as do large-scale foreign and domestic industrial entrepreneurs in the industrialization era. Their accumulation of capital is important in rural areas, but small scale rural entrepreneurship is rarely studied.[11] Soviet Marxist historians used quantitative methods to explore the differentiation of peasant households, with a view toward understanding factors in the revolution, that is, polarization of social groups from the 1870s through the 1900s.[12] The term differentiation, however, does not go a long way toward identifying rural entrepreneurs in imperial Russia. In the contemporary era, the identification is simpler from the statistical category provided by the official statistical agency, Roskomstat – it distinguishes "farmers' operations" from other kinds of agricultural firms. However, Roskomstat does not yet provide statistics regarding their relative efficiency by comparison with large corporate entities.

Understanding the rise of rural entrepreneurship requires following the transformation of peasants into commercial operators. By definition, peasants are not entrepreneurs.[13] In the developing world, where peasants are a majority of rural dwellers, entrepreneurship is stifled because the inward-oriented farming culture pools risks and secures household well-being by nonmarket transactions. A system of reciprocal guarantees is common to protect against unfavorable climatic conditions and the frequent shortfall of credit and equipment in a capital-intensive sector. In farming, since inputs have to be allocated well before harvests and product prices can be known, producers must therefore allocate resources for the future on the basis of highly uncertain expectations. Although peasants can obtain credit from landlords, merchants, and money lenders, the interest charged reflect the high costs of information and levels of uncertainty. Peasants fall into debt, and credit is then interlocked with factor markets by a dependent economic relationship. Obtaining market information may be so costly that

[11] On industry, see Anan'ich (1983); Berliner (1957, 1976); Crisp (1978); McKay (1970); Guroff (1983); Gerschenkron (1963, 1970); Laird (1978); O'Brien (2000, 2002); Owen (1983); on agriculture see Stuart (1972) and others.

[12] See reviews in Leonard (1989); Gregory (1982).

[13] Risk-reduction strategies explain peasant behavior according to Popkin (1979), who sees peasants as rational. Models of rational behavior draw on individual decision making and strategic interaction. The distinction between this view and that of the moral economy, however, is overdrawn. Peasants can only be found in high-risk, not highly commercial agriculture, and their access to markets is limited. Their behavior can be explained fully as insurance against risk, but this would not rule out some dynamics of the moral economy framework. On the moral economy interpretation, see Scott (1976), Migdal (1974), Wolf (1969), Clapp (1994), Root (2001), Fafchamps (1992), and others.

contractual forms, such as sharecropping, dominate over market transactions in land.[14]

Peasants can smooth their income by purchases and sales of real capital assets, including livestock and consumer durables, inventories that they maintain collectively. Buffer stocks and credit, in combination with currency and crop inventories, do not amount to full insurance, however. They must also sell produce from gardens, and where possible, allocate some labor off the land for the sake of remittances sent home from urban wages. Finally, nonmarket forms of reciprocity are exchanged, typically within the rural community.[15] These kinds of insurance are nonreplicable from one event to the next and not always pecuniary: barter of unlike goods and services and sharing and redistribution. Universal marriage and high fertility can also be seen as a form of insurance in labor-intensive agriculture.

Entrepreneurship spreads as per capita income rises, and it assists that rise by factor mobilization. As the spread of education and skills leads to permanent jobs off the farm, those who are successful at farming stay on. Remittances permit some capital investment in farming, while industrial manufacturing leads to the decline of local crafts that had previously been symbiotic with the highly seasonal production schedule. When the household fully commits to grain markets, in other words, peasant production ends.[16]

Small-Scale Rural Entrepreneurship in Tsarist Russia

Even under serfdom in nineteenth-century Russia, northern industrial expansion and southern grain production encouraged rural entrepreneurship in both regions on some scale. In the North, households could grow wealthy from earnings of outwork, from the sale of crafts and from marketing vegetables.[17] Opportunities outside of agriculture were less common in southern agricultural regions, where conditions of serfdom were more confining. After serf emancipation, too, growth had a strongly regional character.

Conditions were particularly difficult everywhere after serf emancipation, however. Excluding the year 1868, the price of rye, declined by 0.2 percent per annum in the 1860s. Price stagnation in St. Petersburg in the early years after reform may have been worsened for producers by moderate protectionism introduced in the 1850s and lasting through the 1870s into the 1880s.

[14] Binswanger (1981, 1986, 1995); Braverman (1992); Newbury and Stiglitz (1981), and others.

[15] Townsend (1995) points out that in areas of unusual climatic risk, where insurance was particularly needed, the forms of risk-pooling multiplied and became interlocked with mechanisms for redistribution. Where households were less in need from unanticipated emergencies, forms of community-wide risk-pooling were less widespread.

[16] See Ellis (1993).

[17] Dennison (2003); Rosovsky (1954).

Tariffs discouraged trade at ports by a 50 percent reduction on goods imported overland, advantageous for the western provinces of European Russia.[18] Price conditions turned positive in the early 1870s: between 1871 and 1880, the average nominal annual increase in the price of rye flour was 6.2 percent in a period of low inflation.[19] To be sure, Russia experienced resonance of the significant grain price convergence across Europe and North America in the late nineteenth century, when grain was in surplus in Europe.[20] Mironov (1985), p. 163 (Table 39) shows the overall correlation between grain prices in western Europe and in Russia in the second half of the nineteenth century, and in particular, from 1887-1914.[21] There was a gap between Russian and world prices, however, although they tended to move together. The further from the ports, the more domestic factors played a role, depending on the costs of transport (which were dramatically falling in late-nineteenth century Russia due to railroad construction),[22] There was profit for Russian traders and producers in wheat exports, in other words, despite a fall in world prices sufficient to create rural unemployment in some countries.[23] By Strumilin's (1960) assessment, from the mid-1880s, domestic cereals prices followed a gentle upward trend until the turn of the twentieth century.[24] That is, despite the fall of prices in western Europe, Russian urbanization in that period meant that prices rose somewhat to meet consumption needs of rapidly expanding urban areas. Strumilin's indices of real agricultural and industrial prices provide terms of trade, the ratio of agricultural to industrial prices, showing improvement in price conditions after a period of decline. Figure 5.1 shows terms of trade between sectors from 1867 to 1916. Although the ratio shows volatility, there is a distinctive upward movement after 1880, and the ratio rises to parity after 1907.

Before the 1880s, rural entrepreneurs faced stiff non-price barriers, primarily restrictions on their mobility and access to capital, both of which were eased by the reform process, including the establishment of financial institutions for peasants. Difficulties began immediately after serf emancipation. If former serfs chose to wait for a minimum of allotment land, they had to remain temporarily obligated to landlords after their personal liberation, as discussed in Chapter 1, until such time as redemption contracts were reached with landlords on the fees owed and the allocation of land. Figure 5.2 shows the sharp regional dimensions of that process. The ranges

[18] Shepelev (1981), pp. 64–7.

[19] Calculated from Rykachev (1911).

[20] Harley (1980); O'Rourke (1997) and others.

[21] A correlation coefficient (Pearson's r) of 0.81.

[22] A cost reduction of some 18 percent in the second half of the nineteenth century for local traders (Mironov, 1985, p. 159).

[23] O'Rourke (1997).

[24] Rykachev (1911). See agricultural prices in Strumilin (1960), p. 90.

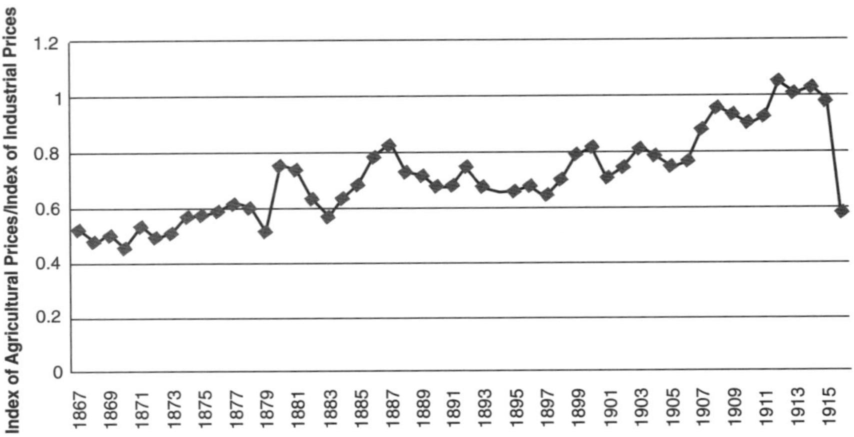

FIGURE 5.1. Agricultural Terms of Trade, 1867–1916.
Source: Strumilin (1960), p. 116.

in the figure consist of the percent of redemption contracts completed by 1871.

With the exception of Astrakhan, the map shows that the southern regions experienced a more rapid completion of the reform process than the northern. In the Northwest and North, where serfdom scarcely existed, the figures show that there was no process to complete. In areas to the Southwest,

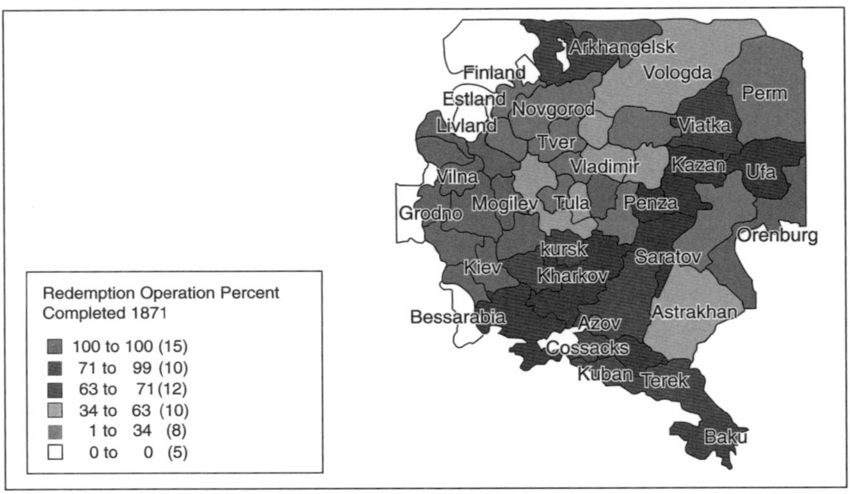

FIGURE 5.2. Geographic Spread of Reform in Tsarist Russia: Percentage Redemption Contracts Concluded by Region, 1870.
Source: Data from Obruchev (1871)1:194.

100 percent of the land had been redeemed by 1871. In Perm, where nobles estates were particularly large and land highly concentrated, the percent redeemed was low, as it tended to be in the central agricultural regions, where the process had barely begun in some provinces.

For some peasants, a small category of emancipated serfs, these numbers did not apply because they were not liable for redemption fees. Former serfs who wanted immediate resolution of their status, that is, to have no further obligations to landlords nor pay redemption fees, chose the option of receiving one-fourth of the minimum *nadel.* In 1870, the government determined that out of a total emancipated in 1861 (almost 10 million male serfs), some 600,000 chose this option, including former house serfs, now peasant landowners (*darstvenniki*).[25]

The *darstvenniki* tended to be poor, but this category also included some entrepreneurs in the late nineteenth century. From a survey conducted in 1906–1907, the *darstvenniki* were found to have settled mainly in the blackearth provinces – Saratov, Simbirsk, Voronezh, Kursk, Kazan, and Samara – and along the Volga River. Although they had small amounts of arable, they rented and bought extra parcels. Over a tenth of the *darstvenniki* were impoverished, and many were landless, according to a ministerial circular of May 26, 1881, but some 14 percent had their own farms.[26]

Representing *darstvenniki* as rural entrepreneurs is at best arguable; a more satisfying statistic is the number of "edinolichniki" or wealthier peasants, who were able to purchase their land outright at the time of serf emancipation. These probably numbered almost 45,000 (household heads).[27] They settled in the North and South. Much wealth was accrued by peasants in the North, since off land earnings were substantial, and the price of land (presumably because it was developed) was higher in the North than the South. Peasant off-farm opportunities for employment expanded; wheat went entirely out of cultivation in some western areas.[28] Some indication of the spread and solidity of rural entrepreneurs can be found by mapping the quantity of land accumulated as "non-nadel" rented land in Figure 5.3.

Rural entrepreneurship is even visible in a second map which shows the average amount of land rented (average holding in desiatiny) by the peasant household. The largest size holdings were located on trade routes in regions where the land was fertile, shown in Figure 5.4. These figures, again, are for households, excluding land rented by peasant associations or communes.

Suggestive of the potential emergence of capital invested in farming, the map in Figure 5.5 shows the regionalization of yields at the beginning

[25] Ministry of Internal Affairs data, cited in Druzhinin (1987), p. 303; Budina (1996).
[26] Druzhinin (1987), p. 304.
[27] Druzhinin (1987), p. 305.
[28] Pintner (1959).

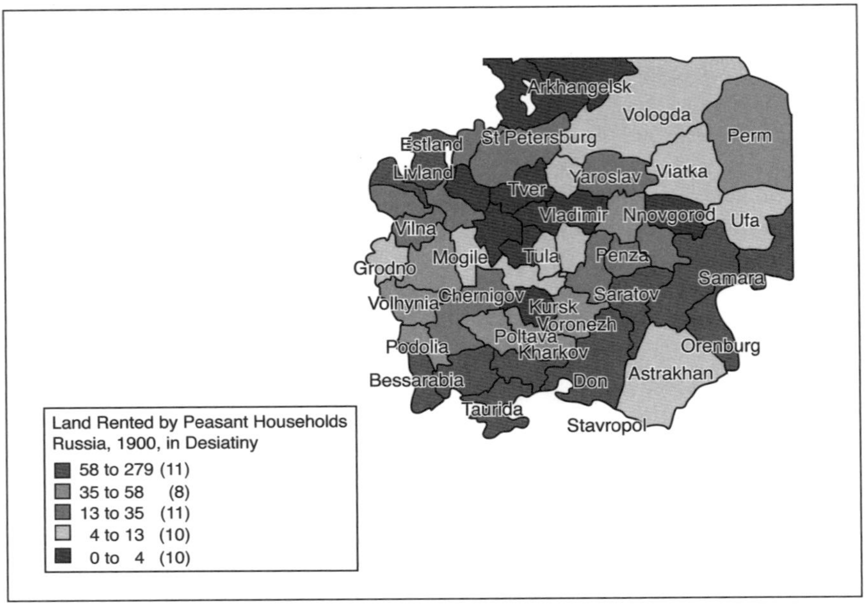

FIGURE 5.3. Non-nadel Land Rented by the Peasantry (individual households) by Province (*Guberniia*) in Russia, 1900, in Desiatiny.
Source: "Arendovanie Krest'ianami vne nadel'nykh zemel' i sdacha im nadel'nykh po 50 gub. Evrop. Rossii v 1901 god (po soobshcheniiam volost. Pravlen.," *Svod Statisticheskikh svedenii po sel'skomu khoziastvu Rossii k kontsu XIX veka* (St Petersburg 1902), Chapter XIV, pp. 113–53.

of the reform period, 1861–1863. Although yields were just above subsistence in most northcentral provinces, in the South and Northwest along trade routes they were somewhat higher in the immediate post-reform period.

The map for 1900, Figure 5.6, shows clearly when compared to the previous map the route of improvement of yields between the 1860s and 1900, from the southern ports to trade centers, such as Nizhnii Novgorod.

Looking more closely at Figure 5.6 reveals the considerable spread of higher yields eastward to the frontier and into Siberia made possible by the railroads and other transportation networks improved in this period. These maps provide clear evidence of significant biological learning among peasants about advanced techniques. There is little evidence of the widespread adoption of expensive equipment, however. Improvements advances were based, presumably, on the advancement of crop rotations and planting of forage crops. Given the overlap of regions where rural entrepreneurs clustered with areas where yields were significantly higher than elsewhere,

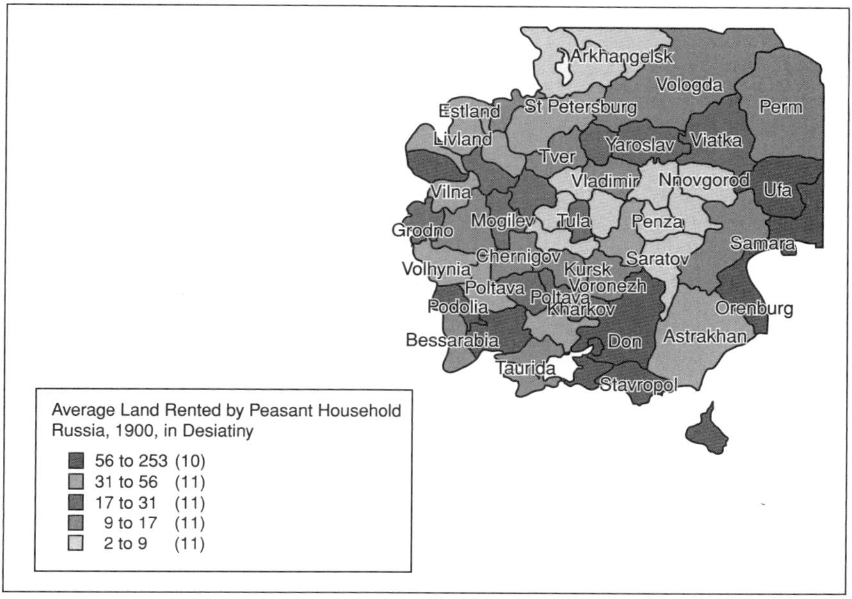

FIGURE 5.4. Average Land Area of Non-nadel Land Rented by Individual Peasant Households by Province (*Guberniia*) in Russia, 1900, in Desiatiny.
Source: See source for Figure 5.3.

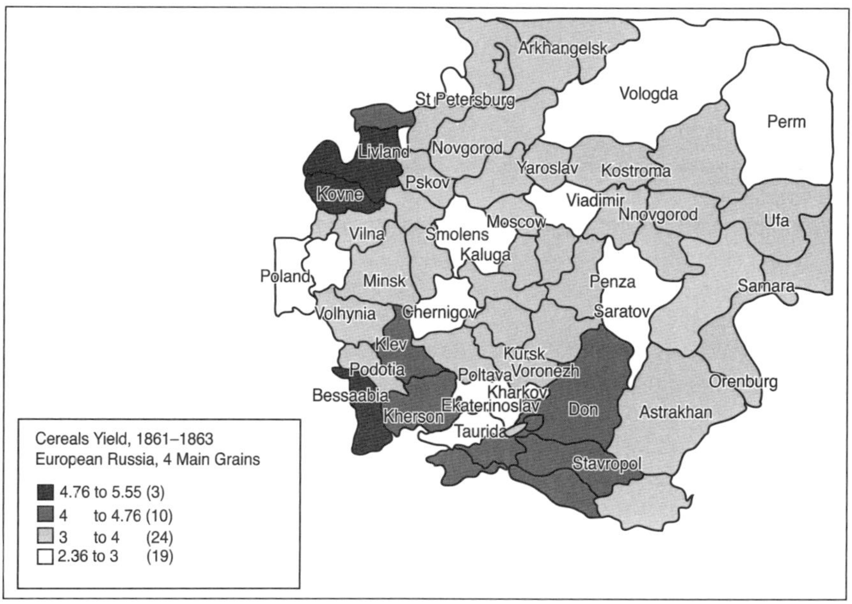

FIGURE 5.5. European Russia: Crop Yields in 1861–1863.
Source: "Posev i sbor khlebov i kartofelia u krest'ian na nadel'nykh zemliakh i u chastnykh zemlevladel'tsev po 50 gub. Evrop. Rossii c 1861 po 1900 g.," *Svod Statisticheskikh svedenii po sel'skomu khoziastvu Rossii k kontsu XIX veka* (St Petersburg 1902), Chapter XV, pp. 155–177.

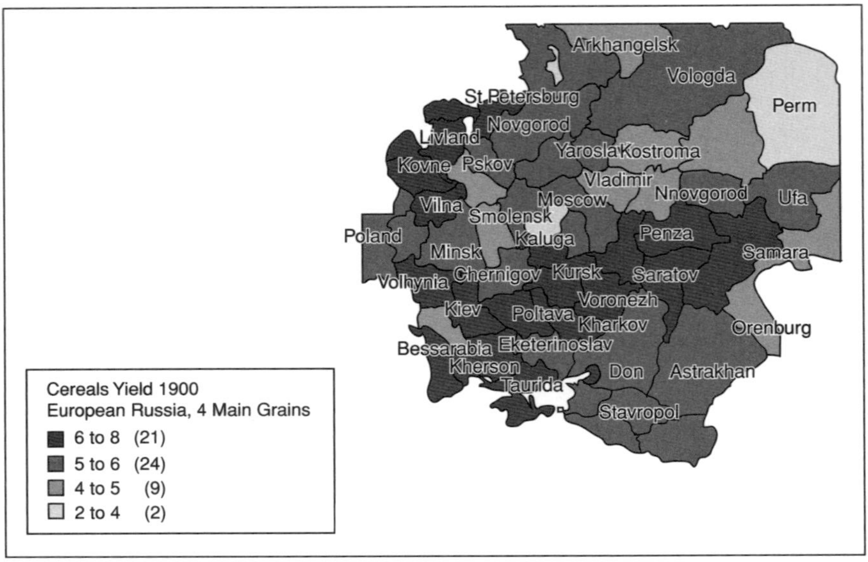

FIGURE 5.6. European Russia: Crop Yields in 1900.
Source: See source for Figure 5.5.

it would also be possible to speculate that it was rural entrepreneurs who brought this advancement to the internal provinces of Russia.

One might expect that the numbers of peasant entrepreneurs could be taken entirely from archival records of the Peasant Land Bank. However, borrowing was constrained at the Bank: peasants were required to supplement credit transactions for land by considerable cash payments, and interest rates on credit were high. These archives would not have captured all entrepreneurs. Even so, during the first twelve years of the bank's activity, 1883–1895, a substantial amount, some 2.4 million desiatiny, were transferred to peasants.

In the mid-1890s, the Bank was particularly active. After the harvest failures of 1891 and 1892 the rates of interest charged by the Peasants' Land Bank were reduced in a measure to appease the peasants. The bank extended its operations, doubling the previous level of loans for the purchase of land.[29] In 1905, the bank began an operation for poor peasants, extending loans for the full value of the land purchased, and, after 1906, extending loans to clients upon the mortgage of their original allotments with subsidized interest rates and loans repayable over fifty-five years at 4.5 percent annually. After 1906, among effects of a twenty-fold increase of the price of rye on domestic markets between 1901 and 1912 and rise in the price of wheat for export at

[29] Antsiferov et al. (1930), pp. 304–09.

southern ports, the average annual land purchases by peasants rose to more than one million desiatina, double the average from the decade before.[30]

However, three times that much was lent by informal credit mechanisms in the village for land purchases by peasants.[31] Informal finance can be small in average amount, although as J. Von Pischke *et al.* write, agricultural technologies are divisible rather than lumpy. Informal credit can be adequate also for working capital:

> In view of the large strides made by agriculture in developing countries, and the relatively small number of farmers who have received formal credit, it seems reasonable to conclude that most agricultural innovations in these countries have not depended directly on formal credit. The relation between innovation and credit has not been realistically viewed in part because credit tends to support large, lumpy investments in highly visible innovations such as tractors, as opposed to the small, divisible investments in much more numerous and widely spread innovations such as improved seeds.[32]

Wealth accumulation was assisted by an astonishing rise in credit cooperatives and associations. In the 1870s, surveys reported only isolated cooperatives, mostly started up by populist agitators living in villages.[33] But within decades credit cooperatives spread across Russia with remarkable speed, as frequently occurs in developing countries. Loan associations were created by the investment of shares, attracting mainly the wealthier strata of peasant society. Mutual associations were created under the terms of the credit act of 1895 by which the state bank issued loans to small producers, carefully supervising the activities of the mutual associations.

By 1916, the amount accumulated through savings in credit cooperatives was five times the amount of loans issued from state funds. The total number of associations rose from roughly 25,000 in 1913 to 47,200 in 1917, providing financial assistance for about fourteen million producers.[34] Whereas credit cooperatives generally benefit village elites, in tsarist Russia the numbers involved may indicate a more democratic denouement, in line with the political activism of peasant associations in the post-1905 period.[35] Table 5.1 shows after 1900 actual numbers of supply cooperatives and services in numbers of members.

It should be emphasized, that the Russian repartitional land commune contributed a powerful and positive boost to rural finance, whatever its impact on production routines. There is no research whatsoever on this

30 Anfimov et al. (1968), pp. 270 ff.
31 Antsiferov et al. (1930), pp. 304–09.
32 Von Pischke et al. (1983), p. 7.
33 Podkolzin (1993); Figurovskaia (1993).
34 Belousov 1999, p. 72–3.
35 Mironov (1999); Koval'chenko (1989); Koval'chenko and Milov (1971); Druzhinin (1978); Goriushkin (1983); Ekonomakis (1998); Burds (1998); Bradley (1985), and others.

TABLE 5.1. *Cooperatives and Members in Russia, 1900–1917*

	1901	1913	1917	1905	1912
Credit cooperatives	800	10,600	16,100	181,300	4,384,300
Lending banks				382,000	1,553,300
Local banks				1,776,200	2,129,200
Consumer societies	600	7,300	20,000		
Agricultural societies	140	4,000	6,000		
Oil-processing guilds	50	2,600	3,000		

Source: Belousov (1999), p. 72; Kozlova (1993), p. 32.

topic, but logic suggests, that as a private-order institution, it was a guarantor of contracts concluded with the bank. It guaranteed the credit reputation of its members individually and as a whole; the peasant commune was the major purchaser of land in tsarist Russia.[36] Where legal proceedings were costly, that is, where informal finance is widespread, the commune could use its members as "hostages" to generate exchange.[37] Such a peer organization can screen the provision of access to information about reputation, and screening is useful in enforcing exchange.[38] As would seem from the sharp rise in all sorts of lending, private-order institutions can be explosively developmental. The macroeconomic indicators for 1913 show Russia to have still been overwhelmingly, like France, an agrarian country, with at least one-half of domestic and five-sixths of foreign trade in primary commodities.[39] However, peasant production was becoming more commercial and export oriented.

With this evidence of spreading wealth, how can one reconcile the sliding *nadel* figures, pointing to the significant decline of average allotment land by household in the late nineteenth century? The nadel declined on average per male "soul" from 4.8 desiatiny (1 desiatina = 1.092 hectares) in 1860 to about 2.6 desiatiny in 1900, an amount of land insufficient for subsistence, let alone commercial production. This dramatic decline seems evidence of a failing rural economy and highly fragmented land holdings, worsening over time, and justifying social historians' rejection of the revisionist picture about tsarist Russia. The answer is that the figures are misleading. Among artifacts of the statistical figures is the rate of population growth in the crowded central blackearth regions and the registration in villages of migrants no longer actually living there. Another reason that figures may be misleading is taxation. It is important to remember that the *nadel* was subject to a land tax, replacing the poll tax. Although the land tax was more

36 Williamson (1983, 1985).
37 Greif (1995), pp. 293–94.
38 Milgrom et al. (1990) and Greif (1993, 1994, 1995, 1996, 1997).
39 Antsiferov (1930), p. 46.

rational for the development of local government and thus appropriate to a market economy, it presumably also had the effect of discouraging accurate reporting. S. Hoch (2004) has written persuasively that official figures on the *nadel* for many other reasons should be treated with caution.

There can be little doubt that toward the end of the nineteenth century, peasants' private landholding was widespread. Publications by I. Koval'chenko show, from a sample of peasants' and nobles' farming from the 1880s in Tambov, Kaluga, Voronezh, and Penza, and a larger sample from thirty-four provinces *(gubernii)* in 1916–1917, based on the agricultural census, that peasants share of local holdings was huge. The nobles share of harvested fields averaged only 7.7 percent, with the highest share in Ukraine (15.4 percent) and Belarus (13.3 percent) and in the black earth central region (11.6 percent). Nobles' presence in agriculture was negligible in the north (0.7 percent), Volga-Viatka (1.2 percent), and Southern Urals (2.4 percent). Nobles rented out some of their land to peasants, on average, a quarter of their arable: the range was 15 to 17 percent in Belarus and the industrial center to 40 to 50 percent in the Volga and southern steppe.[40]

By the end of the century, nobles in some areas no longer were the only agents introducing agricultural machinery on farms: they averaged about 7.7 percent of harvested area and about 5.6 percent of iron plows in use, although 8.2 percent of the more advanced machinery.[41] Koval'chenko explained the surprisingly limited noble entrepreneurship observed in one region, Tambov, at the end of the nineteenth century (30 estates). Given the available labor at low cost, net revenues on noncapital intensive estates were twice as great as net revenues of those that were more capital intensive.[42]

A caution in accepting Koval'chenko's estimates is that they draw on a period (1917) when there was a very rapid decline of inventories of all kinds and panicked sales by noble landlords. Wartime requisitions had affected livestock herds and crops, and from 1914–1916, due to a wartime shortage of labor, the conditions on landlords estates worsened. Late in the war, the land, implements, livestock, and other property began to be seized and distributed among peasants. Koval'chenko acknowledges in the introduction that the data are difficult, and this should be kept in mind.[43] With qualifications, he argues for relatively advanced small farming in Astrakhan, Don, Ekaterinoslav, Orenburg, Perm, Samara, and Ufim.[44] The maps presented here support his understanding, and they show the regions where rural entrepreneurship was strong in the late nineteenth and early twentieth century.

[40] Koval'chenko et al. (1982), p. 120.
[41] Koval'chenko et al. (1982), p. 123.
[42] Koval'chenko et al. (1982), pp. 83–5.
[43] Koval'chenko et al. (1982), Ch. 2; Wheatcroft and Davies (1994), p. 112.
[44] Koval'chenko (1988), Tables 54, 55, and 56, pp. 210–15.

Rural Entrepreneurship and the Organization of Farming in the Russian Transition from Communism

Independent Peasant Farms. The last years of the Soviet Union witnessed the voluntary formation of contract brigades, which multiplied in number during Perestroika, or the era of renewal and reconstruction under Gorbachev. The peasant farms law of the Russian Soviet Federative Socialist Republic (RFSFR) in 1991 then dramatically started up peasant farming, which flourished even without secure property rights in land. Although instruments for long-term investment were unavailable, preventing returns to equity, numerous small farmers were willing to leave the former state and collective farms.[45] Another corner was turned in 1993, when by a constitutional guarantee of the right of individuals to own land (1993), Yeltsin even more vigorously fostered small farming, and he granted subsidies to the independent sector lasting through the mid-1990s. Since the overwhelming share of land continued to be owned and cultivated by large producers, however, since property rights proved to be unenforceable in some regions, and since adverse macroeconomic conditions lingered, both the small farm and large farm sectors seemed to be faring equally badly; the small farms ceased to grow in number, and production recovery after initial shocks was slow. All hope of breaking up the huge farms faded. The lack of mobility and low level of skills in the rural populace, along with price reform, put acute downward pressure on rural wages, and the populace turned to alternative sources of income. The most intensive activity in the early stage of transition was not among the independent farms but the household plots. These had survived the entire Soviet era and were revitalized in the transition era, when demand for fodder crops fell and for potatoes rose and farm employees marketed their produce. Tax-free, these plots were attractive for all kinds of households as recession deepened.

Beginning in the post-privatization era in Russia, therefore, rural entrepreneurship was forced to emerge within the largely unreformed large farm world. Separated but still dependent on the weakened foundation of large farms, the small farm and household sectors were subject to the same volatile conditions and lack of clear laws. All three sectors, the cereals producing fields governed by newly elected management of the employee-owners, the cereals producing but credit-starved small farms, and the relatively profitable but miniscule vegetable and livestock sector dependent entirely on inputs from the farm, shared a chaotic environment. Small farms survived this punishing period relatively well. The numbers of independent farms, the average size of their landholdings, and the total arable grew as follows in Table 5.2.

[45] Boone and Fedorov (1997), p. 163.

TABLE 5.2. *Number and Size of Peasant (Independent) Farms, 1991–2006 (Based on Data for the Beginning of the Year)*

Year	Number of Farms	Average Size of Land Allotment in Hectares	Cultivated Land (Thousands of Hectares)
1991	4,400	41	
1992	4,900	42	2,068
1993	182,800	43	7,804
1994	270,000	42	11,342
1995	279,200	43	11,870
...			
1999	270,200	52	13,845
2000	261,100	55	14,384
2001	265,500	62	16,525
2002	265,500	62	16,525
2003	263,900	69	18,326
2004	261,400	73	19,200
2005	257,400	75	19,246
2006	285,100	103	29,400

Sources: Regiony Rossii (2001); *Rossiiskii statisticheskii ezhegodnik*, including the Russian agricultural census of 2006 (2006, 2008).

The above table shows, however, that most small farms were formed early in transition. A sampling survey in 1998–1999 found that 83 percent of independent farms at that time had been founded by 1995. The Table 5.2 displays evidence that the numbers peaked by the mid-1990s.[46]

There was little clarity initially about whether these farms would last. Out of 10.5 million workers in agriculture in 1991, for example, only 4,000 chose to set up farms. Of these, 75 percent were individuals from urban areas returning to the land. In the words of the farmers themselves, surveyed in 1998–1999, the factor that more than any other inhibited their operations was the lack of cash and capital.[47] This helps explain that 31 percent of small farmers said they resorted to barter in the marketing of their output.[48] Other factors that they counted as obstacles to success were as follows: ineffective state assistance; high interest rates on credit; and the weakness of the laws. In responding to questions regarding their access to equipment, 55 percent said that they obtained their equipment from the large corporative farms; 8 percent by leasing; 10 percent directly from the factory; and 24 percent from retail enterprises.[49] To summarize, both the harsh economic conditions, including the countryside's partial reversion to a natural

[46] *Sel'skokhoziastvennaia* (2000), p. 39.

[47] *Sel'skokhoziastvennaia* (2000), pp. 40–41.

[48] *Sel'skokhoziastvennaia* (2000), pp. 42.

[49] *Sel'skokhoziastvennaia* (2000), pp. 40–41.

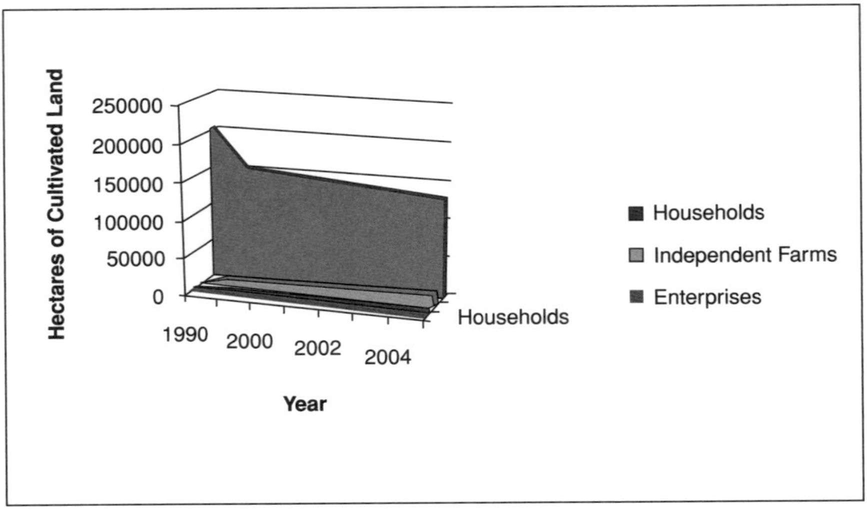

FIGURE 5.7. Cultivated Land by Type of Farm (Thousands of Hectares), 1991–2006, %.
Source: Rossiiskii Statisticheskii Ezhegodnik (2006).

economy, and necessary continued dependency on the large farms, were the characteristic challenges faced by small farmers. Figure 5.7 shows by comparing numbers of farms by type from 1991 to 2006 that independent farms remained a small sector by comparison with the large farm organization. The latter declined in number but held on to production share.

On the whole, independent farms economically were in good shape by 2000, although not a large or perceptibly growing sector. In a national survey of independent farmers conducted jointly in 2000 by the National Agricultural Statistical Services (NASS) of the United States Department of Agriculture (USDA) and the Russian Federation State Statistical Agency (Roskomstat), the surveyors captured information for all large independent farms and 15 percent of the smaller farms in all regions. Although in 1999 12 percent of all independent farms surveyed viewed their circumstances as "on the edge of bankruptcy," an increasing number perceived their situation as satisfactory (44 percent in 1998 and 46 percent in 1999, and almost 70 percent anticipated that in 2000 their situation would be either satisfactory or good.[50]

The independent farmers are potentially significant as a managerial force in agriculture.[51] The typical family farm is not a subsistence farm. Early on, it demonstrated greater efficiency than corporative farms. Between 70 and

[50] *Sel'khoz* (2000), p. 42.
[51] Serova (2000).

80 percent of sales were of crop products by 1992, by contrast with corporative enterprises, which, at that time, still sold mainly (over 40 percent) livestock products, despite the general knowledge that livestock production must fall. Crop yields, according to a survey by Brooks and Lerman in 1992, were indistinguishable on private farms and farm enterprises, but milk yields achieved by private farmers were significantly higher than those achieved by collective farm enterprises.[52] The finding of good management and clear profit orientation by Brooks and Lerman was confirmed by official government data published in 1997 by the Working Centre for Economic Reform (WCER) in Moscow. According to the WCER, the allocation to cash crops increased on independent farms from 61 percent of arable land in 1991 to 71 percent in 1996.[53] As noted, from Roskomstat publications, efficiency of the independent farms cannot be compared with that of the corporative farms – no surveys were taken of independent farms by Roskomstat until 1999.[54] A survey by Roskomstat (2000), permits a glimpse into relative expenditures. Livestock, for example, was costly to large farms, and this expense was lacking on small farms. Small farms tended to devote more substantial resources to seed improvement, which is suggestive of management orientation toward improved yields. Finally, small farms spent less on energy, whose variable costs heighten risk.

The map, Figure 5.8, adds to the understanding of independent farms as a hardy sector. By 2001, independent farmers settled and spread into substantial and larger farms in the highly fertile southern and eastern areas of Russia. This means that it is misleading to assess the future of the typical farm, since the range is so large. A regional focus shows farms not as a struggling third force but a well established part of the agricultural landscape in some regions. The average farm nationally is 76 hectares, but in the south, 339 hectares. This regional picture shows the evidence of continuing drive for competitiveness and enlargement by entrepreneurial farms.

Corporative Farm Enterprises

Entrepreneurship is not limited to small farming. The large farms have made considerable progress in recent years, as shown in Chapter 3. There is, however, clear evidence that learning has been slow among managers of large farms. The Table 5.3 shows the extent of bankruptcy and slow emergence from that state by large farms in the Russian Federation. Without requiring restructuring, the design of reform did not assist or stimulate these managers of large farms to acquire knowledge and skills. The crisis in Russian farming spread from large farms to the others: Table 5.3 shows

[52] Brooks and Lerman (1994), pp. 77–89.
[53] *SPR* (1997), p. 11.
[54] Manellia (2000).

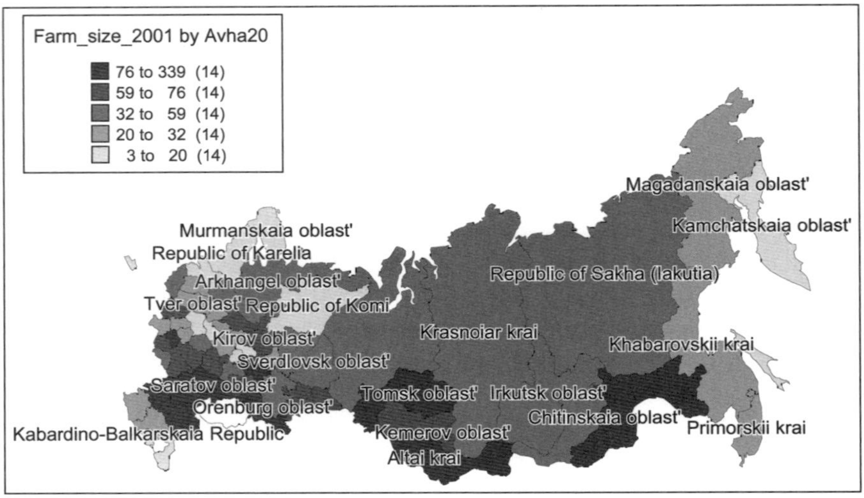

FIGURE 5.8. The Average Size of Independent Farms by Region in the Russian Federation, 2001.
Source: Data from Roskomstat, provided to the University of Oxford by Eastview, at http://www.eastview.com/ (2006).

that some fifteen years after the beginning of mass privatization, 40 percent of all large farm enterprises were still bankrupt. Among other reasons, their size and hence employment numbers made the bulk of them too big to fail. The government supported their recovery, or, rather, allowed most to coast without disappearing; over 10,000 did disappear, as shown in Table 5.3.

This aid to large farms may be precisely what interfered with their recovery. Their dependency on the subnational government and endebtedness was in part a consequence of how local authorities treated them. Amelina (2002) described the role of regional authorities, selecting as a case study Saratov oblast', the grain basket of modern Russia. In that oblast', there is extensive interference and assistance by the regional government. One form of intervention is commodity credit. Food corporations provide input suppliers with tax relief in return for the delivery of inputs at the time of sowing, and in return the producers pay debts in cash or kind after the harvest. This kind of assistance was abandoned by the federal government in 1997, because it was costly and producers did not repay their debts. However, subnational units maintain this kind of aid to ensure that farms retain services needed by the rural populace.[55]

[55] Amelina (2002), pp. 272–73.

TABLE 5.3. *Loss-Making Enterprises, Employment, and Assets in the Corporative Farm Sector, 1990–2007*

	1990	1995	2000	2001	2002	2003	2004	2005	2007
Number of farms (th)	25,800	26,900	27,600	24,800	24,200	22,100	20,600	19,000	15,200
Percentage loss-making farms of total	3	57	51	46	55	49	35	40	22
Average number of employees	322	248	170	171	159	149	139	132	125
Average cultivated land (th ha)	4,300	3,200	2,500	2,600	2,600	2,600	2,600	2,600	3,000
Average herd of cattle	1,756	976	574	600	583	571	547	535	604
Including cows	578	371	226	231	219	216	209	205	230

Source: Rossiiskii statisticheskii ezhegodnik (2008).

TABLE 5.4. *Land Use by Households, All-Russian Agricultural Census 2006 (July 1)*

	Number of Units	Total Land, mlns ha.	Average per Plot, ha.	% Total Land Used for Agriculture
Non-commercial associations:	80,300	1.2	15.5	0.400
Gardens	73,600	1.1	14.9	0.320
Vegetable production	5,400	0.07	11.4	0.020
Livestock production	400	0.04	155.0	0.020
Dach'	900	0.02	15.8	0.004
Private and other plots (*lichnye podsobnie i drugie khoziastva*)	22,799,400	9.7	0.48	2.500
of these, private plots	17,462,600	8.9	0.52	2.400

Source: Rossiiskii statisticheskii ezhegodnik (2008).

Household Subsidiary Plots

The final one of the three kinds of rural entrepreneurial forms in post-reform Russia is the household plot. As in the Soviet era, when they were limited to less than .5 hectares, household subsidiary plots, or *lph* (*lichnye podsobnye khoziastva)* have remained small. The size and number of households' subsidiary plots in 2006 are given in Table 5.4.

Table 5.5 displays the large variety of household operations, but the overwhelming number are in the category of subsidiary plots, which produce vegetables, potatoes, milk, eggs and meat on a large scale. Subsidiary plots have not yet outlasted their usefulness to family income in the sale of vegetables, potatoes, and livestock and meat products. Table 5.5 shows how

TABLE 5.5. *Household Production in Russia (Millions of Tons), 1976–2007*

On Average, Annually	1976–1980	1981–1985	1986–1990	1991–1995	1996–2000	2001–2005	2007
Potatoes	25.3	22.8	21.4	30.3	31.5	32.8	32.8
Vegetables	3.0	3.7	3.1	6.3	8.9	11.4	12.2
Fruit and berries	1.1	1.4	1.3	1.7	2.3	2.8	3.5
Cattle and poultry	2.1	2.2	2.4	2.9	2.7	2.6	2.6
Milk	12.9	12.7	12.7	15.4	16.2	16.8	16.7
Eggs	10.8	10.5	10.2	10.7	9.8	9.6	9.2
Wool	41.0	44.0	48	51.0	28.0	26.0	28.0
Honey, th tons	31.0	28.0	31	39.0	44.0	46.0	51.0

Source: Rossisskii statisticheskii ezhegodnik (2006, 2008).

sturdy these farms have been in difficult times. Also, in tonnage, it shows the general volume that they contribute to agricultural output (GAO), of which their share of output was 49 percent in 2007.[56]

As argued in the previous chapter, household plots were attractive to farm employees because historically they had been important for income support. To this historical utility was added in transition that they became a secure form of property. That is, the plot could safely be developed for income without threat of confiscation by the government or the farm community. This exceptional combination of positive stimuli at a time when parliamentary obstruction to the clarification of land rights made other forms of landownership relatively less secure, fostered the expansion of this sector. Long after the large farm sector started to turn around after the recession of the 1990s, household plots persisted as a viable form of farming.[57]

There was some inherent subsidy from the government, as well, that helped their survival. In some locations the large farm is essentially a shell organization, with inputs going mainly into the household sector Debt write-off subsidizes both forms of production. There was a subsidy in tax exemption on earnings from the plot, although there is an upper limit on the size of the plot fixed by local administrations (usually six to twelve hectares) to contain their commercial orientation. The tax loophole was used by independent farmers as well as corporative farm employees by expanding the plot and reallocating labor to this lucrative activity. On average households provide some 30 percent of their labor to the production of vegetables for consumption and sale in urban markets. Clearly, there are some perverse outcomes despite the benefits. With the loss of labor to the farm, the wage cost of farms falls, but the shift of high-valued output to the subsidiary plot is a loss in profits for the farm. Also, since the household production of livestock is inefficient and lacking in quality guarantees, it lowers the production potential of the farm. In the short run, however, the household gains some benefit in vegetable markets.[58]

56 *Rossiiskii statisticheskii ezhegodnik* (2008).

57 Acemoglu (2002) argues that historical institutions can have a powerful influence. Among countries colonized by European powers during the past 500 years, those that were relatively rich in 1500 are now relatively poor. He argues that the reversal reflects changes in the institutions resulting from European colonialism. The European intervention appears to have created an institutional reversal among these societies, meaning that Europeans were more likely to introduce institutions encouraging investment in regions that were previously poor. This institutional reversal accounts for the reversal in relative incomes. He argues that the reversal in relative incomes took place during the late eighteenth and early nineteenth centuries and resulted from societies with good institutions taking advantage of the opportunity to industrialize.

58 Kiselev (2002) observes that the cost of wages and support for social security fell from 29 percent of farm costs in 1990 to 17 percent in 1999, but this is not the whole of the cost to the farm in view of the large in-kind benefits paid to retain labor.

TABLE 5.6. *Shares of Land and Output by Farm Type, Russian Federation, 2008*

Farm Types	Cultivated Land, Ths Hectares, %				Volume of Ouptut, %			
	Cereals	Technical Crops	Potatoes	Forage	Cereals**	Sunflower Seeds	Potatoes	Cattle and Poultry***
All	100	100	100	100	100	100	100	100
Corporative entities	76	70	10	90	78	71	11	54
Household plots	1	0	82	2	1	0.4	84	43
Individual farms	23	30	8	8	21	29	5	3

Source: Rossisskii statisticheskii ezhegodnik (2009).
** Barn weight
*** Live weight

To summarize, Table 5.6 shows the weight of all sectors, in production of agricultural outputs in 2008. Small farms are producing significant amounts of cereals, competing with the larger farms, and households are producing significant amounts of meat products, although forage is produced almost entirely on large farms.

3 CONCLUSION

Russian rural markets are distorted in favor of household production. "Peasant"-style production, particularly vegetables grown on household plots, has been a growth activity in the 1990s. The incentive was in part the tax-free status of household production, aimed to shelter household production in the difficult transition environment. By contrast, independent farming, at first subsidized, was later taxed at the level established for small enterprises. While small farmers struggled, households could appropriate inputs from the corporative farm, including the use of machinery and fertilizer, and they could claim a portion of the herd as their personal property at the time of enterprise privatization.[59] Anecdotal evidence suggests that the SME tax on farming resulted in a large flow of independent farmers into the category of private subsidiary plot owners. With the revision of the tax code in 2007, making independent farms, corporative farms and household plots all liable to the same tax, the numbers of household production units may begin to decline, along with their share in agricultural output.

The idea that the rise in household production was primarily a response by potential farmers to tax incentives, however, is hard to accept. Roughly half of the shareowners (2002) on corporative farms are pensioners and local administrative officials, who have no interest in farming the land or overseeing management.[60] Of 11.9 million owners of land (embracing 29.3 percent of the four hundred six million hectares of agricultural land in Russia in 2002), those who have nothing to do with agriculture and lease their holdings comprise 71 percent. Of these, only 26 percent invest in the farm enterprise.[61] These owners will disappear as their tax liabilities grow, but it is not clear that the assets of entrepreneur-farmers will grow in proportion.

In the course of market turbulence in 2007 and 2008, household gardening has remained stable. Russian agriculture is now through its transition, large-farm bankruptcy continues to fall, commodities prices are expected to rise, and Russian grain exports to expand. This chapter has argued that

[59] Praust (1999), pp. 67–9.
[60] Volkov (2002), pp. 7–8.
[61] Volkov (2002), pp. 7–9.

markets will remain distorted until large farms lose their subsidies. It is way too soon to talk about the demise of smaller independent farms, however even though the corporative farm sector is strengthening. A similar situation existed in the early twentieth century, when small farming was coming to life well before the Stolypin reforms.

PART III

RUSSIAN AGRICULTURAL PERFORMANCE, 1861–2010

6

Technology and Farming Culture

The pace of change in agriculture is determined mainly by the application of knowledge and technological modernization within the sector. Improvement rests on skill levels and industrial advancement; but technologies used are also affected by the terms of trade, determining whether producers can afford new machinery. Technological diffusion in agriculture depends, further, on the strength of capital and labor markets in rural areas to help integrate more isolated communities with the knowledge-based farming systems of the more advanced core. Knowledge transfer from research scientists to the village was the critical constraint in the technological advancement of Russian agriculture. The contributions of Russian, German, other European and US agricultural researchers in the nineteenth and twentieth century were considerable, but their diffusion from Russia's centrally located institutes was held back by weak rural markets, restrictions on population movement, and incentive systems with weak rewards for producer investment.

Physical technologies used in Russian farming co-evolved with the social technologies in four different economic regimes: serfdom, communal peasant production, collectivized and state farming, and post-Soviet market-based agriculture.[1] Across these regimes, new technologies led to improvement in yields, but always there was some legacy of the old routines and farming culture, especially in the widespread use of the three-field cultivation regime. The most evident discontinuities are those produced by the introduction of advanced farm equipment, but there can also roughly be traced a diffusion of new biological knowledge from the port cities inward. Knowledge moved inland in the imperial era from the Baltic ports and from the southern ports opening to the Black Sea, further and further inland, as the yield maps in the previous chapter clearly show for Russia.

Knowledge moved inland, as transportation expanded. Once isolated farming communities were linked to regions near ports, Technology and

[1] See Nelson (1993) for the co-evolutionary nature of technological and social development.

social change can be traced in the rise of regional output and the changing systems of cultivation by following the strengthening channels of trade and migration. The spread of knowledge was from West to South and East, as travel between the more settled central areas and the frontiers increased both with the relaxing of regulations in the imperial period and the opening up of land for settlement in Siberia. The data introduced in this chapter assesses both the weight of political opening and geographic factors in the diffusion of knowledge and other kinds of technology.

The chapter begins with the regional complementaries, greatly strengthened by investment in transportation after the serf emancipation. Sufficient to stimulate considerable non-agricultural outwork by serfs in the North of Russia, complementarities that allowed the South to become the major producer of cereals and the north, the purchaser in the era of serfdom, led to rapid and visible social and technological change serfdom few decades after reform. The areas most early affected by trade, naturally, were around the Baltic ports, where, transformation began well before the abolition of serfdom in the 1830s. The chapter looks more closely at the impact of industrialization in the late tsarist and early Bolshevik period, then, in Part 2, at policies and technological diffusion after collectivization. Part 3 assesses technological change, the regime and farming culture in transition.

1 TECHNOLOGICAL INNOVATION FROM 1861 TO 1928

Regional Complementarities

The level of agricultural technology in market economies is a function of the level of knowledge passed on from one generation to the next, with older techniques being already tested for security against risk and uncertainty. Even if their yields barely suffice for their subsistence, after payments to their landlords, peasants will persist with traditional cultivation techniques. T. Schultz showed that the low level of knowledge and skills dictates the course of development where the marginal productivity of resources is viewed as an investment in permanent income streams and the net savings of the household approach zero. With constant returns to scale in traditional agriculture, peasant societies rarely change the techniques they use without new learning, and low-level equilibrium is thus an inevitable result of isolation, preventing communities from overcoming the challenges in their environment.[2]

Climate and soil conditions in Russia have represented a special source of downside risk in Russia. In the tsarist era, in the North and West, producers had to deal with excessive moisture and drain the marshes, and they had to accumulate fertilizer for the rocky, sandy soils. In the South, they

[2] Schultz (1964), p. 30.

met challenges of frequent drought, although soil conditions were better. Across European Russia, they faced lengthy and cold winters reducing possible harvests, in view of their low-yielding technologies, to two a year. As in other land abundant countries, the United States, Canada, and Australia, they practiced mainly extensive means of farming.[3] However, Russian producers had few of the compensating advantages of these other countries, as D. Whitehouse and J. Havelka explain:

> The USSR ... is less favorably situated because of its more northerly location and because much of its "high plains" is marginal from the standpoint of rainfall. The USSR, moreover, has no cropland corresponding to the American corn belt. The combination of fertile soil, adequate moist, and a reasonably long growing season which characterizes the US corn belt is not found in the USSR, where low temperature over moist lands prevail in the north and aridity penalizes the south ... annual fluctuations in the level of farm output in the USSR are larger than in the US.[4]

Russian producers could farm only 25 percent of the 1.7 billion hectares in Russia, because the rest was located in areas too cold for settlement. That means they settled on 222 million hectares, roughly 13 percent, which were located in areas suitable for agricultural production. At present, 8 percent of the land is cultivated.

Of that 8 percent, much of the land is flat, its uniformity promoting similar land regimes across space. This is in contrast with western and central Europe, whose natural relief is more varied and extremes of weather less violent. In Europe, localized adoption of farming techniques – and the independence of small states – strengthened community innovation and diversity of market exchange. In Russia the range of farming practices was narrow by widespread custom tracing to the constraints of a servile regime, lasting hundreds of years. In Europe, a variety of cereals were important; in Russia, grains for human consumption were dominated by low-yielding but sturdy rye.

Across the flat, uniform space, were two very different types of soil.[5] The less fertile were the non–black earth soils of the North, where the general agricultural environment was weak. From the north of Russia to about 200 miles south of Moscow, the soils are highly acidic, some with iron pan but most without.[6] In the mixed forests, soils are of such poor quality that agriculture is possible only under a heavy snow cover, a result of Atlantic air currents and the relative proximity of the Gulf Stream. In the

[3] See Shanin, 1 (1985), 133–49.

[4] Whitehouse and Havelka (1971), p. 342.

[5] For a historical geography of Russia, with particular reference to agricultural development, see Pallot and Shaw (1990), Ioffe and Nefedova (1997, 2001), French and Bater (1983), Gromyko (1991), Granberg (2000), among others.

[6] This discussion draws on the geographic description provided in Pallot and Shaw (1990) and Obruchev (1871).

northern edge of non–black earth Russia, the land north of the Dneister, the average temperature ranges from 0 to +4°C, and the layer of the soil containing humus is thin and poor; the average growing season is about 150 days. Somewhat farther south, in the provinces of Novgorod, Yaroslav, Kostroma, Riazan, and in western Russia and northern Ukraine, the average temperature is higher, varying from 4 to 7°C, but the soil ranges from fairly poor, sandy, and clay loams of various quality to marshes or peat bogs, which are rich, but they require drainage. In all of these areas, there is an excess of moisture. In the southeast of this middle Russian area, in the same latitude, the climate is far colder and drier and the land somewhat more productive. The clay soils of the mixed forest and northern steppe areas provide an adequate yield, but only with fertilization. The growing season can last from 180 to 200 days.

In the South, by contrast, the soils provide a far richer agricultural endowment. They include the black earth soils, or *chernozems*, formed by the decay of the close matted roots of the grasses.[7] Black earth and chestnut soils extend through southern parts of the provinces of Kiev, Orel, Tula, Riazan, Nizhnyi-Novgorod, and Ufa to include Kherson, Rostov-on-Don, and parts of Saratov and Samara. The variation in these soils is moderate. They range from clay and sand loams of central areas to the thick humified strata of the more southern areas. The risks to cultivators are not lower in the South, however. The general lack of moisture, except in the western parts, makes this region susceptible to soil erosion, especially across the eastern and southern areas, which turn into an arid zone with under twelve inches of precipitation annually, beyond which lay the deserts of Central Asia. Beyond the endowment of soils, the harshness and fluctuations of weather produced a general adversity, even after mechanization and investment in the Soviet era.[8] Only in the western parts of black earth areas, in parts of Ukraine and southern Russia, is the moisture adequate to produce high yields on soils rich enough not to need fertilizer.[9]

With low-yielding technologies, the rural community lacked access to the means of acquiring education and skills and was separated from urban markets. In a vicious cycle, isolation was the cause and result of low productivity of agriculture.

[7] Pallot and Shaw (1990).

[8] Desai showed a modest impact of weather fluctuations on yields for 1955–1982, 55 percent of the variation, with input variation constituting the rest. Climate and weather are separable in concept. Climate consists of a long-term trend of weather in a region affecting the selection of crops; by contrast, weather consists of a short-term phenomenon related to short-term trends in yields. See Desai (1987), n. 1 p. 196, p. 222.

[9] For a closer look at the economic geography of the nineteenth century, see Tegoborskii (1855); Baranskii (1950); Shuvalov et al. (1965); Shabad (1951).

Trade and Complementarities: Historical Foundation

The foundation for change lay in the regional differences, which encouraged trade between North and South. In the North, most of the time agriculture failed to produce even subsistence-level yields, while the South produced more than enough grain to supply northern populations as well as southern. The flow of Russia's rivers north–south enhanced exchange, but transportation was costly and slow. Rivers emptied into locations disadvantageous for trade: the land-locked Caspian and Aral seas in the South, and in the North, the Arctic Ocean. Overland hauls were required before grain reached central areas for reshipment to St. Petersburg. In the winter, when roadways hardened, the rivers were frozen; in the spring, the rivers flooded and the roads became impassable.[10] Where reloading was frequent, high dependence on roads was a critical constraint. The low ratio of coastline to inland frontier was another disadvantage in Russia's economic development.[11]

Yet even fairly weak complementarities can foster trade and infrastructure development. After 1822, storage for emergency situations in northern villages was monetized, showing that even under serfdom there were plentiful reserves in the South, and that these were marketed. Serf elders in northern villages were given special accounts for emergency purchases of grain through traders from producer regions around Moscow, St. Petersburg, and the Baltic ports.[12] B. Mironov has traced a steady development of retail trade in towns and urbanization across the north and central parts of Russia from the eighteenth through the early nineteenth century.[13] This expansion emerged from and improved the natural complementarities and supported the increasing export of grain.

This book has argued that the timing of the decision to end serfdom was more a matter of events, political strategies and budgetary pressures than economic development objectives. Complementarities and population growth, in other words, were not sufficient in their effect on wages to encourage a regime change. The costs of maintaining and feeding servile labor remained well below the cost of hiring labor in a land abundant, labor scarce, country such as Russia.[14] By contrast, in England, complementarities and regional specialization played a strong role in English economic history. Showing up in settlements, crafts, and patterns of marriage,

[10] See Symons and White (1975).

[11] Among historians of the Russian peasantry, Milov (1998) particularly emphasizes the importance of geography in technological and social advancement.

[12] *Gubernatorskii otchet* 1841, f. 592, l. 5.

[13] Mironov (1981, 1990, 1999).

[14] Evsey Domar (1970) explains the persistence of serfdom in Russia, despite land abundance, as a consequence of interactions between factor endowments, low-yielding production technologies, and the initial distribution of property rights over land.

inter-regional trade exposed local communities in England to supraregional or international markets and allowed interdependence among English villages far earlier than in Russia.[15]

The slow rate of rural transformation in early modern Russia meant a long adjustment by settlements to their relative isolation. With their low-yielding technologies and extensive cultivation techniques, whole villages in areas of two-field cultivation were in continual movement to new lands. Under serfdom, as soils were exhausted, some landlords sometimes moved villages from region to region rather than, or in addition to, permitting work off the land and income from sources other than agriculture.[16] Much of the movement of villages and households was North/South, because of the direction of the flow of rivers. Russia's waterways impeded movement eastward, a direction of potentially useful migration.[17] Through the sixteenth and early seventeenth century, in the so-called Time of Troubles, political strife and social distress had led to migration of households that fled conditions close to bondage on estates of wealthy boyars and the church. In any case, when serfdom became fixed in the late sixteenth century,[18] voluntary migration slowed considerably, and was limited to the state peasantry.The law code of 1649, which gave considerable authority to the landlord over the peasant household, formalized serfdom and merged the states of personal bondage, or slavery, and attachment to the land. The migratory flow for the servile population was transformed into involuntary transfers, when nobles moved villages to the south to be closer to southern ports.[19]

Land, not labor, was the least costly means of adjustment to population change. In response to demographic events, land was partially partitioned, sometimes fully repartitioned, and fields were added for well-endowed households to meet general consumption needs. Land abundance reduced concern over boundaries of the arable for much of Russian history. 89.9 percent of European Russia's land area had a population density of two or fewer persons per square mile, and 70 percent of Russia's total population lived within this area in 1870. Comparable figures in 1870 for density in Germany were 9 percent (of land area) and 3.5 percent (of population); for France, 6.8 percent and 3 percent; for Great Britain, 22 percent and 4 percent.[20] Lack of demand, in other words, made the drawing of

[15] For regional growth in England, see Kussmaul (1990).

[16] Bohac (1989).

[17] For a discussion eastward movement, see LeDonne (1984, 2004).

[18] This is a point of controversy, reviewed in the introductory chapter to Hellie (1971), whether it was established by a no longer extant decree in 1592, prohibiting on all peasant departures, or by the gradual extension of "prohibited years."

[19] The state and crown peasants were not prohibited from resettling on state lands in Siberia or elsewhere, but only when settlements gained in population density and there was pressure on the land. For a history of the state peasantry, see Druzhinin (1946).

[20] Ioffe and Nefedova (1997), p. 31.

boundaries expensive. Costs were imposed by agency intervention, but local authorities did not enforce them. Little priority was given by imperial committees in the tsarist regime or by administrators in the Soviet collectivized regime to *zemleustroistva*, whose translation includes concepts of irrigation and land improvement as well as land registry and valuation. Priority would have necessitated expenditure on local governance and even transfer of funds to local governments, which was discouraged in the tsarist autocracy.[21]

After the End of Serfdom: Infrastructure Improvements

Between the 1860s and 1913, with the impact of the new land market, the divergence of regions into producer and consumer accelerated.[22] By 1913, in the Russian North, roughly 14 percent of the arable land was cultivated, with the rest either left under forest cover or pasturage. In the South, the arable reached between 60 and 73 percent of the land depending on the province.[23] Commercialization broadened the knowledge and skills of peasants and increased income inequality.[24] Railroad construction was important in generating greater volumes of trade and diffusing new technologies.

Beginning in the second quarter of the nineteenth century an investment initiative in construction of railway lines produced the freighting system of the 1860s. The first rails laid were in the vicinity of St. Petersburg, and between 1842 and 1851 lines were laid between St. Petersburg and Moscow to re-route grain shipments and bypass the previous gateway provinces of the north and middle Volga areas, Iaroslav, Kostroma, and Tver', and Simbirsk and Samara, and to directly reach southern ports. Railroads, which replaced barges, improved the trade and production on large southern estates. This assisted in the concentration of production in gateway provinces, where villages close to rail lines prospered. Shifting transportation costs across the economy helped economic growth, particularly in the 1870s and 1880s, the falling cost of shipping coal from the Ural mountains and iron from Krivoi Rog in Ukraine to Moscow and St. Petersburg. The price of cotton shipped from newly acquired territories in Central Asia to the mills of central industrial towns of Vladimir and Iaroslavl' was cheaper after the rails were

21 Starr (1972); Weissman (1981).

22 Rubinshtein (1957); for a review of the historiographic issues, see Leonard (1989); Wheatcroft (1991) provides a careful statistical treatment of regional differences; Gregory (1982) documented the higher agricultural output and marketing figures, evidently in frontier areas, for this period.

23 Pavlovskii (1969), p. 60.

24 On the extent of development, see Koval'chenko (1971, 1989), Koval'chenko, Moiseenko, and Selunskaia (1988); cf Anfimov (1969, 1980), Shanin (1972); on differentiation in the south, see a quantitative examination in Field (1989).

laid.[25] The mid-1870s witnessed a huge jump in exports without affecting the net retained surplus.

Railroad development enhanced complementarities and produced opportunities for greater integration and growth in tsarist Russia (Metzer 1977, 1984). Railways contributed both to agricultural production and the release of surplus labor from the village.[26] Migrants left seasonal jobs in overland cartage for employment in construction and industries, both assisted by railroad development. By 1913, there was a substantial casual and permanent urban labor force.[27] Transportation of inputs improved yields of animals with livestock feed and soil nutrients. Soils could be treated to increased supplies of manure and fixation through the cultivation of leguminous plants. Seeds that produced more from the soil nutrients were substituted for those that were inferior. Russian space was now more clearly dividing into a northern urban and industrial region and a southern and southeastern agricultural region across a frontier that attracted migration.[28]

Large-scale migration to Siberia began within decades after the abolition of serfdom. Before then, only state peasants could easily leave their villages, providing they had no debt and too little land. State peasants with small landholdings (less than five desiatiny, roughly 5.1 hectares or 13.5 acres) were encouraged to resettle in the southern steppe and farther south. After the abolition of serfdom, the government feared the social consequences of the movement out of agriculture by landless peasants and therefore, for nine years after 1861, peasants on estates of small landowners were permitted to resettle freely in southern provinces. The movement off privately owned lands seemed to build into a substantial mass, and in the 1880s the Peasant Land Bank helped peasant communities buy additional land. After the abolition, state peasants temporarily lost their relative freedom of movement. Like other peasants, except those with particularly small sized allotments, they were subject to restrictions imposed to prevent illegal and uncontrolled migration. Among other restrictions, debts had to be paid; one-half of the capital owed on the household's land had to be paid.[29] The government then issued restrictive laws to control family partitions (1886), eliminate partial partitions, and subject all departures to approval of the commune and the local authority, the land captain (1893). The impact of policy on migration, however, cannot easily be judged by the direction of laws and ministerial circulars, which contradicted each other. One statistician, writing in the late 1870s, commented that the constraints were ineffective, since they slowed

[25] Symons (1975).

[26] White (1975), p. 14.

[27] Rashin (1940).

[28] On internal migration, see Burds (1998); Anderson (1980); Ianson (1881); Treadgold (1957); Macey (1987), chapter 1 note 81, with references to additional literature.

[29] Ianson (1881), pp. 30–43.

migration of households but permitted migration of entire communes for resettlement in Orenburg and Samara.[30]

Pressure on the land was strong mainly in central areas by the end of the nineteenth century. Until transportation costs were eased, agriculture had to be conducted in and around settled areas, particularly large cities.[31] Even after the serf emancipation, the rural population was crowded into the central regions, where their allotment land was not only small but also, often, without access to the forests and streams that were granted to the nobles. The allotment land per peasant (*nadel*) on average in 1891–1895 was 65 percent of what it had been, in the central agricultural region, it was 56 percent of what it had been three decades earlier.[32]

To summarize, *the sum of developments as* Russia's industrialization in the late tsarist era began with significant population increase and, after serf emancipation, the movement of some of that populace to the frontier in the Southeast. The government initially attempted to slow that movement, but it seems clear from migration data that, although slow at first, migration significantly picked up with whole villages determining to leave central areas. To be sure, crowding remained in the blackearth areas near cities.

Coinciding in timing with new migration flows was another very important development for Russian agriculture, the effort by scientists (mirrored in the US and western Europe) to build up new knowledge and research for the improvement of cultivation practices, to which this chapter now turns.

Research and Extension

Russian agricultural science was established in the eighteenth century roughly at the same time as in Europe and the United States. Agricultural science was taught at Moscow University under the title of agro-chemistry. In 1829, it was also taught at Khar'kov and Kazan universities, and after 1836, at every university. In 1884, these departments were renamed so that researchers previously doing "agrochemistry" were called agronomists. In Europe and the United States, beginning in the 1850s, agronomic education was complemented by extension. In Russia, the extension aspect of agronomy was slower to develop. In the United States, experimentation on a wide scale began in the 1850s and 1860s, with support in the USDA-SAES for the research-teaching-extension system and in the Land Grant College Act of 1862. In Europe, an experimental station model developed in the 1850s, and it spread to the United States in 1887.[33]

[30] Ianson (1881), pp. 46–53.

[31] Ioffe and Nefedova (1997).

[32] Ioffe and Nefedova (1997), p. 40.

[33] See Huffman and Evenson (1993); Atack (1989).

The Russian central and provincial (*zemstva*) governments invested in experiment and research beginning in the 1880s and 1890s. A major step in their support was taken in 1894 with the creation of the Ministry of Agricultural and State Domains; its major concern was to address technical issues. The amount of government activity immediately expanded.[34]

Researchers were sent to farms to conduct experimental trials in local fields.[35] Experiment stations were founded in Samara, Saratov, Archangel, Simbirsk, Tula, Smolensk, Rostov-on-Don, Vladimir, and Viatka. There was a genetic breeding station in Moscow at the Agricultural Institute, headed by the distinguished geneticist D. Rudzinskii. After the revolution of 1905, concern with technological progress became a vital state policy and investment in agricultural research and extension grew. With support from the Duma, appropriations for the Ministry of Agriculture went from 15.3 million rubles between 1898–1902 to 58.7 million between 1908 and 1912. During that time, allocations by local government increased from 2.3 million in 1900 to 13.1 million in 1912.[36]

Farming Systems

The technologies used in the 1860s and 1870s, it has been argued, were driven to a large extent by resource endowment.[37] In the immediate post-servile period, agricultural systems in Russia were thought of as either free standing – which produced cereals without the requirement of livestock – or livestock-dependent systems.[38] The fundamental geographic determinants of choice between these two systems were the quality of hayfields and their ratio to arable, the extent of forests, and the extent of the available arable. To feed two to three head of cattle, one desiatina (1.09 hectares, or 2.7 acres) of meadow was necessary, and six or more head of cattle were seemingly required per desiatina of arable for three-field rotation.[39] Over much of northern Russia in the 1860s, on average, there were one or two head of cattle per desiatina. Cereal crops on peasants' land were therefore poorly fertilized, if at all. Fertilizer was reserved for commercially grown hemp, flax, and vegetables planted in the households' plots.

34 Macey (1987), p. 31.

35 Nikonov 1995, pp. 112–20; Masal'skii (1899) and Viner (1922).

36 Volin (1970), p. 107.

37 A key source of information lies in statistical materials collected by the military-statistical apparatus. Obruchev (1871).

38 For categorization of farming technologies into those with and those without horses, see, Vil'son (1857) and Obruchev (1871).

39 To fertilize one desiatina of ploughland (1.0902 hectares), sixty carts or 20,000 kilos of livestock manure per annum were needed for the three-field system of crop rotation. One head of cattle equalled 3,266 kilos per annum. See Ianson (1881).

Where meadows were sufficient across northern and central Russia to sustain herds, producers used the three-field system with the complementary *sokha* (wooden plough). The *sokha* scratched the soils and allowed the planting of rye. Producers did not turn the soil over: the *sokha* was designed to decrease need for fertilizer – and reduce weeds.[40] Weeding would have required excessive labor in the season when males were released from the village for outwork. Manure was used in the vegetable gardens on the household plot.

The inefficiencies of the three-field system included excessive intermingling of strips, leaving a substantial amount of the arable – perhaps as much as 7 percent – inaccessible. Intermingling, or strip farming, was a powerful disincentive to invest in the quality of the land.[41] The temporary nature of tenure of any parcel discouraged fertilization and weeding, and waste occurred in travel between strips. In the non–black earth regions, there were fifty to eighty strips per household, and in the black earth areas of the central south, twenty to thirty strips. Only in parts of the south where the land was particularly rich was there no strip farming.

Where meadows were insufficient but land was abundant, producers used their wooden plough, the *sokha*, in a two-field rotation (*perelog*), the two-field fallow system. The *perelog* required that in year one, flax and millet, sometimes corn (most often flax) were grown, and in year two, hard wheat (*arnautka*), with rye in the fallow. In the third year, winter wheat with barley or oats in the fallow was sown, and in the fourth year, rye, barley, or oats. Under this system, soils were quickly exhausted, and the community had to find other locations for planting.[42] Two-field fallow was widespread in the 1860s and 1870s in the South, where there were few forests and abundant sparsely settled steppe.

Where the land was heavily forested, or largely brush, and the population scarce, a modification of the fallow regime was used, one also independent of livestock raising, the ancient system of slash/burn. In the spring, the land cover was burned and then allowed to lie under snow until the following spring, when it was burned. Once cool, in the second spring, the land was sown with barley or sometimes rye to an abundant harvest for two or three years. The planted half, rich in nutrients in the first year, might have yield/seed ratios of eleven and twelve, although they diminished by the second and third year to three or less. The procedure had to be repeated after some seven to ten years. In the 1870s the slash/burn system of agriculture was still dominant in the northern regions of Archangel, Vologda, and Olonetsk,

40 The importance of this issue was emphasized in discussions with L. V. Milov, professor of agrarian history, Moscow State University, Russia.

41 McCloskey (1976).

42 Obruchev (1871), pp. 233–37.

and still practiced in the neighboring non–black earth northern provinces of Kostroma, Viatka, Novgorod, and Perm.[43]

After the 1870s, the two-field fallow system began to be replaced in the South by three-field crop rotation, as noted above. The three-field system reached Russia from Europe in the fourteenth and fifteenth centuries. The three field system was an improvement in that peasants could use more of the land for crops, while still setting aside significant amounts of clean fallow, and thus permitting the production of wheat. However, its limitations were widely recognized in the eighteenth century at the time of the French Revolution, let alone the nineteenth century, when cultivation regimes were of intense concern in periodicals. The three-field system, where three adjoined unhedged fields are sequentially sown with winter grain, spring grain, and fallow, had no capacity to improve yield ratios much beyond the three to five range. Three-field cultivation exhausted the soil and required continual incorporation of fresh reserves of land. In western Europe, the three-field system was replaced by multiple crop rotation, reducing the need for clean fallow by the end of the sixteenth century. Multiple cropping helped rationalize the use of labor, reduced dependence upon hay for feed, and replenished the soils, slowing their exhaustion by cultivation.

Multiple crop rotation was more widely adopted in Russia beginning in the Baltic area at mid-century. In central Russia, as the military–statistical companion to the *Atlas of European Russia* described, there were attempts at multiple crop rotation in the early 1800s, but these efforts were defeated in central Russia by general conditions – the lack of roads, low prices for grain, and immobility of the labor force under serfdom. In the Baltic provinces conditions were far better. By the 1830s, in areas so close to port cities in the Baltic, grain prices rose higher and the servile regime was gone.[44]

The following map summarizes the spatial dimension of the above narrative. Drawn on a database on Russia's regions, it combines a map of Russia's provinces with information from the military–statistical collection (Obruchev 1871) on the location of various field cultivation systems. The data for systems of farming for the Russian empire fall roughly into the decade following the emancipation of the serfs. The digitalized map in Figure 6.1 shows the boundaries of gubernii as they were in the nineteenth century.

Spatial dynamics can be used to trace the change in farming technique as migrants travelled West to East. Multiple crop rotation began in the western region of the empire. After the 1860s it went with settlements to Siberia. The technology of Siberian farming during the nineteenth century responded strongly to colonial intervention. Colonists introduced field rotations and farm implements in host villages, where they had access to lands on

[43] Obruchev (1871), pp. 48–50.
[44] Obruchev (1871), pp. 234–236.

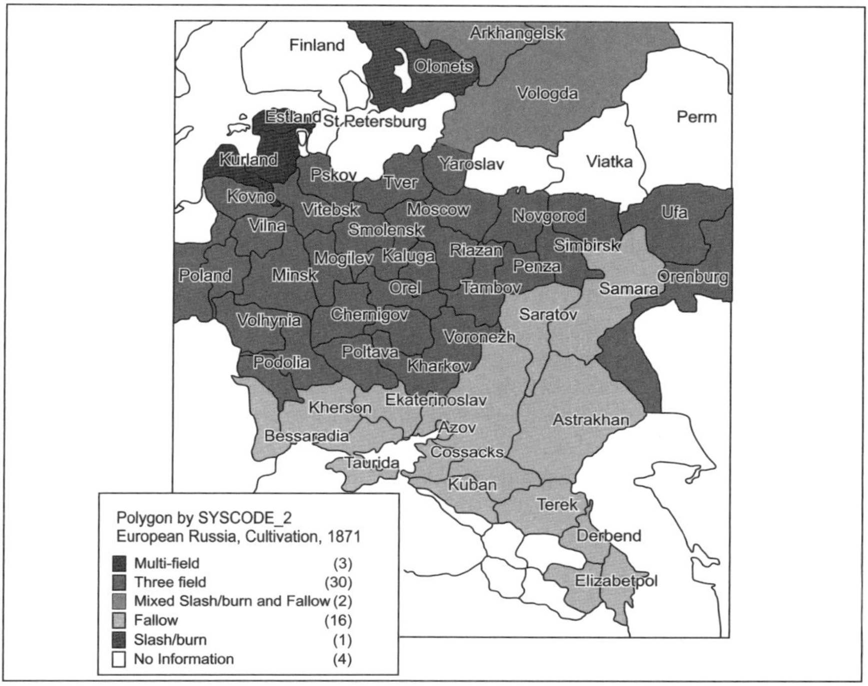

FIGURE 6.1. Farming Production Regimes in 1871 in Tsarist Russia.
Source: Obruchev (1871).

long-term leasing from the state. The state was the owner of much of the land in Siberia before the revolution, but peasant settlers exercised rights relatively undisturbed by state interference. By the 1890s, the transformation of Siberian agriculture by the addition of manure, the replacement of fallow regimes, the introduction of new seeds and varieties of plants, and the Russian iron plow (*plug*), moved from the northern districts of Siberia through Tomsk and Tobolsk farther south.[45] Across the country regions benefitted from the more widespread adoption of the *plug*, made affordable by rapid industrialization.

To summarize, fundamental improvements in Russian agriculture spread after the serf emancipation and accelerated particularly during industrialization. Two factors most powerfully contributed to change: the substitution of the *sokha* by the *plug* and the two transitions in cultivation, from the fallow to the three-field system of rotation in the steppe and from the three-field to multiple-field rotation in the West and central Russia. This is a timeline well behind that of England, where yields were improved by technological means

[45] Goriushkin et al. (1983), pp. 49–54.

much earlier, from the prevalence of the open-field system in 1200 to enclosure in 1650 to four course rotation in 1850 and the further modernization and introduction of new fertilizers and seed varieties from roughly 1920.[46] Technological development in farming across much of western Europe, as in Russia, did not approach levels found in England until well after nineteenth-century industrialization.

Technological Innovation and Industrialization to 1917

There has been some controversy over the technological impact of the Stolypin reforms. One trend in scholarship finds a powerful impact and clear contrasts to the previous era.[47] A more cautious review of the output data by Wheatcroft draws the conclusion that the unusually good weather conditions affecting harvests post-1906 were probably responsible for observed increase.[48] A more extreme view is that of V. A. Bovykin, that the technological impact of the changes in Duma financing and new Duma programs, along with the property rights spread by the Stolypin measures, was negligible:

> Although it aimed to complete the capitalist transformation of the countryside, in its entire conformity with the interests of noble landowners, it was almost without influence on the general technological level of agriculture in the country.[49]

The resources given to extension would have enhanced at least the use of equipment after 1906. It can be seen from the few reliable numbers that there is a trend, as in Figure 6.2.

The chart shows an enormous gap in data points, but general research confirms the late trend.[50] Gregory shows the average annual growth in agricultural equipment between 1891–1893 and 1911–1913 was 9 percent, and at the same time industrial equipment grew by 8 percent annually.[51] Our rough estimate of the increase in the net value of the inventory of agricultural machines, both domestically produced and imports, minus depreciation, shows a doubling between 1876 and 1890 from 14.4 to 30.6 million rubles, and an increase of more than twenty times to 656.6 million rubles by 1913.[52] Over the course of roughly sixty years, moreover, agricultural machinery production moved from North to South, following the regionalization of farming.

46 Austin and Arnold (1989), p. 101.
47 See Macey (1987, 1998); also a review of the literature in Pallot (1998).
48 Cf. Macey (1981).
49 Bovykin (1989), p. 172.
50 Ibragimova and Leonard (2002); Gregory (1994); Kafengauz (1910).
51 Gregory (1982), p. 274.
52 Calculation from Lenin (1952), Vainshtein (1967), Obruchev (1871), and Oganovskii (1923).

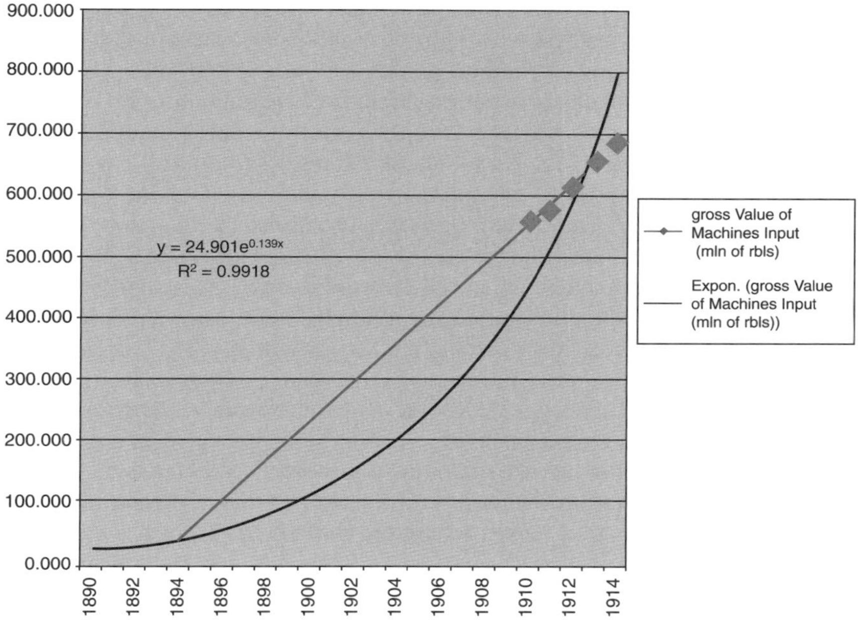

FIGURE 6.2. Mechanization of Agriculture in the Nineteenth Century, Machines in Use (Millions of Rubles), 1890–1914.

Just after the serf emancipation, agricultural machine production was mainly located in northwestern and central Russia, more than in the middle Volga and other regions.[53] The provinces surrounding Moscow[54] industrialized first in Russia, and they were the locus of textile production. Machinery of all kinds was produced both in St. Petersburg and Moscow, but mainly the former. Ukraine, where much of Russia's metal and coal was produced, experienced a surge of growth in machines immediately upon the completion of the railway line linking Krivoi Rog iron to Don Bas coal in 1885. Between 1887 and 1900 output of agricultural machinery grew, supplying the rich agricultural region surrounding the railroad lines.[55] The relatively high cost of rail transport helped the relocation of production of agricultural machinery closer to production areas. The central industrial region, which had produced 39 percent of agricultural machinery at the time of serf emancipation, produced 12 percent in 1900. In 1914, the South produced 52.5 percent of all agricultural machinery.[56] The production of machines

[53] Spechler (1980).
[54] Moscow, Vladimir, Kaluga, Kostroma, Riazan, Nizhnyi-Novgorod, Tula, Tver, and Iaroslav.
[55] Spechler (1980).
[56] Kafengauz (1910), cited in Spechler (1980), p. 412.

followed not only the path of railways but also the direction of concentration, toward the large estates.

A substantial amount of the equipment was used on nobles' estates in a few regions of unusual prosperity, including, among non–black earth provinces, Ekaterinoslav and the Don, which were better supplied with advanced implements. I. D. Koval'chenko's research on the revolutionary era shows that by then, equipment was widely used in the following provinces: Astrakhan, Don, Ekaterinoslav, Orenburg, Perm, Samara, and Ufa.[57] Nobles had a somewhat larger share of more advanced machinery (8.2 percent) than was their share of harvested area, about 7 percent.[58] Nevertheless, Koval'chenko finds, surprisingly, that nobles' production remained, on the whole, labor rather than capital intensive, as discussed in Chapter 5.[59]

On peasant lands, livestock feed was still the operative constraint. An example can be seen from the history of Simbirsk province in 1901.[60] A province with rich black earth soils and access to export markets via the Volga River, bordering on the frontier area Saratov and Samara, Simbirsk belonged in the 1870s to a region where the three-field rotation system was replacing the two-field fallow.[61] By the end of the nineteenth century, local reporters observed the extensive, but not yet dominant, use of the *plug*, the iron-tipped plow. Horsepower was still insufficient in some parts of Simbirsk. The *sokha*, or wooden plow, required one horse, while the *plug* required three, local observers reported. By 1900, they wrote, the plug was still not used in all districts, and the need for it was still hotly debated. Peasants' arguments in defense of the *sokha* were as follows: plowing twice with the *sokha* had the same results as using the *plug*, some said. Most admitted that it was necessary to move to the *plug* in order to turn more soil more deeply. They reported, however, that they could not make the substitution because of the size, weakness, and numbers of their horses. Rumors spread in Simbirsk in 1900 about a *plug* that could be drawn by one horse. Experts found no remaining reason for the rejection of the *plug*. Peasants increased output in this land abundant province as before,

[57] Koval'chenko (1988), Tables 54, 55, and 56, pp. 210–15.

[58] Koval'chenko et al. (1982), p. 123.

[59] Given the available labor at low cost, from a survey of thirty nobles' estates in Tambov guberniia at the end of the nineteenth century, he finds net revenues on noncapital intensive estates were twice as great as net revenues of those that were more capital intensive. Koval'chenko et al. (1982), pp. 83–5.

[60] Simbirsk (1901).

[61] Now called Ulianovsk in the Volga area highlands, bordering on the republics of Mordovia, Chuvashia, and Tatarstan in the northwest and north, respectively, and Samara, Saratov, and Penza Oblast in the southeast, south and southwest, respectively. Mainly an agricultural region historically, it was transformed in the Soviet era into a center for metalworking, automotive, and light industries.

by bringing new lands into cultivation, and that task, they noted, was easier with the *plug*.[62]

In the north, where weeds thrived in the damp soils, some peasants continued to scrape soil with the *sokha* at the turn of the century. However, according to the census of farm implements in 1910, the *plug* adoption rate was roughly 90 percent of all peasants.[63] This certainly explains steady improvement in output documented by Gregory's national estimates and the spread of three-field and multiple-crop rotation systems. To be sure, population pressure was also important in shifting farm regimes toward higher productivity systems. It combined, however, with the use of many kinds of machines on nobles' land, and the spread of the *plug* on peasants' lands.

Roughly half of nobles' and peasants' demand for agricultural machinery, especially the simpler types of mass-produced agricultural machinery based on well-established technologies, was met by domestic producers, since the industry was protected by tariffs and supported by government orders.[64] On balance, Russia was not a large producer of agricultural machinery before World War I. J. Cooper and R. Lewis show that machine building was a weak sector until the war provided a stimulus for large batch production of machine tools. In quantity and quality, machine tools experienced substantial improvement from 1913 to 1917.[65] Imports of more sophisticated machinery continued to be important for rural production, since, as M. Dohan (1991) observes, there were lags in technology transfer and a scarcity of skilled personnel relative to unskilled labor during the surge of industrialization at that time.[66] Indeed, importing recently developed products helped fuel industrialization and remained a model for technological development under the Bolsheviks after the revolution of 1917.

Summary: Technological Development in Tsarist Russian Agriculture

After the serf emancipation, the potential for the development of technology grew at newly established research centers. The industrialization period witnessed the more widespread use of farm machinery and fertilizer in Russia, on state and nobles' lands and in areas where off-farm labor was so extensive that there were sufficient resources in villages for investment. The main innovation until the early twentieth century was the *plug*, along with multiple crop rotation in central and southern areas.

[62] Simbirsk (1901), pp. 360–61.

[63] Calculation from Lenin (1952), Vainshtein (1967), Obruchev (1871), and Oganovskii (1923).

[64] Dohan (1991), p. 216.

[65] Cooper and Lewis (1991), pp. 198–99.

[66] Dohan (1991), p. 216.

2 THE SOVIET ERA

The NEP

The New Economic Policy (NEP) was designed to help peasants recover from the destructive effects of revolution and "War Communism." In the NEP, the mechanization and use of horsepower increased on peasant farms. Some 6.7 million peasants by 1926 participated in cooperatives for marketing or credit, and informal cooperation governed production with cooperation in the use of animals, implements, and land.

The prerevolutionary advance from the two-field to the three-field system continued, but much of the land in the Northwest where multi-field rotation had begun to dominate was lost to Soviet territory in the 1920s. The overwhelming presence of three-field agriculture scarcely met the goals of the new government to use modern science and technology for the rapid advancement of economy and society. It was attacked as primitive and feudal by the Bolsheviks.[67] With little investment resources, not much technological progress was achieved, and yields were only just restored to prewar levels by the end of the 1920s. For a number of reasons – terms of trade for the peasants worsened, nobles' estate operations had been eliminated, and pressure on peasants was reduced by lowering direct taxation – the amount of grain marketed dropped as a percentage of production, and exports suffered. The contribution to industrialization by the peasantry was less than it had been in tsarist times.[68]

Initially retaining the tsarist foreign trade framework, the Bolshevik government sought to import new technologies and rely on import substitution for mass-based production, with a priority given to tractors. However, the shortage of marketed surpluses of grain changed the export structure and led to sharp decline. On average, imports of agricultural machinery between 1923 and 1928 were half the level of prerevolutionary imports, although in individual years, such as 1925, imports more than doubled the average annual amount spent in the late tsarist era (1909–1913). Most tractors produced went to the military, and the overwhelming volume of tractors for use in agriculture were imported until the late 1920s, when the embryonic Soviet factor industry was boosted by a new large capacity factory in Stalingrad.[69]

Technology policy of the NEP was ambitious, however. The science research institutions grew. Before the revolution, science and extension had been under the Ministry of Agriculture, and the Vol'noe Ekonomicheskoe Obshchestvo (VEO, or Free Economic Society) published much of the research and provided a forum for scientists, policy-makers, and practitioners

[67] Male (1971), pp. 7–8.

[68] For a conceptual analysis and rethinking of the data see Harrison (1991); see also Barsov (1969), Allen (2003), and others.

[69] Davies (1991); Dohan 225–27; Cooper and Lewis (1991), pp. 205–06.

of technological experimentation in agriculture. The VEO was closed by the Bolsheviks and agronomic research transferred to the Central Science Institute for Agriculture, founded in 1922, with a center in Moscow and branches in the republics. In the republics, large extension and research institutes were founded in 1924. In Moscow, the Institute for Applied Botany and New Crops (from 1930, All-Union Crop Institute) was founded in 1925 under the famous geneticist Nikolai Vavilov. Research institutes for soil sciences, and in 1929, the All-Union Academy of Agricultural Sciences (named after Lenin), were founded.[70] Research and extension in the NEP was more than a bridge between the fragile recovery of traditional agriculture and the mechanization of the 1930s, it was a new foundation upon which the new state established its scientific credentials.

Innovation after Collectivization

Collectivization, wrote Merle Fainsod, was "a record of 'storm' tactics and stubborn peasant opposition, of grandiose projects and 'paper' victories.'"[71] For agriculture, however, in the long run it was also a record of visible advancement in mechanization, irrigation, drainage of marshes, and, initially, gains by economies of scale.

The slogan "tractorization" of Russian agriculture became popular in the 1930s. Along with now permanent emergency measures to maintain control over agricultural output, there were mass deportations and summary executions.[72] The state centralized investment and mechanized some 250,000 collective farms (*kolkhozy*) and 4,200 state farms (*sovkhozy*) in September 1930 by establishing Machine Tractor Stations (MTS), authorized as the main channel of technological assistance by the state to agriculture. The *kolkhoz* were still under the control of local governmental organs, but they turned for their horsepower to the MTS. In 1928, there was one tractor with ten horsepower for every 3,700 hectares of sown area; in 1929, one for every 2,850; in 1930, one for every 1,610 hectares; and in 1931, one for every 690 hectares.[73] By the late 1930s, the MTS grew from an experiment to a stable supply of tractors to the entire sector.

The role of the MTS was important in the early years of Soviet power, since one station could service a number of farms and equipment was scarce. The MTS was a way to pool power, machinery, and repair stations, and to attach supervisory skills to the farm; individual households had been too poor to purchase tractors. The MTS also provided other key resources,

70 For a detailed treatment of the 1920s and other periods, see Nikonov (1995), pp. 199–203.

71 Fainsod (1989), p. 254.

72 Davies (1994), chapter 1; (1980, 1980, 1989).

73 "The Agricultural situation in 1931–1932," *Economic Commentary on the International Yearbook of Agricultural Statistics for 1931–1932* (Rome: International Institute of Agriculture, 1933), p. 493.

such as horses, in the 1930s during waves of collectivization.[74] It cannot be said that the MTS were a highly positive innovation in all respects, since the coercion of the peasants who had to use the machines and subsequent slaughter of livestock contributed to the initial collapse of farming during collectivization, and over the next decade there was no net agricultural surplus for export.[75] Rural consumption and agricultural output declined in the 1930s.[76] The MTS did, however, prevent productivity from falling as farms were mechanized and labor left agriculture.

Later on, the MTS introduced clear inefficiencies, critically important timing delays in the use of finely calibrated machines, whose correct use required spot decisions of local decision-makers on the basis of small changes in the weather. Use of such combines was now planned long in advance by Soviet managers. The *kolkhozy*, by contrast with the *sovkhozy*, had no control over the timing and use of agricultural machinery. They made no decisions on crop rotations or the purchase of equipment, and they paid for the use of machinery in kind, between 10 and 20 percent of gross yield.[77] Instead, the MTS drew up annual agreement with the *kolhoz* through the rayon administration, based on centralized requirements for successful fulfillment of the Five-Year Plan. This agreement followed the form of the model contract of 1939 between the MTS and the *kolkhoz*, which laid down the precise area of land to be ploughed, cultivated, and harvested, the depth of furrows, the dates when each task was to be completed, the number of workers, and the kinds of small machines the *kolkhoz* would provide for each task. Depriving the producers of the incentives of making such decisions and bearing responsibility for them prolonged the time spent using the machines. The centralized plan also stipulated the use of machinery for which knowledge on farm was inadequate. Finally, in taking away from the farm level the task of making major planning decisions, it deprived the planners of local knowledge of what might go wrong, and it led to supply bottlenecks for parts and a lack of adequate repair services.

Khrushchev's Reforms and After

In February 1958, the Central Committee under Khrushchev's leadership eliminated the MTS and sold the machines to the *kolkhozy*. It transformed the MTS to significantly downsized RTS (repair-technical stations). Khrushchev aimed to end the system by which there were two managers, one on-farm and the other at the MTS, deploring, in his words, having "two bosses on the land." The closure had a political objective of restoring on-farm party organs to serve as an ideological force in the countryside, but it

[74] Volin (1959).
[75] Barsov (1969), Millar (1970, 1974), and Ellman (1975, 1978).
[76] Allen (1998).
[77] Hubbard (1939), p. 150.

had large long term economic consequences. It brought together skilled and unskilled personnel, improved the efficient use and selection of machinery, and increased opportunities for spillovers in daily farm operations. It had steep financial costs, however. *Kolkhozy* were forced in one year to spend 17.2 billion rubles, roughly one-seventh of their record total income in 1958, on machinery purchases. Moreover, no new core of skilled employees was readily available on the *kolkhoz* in the short run.The farm sector underwent a punishing loss of personnel and equipment.

The elimination of the MTS resulted in several years of drastically lowered harvests, although there were good harvests, too. Khrushchev's higher procurement price policies combined with greater farm autonomy succeeded on the whole in improving average yields. His reinvestment in science, including at major agricultural science centers, resulted in the advance of discoveries after a period of when innovative research was suppressed. After the successful harvest of 1958, the government launched a seven-year plan with optimistic targets for agricultural improvement but provided less funds for fertilizer and agricultural machinery; domestic production of grain combines dropped from 134,000 in 1957 to 53,000 in 1959.[78] Without adequate fertilization and moisture, and with continuous sowing, the cultivation of corn caused soil erosion. The low harvest in 1962 was no doubt a consequence of numerous policy failures, including mandatory elimination of fallow in the virgin lands, soil erosion caused by lack of appropriate moisture and fertilizers, and, as always, poor weather conditions.

Khrushchev's reforms were also known for their eccentricity as well as policy failures. He tried to eliminate the practice of annual summer fallowing, so that even in semiarid areas, fallowing would be done only after a few croppings. It is well known that annual summer fallowing is essential on semiarid land as is practiced in the United States and Canada. For 1980, Brooks observes higher seeding rates and lower fertilizer responsiveness in Soviet regions than in comparable areas of the United States, and she reports low fallow rates of about 10 percent.[79] Another policy failure was

[78] Hahn (1972), p. 2.

[79] Brooks (1983), p 161. Clean fallow rates for the Soviet Union and Russian Federation (from World Bank Development Indicators and *Sel'khoz* (2000), p. 53.

Fallow in Russia	% of Sown Area*
1960–1965	6
1965–1970	8
1970–1975	7
1975–1980	6
1980–1985	8
1985–1990	10
1990–1995	14
1995–1999	19

to grow green corn for silage in places where corn could not mature. He substituted pulses for leguminous hay for feed, planning further reductions in hay. Pulses are expensive and used only as food in limited amounts in market economies because they are relatively low in nutrient content needed by livestock. This contrasts with leguminous hay, which is an excellent and cheap source of protein food. Khrushchev advised using sugar beets for feed, although in market economies they are too expensive to be used for purposes other than human consumption. Finally, Khrushchev reduced the planting of oats, even though oats are valued as an important rotation crop and one of the best concentrates for horses and other animals. Khrushchev forced the reduction of the size of private plots and relocated many settlements. Along with mixed effects of new lands and corn campaigns, the overall result of his eccentric policies was a failure to produce steady output improvement, constituting one of the reasons he was removed. After Khrushchev, the Kosygin-Brezhnev regime turned to a policy of reinvestment. The Soviet Union became the world's largest tractor producer. In 1975, the USSR produced about 550,000 tractors, about double the production of the United States. However, the Soviet plan had a problem with the supply of parts and with repairs, which were well below target. Also, it had a relatively high rate of retirement of tractors, roughly 12 percent, reflecting deficiencies in machine quality and durability. By contrast with western economies, finally, the Soviet Union had no used tractor market, and so once tractors were removed from the field, they were scrapped.[80]

Technology and Productivity

Technologically, the USSR's achievement in agricultural production was measured in Soviet statistics in a way that reflected gains from mechanization without considering opportunities lost. The points of comparison in western reporting were the countries of western Europe, the United States, and Canada. The measure classically used in western analysis was and is an estimate of total factor productivity (TFP), taken as the ratio of an index of agricultural output divided by an aggregate input index including labor, land, and capital goods.[81] TFP, generally a residual that cannot be explained by increased input, is assumed to measure technological change, along with other factors in production, such as economies of scale. Its application to Russian agriculture is the subject of the next chapter.

Technological progress in comparative study is difficult to measure directly and accurately,[82] especially given the challenge of comparing market and nonmarket economies. However, rough as the data and assumptions

[80] Rubenking (1976), pp. 609–10.
[81] Gardner (1992), p. 69.
[82] Griliches (1958, 1960).

TABLE 6.1. *Comparative Agricultural Indicators, 1985*

	Russia	U.S.	France	Canada
Yield, cereals in centners per hectare	14.5	47.4	57.1	22.2
Yield, wheat in centners per hectare	15.2	25.2	60.1	17.7
Fertilizer nutrients applied to crops (kg/hectare of arable)	78	110	298	52
Production of meat/head of cattle (kg)	60	111	98	110
Milk per cow (kg)	2,334	5,894	3,284	4,654

Source: Seklhoz (1995), pp. 135–45.

must be, comparison does show a large productivity gap between the Soviet Union and Western advanced countries by a variety of measures. The components of this gap differed over time, and efforts were made to close the gap without lasting success.

The significant slowdown became visible in the 1970s. Soviet agriculture, D. Diamond and W. Davis found, had a growth rate of TFP of 1.0 percent per year for 1961–1970 and 0.4 percent annually for 1971–1977.[83] D. Johnson and K. Brooks found the comparison with the United States in the 1970s to show for the Soviet Union a gap of about one-half to two-thirds of the growth rate, when comparable areas were selected for estimates. The gap was also evident in output per farm worker, with the Soviet Union at 11 percent of that in the United States in 1970.[84]

In the early 1970s, the gap narrowed somewhat. However, shifts in investment policy and unreliable delivery resulted in planning failure and on-farm management problems. Managers could not develop stable expectations of the assignment of resources and availability of repairs, parts, and other inputs. Weather presented unusual risk not eased by investments. The impact of these factors was severely damaging to predictability. After the 1970s, high investments produced almost no gain in TFP.

A major bottleneck for Soviet agriculture, as before in the tsarist era and as later in the post-Soviet era, was the livestock and dairy sector. Measured by cost and results, Table 6.1 shows the comparisons for 1985.

The troubles with collectivized agriculture, even after reinvestment, show up in the preceding table. The 1980s brought new developments in biotechnology, successfully improving productivity in the U.S. and European farming systems. Lack of such biological innovation in Soviet production is a main reason the comparisons of cereal yields are so stark.

[83] Johnson and Brooks p. 151, who cite Diamond and Davis (1979), p. 32.
[84] Whitehouse and Havelka (1973), p. 354.

Soviet Research and Extension

After the development of an ambitious agricultural research program in the 1920s, the decline of agricultural science from the 1930s is striking. The application of research to agricultural production was stymied during Stalin's era by his support for the scientist Trofim Lysenko (1898–1976), a Lamarckian researcher who rejected the idea and empirical evidence of genetic inheritance. Empirical research was stopped in favor of a more theoretical approach. Theoreticians used linear programming to develop models or optimal plans for the sector. At the time of Khrushchev's ascent to power in the Soviet Union, Soviet agronomy was significantly behind in empirical understanding.

Lysenko and his colleagues opposed the acceptance of the revolutionary research findings of genetic crop improvement.[85] Hybridization had first been explored in a 1865 paper by G. Mendel (1822–1884) on the heritability of seven characteristics in garden peas. His research findings were confirmed by considerable research, and in 1909 the Danish botanist and geneticist W. Johannsen (1857–1927) named the bearer of inheritance, the gene. In 1911, the American geneticist and biologist T. Morgan (1866–1945) established a chromosome theory of heredity. Experimentation on a large scale occurred in the United States in the 1920s and 1930s.

Lysenko's writings about hybridization turned the use of inbred lines into a political fallacy of "Morganism," injurious to a plant's "biology." He advocated intervarietal and vegetative hybridization, which involved planting crops such that by selection of the fittest they would improve. The defense by the geneticists, whose research was cautious, rested on prior Western empirical findings, and this Lysenko represented as a political threat. The eight Russian centers for the teaching of genetics were closed, and seventy-seven geneticists and agronomists were arrested and shot.[86]

Russian agricultural science was severely damaged as a result, although a small center for the study of genetics at the Moscow Pharmaceutical Institute continued to exist. L. Belin has described that institute and a network of researchers who produced double-crosses eventually incorporated into Khrushchev's corn program.[87] The researchers introduced hybrid seed production, although Khrushchev was more inspired in his support for it by the idea of mass distribution than improved quality of output, and Russian hybridization tended to be encouraged for all breeds, including those that

[85] See the monograph on genetics and its fate in Stalin's rule, Sofer (1993).

[86] Among those arrested and shot without trial included, beginning in December 1929, the economists, including Nikolai Kondratieff, the "neonarodniks," including Aleksandr Chayanov, who was shot in 1937, and the geneticists, including Nikolai Vavilov; see Nikonov (1995), pp. 216 ff.

[87] Belin (1991).

were inferior.[88] Khrushchev's policy was inconsistent. He also maintained government support for Lysenko's work, thereby undercutting advances in theoretical knowledge. Moreover, although important in improved crop yields, Russian advances remained within a narrow research circle, and much research was done that could not be published.[89] Khrushchev did not much consult professional agronomists in policy-making. His campaign to produce corn in the virgin lands was uninformed. Although corn is a high-yield product and invaluable source of feed for livestock, and it is a crop that could be planted on the virgin lands, the project moved forward by forcing farms to reduce other crops which were, no doubt, more suitable to local conditions. Even the weak yield of corn produced in this campaign revealed the lag with the West, it showed weak progress in using inbred seed for crosses.

The significance of continued Lysenkoism in Russia went beyond poor research. As summarized in a report by the U.S. Department of Agriculture, it represented the subordination of research results to political demands:

> The most detrimental features of Lysenkoism were not only the theoretical propositions put forward, but also the improper verification of experiments and Lysenko's political power to impose his ideas upon Soviet biology and to hamper other research. When it was expedient, he adapted his theories to fit the preferences of Soviet leaders. For example, he downgraded the benefits of mineral fertilizer when the government was unwilling to increase the supply.[90]

The impact of Stalinism on Russian agronomic research can scarcely be overstated. In an administrative and human sense, it is the history of the elimination of institutes and the distinguished biologists, botanists, and geneticists who worked in them, beginning in 1929. In a scientific sense, it is the history of agronomic science in the Soviet Union. The impact of Lysenkoism could be felt through the 1980s. Under Khrushchev, Russian textbooks for instruction of younger agronomists still carried the views of Lysenko. After 1965, he was fully discredited, but Russian agronomic science was not restored to its prior brilliance and certain topics were avoided, although by then, the necessity of supporting theoretical understandings with research experiments and extension, was well understood. Alexander Nikonov described one critical example of the gap in research on cultivation in arid climates:

> In 1931, from 26 to 31 October, the All-Union conference on the fight against drought took place. Practically the entire scientific establishment was represented.... There were more than 80 papers.... The main ones were – in sessions

[88] See manuscript by L. Belin (1991) for a close study of Khrushchev's crop experimentation.

[89] This controversy was examined in Belin (1991); Hudson and Richens (1946); Popovsky (1984); Joravsky (1970).

[90] USDA, *Outlook* (1966), p. 16.

> organized analytically – on the cause of drought and erosion by Professor A. F. Vangengeim . . . on agrotechnology by Professor N. M. Tulaikov . . . on selection, by N. I. Vavilov . . . on access to water by Professor A. N. Kostiakov. . . . Ten recommendations were made. . . . VASKhNIL [The Lenin All-Union Academy of Agricultural Science] never again returned to the problem of drought, not in the 1940s, 1950s, 1960s, 1970s or 1980s.[91]

This means little was done to correct problems caused by Khrushchev's intervention in the virgin lands, where wind and water erosion affected about two-thirds of all arable and more than 50 percent of permanent grassland, causing substantial losses of soil and plant nutrients.

Through the late Soviet decades, Russian agricultural research and extension was not given a free hand regarding the incorporation of results of U.S. and western European research. Reports by public and private firms on biotechnological innovation, which pushed up yields enormously in the 1970s–1990s, were not available in Russia. Technological deepening in Russia drew not on the linkage between Russian science and practice, nor on linkages to world science or global markets.

Isolation was a significant factor in slow progress of Soviet agronomic science. Experimental agricultural researchers remained at risk in their association with foreign research institutes, and they could not lobby effectively. Not only discouraging global linkages, Russian policies failed to allow clear institutional direction and coordination of policy views.[92] In western market economies, valuable investments – providing for an adequate amount of clean fallow, guaranteeing the quality of seed and agronomic practices, and manufacturing equipment and fertilizer – were self-organized. Research and extension and its lobbyists tend to foster a sustained and ample government program of research grants which require demonstration of applications for continued funding.

In Russia, there were numerous reasons for the slow diffusion of innovation. Hybrids in the Soviet era, for example, were imposed selectively on farms, after their production in government laboratories, and this did not stimulate diffusion. Since the mid-1980s, in advanced market economies, private firms have dominated research as well as dissemination of inbred seed lines. The average yield of patented single crosses now exceeds that of widely available seed, and results are visible in comparative yields of western advanced countries, where such seeds are used. Soviet production and diffusion were constrained.

In summary, due mainly to the success of biotechnological achievements, the rate of return to investment in agricultural research in market economies

91 Nikonov (1995), p. 206.
92 Ruttan and Stout (1960), Binswanger (1974), Huffman and Evenson (1989).

exceeded the rate of return to investment in Russia.[93] The contribution of technology to TFP is large: in the United States, agricultural productivity growth continued to rise in the 1970s and 1980s as growth in other sectors slowed down. Returns to agronomic research, as demonstrated by comparative data, make the investment and open science critical to the rural economy. The Soviet economy was able to take advantage of state capacity to increase investment in agricultural research and technology. Under Kosygin and Brezhnev, investment in science rose to significant levels. By the time of the collapse of communism, there were five major agricultural academies with more than 100 branch institutes, as well as agricultural universities in each of the fifteen former republics. Nevertheless, the biogenetic revolution failed to make a mark on Russian agriculture in the 1980s.

Railroads and Grain Transport in the Soviet Era: The Investment Bottleneck

Transport was another investment project that was less successful than it might have been for the agricultural sector. Soviet-era rail networks mostly accommodated industrial rather than agricultural shipments. Transportation routes were redesigned to trace outward from nodes, leading early on from the metallurgical bases of the 1930s and, later, from territorial industrial complexes (TIC), which were located to take advantage of sourcing the required raw materials and the expansion of particular industrial sectors. The agricultural sector was relatively isolated in Soviet economic networks, and it was not the only sector so positioned. The TIC targeted regional self-sufficiency in part for strategic reasons and in part to save on wasteful cross-hauls over the enormous territory of the Soviet Union. Transportation networks across the country favoured heavy bulk freight traffic – coal, coke, ore, and petroleum or timber. Agriculture was expected to feed a more limited population; it relied on regional outlets and East/West transport.

A decision was made in the 1920s for the base of Russian transport to be rail rather than roadways. Increasing traffic made heavier trains a necessity over long distances, and the growth of diesel and electric traction was steady. The shipments moved between consumers and producers in an East/West direction. The benefit was that the historical constraint on East/West trade, that is, the fact of rivers flowing North and South, was broken. The disadvantage was that roadways were a lower priority. Sunk cost diverted production into goods for which railroads were the most efficient means of transport. Through the 1960s, bulk goods still comprised 80 percent of shipments by tonnage, chiefly by rails. Although roadways are far more efficient for manufactured goods and agricultural output, and far more useful

93 Gardner (1998).

TABLE 6.2. *Percentage Share of the Prime Haulers in Total National Transport, 1913–2007*

	1913	1928	1940	1950	1960	1970	1980	1990	2000	2007
	Goods transport, traffic (blns of ton-kilometers)									
Railroads	60	73	84	83	79	64	53	53	38	43
Roads	0.5	0.1	2	3	4	4	5	6	4.2	4.3
Shipping	16	...	4	5	6	16	12	11	3.4	1.3
Internal waterways	23	27	10	9	8	6	5	4	2	1.7
Pipelines	0.5	0.1	0.4	1	4	9	25	26	53	50
Air	...	...	...	...	...	...	0.001	0.000	0.1	.1
SUM	100	100	100	100	100	100	100	100	100	100

Sources: Mellor (1974), updated and corrected, *Rossiiskii Statisticheskii Ezhegodnik* (1998, 2001, 2008).

for rural development, the lagging development of road infrastructure was another force for the relatively slow progress of agriculture i the Soviet era.

Table 6.2 shows the priorities. Pipelines expanded in tonnage since the 1960s. Since the transition began, pipelines have more than doubled in percentage of traffic. Meanwhile, asphalted roads have fallen even further in priority.

The share of bulk trade makes the relative inadequacy of roads stand out among bottlenecks in central planning. In the Soviet era, the western transportation system, which is adapted to local needs, was thought to be irrational and an enormous waste of public wealth.[94] In consequence, in the Soviet Union, the small trade important for farming declined with underdeveloped roadways, a common legacy of highly centralized states in the developing world. The lack of roadways is related to the lack of local services, and this is a problem of most less developed economies.[95]

Sectoral Technological Bottlenecks

There are also sectoral technological bottlenecks that illustrate the importance of the isolation of scientific researchers in the Soviet era even in an era of abundant resources for the sector. This is another example of how carefully planned and extravagant investment projects could fail. The sector that was probably one of the most difficult challenges in agriculture was the production of livestock, important because of Soviet objectives of raising per capita meat consumption. The World Bank review of conditions

[94] Mellor (1974), p. 76.
[95] See the review of the literature by Bardhan (2002).

in the livestock sector showed a variety of problems. In a sector where knowledge and updated techniques for breeding are essential to maintaining competitiveness, investment did not produce expected results:

> Improper feeding and shortcomings in pure-strain stock breeding have led to the inefficient use of the cattle's genetic potential. Only 65–70 percent of genetic potential is used in milk production, 45–50 percent in beef production, and 40–60 percent in pork production.... The deficiencies in pure-strain cattle breeding prevent improving the quality of the cattle.... The public sector misuse of the cattle's biological potential resulted in a 30–35 million-liter shortfall in planned milk production and a 3.5–4.0 million-ton shortfall in planned meat production given the available cattle population and available fodder.[96]

The expenditure on livestock sheds and expensive complexes without matching efforts in pure-strain stock breeding resulted in an abundance of cattle with low biological potential and squandered farm investment.

Fertilizer usage, also, tended to be a challenge because investment strategies were centralized, and on-farm monitoring was insufficient.[97] Technical standards in land reclamation projects were not maintained because local skills were found to be insufficient, according to the World Bank.[98] Its review in 1992 found the central issue in all these sectors to be the lack of effective coordination at local levels between planners, agronomic experts, and farm managers. It is important to qualify this conclusion by saying that inter-*kolkhoz* cooperation and regional coordination were an important part of Soviet output plans. Between the 1960s and 1980s, the agro-industrial complex (AIC) represented a network of regional complexes that integrated the entire food chain with industry: input supply, cereals and livestock production, and downstream or processing activities, including storage facilities. Coordination and integration within regions and across farms were a priority in the plan. The AIC consisted of three or four spheres: (1) production of equipment, fertilizers, herbicides, microbiological research and production, and sometimes separately listed: rural infrastructure (including inter-*kolkhoz* roads), community structures, and agricultural education; (2) production of cereals and other crops and livestock; and (3) processing and the food industries, including specialized transport and storage facilities (elevators, refrigeration).[99] It is difficult to assess exactly at what place in the AIC coordination did not work and investment failed to stimulate appropriate levels of innovation. Perhaps the flaw lay in the export priorities of the system. Large-scale benefits were for exportable commodities. The AIC represented huge fertilizer and equipment factories,

96 WBWP (1992) 3: 11.

97 The application of fertilizers was 15 percent of demand in 1986–1990, and 60–70 percent of the required fertilizer machinery was available (WBWP 3 [1992]), p. 6.

98 WBWP (1992), 3: 7.

99 Smetanin, Tikhonov, Lemeshev, Belov (1980).

TABLE 6.3. *Purchase of Oil Products by Agricultural Enterprises (Millions of Tons), 1985–2000*

	1985	1990	1995	1998	2000
Gasoline for automobiles (total)	18.5	11.3	3.3	2.4	1.8
Including by direct trade	–		0.4	0.1	0.1
Diesel energy (total)	23.5	20	7.1	6.2	4.0
Including by direct trade	–	–	0.8	0.3	0.4

Source: Rossiiskii Statisticheskii Ezhegodnik (2001), p. 404.

and fertilizer amounted to 60 percent of agricultural inputs as well as a substantial portion of exports (see Appendix 7).[100]

3 AFTER COMMUNISM: AGRICULTURAL INNOVATION IN THE RUSSIAN FEDERATION

In transition, the collapse of input sectors, especially agricultural machinery, was devastating to equipment renewal, and this held back agricultural recovery. Without financial instruments and lacking the skills to evaluate real costs of depreciation and purchases, farm directors found their choice of inputs dictated by nonmonetary opportunities, a form of soft-budget constraints.[101] The number of farms operating at a loss grew, as discussed in Chapter 5.

Soft-budget constraints perpetuated loss-making corporative enterprises, which did not purchase inputs. This contributed to collapse of their production.[102] Mineral fertilizer production fell by 17 percent and herbicide production by 21 percent between 1991 and 1995.[103] The share of land sown with mineral fertilizers declined from 66 percent in 1990 to 25 percent in 1996, and share of land sown with organic fertilizers declined from 7.4 percent in 1990 to 2.9 percent in 1996.[104] Tractor and agricultural machine production fell by 41 percent, and there was a dramatic fall in the consumption of energy on farm, as Table 6.3 shows.

Agricultural machinery began to increase in production in the late 1990s, although in 2000 and 2001, numbers grew slowly, and tractor production even declined. The production of combines was less than a fourth in 2004 the number produced in 1990.[105] One reason for this is continued fall in demand due to reorganization of the system of federal leasing in 2001 to help

[100] *Sel'skoe khoziastvo Rossii* (1988), p. 9; Nikonov (1995), p. 355.
[101] Voigt (2001).
[102] Serova (2000).
[103] *Russian Economy in 1996* (1997), p. 77.
[104] OECD (1999), p. 55.
[105] *Rossiiskii statisticheskii ezhegodnik* (2005), p. 408.

farms avoid equipment purchases. Another is that domestically produced equipment lost its price advantage over imports after the early 1990s, and the import sector continued to grow, crowding out domestic production. It may also be that the "asphalt farmers," or vertically integrated holding companies that now dominate high-end farms, have depressed machinery production by using mainly imported equipment.[106] However, after 2005, with the sharp rise in oil prices, agriculture began to receive special support for the purchase of energy inputs.[107] Fertilizer production alone among inputs to the sector significantly increased, encouraged by export expansion (80 percent is exported). After the mid-1990s, usage increased on a per hectare basis, with a relatively faster decline of the amount of land under crops than of fertilizers used. Per hectare, mineral fertilizer usage increased in Russia between 1995 and 2004 from 17 to 23 kg per hectare, in line with applications in Latvia and Estonia but still well below European levels, as Table 6.4 shows for 1996–1998.

In Europe, the highest application rates for mineral fertilizer are found in the Netherlands, Belgium, Finland, and France. Generally, application rates are adjusted to local soil and weather conditions and the kind of crops that these favor. The grassland and arable crops of some northern countries in Europe typically require more fertilizer than the vineyards and olive plantations of some southern countries. The consequence of extremely low fertilizer application in Russia is that the soil has been damaged; long-term damage through soil depletion and loss of fixed capital is advanced. In 2005, the figure for Russia is 25 kg and 0.9 kg of organic fertilizers per hectare of arable.[108]

After 1999, the government included tractors in its leasing programs, which improved numbers, as seen in Table 6.5. However, this partial compensation diminishes in importance as the drop in overall state investment in the sector is considered. Investment in public sector projects was cut for fiscal reasons in the early 1990s, and agriculture's share of private-sector fixed capital investment funds, allocated by efficiency of production, fell from 16 percent in 1990 to 4 percent in 2004.[109] The food industry has the lion's share of sectoral funds, with eight times the amount of short-term funds and four times the amount of long-term resources in 2004.[110]

The slow pace of restructuring and farm survival, despite loss-making, slowed the downsizing as well as disappearance of the collective entities.

[106] "Russian Agrifood Sector," in *Russian Economy in 2001: Trends and Perspectives*, No. 23 (Moscow: April 2002).
[107] OECD (2007).
[108] *Rossiiskii Statisticheskii Ezhegodnik* (2006).
[109] Rossiiskii statisticheskii ezhegodnik (2005), p. 661.
[110] *Rossiiskii statisticheskii ezhegodnik* (2005), p. 669.

TABLE 6.4. *Fertilizer Consumption in kg per Hectare, Selected Countries (1996–1998)*

Belgium-Luxembourg	383
Denmark	24
Germany	242
Spain	147
France	271
Ireland	514
Italy	217
Netherlands	554
Finland	144
Sweden	107
United Kingdom	358
European Union (15)	232
Russian Federation	17
Hungary	93
Poland	115
Romania	39
Slovakia	75
Latvia	19
Estonia	25
Lithuania	45
Bulgaria	42
Czech Republic	105

Source: FAOSTAT (2001).

TABLE 6.5. *Government Investment in Agriculture, 1991–2000*

	1991	1992	1993	1994	1995	1999	2000
Government capital investment in agriculture in constant prices, base year 1991 (billions of rubles)	37.4	13.0	8.1	3.9	Na	Na	Na
Government investment in agriculture as a percentage of total capital investment	17.8	10.8	7.9	5.0	3.5	3.0	3.0
Tractors supplied to agriculture (thousands)	131.4	65.4	39.5	22.1	8	17	23
Grain combines supplied to agriculture (thousands)	31.7	17.3	14.3	9.1	4.4	3	1

Sources: Sel'khoz (1995), pp. 34, 37; (1998), p. 19; (2000), p. 21; *Agropromyshlennyi kompleks* (2001), pp. 16–17.

The number of corporative farms decreased from 25,800 in 1990 to 19,000 in 2005. The average work force diminished from 322 to 139 per farm. Average size, in hectares of arable, shrank from 4,300 to 2,600, still very large. Further rationalization is the key task continuing to be important for the government.

One reason that large-scale farms continue to exist is that support policies are still tailored to the needs of large farming and to channels of centralized supply. The tractor leasing scheme is an example. Leasing funds in 1996 were used to distribute fertilizer, seeds, and pedigree cattle, in addition to tractors, crowding out competition in highly profitable upstream activities.[111] Another is that no technology for more modest-scale farms was generally available. The provision of new capital throughout the Soviet era was designed for large-scale farming. By creating larger-scale production capacity, the regime relied on the integration of capacity for producing large machinery and output of ever-larger machinery and larger-capacity plants while eliminating production of small and medium-scale machines. Management was also geared toward large scale.

A third factor for the tenacious hold of very large farms on production is their technological dependence on subsectors supplying them, particularly machinery inputs. This means dependence on branch orders rather that demand. In a market economy, the firm, or farm, not the state, does the purchasing, and technologies are purchased that can be used across the firm's activities. The farming sector functions in market economies under conditions of on-farm diversification. When purchasing equipment is unrealistic, there is close integration through cooperative input supply and inter-farm cooperation. For example, there is integration of dairy and crop production, cooperative banking, and tailoring of seed production across counties to on-farm experimentation.

In other words, by technological legacy in agriculture, input supply is still separated by production unit. Since cost advantage for cereals production dictates planning for other parts of farming, this means that critical knowledge spillovers from one branch of farming to another are diminished, since different branches are supplied by different factors to different farm locations. This legacy is particularly damaging to production efficiency in transition.

Agricultural Research and Extension in Transition. Research and extension were initially treated dismissively in transition. Agricultural research and extension were a previous priority now to be cut, along with other branches of state-supported science. In general, innovation was initially funded mostly by a voluntary tax on firms, while the total budget for science was dramatically reduced from what it had been in the Communist regime,

111 Leonard and Serova (2000).

and this affected academic agricultural research as well as linkages between farms and laboratories. In addition to being a low priority, the government did not have a sense of what public and private benefits should be weighed in support for the sector. For example, not only seed research but also seed multiplication remained a government-funded area.[112]

Slowly, policy leaders are focusing on how to foster biotechnological innovation. Inappropriate levels of current funding prolong its failure to be applied as a priority for development of Russian seeds and breeds. The power of biotechnology to enable rapid and precise manipulation of plant and animal genetics has increased remarkably. To be sure, the global promise of biotechnological discoveries beginning in the early 1980s was not entirely borne out by subsequent research, but there is considerable progress in upstream biological sciences and the pretechnology agricultural sciences in locating genes for particular characteristics. In field crops, insect resistance and herbicide tolerance/resistance were achieved, especially after the 1987 ruling in the United States that nonhuman animals were patentable. In the United States there was legislation to assist transfer of technology between federal laboratories and private industries. However, many innovations have externalities, such as air and water pollution, soil erosion, genetic vulnerability, and loss of diversification.[113] In Europe, as in Russia, widespread concern over the nature of applications halted much research into genetic modification. In Russia, only in the past few years has the Ministry of Agriculture actively begun to organize conferences and encourage linkages between biotechnological experts and agribusiness.[114]

4 CONCLUSION AND SUMMARY: THE SOVIET AND POST-SOVIET TRANSITIONS IN TECHNOLOGY

The Soviet farming experiment was technologically driven, from tractorization to territorial industrial complexes. Labor productivity responded well to this approach. Under labor-augmenting technologies, especially during the massive reinvestment under Brezhnev, there was continual output increase. However, the investment in technological improvement failed to exert much upward pressure on TFP, and the Soviet system was criticized widely for lacking an adequate incentive system for innovation and bottom-up decision making. Was this critique right?

One problem with Soviet farming is that the linkage between households and innovation was entirely broken. This linkage, imparting skills and knowledge across generations, is critically important for factor productivity

112 "O semenovodstve," Federal'nyi Zakon, No 149-FZ, December 17, 1997.
113 Huffman and Evanson (1993), pp. 254–56.
114 V. Vladimirov, "Bioprogress," Sankt-Peterburgskie vedomosti, April 8, 2003, p. 4.

and thus for the pace of agricultural growth. The responsibility for finding innovations was given to farm managers during the era of state and collectivized production, turning households into more limited operators in the village.

Another problem was the ideological suppression of biological research. Under Stalin, farm experimentation was directed in non-genetic directions. To this problem was added the spatial dimension that agricultural research was being tested in sites remote from local decision making, and extension did not adequately bridge that spatial gap. Original biological research, suppressed under Stalin, did not recover independence under Khrushchev. Russian farm experimentation remained apart from world developments, including the biotechnological methods for improving agriculture, methods that had a revolutionary impact on yields in the West.

The Khrushchev era did remove some barriers in the realm of price incentives. However, ill-advised experiments with large-scale crops and the continuation of Stalin's centralization of command in farming were not helpful. The 1970s and 1980s reinvestment policies did not succeed in easing major coordination problems. Markets were fostered, not for the main commodities, cereals and industrial crops, but for vegetables and livestock. Most important, central plans emphasized the modernization of existing facilities over new plants and improved equipment. The development of natural resources as renewable and sustainable was not part of economic planning; the economy was led into a Ricardian trap.[115]

This chapter has shown the degree to which both the technological benefits and drawbacks of Soviet central planning left a long shadow on Russian agriculture in transition. The link between households, cereals production, and the market has not been restored after decades of central planning. Inherited patterns of farm machinery production and use encourage the preservation of corporative farms. Dependencies along the production chain dominate new supply relations, tightly network the farm lobby, and exclude prospective small farmers.

The vertically integrated corporations, the so-called asphalt farmers such as Gazprom, which have access to capital and land, have flourished in this context. These companies introduce foreign technology and highly effective production routines.[116] The advances of these farms and their increasing share of the agricultural sector output will affect numerous other developments across the sector, crowding out smaller farms and encouraging even

115 See Allen (2001) for a recent review. Research was not directed at meeting the needs of business, firms did not gain from innovation due to pricing that passed on gains to consumers, that the emphasis of production was output targets, leaving weak incentives to innovate. Allen emphasizes positive results of experimentation in the period before Brezhnev: when spending on the military increased during the Brezhnev era, TFP began to decline.

116 Dmitrii Rylko, "Nastuplenie Asfaltovyikh Fermerov," *Ekspert*, November 15, 1999.

more the demand for farm equipment that meets the needs of super farms while also meeting consumers' needs for cheaper food.

These giant corporations make general prospects for Russian technological improvement very positive, whatever the distributional consequences. Moreover, since the economy is increasingly open – negotiations toward World Trade Organization (WTO) membership improve enforcement of regulations and allow only a small measure of protectionism, at a relatively low level by comparison with levels in Europe and the United States. Russian technological advancement will benefit from exchange and competition. Intensive borrowing of agricultural research results in the European market economies between 1973 and 1993 led them to convergence, and the same source will produce convergence in Russian performance to European levels. Finally, the Russian government, especially under President Medvedev, has made efforts to apply bankruptcy laws and impose restructuring requirements on large corporative entities; the challenge will be for the government to find nondistortive ways to assist access to technology for others.

7

Reform and Long-Run Productivity Growth, 1861–2010

INTRODUCTION

Were Russia's agrarian institutions resistant to change in periods following reform? One way to address this question is by examining the numbers: what information do indicators of agricultural performance provide about rates of change before and after reforms? By assessing institutional response one may ask, for example, was the second major reform as necessary as it seemed to Stolypin? That is, were Russia's transformed agrarian institutions after serf emancipation adjustable and effectively responding to markets? Using total factor productivity (TFP) as the main performance indicator, this chapter presents new evidence for the tsarist period and reviews published estimates for the Soviet and post-Soviet eras to assess the pace of change over the short and long run.

The annual rate of change in TFP is used here because it is comparable over time – a valuable quality for such different regimes – and it is revealing of the potential of skills, new knowledge and organizational change to bring about improvements in the sector. Positive agricultural TFP growth lowers food prices, thereby stabilizing welfare as economies grow, while releasing resources for use in more productive sectors and bringing capital into the country via exports of grain. Partial factor productivities – the ratio of total output to a single input, generally land or labor, can be used when there is concern with specific processes.[1] The productivity of labor and land, for example, can be estimated by using, respectively, labor-hours and sown acreage as input variables in the ratio with output. Partial productivities without reference to factor endowments and available technologies,

[1] Yields, the partial productivity of land (see Appendix 3), are widely published and used in estimates.

however, can be misleading.[2] This chapter therefore introduces TFP estimates allowing comparisons of performance over countries and across time.

TFP in agriculture is an embracing measure generally associated with a translog production function, in which improvement caused by changes in efficiency, the scale of production and/or technical change, that is, the increase in production not accounted for by the growth in the quantity of inputs used is counted as a residual. For modern agriculture, it is a standard measure; it has been reported by the United States Department of Agriculture (USDA) for US agriculture annually since 1960.[3] Most recent studies of agricultural TFP (Ali 2004, Evenson, Pray and Rosegrant 1999) use the Tornqvist-Theil Index (TTI), which is a discrete approximation of the Divisia Input Index based on a time varying weighting scheme. There are many advantages of the TTI. It imposes no restrictions on substitution possibilities between inputs, and, since it employs current factor prices in constructing weights, it accounts for changes in quality of inputs. The statistical methods used here are discussed in more detail in Appendix 1.

The challenge in estimating long run TFP for Russian agriculture lies in the data requirements. For many periods of Russian history, as in the contemporary developing world, information about costs and quantities is fragmentary. The gaps in data and solutions used here for the tsarist period are elaborated in greater detail in Appendix 1.[4] For the Soviet era, the key data problems also include reliability. Efforts to find solutions are explained in works cited by period below. For the latest period, that of the Russian Federation, or the transition to a market economy, gaps and reliability of all aggregates are severe problems. Volatile macroeconomic conditions in the early Yeltsin period make the longitudinal series dependent upon the base year. Indicators of land use and many other aggregates are still not highly reliable. Analytical works, cited below, provide various estimates, which are presented as a reasonable range.

[2] An example from Clalyton (1980), p. 452, is for the Soviet era. Partial productivity estimates will result in contrasting pictures: that private agriculture was more productive than socialized labor because output per hectare was higher, and the reverse, that private agriculture was less productive because output per worker was lower. Both judgments should be qualified by the circumstance that raising livestock on private plots was a land-saving production choice determined in large part by the land constraint (0.5 hectares), and cereals in the socialized sector were land-using and labor-saving, and they were exported to the private sector.

[3] The USDA Economic Research Service (ERS) provides factor productivity (TFP) measures based on a system of farm production accounts (see www.ers.usda.gov/Data/AgProductivity. Its TFP model uses the transcendental logarithmic (translog) transformation frontier. It relates the growth rates of multiple outputs to the cost-share weighted growth rates of labor, capital, and intermediate inputs. See Ball (1997, 1999) for a complete description of the USDA model.

[4] The author gratefully acknowledges research assistance by Dr. Dilyara Ibragimova of the Moscow Institute of Social Research who provided initial estimates of labor, land, agricultural equipment, and fertilizer for the years 1870 to 1913.

To summarize the conclusions, this chapter finds a strong although delayed effect of the two major "incentive" reforms, serf emancipation and privatization in the 1990s. Three others likely had a weaker but still visible effect: the Stolypin reforms, the NEP and the Khrushchev era reforms. None of the latter three regimes lasted very long – in part due to the perceived failure of reforms – which permits only short-run indicators, which are not very satisfying. They point to the impact of technological change or price shifts, or both, but it would be difficult to determine exactly in the short run.

This chapter, like those preceding it, follows a chronological order. The first part concerns tsarist agriculture, the second the Soviet-era performance and the last, agriculture in the transition period.

I DYNAMICS OF TSARIST AGRICULTURAL PERFORMANCE

Controversy over Russia's Rural Backwardness: The Tsarist Era

The crop output dynamics for the entire empire are as clear to economic historians as they will ever be. P. Gregory (1980, 1982) shows a high rate of growth of grain output relative to contemporary countries in Europe of 3.1 percent annually between 1885 and 1913.[5] He finds that Russia produced more grain than any other country in 1861, and in 1913, was second only to the US.[6] Urban consumption was rising at 4.2 annually, and rural consumption by 2.6 percent between 1885 and 1900 (1980, pp. 56–57, 162, 127–129, 131).[7] J. Metzer (1974) shows from trade data that price gaps were falling at that time between Russia's ports and that there was an increasing dispersion of the production of wheat and rye after the 1870s in Russia. From trade data, Goodwin and Grennes (1998) show evidence of Russia's integration with world cereals markets. Finally, B. Mironov and B. A'Hearn (2008) and Mironov (2010) use anthropometric evidence to show from heights that there could scarcely have been an agrarian crisis in the 1890s (Mironov and A'Hearn 2008). Other scholars who made substantial contributions and concur with this view include O. Crisp (1976), J. Simms (1977), P. Gatrell (1986), S. Wheatcroft (1990), M. Harrison (1990), and S. Hoch (1991, 1994, 2004).

This bright picture of Russian agriculture at the end of the century rests on such persuasive quantitative economic estimates, that Hoch (1994, pp. 52–53) summarizes the state of the controversy among economic historians as follows:

[5] Some of this was presumably the reduction of waste, that is, the increase in the ratio of net to gross production; see Gregory (1982), pp. 75–76.

[6] Gregory (1982), p. 158.

[7] See also Mironov (2006), pp. 541–546.

The evidence is now overwhelming regarding long-term trends in peasant grain production and yields-leaving little life in the pessimist view. Increased per capita cereal production during the last 30 years of the empire has been demonstrated by Goldsmith, Nifontov, Gregory, Lowe and Wheatcroft. Their findings are supported by Kahan, Bideleux and Gatrell, though these studies are not based upon original analysis. The position of Gerschenkron and Volin among others is no longer tenable, and the recent attempt by Shanin to resurrect it has been properly criticized by Bushnell. Nor is the seemingly more optimistic view new. As many of the above scholars have pointed out, both V. M. Obukhov and V. G. Mikhailovskii, writing in the 1920s, were in accord.

In the view of social historians, however, this was an era of revolutionary ferment. Social historians are still likely to characterize peasants' experience by deepening poverty and landlessness, which contributed to rural unrest and led to the revolutionary environment in the summer of 1917. Their sources for this view represent the writings of government officials, social historians, memoirists and populist writers, who depict a worsening "agrarian crisis" beginning in the 1890s. V. I. Lenin in *The Development of Capitalism in Russia* (1899) blamed "rural capitalism" for the crisis, focusing on the income gap, the emergence of class divisions or polarization as markets strengthened.[8] Lenin and later Soviet Marxist historians compiled evidence of a restive peasantry in their works, drawing together relatively fragmentary data on social history. To most social historians, the analysis presented by Goldsmith and Gerschenkron, even if only for the fifty provinces of European Russia, is essentially right in this regard.

The first part of this chapter reviews the Goldsmith-Gerschenkron data for the fifty provinces of European Russia and introduces adjustments based on Nifontov (1974) and contemporary sources. It notes, as Hoch and Gregory do, the Soviet-era works that undermine the gloomy view of the rural economy, such classics as Kafengaus and Varzar (1994 [1929]); Strumilin (1960); Nifontov (1974); Koval'chenko and Milov (1974); Bovykin et al. (1984, 1989); Rashin (1940). Perhaps best known among these scholars, I. D. Koval'chenko in particular showed the regional and structural variance of tsarist Russia's bimodal agriculture that explains the positive direction of change. Russian agriculture was increasingly dominated by a commercialized sector driven by large and fairly advanced "Prussian style" estates, in contrast with the still backward small peasant farming.[9] Many Soviet historians, in other words, argued for a more complex picture of agricultural expansion than was customarily produced. To be sure, on a per capita basis, the Russian peasant economy lagged far behind that of US and

8 Leonard, "Postscript" (1989), pp. 507–514.
9 See Koval'chenko (1982).

TABLE 7.1. *Annual Quantity Growth Rate of Output in Tsarist Russia by Decade, Cereals, Potatoes (in puds), and Livestock (head, slaughter rate, 40%), Fifty Provinces of European Russia (%)*

	4 Main Grains and Potatoes	4 Main Grains, Excluding Potatoes	Livestock
1860s	1.20	0.70	0.00
1870s	2.62	2.34	0.54
1880s	0.97	0.94	1.36
1890s	2.12	0.67	2.34
1900s	3.73	2.97	−0.28

Western Europe in 1913.[10] Therefore, agriculture grew from a low base. However, this condition meant that technological change of even a limited kind was of paramount importance for welfare.

The objective here is to attempt to establish levels of outputs and inputs in order to explore the nature of change. Robert Allen (2003) observes that even if agricultural output rose after the 1890s, agriculture remained a bottleneck in overall growth. Output increase by itself, naturally, does not necessarily show that agricultural productivity growth was strong or self-sustaining in late pre-revolutionary Russia.[11] The following discussion of the data tests that assumption.

The Fifty European Provinces of Russia: Long-run Outcomes of Serf Emancipation

For the decade of the 1860s, the cereals sector stagnated and thereafter followed an uneven course before picking up in the late 1880s through the 1900s. Regions of particularly strong growth, such as southern Russia, made up for the weaker and unreliable harvests of the central and northeastern parts of the country.[12] The increase in biological learning along trade routes from South to North seems the obvious pattern.

Table 7.1 shows aggregates representing the annual rate of quantity growth for cereals and livestock output by decadal averages.

The Table 7.1 shows a striking rise in cereals output growth rates for the 1870s and then, again, in the 1890s and after 1900s. Livestock production was characteristically weak except in the 1880s and 1890s, with figures

[10] Gregory (1982), p. 158.

[11] Allen (2003, p. 34): "The nineteenth century sources of growth had run their course, and the most important had reversed direction. The prime mover behind the agricultural expansion had been the rise in the price of wheat."

[12] Friesen (2004).

TABLE 7.2. *Annual Rate of Quantity Growth in Tsarist Russia of Cereals (by Crop) and Potatoes (in puds), Fifty Provinces of European Russia, 1861–1911 (%)*

Decade	Wheat	Rye	Oats	Barley	Potatoes
1860s	0.70	0.70	0.70	0.70	4.54
1870s	2.67	1.39	3.72	2.55	4.00
1880s	1.43	0.59	0.85	2.16	1.08
1890s	3.21	0.41	−2.49	4.66	7.04
1900s	4.41	1.67	3.04	4.17	5.40

adjusted for the change in the method of reporting. The Table 7.2 shows estimates by crop.

The rate of increase in wheat output, according to Table 7.2, accelerated during a period of a steady fall in European prices in the late nineteenth century, showing the importance for wheat production of inter-regional price variance (Mironov 2010). The increase in production of oats suffered a major downturn in the 1890s; rye, like oats, underwent two decades of relative stagnation, but the other grain export, barley, grew steadily across the decades, and potato production mostly boomed. To summarize, with the exception of potatoes, for a decade following the great reform, conditions were punishing, but the 1870s brought an upturn, and at the turn of the century, improvement was marked. Averages for the 1890s are brought down by the severe famine in 1891 and drought in 1892 and 1892, affecting the central blacksoil, the lower Volga, North Caucasus and Ukraine (Kahan 1989, p. 140).

The Data

A study on the long run requires data for the entire period, not just from 1883, which is the starting year for most statistical work because of the improved quality of the reports. For the database here, missing data for early years are eased by taking averages around decades: 1860s, 1870s, through 1911 and by further reasonable adjustments. Net crop output for 1911, for example, is an average of 1909–1913, instead of 1910–1912, because of the unusually low harvest of 1911, and a similar treatment adjusts for harvest failure in 1891. Some extrapolations follow the approach set out in Gallman (1972), whose assumptions about early to mid-nineteenth century US agricultural production are also useful for nineteenth-century Russia.

Data issues are treated in Appendix 1, but general remarks here are needed for background. The key issue is data for the 1860s and 1870s, when grain output figures must be drawn from appendices to the governor general annual reports, not as reliable a source as the agricultural survey data available after 1881.[13] Another problem is finding data on farm input cost and output by product throughout the nineteenth century. What is available for European and US farming in the 1860s and 1870s is a minimum: gross production (net of seed), value-added for all farm activities, livestock raising and sales, and sales of other products produced by the farm. For the US, surveys provide exacting accounts of income, including returns from cleared and uncleared land and farm investment, beginning roughly in 1840.[14] For Russia, income data has only two components: gross production of crops (including the four main grains (wheat, rye, oats, barley) and potatoes, from which seeds and waste are subtracted for net production,[15] and livestock sales. The slaughter and sale of livestock are estimated at 40 percent of heads of mature cattle, as is done elsewhere.[16] Livestock herds are estimated by regression from numbers provided for the last decades of the tsarist regime by Vainshtein (1960).[17] For Russia, input costs can be estimated for land, labor, machinery, fertilizer, and livestock and crop inventories (valued by rental rates). Cereal prices were taken from Mironov (1985); animal prices were from Koval'cheno and Milov (1974), and other prices from published sources and secondary works as noted in the Appendix.

One issue emerging from data limitations is that the production process cannot be fully captured in a model of Russian agriculture. The typical farm? There is enviable clarity in the following note by a US historian:

> To derive an index of labor inputs consistent with our capital and land indexes, we must consider the trend of labor inputs per average farm. Because the typical farm was a family concern, average labor input per farm was dominated by family size.[18]

In Russia, peasant production was still communalistic, reflecting economic and social dependency and incomplete household control over production

[13] From 1883 to 1915, the Central Statistical Committee (TsSK) sent two sets of forms to each locality, requesting information about yields and sown areas by crops from both peasants' allotments and nobles' fields. From this information, the TsSK estimated harvests, or gross output, using population data to provide information on per capita yields. Obukhov (1927), p. 1.

[14] See, for example, Towne and Rasmussen (1960).

[15] For 1861, from Vil'son (1869, pp. 107–112); for 1871, 1881, 1891, 1900, from Nifontov, and for 1911, from the source [*Svod statistiko-ekonomicheskikh.*] and Nifontov's estimate of seed ratios for 1900; see Nifontov (1974), pp. 155, 157, 183, 185, 187. This estimate was compared with Dubrovskii's (1975, p. 220) lower "net" production crop figures, showing that taking the seed/yield ratio from Nifontov for 1900 did not understate net harvests.

[16] Gallman (1972), p. 204, n. 25, cites Samuel Blodgett *Economica, A Statistical Manual for the United States of America* (1806; reprint ed., New York: Augustus M Kelley, 1964), p. 90, for his estimate of a 40 percent slaughter rate. This nineteenth century estimate is plausible for Russia at a similar period.

[17] Hoch (1994), n. 35, cites the literature on the dispute over the number of livestock in tsarist Russia.

[18] Ball and Walton (1976), p. 108.

TABLE 7.3. *Historical Rates of Average Annual Change in Total Factor Productivity in Agriculture, Selected Countries*

Area	Year	Number of Countries	Average
After 1700			
US[a]	1700s	1	0.2–0.3
Britain[b]	1790–1815	1	0.2
Britain[c]	1800–1850	1	0.5
Britain[c]	1860–1914	1	0.4
France[d]	1789–1840	1	0.45
France[d]	1840–1870	1	0.81
France[d]	1815–1914	1	0.85
US[e]	1800–1850	1	0.14
US[e]	1850–1900	1	0.80
Africa	1821–1875	1	3.41
After 1870			
Europe	1870–1910	15	0.78
Europe	various	10	0.71
Western settlement	various	2	0.70
Asia	various	3	1.24
Africa	1875–1912	1	0.83

[a] Ball and Walton (1976).
[b] Hueckel (1981), p. 192.
[c] Allen (1994), O'Grada (1994), cited in Grantham (1997), p. 389.
[d] Grantham (1997), p. 391.
[e] Gallman (1972).
Sources: G. Federico (2005), p. 77; Ball and Walton (1976); Hueckel (1981), p. 192; Allen (1994); O'Grada (1994); Grantham (1997); Gallman (1972).

decisions. This means that the typical unit for sampling would be a commune. However, an autonomous form of farming was rapidly emerging, and a sampling of communes would not capture this complexity.

Comparisons

Agricultural modernization was well on its way in Europe and North America by the third quarter of the nineteenth century. Some comparison is useful to place the pace of change in Russia in a broader context. Table 7.3, drawn on data from various sources, shows the range by countries and time periods.

Annual rates of change for the period examined here, as seen in Table 7.3, were about .78 percent in Europe and the US. Before 1870, the change in the US and Europe is attributed mainly to the introduction of multiple crop

TABLE 7.4. *Cereals and Potato Shares in Quantity (Weight) of Crop Output (in puds), Fifty Provinces of European Russia, 1861–1911 (%)*

	Crop					
Years	Wheat	Rye	Oats	Barley	Potatoes	Total
1859–1861	14	44	23	07	11	100
1869–1871	14	42	22	07	16	100
1879–1881	14	37	25	07	18	100
1889–1993	14	36	24	07	18	100
1899–1901	16	30	15	09	29	100
1909–1913	17	25	14	10	34	100

rotations, better plowing and greater knowledge about seeds and soils.[19] After 1870, productivity improvement is also due to wider use of fertilizers and more advanced equipment.

Outputs

Goldsmith reported no significant shift among crops. Here, the shift is fairly clear toward the production of more wheat and barley from 16 percent in the 1870s and the 1880s to 26 percent by the end of the first decade of the twentieth century.[20] Strengthening grain markets encouraged less production of rye. Regions that could produce only rye declined steadily in agricultural importance. The nutritious (and heavy) potato climbed to 34 percent in weight of the quantity of crop outputs. Table 7.4 shows production shifts by crop shares including potatoes.

The Table 7.5 excludes potatoes to emphasize shares of the four main grains, showing the proportion of rye dropping by 12 percent and that of wheat and barley rising.

In regard to income, or revenue shares of output, a determination generally requires budget surveys, but one can roughly say for these data, that estimates for earnings from the slaughter of livestock attain an average of 35 percent of peasant income, which fits closely with published estimates of 31 percent in household budget surveys the late tsarist era.[21] A highly variable but valuable asset, livestock's share had a substantial weight in overall performance indicator, as shown in percentages in Table 7.6.

[19] Grantham (1997).

[20] Goldsmith's failure to find the evidence, introduced here, of production shifts contributed to his pessimism, as in the following remark Goldsmith (1961), p. 445: "Although there are no reliable figures to measure the extent of the shift in the relative importance of crops between 1860 and World War I, it does not appear that it was spectacular."

[21] Dubrovskii (1975), p. 258.

TABLE 7.5. *Cereal Output Shares, Excluding Potatoes, Quantity (Weight) of Crop Output (in puds), Fifty Provinces of European Russia, 1861–1911 (%)*

	Crop				
Year	Wheat	Rye	Oats	Barley	Total Cereals
1859–1861	16	50	26	08	100
1869–1871	16	50	26	08	100
1879–1881	17	45	30	08	100
1989–1893	17	44	30	09	100
1899–1901	22	43	22	13	100
1909–1913	26	38	22	15	100

These output and income share estimates are missing yet one further source of support for the household, which in the developing world can be critical for the household: remittances of migrant workers. Throughout the period, households derived considerable supplementary income from outwork. P. Ryndziunskii (1978, p. 172) calculates for the rich agricultural region, as much as one-third to one-half of household income from outwork, and in the northern parts of the country almost all of income was from that source. As in the developing world, this would have encouraged the extended family dwellings and high fertility rate observed in Russia. The estimates from the database compiled for this study show this striking dynamic, as in Figure 7.1.

With the internal market for grain rapidly accelerating, the depiction of rural Russia in crisis and households unable to purchase grain does not, for many regions, hold up.

Remarks about the Standard of Living

The classical study on the living standard in tsarist Russia is by Stephen Hoch (1994), who cautions against assuming Malthusian growth. The growth of

TABLE 7.6. *Revenue Shares of Output, Fifty Provinces of European Russia, 1861–1911 (Current Rubles, %)*

Year	Cereals and Potatoes	Livestock, Slaughter Rate, 40%
1859–1861	61	39
1869–1871	66	34
1879–1881	73	27
1889–1893	71	29
1899–1901	53	47
1909–1913	65	35

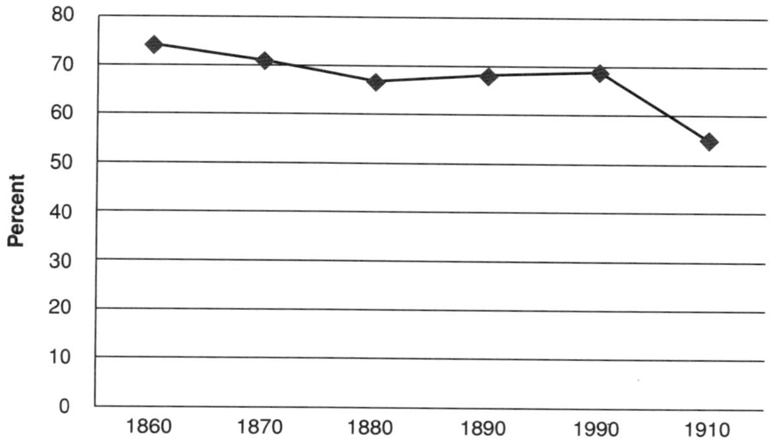

FIGURE 7.1. Off-Farm Earnings as a Percent of Farm Income in Russia, 1860–1910.

population (European Russia) was on average 1.5 percent a year rising to 2 percent by the end of the period under study. In the last two decades, the rate of growth of agricultural production as estimated by Gregory by far exceeded the rate of growth of the population, whereas Gerschenkron and Goldsmith's estimates for the smaller territory of European Russia show it failed to keep up with population increase. Here, for the smaller territorial unit covered by the data, rates of growth for some decades lie between those of Gregory and those of Goldsmith and Gerschenkron. There are so many questions regarding the data for this epoch, however, that a close regional analysis is required.

Inputs – Labor

Labor estimates are derived from percentages of the number actually engaged in agriculture out of those employed in the sector. Those "engaged in agriculture" compared roughly to estimates used by Goldsmith, from whom we took the number of agricultural labourers for 1881. Number of days worked per year, for selected years, we took from B. Mironov,[22] and for 1907 from A. Chayanov, and from A. Chelintsev we derived information about actual expenditure of time on agriculture, from which we constructed a trend.[23] Then we take the average daily wage (for sowing, hay making and threshing) from Strumilin in kopecks per day.[24]

22 1855, 1872, 1902, from Mironov (2003), 2:308.

23 For 1907, Chayanov et al. (1966), pp. 73–77 and Chelintsev (1919), p. 126. The trend for working days spent per year in agriculture estimated from the polynominal regression model, y = −0.0096*t^2 − 0.2226*t + 134.3.

24 Strumilin (1958), p. 277.

TABLE 7.7. *Labor Quantity (Average Annual Increase by Decade), Fifty Provinces of European Russia, 1860s–1900s (%)*

Decade	Rate of Growth of Labor Days
1860s	1.1
1870s	0.6
1880s	0.2
1890s	−0.3
1900s	−0.5

Estimating wages, which we assume to be an adequate reflection of the factor share of income, would ordinarily require some discussion of problems with cost-of-living indexes. However, since our method rests on current prices, deflaters are not of concern here. In terms of quantity (labor days), the Table 7.7 shows the annualized growth rate of agricultural labor, which began to decline in the 1890s.

Equipment and Capital Structures

Agricultural equipment includes imported and domestically produced machines. Data on the value of imported agricultural machinery exists for almost the entire period in current prices.[25] Far more fragmented, for domestic agricultural machinery production, we used Lenin (1876, 1879, 1890 and Obruchev for the 1860s), Khromov (1950), Kaufman (2000 [1915]) and Kafengauz (1910) for later periods. The Table 7.8 shows the rate of growth of the value (rubles) of equipment in the imperial period deflated by the TTI.

The table may tentatively be used to show the dramatic introduction of improved equipment following serf emancipation, although until the last years of the century, this surely reflected mainly the adoption of the iron-tipped plow. After the turn of the century, the improvement of equipment included more advanced instruments for improvement of the soil and the production process. For capital structures, Gregory's estimates of the value of capital structures in agriculture are an overestimate for the fifty provinces; in any case, structures were very limited in number and quality. Procedures

[25] For 1865–1867 we used data from Obruchev (1871); for 1869–1896 we relied on Lenin's figures Lenin (1952), 1: i; for 1901–1913, Oganovskii and Kondratiev (1923). To construct a trend (based on a regression model), we used Vainshtein's data for 1910–1913 as a baseline.

TABLE 7.8. *Annual Rate of Growth by Decade of Equipment Consumption, Fifty Provinces of European Russia, 1861–1911 (%)*

Decade	Annual Rate of Growth, %
1860s	10.0
1870s	6.4
1880s	5.1
1890s	5.4
1900s	23.5

for estimating quantity when only aggregate value is known (Gardner 2002, p. 39), I derive a price index from early and late period ruble amounts spent on the same structures used in production, and, from the formula (PQ/P = Q), derive quantity. The rate of increase that appears plausible is as follows in Table 7.9.

Mineral Fertilizers

By the 1840s, experiments with guano were carried out in Europe, and although they remained expensive until the 1890s, mineral fertilizers also supplemented natural fertilizer in Europe after the 1890s, including in Russia. It was used especially on industrial crops. By 1913, the 6.9 kilograms per hectare were far less than levels used in 1913 in Belgium (65), Germany (47) and the Netherlands (146) (Van Zanden 1991, p. 231) Dubrovskii

TABLE 7.9. *Annual Rate of Growth by Decade of Capital Structures, Russian Empire, 1861–1911 (%)*

Decade	Rate of Growth
1860s	0.000
1870s	−1.698
1880s	5.603
1890s	9.872
1900s	0.045

Source: Extrapolated from tables in Gregory (1982), Appendix J, pp. 289–91.

TABLE 7.10. *Annual Rate of Growth of Consumption of Mineral Fertilizers (Imported and Domestically Produced, Tornqvist-Theil Price Index), Fifty Provinces of European Russia, 1860s–1900s (%)*

Decade	Annual Rates of Growth, Consumption of Mineral Fertilizers in Russia
1860s	0.0
1870s	0.0
1880s	50.9
1890s	22.4
1900s	15.0

(1975, p. 266).[26] However, Russian estimates are less in contrast to 8 for the US, another land abundant country.

Prices of different mineral fertilizers can be obtained from trade and customs records for 1900 to 1913, but for this study, the distinction is not made. In further research, these kinds of fertilizer (like machinery) would be disaggregated.[27] In 1900, the value of imported fertilizer was 4.1 million rubles (1913 prices), and by 1913, in fixed prices, 15.2 million rubles, an average annual rate of growth of 12 percent. The annual average rate of increase of mineral fertilizers used is, by decades, in Table 7.10, reflects falling prices as well as rising consumption.

Crop and Animal Inventories

It is a mistake to exclude crop and animal inventories among capital inputs, as do most tsarist Russian statistical surveys do. Standard technique requires assessing the rent typically charged by item. I used estimates of the percent of crops in inventories (Vil'son's estimates [Vil'son 1869, p. 112] of 11 percent of net output of crops for the 1860s, extended forward). According to standard methods, capital is broken down by quantity and price and then a standard rate of return is used across categories (gross of capital consumption). As in Gallman, I used 5 percent for inventory cereals and livestock stocks (and 5 [for 1861] and 6 percent for later years, in accord with the cost of land in the period)[28], 7 percent for long-lived capital structures, and

[26] Liashchenko (1956), p. 278; see Van Zanden (1991) and O'Brien et al. (1992).
[27] Khromov (1950), p. 164; Oganovskii (1923), pp. 307–308.
[28] Ananich et al. (2005), p. 416.

10 percent for equipment, the differentials expressing roughly the importance of capital consumption. In general, no allowance was made here, as in Gallman, for changing rates of return, due to monetary or real phenomena and due to its presumed lack of importance for this purpose. For the land, since the interest rate was available, I used 5 percent through 1900 and 6 percent afterwards.[29]

Livestock

Livestock data are extremely fragmented, since they were not systematically gathered before the 1880s. In view of the substantial part of cereals, potatoes and industrial crops in Gross Agricultural Output (70 or more percent), the fragility would seem unfortunate but tolerable for the early years. However, the numbers of animal stock probably became more crucial over time. Horsepower was particularly important in production for introducing the three-field and multicrop rotations.[30] Because of the speed of planting and harvesting induced by the high seasonality of production, oxen were almost useless in much of Russia, and horses were the main productive force.

A sense of the state of information about livestock production, based on all the available sources, can be felt in the summary remarks by Davies and Wheatcroft, remarks cited in full because of the importance of the issue to growth calculations:

> Livestock farming was the second most important sector, providing some 34 percent of agricultural production. Our knowledge of its rate of growth in pre-war decades is imperfect. Neither the absolute numbers of livestock nor their rate of increase are known with certainty; and no data are available about changes in the average weight of farm animals in this period. It seems reasonable that livestock numbers increased by only about one percent a year between 1900 and 1914, or more slowly than the growth of population.[31]

Goldsmith also believed that there was so little information on livestock figures that a series could not be supplied.

Actually, as Vainshtein remarked in his article about pre-revolutionary livestock inventories, "statistics regarding livestock numbers for pre-revolutionary Russia suffer not from insufficiency but from an abundance of contradictory materials."[32] In data published after 1908, including a retrospective statistics for the post-Emancipation period, there is a conflict between information gathered by the Veterinary Administration and that gathered by the Central Statistical Committee. A leap in the series occurs at 1896. In 1895, this retrospective series gives 24.5 million heads of cattle,

29 Gallman (1971), p. 205, n. 29;
30 Obruchev (1871), p. 233.
31 Davies and Wheatcroft (1994), p. 109.
32 Vainshtein (1960), p. 87.

TABLE 7.11. *Annual Increase in Quantity of Horses and Livestock, Fifty Provinces of European Russia, 1860s–1900s (%)*

	Annual Rate of Quantity Index	
Decade	Horses	Livestock
1860s	0.0	0.0
1870s	0.1	0.6
1880s	0.2	1.5
1890s	1.4	2.6
1900s	0.7	−0.3

and in 1896, 29.5, or an increase in one year of over 20 percent. We take this to be an error due to the introduction of a new method of counting or statistical problems; Gregory, like Vainshtein, accepts the larger number.[33] Table 7.11 shows the annual average increase in quantity of horses and livestock in our database.

Land

Only after 1884 was the privately owned land, measured in *desiatiny* (see Appendix 1), adequately captured by surveys. Even then, however, estimates were challenged, since peasant communal holdings (including fields rented from the state) were not included in surveys of peasant production; the area of arable presented here is therefore too small, but in view of the necessity of using published sources (see references), it is necessary to use these estimates. Land prices were taken for estimates here from Koval'chenko and Milov.[34] Table 7.12 shows the quantity increase during the period.

Settlement of new lands, as expected, rose rapidly during the decade after the serf emancipation, then slowed as the land in use was improved for two decades. By the 1890s new settlements again pushed forward, slowing somewhat after the turn of the century.

Input Cost Shares

The Table 7.13 presents the cost shares in production of land, labor and capital at current prices for the decadal averages from the serf Emancipation to 1911, after the completion of the Stolypin reforms.

33 For further a discussion of this issue, see Goldsmith (1955) and Gregory (1981), pp. 265–267.

34 1863–1909, Koval'chenko and Milov (1974), pp. 259–267.

TABLE 7.12. *Annual Increase by Decade in Quantity of Land, Fifty Provinces of European Russia, 1860s–1900s (%)*

Decade	Quantity of Land: Annual Rates of Growth (%)
1860s	1.5
1870s	0.3
1880s	0.2
1890s	1.0
1900s	0.8

Increasing amounts of land and capital were brought into the production process, while the cost share of labor fell. Although the initial share of labor seems high, it is not an uncommon estimate for the developing world, where labor intensive agriculture dominates. By the end of this period, resulting from obvious structural changes, the estimates for labor's share are about the same as in nineteenth century US agriculture, and those of land and capital are moving toward the averages in other countries, which itself is suggestive of the amount of change that had occurred. Table 7.14 shows the sources of growth, highlighting the importance of TFP in growth, especially toward the end of the tsarist period.

Conclusion

Table 7.14, based on data that are fragile but consistent in what they represent over time, may be viewed tentatively as evidence of structural change well in advance of the Stolypin reforms, and there is a surge of TFP growth in the 1900s. Across the entire period, the rate of TFP growth per annum averaged roughly 1 percent, which is within the range of rates of growth in Europe and the US presented in Table 7.3. The output growth in the 1870s, 1890s and 1900s is very substantially due to the cultivation of new land,

TABLE 7.13. *Input Cost Shares in Agriculture, Fifty Provinces of European Russia 1861–1911 (%)*

Decade	Capital Share	Land Shares	Labor Shares	
1861	13	05	82	100
1871	11	05	83	100
1881	11	06	83	100
1891	11	10	78	100
1901	13	13	73	100
1911	12	18	70	100

TABLE 7.14. *Sources of Growth in Agriculture, Fifty Provinces of European Russia, 1860s–1900s, Annual Rate of Change in %*

	Decade				
	1860s	1870s	1880s	1890s	1900s
Output Growth	0.56	1.87	1.05	1.62	1.87
Sources of Growth					
Labor	0.76	.04	0.12	−0.21	−0.31
Capital[a1]	0.01	0.07	0.12	0.34	0.13
Land	0.07	1.4	0.10	0.86	0.84
TFP	−0.03	1.40	0.80	1.41	1.97
Average Output Growth, 1861–1910				1.54	
Average Input Growth, 1861–1910				0.34	
Labor				0.15	
Capital[a1]				0.13	
Land				4.02	
Average TFP Growth, 1861–1910				1.06	

Note: Production equals gross farm product minus seed, livestock sales (estimated 40 percent of livestock (as in Gallman 1972).

[a1] Crop inventories were taken as a percent, based on Vil'son (1869, p. 112), and assumed to be constant through 1911, with rent estimated as 5 percent (Gallman 1972). Livestock inventories (horses and 60 percent of production of mature cattle), rental rate estimated at 5 percent for the 1860s, 6 percent thereafter. For 1881–1895, the trend is extrapolated from Vainshtein's (1960, p. 115) estimates by linear regression ($y = 37.667t + 2818.3$); for the 1861 and 1871 period, from the rate of change in Khromov (1950) P.466–67, whose source is *Sborniki statistiko-ekonomicheskikh svedenii po selskomu khozyaistvy Rossii I inostrannykh gosudarstv* (1915, 1917). Equipment consisted of imported and domestically produced farm machinery. Data on equipment was taken from Khromov (1950, pp. 164–5), Kaufman (2000 [1915]), pp. 602–3; and Sbornik (1915), at a return estimated at 10 percent (Gallman 1972). Sources for data on fertilizer, Khromov (1950), pp. 164; Sborniki (1915, 1917), and as noted above. The return on fertilizer, like equipment, is estimated at 10 percent (Gallman 1972).

presumably on the frontier, for the costs of clearing the land must have consumed profits in the early years. The land market grew in the 1870s and again beginning in the 1890s, and peasant households also added rented fields to their meadows and plots.

In this rough depiction of TFP growth, the important point from the perspective of this book is that reform clearly played an important role in agriculture, although with a delay. As can be seen in the timing of the acceleration of TFP growth, industrialization boosted the potential of agriculture, as the cost of capital used in production fell. The unexplained residual, presumably technological change, in agricultural production benefitted in a classic way from general economic growth. It is important, too, that the Russian average annual contribution for TFP over the entire period of roughly 1 percent shows the production process to have been improving in roughly the same pattern at the same time that it was improving in Europe. The spread of new technologies, including biological innovation, was also affecting Russian farming custom.

2 POSTREVOLUTIONARY RUSSIA AND THE SOVIET ERA

The NEP

The drastic effects of revolution, civil war, and famine of 1921–1922 on agriculture are well known. They were only ameliorated well into the new regime when forced requisitions and other harsh measures were relaxed during the New Economic Policy (NEP). Exact estimates of agricultural growth during the NEP cannot be supplied, but gross output would seem to have recovered by 1927; grain output did not. From 1916 to 1920, grain production had declined by about 66 percent of average output between 1913 and 1916, with loss in both sown areas and yields.[35] By 1926, total loss in production of grain per capita from the 1913–1916 average was between 3–6 percent.[36] By 1922, livestock herds had fallen by 30 percent, and livestock previously cultivated on large landlords' estates were reallocated to communes, along with the land, which was nationalized. The loss of horses and draft power in two important producer regions during the famine diminished grain output. From a low base, recovery for some sectors showd rapid progress. Household production, particularly, rapidly recovered.

The rural order under the NEP did not resemble that of late imperial Russia. It was shaped by the massive redistribution scheme, supported by the Bolsheviks in 1918 and begun by the peasants in September and October 1917, who did not wait for the promised socialist land reform to seize lands and burn manorial homes.[37] The communes succeeded in attracting back to their midst the "separators," who had removed their holdings and formed small farms in the Stolypin era. From possibly as much as one/third of all households in 1916, the number of separators shrank in the main agricultural areas of Russia to less than two percent by 1922 (Figes [1991), p. 383). No framework of laws protecting property rights bound the peasantry in the NEP. Its stimulus was not that of the restoration of the Stolypin reforms but the restoration of greater leeway for customary law.

35 Davies and Wheatcroft (1994), p. 110.

36 Wheatcroft (1994), p. 111.

37 Figes (1991), pp. 378–388. In Penza province, one-fifth of the manor houses were destroyed in those two months.

Grain exports grew under this regime from well below the pre-war level in 1921 to more than six million tons in 1923, 1925 and 1926.[38] By 1926–1927 non-grain output probably exceeded its prewar level, with livestock up 17 percent on 1909–1913 levels. High value non-grain output was also increasingly marketized.[39] This development shows, again, as in the tsarist era, that communal agriculture was flexible in response to markets.

It does not show, however, great strides forward, lacking the institutional environment for finance, landownership and labor mobility that led to favorable conditions in the pre-war era Marketings of grain failed to live up to expectations; a domestic grain market did not flourish under the NEP. Government intervention constrained markets. The government taxed well-off peasants, controlled the extent of hired labor and rental agreements between households, and followed an industrial policy that caused peasants to withhold grain from the market or market it in livestock. Grain marketings fell to 17 percent by 1926 from 22 to 25 percent of output.[40] Low official prices further weakened rural participation in rural/urban trade from 1927 on.[41] To be sure, the net resource transfer was probably positive owing to peasant earnings in nonagricultural wage employment and employment in handicrafts and peasant trade. Peasant communities participated widely in the migrant labor market by 1928.

Despite the discouraging level of marketings the NEP produced more than a survivalist response to relaxed conditions after war communism. Output improvement was steady.[42] Improved technologies owed something to past investments of the Stolypin era which had added to effects of the industrial boom on TFP growth. However, the evidence of reduced marketings does suggest a fixed focus by households on sources of income, and this leaves open the verdict on the promises of the NEP for the future. The future role of improved plows and crop rotations cannot be ascertained from NEP conditions. In a more practical sense, for the objectives of this chapter, productivity following the NEP reforms cannot be estimated because of the unreliability of the data.

Collectivization

The relocation of production into large collective and state entities failed to improve production much in the short- and medium-term. A destructive force of farm reorganization swept away successful small farms along with

[38] Hubbard (1939), p. 90; Harrison (1991), p. 110.

[39] Harrison (1991), pp. 110–11.

[40] These figures are from Davies and Wheatcroft (1994), pp. 110–11; see also Gregory (1994), pp. 104–05; Danilov (1977, 1988), Sedik (1994), and Allen (1997).

[41] Harrison (1991), p. 117.

[42] Harrison (1991), pp. 122–23.

the weak more fragmented holdings. The veiled attack on peasant agriculture in general was carried out by slogans regarding, "dekulakization" in 1929–1931. For the first decade of collectivization, output levels were not encouraging.

By the end of the 1930s, however, gross output seemed to have recovered to the level achieved in the mid-1920s. Exact numbers are unavailable, because official declarations were based on correction coefficients and artificially estimated yields, which changed the comparator to offset the decline.[43] The consensus is that by 1940, gross agricultural output (GAO) exceeded production in 1928 by 2.5 percent.[44] Livestock was slower to recover. In the 1930s, herds declined. By 1933, after five years of forced collectivization, herds were only at 64 percent of their 1928 level. In respect to horse power, tractors introduced in the 1930s made up for the loss of working horses: Davies and Wheatcroft estimate from the drop in actual horsepower from twenty-seven million in 1928 to sixteen million in 1933, that recovery reached 26–32 million by 1938.[45] Centralization and expansion of resources also added to the power of knowledge: tens of thousands of personnel, including agronomists and technicians with higher education, were added to the administrative personnel in agriculture. Neither the tractors nor the experts, however, available only as rationed centralized resources, could make up for the loss of on-farm knowledge and initiative after collectivization. The potential for skilling of the actual work force on farm was a largely unrecognized resource, except under Khrushchev, throughout the Soviet era.[46]

By 1940, overall productivity gains were evident in the augmentation of land and labor through mechanization and fertilization. Mechanization augmented the efficiency of labor, since each worker can work more land, and fertilizer application augmented the land supply. The land/labor ratio initially fell, because each worker can produce more output but manage less land. After the 1950s, with far more substantial improvement in fertilization, collectivized agriculture was both labor and land saving, and output per worker rose sharply as the land/labor ratio continued to rise. The figures on output per labor day by N. Nimitz show an increase annually of labor productivity of 2.5 percent, while the standard yield figures for the era, adjusted by R. Davies and S. Wheatcroft estimates for the early 1930s, show the productivity of the land in centners per hectare increasing by 3.6 percent per annum, a momentum maintained at a somewhat lower level for some years afterward.[47]

43 Davies and Wheatcroft (1994), p. 115.
44 Wheatcroft (1994), p. 285.
45 Davies and Wheatcroft (1994), p. 11.
46 Davies and Wheatcroft (1994), p. 123; Clayton (1980).
47 Nimitz (1967), pp. 189–96; Davies and Wheatcroft (2004), Appendix I.

TABLE 7.15. *Average Annual Rate of Growth of Net Agricultural Output, Soviet Union, 1951–1975 (%)*

Year	Straight Annual Average	Three-Year Moving Average
1951–1964	3.8	3.7
1954–1955	2.0	2.4
1956–1959	9.2	8.7
1960–1964	4.2	4.8
1961–1965	2.8	2.8
1966–1970	4.5	3.4
1971–1975	−0.6	...

Sources: Diamond (1966), p. 352; Carey (1976), p. 580.

Khrushchev Reforms and Kosygin/Brezhnev Investment Strategy

Between 1953, the year of Stalin's death, and 1964, the year of Khrushchev's ouster, output significantly expanded. Between 1950 and 1965, it grew by 70 percent, with most of the growth taking place during the second half of the 1950s.[48] D. Diamond (1966) presents the following rates of growth during this key period using a three-year moving average to reduce the effect of annual variations in Table 7.15.

Between 1956 and 1959, the Soviet rate of growth of agricultural output was well above the 2 percent average in the rest of the world and almost twice the rate of growth of U.S. agriculture at that time.[49] Between 1955 and 1963, according to Nimitz, whose calculations embraced labor allocated to subsidiary plots, gardens, and services, as well as to collective and state farms, output per worker improved by 5.3 percent annually. The productivity of land rose almost as steeply as during collectivization. Total land in use increased by 8 percent between 1960 and 1975, although the overall quality probably deteriorated due to the expansion of farming onto marginal soils.[50] Factor productivity rose by 3 percent per annum from 1954 through 1960.

After 1960, however, advancement seriously slowed, and costs of production increased. From 1954–1955, inputs increased by 5 percent per year due in large part to the virgin lands program. Seeking to demonstrate the impact of incentive programs, Khrushchev reduced inputs from 1955 from 5 percent to 1.5 percent per annum, and between 1956 and 1960, output, indeed, rose by 47 percent with only 17 percent more resources. These early gains under Khrushchev possibly were in part due to improved schooling of

48 Diamond (1966), p. 346.
49 Diamond (1983), p. 144.
50 Clayton (1980), p. 453.

the farm labor force, a development particularly marked between 1950 and 1958.[51]

In 1959 and 1960, however, performance faltered. Khrushchev restored high levels of inputs and called for shifts in cultivation techniques, that is, the reduction of clean fallow and intensification of the production of small crops. The reduction of clean fallow had perverse effects, and there was continued weakness in the farm sector, an average decline in productivity between 1961 and 1964 by about 0.2 percent per year. It can be demonstrated that the slowdown from 1960 to 1965 had little to do with weather.[52]

Khrushchev retreated after 1960 from his more liberal policies encouraging the collective farmers. He launched a vigorous new campaign in 1958 against the small private subsidiary plots in the *kholkhoz* sector, possibly convinced that there was no further need to adjust living standards of rural and urban dwellers.[53] Suppressing profit incentives for the *kolkhoz* market, he dampened the production of produce that had reached one-third of GAO. He also eliminated the Machine Tractor Stations, temporarily halting repair services and maintenance and forcing collective farms to purchase their machinery. Retreat from reform was blamed for the failure of the early productivity gains to be sustained under Khrushchev, but decline was a consequence of many factors.[54]

The Kosygin-Brezhnev regime renewed commitment to investment, aiming to improve welfare through support for the food industries. The 1965 reforms, originally designed by Kosygin, used reinvestment to improve the quality of capital stock and to renew high growth in the agricultural sector.[55] As Khrushchev accomplished by his incentive programs, Kosygin and Brezhnev saw substantial initial gains (1966 to 1970), and they rewarded the peasants by further tolerance of the private sector. In a miscalculation, repeating the mistake of the Khrushchev era, however, Brezhnev saw early success as an opportunity to cut inputs for 1967–1969, and disappointing results in 1969 led to higher levels of investment. Inputs increased in 1970 by almost 2.5 percent. Decline continued, however, and in 1971 and 1972 output declined on average by 1.9 percent, and TFP by 3.8 percent.[56] In 1972, output declined further by 6.5 percent. In 1973, there was a record high import of farm products in response to increasing demand.[57] The harvest in 1975 was so poor it complicated the flagship livestock program's feed requirements.[58]

[51] Clayton (1980).
[52] The discussion that follows is from Diamond (1966), pp. 353–55.
[53] Karcz (1966), p. 413.
[54] Diamond (1966), p. 364.
[55] Schroeder (1991), p. 36.
[56] Diamond and Krueger (1973), pp. 317–19.
[57] Net exports, twenty-one million tons, Diamond and Krueger (1973), p. 327.
[58] Carey (1976), p. 581.

TABLE 7.16. *Agricultural as a Percent of Total Employment, Soviet Union, 1913–1950*

	1913	1928	1937	1940	1950
Soviet Union/Russia	75	80	56	54	48

Sources: 1913–1950: *Trud* (1988).

There were no further cuts in inputs under Brezhnev. From 1971 to 1975, investment in agriculture grew two-thirds faster than in other sectors of the economy.[59] By 1975, Russia was the largest producer of tractors in the world.[60] Agricultural advancement was important: it contributed roughly one-fifth of GDP.[61] The early positive supply response under Brezhnev, however, stopped. The Tenth Five-Year Plan (1976–1980), Carey writes, began "with shattered momentum in the agricultural sector, depleted reserves, a population unhappy about food shortages, and an economy that is vulnerable to further setbacks."[62]

Why did agriculture stagnate? Weather, P. Desai wrote, was an important factor, as always, in the volatility of harvests.[63] More important was a failed investment plan. As compared to thirty-eight other countries evaluated in 1970 by Y. Hayami and V. Ruttan, E. Clayton shows the marginal value[64] of land and fertilizer in the Soviet Union to be relatively considerably higher (0.20 compared with 0.06; 0.21 compared with 0.16).[65] For example, if output increased by one unit, fertilizer would increase by 0.21. The marginal value of livestock was less, however (0.05 compared with 0.19), of the average for other countries. Clayton draws the conclusion that the investment strategy was poorly designed.

Factor intensity, Clayton comments, led, in effect, to a full employment program in agriculture. The retention of labor in the traditional sector is visible in Table 7.16 and in comparative perspective in Table 7.17. Percentage employed in agriculture fell sharply between 1928 and 1930 from 80 to 56 percent of employment. They then stabilized and began to decline again after 1950. The following is a general timeline showing period levels of the percentage employed in the sector.[66]

59 Carey (1976), p. 585.
60 Carey (1976), p. 585; the quality of the average tractor was less powerful, to be sure, than U.S. tractors Rubenking (1976), p. 601.
61 Carey (1976), p. 584.
62 Carey (1976), p. 588.
63 Desai (1986).
64 Equal to the regression coefficient, evaluated at the means.
65 Clayton (1980), p. 455; Hayami and Ruttan (1970), p. 901.
66 Narkhoz (1961), p. 567; *Istoriia Krestianstva* (1988); Hunter and Szyrmer (p. 48); Zelenin (1969); Davies (1994) p. 322 (cf. the larger numbers for the rural populace in Davies (1994), p. 277).

TABLE 7.17. *Agricultural as a Percent of Total Employment, Selected Countries, 1950–2010 (Projected)**

	1950	1960	1970	1980	1990	2000	2010
France	31	22	14	8	5	3	2
Germany	23	15	9	7	4	3	2
UK	6	4	3	3	2	2	1
U.S.	12	7	4	3	3	2	2
Soviet Union/ Russia	48	39	35	20/15**	13	10	8

* FAOStat (2008).
** Soviet Union/Russia.

The labor force dramatically diminishes in agriculture in developed market economies, as shown above for the post-World War II era. Technological change is the dominant force in agricultural growth in the United States and Europe, and this allows the release of labor. In the non-market Russian economy, instead, the labor force expanded with modernization of the sector; the working day grew. On state farms, 180–182 days per year per worker was average, but on collective farms, excluding private sector activity, days worked were between 192 and 208.[67] Soviet farms used a far larger labor force than was typical in Western advanced economies.

Khrushchev had hoped to improve labor productivity and to encourage investment. He used Russia's comparative weakness in labor productivity in his 1956 statement to the Central Committee by the reference to comparisons with the United States in regard to labor requirement (hours per "centner") for output of crops and livestock products. In the production of grain, collective farms required more than seven times as much labor, and in the production of cattle (live weight gain), more than sixteen times as much labor.[68]

However, he could not bring down the costs of agriculture while attempting reforms requiring investment. Moreover, his ambitious goals required considerable skilling in agriculture, along with greater farm autonomy, and the latter he did not embrace. So, costs rose, and huge state subsidies resulted in inefficient resource allocation, in view of the relative size of the agricultural sector in the industrialized economy.[69] In regard to state finance, investments resulted in higher yields, still insufficient to meet demand, continually growing in the consumer society. From 1981 to 1985, imports of grain were up to an annual average of forty million tons – despite the

[67] Nimitz (1967). Labor force participation in the state sector was measured in synthetic accounting units, or labor days, which assessed pay on the basis of the arduousness, importance, and skill requirements of tasks. Private-sector activity, although taken down in surveys, was not published along with state-sector data by the Soviet statistical agency.

[68] Khrushchev, cited in Volin (1960), p. 317.

[69] Gray (1987), p. 10.

increase in combines by 19 percent, tractors by 30 percent, and fertilizer by 46 percent for 1981–1985 over 1976–1980.[70] The Twelfth Five-Year Plan, beginning in 1985, marked the time for more vigorous reforms and the beginning of the brief but impressive era of Gorbachev.

Gorbachev's Reforms

Gorbachev's reforms, to review, introduced a new contract system and a new marketing structure for agriculture, modeled in part on the NEP (*prodnalog*). Intensification of agricultural production signified more emphasis on improvement of yields than putting new land into cultivation. That 1986 was a record harvest seemed to vindicate the program with wheat yields on experimental farms, which were doing exceptionally well. Western and many Soviet analysts were skeptical, however, saying that reform effects had not been measured by a properly representative survey.[71] Their criticism was borne out.

Viewed as a failure in hindsight, the agrarian reforms of Gorbachev making contract fulfillment a success indicator seem not very different from ideas for agriculture developed in 1965. Although contracting was a force of potentially of enormous significance for transparency, neither firms nor consumers could choose their suppliers, and so the stimulus to competition was weaker than expected.[72] Similarly, although expansion of the private and cooperative sector promised an impact on legal market development, sanctions against unearned income were retained, providing little incentive for the diminution of the black market.[73] In retrospect, much of the burden of what went wrong in agriculture in the Gorbachev era, as in the other sectors of the economy, can be attributed to the continued prevalence of systemic weakness. Kornai (1980) identified that central weakness as a soft-budget constraint: the norm-oriented production system could not succeed in shifting emphasis to cost and profitability. However, two experts caution that the understanding of what went wrong in agriculture under Perestroika is still not entirely clear. They describe the three hypotheses: that climate was a handicap, that the scarcely reformed institutional framework continued to impose perverse incentives – i.e., that reform was not radical enough – and that the excessive regulatory environment of the larger economy dominated the new on-farm incentives.[74] Certainly, the rise in numbers of independent farmers under Gorbachev shows the potential response to reform, but the regime ended in the collapse of Communism.

70 Gray (1987), p. 14.
71 Gray (1987), pp. 12–13.
72 Schroeder (1991), p. 44.
73 Schroeder (1991), p. 45.
74 Brooks and Gardner (2004), p. 574.

TABLE 7.18. *Russian Federation Agricultural Output (1992 = 100)*

	1992	1996	2000	2004	2007
Cereals	100.0	65	62	62.8	78
Cattle	100.0	73	51	46	39
Chickens	100	65	53	51	56
Pigs	100.0	64	52	45	45

Source: FAOStat (2009).

Trends under Gorbachev led to an average annual rate of growth of grain production of under 1 percent (Zhang 1996, p. 207). However, the partial productivities of labor and land were both improving. Following the enormous expenditure on fertilizer and machinery in the 1960s and 1970s, the reduction of these inputs in the 1980s was prudent. Even this low rate of growth under Gorbachev, however, is more generous than the general view that agricultural productivity before 1992 was stagnant.[75]

3 TRANSITION REFORMS

Macroeconomic conditions discouraged agricultural recovery after the price shocks of the early 1990s. Adverse terms of trade, withdrawal of producer and consumer subsidies, stalemated institutional reform, the fall in income and a shift away from meat consumption, and production variability due to weather and undeveloped factor markets are causes most often noted for the severe decline in the sector in the 1990s.[76] A severe decline in capital input after the end of Communism resulted, to be sure, in a one-time gain in productivity in 1992. For years afterwards, however, productivity growth was not the force it was expected to be in a transition economy.[77] The adjustment costs of transition reforms in agriculture are generally acknowledged to have been more extreme than in other sectors of the economy.[78] The average annual decline of cereals production between 1992 and 1995, according to Zhang, was more than 11 percent.[79] Output growth began to recover only after 1996. It should have benefited from more advantageous terms of trade after devaluation in 1998, but opportunities were missed, and in some sectors, such as livestock, trends remained weak. Table 7.18 shows the estimates.

[75] Review of the literature in "Agricultural Productivity and Efficiency in Russia and Ukraine," USDA, Economic Research Service/AER 813, p. 10.

[76] Liefert (2001, 2002, 2005, 2008); Serova (2000); for a review of literature, see Bokusheva and Hockmann (2006).

[77] Lermon (2001, 2003).

[78] Brooks and Gardner (2004), p. 577.

[79] Zhang (1997), p. 202.

Economic research has produced an impressive body of work assessing agricultural productivity after the transition reforms.[80] W. Liefert et al. (2005) and K. Macours and J. Swinnen (2000) find a decline in labor productivity from an index value of 100 in 1991 to 61 after five years, in agreement with an estimate by Serova in 2000 for 1991 to 1996.[81] However, for TFP, the findings are moderately optimistic for the later periods once the initial shocks forced an adjustment and the economy began to recover. Productivity rise is seen in results by Lerman in 2003, who finds a multifactor productivity growth of 1.5 percent annually between 1992 and 1997.[82] Unfortunately, using 1993 as the base year provides a different result. In 1992, as noted, there was a one-time rise in productivity due to the decline in 1992–1993 of inputs, and without that year, TFP growth was negative.[83] This decline in productivity particularly affected the cereals sector.[84] Where the Soviet regime had been making significant progress in yields (ignoring cost), which were beginning to converge with those in advanced market economies – trends to 2002 show falling yields and a widening gap with Western countries.[85]

To be sure, between 2006 and 2008, during the commodities price boom, Russian cereals output rose by about 5 percent (Liefert, Liefert and Serova 2009). From 2001 to 2008, yields rose by 38 percent.[86] Recent official figures on labor productivity in the farm sector for the years between 2000 and 2008 show significant ongoing improvement.[87] Analysts predict that another sustained rise in grain prices and extensive investments to improve physical and commercial infrastructure would lead to further acceleration in output growth.[88] Moreover, by no means are all corporative farms unprofitable, as the small sector of entrepreneurial 300 Club farms discussed in Chapter 3 prove. The Golitsino papers, published in *Comparative Economic Studies* in 2005, find that about half are operating close to the efficiency frontier. However, the other half lie considerably below it.[89]

The corporative farms that dominate production have shown uneven performance. Most are not restructured (Brock et al., 2008). One problem is that even the efficient farms seem to lack highly skilled management. Among problems he found in the Soviet era agriculture, Bruce Gardner attributes

[80] See a general review of this literature by Bokusheva and Hockmann (2006), and a more technical review by Liefert (2008).
[81] Cited in Brooks and Gardner (2004), p. 578.
[82] Lermon (2001).
[83] Trueblood and Osborne (2002); Voigt and Uvarovsky (2001); Trueblood (1996).
[84] Trueblood and Osborne (2002).
[85] Trueblood and Osborne (2002).
[86] Roskomstat, cited in Liefert, Liefert and Serova (2009).
[87] Roskomstat (2010).
[88] Liefert, Liefert and Serova (2009).
[89] Gardner (2005), p. 227.

problems in Russian Federation agriculture in general to the lack of skills in the labor force (Gardner 2005). The relative shortage of well-educated farm management remains a major factor holding back competitiveness of Russian farming.[90] The Organization for Economic Co-operation and Development OECD economic survey of Russia in 2006 finds agricultural progress "is mediocre and its long term prospects in the absence of further reforms are uncertain."[91] The weak prospects for the sector, reflected in continued degradation of the soils, the report continues, is due to low investment levels, dampened by a weak land market and cumbersome regulations.

4 SUMMARY

The following summary highlights the numbers provided in the chapter above. The Table 7.19 is used to organize the long-run picture.

By period, as illustrated in Table 7.19, TFP is not, on the whole, the driver of growth in agriculture in the past century and a half. In particular, although it had become significant by the end of tsarist Russia, TFP sources of growth do not show up again until the restoration of the market economy in the Russian Federation. Collectivization resulted in dramatic capital investment, and this level of investment was maintained for a long period, with predictable results for labor productivity but little benefit for TFP growth. Under Putin and Medvedev, the development process is improving agriculture with certainty. However, analysis has not yet produced a clear understanding of the rate and sources of change.

Summarizing the data for the first reform, trends identified in Table 7.19 show that obstacles to the introduction of new technologies and growth in general diminished after serf emancipation. After several decades, the institutional changes across the economy went a long way toward transformation of peasants' routines. To be sure, observers continued to point out the frequency of famines, or "hunger" in the land of the tsars, as Kahan (1989, p. 108) entitled his famous essay. Observers, including government officials, perceived these repeated episodes as a challenge the government failed to master. This was certainly the case: the government lacked adequate administrative services, and famine areas were not well served by the country's transportation networks.[92] Steadily, however, in good years, yields were improving.

The second reform studied here, the Stolypin reforms, can be associated with continuing transformation from the data trends in Table 7.19. The strong rate of productivity growth was undisturbed by major disruptions, such as caused by the Russo-Japanese War, urban revolt, and industrial

[90] Gardner (2005); Clayton (1980).

[91] OECD Economic Survey of Russia (2006), p. 72.

[92] Simms (1977); Robbins (1975).

TABLE 7.19. *Total Factor Productivity in Russian Agriculture by Period (Annual Rate of Growth, %), 1801–2007**

Regime	Pre-1861	1860s	1870s	1880s	1890s	1900s	
	Imperial Russia						
Servile Russia	NA						
Post-Emancipation Russia		−0.35**	1.40				
Industrialization				0.803	1.41	1.97	
	Soviet Union						
	1920s	1930s	1953–1991				
			1955–1965	*1960–1975*	*1965–1975*	*1961(60)–1989(91)*	*1965–1990*
NEP	NA						
Collectivization		NA					
Khrushchev Reforms			1.2[DD]				
Kosygin-Brezhnev Reinvestment				0[C]	0.6[DD]		
Gorbachev Reforms						−0.4[P]–1.1[Z]	0.12[LKB]
	Russian Federation						
	1992–						
	1992–1995		*1993–1998*		*1992–1997*		
Transition Reforms	3.48[Z]		−1.7[T]		1.7[Lo1]; 7.4 (interval)[Lo3]		

* Output = Gross production (see Appendix 1 for tsarist Russia) minus intermediate inputs, unless otherwise indicated.
** Negative total factor productivity is not an unusual result in estimates for developing countries.
[B] Brooks and Gardner (2004).
[C] Clayton (1980), p. 455.
[d] Data represent official estimates of yields as adjusted (see appendix).
[DD] Diamond and Davies (1979), p. 50.
[Lo1] Lerman (2001).
[Lo3] Lerman (2003).
[LKB] Lerman, Biton, Kislev (2003).
[N] Nimitz (1967), p. 189, 196.
[G] Official government estimates (for Soviet Union, socialized sector).
[P] Pitzer and Baukol (1991), p. 55, 67.
[T] Trueblood and Osborne (2002), Fig. 6.
[Z] Zhang (1997), p. 207, output = cereals.

recession. Rapid improvement of the sector at the turn of the century was sustained and self-organizing. The use of fertilizer and equipment was increasing, and rural financial institutions were dramatically spreading. The land market continued to strengthen. The Stolypin reforms significantly loosened constraints on migration, shored up property rights and promoted rural finance. There seems adequate evidence to suggest that, had Russia not entered World War I, nor been kept from concluding a separate peace by the allies, the peasant demands for more land might have been reconciled with the nobles' resistance to change.

Another finding from Table 7.19 is that the 1950s and 1960s were promising years for agriculture with an annual rate of TFP increase of 1.2 percent. That this rate of growth of TFP was not sustained in later years is generally explained by the lack of incentives in the system as well as long term effects of soil erosion and other unintended consequences of Khrushchev's virgin lands campaign. Finally, Table 7.19 shows trends from recent research assessing change after the end of central planning in agriculture. Transition agrarian reforms did not impart a sense of clear performance gains by the late 1990s, since harvests are still highly influenced by climatic conditions. However, there is improvement in efficiency and estimates of steadily growing TFP. The dramatic increase in yields from 2001 to 2008 by 38 percent show, that as after the serf emancipation, the second decade has proved far more promising than the first.

Conclusion: The Present from the Perspective of the Past

There are many ways of looking at the history of Russia's agrarian reforms. One may see them in light of industrial policy: evidence of the government's determination to break with rural backwardness, or one may trace the process of decision-making for a study of governance. One may see them in light of their effect on agricultural performance or the evolution of agrarian institutions. But one can hardly fail to identify in each way of looking the close cooperation even in eras of reform between the state and rural elites. Ordinarily, the influence of vested interests was sufficient to block legal change to their exclusive prerogatives in the rural economy. Even in conditions of crisis, elite interests were conciliated by compromise. Cooperation on one reform was coordinated with concessions on another, and those who opposed reforms were assured of retained power in government. The crisis-reform pattern in agriculture survived for a century and a half because it was collectively stable and deliberately constructed to stimulate the economy without causing extensive social disruption.

BREAKING WITH BACKWARDNESS

Generally concerned more about stability and order, the Russian government was nevertheless particularly concerned about the consequences of rural backwardness in times of crisis. Rosenberg (1993, p. 841) explains perceptions about the necessity of agrarian reform in the late nineteenth century:

> . . . a major reason the countryside had to change if Russia was to move forward had to do with the simple ignorance of peasant lives, which populists romanticized and Marxists scorned, and was thought by almost everyone to be a barrier against what was variously understood as Russia's place in the Western community.

Changing the economy was about improving the behavior of Russian peasants. Y. Kotsonis (1998, pp. 17–18) describes the disparaging of peasants as linked to elite self-image in his work on the "othering" of the peasantry;

> By the late nineteenth century, the division between educated elite and masses was firmly structured as a dichotomy of progress and backwardness, and the agrarian question as a debate over what elites should do about the backwardness of peasants. In this sense, the agrarian question was not even about peasants as such – few studied peasants for the sake of understanding them – but about the place of peasants in a social order to be defined by the competing visions of non-peasants. The main difference dividing these groups was not whether peasants fell outside notions of culture and civilization (all assumed that they did), or whether peasants required transformation (all offered strategies to effect it), but who would represent peasants and what future polity they had in mind.

After serf-emancipation, peasants were given almost a probationary status. Assigned to separate courts by law, where customary law was consulted rather than the civil codes, peasants did not enjoy the same rights as other subjects and were at the bottom of a caste-like hierarchy. They could not as individuals, for example, purchase and sell arable land, unless they had paid off the full redemption fees on their plots – an obligation designed to last forty-nine years from the signing of the contract. Peasants did not become full citizens until the Stolypin reforms just before World War I.

The representation of peasants as inferior and set apart in civil society, discussed in Kotsonis, Rosenberg and many other works, was invariably linked to perceptions of Russia's image abroad and power in the world. The policy imperative of breaking with rural backwardness thus drew on closing the gap with the West. In that sense, agrarian reform seemed almost necessary for Russia to succeed and justified even the use of force in order to catch up with western countries. A graph can be used roughly to illustrate the performance gap in terms of yields of wheat between 1800 and roughly the late 1980s, in Figure 8.1.

This book has argued that the historical yield trends depicted in Figure 8.1 show a sustained gap with western economies. The gap opens wide during the era of collectivization, followed by World War II, and shows slow post-war recovery, but it strikingly narrows in key historical periods, highlighted in this book. The late nineteenth- and early twentieth century showed a narrowing of the gap, as did the post-war period partway through the 1970s (see Appendix 3). The data showing a gap in dairy yields in the Table 8.1 represents a greater lag despite progress.

Although it did not achieve the level of productivity achieved in more advanced market economies, agricultural performance in eras of industrial advancement can favorably be compared with growth rates in less developed nations in Latin America, Asia and the Middle East (Allen 2003).

Russia's sustained effort to defeat persistent rural backwardness did not, nevertheless, meet the goals which the government itself set. It was so far off

TABLE 8.1. *Dairy Yield in Selected Countries, 1887–2005, kg of Milk per Cow*

Country	1887	1913	1929	1939	1953	1970	1987	2005
Russia	*850*	*875*	*980*	*1,185*	*1,389*	*2,110*	*2,508*	*2,991*
Canada				1,872	2,419	3,259	4,601	7,324
Britain	1,870		2,234	2,532	2,910	3,929	4,936	7,116
U.S.	1,382	1,413	2,001	1,969	2,514	4,423	6,169	8,862

Sources: Mironov (1992), p. 152; FAOStat (2007); World Dairy Products: FAPRI 2006, *Outlook* [http://www.fapri.iastate.edu/outlook2006/text/16Dairy.pdf]; Department of Agriculture and Rural Development UK, Trends in Dairy Herd Performance, http://wwwruralni.gov.uk/index/publications/press_articles_dairy/trends.htm, 07/09/2006.

from those goals at the time of the collapse of the Soviet central planning regime, that there was a reckoning with long run policy failure in agriculture as well as other sectors.

Regime collapse, however, was not the time for rural reform. Opportunities for carefully crafted, pro-cyclical and incentive-oriented policies had existed, but the government did not act to take advantage of these moments. In this vein, it is appropriate for illustrative purposes to give some weight to Witte's criticism of the equally ill-timed Stolypin reforms as too much a policing measure and too late. His own more timely proposals in the 1890s

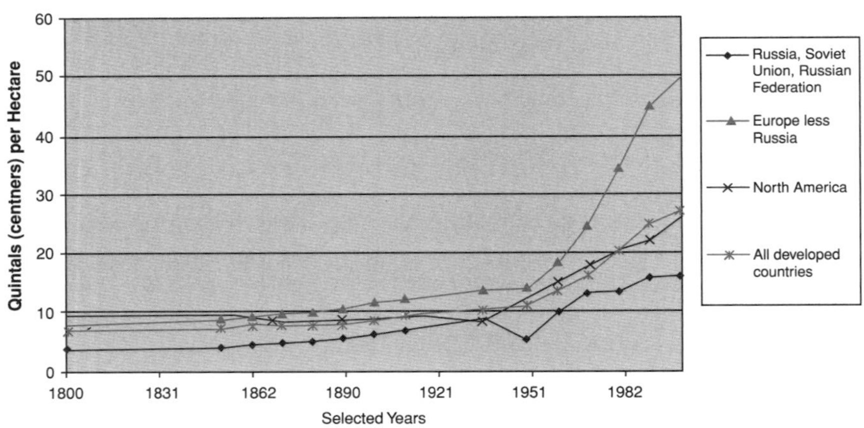

FIGURE 8.1. Wheat Yields, 1800–2004 (Five-Year Averages): Russia in World Perspective.
Sources: Data for Russia and the Soviet Union to 1960 see Appendix; for post-1960 Soviet Union and Russian Federation, Europe, North America, and developed countries FAOStat; for pre-1960 Europe, North America, and developed countries, Baroch (1997).

were not approved. On the whole, the Russian government chose the worst possible circumstances for the production of agrarian reform, times in which there were few alternatives to debate. One example can be drawn from remarks by L. Lih (1990) in his work on chaos and crisis in the food supply in 1917. In principle, as an alternative to forced requisitions under War Communism, the government might have chosen an "enlistment" strategy to draw in the Russian public into discussion of how to gain food security. Lih sees the path ultimately chosen, that of forced requisitions, as virtually mandated by the chaos and threat of instability.

In a crisis, the agricultural sector can seem a deadweight burden on a pre-modern economy. Agriculture in the late tsarist regime and 1920s was perceived to be conducted by a mass of traditional cultivators, and the pressing need for adjustment assistance was taken as a permanent need for external direction and assistance in modernizing both cultivation practices and in marketing of output. This reasoning encouraged the view that agriculture was not the way forward for this economy.

DECISION-MAKING: ELITE SETTLEMENT

The government's sustained commitment to eradicate rural backwardness showed up in peaks of concentrated reform activities, among which it bundled agrarian reform with other liberalizing measures. Enhancing the value of redistributional measures by bundling is a well known tactic of "enlarging the shadow of the future" to gain cooperation.[1] Alexander II used such conciliation tactics in his serf emancipation in 1861. Serf emancipation was the first of a series of "Great Reforms." The others that followed included a property tax to replace the capitation, a reform of the military, liberalization of higher education, the expansion of provincial government and the weakening of the power of the censors. Following his example in the second great reform era after the revolution of 1905, the government of Nicholas II packaged agrarian reform with the creation of a parliament (the Duma) as the basis of a new semi-constitutional regime and promised sweeping social legislation and fiscal reform. Again, in the 1920s, in the New Economic Policy (the NEP), the Bolshevik government embraced liberalization across the economy along with agrarian reform. Once more, collectivization formed part of a major revolutionary package of plans to serve the ambitious targets of the First Five Year Plan in 1929. Finally, Russia's farm privatization in the 1990s accompanied a new constitutional order based on broad property rights and a "big bang" program, which included price and trade liberalization and the consolidation of a democratic order.

[1] Axelrod (1984), p. 129.

More specifically, the government's bundling of redistributional reforms with supplementary benefits for elites helped those elites achieve benefits from the new order. For example, Alexander II's serf emancipation required noble landlords to use hired rather than bonded labor, but by doing so in the context of military reforms, the government also ended nobles' obligation of providing military recruits and social services in the village. In another example, the government's simultaneous price liberalization in 1992 and farm privatization (1991–1993) gave former collective and state farm directors a distinct advantage in overseeing the restructuring of enterprises. Price liberalization strengthened the value of their lobby for continued subsidies, and it protected them from competition at a time when the economic productivity of the asset was low but the political productivity was high – the state was prepared to accommodate lobbying for subsidies.[2] The agrarian lobby, which consisted mainly of farm directors, was powerful before and after reform. V. Gel'man describes the forms of cooperation that knit together the regional party leadership and farm enterprise directors, "a largely closed, homogenous, hierarchically structured corporatist group."[3] Regional rural elites continue to be well represented in Russian Federation government in the industrial ministries and parliamentary blocs.[4]

Elite settlements were visible in the reform process as well as afterwards. One reference here illustrates the atmosphere in which reform decisions were taken and elites consolidated behind reform. D. Field describes the cautious and long preparation for the serf emancipation enactment in the late 1850s through 1861. Extensive negotiations were so conciliatory of elite interests, that, as Dan Field writes, until the actual announcement of reform, the reformers were not aware that they had actually won:

> New policies were officially adopted, but the old policies were never renounced; the sanovniki were made to accept these new policies, but they continued to enjoy their offices and, apparently, the tsar's confidence. The nobles persisted in their illusions, and there was no Fronde or conspiracy of oligarchs.[5]

To understand more exactly how a government so closely allied with elite interests ever determines to move forward with re-distributional reform, it is important to draw not only on crisis conditions. The bureaucratic style of governance both prevented reform in ordinary times and eased compensation of elites in bad times.

[2] Frydman and Rapaczynski (1994), p. 193, cited in Jones (1997), p. 72; preservation of the large farm enterprises had political as well as economic objectives; the percent of large farms remains significant in Central and Eastern Europe (CEE): 89 per cent in Slovakia, 62 per cent in the Czech Republic, 48 per cent in Bulgaria, 46 per cent in Hungary, Bezemer (2002), p. 723; Czaki and Lerman (1994), pp. 566, 573; Lerman et al (2002).

[3] Gel'man (2003), pp. 48–49.

[4] Chaisty (2006).

[5] Field (1976), p. 362.

Management literature has a special framework for understanding why corporate culture tends to be conservative, and this framework also applies to bureaucratic governments, where reformers rarely gain a voice in policy. In crises, however, more opportunities emerge for reformers to persuade colleagues to cooperate. Crisis is a a punctuating event, which disrupts equilibrium in the operation of a large enterprise. Another is the transfer of the firm to new leadership, which allows a challenge to even the most conservative culture of the largest firms. Punctuating events can lead to innovation in organization, sales, design or the production process. An example of a punctuating event would be a serious and sustained threat to market share, forcing managers to focus seriously on new insights and take advantage of opportune moments to win over investors. Such corporate breakthroughs, like government reforms, characteristically show the marks of pressured deals. Just as political breakthroughs historically tend to be weakened by compromise, corporate change can lead to little real gain.

CARRYING OUT REFORM: JUSTIFICATION OF COERCION

By contrast with conciliatory treatment of elites, the governments tended to use force to gain the compliance of the peasantry. For example, although settling up between landlords and village communes after serf emancipation was voluntary for noble landlords, it was not for peasants. Many villagers attempted to resist disadvantageous settlements that they were offered. 89.4 percent of all redemption contracts were concluded by means of government intervention.[6] Similarly, in 1906, after choking off dialogue by enacting an imperial decree when the Russian parliament (Duma) was not in session, Prime Minister Peter Stolypin aggressively implemented his reforms in the village. Again, crisis was an excuse for violence against the peasantry under Bolshevik leadership, who sustained their armies in the civil war by means of forced requisitions and broke resistance among the peasantry. In this regard, the NEP brought relief from the use of force. But it proved only temporary. Extreme force was used to resettle peasants during the "dekulakization," accompanying the collectivization of Russian agriculture. Khrushchev too took an interventionist approach, especially in regard to the forced resettlement of villages during a period when the size of collective farms was increased. After Khrushchev, the cycle of violence and resistance diminished, and it was set to rest under Gorbachev and Yeltsin, whose successive governments both refused to carry out "Bolshevism in reverse." Under Putin and Medvedev, the ongoing reform process is carefully designed and carried out in the style of OECD initiatives, with productive investments rather than mobilization of labor resources.

[6] Druzhinin (1987), p. 304.

Historically, the coercive impact of policy fell mainly upon peasants. In the era of serfdom, local authorities and landlords could call upon the army to assist them to maintain order on their private estates. However, the military was a strong presence in the Russian government, and, at times of crisis, the military could exerted influence across sectors of the population. Boris Yeltsin, President of the Russian Federation (1991–1999), remarked in his memoirs that it was the elevation of generals to politicians that accounted for the violence in the early Bolshevik regime. He wrote,

> If earlier in the century, the famous Red generals hadn't executed the civilian population, if they had not declared total terror against rebellious peasants and Cossacks, if they hadn't purged and eradicated entire social classes . . . .I began to reflect deeply on this phenomenon of the general-politician."[7]

Setting to one side his scarcely concealed justification of his own showdown in 1993 with Alexandr Rutskoi, Vice President of the Supreme Soviet, hero of the Afghan war, and champion of reconstituting the Soviet Union, his observation has much merit. It was the case, that at times of reform, the state of crisis combined with the military presence to produce the campaign-like character of agrarian reform.

As in military campaigns, political leaders' reputations were made or broken in attempts to modernize agriculture. In Khrushchev's ouster, for example, one finds clear evidence that failed agrarian reform was a political liability. In this regard, Russian experience mirrors that of other countries in the developing world. Strong government intervention in Asia was commonly perceived as necessary in the reform of agriculture. As in Russia, peasant rebellions could threaten the success of agrarian reforms, which could end in the occupation of private lands. Regimes that fail at land reform are vulnerable for years to come.

POST-REFORM REGULATION

There was also some coercion in the regulatory regime always imposed on producers for the post-reform order. Effectively subordinating producers to new laws and taxes required new agencies and monitoring. The monitoring of movement in particular was coercive and constraining, and it had a large economic impact on labor markets. For example, the restrictions imposed on former serfs after 1861 significantly slowed migration.[8] In the first years of reform, peasants could choose to leave the community and reject the settlement. But they were left a beggar's share of the land, or less than a minimum amount considered necessary for survival, and if they did not

[7] Yeltsin (2000), pp. 52–3.

[8] On the passport regime and peasant migration, see Matthews (1993); Matthews and Burds (1996); Moon (1997); Burds (1998); Bohac (1989); Anderson (1980).

exercise this right by the time of the settlement, afterwards, they could not do so. All former state as well as privately owned peasants were subjected to a passport regime after reform. This guaranteed that voluntary migration was controlled, along with seasonal departures from the land for work in the cities. In 1906, Stolypin relaxed this harsh requirement, making peasants full citizens with rights to leave their village and go elsewhere, and they were encouraged to resettle in Siberia. But in the Soviet era, controls over movement were again imposed. Although in the Soviet era, all citizens were required to carry passports and were restricted in their residence, as in the tsarist era, rural dwellers faced especially restrictive conditions. For many years, collective and state farm employees were unable to obtain domestic passports. The gulf between rural and urban dwellers diminished in the late Soviet era. Brezhnev changed the passport regime, so that rural and urban citizens were treated equally, and he subsidized wages on collective farms to increase them almost to the level of those in industrial sectors.

Much of the Soviet era was also a step back to pre-reform tsarist Russia in regard to another key expected outcome of traditional agrarian reform: producer autonomy. Neither rural producers nor their managers, D. Gale Johnson writes, were really in charge of production. The guiding principle of the collectivized system was that farms could not be trusted to make the appropriate decisions.[9]

In this sense, that of producer autonomy, the Russian village has experienced in transition reforms relief from the previous monitoring of their production activities and their travel off the farm. In some respects, de facto, however, their choice to leave the farm has been constrained. Where former state and collective farm employees privatized their enterprises, before the land market came into being and the land registry was created, they had difficulty disposing of their shares of land. Because of parliamentary opposition to land reform, producers could not buy and sell arable land until the turn of the twenty-first century or use arable as collateral for long-term investment, a prohibition removed by Putin. The slowing of their departure from the land may have served to ease fears of food security in an environment of widespread unemployment after price and trade reform. Household gardening in particular created a buffer protecting rural income throughout the transition. Relocation became easier over time, and the rural population has dramatically shrunk in the 2000s.

The state's tendency closely to monitor peasant movement, at least in the tsarist era, was due not only to the desire for order and stability. The main lesson some officials learned from serf emancipation was that it worked as a fiscal reform. The weight of tax collection in the reasoning behind reform was powerful enough to override every other argument. A letter by Sergei Witte, at that time Finance Minister, to Emperor Nicholas II from

[9] Cited in Brooks and Gardner (2004), p. 575.

October 1898, argued that this benefit could be achieved, again, by another large reform. "Before the emancipation of the peasants, our budget was 350 million rubles," he wrote, "and emancipation gave us the possibility of increasing that to 1400 million rubles."[10] Agrarian reform, in summary, was timed in a crisis not only because it provided the opportunity for elite settlement on a large scale but also because it promised greater fiscal stability, and the army could be used to subdue the peasantry if unrest occurred.

THE EFFECTS OF REFORMS

Apart from long run fiscal benefits, it is difficult to link all the historical reforms to particular effects. V. Treml' (1982, p. 176) argues that in Russia, there was never any clear pattern of relationships between agricultural performance and the policies of reform. A downturn in the immediately following period, for example, might be followed by an upturn later, or the reverse. This book supports his understanding, and documents it in Chapter 7. A brief summary here of the findings is warranted.

The first decade after serf emancipation showed growth of production (fifty provinces of European Russia, livestock and net production of cereals) at less than 1 percent per annum in real prices. Growth thereafter was unsteady, in the 1870s, 1.8 percent per annum, and in the 1880s, 1 percent. Growth accelerated in the 1890s (1.6 percent) and again in the 1900s (1.9 percent). Gregory's data, beginning in the mid-1880s, show a considerably larger output estimate for the period beginning in the 1880s for the larger territory of the entire empire. Productivity estimates in Chapter 7 show that structural changes in production routines were well underway by the 1890s.

Positive trends were sustained through the 1920s, when liberalizing policies of the New Economic Policy (NEP) resulted in recovery after the difficult years of civil war. Non-grain output under the NEP exceeded its prewar level by 1926, and grains probably came close to that level. However, private agriculture was crushed during collectivization, which destroyed the productive along with the unproductive farms under the NEP. In the first decade of collectivized agriculture, recovery was slow, and in the next entirely interrupted by the outbreak of World War II.

After World War II, trends turned positive, but too slowly and with too few results to match expectations of the Soviet leadership. Khrushchev raised producer prices and this resulted in a short-term improvement, an annual growth rate between 1951 and 1964 of an impressive 3.7 percent, peaking from 1956 to 1959, at a stunning 8.7 percent. However, the slowing of these growth rates in the early 1960s produced the impression that his

10 Witte (2003 [1898]), 1 (2), p. 538.

reforms had failed. Under Brezhnev and Kosygin, plans for reinvestment were revived. On the whole, the Kosygin-Brezhnev reforms had moderately positive results, although between 1971 and 1975, there was a sharp decline and Russia actually began to import grain. With the system introduced in the 1930s seeming incapable of a sustained competitive growth rates, more reforms ensued. After the Gorbachev reforms, however, the growth rate of output was unimpressive, less than 1 percent per annum, although partial productivities of land and labor may have been improving.

The final decade of modern agrarian reform in Russia, 1990s, resulted immediately in a severe decline, from which some agricultural sectors have still not fully recovered. Cereals production in 2007 was still only 78 percent of what it was in 1992, and livestock declined to 39 percent of its level in 1992, poultry to 56 percent and pigs to 45 percent. Output stagnation owed much to macroeconomic volatility in the 1990s. Effects of inflation – particularly harsh for capital-intensive sectors such as agriculture – were felt in the psychological response of rural dwellers, dampening expectations for the value of their cash resources in the future.[11] As recession deepened, a decline in consumption of high-valued products worsened effects in the cereals sector, which suffered from falling demand for livestock feed.

In the 1990s, small farms faced special challenges. Large farms continued to be highly dependent upon public resources, which were partially supplied, but independent farmers required financial resources that were not supplied.[12] Assistance was finally available in Putin's second term in the national project for rural development. Until then, farms of all sizes were crippled by a lack of access to market-based technical assistance, specialist seed and breed research, and, especially, price information systems, which comprise a part of the national project.

Assistance after agrarian reform can in principle be supplied by voluntary social organizations, which in market economies are among the most powerful instruments of aid to agriculture. In Western market economies, associations and unions provide considerable support for extension and innovation. For example, the quasi-official Farm Bureaus, drawn together in 1919 in the United States as the Farm Bureau Federation, promoted financial and technical assistance to farmers.[13] Why voluntary social organization in the Russian rural environment has not historically played a strong role in the adjustment process after reforms maps into the history of local government. Young and Wilson use the long-run perspective to underscore the historical as well as contemporary weakness of local government and its critical importance for governance, and this had a large effect on the implementation of reforms:

[11] See, for an assessment over the past thirty years, Laeven, Klingebiel and Kroszner (2002).

[12] Amelina (2000, 2002).

[13] Olson (2000), pp. 150–159.

Governments experimented repeatedly with local administration reforms that consistently failed because of the inherent conflict between local accountability and effective subordination. From the late nineteenth century through to the collapse of the Soviet Union, local reforms aimed at two distinct ends: a simultaneous extension and retraction of the state. The subsequent and repeated failures that followed are key to understanding the implosions of both the Tsarist and Soviet administrations.[14]

Russia's rural communities continue to reside in relative isolation. Combined with effects of Russia's low population density, village isolation from market information systems discourages the diffusion of skills and the results of research and extension.[15]

In the longer term, Russian agriculture promises to continue improving if commodity prices rise. A profitability gap between many of Russia's corporative entities and advanced farms in other countries may persist for some time. However, the operations of the vertical holding companies, like Gazprom, which imports equipment for its agricultural production and has adequate resources to hire skilled managers, are a new entrepreneurial force present in the countryside. Russia now exports substantial volumes of grain, as it did in the tsarist period. Reports from the 2009 harvest indicate a sustained improvement in grain yields after 2007 and a steady improvement in wheat quality.[16] Indicators, in Table 8.2, show the distance that Russian agriculture has come since the early 1990s.

RUSSIA'S AGRARIAN INSTITUTIONS[17]

Throughout the nineteenth and twentieth century, Russia's rural institutions seemed resistant to change. The impression was, as Rosenberg (1993, p. 841) puts it, "peasant agriculture seemed both figuratively and literally mired in primitive techniques of production." To explain the endurance of some parts of rural tradition over several centuries in Russia, through several different production regimes, it is not sufficient to talk about rational behavior toward risk or the functionality of these different regimes. A main source of persistence of routines was the dependency created among households as certain practices were perpetuated in times of need. Dependency is an incentive for the construction of lasting social rules, or institutions,

[14] Young and Wilson (2007), p. 1072.

[15] Johnston and Mellor (1961); Ruttan (2001); David (1991), p. 197.

[16] August 31, 2009, http://gain.fas.usda.gov.

[17] Ruttan (2001), p. 119, n. 9, the term institutions "is employed so as to be able to consider changes in the rules of conventions that govern behavior (1) within economic units such as families, firms, and bureaucracies, (2) among economic units as in the cases of the rules that govern market relationships, and (3) between economic units and their environment, as in the case of the relationship between a firm and a regulatory agency. Thus organisations are defined as a subset of institutions involving deliberate coordination...." The term institutions is generally used to distinguish behaviors and rules from policies that tend to change more often. Easterly and Levine (2002).

TABLE 8.2. *Main Agricultural Indicators, Selected Countries, 1990–2007*

	Exports[a]			Yield[b]			% GDP[c]			Employment[d]		
	1995	2000	2007	1995	2000	2007	1990	2000	2007	1997	2000	2005
Australia	8.53	6.06	3.44	18.7	19.6	11.7	4.92	3.51	2.41	5.10	5.00	3.60
Canada	9.24	6.19	4.27	27.0	28.0	29.6	2.86	2.28	2.2(04)	3.90	3.30	2.70
Finland	8.36	6.33	5.32	34.0	35.0	36.5	6.33	3.53	3.19	6.90	6.00	4.80
France	1.46	1.10	0.92	64.6	72.4	65.5	3.77	2.84	2.20	...	...	3.80
Germany	1.09	0.90	0.83	61.1	64.5	61.8	1.49	1.26	0.92	2.90	2.70	2.40
Russian Federation	...	3.10	2.87	12.2	15.6	19.9	16.61	6.43	4.76	12.20	14.50	10.20
United Kingdom	0.74	0.48	0.67	68.7	71.6	66.3	1.89	1.04	0.94	1.80	1.50	1.40
United States	3.93	2.33	2.42	46.4	58.5	67.0	2.06	1.23	1.08(06)	2.70	2.60	1.60

[a] Agricultural raw materials exports, % merchandise exports.
[b] Cereal yield (Hg (thousands)/ha).
[c] Agricultural value added (% GDP).
[d] Employment in agriculture (% total employment).
Source: World Bank Development Online Indicators (2009); FAOStat (2009).

which facilitate coordination of relationships and help rural dwellers form expectations for dealing with each other and with downside risk.

Dependency can actually be encouraged rather than eliminated at times of reform. Without the provision of adjustment costs, without laws clearly limiting control over reform implementation by elites, and without post-reform rights to move freely from rural areas, dependencies are likely to persist. Dependency is not the whole story, to be sure. At times of reform, coordinated to coincide with crisis conditions, the need for traditional institutions of self-insurance can be intense.

Historically in Russia, the household's arable (*nadel*) was claimed by the collective or commune, a claim guaranteed by custom and after 1861 by law. After 1861, the plots of land worked by each household after serf emancipation belonged to the commune until they were fully redeemed. This meant that well into the early twentieth century – since complete and partial repartitions were not always in the power of households to resist – there was less than full security of land rights over the nadel and less than strong incentives to improve that land. There was an additional source of land, however. Rented and purchased land, which was not repartitioned, was therefore more secure. This land, expanding considerably in the 1870s, would have been the source of some of the strong yield improvement in agriculture in the late nineteenth century.

Households' rights to the *nadel*, that is, to consolidated plots of land, were finally granted after the abolition of redemption payments in 1905 and by legislative enactments of the Duma after Stolypin's edict of 1906. The widespread land titling after the grant of property rights brought consolidation to Russia's peasant plots; a large part of Russia, the size of England, came to be cultivated on enclosed lands. This means that purchased and rented land could be added to the *nadel* for a sizable and commercially profitable enterprise. The Russian revolution of 1917 cut off this historical growth path by eliminating secure rights to the arable and socializing, then nationalizing the land. These revolutionary acts tended to favor, at least initially, communal agriculture, including grazing and some collective cultivation.

In view of the insecurity of rights to the *nadel* for much of tsarist history, a number of practices arose in the villages for self-insurance against risk. In addition to the collective practices that helped pool arable and other resources, the most important was the household's cultivation of a garden plot. It remained a valued source of income over many centuries, and for some members of the household, a job more fundamental than cultivation of the fields. The garden plot was largely secure against other households' claims, and it was passed on across generations by customary laws of inheritance.

In their effort to appeal to the peasantry, in the 1920s the Bolshevik government did not remove the households' guarantee of rights to a garden plot. Nor did Stalin end the idea of inheritable property. Instead, the leadership attempted to encourage gardening, while controlling it, that is, limiting *kolkhoz* (collective farm) private subsidiary plots to 0.5 hectares. This would avail consumers of vegetables and fresh meat at special urban markets, organized by the government, without creating a political or ideological threat to the regime. Indeed, in the Soviet era, vegetable production on *kolkhoz* plots amounted to nearly a quarter of gross agricultural production. The flourishing vegetable market in Soviet Russia is evidence that the garden remained a valued source of supplementary household income (Pallot and Nefedova 2007).

By the mid-1980s, the traditional forms of village insurance against risk, including barter arrangements and the garden plot, were no longer a necessity. Per capita income had risen: subsidies were provided to *kolkhoz* members so that they were paid the equivalent in wages to state farm workers. By that time, however, a symbiotic relationship had grown up between household plots and the larger farms. Inputs–fuel, fertilizer and equipment – purchased for the fields were also used on the plot. The interlocking of households with factor markets through these dependent economic relationships powerfully contributed to the perpetuation of traditional practice, even when it was no longer essential to livelihood. The tradition of cultivation of the plot has thus survived and been reshaped during numerous episodes of accelerated growth.[18] Parallel situations can be found in the developing world, where traditional farming practices survive even radical episodes of effective reform and improved production.[19]

It is important to ask whether the survival of household plots and their transformation into a main source of household income is an efficient use of labor and land on the large corporative farms. That these plots were not taxed during the transition, by contrast with independent farms, increased their relative security and profits while drawing labor from more productive activities. For example, well after the sector began to recover after devaluation in 1998, the numbers of urban and rural producers cultivating household plots did not diminish. Bogdanovsky (2005, p. 144) estimates that the labour input of the 23.7 million "shadow farmers" at about 12 percent of the labour input of the entire Russian population."

The survivals across regime of customary practice are depicted in Table 8.3. It emphasizes the powerful place of household traditions and rights throughout the period under study. The family farm, far more promising commercially than a household plot, has yet to become an institution as fundamentally important in Russia as it is in western Europe and the United States.

[18] Bardhan (1989), p. 9, observes that this is often the case in the developing world, drawing an analogy to biology and arguing for the force of path dependence against the operation of natural selection in social institutions.

[19] De Janvry (1981); Bardhan (1989), pp. 10–11, cited in Swinnen (2002), p. 373.

TABLE 8.3. *Household Custom and Rights in Russia, 1800–2008*

Period	Collective Cultivation of the Arable	Household Control over Factors of Production and Assets	Subsidiary Plot as the Main Source of Supplementary Earnings
SERFDOM	High	Low	High
Post-abolition	High	Medium	High
Stolypin era	Medium	High	High
The NEP	High	Medium	High
Collectivization	High	Low	High
Mid-1950s–1980s	High	Low	High
TRANSITION	Medium	High	High

GOVERNANCE AND RURAL INSTITUTIONS

Crisis-induced reform was a policy instrument used in Russia to resolve severe agricultural sector problems without significantly weakening support by elites for the government. The achievement of consensus about reform was very difficult in a regime dominated by special interests, and once it was achieved, it was sustained by repeating the process. A consensus would decay, for example, in part because agriculture had not improved much, and both farm sector problems and consolidation of elite support required renewal of the consensus. Resolving contentious re-distributional issues by weak reforms in a crisis did not provide a lasting coalition of powerful interests, but it did break deadlocks and preserve stability.

Because of the power of vested interests to undermine reform, effective policies require targeted action to encourage the new order. One highly effective historical reform can be used as an example. In France, at the time of the revolution of 1789, notions of agrarian reform were infused with a high regard for individual landownership and concern to make production more efficient. Compulsory rotation, M. Bloch (1966) writes, was considered "too repugnant to the new and totally individualistic notion of liberty for anyone to want to retain it." The French assemblies thus devised numerous other reforms, complementary to the abolition of the feudal order, to help peasants to change their routines. For example, taxes and seigniorial fees were abolished, proprietors were restricted in their access to collective grazing, and forage crops were promoted. The triumph of the peasants in France, Bloch writes, owed to the sweeping loss of privileges by rural elites and to the revolutionary assembly's effort to reduce the fallow and foster new routines in farming (pp. 235–37).

Without such stimulus to change, there would have been no restructuring of farming techniques, Arthur Young observed in 1789. Government efforts to promote peasant proprietorship, to remove elites' privileged access to the best land resources, and to provide assistance for technological innovation to peasant communities in early modern Europe were one way to end a system of land use of such long standing.

This book uses as case studies several agrarian reforms that lacked such instruments for more effective reform. It emphasizes the problem as a constraint on governance, in particular, on redistributional policies. The lack of instruments shows up in weak systems of law enforcement, poorly funded local government, lack of commitment and budgetary resources to cover the costs of transformation, and social barriers standing in the way of effective reform. In the longer run, these constraints sometimes diminish in importance as the rural economy strengthens. But other constraints appear. Governments that enjoy success in reform tend to remove barriers to reallocation as an ongoing process.[20] In its major reforms, the Russian government lacked the capacity to carry out follow-on monitoring and policy adjustment. D. Orlovsky (1981, p. 2) explains that this was an observable weakness of nineteenth-century bureaucratised government. Bureaucratic institutions lacked the flexibility and authority to develop and implement policies targeting specific political and social problems.

This conclusion summarizes the common features of these reforms and their similar effects on the Russian rural economy. It shows the power in policy decisions of historical tradition, social conventions and perceptions, along with the development objectives of Russia's agrarian reforms. Rural development goals were a significant shaping force in government decision-making; agrarian reform in Russia was part of a vigorous industrial policy.

This book identifies major challenges that face agrarian reformers. The first challenge is to stop government routines from slowing down the pace of necessary actions and policies. The second is to strengthen the ability of rural dwellers to resist dependency and to reduce interference by local elites. But – as the case studies in this book have shown – these goals can be hard to achieve. Other challenges draw on economic policy lessons. Agrarian reform should treat all producers equally (and allow them to operate autonomously). It should assist in developing the market infrastructure that allows households to repay their debts and to take advantage of opportunities that arise. But all reforms will face problems from the historical legacies of rural communities. In Russia, the key legacy is the bimodal structure of farming; the agricultural sector is dominated by very large cooperative farms, locked in a symbiotic relationship with very small household plots. Because there is no suitable, scaled-down infrastructure, small farmers remain dependent. This market structure has a strong (though distant) historical foundation on the road traveled from serfdom.

[20] Eslava et al. (2004).

APPENDIX 1

Construction of Total Factor Productivity for Russian Agriculture in the Tsarist Period, 1861–1911*

METHODS

The use of the Tornqvist-Theil Index of TFP (TT TFP) follows the approach of Capalbo and Antle (1988), Thirtle and Bottomley (1989), Caves, Christenson and Diewert (1982), Ali (2004), Evenson, Pray and Rosegrant (1999) and Coelli et al. (2005). An approximation to the Divisia index with a time varying weighting scheme, TT TFP has come to be viewed as superior to other indices. A theoretical appeal of this indexing procedure is its association with a less rigid production structure than either the arithmetic or geometric indices. The TT index imposes no restrictions on the substitution possibilities between inputs, adjusting implicitly for the relative productivity of each input in the aggregation of input growth by using the cost shares as weights. It is an exact specification for the linear homogeneous translog production function, which represents a second order, local approximation to an arbitrary functional form. If the existence of technical inefficiencies for the given farm regime is ruled out, TFP growth is equal to the rate of technical change. The change from period *t*-1 to period *t*, the TT TFP index is expressed and applied in logarithmic form as follows:

$$\ln(TFP_t/TFP_{t-1}) = \frac{1}{2}\sum_j (R_{jt} + R_{jt-1})\ln(Q_{jt}/Q_{jt-1}) - \frac{1}{2}\sum_i (S_{it} + S_{it-1})\ln(X_{it}/X_{it-1}). \qquad (A.1)$$

Where R_{jt} is the share of output *j* in total revenue, Y_{jt} is output j, S_{it} is the share of input i in the total input cost, X_{it} is input i, all in period *t*. In this

* The author is indebted for research assistance to Dilyara Ibragimova, a researcher at Moscow Institute of Social Research, who assisted in estimates of labor, land, agricultural equipment, and fertilizer for the years 1870 to 1913.

specification and in this study, revenue shares for the output index and cost shares for the input index are updated over time.

Further decomposition of causal factors in Russian productivity growth or closer examination of the residual above would require additional procedures, using estimated TFP as a dependent variable in regression analysis. Performance is thus measured for each time period against an estimated production frontier, the non-parametric Data Envelopment Analysis (DEA) or the parametric Stochastic Frontier Analysis (SFA).[1] However, for the purposes of this work, in view of the deficiencies of the data and the main objective of rough cross-country comparisons, the TFP is the indicator of interest.

DATA

Three of the four published output series for the tsarist era draw on data published by Russian statistical agencies from the late nineteenth through the early twentieth century, which include the following:

Tsentral'nyi Statisticheskii Komitet Ministerstva Vnytrennykh Del (1884). Raspredelenie zemel' po ugod'iam v Evropeiskoi Rossii za 1881 god. *Statisticheskii Vremennik Rossiiskoi Imperii*. Seriia III. Vyp. 4. St Petersburg.

Tsentral'nyi Statisticheskii Komitet Ministerstva Vnytrennykh Del (1892–1901) *Statistika Rossiiskoi Imperii XXII. Glavneishiia dannyia pozemel'noi statistiki po obsledovaniiu 1887 god.* St Petersburg.

Tsentral'nyi Statisticheskii Komitet Ministerstva Vnytrennykh Del Statistika Rossiiskoi Imperii XXVIII, XLI, LI. *Urozhai khlebov 1893, 1899, 1900.*

Departamenta Sel'skago Khoziastva Ministerstva Gosudarstvennykh Imushchestv (1869). *Ob'iasneniia k khoziastvenno-statisticheskomu atlasu Evropeiskoi Rossii.* St Petersburg.

Materialy vysochaishe uchrezhdennoi 16 noiabria 1901 g. Kommissii po issledovaniiu voprosa o dvizhenii s 1861 g. po 1900 g. Blagosostoianiia sel'skago naseleniia srednezemledel'cheskikh gubernii, sravnitel'no s drugimi mestnostiami Evropeiskoi Rossii, 1 Chast' (razrabotano Departamentom Okladnykh Sborov) (1903). St Petersburg.

XV Posev i sbor khlebov i kartovelia u krest'ian na nadel'nykh zemliakh i u chastnykh zemlevladeltsev po 50 gyb. Evropeiskoi Rossii s 1861 po 1900 g.

[1] For a discussion of the methodological differences and limitations, see Voigt and Hockmann (2008); Coelli (2005).

Ministerstvo Zemledelii i Gosudarstvennykh Imushchestv, otdel sel'skoi ekonomiki i sel'skokhoziastvennoi Statistiki (1902). *Svod Statisticheskikh Svedenii po sel'skomu khoziastvu Rossii k kontsu XIX veka.* Vyp. 1: III. Ugod'ia i posevnyia ploshchadi pp. 35–73; IV Urozhainost' 76–153. St Petersburg.

Sbornik statistiko-ekonomicheskikh svedenii po sel'skomu khoziastvu Rossii i inostrannykh gosudarstv 1917 g. [Veterinary Department].

Sel'skokhoziastvennaia perepis' 1916 g. In Statisticheskii sbornik za 1913–1917 gg. Vyp. 1, Moscow 1921.

Obukhov's 1927 series for the fifty European provinces of Russia, Raymond Goldsmith's 1955 unpublished series for 1860–1913 also covering European Russia, and Paul Gregory's 1982 estimates of the value of net agricultural output in his comprehensive study of national income across the entire territory of the empire, all use these data. They are three of the main analytic works on Russia's agricultural markets in the late nineteenth century. The fourth is A. Nifontov's 1974 work on Russian grain output using archival appendices from the above published tables.

Goldsmith's unpublished manuscript (1950) uses materials from the 1860s, but in his 1961 published work, he, like Obukhov and Gregory, avoids the most severe data issues *in their publications* by focusing on the period after the early 1880s, when countrywide uniform standards were imposed and surveys aimed for accuracy and completeness. Crop production data begins in 1884 from surveys taken by the Central Statistical Committee (the Ministry of Interior) (the volume in *puds* [36 lbs, or 16.33 kgs] of wheat, rye, oats, barley, and potatoes; *chetverti*[2] were converted to puds at ratios provided by the source for the earlier periods).[3]

There is so little work on the 1860s that the decade is a clear roadblock to growth accounting for the entire tsarist era. Gaps for that and the next decade, the 1870s, include such fundamentals as the extent of cleared and uncleared land, net harvest figures by crop, reliable livestock estimates, and capital input series: land rental, insured structures, the production and application of domestically produced mineral fertilizers, the use of mechanized equipment, exacting livestock and crop inventories, and producers prices for some of these years. Blame probably falls on weak and poorly financed institutions of local government. I. Vil'son, Russia's leading agricultural expert, writes in 1869,

[2] See Appendix 2.

[3] Through 1915, the TsSK sent two sets of forms to each locality, requesting information about yields and sown areas by crop from both peasants' allotments and nobles' fields. From this information, the TsSK estimated harvests, or gross output, using population data to provide information on per capita yields. Groman (1927), p. 1.

the amount of land under crops is unknown; exacting and well defined household surveys do not exist, or, at least, did not exist before the introduction of zemstva institutions [1864 – csl], therefore, the evidence collected by committees for the public supply of food can be accepted only with extreme caution . . . we have as rough indicators . . . from reports by landowners the general extent of plowed land, the level of the harvest of every year, and so forth.[4]

Non-agricultural output of the household, a possibly significant source of income from trade, is not reported.

After 1870, coverage improves considerably. The arable was separated by crop, and the volume of seeds sown and produced by field were recorded for the first time in a joint upgrade project of the Central Statistical Committee (TsSK) and the Ministry of State Domains. There was no further progress, however, until after 1880. In 1881, the TsSK produced its own estimates based on the first agricultural census. At that time, registry institutions for formal land markets reported actual land use by individual peasant *khoziastva* (households). Together, the Department of Agriculture and Rural Industry of the Ministry of State Domains produced a considerably improved survey after 1880, a close accounting of cereals and industrial crop output, livestock, and conditions of agricultural production. Beginning in 1881, Russian surveys compare in structure with those in the United States, Prussia, and England.[5]

Gaps remain, for example, for non-agricultural output of peasant farms and gardens and actual arable in use.[6] Data captured the original allotment land (upon which redemption fees after the end of serfdom were based), an area of arable that may have included rented croplands but not purchased land. We concur with Goldsmith in regard to output and land in that although absolute levels, even after 1884, are not entirely reliable for any given year, the movement of production over time will reflect a consistent collection technique over a territory where officials practiced familiar routines. For consistency over time, we embrace only the fifty European provinces of Russia, for which estimates exist through 1913.

GROSS PRODUCTION

Cereals (Four Main Grains) and Potatoes

Gross production for the fifty provinces of European Russia embraces mainly crop output: consumption and sales of the four main grains, potatoes, and industrial crops. The four grains accounted for 90.3 percent of all

[4] Vil'son (1869), pp. 75–6.
[5] Timiriazev (1902), pp. ix–xi.
[6] Ivantsov (1915).

net grain production in 1896–1900, according to Prokopovich's estimates.[7] Goldsmith believed that for 1861 and 1864–1866 there are no figures on grain production.[8] This is not right. Information for all years through the early 1880s is available in governor general reports. The data are not missing. The problem is that for the 1860s, crops are distinguished only as "winter" and "spring," and harvest size must be estimated from crude seed/yield and yield/desiatina (one desiatina = 2.7 acres) ratios. Through the 1860s, yield/seed estimates were based in landlords' reports of harvest yields, which also provided the base for estimates of sown arable. For the 1860s, our data are from Vil'son, also reported in Khromov.[9] We also estimated production net of seed, averaging the regional data in provincial sources for "yield" and taking the percentage required as the minimum net volume.

In the determination of value, Goldsmith took price estimates from Prokopovich, who then derived net value by excluding expenditure on seed in output. Since this approach leads to no important difference for Goldsmith's purposes, the relative weight attached to individual crops, Goldsmith's indexes are based on gross value.[10] For assessing the growth rate of aggregates, however, this is a drawback.[11] For this study of gross production including marketings, to examine productivity we first disaggregated the crops and used annual yields by crop to determine seed, and for the 1860s, used I. Vil'son's breakdown for aggregate consumption and seed.[12]

For the value of cereals and potatoes output, prices are regional aggregates from Mironov (1985), which are useful despite large regional differences across European Russia.[13]

a) Rye and oats. We used regional retail prices for 1860–1880s and procurement prices for European Russia, 1881–1913.
b) Wheat and barley. We used Mironov's procurement prices for 1881–1913. For the earlier period, we reconstructed the price data, assuming a constant price ratio for crops.
c) Potatoes. Price information for potatoes is relatively scarce until the twentieth century, when the standard statistical sources listed above include prices. We used Gregory's price data for the 1880s and 1890s

[7] Prokopovich (1918), p. 7.
[8] Goldsmith (1955), p. A-2.
[9] For 1857–1866 from Obruchev (1871), pp. 247–53, and these data are much the same as in the earlier publication by Vil'son, who essentially wrote the text of the *Voenno-statisticheskii sbornik* edited by Obruchev. The other years are from Goldsmith for the fifty provinces of European Russia, checked for accuracy against Obukhov (1927); Khromov (1950).
[10] This assumption has been challenged (see Gregory [1982], pp. 75–6.
[11] See Gregory (1982).
[12] Vil'son (1869), p. 112.
[13] Mironov (1985).

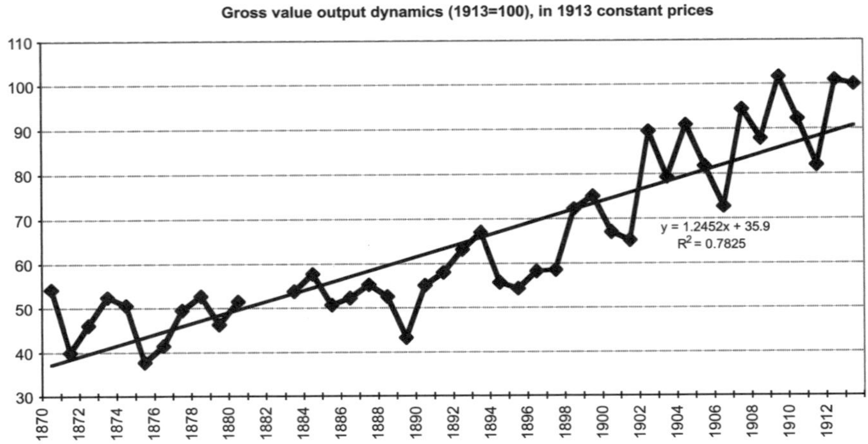

FIGURE A1.1. Gross Value of Production of Cereals and Potatoes, 1870–1913, in 1913 Prices.

(which are in part reconstructed, based on the price ratio of potatoes and barley for fragmentary years) and similarly reconstructed prices for potatoes for the earlier years. Beginning late in the 1890s, price data for potatoes is more readily available.

The TFP estimates do not require constant prices. However, for comparison, one price index can be found in Strumilin, with 1913 as the base year. By that estimate, value rose as shown in Figure A1.1.

Gross Production: Inclusion of Livestock Sales. Production here is cereals and livestock (the slaughter rate is estimated at 40 percent of output, as in Gallman [1972]).[14] To this we should add changes in the value of land through improvements. Information for cleared land for Russian data is not available, however. For gross production, it would be a substantive deficiency to ignore sales receipts from home production (Carlin and Handy 1974). Non-agricultural labor was highly productive, earning some 40 to 50 percent of household income by the end of the nineteenth century, for those households with local sales of home-produced items, there may have been a small but significant income.[15] For these aggregate estimates, however, no proxies are currently available.

[14] Gallman (1972), p. 204, n. 25, cites Samuel Blodgett *Economica, A Statistical Manual for the United States of America* (1806; reprint ed., New York: Augustus M. Kelley, 1964), p. 90, for his estimate of a 40 percent slaughter rate.

[15] Towne and Rasmussen (1960), p. 256.

Remarks about Output Estimates. Unresolved controversy over estimates produced for the year 1913 by the Tsarist Central Statistical Committee officially corrected in 1925, create problems in taking the data through 1913. It was thought that yields and sown area were both underestimated by as much as 19 percent – and then corrected again in the 1930s, downward, and again in the 1960s so that Soviet achievement in agriculture would appear more significant.[16] We stay with the original estimates, even though they are likely to underestimate production. Counterbalancing this estimate is the inherent overstatement of gross harvest figures, which, through the Soviet era, include the waste.[17] Crop output is not rendered in barn weight, by contrast with estimates for other countries, where gross production means net of waste. In these data, there is no doubt that gross production is understated somewhat, but the estimates are consistent over time.

Once again, the break in the quality of the data, improving in the last two decades of the nineteenth century, makes longitudinal series difficult. Internal Ministry documentation shows that the method of gathering harvest statistics changed in the 1880s and again in the late 1890s, each time boosting the figures. This means, however, as Goldsmith (1951) remarked in his unpublished work, that the corrected figures should be incorporated back into the series in an integrated way without such a sharp rise for the late 1890s. Although the growth of agricultural output was more significant in the last several decades of the tsarist regime, when the figures are adjusted properly for the change in methods of calculation we find the rate of growth for the entire period, as in Goldsmith, is adjusted downward, not upward, by this irregularity.

Finally, there is an additional special feature of Russian data to be considered. Official tsarist Russian (and current) data capture weight rather than volume in reporting quantity of crop output. Weight was measured in centners (one centner equals a quintal, 100 kilograms), and it formerly was measured in puds. This is different from estimates elsewhere, which are in volume. The difficulty in using weight for product of the arable (rye, wheat, oats, and potatoes) lies in the mix. Output in pre-modern times differs considerably from that in modern agriculture, and the weight of output will generally be insufficient to show structural transformation. The Figure A1.2 for example, shows the increasing relative volume weight of potatoes in output across the period. To this is contrasted in Figure A1.3 the relative value in current prices.

Potatoes grew in importance for consumption after the mid-1880s, as seen in both figures. There was some structural change in output across the decades. The bulk of production in rye shrank somewhat relative to wheat. In other countries, such as the United States, this variability would

[16] Wheatcroft and Davies (1994), p. 108.
[17] Prokopovich (1918), p. 44.

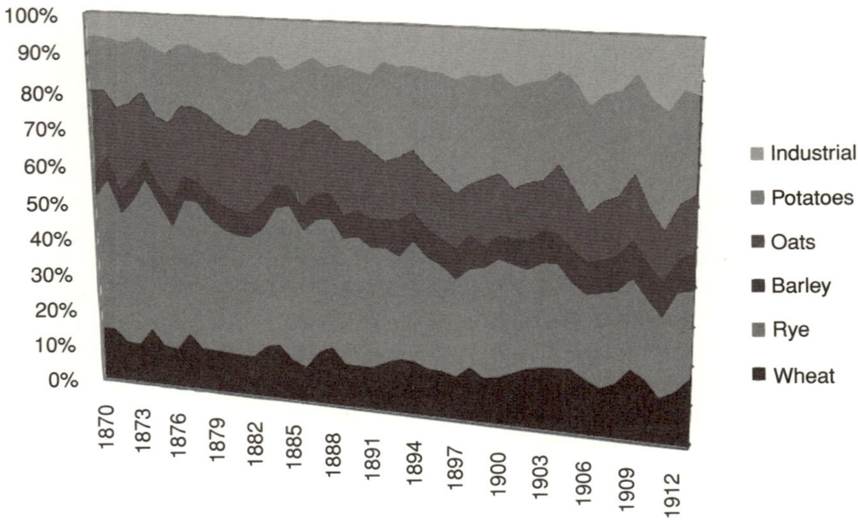

FIGURE A1.2. Output of Crops and Potatoes, puds (% of Total), 1870–1913.

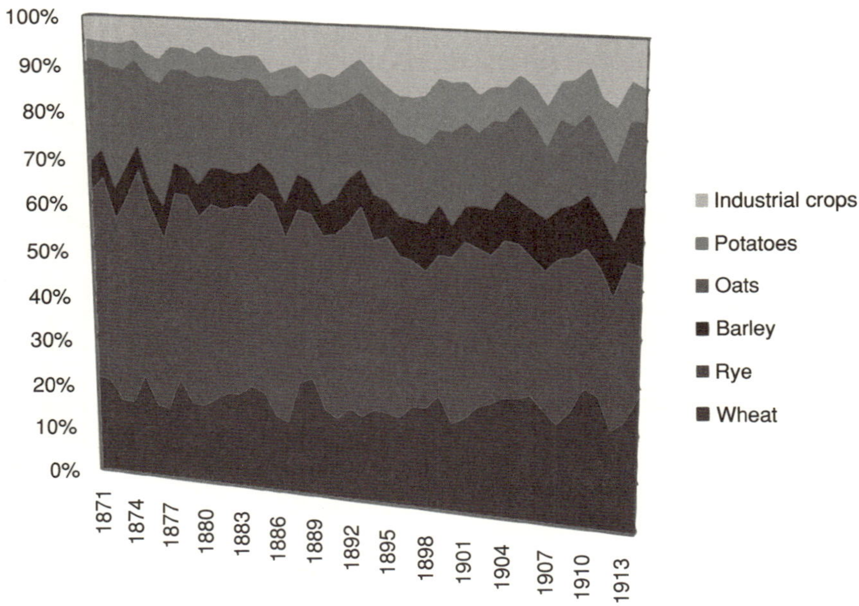

FIGURE A1.3. Output of Crops and Potatoes, Millions of Rubles (% of Total), 1870–1913, Current Prices.

encourage researchers to use volume of output rather than weight, as in the United States, where the measure used is bushels. A bushel of wheat, white potatoes, and soybeans weighs 60 lbs; a bushel of corn, rye, sorghum grain, and flaxseed weighs 56 lbs; a bushel of barley and buckwheat weighs 48 lbs, and oats 32 lbs. The weight of the potato crop is heavier than rye. Weights are fragile, and they depend upon acceptance of numbers not based on the output of various fields.

There are a number of reasons, however, for staying with weight. For one thing, in Russia, the weight of output per unit of land is traditional as the measure of yields. For another, in regard to variability, the product mix does not change too much. This is the main reason weight is retained as the measure used. Regarding the inclusion of potatoes, the benefit is that this high-valued crop is of great nutritional value, even though it is considered a low-valued product for statistical purposes. A measure of volume will not reflect actual utility, and weight will. The figure used here, weight, reflects value as well as gross output (food and feed crops, including potatoes) per hectare.

INPUTS

Labor

To establish estimates of labor, as noted in Chapter 7, we estimated the number employed in agriculture drawn from the population census of 1897. For earlier years take standard population data. We take 1858 as representative of 1861 (Mironov [1999], 1: 20; de Livron [1874], p. 26). and for later dates from published series.[18] The ratio between engaged in agriculture and able to work was calculated based on the census of 1897. Days worked was from Mironov,[19] and from Chayanov and Chelintsev, actual expenditure of time on agriculture, from which a trend was constructed.[20] Then we take the average daily wage (for sowing, hay making, and threshing) in kopecks per day and assume that all labor in agriculture is paid at its marginal value.[21]

Capital. Agricultural equipment includes imported and domestically produced machines. Data on the value of imported agricultural machinery exist

[18] The rural population in 1863, from Obruchev (1971), v. 4, pp. 36, 132; rural population and percentage of rural population engaged in agriculture in 1860 and from 1871 from Goldsmith (1955), p. 32, no. 45; rural population and percentage engaged in agriculture, for 1897 from census data, see Strumilin (1964), vol. 3, pp. 304–06.

[19] 1855, 1872, 1902, from Mironov (2003), 2:308.

[20] For 1907, Chayanov et al. (1966), pp. 73–7 and Chelintsev (1919), p. 126. The trend for working days spent per year in agriculture estimated from the polynominal regression model, $y = -0.0096*t\hat{}2 - 0.2226*t + 134.3$.

[21] Strumilin (1958), p. 277.

for almost the entire period in current prices.[22] For domestic production we used data as cited in Chapter 7. For comparison, we also show trends in constant 1913 prices. From this perspective, the value of agricultural equipment for 1867 through 1913 rose, in our estimate, 36.5 times, with an average annual rate of growth of 8.6 percent, that is, 7.1 percent for the first twenty years and 10 percent for the remainder of the period.

Mineral Fertilizers

Other researchers have ignored mineral fertilizers on the assumption that the Russian rural producers used, almost entirely, natural fertilizer. This assumption is fair for the peasants' allotment land (*nadel*) in the early period, but mineral fertilizers were beginning to be used at this time on large nobles' farm enterprises, especially for industrial crops, a trend that increased after the turn of the century. We have data for 1900 to 1913.[23] These estimates were deflated by Strumilin's price index for industrial products (which we assume is close, although not exacting). In 1900, the value of imported fertilizer was 4.1 million rubles (1913 prices), and by 1913, 15.2 million rubles, an average annual rate of growth of 12 percent.

Livestock

Livestock data are extremely fragmented, since they were not systematically gathered before the 1880s. In view of the substantial part of cereals, potatoes, and industrial crops in gross agricultural output (70–80 percent), the fragility would seem unfortunate but tolerable. However, toward the twentieth century the numbers of animal stock were probably crucial. Estimates from Prokopovich in 1913 find about one-fourth of the income of agriculture derived from the sale, or self-consumption by farmers, of meat, dairy products, or other livestock products; we cannot reproduce this information, but our estimates are higher.[24]

For the earlier years, livestock inventories were entirely determined by the amount of meadowlands and hay available to feed cattle in sufficient numbers to fertilize the land. As observed in Chapter 7, one could still describe Russia as a country split between two kinds of agriculture, that which was higher yielding, the three-field and multicrop rotation, was a production process only available to households with meadowland.[25] The

[22] For 1865–1867 we used data from Obruchev (1871); for 1869–1896 we relied on Lenin's figures Lenin (1952), 1: i; for 1901–1913, Oganovskii and Kondratiev (1923). To construct a trend (based on a regression model), we used Vainshtein's data for 1910–1913 as a baseline.

[23] Khromov (1950), p. 164; Oganovskii (1923), p. 307–08.

[24] See Prokopovich (1918).

[25] Obruchev (1871), p. 233.

exclusion of livestock at any point in this period of history would therefore be a problem for understanding cereals growth in Russia's nineteenth century.

A sense of the state of information about livestock production, based on all available sources, can be felt in the summary remarks by Davies and Wheatcroft, remarks cited in full because of the importance of the issue to growth calculations:

> Livestock farming was the second most important sector, providing some 34 percent of agricultural production. Our knowledge of its rate of growth in pre-war decades is imperfect. Neither the absolute numbers of livestock nor their rate of increase are known with certainty; no data are available about changes in the average weight of farm animals in this period. It seems reasonable that livestock numbers increased by only about one percent a year between 1900 and 1914, or more slowly than the growth of population.[26]

Goldsmith also believed that there was too little information at all on livestock figures, and he refused to supply a series.

Actually, as Vainshtein remarked in his article about prerevolutionary livestock inventories, "Statistics regarding livestock numbers for prerevolutionary Russia suffer not from insufficiency but from an abundance of contradictory materials."[27] In data published after 1908, including a retrospective statistics for the post-emancipation period, there is a conflict between information gathered by the Veterinary Administration and that gathered by the Central Statistical Committee. A leap in the series occurs at 1896. In 1895, this retrospective series gives 24.5 million heads of cattle, and in 1896, 29.5 million, or an increase in one year of more than 20 percent. We take this to be an error due to the introduction of a new method of counting or statistical problems; Gregory, like Vainshtein, accepts the larger number.[28]

Production of livestock is such an important part of farming in Russia that we cannot exclude it among factors of production or sources of income. However, because of the speed of planting and harvesting induced by the high seasonality of production, oxen were almost useless in much of Russia, and horses were the main productive force. The weight of horses would be important, then, were it available, allowing detection of age, we take for input the horses more than four or five years of age, or those used for plowing.

We cannot use Gregory's figures for the value of livestock in investment. For our data range, his bias is upward due to his use for the pre-1900 period

[26] Davies and Wheatcroft (1994), p. 109.
[27] Vainshtein (1960), p. 87.
[28] For further discussion of this issue, see Goldsmith (1955) and Gregory (1981), pp. 265–67.

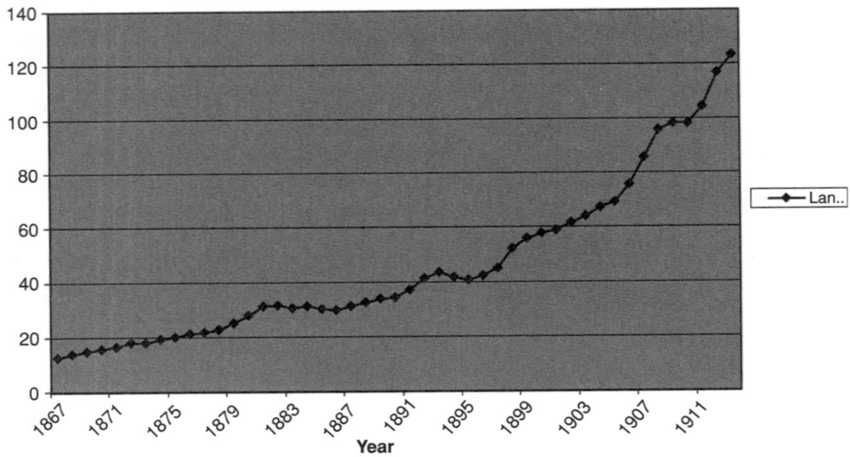

FIGURE A1.4. Real Land Prices, 1867–1913 (Rubles/Desiatina, 1913 = 100).

of additional estimates for Poland, Siberia, and Asia with reference to the population series.

Land. The estimates of land used in farming for the period before 1870 were taken from records of the eighteenth-century General Land Survey. Entries show that, where there were numerous owners of one estate, the survey did not distinguish separate boundaries but instead the number of serfs belonging to individually owned parcels of the *dach'*, often mixing even state and church property together with privately owned land.[29] This practice lasted officially to 1861, and the reporting routines much longer. Also a carryover through 1870 from the era of serfdom, where it still existed, the extent of the demesne, interleaved with allotment land, cannot be determined for that era.[30]

The measure for land is obtained by weighting total sown acreage by an index of weighted yields to which meadows and pasture lands were added. Land prices were taken from Koval'chenko and Milov.[31] For a look at estimates of real prices, based on the Strumilin price index, Figure A1.4 is shown.

VALUE OF OFF-FARM LABOR. This was estimated not for input into the productivity model but for information only. The data for income (in current prices) were estimated as follows. For decadal averages, from the data base compiled for this book, the number of passports (in full year equivalents) was used to derive the percent of outworkers among all agricultural

[29] Milov (1965); Ivanov (1846); Kavelin (1914).
[30] Confino (1969).
[31] 1863–1909, Koval'chenko and Milov (1974), pp. 259–267.

workers (Rashin [1958], pp. 327–8; Khromov [1967, p. 326). Days worked in urban jobs were estimated at 270 per annum at nominal wages estimated by Strumilin (1966, p. 82). Net farm income in current prices was estimated from the database as output net of seed, sales of livestock (40 percent of production). From this redemption payments and taxes were subtracted (Neupokov [1987], pp. 249–250; Hoch [1994]; Khromov [1950], pp. 498, 504, 507, 511; [1957], p. 494).

APPENDIX 2

Measures

Item	Old Russian	New Russian	U.S./British	Metric
1 bushel (wheat)			56 lbs	25.4 kilograms
1 pud		.1638 centners	36 lbs	16.33 kilograms
Pud per desiatina		.1499 centners per hectare		
Chetvert winter wheat	9.63 puds	1.577 centners		
Chetvert spring wheat	9.17 puds	1.502 centners		
Average for winter and spring wheat chetverts to puds	9.34, assuming share of spring in total harvest 62.5%	1.529 centners		
Chetvert rye	8.85 puds			
Chetvert oats	5.63 puds			
Chetvert barley	7.42 puds			
Chetvert potatoes	8.97 puds			
1.5771 metric ton	.984 long tons 1.1023 short tons		36.74 bushels	1,000 kilograms
1 short ton			33.33 bushels	.907 metric tons
1 long ton		1.12 short tons	37.33 bushels	1.016 metric tons

(*continued*)

(*continued*)

Item	Old Russian	New Russian	U.S./British	Metric
1 kilogram			2.205 lbs .0367 bushels	.001 metric tons
1 centner		100 kilograms	45.3 kg/ 50.6 kg 1 quintal	100 kilograms
1 metric quintal			220.4622 pounds	3.674 bushels
1 centner per hectare			89.2 lbs per acre 2.48 puds per acre	
1 bushel per acre				62.76 kg per hectare 138.38 lbs per hectare
1 hectare	0.914 desiatiny		2.471 acres	
1 desiatina	1.092 hectares		2.7 acres	
1 square kilometer				100 hectares
1 mile			5,280 ft	1.6093 km
1 acre			43,560 ft(2)	.4047 hectare
1 versta	500 sazhen			1066.78 meters
1 desiatina			2.7 acres	1.093 hectares
1 chetvert	.25 desiatina 9 puds (8.34)			
1 sazhen				2.13 meters
1 kilogram			2.205 lbs	.001 metric tons
1 pound			453.59 grams	.453 kg
1 stone			14 lbs	6.35 kg

APPENDIX 3

The Yield of Arable Land (Ratio of Harvest to Arable Land)

THE LONG RUN TREND AND MEANS BY PERIOD

The data below, in Figure A3.1, show official Russian statistical reports of output per hectare from 1800 to 2005 (the latest year available), compared with my compilation, which I have transformed into a 3-year moving average. The denominator is total arable (hectares) in rotation, excluding the waste, or unused land. The numerator is gross output in centners (see Appendix 2 on measures), including all grains and potatoes, the "vysev," or harvest, calculated as indicated in Appendix 1.[1] For much of the Soviet period, the data is not barn weight but truck weight, which includes moisture and waste matter; this makes it comparable to the pre-revolutionary information.

Official records of yields broke off only during the first and second world wars. Observations for the war years are missing, given that there are no published figures. Judging by immediately post-war years, effects were devastating but recovery was rapid, leading to restoration of pre-war levels within a few years. The main difference above is the higher estimates for the period of serfdom in official data. Both series show the lack of growth, however, over sixty years.

Table A3.1 allows a rough comparison of the means of annual rates of growth of yield and of land under cultivation by historical epoch and reform period. The periods are as follows: pre-1862 era of serfdom; the 20-year post-emancipation era (1861–1884), which ends with the beginning of the era of industrialisation in 1883; industrialisation to the first revolution following the Russo-Japanese conflict (1885–1905); the Stolypin era (1906–1917); New Economic Policy in the 1920s, the collectivisation that followed it (1929–1940). Following World War II, the post-war era of Khrushchev (1956–1964) and then Kosygin and Brezhnev expansion

[1] De-Livron (1871); Obukhov (1927); *Tsentral'noe Statisticheskoe Upravlenie SSSR* (1940–).

TABLE A3.1. *Period Means Annual Growth Rates of Yield*

Period	Df	Estimate	F	Sigf
Serfdom	58	−.0004	.23	.633
Emancipation	22	.0056	7.28	.013
Industrialisation	18	.0105	10.43	.005
Stolypin Era	9	.0155	5.31	.047
NEP	7	.0245	5.67	.049
Collectivisation	10	.0149	9.33	.012
Khrushchev	10	.0129	5.67	.038
Kosygin	18	.0042	3.80	.067
Gorbachev	4	.0059	.36	.582
Transition	9	.0053	.90	.367

programs (1965–1984) comprise two periods, followed by the brief era of Perestroika, 1985 through 1990. The last period covers the 11-year period from 1991 through 2001.

The annual growth rates of the yield, broken down by period, show the curve fitted to each segment, providing estimates of the period mean in the column "Estimate." Only three of the estimates are not significant, with the underlying series of indicators for the first and last two periods of such volatility to lower the significance of the differences in period means.

From these results, the freedom from servitude was the single most important event in Russia's agrarian economy. It marked a dividing line between stagnation and growth. It is important, however, that the estimate for the period of years around Emancipation shows a very gradual new trend, making clear that the reform was not immediately and visibly a success. It took several decades for the pace in growth of yields to accelerate.

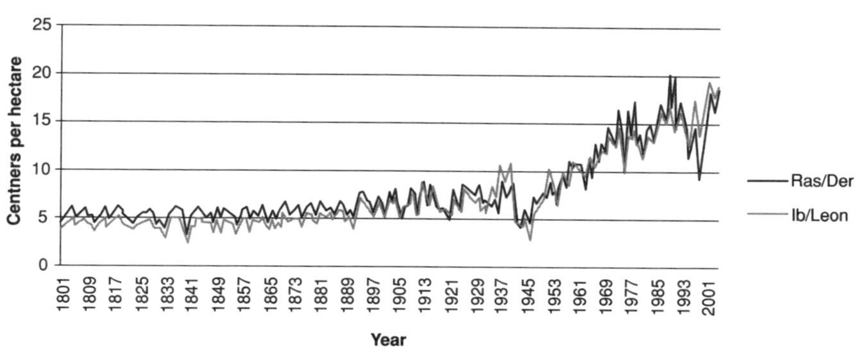

FIGURE A3.1. Comparison of Yields (Major Grains and Potatoes) (cnt/ha): Ibragimova/Leonard (2007) and Rastiannikov/Deriugina (2005), 1801–2005.

TABLE A3.2. *Annual Growth Rates of the Arable in Russia*

Period	Minimum	Maximum	Mean	Std. Deviation
Post-Emancipation	−0.00	0.01	.008691	2.671E-03
Industrialisation	−0.00	0.02	.013723	5.394E-03
NEP	0.01	0.02	.000128	9.76E-03
Prewar	−0.01	0.04	.014284	1.517E-02
Khrushchev	−0.02	0.19	.015548	5.4032E-02
Kosygin/Brezhnev	−0.02	0.02	−.00163	1.15429E-02
Perestroika	−0.01	−0.01	−.027462	3.5492E-02
Post-Command	−0.17	−0.03	−.06929	5.4779E-02

Far more marked and steady climbs were associated with each period of intense industrialisation. As rates of growth in industry increased, so too did the trend in agriculture, building during the Stolypin reforms, the NEP and Collectivization. Mechanisation and expansion of fields onto new lands improved output substantially, as Gregory (1982) has shown. As is documented, in Table A3.2, sown lands expanded; they increased by 45 percent between 1861 and 1913.[2]

From the figures above, the fastest growth rate of the yield was achieved during the NEP, as the peasantry recovered from the devastations of war. Collectivisation and the Khrushchev era had a roughly equivalent effect, which slowed under Kosygin and remained steady thereafter. As explained above, the effects of Emancipation were moderate but highly significant, given the record of the previous sixty years.

It is useful also to look at the expansion of the arable for a rough summary of periods after 1861, as follows.

In four periods, there was aggressive expansion of the arable: post-emancipation, industrialisation (through the Stolypin era), collectivisation and the Khrushchev era. The period of most expansion led between 1958 and 1962 to the addition of more than 60 million hectares to cultivated fields and a radical restructuring of crop patterns. Crop yields in the 1960s and 1970s averaged about 45 and 70 percent above a 1949–1953 base period, which is clearly evidence for this period of both extensive and intensive growth.[3] The locational shift, with a new lands programme in the relatively low-yielding areas of the Volga Valley, Kazakhstan and West Siberia, and a contraction on high yielding soils, such as Ukraine, reduced what would have been an even higher jump in yields.[4]

In the late 1970s and 1980s, policies shifted toward greater investment. As the government spelled out in its 1982 Food programme, the aim was

[2] Karnaukhova (1951), p. 77.
[3] Diamond (1983), p. 149.
[4] Diamond (1983), note 8, p. 173.

to improve yields by increasing investment significantly. As that programme was being implemented Johnson and Brooks (1983) concluded that with the same bundle of resources invested in land of roughly the same climatic condition, output in the Soviet Union was about half that in the US.[5] To be sure, arable and labour inputs decreased, as capital inputs increased, but yields rose only modestly. Under Perestroika and in transition, the arable shrank considerably, as yields rose steadily following a severe output decline.

[5] Johnson and Brooks (1983), p. 196.

APPENDIX 4

Land/Labor Ratio, Tsarist Russia, 1913 = 100

Year	Land/Labor Ratio	Year	Land/Labor Ratio
1860	0.63	1887	0.65
1861	0.61	1888	0.65
1862	0.60	1889	0.66
1863	0.60	1890	0.70
1864	0.60	1891	0.71
1865	0.60	1892	0.70
1866	0.60	1893	0.71
1867	0.59	1894	0.72
1868	0.59	1895	0.72
1869	0.59	1896	0.76
1870	0.59	1897	0.77
1871	0.59	1898	0.77
1872	0.59	1899	0.79
1873	0.59	1900	0.82
1874	0.59	1901	0.84
1875	0.60	1902	0.84
1876	0.60	1903	0.86
1877	0.60	1904	0.89
1878	0.60	1905	0.88
1879	0.61	1906	0.90
1880	0.61	1907	0.89
1881	0.62	1908	0.89
1882	0.62	1909	0.91
1883	0.63	1910	0.95
1884	0.64	1911	0.97
1885	0.64	1912	0.96
1886	0.65	1913	1.00

APPENDIX 5

Exports and Imports, Cereals, Meat, Chicken, Selected Countries, Years (Transition Era)*

	1992	1995	1996	1998	1999	2000	2002	2003	2004	2005
			Export Quantity (inc. food aid) (1,000 tons) | Cereals, nec +							
Argentina	45	34	29	70	64	63	54	105	620	571
Australia	49	90	100	86	117	78	71	74	99	26
Canada	237	422	380	493	565	574	649	714	744	475
France	325	391	404	505	499	582	623	681	741	241
Germany	312	365	445	734	700	793	954	908	929	335
Poland	78	30	26	24	33	48	40	49	73	82
Russian Federation	9	17	6	37	22	63	67	367	85	49
Ukraine	1	16	34	102	1	28	56	61	81	47
United Kingdom	147	186	231	237	291	272	285	292	295	60
United States of America	791	1,507	1,458	1,805	1,881	1,887	3,231	4,872	4,838	1,010
			Import Quantity (inc. food aid) (1,000 tons) | Cereals, nec +							
Argentina	6	7	12	19	18	21	10	8	9	1
Australia	6	74	2	56	38	59	62	66	90	18
Canada	140	201	207	271	346	356	432	488	441	122
France	246	281	299	372	383	437	447	492	489	109
Germany	286	293	330	363	405	407	455	438	475	115
Poland	45	68	123	77	84	107	101	117	95	30
Russian Federation	80	158	231	352	147	221	230	528	360	97
Ukraine	3	19	22	24	18	20	21	304	28	28
United Kingdom	182	262	232	319	347	386	423	489	540	241
United States of America	123	472	535	727	776	841	1022	1087	1,194	198

(continued)

(continued)

	1992	1995	1996	1998	1999	2000	2002	2003	2004	2005
			Import Quantity (inc. food aid) (1,000 tons) | Meat, nec (inc. camel, game) +							
Argentina	3.23	0.09	0.11	0.32	0.31	0.14	0.07	0.02	0.12	0.1
Australia	0.69	0.47	0.3	0.39	0.39	0.53	0.28	0.34	1.12	1.68
Canada	1.19	1.25	0.97	2.27	2.1	2.54	3.86	2.81	2.9	2.18
France	19.97	22.5	25.35	21.01	20.81	24.22	24.01	28.68	29.54	35.54
Germany	22.15	18.56	22.63	36.66	56.26	100.8	113.38	163.13	23.02	26.26
Poland	1.06	0.8	0.26	0.34	0.31	0.38	0.19	0.29	0.59	0.8
Russian Federation	53.07	3.2	5.48	32.92	60.31	7.69	4.23	2.9	3.76	5.32
Ukraine	0.1	40.17	0.37	0.1	0.06	0.18	0.66	0.27	0.21	231.94
United Kingdom	11.63	3.8	4.23	6.09	8.93	16.46	63.87	38.22	25.66	20.07
United States of America	2.37	3.78	6.44	6.83	6.71	6.12	8.14	7.37	7.09	6.62
			Import Quantity (inc. food aid) (1,000 tons) | Chicken Meat +							
Argentina	42.97	20.52	30.28	79.3	72.93	44.78	1.63	8.85	2.25	3.96
Australia	0.3	1.34	0.16	0.56	0.41	0.28	1.02	0.87	0.51	0.47
Canada	68.22	85.29	96.93	131.18	134.01	151.22	155.25	144.42	150.71	130.63
France	94.88	104.81	132.73	179.57	189.39	192.65	207.74	211.91	223.14	228.97
Germany	332.74	350.55	416.73	372.72	296.3	300.96	363.8	458.34	544.25	495.9
Poland	55.36	30.58	32.84	88.89	53.17	18.97	29.48	15.41	140.44	112.9
Russian Federation	33.01	851.25	1,062.50	626.03	76.01	605.07	1,209.87	1,085.23	1,054.80	1,156.29
Ukraine	1.11	26.24	53.01	41.35	74.79	16.2	64.6	87.75	289.6	158.75
United Kingdom	199.26	221.81	236.54	330.44	356.79	378.06	424.81	482.96	570.83	623.37
United States of America	3.99	4.33	5.56	12.86	18.33	21.61	36.19	42.02	49.01	54.61

* FAOSTAT | © FAO Statistics Division 2007 | July 06, 2007.

APPENDIX 6

Fertilizer Use in the Post-Khrushchev Era, 1970–1990

Kilos Mineral Fertilizer Per Hectare Arable	
Year	Fertilizer Applied
1970	32.9
1971	37.2
1972	37.2
1973	41.2
1974	44.6
1975	47.5
1976	59.9
1977	63.2
1978	63.8
1979	65.6
1980	62.2
1981	67.5
1982	70.8
1983	74.1
1984	85.4
1985	87.9
1986	96.0
1987	103.5
1988	106.7
1989	105.3
1990	95.6

APPENDIX 7

Agrarian Reform: Crises and Short-Run Outcomes in Russia, 1861–2010

Reform Design	Crisis Conditions	Short-Run Outcomes
Emancipation statutes (1861)		
Personal freedom	Banking crisis	Decline, then slow growth
Transfer of tax from households to land	Military defeat	Rising peasant debt
Minimum subsistence allotments allocated	High levels of state debt	Formal credit
Redemption of land (forty-nine yrs)		Constraints on labor
Repartitional land commune given broad authority		Seasonal factory closures
Stolypin acts (1906–1910)		
Citizenship	Banking crisis	Moderate growth
Enlargement of tax base	Military defeat	Farm formation
Transfer of tax payments from commune to household	High levels of foreign debt	Peasant landownership
Farm productivity	Labor disturbances	Expanded migration
Enclosures and titling	Industrial slump to 1908	Mechanization
Financial infrastructure		Credit expansion
Rural emigration		
Collectivization (1928–1937)		
Mechanization	Grain procurement crisis	Decline followed by slow recovery
Industrialization	Foreign debt refused	Mechanization
Ideological conformity	War scare	Mass migration to cities

(continued)

(*continued*)

Reform Design	Crisis Conditions	Short-Run Outcomes
Khrushchev incentives reform (1954)		
Greater farm autonomy Larger farm size Expanded state production Incentives (price reform) Investment rise and fall Use of marginal lands Reduction of clean fallow	Demographic outcomes of World War II Internal political struggle	Dramatic initial output improvement Rise in farm income Cost increase Later decline in growth
Privatization of farm enterprises and property rights in land (1991–2010)		
Privatization of farm assets Reduction of subsidies Market incentives Food security	High foreign debt Severe inflation State transformation	Decline followed by slow recovery Drop in farm income Limited independent farming Stalled arable land market

References

Abramovitz, M. (1989). *Thinking about growth and other essays on economic growth and welfare*. Cambridge: Cambridge University Press.

Abramovitz, M., & David, P. (1998). American macroeconomic growth in the era of knowledge-based progress: the long-run perspective. In S. L. Engerman & R. E. Gallman (Eds.), *An economic history of the United States*. Cambridge: Cambridge University Press.

Abriutina, M. S. (1965). *Sel'skoe khoziaistvo v sisteme balansa narodnogo khoziaistva*. Moskva.

Acemoglu, D., Johnson, S., & Robinson, J. A. (2002). Reversal of fortune: geography and institutions in the making of the modern world income distribution. *Quarterly Journal of Economics*, 117(4), 1231–94.

Acemoglu, D., & Robinson, J. A. (2004). Why did the west extend the franchise? Democracy, inequality, and growth in historical perspective. Cheltenham, U.K., and Northampton, MA: Elgar. (pp. 622–54).

Acevedo, C., Barry, D., & Rosa, H. (1995). El Salvador's agricultural sector: macroeconomic policy, agrarian change and the environment. *World Development*, 23(12), 2153–72.

Acheson, J. M. (1993). Capturing the commons: legal and illegal strategies. In T. L. Anderson & R. T. Simmons (Eds.), *The political economy of customs and culture: informal solutions to the commons problem* (pp. 69–84). Lanham, MD: Rowman & Littlefield.

Acs, Z. J., Carlsson, B., & Karlsson, C. (1999). The linkages among entrepreneurship, SMEs and the macroeconomy. In Z. J. Acs, B. Carlsson, & C. Karlsson (Eds.), *Entrepreneurship, small and medium-sized enterprises and the macroeconomy* (pp. 3–42). Cambridge: Cambridge University Press.

Afanasev, I. N., & Ivnitskii, N. A. (1995). *Derevnia v nachale veka: revoliiutsiia i reforma*. Moscow: RGGU.

Afanasev, M. N. (1990). *Bureaucracy, triumph and crisis: new thinking*. Moscow: Progress Publishers.

Aganbegyan, A. G. (1991). Basic directions of perestroyka. In E. A. Hewett & V. H. Winston (Eds.), *Milestones in glasnost' and perestroyka* (pp. 104–21). Washington, DC: Brookings Institute.

Aghion, P., & Blanchard, O. J. (1998). On privatization methods in Eastern Europe and their implications. *Economics of Transition*, 6(1), 87–100.

Aghion, P., Caroli, E., & García-Peñalosa, C. (1999). Inequality and economic growth: the perspective of the new growth theories. *Journal of Economic Literature*, 37(December), 1615–60.

Agrarian Institute of the Russian Academy of Agricultural Science (1993). Agrarnaia reforma v rossii. *Zemlia Rossii*, 1(93), 1–80.

Ahrend, R., & Tompson, W. (2005). Fifteen years of economic reform in Russia: what has been achieved? What remains to be done? *Organisation for Economic Co-Operation and Development. Economics Dept. Working Papers*, No. 430, 1–71.

Akimov, V. V. (1913). Semeinaia sobstvennost' u krest'ian i narodnoe pravo. *Trudy Iuridicheskago Obshchestva (1911)*, 5, 509–23.

Aksenenok, G. A. (1960). *Pravo gosudarstvennoi sobstvennosti na zemliu v SSSR*. Moscow: Nauka.

Albach, H. (1994). *The transformation of firms and markets–a network approach to economic transformation processes in East Germany*. Stockholm: Alquis & Wiksell.

Aleksandrov, V. A. (1976). *Sel'skaia obshchina v Rossii: (XVII-nachalo XIX v.)*. Moscow: Nauka.

Aleksandrov, V. A. (1984). *Obychnoe pravo krepostnoi derevni Rossii XVIII-nachalo XIX v*. Moscow: Nauka.

Alekseev, P. F., Rozygraev, S. A., & Pannikov, V. D. (1967). *Sel'skoe khoziaistvo SSSR*. Moscow.

Alekseeva, G. D. (2003). *Istoricheskaia Nauka v Rossii: ideologiia, politika, 60–80 -e gody XX veka*. Moscow: Institut Rossiiskoi Istorii RAN.

Alesina, A., & Drazen, A. (1998). Why are stabilizations delayed? In F. Sturzenegger & M. Tommasi (Eds.), *The political economy of reform* (pp. 77–103). Cambridge, MA: MIT Press.

Alexeev, M., & Kurlyandskaya, G. (2003). Fiscal federalism and incentives in a Russian region. *Journal of Comparative Economics*, 31(1), 20–33.

Ali, S. (2004). Total Factor Productivity Growth in Pakistan's Agriculture: 1960–1996. *Pakistan Development Review*, 43, pp. 493–512.

Allen, P. (1999). Reweaving the food security safety net: mediating entitlement and entrepreneurship. *Agriculture and Human Values*, 16(2), 117–29.

Allen, R. C. (1997). Agricultural marketing and the possibilities for industrialization in the Soviet Union in the 1930s. *Explorations in Economic History*, 34(4), 387–410.

Allen, R. C. (1994). Agriculture during the Industrial Revolution, 1700–1850. In R. Floud & D. McCloskey (Eds.), *The economic history of Britain since 1700*. Cambridge: Cambridge University Press.

Allen, R. C. (2003). *Farm to factory: a reinterpretation of the Soviet Industrial Revolution*. Princeton, NJ: Princeton University Press.

Allen, R. C. (2003). Progress and poverty in early modern Europe. *Economic History Review*, LVI(3), 403–43.

Allen, R. C. (2001). The rise and decline of the Soviet economy. *Canadian Journal of Economics*, 34(4), 859–81.

Allen, R. C. (1998). The standard of living in the Soviet Union, 1928–1940. *Journal of Economic History*, 58(4), 1063–89.

Allen, R. C. (1999). Tracking the agricultural revolution in England. *Economic History Review*, 52(2), 209–35.

Alston, L. J., Libecap, G. D., & Mueller, B. (1999). *Titles, conflict, and land use: The development of property rights and land reform on the Brazilian Amazon frontier*. Ann Arbor: University of Michigan Press.

Amelina, M. (2000). Rural interactions in the post-Soviet era. In L. A. Norsworthy (Ed.), *Structures, policy outcomes, and adaptive responses: Russian views of the transition in the rural sector* (pp. 16–24). Washington, DC: The World Bank.

Amelina, M. (2000). Why Russian peasants remain in collective farms: a household perspective on agricultural restructuring. *Post Soviet Geography and Economics*, 41(7), 483–511.

Amelina, M. (2002). What turns the kolkhoz into a firm? Regional policies and the elasticity of budget constraint. *Rural reform in post-Soviet Russia* (pp. 264–97). Washington, DC: Woodrow Wilson Center Press.

Amiel, Y., & Cowell, Y. (1994). *The measurement of poverty: an experimental questionnaire investigation*. London: Suntory-Toyota International Centre for Economics and Related Disciplines, London School of Economics.

Anan'ich, B. V. (1983). The economic policy of the tsarist government and enterprise in Russia from the end of the nineteenth through the beginning of the twentieth century. In G. Guroff & F. V. Carstenson (Eds.), *Entrepreneurship in Imperial Russia and the Soviet Union* (pp. 125–39). Princeton, NJ: Princeton University Press.

Anan'ich, B. V., Aref'eva, M. I. Beliaev, S. G., Burgov, A. V., Dadykin, M. M., Dragan, O. V., Dmitrieva, Z. V., Lebedev, S. K., Lizunov, P. V., Morozen, V. V. Petrov, Iu. A. & Salomatina, S. A. (2005). *Kredit i banki v Rossii do nachala XX veka: Sankt-Peterburg i Moskva*. St Petersburg: Izd-vo S.-Peterburskogo Universiteta.

Anderson, B. A. (1980). *Internal migration during modernization in late nineteenth-century Russia*. Princeton, NJ: Princeton University Press.

Anderson, J., & Cochrane, A. (1989). *Restructuring Britain – a state of crisis – the changing face of British politics*. London: Hodder and Stoughton.

Anderson, J. R., & Hazell, P. B. R. (1989). *Variability in grain yields: implications for agricultural research and policy in developing countries*. Baltimore, MD: Published for the International Food Policy Research Institute [by] the Johns Hopkins University Press.

Anderson, K. M. (2001). The politics of retrenchment in a social democratic welfare state: reform of Swedish pensions and unemployment insurance. *Comparative Political Studies*, 34(9), 1063–91.

Anderson, K., & Josling, T. (1993). The challenge to economists of multilateral trade negotiations on agricultural protection. *Food Research Institute Studies*, 22(3), 275–304.

Anderson, T. L., & Hill, P. J. (1975). The evolution of property rights: a study of the American West. *Journal of Law and Economics*, 18(1), 163–79.

Anderson, T. L., & Simmons, R. T. (1993). *The political economy of customs and culture: informal solutions to the commons problem*. Lanham, MD: Rowman & Littlefield.

Andriushina, I. A. (2002). Formiruiushchiisia zemel'nyi rynok Rossii, *Vlast', biznes i krest'ianstvo: mekhanizmy effektivnogo vzaimodeistviia: Nikonovskie chteniia–2002* (pp. 135–36). Moscow: Rossiiskaia Akademiia Selskokhoziastvennykh Nauk, Vserossiiskii Institut Agrarnykh Problem i Informatiki, Fond Podderzhki Agrarnoi Reformy i Sel'skoto Razvitiia.

Anfimov, A. M. (1959). K voprosu o kharaktere agrarnogo stroia Evropeiskoi Rossii v nachale XX v. *Istoricheskie Zapiski*, **65**, 119–39.

Anfimov, A. M. (1961). *Zemel'naia arenda v Rossii v nachale XX veka*. Moscow: Nauka.

Anfimov, A. M. (1962). *Rossiiskaia derevnia v gody pervoi mirovoi voiny, 1914-fevral' 1917 g*. Moscow: Izd-vo sotsial'no-ekon. lit-ry.

Anfimov, A. M. (1969). *Krupnoe pomeshchiche khoziaistvo Evropeiskoi Rossii: konets XIX-nachalo XX veka*. Moscow: Nauka.

Anfimov, A. M. (1980). *Krest'ianskoe khoziaistvo Evropeiskoi Rossii*, 1881–1904. Moscow: Nauka.

Anfimov, A. M., Danilova, L. V., & Koroleva, S. I. (1993). *Sistema gosudarstvennogo feodalizma v Rossii: sbornik statei*. Moscow: Rossiiskaia Akademiia Nauk RF.

Anfimov, A. M., Volobuev, P. V., & Gindin, I. F. (1968). Sotsial'no-ekonomicheskoe razvitie Rossii v nachale XX v. *Istoriia SSSR*, 257–338.

Anisimov, E. V. (1989). Changes in the social structure of Russian society at the end of the 17th and the beginning of the 18th century: the final page in the history of Russian slavery. *Soviet Studies in History* (September), 33–58.

Antonelli, C. (2007). The system dynamics of collective knowledge: from gradualism and saltationism to punctuated change. *Journal of Economic Behavior and Organization*, **62**(2), 215–36.

Antsyferov, A. N., Bilimovich, A. D., Batshev, M. O., & Ivantsov, D. N. (1930). *Russian agriculture during the war*. New Haven, CT: Yale University Press.

Aoki, M. (2000). Institutional evolution as punctuated equilibria. In C. Ménard (Ed.), *Perspectives from new institutional economics: institutions, contracts and organizations* (pp. 11–33). Cheltenham: Edward Elgar.

Aoki, M., & Hayami, Y. (2001). *Communities and markets in economic development*. Oxford [UK], New York: Oxford University Press.

Aoki, M., & Kim, H. K. (1995). *Corporate governance in transitional economies: insider control and the role of banks*. Washington, DC: The World Bank.

Arce, M. (2005). Market reform in society. Post-crisis politics and economic change in authoritarian Peru: University Park, PA.

Arnade, C., & Gopinath, M. (2000). Financial constraints and output targets in Russian agricultural production. *Journal of International Development*, **12**(1), 71–84.

Arnade, C., & Trueblood, M. A. (2002). Estimating a profit function in the presence of inefficiency: an application to Russian agriculture. *Journal of Agricultural and Resource Economics*, **27**(1), 94–113.

Arnade, C., & Vasavada, U. (1995). Causality between productivity and exports in agriculture: evidence from Asia and Latin America. *Journal of Agricultural Economics*, **46**(2), 174–86.

Arnott, R., Greenwald, B. C. N., & Stiglitz, J. E. (1993). *Information and economic efficiency* Cambridge, MA: National Bureau of Economic Research.

Arnott, R., & Stiglitz, J. E. (1990). *The welfare economics of moral hazard*. Cambridge, MA: National Bureau of Economic Research.

Arriagada Herrera, G., & Dornbusch, R. (1991). *Eastern Europe, Latin America and comparative politics*. Washington, DC: Latin American Program Woodrow Wilson Center.

Arrow, K. (1951). *Social choice and individual values*. New Haven, CT: Yale University Press.

Arrow, K., Colombatto, E., Perlman, M., & Schmidt, C. (1996). *The rational foundations of economic behavior: proceedings of the IEA Conference held in Turin, Italy*. London: Macmillan Press.

Arsenev, K. (1848). *Statisticheskie ocherki Rossii*. St. Petersburg: Nauka.

Arthur, W. B. (1989). Competing technologies, increasing returns, and lock-in by historical events. *Economic Journal*, **99**(394), 116–31.

Arthur, W. B. (1994). *Increasing returns and path dependence in the economy*. Ann Arbor: University of Michigan Press.

Asalkhanov, I. A. (1975). *Sel'skoe khoziaistvo Sibiri kontsa XIX-nachala XX v.* Novosibirsk: Nauka.

Asaturov, G. B., & Florentiev, L. I. A. (1967). *Sel'skoe khoziaistvo Rossii*. Moscow: Nauka.

Ascher, A. (1988). *The Revolution of 1905*. Stanford, CA: Stanford University Press.

Ascher, A. (2001). *P.A. Stolypin: the search for stability in late Imperial Russia*. Stanford, CA: Stanford University Press.

Åslund, A. (1994). *Economic transformation in Russia*. New York: St Martin's Press.

Åslund, A. (1995). *How Russia became a market economy*. Washington, DC: Brookings Institution.

Åslund, A. (1997). *Russia's economic transformation in the 1990s*. London, Washington DC: Pinter.

Åslund, A., & Layard, P. R. G. (1993). *Changing the economic system in Russia*. New York: St. Martin's Press.

Asmus, R. D. (2008). Europe's eastern promise. *Foreign Affairs*, **87**(1), 95–106.

Aspe Armella, P., Dornbusch, R., & Obstfeld, M. (1983). *Financial policies and the world capital market: the problem of Latin American countries*. Chicago: University of Chicago Press.

Atack, J., & Bateman, F. (1989). Land and the development of mid-nineteenth century American agriculture in the northern states. In G. Grantham & C. S. Leonard (Eds.), *Agrarian organization in the century of industrialization: Europe, Russia, and North America* (pp. 279–312). Greenwich, CT: JAI Press.

Atkinson, A. B. (1970). On the measurement of inequality. *Journal of Economic Theory*, **2**, 244–63.

Atkinson, A. B. (1991). *Modern public finance*. Aldershot, Hants, England; Brookfield, VT: Elgar.

Atkinson, A. B., & Micklewright, J. (1992). *The economic transformation in Eastern Europe and the distribution of income*. Cambridge; New York: Cambridge University Press.

Atkinson, D. (1990). Egalitarianism and the commune. In R. Bartlett (Ed.), *Land Commune and peasant community in Russia: communal forms in imperial and early Soviet society* (pp. 7–19). London: Macmillan.

Atkinson, D. (1983). *The end of the Russian Land Commune, 1905–1930*. Stanford, CA: Stanford University Press.

Aturupane, C., Djankov, S., & Hoekman, B. (1997). *Determinants of intra-industry trade between East and West Europe*. Palo Alto, CA; Ann Arbor, MI; Washington, DC:World Bank, Development Research Group.

Austen-Smith, D. (1997). Interest groups: money, information, and influence. In D. C. Mueller (Ed.), *Perspectives on public choice: a handbook* (pp. 296–321). Cambridge; New York; Melbourne: Cambridge University Press.

Austin, R. B., & Arnold, M. H. (1989). Variability in wheat yields in England: analysis and future prospects. In J. R. Anderson & P. B. R. Hazell (Eds.), *Variability in grain yields: implications for agricultural research and policy in developing countries* (pp. 100–06). Baltimore, MD: Published for the International Food Policy Research Institute [by] the Johns Hopkins University Press.

Aven, P. (1997). Problems in foreign trade regulation in the Russian economic reform. In A. Åslund (Ed.), *Russia's economic transformation in the 1990s* (pp. 56–67). London: Pinter.

Avrekh, A. I. (1968). *Stolypin i Tret'ia Duma*. Moscow.

Avrich, P. (1970). *Kronstadt, 1921*. Princeton, NJ: Princeton University Press.

Axelrod, R. (1984). *The evolution of cooperation*. New York: Basic Books.

Bairoch, P. (1997). New estimates on agricultural productivity and yields of developed countries, 1800–1990. In A. Bhaduri, & R. Skarstein (Eds.), *Economic development and agricultural productivity* (pp. 45–64). Cheltenham: Edward Elgar.

Baland, J. M., & Platteau, J. P. (1996). *Halting degradation of natural resources: is there a role for rural communities?* New York: United Nations Food and Agriculture Organization.

Balcerowicz, L., Blaszczyk, B., & Dabrowski, M. (1997). The Polish way to the market economy 1989–1995. In S. Parker, W. T. Woo, & J. D. Sachs (Eds.), *Economies in transition: comparing Asia and Europe* (pp. 131–60). Cambridge, MA: The MIT Press.

Baldwin, R. E., & Martin, P. (1999). *Two waves of globalisation: superficial similarities, fundamental differences*. Cambridge, MA: National Bureau of Economic Research.

Balfour, S. (1995). Riot, regeneration and reaction: Spain in the aftermath of the 1898 disaster. *Historical Journal*, 38(2), 405–24.

Ball, D. E., & Walton, G. M. (1976). Agricultural productivity change in eighteenth-century Pennsylvania. *The Journal of Economic History*, 36(March), 102–17.

Ball, V. E. (1997). Agricultural productivity revisited. *American Journal of Agricultural Economics*, 79, 1045–63.

Ball, V. E. (1999). Patterns of state productivity growth in the U.S. farm sector: linking state and aggregate models. *American Journal of Agricultural Economics*, 81, 164–79.

Ball, V. E., Bureau, J.-C., Butault, J.-P., & Nehring, R. (2001). Levels of farm sector productivity: an international comparison. *Journal of Productivity Analysis*, 15, 5–29.

Ball, V. E., Butault, J.-P., & Nehring, R. (2001). U.S. agriculture, 1960–96: a multilateral comparison of total factor productivity. *Technical Bulletin*. Washington, DC: USDA.

Balmaceda, M. M. (2008). *Energy dependency, politics and corruption in the former Soviet Union: Russia's power, oligarchs' profits and Ukraine's missing energy policy*, 1995–2006. London: Routledge.

Bandow, D., & Vásquez, I. (1994). *Perpetuating poverty: the World Bank, the IMF, and the developing world*. Washington, DC: Cato Institute.

Banerji, A. (1997). *Merchants and markets in revolutionary Russia*, 1917–1930. London: Macmillan in association with the Centre for Russian and East European Studies, University of Birmingham.

Bardhan, P. (1989). Alternative approaches to the theory of institutions in economic development. In P. Bardhan (Ed.), *The economic theory of agrarian institutions* (pp. 1–17). Oxford: Clarendon Press, Oxford University Press.

Bardhan, P. (1993). Symposium on management of local commons. *Journal of Economic Perspectives*, 7(4), 87–92.

Bardin, I. P. (1960). *Sel'skoe khosiaistvo*. Moscow: Nauka.

Barkai, H. (1973). The macro-economics of tsarist Russia in the industrialization era: monetary developments, the balance of payments and the gold standard. *Journal of Economic History*, 33(June), 339–71.

Barnett, V. (1995). Soviet commodity markets during NEP. *Economic History Review*, 48(2), 329–52.

Barry, R. A., & Cline, W. R. (1979). *Agrarian structure and productivity in developing countries*. Baltimore, MD: The Johns Hopkins University Press.

Barsov, A. A. (1969). *Balans stoimostnykh obmenov mezhdu gorodom i derevnei*. Moscow: Nauka.

Bartlett, R. P. (1984). *Russian thought and society*, 1800–1917: *essays in honour of Eugene Lampert*. Staffordshire: University of Keele.

Bartlett, R. P. (1990). *Land commune and peasant community in Russia: communal forms in imperial and early Soviet society*. New York: St. Martin's Press.

Bartlett, R. P. (1994). Defences of serfdom in eighteenth-century Russia. In L. A. J. Hughes & M. di Salvo (Eds.), *A window on Russia* (pp. 67–74). Rome: La Fenice Edizioni.

Bartlett, R. P. (2003). Serfdom and state power in Imperial Russia. *European History Quarterly*, 33(1), 29–64.

Bartlett, R. P., & Lampert, E. (1984). *Russian thought and society* 1800–1917: *essays in honour of Eugene Lampert*. Staffordshire: University of Keele.

Baryshnikov, M. (2005). The family in the institutional space of Russian entrepreneurship (an attempt at historical study). *Voprosy ekonomiki*, 7, 150–56.

Barzel, Y. (1989). *The economic analysis of property rights*. New York: Cambridge University Press.

Barzel, Y. (2000). Property rights and the evolution of the state. *Economics of Governance*, 1(1), 25–51.

Barzel, Y., & Kochin, L. A. (1995). Ronald Coase on the nature of social cost as a key to the problem of the firm. In Y. Barzel (Ed.), *Productivity change, public goods and transaction costs: essays at the boundaries of microeconomics*. Aldershot: Elgar.

Bater, J. (1976). *St Petersburg: industrialization and change*. New York: Edward Arnold.

Bates, R. H. (1990). Macropolitical econcomy in the field of development. In J. E. Alt & K. A. Shepsle (Eds.), *Perspectives on positive political economy* (pp. 31–56). Cambridge, MA: Cambridge University Press.

Bates, R. H., & Krueger, A. O. (1993). Introduction. In R. H. Bates & A. Krueger (Eds.), *Political and economic interactions in economic policy reform: evidence from eight countries* (pp. 1–26). Cambridge and Oxford: Blackwell.

Batkibekov, S., & Sharipova, E. (2002). *The state budget*. Moscow: Institute for the Economy in Transition.

Batsaev, I. D. (1997). *Sel'skoe i promyslovoe khoziaistvo Severo-Vostoka Rossii 1929–1953 gg*. Magadan: Rossiiskaia akademiia nauk Dal'nevostochnoe otd-nie Severo-Vostochnyi nauch. tsentr Severo-Vostochnyi kompleksnyi nauchno-issl. in-t.

Bautista, R. M., & Jayasuriya, S. (1996). Effects of macroeconomic policy reforms on agriculture and the rural sector: a critical survey of the empirical literature. *Asian Journal of Agricultural Economics*, 2(1), 67–78.

Bautista, R. M. et al. (2002). *Macroeconomic policy reforms and agriculture: towards equitable growth in Zimbabwe*. Washington, DC: International Food Policy Research Institute.

Bayar, A. H. (2001). Entry and exit dynamics of "excessive deficits" in the European Union. *Public Finance and Management*, 1(1), 92–112.

Beenstock, M. (1984). *The world economy in transition*. London; Boston: Allen & Unwin.

Belin, L. (1991). Secret Agents 301, 329 and 345: the introduction of hybrid corn in the USSR. *Department of history and literature*. Cambridge, MA: Harvard University.

Belousov, R. (1999). *Ekonomicheskaia istoriia Rossii: XX vek: Na rubezhe dvykh stoletii*. Moscow: Izdat.

Belousov, R. (2000). Gosudarstvennyi biudzhet dorevoliutsionnoi Rossii. *Ekonomicheskaia istoriia Rossii XIX–XX vv; Sovremennyi vzgliad* (pp. 37–52). Moscow: ROSSPEN.

Benácek, V., Shemetilo, D., & Petrov, A. (1997). Efficiency under restructuring from a microeconomic perspective. In S. Sharma (Ed.), *Restructuring Eastern Europe: the microeconomics of the transition process* (pp. 58–71). Cheltenham, UK: Edward Elgar.

Bennett, R. J. (1990). *Decentralization, local governments and markets*. Oxford: Clarendon Press.

Berelowitch, A., & Danilov, V. A. (1998). *Sovetskaia derevnia glazami VChK-OGPU-NKVD, 1918–1939: dokumenty i materialy v 4 tomakh*. Moscow: ROSSPEN.

Bergson, A. (1989). Economics of perestroika: an inauspicious beginning. *Challenge*, **32**(3), 10–15.

Bergson, A. (1985). Gorbachev calls for intensive growth. *Challenge*, **28**, 11–14.

Bergson, A. (1997). How big was the Soviet GDP? *Comparative Economic Studies*, **39**, 1–14.

Bergson, A. (1995). The big bang in Russia: an overview. *Harvard Institute of Economic Research. Discussion Paper Series*, No. 1730, 1–27.

Bergson, A. (1989). *Planning and performance in socialist economies: the USSR and Eastern Europe*. Boston: Unwin Hyman.

Bergson, A. (1961). *The real national income of Soviet Russia since 1928*. Cambridge, MA: Harvard University Press.

Bergson, A. (1944). *The structure of Soviet wages: a study in socialist economics*. Cambridge, MA; London: Harvard University Press; Oxford University Press.

Bergson, A., & Kuznets, S. (1963). *Economic trends in the Soviet Union*. Cambridge, MA: Harvard University Press.

Bergson, A., & Levine, H. S. (1983). *The Soviet economy: toward the year 2000*. London; Boston: G. Allen & Unwin.

Berkowitz, D., & DeJong, D. N. (2001). The evolution of market integration in Russia. *Economics of Transition*, **9**(1), 87–104.

Berkowitz, D., & DeJong, D. N. (2002). Accounting for growth in post-Soviet Russia. *Regional Science and Urban Economics*, **32**(2), 221–39.

Berkowitz, D., & DeJong, D. N. (2003). Regional integration: an empirical assessment of Russia. *Journal of Urban Economics*, **53**(3), 541–59.

Berkowitz, D., & DeJong, D. N. (2003). Policy reform and growth in post-Soviet Russia. *European Economic Review*, **47**(2), 337–52.

Berkowitz, D., DeJong, D. N., & Husted, S. (1998). Quantifying price liberalisation in Russia. *Journal of Comparative Economics*, **26**, 735–60.

Berlin, I. S. (1978). *Russian thinkers*. London: Hogarth Press.

Berliner, J. S. (1957). *Factory and manager in the USSR*. Cambridge, MA: Harvard University Press.

Berliner, J. S. (1972). *Economy, society, and welfare: a study in social economics*. New York: Praeger.

Berliner, J. S. (1976). *The innovation decision in Soviet industry*. Cambridge, MA: MIT Press.

Bernanke, B. S., Laubach, T., Mishkin, F. S., & Posen, A. S. (1999). *Inflation targeting: lessons from the international experience*. Princeton, NJ: Princeton University Press.

Bertero, E. (1997). Restructuring financial systems in transition and developing economies: an approach based on the French financial system. *Economics of Transition*, **5**(2), 367–94.

Besley, T. J., & Rosen, H. S. (1998). Vertical externalities in tax setting: evidence from gasoline and cigarettes. *Journal of Public Economics*, **70**(3), 383–98.

Bespakhotnyi, G. V. (2002). Izmennie napravlenii biudzhetnogo finansirovaniia sel'skogo khoziastva, *Vlast', biznes i krest'ianstvo: mekhanizmy effektivnogo vzaimodeistviia: Nikonovskie chteniia–2002* (pp. 97–9). Moscow: Rossiiskaia Akademiia Selskokhoziastvennykh Nauk, Vserossiiskii Institut agrarnykh problem i informatiki, Fond Podderzhki Agrarnoi Reformy i Sel'skovo Razvitiia.

Bezemer, D. J. (2002). De-collectivization in Czech and Slovak agriculture: an institutional explanation. *Journal of Economic Issues*, 36(3), 723–46.

Bezemer, D. J. (2002). Microeconomic institutions and the transformation of agribusiness. *Journal of Economic Issues*, 36(3), 723.

Bezes, P. (2007). The hidden politics of administrative reform: cutting French civil service wages with a low-profile instrument. *Governance*, 20(1), 23–56.

Bhaduri, A., & Skarstein, R. (1997). *Economic development and agricultural productivity*. Cheltenham: Edward Elgar.

Bhagwati, J., & Ramaswammi, V. K. (1963). Domestic distortions, tariffs, and the theory of optimum subsidy. *Journal of Political Economy*, 71(February), 44–50.

Bhaumik, S., & Estrin, S. (2002). *Why transition paths differ: Russian and Chinese enterprise performance compared*. London: London Business School.

Bialer, S. (1987). *Soviet paradox: external expansion, internal decline*. New York: Random House, Vintage Books.

Bialer, S., & Gustafson, T. (1982). *Russia at the crossroads: the 26th Congress of the CPSU*. London; Boston: Allen & Unwin.

Bideleux, R. (1990). Agricultural advance under the Russian village commune system. In R. Bartlett (Ed.), *Land commune and peasant community in Russia: communal forms in imperial and early Soviet society* (pp. 196–218). London: Macmillan in association with the School of Slavonic and East European Studies, University of London.

Binswanger, H. P. (1974). The measurement of technical change biases with many factors of production. *American Economic Review*, 64(6), 964–76.

Binswanger, H. P. (1979). Risk and uncertainty in agricultural development: an overview. In J. A. Roumasset, J.-M. Boussard, & I. J. Singh (Eds.), *Risk, uncertainty and agricultural development*. Laguna, Philippines: ADC and SEARCA.

Binswanger, H. P., Deininger, K., & Feder, G. (1995). Power, distortions, revolt and reform in agricultural land relations. In T. N. Srinivasan & J. Behrman (Eds.), *Handbook of development economics*. North Holland: Amsterdam.

Binswanger, H. P., & Elgin, M. (1984). Reflections on land reform and farm size. In C. K. Eicher & J. M. Staatz (Eds.), *Agricultural development in the third world* (pp. 342–54). Baltimore, MD: The Johns Hopkins University Press.

Binswanger, H. P., & Ruttan, V. W. (1978). *Induced innovation: technology, institutions, and development*. Baltimore, MD: The Johns Hopkins University Press.

Bird, R. (1991). Tax administration and tax reform: reflections on experience. In J. Khalilzadeh-Shirazi & A. Shah (Eds.), *Tax policy in developing countries* (pp. 38–56). Washington, DC: The World Bank.

Black, B. S., Kraakman, R., & Tarassova, A. S. (1998). *Guide to the Russian law on joint stock companies*. The Hague: Kluwer Law International.

Blackbourn, D. (1998). *The long nineteenth century: a history of Germany*, 1780–1918. New York: Oxford University Press.

Blackwell, W. (1970). *The industrialization of Russia: an historical perspective*. New York: New York University.

Blackwell, W. L. (1974). *Russian economic development from Peter the Great to Stalin*. New York: New Viewpoints.

Blair, M. M. (1995). *Ownership and control: rethinking corporate governance for the twenty-first century*. Washington, DC: Brookings Institution.

Blanchard, O. (1997). *The economics of post-communist transition*. Oxford; New York: Clarendon Press; Oxford University Press.

Blasi, J. R. (1996). *Corporate ownership and corporate governance in the Russian Federation*. Washington, DC: Federal Commission on the Capital Markets.

Blasi, J. R., Kroumova, M., & Kruse, D. (1997). *Kremlin capitalism: privatizing the Russian economy*. Ithaca, NY: Cornell University Press.

Bliokh, I. S. (1890). *Melioratsionny krediti i sostoianie sel'skogo khoziastva v Rossii i inostrannykh gosudarstvakh*. St. Petersburg.

Bloch, M. (1966). *French rural history: an essay on its basic characteristics*. Berkeley: University of California Press.

Block, S. A. (2001). Does Africa grow differently? *Journal of Development Economics*, 65(2), 443–67.

Blommestein, H. J. (1993). Financial sector reform and monetary policy in Central and Eastern Europe. In D. E. Fair & R. J. Raymond (Eds.), *The new Europe: evolving economic and financial systems in East and West* (pp. 145–67). Boston, MA: Kluwer Academic Publishers.

Blum, D. W. (2003). Perspectives on the Caspian Sea dilemma: a framing comment. *Eurasian Geography and Economics*, 44(8), 617–22.

Blum, J. (1961). *Lord and peasant in Russia: from the ninth to the nineteenth century*. Princeton, NJ: Princeton University Press.

Blum, J. (1978). *The end of the old order in rural Europe*. Princeton, NJ: Princeton University Press.

Boediono, & Sarwono, H. A. (1999). Macroeconomic policy: a foundation for Indonesia's sustainable economic development. In F. Adams & W. James (Eds.), *Public policies in East Asian development: facing new challenges* (pp. 185–201). Westport, CT.

Boev, V. i. R., & Gabov, V. i. M. (1981). *Sel'skoe khoziaistvo v raionakh promyshlennogo osvoeniia Sibiri: Opyt, problemy*. Moscow: Ekonomika.

Bogdanovsky, V. (2000). Land reform: expectations and social consequences. In L. A. Norsworthy (Ed.), *Russian views of the transition in the rural sector: structures, policy outcomes, and adaptive responses* (pp. 57–66). Washington, DC: The World Bank.

Bohac, R. (1989). Agricultural structure and the origins of migration in central Russia, 1810–1850. Agrarian organization in the century of industrialization: Research in Economic History series. In G. Grantham & C. S. Leonard (Eds.), *Europe, Russia, and North America* (pp. 369–87). Greenwich, CT: JAI Press.

Bohac, R. (1991). Everyday forms of resistance: serf opposition to gentry exactions, 1800–1861. In E. Kingston-Mann & T. Mixter (Eds.), *Peasant economy, culture, and politics of European Russia, 1800–1921* (pp. 236–60). Princeton, NJ: Princeton University Press.

Bokusheva, R., & Hockmann, H. (2006). Production risk and technical inefficiency in Russian agriculture. *European Review of Agricultural Economics*, 33(1), 93–118.

Bol'shakova, O. V. (1996). *Bìurokratiia i velikie reformy v Rossii, 1860–70-e gg; sovremennaia anglo-amerikanskaia istoriografiia: nauchno-analiticheskii obzor*. Moscow: Rossiiskaia akademiia nauk.

Boone, C. (1990). The making of a rentier class – wealth accumulation and political control in Senegal. *Journal of Development Studies*, **26**(3), 425–49.

Boone, P., & Federov, B. (1997). The ups and downs of Russian economic reforms. In S. Parker, W. T. Woo, & J. D. Sachs (Eds.), *Economies in transition: comparing Asia and Europe* (pp. 161–88). Cambridge, MA: The MIT Press.

Boone, P., Gomulka, S., & Layard, P. R. G. (1998). *Emerging from communism: lessons from Russia, China, and Eastern Europe*. Cambridge, MA: MIT Press.

Borders, K. (1927). *Village life under the Soviets*. New York: Vanguard Press.

Bornefalk, A. (1998). *Democratization, rent seeking, and economic transition*. Stockholm: SITE [Stockholm School of Economics].

Bornstein, M. (1997). Non-standard methods in the privatization strategies of the Czech Republic, Hungary and Poland. *Economics of Transition*, 5(2), 323–38.

Borodkin, L. I. (2006). O promyshlennom roste dorevoliutsionnoi Rossii. *Ekonomicheskaia istoriia, Obozrenie*, 12, 184–200.

Borodkin, L., Granville, B., & Leonard, C. (2008). The rural urban wage gap in the industrialization of Russia, 1885–1910. *Economic Review of European History*, 12(1).

Borodkin, L., & Leonard, C. (1994). The Russian land commune and the mobility of labour during industrialization, 1885–1913. Economics in a changing world: Volume 1. System transformation: Eastern and Western assessments. In A. Aganbegyan, O. Bogomolov, & M. Kaser (Eds.), *Proceedings of the Tenth World Congress of the International Economic Association, Moscow* (pp. 1167–1978). London: Macmillan Press, in association with the International Economic Association.

Borodkin, L. I., & Valetov, T. I. (1999). Dinamika differentsiatsii v oplate truda rabochikh-tekstil'shchikov i metallistov v Rossii v period dorevoliutsionnoi industrializatsii, *Ekonomicheskii istoriia. Ezhegodnik* (pp. 111–51). Moscow: ROSSPEN.

Borodkin, L. I., & Valetov, T. I. (2001). Mikroanaliz dannykh o kvalifikatsii i dinamike zarabotnoi platy rabochikh-tekstil'shchikov Tovarishchestva manufaktur N. N. Konshina (konets XIX-nachalo XX v.). *Ekonomicheskaia istoriia, ezhegodnik*. Moscow: ROSSPEN.

Borovoi, S. I. (1958). *Kredit i banki Rossii: seredina XVII v.–1861 g.* Moscow: Gosfinizdat.

Borrero, M. (2003). *Hungry Moscow: scarcity and urban society in the Russian Civil War*, 1917–1921. New York: Peter Lang.

Bosworth, B., Dornbusch, R., & Labán, R. (1994). *The Chilean economy: policy lessons and challenges*. Washington, DC: Brookings Institution.

Botosh, N. N., & Fauzer, V. V. (1997). *Sel'skoe naselenie v etnoterritorial'nykh obrazovaniiakh Rossiiskogo Severa*. Syktyvkar: Syktyvkarskii gosudarstvennyi universitet.

Bovykin, V. I. (1997). *Foreign entrepreneurship and foreign investment in Russia*. Moscow: ROSSPEN.

Bovykin, V. I., & Laverychev, V. I. A. (1984). *Formirovanie finansovogo kapitala v Rossii: konets XIX v.–1908 g.* Moscow: Nauka.

Bovykin, V. I., Naumova, G. R., & Petrov, I. U. A. (1989). *Monopolisticheskii kapitalizm v Rossii: sbornik nauchnykh trudov*. Moscow: Nauka.

Bovykin, V. I., & Nussbaum (1986). *Proizvoditel'nye sily i monopolisticheskii kapital v Rossii i Germanii v kontse XIX-nachale XX vv*. Moscow: Nauka.

Bowler, I. R., Bryant, C. R., & Nellis, M. D. (1992). *Contemporary rural systems in transition*. Wallingford, Oxon; Tucson, AZ: CAB International.

Bowman, L. (1993). Russia's first income taxes: the effects of modernized taxes on commerce and industry, 1885–1914. *Slavic Review*, 52(2), 256–82.

Boycko, M. (1995). Russia's struggle with stabilization: conceptual issues and evidence: comment. In M. Bruno & B. Pleskovic (Eds.), *Proceedings of the World Bank. Annual Conference on Development Economics, 1994. Supplement to The World Bank. Economic Review and The World Bank. Research Observer* (pp. 86–9). Washington, DC: World Bank.

Boycko, M., Shleifer, A., & Vishny, R. W. (1994). The progress of Russian privatization. In A. Åslund (Ed.), *Economic transformation in Russia* (pp. 101–110). New York: St Martin's Press.

Boycko, M., Schleifer, A., & Vishny, R. (1995). *Privatizing Russia*. Cambridge, MA: The MIT Press.

Boycko, M., Shleifer, A., & Vishny, R. (1996). Second-best economic policy for a divided government. *European Economic Review*, 40(3–5), 767–74.

Boyer, G. R., & Hatton, T. J. (1994). Regional labour market integration in England and Wales, 1850–1913. In G. Grantham & M. MacKinnon (Eds.), *Labour market evolution: the economic history of market integration, wage flexibility and the employment relation* (pp. 84–106). London and New York: Routledge.

Brabant, J. M. v. (1996). *Integrating Europe: the transition economies at stake*. Dordrecht; Boston: Kluwer Academic Publishers.

Brabant, J. M. v. (1998). *The political economy of transition: coming to grips with history and methodology*. London and New York: Routledge.

Brada, J. C. (1996). A skeptical note on the usefulness of a tight fiscal policy applied to the Czech case: a response to Bruno Sergi. *Eastern European Economics*, 34(6), 89–91.

Brada, J. C. (1996). Privatization is transition – or is it? *Journal of Economic Perspectives*, 10(2), 67–86.

Brada, J. C. (2000). Fiscal policy in transition economies: a postscript. *Post Soviet Geography and Economics*, 41(8), 599–604.

Brada, J. C., Hess, A., & Singh, I. (1996). Corporate governance in Eastern Europe: findings from case studies. *Post Soviet Geography and Economics*, 37(10), 589–614.

Brada, J. C., King, A. E., & Kutan, A. M. (2000). Inflation bias and productivity shocks in transition economies: the case of the Czech Republic. *Economic Systems*, 24(2), 119–38.

Brada, J. C., & Singh, I. (1999). *Corporate governance in Central Eastern Europe: case studies of firms in transition*. Armonk, NY: M. E. Sharpe.

Brada, J. C., & Wädekin, K. E. (1988). *Socialist agriculture in transition: organizational response to failing performance*. Boulder, CO: Westview Press.

Bradley, J. (1985). *Muzhik and Muscovite: urbanization in late Imperial Russia*. Berkeley, CA: University of California Press.

Bradshaw, M. J. (1991). *The Soviet Union: a new regional geography?* London; New York: Belhaven Press; Halsted Press.

Bradshaw, M. J. (1997). *Geography and transition in the post-Soviet republics*. Chichester; New York: Wiley.

Bradshaw, M., & Hanson, P. (1999). The territories and the federation: an economic perspective. *The territories of the Russian Federation* (pp. 3–21). London: Europa.

Bradshaw, M., & Prendergrast, J. (2005). The Russian heartland revisited: an assessment of Russia's transformation. *Eurasian Geography and Economics*, **46**(2), 83–122.

Bradshaw, M., & Treyvish, A. (2000). Russia's regions in the "triple transition." In P. Hanson & M. Bradshaw (Eds.), *Regional economic change in Russia* (pp. 17–42). Cheltenham; Northampton, MA: Elgar.

Bradshaw, M. J., & Vartapetov, K. (2003). A new perspective on regional inequalities in Russia. *Eurasian Geography and Economics*, **44**(6), 403–29.

Braithwaite, J., Grootaert, C., & Milanovic, B. (2000). *Poverty and social assistance in transition countries*. New York: St. Martin's Press.

Bramall, C. (2000). *Sources of Chinese economic growth, 1978–1996*. Oxford: Oxford University Press.

Brassley, P. (1997). *Agricultural economics and the CAP: an introduction*. Oxford: Blackwell Science Ltd.

Braverman, A. (1992). *Commodity price stabilization and policy reform: an approach to the evaluation of the Brazilian price band proposals*. Washington, DC: World Bank.

Braverman, A., & Guasch, J. L. (1993). Administrative failures in government credit programs. In K. Hoff, A. Braverman, & J. E. Stiglitz (Eds.), *The economics of rural organization: theory, practice, and policy* (pp. 53–69). Oxford: Oxford University Press.

Brazelton, W. R. (1996). A selection of early Soviet economic reforms: the Khrushchev era. *Journal of Economics (MVEA)*, **22**(1), 7–13.

Brenton, P., Gros, D., & Vandille, G. (1997). Output decline and recovery in the transition economies: causes and social consequences. *Economics of Transition*, **5**(1), 113–30.

Breslauer, G. W. (1991). *Dilemmas of transition: in the Soviet Union and Eastern Europe*. Berkeley, CA: University of California at Berkeley International and Area Studies.

Brewster, D. E., Rasmussen, W. D., & Youngberg, G. (1983). *Farms in transition: interdisciplinary perspectives on farm structure*. Ames: Iowa State University Press.

Brianskii, A. M. (1960). Statistika sel'skogo khoziastva. *Istoriia sovetskoi gosudarstvennoi statistiki, sbornik statei*. Moscow: Gosudarstvennoe statisticheskoe izd-vo.

Bristow, J. A. (1996). *The Bulgarian economy in transition*. Cheltenham, UK; Brookfield, VT: Edward Elgar.

Broadberry, S. (1994). Comparative productivity in British and American manufacturing during the nineteenth century. *Explorations in Economic History*, 31(4), 521–48.
Broadberry, S. (1997). The long run growth and productivity performance of the United Kingdom. *Scottish Journal of Political Economy*, 44(4), 403–24.
Broadberry, S. N., & Irwin, D. A. (2006). Labor productivity in the United States and the United Kingdom during the nineteenth century. *Explorations in Economic History*, 43(2), 257–79.
Broadberry, S., & O'Mahony, M. (2004). Britain's productivity gap with the United States and Europe: a historical perspective. *National Institute Economic Review*, 189(July), 72–85.
Brock, G. J. (1994). Agricultural productivity in Volgograd province. *Comparative Economic Studies*, 36(1), 33–53.
Brock, G. J. (1996). Are Russian farms efficient? *Journal of International and Comparative Economics*, 5(1), 45–66.
Brock, G. J. (1999). Exploring a regional technical efficiency frontier in the former USSR. *Economics of Planning*, 32(1), 23–44.
Brock, W. A. (2003). Tipping points, abrupt opinion changes, and punctuated policy change. *Wisconsin Madison – Social Systems in its series Working Papers*, 28.
Brock, G., Grazhdaninova, M., Lerman, Z. & Uzun, V. (2008). "Technical efficiency in Russian agriculture." In Z. Lerman (Ed.): *Russia's agriculture in transition* (pp. 353–372). Lanham, MD: Lexington Books.
Broehl, W. G. (1978). *The village entrepreneur: change agents in India's rural development*. Cambridge, MA: Harvard University Press.
Brooks, K. (1990). Agricultural reform in the Soviet Union. In C. Eicher & J. Staatz (Eds.), *Agricultural development in the third world* (pp. 459–79). Baltimore, MD: The Johns Hopkins University Press.
Brooks, K. M. (1990). Soviet agricultural policy and pricing under Gorbachev. In K. R. Gray, *Comparative perspectives* (pp. 116–29). Kennan Institute for Advanced Russian Studies.
Brooks, K. M. (1990). Lease contracting in Soviet agriculture in 1989. In W. Moskoff, *Agricultural reform in the Gorbachev era* (pp. 63–80). Armonk.
Brooks, K. M., & Gardner, B. (1993). How retail food markets responded to price liberalization in Russia after January 1992. *Policy Research Working Paper Series*: The World Bank.
Brooks, K., & Gardner, B. (2004). Russian agriculture in the transition to a market economy. *Economic Development and Cultural Change*, 52(3), 571–86.
Brooks, K., & Lerman, Z. (1993). Land reform and farm restructuring in Russia: 1992 status. *American Journal of Agricultural Economics*, 75(4), 1254–59.
Brooks, K., & Lerman, Z. (1994). Farm reform in the transition economies. *Finance and Development, a Quarterly Publication of the International Monetary Fund and the World Bank*, 31, 25–8.
Brown, R. A. (1994). *Capital and entrepreneurship in South-East Asia*. New York; London: St. Martin's Press; Macmillan Press.
Brown, A. (1996). *The Gorbachev factor*. Oxford; New York: Oxford University Press.

Brownlow, W. R. (1969). *Lectures on slavery and serfdom in Europe*. New York: Negro Universities Press.

Bruk, S., & Kabuzan, V. (1984). Migration of the population in Russia in the XVIIIth–XXth centuries [number, structure, geography]. *Istoria SSSR*(4), 41–59.

Brunt, L. (1999). An arbitrage model of crop rotation in 18th century England. *Discussion Paper in Economic and Social History* No .032. Oxford University.

Brunt, L. (1999). Estimating English wheat production in the Industrial Revolution. *University of Oxford, Discussion Paper in Economic and Social History* No 29. Oxford University.

Brunt, L. (2004). Nature or nurture? Explaining English wheat yields in the Industrial Revolution, c. 1770. *Journal of Economic History*, 64(1), 193–225.

Brus, W. (1982). East European economies facing the "eighties." *Wirtschaft Und Gesellschaft*, 8(2), 405–14.

Brus, W., & Kowalik, T. (1983). Socialism and development. *Cambridge Journal of Economics*, 7, 243–55.

Bucher, G. (2006). *Women, the bureaucracy and daily life in postwar Moscow, 1945–1953*. Boulder, CO: New York: East European Monographs; distributed by Columbia University Press.

Buckberg, E. (1997). *Legal and institutional obstacles to growth and business in Russia*. Washington, DC: IMF Paper on Policy Analysis and Assessment.

Budina, O. (1996). *Krest'iane-darstvennik i v Rossii*, 1861–1907. Moscow: ROSSPEN.

Burbank, J. (2004). *Russian peasants go to court: legal culture in the countryside*, 1905–1917. Bloomington IN: Indiana University Press.

Burds, J. (1998). *Peasant dreams and market politics: labor migration and the Russian village*, 1861–1905. Pittsburgh, PA: University of Pittsburgh Press.

Burger, A. (1994). *The agriculture of the world*. Aldershot, UK: Avebury.

Bush, K. (1966). *Agricultural reforms since Khrushchev*. In J. E. Committee (Ed.), *New directions in the Soviet economy*. Washington, DC: Government Printing Office.

Bush, M. L. (1996). *Serfdom and slavery: studies in legal bondage*. London; New York: Longman.

Bush, R. (1999). *Economic crisis and the politics of reform in Egypt*. Boulder and Oxford: Westview Press.

Bush, R. (2000). An agricultural strategy without farmers: Egypt's countryside in the new millennium. *Review of African Political Economy*, 27(84), 235–49.

Bushnell, J. (1985). *Mutiny amid repression: Russian soldiers in the Revolution of* 1905–1906. Bloomington: Indiana University Press.

Buti, M., von Hagen, J., & Martinez-Mongay, C. (2002). *The behaviour of fiscal authorities: stabilization, growth and institutions*. New York: Palgrave.

Butler, W. E. (2002). *Russian law*. Oxford; New York: Oxford University Press.

Butler, W. E., & Gashi-Butler, M. E. (1993). *Legal aspects of doing business in Russia*. London: Longman.

Buzdalov, I. (2002). Agrarnaia Reforma: opyt desiatiletiia i perspektivy zaversheniia. *Agrarnaia Reforma: Ekonomika i Pravo*, 5(23, Sept–Oct), 1–5.

Cachel, S. (1992). The theory of punctuated equilibria and evolutionary anthropology. In A. Somit & S. A. Peterson (Eds.), *The punctuated equilibrium debate in the natural and social sciences. The dynamics of evolution* (pp. 187–220). Ithaca and London: Cornell University Press.

Callaghy, T. M. (1990). Lost between state and market: the politics of economic adjustment in Ghana, Zambia, and Nigeria. In J. Nelson (Ed.), *The politics of adjustment in the third world: Economic crisis and policy choice* (pp. 257–319). Princeton, NJ: Princeton University Press.

Calvo, G. A. (2002). Globalization hazard and delayed reform in emerging markets. *Economia: Journal of the Latin American and Caribbean Economic Association*, 2(2), 1–29.

Cameron, R. E., Bovykin, V. I., & Ananich, B. V. (1991). *International banking, 1870–1914*. New York: Oxford University Press.

Campbell, A. (2008). State versus society? Local government and the reconstruction of the Russian state. In *Local government in Central and Eastern Europe: the rebirth of local democracy*. London: Routledge.

Campos, N. F. (2004). What does WTO membership kindle in transition economies? An empirical investigation. *Journal of Economic Integration*, 19(2), 395–415.

Campos, N. F., Hsiao, C., & Nugent, J. B. (2006). Crises, what crises? *CEPR Discussion Papers*. London: CEPR.

Capalbo, M. & Antle, C. (1988). Measuring the Components of Aggregate Productivity Growth in U.S. Agriculture. *Western Journal of Agricultural Economics*, 13, pp. 53–62.

Cappoccia, G., & Kelemen, R. D. (2006). The study of critical junctures: theory, narrative and counterfactuals in historical institutionalism. *History papers*. Oxford: University of Oxford.

Caprio, G., Honohan, P., & Stiglitz, J. E. (2001). *Financial liberalization: How far, how fast?* Cambridge; New York; Melbourne: Cambridge University Press.

Carey, D. W. (1976). Soviet agriculture: recent performance and future plans. In U.S.C. Joint Economic Committee (Ed.), *Soviet economy in a time of change* (pp. 575–99). Washington, DC: Joint Economic Committee.

Carlin, T. A., & Handy, C. R. (1974). Concepts of the agricultural economy and economic accounting. *American Journal of Agricultural Economics*, 56(5), 964–75.

Carlson, L. A. (1981). *Indians, bureaucrats, and land: the Dawes act and the decline of Indian farming*. Westport, CT: Greenwood Press.

Carr, E. H. (1963). The Russian revolution and the peasant. *Proceedings of the British Academy*, 49, 69–93.

Cashore, B., & Howlett, M. (2006). Behavioral thresholds and institutional rigidities as explanations of punctuated equilibrium processes in Pacific Northwest forest policy dynamics. In R. Repetto (Ed.), *Punctuated equilibrium and the dynamics of U.S. environmental policy* (pp. 137–61). New Haven; London: Yale University Press.

Catherine (1859). *Memoirs of the empress*. London: Trübner & Co.

Caves, D. W., Christensen, L. R. & Diewert, W. E. (1982). The economic theory of index numbers and the measurement of input, output, and productivity. *Econometrica*, 50, 1393–1414.

Chai, C. H. (1997). *China: transition to a market economy*. Oxford; New York: Clarendon Press; Oxford University Press.

Chaisty, P. (2006). *Legislative politics and economic power in Russia*. Basingstoke: Palgrave. Macmillan in association with St. Antony's College.

Chamberlin, W. H. (1987). *The Russian revolution, 1917–1921*. Princeton, NJ: Princeton University Press.

Chang, H.-J., & Yoo, C.-G. (2000). The triumph of the rentiers? *Challenge*, 43(1), 105–24.

Chayanov, A. V. (1927). Itogi desiatiletiia sovetskoi vlasti v tisifrakh 1917–1927. Moscow: Tsentral'noe statisticheskoe upravlenie, SSSR.

Chayanov, A. V., Thorner, D., Kerblay, B. H., & Smith, R. E. F. (1966). *The theory of peasant economy*. Homewood, IL: Published for the American Economic Association, by R. D. Irwin.

Cheetham, R. J., Kelley, A. C., & Williamson, J. G. (1974). Demand, structural change, and the process of economic growth. In P. A. David & M. W. Reder (Eds.), *Nations and households in economic growth: essays in honor of Moses Abramovitz* (pp. 239–63). New York: Academic Press.

Chelintsev, A. N. (1919). *Teoreticheskiya osnovaniya organizatsii krest'ianskago khozyaistva*. Khar'kov: Agronomiya.

Chelintsev, A. N. (1924). *Sel'skokhoziastvennaia geografiia Rossii*. Prague.

Chelintsev, A. N. (1928). *Russkoe sel'skoe khoziaistvo pered revoliutsiei* Moscow: Novyi agronom.

Chelintsev, A. N. (1928). *Dinamika krest'ianskogo khoziaistva (po materialam dinamicheskikh perepisei Ts.S.U. za 1920–1926 g.g.)*. Moscow: Knigosoiuz.

Chenery, H. B. (1974). *Redistribution with growth: policies to improve income distribution in developing countries in the context of economic growth: a joint study [commissioned] by the World Bank's Development Research Center and the Institute of Development Studies, University of Sussex*. London: Published for the World Bank and the Institute of Development Studies University of Sussex [by] Oxford University Press.

Chenery, H. B., & Elkington, H. (1979). *Structural change and development policy*. New York: Published for the World Bank [by] Oxford University Press.

Chenery, H. B., Robinson, S., & Syrquin, M. (1986). *Industrialization and growth: a comparative study*. New York: Published for the World Bank [by] Oxford University Press.

Chenery, H. B., & Syrquin, M. (1975). *Patterns of development, 1950–1970*. London: Oxford University Press for the World Bank.

Chernukha, V. G. (1978). *Vnutrenniaia politika tsarizma s serediny 50-kh donachala 80-kh gg. XIX v*. Leningrad: Nauka.

Chesbrough, H. W., Vanhaverbeke, W., & West, J. (2006). *Open innovation: researching a new paradigm*. Oxford: Oxford University Press.

Chiarini, R. (2005). Reasons for a policy change: the reform of public employment in Italy. *Rivista italiana di scienza politica*, XXXV(2), 289–320.

Chubais, A., & Vishnevskaya, M. D. (1994). Privatisation in Russia: An Overview. In A. Åslund (Ed.), *Economic transformation in Russia* (pp. 92–110). New York: St Martin's Press.

Claessens, S., and Peters Jr. R. K. (1997). State enterprise performance and soft budget constraints: the case of Bulgaria. *Economics of Transition*, 5(2), 305–22.

Clague, C. (1992). The journey to a market economy. In C. Clague & G. C. Rausser (Eds.), *The emergence of market economies in Eastern Europe* (pp. 1–24). Oxford: Blackwell.

Clague, C., Keefer, P., Knack, S., & Olson, M. (2003). Property and contract rights in autocracies and democracies. In S. Knack (Ed.), *Democracy, governance, and growth* (pp. 136–80). Ann Arbor: University of Michigan Press.

Clague, C. K., & Rausser, G. C. (1992). The emergence of market economies in Eastern Europe. Cambridge, MA: Blackwell Publishers.

Clarke, R. A. (1972). *Soviet economic facts 1917–1970*. London: Macmillan.

Clarke, S. (1996). *Labour relations in transition: wages, employment and industrial conflict in Russia*. Cheltenham: Edward Elgar.

Clarke, S. (1999). Poverty in Russia. *Problems of Economic Transition*, **42**(5), 5–55.

Clayton, E. (1976). Crop response to price in the Soviet Union. In J. Thornton (Ed.), *Economic analysis of the Soviet-type system* (pp. 351–66). London: Cambridge University Press.

Clayton, E. (1976). Price appropriability and the Soviet agricultural incentives. In J. Thornton (Ed.), *Economic analysis of the Soviet-type system* (pp. 255–68). London: Cambridge University Press.

Clayton, E. (1980). Productivity in Soviet agriculture. *Slavic Review*, **39**(3), 446–58.

Clem, R. S., & Chodakiewicz, M. J. (2004). Poland divided: spatial differences in the June 2003 EU accession referendum. *Eurasian Geography and Economics*, **45**(7), 475–90.

Clements, B. E., Engel, B. A., & Worobec, C. (1990). *Russia's women: accommodation, resistance, transformation*. Berkeley: University of California Press.

Coale, A. J., Anderson, B. A., & Härm, E. (1979). *Human fertility in Russia since the nineteenth century*. Princeton, NJ: Princeton University Press.

Coase, R. H. (1989). *The firm, the market, and the law*. Chicago: University of Chicago Press.

Coase, R. H. (1937). The nature of the firm. *Economica*, **4**, 386–405.

Coelli, T. (2005). *An introduction to efficiency and productivity analysis*, New York: Springer.

Coelli, T., Perelman, S., & van Lierde, D. (2006). CAP reforms and total factor productivity growth in Belgian agriculture: a Malmquist Index approach. *International Association of Agricultural Economists, Annual Meeting*. Queensland, Australia: International Association of Agricultural Economists.

Coelli, T. (2005). *An introduction to efficiency and productivity analysis*, New York: Springer.

Cohen, J. M. (1975). Effects of green revolution strategies on tenants and small-scale landowners in the Chilalo region of Ethiopia. *Journal of Developing Areas*, **9**(3), 335–58.

Cohen, W. M., & Levinthal, D. A. (2000). Absorptive capacity: a new perspective on learning and innovation. In B. R. Martin & P. Nightingale (Eds.), *The political economy of science, technology and innovation* (pp. 499–523). Cheltenham; Northampton, MA: Edward Elgar, distributed by American International Distribution Corporation.

Cohen, W. M., & Levinthal, D. A. (2000). Innovation and learning: the two faces of R&D. In B. R. Martin & P. Nightingale (Eds.), *The political economy of science, technology and innovation* (pp. 123–50). Cheltenham; Northampton, MA: Edward Elgar, distributed by American International Distribution Corporation.

Cohen, W. M., & Levinthal, D. A. (1990). The implications of spillovers for R&D investment and welfare – a new perspective. *Advances in Applied Micro Economics Volume*, 5, 29–46.

Cole, W. A. (1981). Factors in demand 1700–1900. In R. Floud & D. McCloskey (Eds.), *The economic history of Britain since 1700* (pp. 36–65). Cambridge: Cambridge University Press.

Collins, J. B. (1988). *Fiscal limits of absolutism: direct taxation in early seventeenth-century France*. Berkeley: University of California Press.

Colton, T. (2008). *Yeltsin: A Life*. New York: Basic Books.

Comisso, E., & Marer, P. (1986). The economics and politics of reform in Hungary. *International Organization*, 40(2), 421–54.

Commander, S., & Mumssen, C. (1999). *Understanding barter in Russia*. London: European Bank for Reconstruction and Development.

Confino, M. (1963). *Domaines et seigneurs en Russie vers la fin du XVIIIe siècle; étude de structures agraires et de mentalités économiques*. Paris: Institut d'études slaves de l'Université de Paris.

Confino, M. (1985). Russian customary law and the study of peasant mentalités. *The Russian Review*, 44(1), 35–43.

Confino, M. (1991). *Société et mentalités collectives en Russie sous l'Ancien Régime*. Paris: Institut d'études slaves.

Confino, M. (1969). *Systèmes agraires et progrès agricole*. Paris: Mouton.

Conquest, R. (1990). *The great terror: a reassessment*. New York: Oxford University Press.

Conquest, R. (1986). *The harvest of sorrow: Soviet collectivization and the terror-famine*. New York: Oxford University Press.

Conroy, M. S. (1998). *Emerging democracy in late Imperial Russia: case studies on local self-government (the Zemstvos), state Duma elections, the tsarist government, and the state council before and during World War I*. Niwot: University Press of Colorado.

Cook, E. C. (1990). Reforming Soviet agriculture: problems with farm finances and equity considerations. In W. Moskoff (Ed.), *Agricultural reform in the Gorbachev era: perestroika in the countryside* (pp. 47–62). Armonk, NY: M. E. Sharpe.

Cooper, J. M., & Lewis, R. A. (1991). Research and technology. In R. W. Davies (Ed.), *From tsarism to the New Economic Policy: continuity and change in the economy of the USSR* (pp. 189–211). Ithaca, NY: Cornell University Press.

Cowan, R. (1990). Nuclear power reactors: a study in technological lock-in. *Journal of Economic History*, 50(3), 541–67.

Cox, T., & Mason, B. (1999). *Social and economic transformation in East Central Europe: institutions, property relations, and social interests*. Cheltenham; Northampton, MA: Edward Elgar.

Crichlow, M. (1994). State, class and agricultural entrepreneurship in Trinidad and Tobago. In S. S. Ryan (Ed.), *Culture, structure, conjuncture: entrepreneurship in the Caribbean* (pp. 53–91): St. Augustine Republic of Trinidad and Tobago: Institute of Social and Economic Research University of the West Indies.

Crisp, O. (1978). *Management of agricultural estates in tsarist Russia*. Washington, DC: Wilson Center Kennan Institute for Advanced Russian Studies.
Crisp, O. (1976). *Studies in the Russian economy before 1914*. London: Macmillan.
Csaki, C., & Lerman, Z. (2002). Land and farm structure in transition: the case of Poland. *Eurasian Geography and Economics*, 43(4), 305–22.
Csaki, C. et al. (2003). The agricultural sector of Slovakia on the eve of EU accession. *Eurasian Geography and Economics*, 44(4), 305–20.
Csite, A., & Kovách, I. (1997). *Institutional, economic, social and political transformation of the post-socialist Central and Eastern Europe*. Budapest: Institute for Political Science of the Hungarian Academy of Sciences.
Csizmadia, M. (1983). New features of the enterprise structure in the Hungarian agriculture and food industry. *Acta Oeconomica: Periodical of the Hungarian Academy of Sciences*, 31(3/4), 225–40.
Csontos, L., Kornai, J., & Tóth, I. (1998). Tax awareness and reform of the welfare state: Hungarian survey results. *Economics of Transition*, 6(2), 287–312.
Czaki, C., & Lerman, Z. (1997). *Land reform in Ukraine: the first five years*. Washington, DC: The World Bank.
Czech Parliamentary Agricultural Committee (1996). *Written evidence, enlargement and common agricultural policy reform* (pp. 80–8). London: Select Committee on the European Communities, House of Lords.
Dabrowski, M. (1997). Dynamics of fiscal developments during transition. *Fiscal policy in transition. Forum Report of the Economic Policy Initiative* (pp. 3–15). Warsaw, NY: CEPR, Institute for EastWest Studies.
Dabrowski, M. (2001). Ten years of Polish economic transition, 1989–1999. In M. I. S. Blejer & M. Skreb (Eds.), *Transition: The first decade* (pp. 121–52). Cambridge and London: MIT Press.
Dabrowski, M., Gomulka, S., & Rostowski, J. (2001). Whence reform? A critique of the Stiglitz perspective. *Journal of Policy Reform*, 4(4), 291–324.
Dagan, H., & Heller, M. A. (2001). The liberal commons. *Yale Law Journal*, 110(4), 549–623.
Dahl, R. V. (1961). *Who governs?* New Haven, CT: Yale University Press.
Daniel, W. (1995). Entrepreneurship and the Russian textile industry: from Peter the Great to Catherine the Great. *Russian Review*, 54(1), 1–25.
Daniels, R. V. (2007). *The rise and fall of communism in Russia*. New Haven, CT: Yale University Press.
Danilov, V. P. (1976). Ob istoricheskikh sud'bakh krest'ianskoi obshchiny v Rossii. *Ezhegodnik po agrarnoi istorii, vyp. VI, Problemy istorii russkoi obshchiny* (Vologda), pp. 103–106.
Danilov, V. (2000). *Plenum TsK VKP(b) 16–24 noiabra 1928 g*. Moscow: Materik.
Danilov, V. P. (1988). *Rural Russia under the new regime*. Bloomington; London: Indiana University Press.
Danilov, V. N. (2002). *Saratovskii kraevedcheskii sbornik: nauchnye trudy i publikatsii*. Saratov: Izd-vo Saratovskogo universiteta.
Danilov, V. P. (1977). *Sovetskaia dokolkhoznaia derevnia: naselenie, zemlepolzovanie, khoziaistvo*. Moscow: Nauka.
Danilov, V. A. (1957). *Sozdanie material'no-teknicheskikh predposilok kollektivizatsii sel'skogo khoziastva v SSSR*. Moscow: Akademiia Nauk S.S.S.R.

Danilov, V. P. (1999). *Tragediia sovetskoi derevni: kollektivizatsiia i raskulachivanie: dokumenty i materialy v 5 tomakh: 1927–1939*. Moscow: ROSSPEN.

Danilov, V. P., Khlevniuk, O. V., & Vatlin, A. I. (2000). *Kak lomali NEP: stenogrammy plenumov TSK VKP(b) 1928–1929 gg*. Moscow: Mezhdunarodnyi fond "Demokratiia."

Danilov, V. P., Kim, M. P., & Tropkin, N. V. (1973). *Sovetskoe krest'ianstvo*. Moscow: Politizdat.

Danilov, V. P., & Milov, L. V. (1996). *Mentalitet i agrarnoe razvitie Rossii, XIX–XX vv; materialy mezhdunarodnoi konferentsii, Moskva, 14–15 iiunia 1994 g*. Moscow: ROSSPEN.

Darrow, D. W. (2002). Statistics and 'sufficiency': toward an intellectual history of Russia's rural crisis. *Continuity and Change*, 17(1), 63–96.

David, C.-C. (1989). Philippines: price policy in transition. In T. Sicular (Ed.), *Food price policy in Asia: a comparative study* (pp. 154–82). Ithaca, NY; London: Cornell University Press.

David, C.-C. (1991). Rural development: problems and prospects. In C. P. Timmer (Ed.), *Agriculture and the state: growth, employment, and poverty in developing countries* (pp. 191–201). Food Systems and Agrarian Change series, Ithaca and London: Cornell University Press.

David, P. A. (1985). Clio and the economics of QWERTY. *American Economic Review*, 75(2), 332–37.

David, P. (2000). Path dependence and varieties of learning in the evolution of technological progress. In J. Ziman (Ed.), *Technological innovation as an evolutionary process* (pp. 118–345). Cambridge: Cambridge University Press.

David, P. A. (1976). *Reckoning with slavery: a critical study in the quantitative history of American Negro slavery*. New York: Oxford University Press.

David, P. A. (1975). *Technical choice, innovation and economic growth: essays on American and British experience in the nineteenth century*. London: Cambridge University Press.

David, P. (1989). *Why and when does history really matter*? Washington, DC: Presidential address, Economic History Association.

David, P. (1994). Why are institutions the 'Carriers of History'? Path dependence and the evolution of conventions, organizations and institutions. *Structural Change and Economic Dynamics*, 5(2), 205–20.

David, P. A., Foray, D., & Dalle, J.-M. (1998). Marshallian externalities and the emergence and spatial stability of technological enclaves. *Economics of Innovation and New Technology*, 6, 147–82.

David, P., & Rothwell, G. (1996). Standardization, diversity and learning: strategies for the coevolution of technology and industrial capacity. *International Journal of Industrial Organisation*, 14, 181–201.

Davies, R. W. (1994). Changing economic systems: a overview. In R. W. Davies, M. Harrison, & S. G. Wheatcroft (Eds.), *The economic transformation of the Soviet Union, 1913–1945* (pp. 1–23). Cambridge; New York: Cambridge University Press.

Davies, R. W. (1989). Economic and social policy in the USSR: 1917–1941, *Cambridge economic history of Europe* (pp. 984–1087). Cambridge: Cambridge University Press.

Davies, R. W. (1990). *From tsarism to the New Economic Policy: continuity and change in the economy of the USSR*. Ithaca, NY: Cornell University Press.
Davies, R. W. (1990). Introduction: from tsarism to NEP. In R. W. Davies (Ed.), *From tsarism to the New Economic Policy: continuity and change in the economy of the USSR* (pp. 1–26). Ithaca, NY: Cornell University Press.
Davies, R. W. (1980). *The Socialist offensive: the collectivisation of Soviet agriculture*, 1929–1930. Cambridge, MA: Harvard University Press.
Davies, R. W. (1980). *The Soviet collective farm*, 1929–1930. Cambridge, MA: Harvard University Press.
Davies, R. W. (1998). *Soviet economic development from Lenin to Khrushchev*. Cambridge; New York: Cambridge University Press.
Davies, R. W., Harrison, M., & Wheatcroft, S. G. (1994). *The economic transformation of the Soviet Union*, 1913–1945. Cambridge; New York: Cambridge University Press.
Davies, R. W., & Wheatcroft, S. G. (2004). *The years of hunger: Soviet agriculture*, 1931–1933. Basingstoke; New York: Palgrave; Macmillan.
Davis, J. R. (1997). Understanding the process of decollectivization and agricultural privatization in transition economies. Edinburgh: Heriot-Watt-University, Department of Economics.
Davydov, M. A. (2003). *Ocherki agrarnoi istorii v kontse XIX-nachale XX vv.: (pomaterialam transp. Statistiki i statistiki zemleustroistva)*. Moscow: Ros. Gos. Gumanitarnyi un-t.
de Brauw, A., Huang, J. & Rozelle, S. (2002). Sequencing and the success of gradualism: empirical evidence from China's agricultural reform. Davis, CA: Department of Resource Economics, University of California at Davis.
de Janvry, A. (1981). The role of land reform in economic development: policies and politics. *American Journal of Agricultural Economics*, 63(2), 384–92.
de Livron, B. (1874). *Statisticheskoe Obozrenie Rossiiskoi Imperii*. St Petersburg: Tovarishchestvennaia Obshchestvennaia Pol'za.
de Melo, M. (2001). Circumstance and choice: the role of initial conditions and policies in transition economies. *World Bank. Economic Review*, 15(1), 1–31.
De Vecchi, N. (1995). *Entrepreneurs, institutions and economic Change*. Aldershot: Edward Elgar.
de Vries, J. (1994). How did pre-industrial labour markets function? In G. Grantham & M. MacKinnon (Eds.), *Labour market evolution, the economic history of market integration, wage flexibility and the employment relation* (pp. 39–63). London and New York: Routledge.
DeBardeleben, J. (1997). The development of federalism in Russia: the emergence of regionalism in post-Soviet Russia. In P. J. Stavrakis, J. DeBardeleben, & L. Black (Eds.), *Beyond the monolith* (pp. 35–56). Washington, DC: Institute of Central/East European and Russian Area Studies.
Deininger, K. (2002). Agrarian reforms in Eastern European countries: lessons from international experience. *Journal of International Development*, 14(7), 987–1003.
Deininger, K. (1995). Collective agricultural production: a solution for transition economies? *World Development*, 23(8), 1317–34.
Deininger, K. (1999). Making negotiated land reform work: initial experience from Colombia, Brazil and South Africa. *World Development*, 27(4), 651–72.

Deininger, K., & Binswanger, H. (1999). The evolution of the World Bank's land policy: principles, experience, and future challenges. *World Bank. Research Observer*, 14(2), 247–76.

Deininger, K. W. (1995). *Technical change, human capital, and spillovers in United States agriculture*, 1949–1985. New York and London: Garland.

Demsetz, H. (1967). Toward a theory of property rights. *American Economic Review*, 57, 347–59.

Denison, E. F. (1962). *The sources of economic growth in the United States and the alternatives before us* [New York]: Committee for Economic Development.

Dennison, T. K. (2003). Serfdom and household structure in Central Russia: Voshchazhnikovo, 1816–1858. *Continuity and Change* 18(3), 395–429.

Desai, P. (1986). *Weather and grain yields in the Soviet Union*. Washington, DC: International Food Policy Research Institute.

Desai, P. (1997). Going global: transition from plan to market in the world economy. Cambridge, MA: The MIT Press.

Desai, P. (1997). *Introduction*. In P. Desai (Ed.), *Going global: transition from plan to market in the world economy* (pp. 1–94). Cambridge, MA: The MIT Press.

Desai, P. (1989). *Perestroika in perspective: the design and dilemmas of Soviet reform*. Princeton, NJ: Princeton University Press.

Desai, P. (1992). Reforming the Soviet grain economy: performance, problems, and solutions. *The American Economic Review*, 82(May 2), 49–54.

Desai, P. (1997). *Russia*. In P. Desai (Ed.), *Going global: transition from plan to market in the world economy* (pp. 317–52). Cambridge, MA: The MIT Press.

Desai, P. (1987). *The Soviet economy: problems and prospects*. Oxford: Basil Blackwell.

Desai, R. M., Freinkman, L., & Goldberg, I. (2003). *Fiscal federalism and regional growth: evidence from the Russian Federation in the 1990s*. Washington DC: World Bank.

Desai, R. M., Freinkman, L., & Goldberg, I. (2005). Fiscal federalism in rentier regions: evidence from Russia. *Journal of Comparative Economics*, 33(4), 814–34.

Deutschmann, P. J., & Fals-Borda, O. (1962). *Communication and adoption patterns in an Andean village*. San José: Costa Rica.

Dewatripont, M., & Roland, G. (1998). The design of reform packages under uncertainty. In F. Śturzenegger & M. Tommasi (Eds.), *The political economy of reform* (pp. 243–68). Cambridge, MA: Harvard University Press.

Di Tella, G., & Dornbusch, R. (1989). *The political economy of Argentina*, 1946–83. Basingstoke: Macmillan, in association with St Antony's College Oxford.

Diamond, D. B. (1966). *Trends in output, inputs, and factor productivity in Soviet agriculture*. Washington, DC: Joint Economic Committee.

Diamond, D. B., & Davis, W. L. (1979). *Comparative growth in output and productivity in U.S. and U.S.S.R. agriculture*.Washington, DC: Joint Economic Committee.

Diamond, D. B., & Krueger, C. B. (1973). *Recent developments in output and productivity in Soviet agriculture*. Washington, DC: Joint Economic Committee.

Dickler, R. (1975). Organization and change in East Prussia. *European peasants and their markets: essays in agrarian economic history* (pp. 269–92). Princeton, NJ: Princeton University Press.

Dimitrii, C., Effland, A., & Conklin, N. (2005). The 20th century transformation of U.S. agriculture and farm policy. *Economic information bulletin*. Washington, DC: United States Department of Agriculture.

Dinar, A., & Keck, A. (1997). Private irrigation investment in Colombia: effects of violence, macroeconomic policy, and environmental conditions. *Agricultural Economics*, **16**(1), 1–15.

Djankov, S., & Pohl, G. (1998). The restructuring of large firms in the Slovak Republic. *Economics of Transition*, **6**(1), 67–86.

Dmitrenko, V. P., Sokolov, A. K., & Neretina, L. A. (1998). *NEP, zavershaiushchaia stadiia: sootnoshenie ekonomiki i politiki*. Moscow: Institut rossiiskoi istorii RAN.

Dmitriev, A. I. (1962). *Statistika produktsii sel'skogo khoziaistva*. Leningrad: Izd-vo Leningradskogo universiteta.

Dmitriev, M. (1997). *Biudzhetnaia politika v sovremennoi Rossii*. Moscow: Carnegie Endowment for International Peace.

Dobrinsky, R. (1996). Enterprise restructuring and adjustment in the transition to market economy: lessons from the experience of Central and Eastern Europe. *Economics of Transition*, **4**(2), 389–410.

Dohan, M. R. (1991). *Foreign trade*. In R. W. Davies (Ed.), *From tsarism to the New Economic Policy: continuity and change in the economy of the USSR* (pp. 212–34). Ithaca, NY: Cornell University Press.

Dolbilov, M. D. (2002). Zemel'naia sobstvennost' i osvobozhdenie krest'ian. In D. F. Aiatsko (Ed.), *Sobstvennost' na zemliu v Rossii: istoriia i sovremennost'* (pp. 45–152). Moscow: ROSSPEN.

Domar, E. D. (1970). The causes of slavery or serfdom: a hypothesis. *Journal of Economic History*, 30(1), 18–32.

Domar, E. D. (1989). Were Russian serfs overcharged for their land by the 1861 emancipation? The history of one historical table. In C. Leonard & G. Grantham (Eds.), *Agrarian organization in the century of industrialization: Europe, Russia, and North America* (pp. 429–39). Greenwich, CT: JAI Press.

Domar, E. D. (1989). *Capitalism, socialism, and serfdom: essays*. Cambridge; New York: Cambridge University Press.

Donath, F. (1986). Hungarian agriculture: achievements and problems. *Journal of Rural Cooperation*, **14**(1), 3–20.

Donnorummo, R. P. (1987). *The peasants of central Russia: reactions to emancipation and the market*, 1850–1900. New York: Garland.

Doolittle, P., & Hughes, M. (1987). Gorbachev's agricultural policy building on the Brezhnev Food Program. *Gorbachev's economic plans* (pp. 27–43). Washington, DC: U.S. Congress, Joint Economic Committee.

Dornbusch, R. (1986). *Inflation, exchange rates, and stabilization*. Princeton, NJ: International Finance Section Department of Economics, Princeton University.

Dornbusch, R. (1993). *Policymaking in the open economy: concepts and case studies in economic performance*. Oxford; New York: Oxford University Press.

Dornbusch, R., & Edwards, S. (1995). *Reform, recovery, and growth: Latin America and the Middle East*. Chicago: University of Chicago Press.

Doroshenko, P. E. (1959). *Sel'skoe khoziaistvo SSSR v 1959–1965 godakh*. Moscow: Gos. izd-vo sel'khoz lit-ry.

Dovring, F. (1980). Capital intensity in Soviet agriculture. In R. A. Francisco, B. A. Laird, & R. D. Laird (Eds.), *Agricultural policies in the USSR and Eastern Europe* (pp. 5–26). Boulder, CO: Westview Press.

Dowling, E. T., & Hilton, F. G. (1992). Oil in the 1980s: an OECD perspective. In S. Shojai & B. Katz (Eds.), *The oil market in the 1980s: a decade of decline* (pp. 71–87). Westport, CT: Greenwood.

Drage, G. (1904). *Russian affairs*. London: J. Murray.

Drazen, A. (2000). *Political economy in macroeconomics*. Princeton, NJ: Princeton University Press.

Drazen, A. (1998). The political economy of delayed reform. In F. Sturzenegger & M. Tommasi (Eds.), *The political economy of reform* (pp. 39–60). Cambridge, MA: The Political Economy of Reform.

Drazen, A., & Easterly, W. (2001). Do crises induce reform? Simple empirical tests of conventional wisdom. *Economics and Politics*, 13(2), 129–58.

Drazen, A., & Grilli, V. (1998). The benefit of crises for economic reforms. In F. Sturzennegger & M. Tommasi (Eds.), *The political economy of delayed reform* (pp. 127–42). Cambridge, MA: Massachusetts Institute of Technology.

Dregne, H. E. (1970). *Arid lands in transition [papers]*. Washington, DC: American Association for the Advancement of Science.

Druzhinin, N. M. (1946). *Gosudarstvennye kresti'ane i reforma P.D. Kiseleva*. Moscow: Nauka.

Druzhinin, N. M. (1987). Liquidatsiia feodal'noi sistemy v Rossii pomeshchich'ei derevne (1862–1882 gg.). *Izbrannyie trudy, Sotsial'no-ekonomicheskaia istoriia Rossii*. Moscow: Nauka, pp. 287–319.

Druzhinin, N. M. (1978). *Russkaia derevnia na perelome 1861–1880 gg*. Moscow: Nauka.

Druzhinin, N. M., Ivanov, L. M. (1971). *Problemy sotsial'no-ekonomicheskoi istorii Rossii*. Moscow: Nauka.

Druzhinin, N. M., Sivkov, K. V., Iatsunskii, V. K., & Anfimov, A. M. (1969). Materialy po istorii sel'skogo khoziastva i krest'ianstva SSSR. Moscow: Nauka.

Druzhinin, N. M., & Skazkin, S. D. (1965). *Genezis kapitalizma v promyshlennosti i sel'skom khoziaistve*. Moscow: Nauka.

Dubrovskii, S. M. (1963). *Stolypinskaia zemel'naia reforma*. Moscow: Nauka.

Dubrovskii, S. M. (1975). *Sel'skoe khoziastvo i krest'ianstvo Rossii v period imperializma*. Moscow: Nauka.

Dukes, P. (1967). *Catherine the Great and the Russian nobility: a study based on the materials of the Legislative Commission of 1767*. Cambridge: Cambridge University Press.

Dunn, M. H. (2000). Privatization, land reform, and property rights: the Mexican experience. *Constitutional Political Economy*, 11(3), 215–30.

Dunn, S. (1971). In J. R. Millar (Ed.), *The Soviet rural community* (pp. 325–45). Urbana: University of Illinois Press.

Dunn, S. P., & Dunn, E. (1967). *The peasants of central Russia*. New York; London: Holt, Rinehart and Winston.

Durand, R., & Simon, M. (2008). Beyond greed, fear and the Iron Curtain. *Applied Financial Economics*, **18**(4), 275–93.

Durgin, F. (1978). The inefficiency of Soviet agriculture versus the efficiency of U.S. agriculture: reality or an idol of the mind? *ACES Bulletin*, **20**(3–4), 1–36.

Durgin, F. (1984). USSR in crisis: the failure of an economic system: review article. *ACES Bulletin*, **26**(2–3), 99–110.

Dyba, K. (1996). *The Czech Republic, 1990–1995: an economy in transition* [S.l.]: Needham, MA: Schuster Foundation Press.

Dzhanshiev, G. (1896). *Epokha velikikh reform*. Moscow: Razsviet.

Dzhivelegov, A. K., Mel'gunov, S. P., & Picheta, V. I. (Eds.) (1911). *Velikaia Reforma, Russkoe obshchestvo i krestianskii vopros v proshlom i nastoiashchem*. Moscow.

Earle, J. (1997). Do East European enterprises provide social protection? Employee benefits and labour market behaviour in the East European transition. In M. Rein, B. L. Friedman, & A. Wörgötter (Eds.), *Enterprise and social benefits after communism* (pp. 49–74). Cambridge: Cambridge University Press.

Earle, J. S., & Sabirianova, K. Z. (1998). Understanding wage arrears in Russia: SITE, Stockholm School of Economics, Central European University, and Urals State University.

Easter, K. W. (2000). Asia's irrigation management in transition: a paradigm shift faces high transaction costs. *Review of Agricultural Economics*, **22**(2), 370–88.

Easterlin, R. A. (1996). *Growth triumphant: the twenty-first century in historical perspective*. Ann Arbor: University of Michigan Press.

Easterly, W. (2002). The elusive quest for growth: Economists adventures and misadventures in teh tropics. Cambridge and London: MIT Press.

Easterly, W., & Fischer, S. (1994). The Soviet economic decline: historical and republican data. *NBER Working Papers: 4735:* National Bureau of Economic Research.

Easterly, W., & Fischer, S. (1995). The Soviet economic decline. *World Bank. Economic Review*, **9**(3), 341–71.

Economakis, E. G. (1998). *From peasant to Petersburger*. New York: St. Martin's Press.

Edelman, R. (1980). *Gentry politics on the eve of the Russian Revolution: the Nationalist Party*, 1907–1917. New Brunswick, NJ: Rutgers University Press.

Eggertsson, T. (1990). *Economic behavior and institutions*. Cambridge Surveys of Economic Literature. Cambridge; New York; Melbourne: Cambridge University Press.

Eggertsson, T. (2005). *Imperfect institutions: possibilities and limits of reform* Ann Arbor: University of Michigan Press.

Eggertsson, T. (1998). Limits to institutional reforms. *Scandinavian Journal of Economics*, 100(1), 335–57.

Eggertsson, T. (1999). State reforms and the theory of institutional policy. *Revista de Economia Politica*, **19**(2), 49–63.

Eichengreen, B., & Kohl, R. (1998). The external sector, the state and development in Eastern Europe. London: Centre for Economic Policy Research.

Eicher, C. K., & Staatz, J. M. (1984). Agricultural development in the third world. Baltimore, MD: The Johns Hopkins Press.

Eisen, J. G., Bartlett, R. P., & Donnert, E. (1998). *Johann Georg Eisen (1717–1779): ausgewählte Schriften: deutsche Volksaufklärung und Leibeigenschaft im Russischen Reich*. Marburg: Verlag Herder-Institut.

Eklof, B. (1986). *Russian peasant schools: officialdom, village culture, and popular pedagogy, 1861–1914*. Berkeley: University of California Press.

Eklof, B. (1993). *School and society in tsarist and Soviet Russia: selected papers from the Fourth World Congress for Soviet and East European Studies, Harrogate, 1990*. New York: St. Martin's Press.

Eklof, B., Bushnell, J., & Zakharova, L. G. (1994). *Russia's great reforms, 1855–1881*. Bloomington: Indiana University Press.

Eklof, B., & Frank, S. (1990). *The world of the Russian peasant: post-emancipation culture and society*. Boston: Unwin Hyman.

Eldredge, N., & Gould, S. J. (1972). Punctuated equilibrium: an alternative to phyletic gradualism. In T. J. M. Schopf (Ed.), *Models in palaeobiology* (pp. 82–115). San Francisco: Freeman & Cooper.

Ellis, F. (1992). *Agricultural policies in developing countries*. Cambridge; New York: Cambridge University Press.

Ellis, F. (1993). *Peasant economics: farm households and agrarian development*. Cambridge; New York: Cambridge University Press.

Ellis, F. (1998). Household strategies and rural livelihood diversification. *The Journal of Development Studies*, 35(1), 1–38.

Ellman, M. (1984). *Collectivisation, convergence, and capitalism: political economy in a divided world*. London; Orlando: Academic Press.

Ellman, M. (1975). Did the agricultural surplus provide the resources for the increase in investment in the USSR during the First Five Year Plan? *Economic Journal*, 85(340), 844–63.

Ellman, M. (1993). General aspects of transition. *Economic transition in Eastern Europe*. Oxford; Cambridge, MA: Blackwell.

Ellman, M. (2000). Perestroika economics from the inside. In E. Maskin (Ed.), *Planning, shortage, and transformation: essays in honor of Janos Kornai* (pp. 269–81). Cambridge: Blackwell.

Eltis, D., & Engerman, S. L. (2000). The importance of slavery and the slave trade to industrializing Britain. *Journal of Economic History*, 60(1), 123–44.

Emmons, T. (1968). *The Russian landed gentry and the peasant emancipation of 1861*. London: Cambridge University Press.

Emmons, T. (1970). *Emancipation of the Russian serfs*. New York: Holt Rinehart and Winston.

Emmons, T., & Vucinich, W. S. (1982). *The Zemstvo in Russia: an experiment in local self-government*. Cambridge; New York: Cambridge University Press.

Engel, B. A. (1994). *Between the fields and the city: women, work, and family in Russia*, 1861–1914. Cambridge; New York: Cambridge University Press.

Engelstein, L. (2009). *Slavophile empire: imperial Russia's illiberal path*. Cornell University Press.

Engelgardt, A. N. (1993). *Aleksandr Nikolaevich EngElgardt's letters from the country*, 1872–1887. New York: Oxford University Press.

Engerman, S. (1973). Some considerations relating to property rights in man. *Journal of Economic History*, 33(March), 43–65.

Engerman, S. L. (1999). *The terms of labor: slavery, serfdom, and free labor*. Stanford, CA: Stanford University Press.
Ensminger, J., & Juttan, A. (1993). The politics of changing property rights: dismantling a commons from within. In T. L. Anderson & R. T. Simmons (Eds.), *The political economy of customs and culture: informal solutions to the commons problem* (pp. 85–108). Lanham, MD: Rowman & Littlefield.
Ericson, R. E. (1991). Classical Soviet-type economy: nature of the system and implications for reform. *Journal of Economic Perspectives*, 5, 11–27.
Ericson, R. E. (1983). Difficulty with the "command" allocation mechanism. *Journal of Economic Theory*, 31, 1–26.
Ericson, R. E. (1990). *The Soviet Union*, 1979–1990. San Francisco: ICS Press.
Erlich, A. (1960). *The Soviet industrialization debate*, 1924–1929. Cambridge, MA: Harvard University Press.
Ersado, L. (2006). Rural vulnerability in Serbia. *Policy research working paper series*. Washington, DC: The World Bank.
Eslava, M., Haltiwanger, J., Kugler, A., & Kugler, M. (2004). The effects of structural reforms on productivity and profitability enhancing reallocation: evidence from Colombia. *Journal of Development Economics*, 75(2), 333–71.
Estrin, S., Richet, X., & Brada, J. C. (2000). Foreign direct investment in Central Eastern Europe: Case studies of firms in transition. *Microeconomics of transition economies*. Armonk, NY; London: Sharpe.
Estrin, S., Schaffer, M. I., & Singh, I. J. (1997). The provision of social benefits in state-owned, privatized, and private firms in Poland. In M. Rein, B. L. Friedman, & A. Wörgötter (Eds.), *Enterprise and social benefits after communism* (pp. 25–48). Cambridge: Cambridge University Press.
Europa Publications Limited. (2010). *The territories of the Russian Federation, 2010*. London: Europa Publications.
European Bank for Reconstruction and Development (1994–2010). *Transition reports*. London: EBRD.
Evenson, R. D., Pray, C. E. & Rosegrant, M. W. (1999). Agricultural research and productivity growth in India. *Research Report*, 109.
Eyzaguirre, N. G. (1993). Financial crisis, reform and stabilization: the Chilean experience. In S. Faruqi (Ed.), *Lessons of comparative experience* (pp. 127–46). Financial sector reforms in Asian and Latin American countries: EDI Seminar Series. Washington, DC.
F. A. O. Statistics Office (1988–). *FAOSTAT Statistical Databases*: http://apps.fao.org/default.jsp.
Faaland, J., & Parkinson, J. (1991). The nature of the state and the role of government in agricultural development. In C. P. Timmer (Ed.), *Agriculture and the state: growth, employment, and poverty in developing countries* (pp. 247–74). Ithaca; London: Cornell University Press.
Faini, R., & Portes, R. (1995). *European Union trade with Eastern Europe*. London: CEPR.
Fainsod, M. (1989, 1958). *Smolensk under Soviet rule*. Boston: Unwin Hyman.
Fairchild, G. F. (1991). Analyzing extension's role in macroeconomic policy education: discussion. *American Journal of Agricultural Economics*, 73(5), 1366–69.

Falcetti, E., Lysenko, T., & Sanfey, P. (2006). Reforms and growth in transition: re-examining the evidence. *Journal of Comparative Economics*, 34(3), 421–45.

Falcetti, E., Raiser, M., & Sanfey, P. (2002). Defying the odds: initial conditions, reforms, and growth in the first decade of transition. *Journal of Comparative Economics*, 30(2), 229–50.

Farnsworth, B., & Viola, L. (1992). *Russian peasant women*. New York: Oxford University Press.

Feder, G., & Feeny, D. (1993). The theory of land tenure and property rights. In K. Hoff, B. Avishay, & J. E. Stiglitz (Eds.), *The economics of rural organization: theory, practice, and policy* (pp. 240–58). Oxford: Oxford University Press.

Feder, G., & Zilberman, S. (1985). Adoption of agricultural innovations in developing countries. *Economic Development and Cultural Change*, 33(2), 255–98.

Federal'naia sluzhba gosudarstvennoi statistiki (earlier, Gosudarstvennyi komitet Rossiiskoi Federatsii po statistike) (2001). *Agropromyshlennyi kompleks Rossii: statisticheskii sbornik*. Moscow: Roskomstat (earlier, Goskomstat) (provided by East View).

Federal'naia sluzhba gosudarstvennoi statistiki (earlier, Gosudarstvennyi komititet Rossiiskoi Federatsii po statistike) (1998, 2008). *Finansy Rossii, Statisticheskii sbornik*. Moscow: Roskomstat (earlier, Goskomstat), provided by East View.

Federal'naia sluzhba gosudarstvennoi statistiki (earlier, Gosudarstvennyi komitet Rossiiskoi Federatsii po statistike) (1998). *Naselenie Rossii za 100 let* (1897–1997), *Statisticheskii sbornik*. Moscow: Roskomstat (earlier Goskomstat), provided by East View.

Federal'naia sluzhba gosudarstvennoi statistiki (earlier, Gosudarstvennyi komitet Rossiiskoi Federatsii po statistike) (1997–2009). *Regioni Rossii*. Moscow: Roskomstat (earlier Goskomstat), (1997–2009) provided by East View.

Federal'naia sluzhba gosudarstvennoi statistiki (earlier, Gosudarstvennyi komitet Rossiiskoi Federatsii po statistike) (1996–2009). *Rossiiskii statisticheskii ezhegodnik*. Moscow: Roskomstat (earlier Goskomstat), provided by East View.

Federal'naia sluzhba gosudarstvennoi statistiki (earlier, Gosudarstvennyi komitet Rossiiskoi Federatsii po statistike (2000, 2002, 2004, 2009). *Sel'skoe khoziaistvo v Rossii: statisticheskii sbornik*. Moscow: Roskomstat (earlier, Goskomstat) (provided by East View).

Federal'naia sluzhba gosudarstvennoi statistiki (earlier, Gosudarstvenii Komitet Rossiiskoi Federatsii po statistike) (1996). *Trud i zaniatost' v Rossii*. Moscow: Roskomstat (earlier, Goskomstat), provided by East View.

Federico, G. (2005). *Feeding the world: an economic history of agriculture*, 1800–2000. Princeton and Oxford: Princeton University Press.

Fedorov, B. G. (1997). Macro-economic policy and stabilization in Russia. In A. Åslund (Ed.), *Russia's economic transformation in the 1990s* (pp. 119–26). London: Pinter.

Fedorov, B. (2002). *Petr Stolypin*: "*Ia Veriu v Rossiiu*." St Petersburg: Limbus Press.

Fedorov, V. A. (1974). *Pomeshchich'i krest'iane Tsentral'no-promyshlennogo raiona Rossii kontsa XVIII-pervoi poloviny XIX v*. Moscow: 1974.

Feeny, D. (1982). *The political economy of productivity: Thai agricultural development, 1880–1975*. Vancouver: University of British Columbia Press.
Feeny, D. (1988). The demand for and supply of institutional arrangements. In V. Ostrom, D. Feeny, & H. Pitcht (Eds.), *Rethinking institutional analysis and development: issues, alternatives, and choices*. San Francisco: Institute for Contemporary Studies Press.
Feeny, D., Berkes, F., McCay, B. J., & Acheson, J. M. (1990). Tragedy of the commons: twenty-two years later. *Human Ecology*, 18(1), 1–19.
Fei, J. C. H., & Ranis, G. (1964). *Development of the labor surplus economy*. Homewood, IL: Homewood.
Fei, J. C. H., & Ranis, G. (1997). *Growth and development from an evolutionary perspective*. Oxford: Blackwell.
Feiwel, G. R. (1968). *New currents in Soviet-type economies: a reader*. Scranton, PA: International Textbook Co.
Feiwel, G. R. (1972). *The Soviet quest for economic efficiency: issues, controversies, and reforms*. New York: Praeger Publishers.
Feldbrugge, F. J. M. (1993). *Russian law: the end of the Soviet system and the role of law*. Dordrecht; Boston: M. Nijhoff.
Ferguson, N., & Granville, B. (2000). "Weimar on the Volga": causes and consequences of inflation in 1990s Russia compared with 1920s Germany. *Journal of Economic History*, 60(4), 1061–87.
Fernandez, R., & Rodrik, D. (1998). Resistance to reform: status quo bias in the presence of individual-specific uncertainty. In F. Sturzenegger & M. Tommasi (Eds.), *The political economy of reform* (pp. 61–76). Cambridge, MA: The MIT Press.
Field, D. (1976). *The end of serfdom: nobility and bureaucracy in Russia, 1855–1861*. Cambridge, MA: Harvard University Press.
Field, D. (1989). The polarization of peasant households in prerevolutionary Russia: Zemstvo censuses and problems of measurement. In C. Leonard & G. Grantham (Eds.), *Agrarian organisation in the century of industrialization: Europe, Russia, and North America* (pp. 477–506). Greenwich, CT: JAI Press.
Field, D. (1989). *Rebels in the name of the tsar*. Boston: Unwin Hyman.
Figes, O. (1989). *Peasant Russia, civil war: the Volga countryside in revolution (1917–1921)*. London: Phoenix.
Figes, O. (1991). Peasant farmers and the minority groups of rural society: Peasant egalitarianism and village socil relations during the Russian revolution (1917–1921). In E. Kingston-Mann and T. Mixter (Eds.), *Peasant Economy, Culture, and Politics of European Russia, 1800–1921* (pp. 378–402). Princeton: Princeton University Press.
Figurovskaia, N. K. (1993). Nekotorye istoricheskie uroki razvitiia kooperatsii v Rossii kontsa XIX nachala XX veka. In N. K. Figurovskaia (Ed.), *Kooperatsiia. Stranitsy istorii* (pp. 1–26). Moscow: International Fund for the History of Science.
Fischer, G. (1958). *Russian liberalism, from gentry to intelligentsia*. Cambridge, MA: Harvard University Press.
Fischer, L. A., & Uren, P. E. (1973). *The new Hungarian agriculture [by] Lewis A. Fischer and Philip E. Uren*. Montreal: McGill-Queen's University Press.

Fischer, S. (1994). Stabilization and economic reform in Russia. In A. Solimano, O. Sunkel, & M. I. Bléjer (Eds.), *Rebuilding capitalism: alternative roads after socialism and dirigisme*. Ann Arbor: University of Michigan Press.

Fischer, S., & Sahay, R. (2000). The transition economies after ten years. Washington, DC: International Monetary Fund working paper.

Fischer, S., Sahay, R., & Vegh, C. A. (1996). Stabilization and growth in transition economies: the early experience. *Journal of Economic Perspectives*, 10, 45–66.

Fitzpatrick, S. (1984). *The Russian Revolution*, 1917–1932. Oxford: Oxford University Press.

Fitzpatrick, S. (1994). *Stalin's peasants: resistance and survival in the Russian village after collectivization*. New York; Oxford: Oxford University Press.

Fitzpatrick, S., Rabinowitch, A., & Stites, R. (1991). *Russia in the era of NEP: explorations in Soviet society and culture*. Bloomington: Indiana University Press.

Fleming, W. J. (1979). The cultural determinants of entrepreneurship and economic development: a case study of Mendoza province, Argentina, 1861–1914. *Journal of Economic History*, 39(1), 211–24.

Floud, R., & McCloskey, D. N. (1981). *The economic history of Britain since 1700*. Cambridge; New York: Cambridge University Press.

Floud, R., & McCloskey, D. N. (1994). *The economic history of Britain since 1700*. Cambridge; New York: Cambridge University Press.

Fogel, R. W., & Engerman, S. L. (1974). *Time on the cross; the economics of American Negro slavery*. Boston: Little Brown.

Fortunatov, A. (1893). *Sel'skokhoziastvennaia statistika Evropeiskoi Rossii*. Moscow: I. N. *Kushnerov*.

Foster, C. (1999). The impact of FDI in the upstream and downstream sectors on investment in agriculture in the NIS. *Agricultural finance and credit infrastructure in transition economies* (pp. 198–211). Paris: OECD.

Francisco, R. A., Laird, B. A., & Laird, R. D. (1980). *Agricultural policies in the USSR and Eastern Europe*. Boulder, CO: Westview Press.

Frank, S. (1999). *Crime, cultural conflict, and justice in rural Russia*, 1856–1914. Berkeley, CA: University of California Press.

Frank, S., & Steinberg, M. D. (1994). *Cultures in flux: lower-class values, practices, and resistance in late Imperial Russia*. Princeton, NJ: Princeton University Press.

Frederick, S., Loewenstein, G., & O'Donoghue, T. (2002). Time discounting and time preference: a critical review. *Journal of Economic Literature*, 40(2), 351–401.

Freeze, G. (1986). The soslovie (estate) paradigm and Russian social history. *The American Historical Review*, 91(1), 11–36.

Fridman, M. (1905). *Nasha finansovaia sistema*. St. Petersburg: Obshchestsvennaia Pol'za.

Friedgut, T. H., & Borrero, M. (1997). Iuzovka and revolution. Politics and revolution in Russia's Donbass. *Russian Review*, 56(1), 138.

Friedman, E. J., & Johnson, S. (1996). Complementarities in economic reform. *Economics of Transition*, 4(2), 319–30.

Frierson, C. A. (1990). Peasant family divisions and the commune. In R. Bartlett (Ed.), *Land commune and peasant community in Russia: communal forms in imperial and early Soviet society* (pp. 303–20). London: Macmillan.

Friesen, L. G. (1994). Bukkers, Plows and Lobogreikas: Peasant Acquisition of Agricultural Implements in Russia before 1900. *Russian Review*, 53(3), 399–418.

Frohberg, K., Poganietz, W.-R. (1998). *The importance of institutions for the transition in Central and Eastern Europe: with emphasis on agriculture and food industry*. Kiel: Vauk.

Frohberg, K., & Voigt, P. (2000). Russia's position within the CIS: a cross-country comparison. In P. Wehrheim, K. Frohbert, E. Serova, & J. von Braun (Eds.), *Russia's agro-food sector: towards truly functioning markets* (pp. 39–80). Boston; Dordrecht; London: Kluwer Academic Publishers.

Frohberg, K., & Weingarten, P. (1999). *The significance of politics and institutions for the design and formation of agricultural policies*. Kiel: Wissenschaftsverlag Vauk.

Frydman, R., & Rapaczynski, A. (1994). *Privatization in Eastern Europe: Is the State Withering Away?* Budapest; London; New York: Central European University Press.

Frydman, R., Gray, C. W., & Rapaczynski, A. (1996). Insiders and the state. *Corporate governance in Central Europe and Russia*. Budapest; London; New York: Central European University Press.

Frydman, R., Rapaczynski, A., & Earle, J. S. (1993). *The privatization process in Central Europe: economic environment, legal and ownership structure, institutions for state regulation, overview of privatization programs, initial transformation of enterprises*. Budapest; New York: Central European University Press.

Frye, T. (1997). Russian privatization and the limits of credible commitment. In David L. Weimer (Ed.), *The Political Economy of Property Rights* (84–108). Cambridge: Cambridge University Press.

Fuller, W. C. (1992). *Strategy and power in Russia*, 1600–1914. New York; Toronto; New York: Free Press; Maxwell Macmillan Canada; Maxwell Macmillan International.

Gács, J., Holzmann, R., Wyzan, M. L. (1999). *The mixed blessing of financial inflows: transition countries in comparative perspective*. Northampton, MA: Edward Elgar.

Gaddy, C. G., & Ickes, B. W. (1998). Russia's virtual economy. *Foreign Affairs*, 77, 53–67.

Gaidar, Y. (2003). The inevitability of collapse of the socialist economy. *The Economics of Russian Transition* (pp. 17–30). Cambridge, MA: MIT Press.

Gaidar, Y., & Pyle, W. H. (2006). The economics of Russian transition. *Russian Review*, 65(1), 163–65.

Galbi, D. (1995). *The significance of credits and subsidies in Russian agricultural reform*. Washington, DC: The World Bank, policy research working paper.

Gallman, R. E. (1960). Commodity output, 1839–1899. In W. Parker (Ed.), *Trends in the American economy in the nineteenth century* (pp. 13–72). Princeton, NJ: Princeton University Press.

Gallman, R. E. (1972). Changes in total U.S. agricultural factor productivity in the nineteenth century. *Agricultural History*, 46(January), 191–210.

Gardner, B. (2005). Golitsino papers: summary of findings and implications. *Comparative Economic Studies*, 47, 224–28.

Gardner, B. L. (1992). Changing economic perspectives on the farm problem. *Journal of Economic Literature*, 30(March), 62–101.
Gardner, B. L. (2002). A framework for investigating issues in factor markets and economic organisation of Russian agriculture. *Factor markets in Russsia's agri-food sector frameworks of further analysis* (pp. 5–12). Moscow: IRIS, for USAID.
Gardner, B. L., & Brooks, K. M. (1994). Food prices and market integration in Russia: 1992–93. *American Journal of Agricultural Economics*, 76, 641–46.
Gáspár, P. (1995). *Changes and challenges: economic transformation in East-Central Europe*. Budapest: Akadémiai Kiadó.
Gates, S. (1995). Defense conversion and economic reform in Russia. In E. P. Lazear (Ed.), *Economic transition in Eastern Europe and Russia* (pp. 367–90). Stanford, CA: Hoover Institution Press.
Gatrell, P. (1986). *The tsarist economy*, 1850–1917. New York: St Martin's Press.
Gavetti, G., & Levinthal, D. (2001). Bringing cognition back in and moving forward. *Journal of Management & Governance*, 5(3–4), 213–216.
Gel'man, V. (2003). *Making and breaking democratic transitions: the comparative politics of Russia's regions*. Lanham: Rowman & Littlefield.
Gerschenkron, A. (1963). The early phases of industrialization in Russia: afterthoughts and counterthoughts. In W. W. Rostow (Ed.), *The economics of take-off into sustained growth*. London: Macmillan.
Gerschenkron, A. (1962). *Economic backwardness in historical perspective*. Cambridge, MA: Harvard University Press.
Gerschenkron, A. (1952). An economic history of Russia. *Journal of Economic History*, 12(2), 146–59.
Gerschenkron, A. (1970). *Europe in the Russian mirror, four lectures in economic history*. Cambridge: Cambridge University Press.
Gersick, C. J. (1991). Revolutionary change models: a multilevel exploration of the punctuated equilibrium paradigm. *Academy of Management Review*, 16, 10–36.
Gersick, C. J., & Hackman, J. (1990). Habitual routines in task-performing groups. *Organizational Behavior and Human Decision Processes*, 47(1), 65–97.
Gimpel'son, E. G. (2004). *NEP: novaia ekonomicheskaia politika Lenina-Stalina: problemy i uroki; 20-e gody XX veka*. Moscow: Sobranie.
Gimpelson, V., Lippoldt, D., Hoque, K., & Schwartz, G. (2004). The Russian labour market: between transition and turmoil. *Industrial Relations Journal*, 35(6), 683–86.
Glants, M., Toomre, J. S. (1997). *Food in Russian history and culture*. Bloomington: Indiana University Press.
Gleason, A. (1983). *Young Russia: the genesis of Russian radicalism in the 1860s*. Chicago: University of Chicago Press.
Gleason, W. J. (1981). *Moral idealists, bureaucracy, and Catherine the Great*. New Brunswick, NJ: Rutgers University Press.
Goldberg, V. P. (1989). *Readings in the economics of contract law*. Cambridge; New York: Cambridge University Press.
Goldmann, J. (1968). Fluctuations and trend in the rate of economic growth in some socialist countries. In G. R. Feiwel (Ed.), *New currents in Soviet-type economies: a reader* (pp. 112–21). Scranton, PA: International Textbook Co.

Goldsmith, R. (1955). *Economic growth in Russia, 1860–1913*. Cambridge, MA: National Bureau for Economic Research.
Goldsmith, R. (1961). The economic growth of tsarist Russia. *Economic Development and Cultural Change*, **9**, 441–75.
Golikov, V. A. (1967). *Itogi i perspektivy: sel'skoe khozyaistvo posle martovskogo Plenuma TsK KPSS*. Moscow: Izd-vo politicheskoi lit-ry.
Gomulka, S. (1994). Economic and political constraints during transition. *Europe-Asia Studies*, **46**(1), 89–106.
Goodman, A., Hughes, M., & Schroeder, G. (1987). Raising the efficiency of Soviet farm labor: problems and prospects. *Gorbachev's economic plans* (pp. 100–25). Washington, DC: U.S. Congress, Joint Economic Committee.
Goodspeed, T. (1998). The relationship between state income taxes and local property taxes: education finance in New Jersey. *National Tax Journal*, **60**(2), 219–38.
Goodspeed, T. J. (2000). Tax structure in a federation. *Journal of Public Economics*, **75**, 493–506.
Goodwin, B. K., & Grennes, T. J. (1998). Tsarist Russia and the world wheat market. *Explorations in Economic History*, **35**(4), 405–30.
Goodwin, B. K., Grennes, T. J., & McCurdy, C. (1999). Spatial price dynamics and integration in Russian food markets. *Journal of Policy Reform*, 3(2), 157–93.
Goriushkin, L. M. (1977). *Vvedenie*. In L. M. Goriushkin, M. M. Gromyko, A. N. Kopylov, & T. S. Mamsik (Eds.), *Krest'ianskaia obshchina v Sibiri XVII-nachala XX vv* (pp. 3–13). Novosibirsk: Nauka.
Goriushkin, L. M. (1983). *Krest'ianstvo Sibiri v epokhu kapitalizma*. Novosibirsk: Nauka Sibirskoe otd-nie.
Gorlin, R. H. (1977). Problems of tax reform in Imperial Russia. *Journal of Modern History*, **49**, 246–65.
Gorodskoe upravlenie (1858). *Obshchee kolichestvo zemli v Iaroslavskoi gubernii pp. 5–50b)*. Iaroslavl': Gosudarstvennyi Arkhiv Iaroslavskoi Oblasti.
Gorodskoe upravlenie (1858). *Istoriia Mologskoi strany (ll.1–740b)*. Iaroslavl': Gosudarstvennyi Arkhiv Iaroslavskoi Oblasti.
Goskomstat Rossii (2004). Ob urozhainost' zernovykh khlebov v 1795–1915 gg. *Voprosy statistiki* (31 May).
Goskomstat Rossii (2000). *Sel'skokhoziastvennaia deiatel'nost' krest'ianskikh (fermerskikh) khoziastv v Rossii: Statisticheskii sbornik*. Moscow: Goskomstat Rossii.
Gosudarstvennyi Dvorianskii zemel'nyi bank (1910). *Gosudarstvennyi Dvorianskii zemel'nyi bank*, 1885–1910: St. Petersburg.
Gottschalk, J., & Moore, D. (2001). Implementing inflation targeting regimes: the case of Poland. *Journal of Comparative Economics*, **29**, 24–39.
Government of Poland (1998). *Medium-term strategy for agriculture and rural areas development*. Warsaw: Government of Poland, Council of Ministers.
Government of Russia (1905). *Svod otchetov fabrichnykh inpektorov za 1904 god*. St. Petersburg.
Gow, H., & Swinnen, J. (1999). The impact of FDI in the downstream sector on agricultural finance, investment and production: evidence from the CEEC. *OECD Expert Meeting* (pp. 184–97). Moscow: OECD.

Gow, H., & Swinnen, J. (1998). Up- and downstream restructuring, foreign direct investment, and hold-ups in agricultural transition. *European Review of Agricultural Economics*, 184–97.

Gowdy, J. M. (1994). *Coevolutionary economics: the economy, society and the environment*. Boston, MA: Kluwer.

Gozulov, A. I. (1959). *Statistika sel'skogo khoziaistva*. Moscow. Goskomstat.

Grabher, G. (1993). Rediscovering the social in the economics of interfirm relations. In G. Grabher (Ed.), *The embedded firm–on the socioeconomics of industrial networks* (pp. 1–31). London; New York: Routledge.

Grabowski, R. (1979). The implications of an induced innovation model. *Economic Development and Cultural Change*, **27**(4), 723–34.

Grabowski, R. (1981). Induced innovation, green revolution, and income distribution: reply [The implications of an induced innovation model]. *Economic Development and Cultural Change*, **30**(1), 177–81.

Graham, L. R. (1998). *What have we learned about science and technology from the Russian experience?* Stanford, CA: Stanford University Press.

Granberg, A. G. (2000). *Osnovy regional'noi ekonomiki*. Moscow: TACIS.

Grantham, G. (1989). Agricultural supply during the Industrial Revolution: French evidence and European implications. *Journal of Economic History*, **49**(1), 43–72.

Grantham, G. (1997). The French cliometric revolution: a survey of cliometric contributions to French economic history. *European Review of Economic History*, 1, 353–404.

Grantham, G., & Leonard, C. S. (1989). *Agrarian organization in the century of industrialization: Europe, Russia, and North America*. Greenwich, CT: JAI Press.

Grantham, G., & MacKinnon, M. (1994). *Labour market evolution: the economic history of market integration, wage flexibility, and the employment relation*. London; New York: Routledge.

Granville, B. (1995). *The success of Russian economic reforms*. London and Washington, DC: Royal Institute of International Affairs, International Economic Programme, distributed by the Brookings Institution.

Granville, B. (1997). Farewell, rouble zone. In A. Åslund (Ed.), *Russia's economic transformation in the 1990s* (pp. 101–18). London: Pinter.

Granville, B. (2001). The problem of monetary stabilization. In B. Granville & P. Oppenheimer (Eds.), *Russia's post-communist economy* (pp. 93–130). Oxford: Oxford University Press.

Granville, B., & Oppenheimer, P. (2001). *Russia's post-communist economy*. Oxford: Oxford University Press.

Gray, K. (1987). *Reform and resource allocation in Soviet agriculture*. Washington, DC: Joint Economic Committee.

Gray, C. W., & Holle, A. (1996). Bank-led restructuring in Poland: the conciliation process in action. *Economics of Transition*, **4**(2), 349–70.

Grazhdaninova, M., & Brock, G. (2004). Grain and sunflower on Russian farms in 2001: how efficient is crop production? *Post-Communist Economies*, **16**(3), 297–305.

Graziosi, A. (2005). The Soviet 1931–1933 famines and the Ukrainian holodomor. Is a new interpretation possible, what would its consequences be? *Cahiers du monde russe*, **46**(3), 453–72.

Greenhalgh, S. (1990). Land reform and family entrepreneurship in East Asia. In G. McNicoll & M. Cain (Eds.), *Rural development and population* (pp. 77–118). Oxford: Oxford University Press.

Greenwald, B. C. N., Stiglitz, J. E. (1989). *Toward a theory of rigidities*. Cambridge, MA: National Bureau of Economic Research.

Greenwald, B. C. N., Stiglitz, J. E. (1991). *Information, finance, and markets: the architecture of allocative mechanisms*. Cambridge, MA: National Bureau of Economic Research.

Greenwald, B. C. N., Stiglitz, J. E. (1989). *Financial market imperfections and productivity growth*. Cambridge, MA: National Bureau of Economic Research.

Gref, G. (2000). *Strategiia ekonomicheskoi programmoi*. St Petersburg: Tsentr strategicheskikh razrabotok.

Gregory, P. R. (1994). *Before command: an economic history of Russia from emancipation to the First Five-Year Plan*. Princeton, NJ: Princeton University Press.

Gregory, P. R. (1980). Grain marketings and peasant consumption, Russia, 1885–1913. *Explorations in Economic History*, 17(2), 135–64.

Gregory, P. (2003). *The political economy of Stalinism: evidence from the Soviet secret archives*. Cambridge: Cambridge University Press.

Gregory, P. R. (1986). *Productivity, slack and time theft in the Soviet economy: evidence from the Soviet interview project*. Urbana-Champaign, IL: Soviet Interview Project University of Illinois at Urbana-Champaign.

Gregory, P. (1982). *Russian national income*, 1885–1913. Cambridge: Cambridge University Press.

Gregory, P. R. (1997). Searching for consistency in historical data: alternate estimates of Russia's industrial production, 1887–1913. *Journal of Economic History*, 57(1), 196–202.

Gregory, P. R. (1970). *Socialist and nonsocialist industrialization patterns; a comparative appraisal*. New York: Praeger Publishers.

Gregory, P., & Harrison, M. (2005). Allocation under dictatorship: research in Stalin's archives. *Journal of Economic Literature*, **43**, 721–61.

Gregory, P. R., & Stuart, R. C. (1998). *Russian and Soviet economic performance and structure*. Reading, MA: Addison-Wesley.

Greif, A. (1994). Cultural beliefs and the organization of society: historical and theoretical reflections on collectivist and individualist societies. *Journal of Political Economy*, **102**, 912–50.

Grief, A. (2001). Impersonal exchange and the origins of markets: from the community responsibility system to individual legal responsibility in pre-modern Europe. In M. Aoki & Y. Hayami (Eds.), *Communities and markets in economic development* (pp. 3–41). Oxford: Oxford University Press.

Greif, A. (1993). Institutional infrastructure and economic development: reflections from the commercial revolution. In M. Kaser (Ed.), *Tenth World Congress of the International Economic Association*. London: Macmillan.

Greif, A. (1996). On the study of organizations and evolving organizational forms through history: reflect from the late medieval family firm. *Industrial and Corporate Change*, 5, 473–502.

Greif, A., & Kandel, E. (1995). Contract enforcement institutions: historical perspective and current status in Russia. In E. P. Lazear (Ed.), *Economic transition in Eastern Europe and Russia: realities of reform* (pp. 291–321). Stanford, CA: Hoover Institution Press.

Grekov, B. D. (1946). *Krest'iane na Rusi s drevneishikh vremen do XVII veka*. Moscow: Nauka.

Griffin, K. (1979). *The political economy of agrarian change*. London: Macmillan Press.

Griffin, K. (1989). *Alternative strategies of economic development*. London: Macmillan Press, in association with the OECD Development Centre.

Griffin, K. B. (1995). *Poverty and the transition to a market economy in Mongolia*. New York: St. Martin's Press.

Griliches, Z. (1957). Hybrid corn: an exploration in the economics of technological change. *Econometrica*, 25(4), 501–22.

Griliches, Z. (1960). Measuring inputs in agriculture: a critical survey. *Journal of Farm Economics*, 42(5), 1411–27.

Griliches, Z. (1958). Research costs and social returns: hybrid corn and related innovations. *Journal of Political Economy*, 66(5), 419–31.

Grindle, M. S., & Thomas, J. W. (1989). Policy makers, policy choices, and policy outcomes: the political economy of reform in developing countries. *Policy Sciences*, 22(3–4), 213–48.

Gromyko, M. M. (1991). *Mir russkoi derevni*. Moscow: Molodaia Gvardiia.

Grosh, M., & Glewwe, P. (1996). *A guide to living standards surveys and their data sets*. Washington, DC: The World Bank.

Grossman, G. (1990). Communist agriculture: farming in the Soviet Union and Eastern Europe: foreword. In K. E. Wadekin (Ed.), *Communist agriculture: farming in the Soviet Union and Eastern Europe* (pp. xi–xiii). New York: Routledge.

Grossman, G. (1974). *Economic systems*. Englewood Cliffs, NJ: Prentice-Hall.

Grossman, G. (1971). *The industrialisation of Russia and the Soviet Union*. London: Collins.

Grossman, G. (1968). Thirty years of Soviet industrialisation. In G. R. Feiwel (Ed.), *New currents in Soviet-type economies: a reader* (pp. 41–9). Scranton, PA: International Textbook Co.

Grossman, L. (1991). *Social guarantees in the transition to a market economy in the USSR*. Monterey, CA: Monterey Institute of International Studies.

Gumbell, E. J. (1958). *Statistics of extremes*. New York: Columbia University Press.

Gupta, S., Clements, B., McDonald, C., & Schiller, C. (1998). *The IMF and the poor*. Washington, DC: Fiscal Affairs Department, IMF.

Gur'ev, A. (1904). *Ocherk razvitiia kreditnykh uchrezhdenii v Rossii*. St. Petersburg

Gurko, V. I. (1970). *Features and figures of the past; government and opinion in the reign of Nicholas II*. New York: Russell & Russell.

Gurley, J. G., & Shaw, E. S. (1983). Financial structure and economic development. In J. D. V. Pischke, D. W. Adams, & G. Donald (Eds.), *Rural financial markets in developing countries* (pp. 29–36). Baltimore and London: The Johns Hopkins University Press.

Guroff, G., & Carstenson, F. V. (1983). *Entrepreneurship in Imperial Russia and the Soviet Union*. Princeton: Princeton University Press.

Gustafson, T. (1999). *Capitalism Russian-style*. Cambridge; New York: Cambridge University Press.

Gustafson, T. (1989). *Crisis among plenty: the politics of Soviet energy under Brezhnev and Gorbachev*. Princeton, NJ: Princeton University Press.

Gustafson, T. (1981). *Reform in Soviet politics: lessons of recent policies on land and water*. Cambridge; New York: Cambridge University Press.

Haavisto, T. (1997). *The transition to a market economy: transformation and reform in the Baltic states*. Cheltenham; Brookfield, VT: E. Elgar.

Hadiz, V. R., & Robison, R. (2005). Neo-liberal reforms and illiberal consolidations: the Indonesian paradox. *Journal of Development Studies*, 41(2), 220–41.

Haggard, S. (1990). The political economy of the Philippine debt crisis. In J. M. Nelson (Ed.), *The politics of adjustment in the third world* (pp. 215–55). Princeton, NJ: Princeton University Press.

Haggard, S., Lim, W., & Kim, E. E. (2003). *Economic crisis and corporate restructuring in Korea: reforming the chaebol*. Cambridge; New York; Melbourne: Cambridge University Press.

Haimson, L. H. (1979). *The politics of rural Russia, 1905–1914*. Bloomington: Indiana University Press.

Haimson, L. H. (2000). The problem of political and social stability in urban Russia on the eve of war and revolution. Revisited. *Slavic Review*, 59(4), 848–75.

Haimson, L. H., & Sapelli, G. (1992). *Strikes, social conflict and the First World War: an international perspective*. Milan: Feltrinelli.

Haimson, L. H., & Tilly, C. (1989). *Strikes, wars and revolutions in an international perspective: strike waves in the late nineteenth and early twentieth centuries*. Cambridge; Paris: Cambridge University Press; Maison des sciences de l'homme.

Hainsworth, R., & Tompson, W. (2002). Tax policy and tax administration in Russia: the case of the banking sector. *Post-Communist Economies*, 14(3), 277–300.

Hakansson, H., & Johanson, J. (1993). The network as a governance structure: interfirm cooperation beyond markets and hierarchies. In G. Grabher (Ed.), *The embedded firm – on the socio-economics of industrial networks* (pp. 35–51). London; New York: Routledge.

Hallberg, M. C., & Herendeen, J. B. (1996). Macroeconomic policy and agricultural cycles in Australia and the United States. *Review of Marketing and Agricultural Economics*, 64(1), 45–59.

Halpern, L., & Korösi, G. (1998). Corporate performance in the transition: econometric analysis of Hungarian exporting firms, 1985–1994. In L. Halpern & C. Wyplosz (Eds.), *Hungary: towards a market economy* (pp. 192–211). Cambridge: Cambridge University Press.

Halpern, L., & Wyplosz, C. (1998). *Hungary: towards a market economy*. Cambridge: Cambridge University Press.

Hanson, P. (1994). *Regions, local power and economic change in Russia*. London: Russian and CIS Programme Royal Institute of International Affairs.

Hanson, P. (1991). The shape of Gorbachev's economic reform. In E. A. Hewett & V. H. Winston (Eds.), *Milestones in glasnost and perestroyka: the economy* (pp. 57–68). Washington, DC: Brookings.

Hanson, P. (1992). *From stagnation to catastroika: commentaries on the Soviet economy*, 1983–1991. Westport, CT; London: Greenwood.

Hanson, P., & Bradshaw, M. (2000). *Regional economic change in Russia*. Cheltenham; Northampton, MA; Elgar, distributed by American International Distribution Corporation.

Harberger, A. C. (1993). The search for relevance in economics. *American Economic Review*, 83(2), p. 1.

Hardaker, J. B., Huirne, R. B. M., & Anderson, J. R. (1997). *Coping with risk in agriculture*. Wallingford: CAB International.

Hardin, R. (1982). *Collective action*. Baltimore, MD: Johns Hopkins University Press.

Hardt, J. P. (2003). *Russia's uncertain economic future*. Armonk, NY: M. E. Sharpe.

Hargadon, A. (2003). *How breakthroughs happen: the surprising truth about how companies innovate*. Boston, MA: Harvard Business School Press.

Harley, C. K. (1992). Substitution for prerequisites: endogenous institutions and comparative economic history. In R. Sylla & G. Toniolo (Eds.), *Patterns of European industrialization* (pp. 29–44). London; New York: Routledge.

Harley, C. K. (1980). Transportation, the World Wheat Trade and the Kuznets Cycle. *Explorations in Economic History*, 17(3), 218–250.

Harris, E. (2001). Policy dialogue focuses on links between country ownership and IMF conditionality. *IMF Survey*, 30(13), 218–21.

Harrison, M. (1996). *Accounting for war: Soviet production, employment, and the defence burden*, 1940–1945. Cambridge: Cambridge University Press.

Harrison, M. (2001). *Coercion, compliance, and the collapse of the Soviet command economy*. University of Warwick working papers.

Harrison, M. (1990). The peasantry and industrialisation. In R. W. Davies (Ed.), *From tsarism to the New Economic Policy: continuity and change in the economy of the USSR* (pp. 104–23). Ithaca, NY: Cornell University Press.

Harrison, M. (1985). Primary accumulation in the Soviet transition. In A. Saith (Ed.), *The agrarian question in socialist transitions* (pp. 81–103). London: Cass.

Harrison, M. (1994). The Second World War. In R. W. Davies, M. Harrison, & S. G. Wheatcroft (Eds.), *The economic transformation of the Soviet Union*, 1913–1945 (pp. 238–67). Cambridge; New York: Cambridge University Press.

Harrison, M. (1986). Why did NEP fail? In K. Smith (Ed.), *Soviet industrialisation and Soviet maturity. Economy and society* (pp. 8–22): Routledge and Kegan Paul in associaton with Methuen.

Hatton, T. J., & Williamson, J. G. (1992). What explains wage gaps between farm and city? Exploring the Todaro model with American evidence, 1890–1941. *Economic Development and Cultural Change*, 267–93.

Hatton, T. J., & Williamson, J. G. (1998). *The age of mass migration: causes and economic impact*. New York: Oxford University Press.

Haxthausen, A. F. (1972). *Studies on the interior of Russia*. Chicago: University of Chicago Press.

Hayami, Y. (1984). Assessment of the green revolution. In C. K. Eicher & J. M. Staatz (Eds.), *Agricultural development in the third world* (pp. 416–23). Baltimore, MD: The Johns Hopkins Press.

Hayami, Y. (1997). *Development economics: from the poverty to the wealth of nations.* Oxford: Clarendon Press. Oxford University Press.

Hayami, Y. (1981). Induced innovation, green revolution, and income distribution: comment [The implications of an induced innovation model]. *Economic Development and Cultural Change*, 30(1), 169–76.

Hayami, Y., & Otsuka, K. (1993). Kasugpong in the Philippine rice bowl: the emergence of new labor institutions after the land reform. In K. Hoff, A. Braverman, & J. E. Stiglitz (Eds.), *The economics of rural organization: theory, practice, and policy* (pp. 292–304). Oxford: Oxford University Press.

Hayami, Y., & Ruttan, V. (1971). *Agricultural development: an international perspective.* Baltimore, MD: Johns Hopkins University Press.

Hayek, F. A. (1973). *Law, legislation and liberty.* Chicago: University of Chicago Press.

Heady, C., & Mitra, P. (1987). Designing taxes with migration. *Economic Journal*, 97, 87–98.

Heath, J. A. et al. (2000). The calculus of fear: revolution, repression, and the rational peasant. *Social Science Quarterly*, 81(2), 622–33.

Held, J. (1980). *The modernization of agriculture: rural transformation in Hungary, 1848–1975.* Boulder, CO: East European Quarterly.

Heller, M. A. (1999). The boundaries of private property. *Yale Law Journal*, 108(6), 1163–1223.

Hellie, R. (1999). *The economy and material culture of Russia, 1600–1725.* Chicago: University of Chicago Press.

Hellie, R. (1971). *Enserfment and military change in Muscovy.* Chicago: University of Chicago Press.

Hellie, R. (1965). *Muscovite law and society: the Ulozhenie of 1649 as a reflection of the political and social development of Russia since the Sudbnik of 1589.* Chicago: University of Chicago Press.

Hellie, R. (1988). *The Muscovite Law Code (Ulozhenie) of 1649.* Irvine, CA: C. Schlacks Jr.

Hellie, R. (1982). *Slavery in Russia, 1450–1725.* Chicago: University of Chicago Press.

Hellman, J. S. (1998). Winners take all: the politics of partial reform in post-communist transitions. *World Politics*, 50(2), 203–34.

Hellman, J. S., Jones, G., & Kaufmann, D. (2003). Seize the state, seize the day: state capture and influence in transition economies. *Journal of Comparative Economics*, 31(4), 751–73.

Hellman, J., & Schankerman, M. (2000). Intervention, corruption and capture: the nexus between enterprises and the state. *Economics of Transition*, 8(3), 545–76.

Herrera, Y. M. (2006). *Transforming bureaucracy: conditional norms and the international standardization of statistics in Russia.* Aberdeen, Scotland: Centre for the Study of Public Policy.

Herriott, S. R., Levinthal, D., & March, J. G. (1985). Learning from experience in organizations. *American Economic Review*, 75(2), 298–302.

Heston, A. W., & Lipsey, R. E. (1999). *International and interarea comparisons of income, output, and prices*. Chicago: University of Chicago Press.

Hewett, E. A. (1991). Gorbachev's economic strategy: a preliminary assessment. *Milestones in glastnost' and perestroyka: the economy* (pp. 5–22). Washington, DC: Brookings Institute.

Hewett, E. A., & Winston, V. H. (Eds.) (1991). *Milestones in glasnost' and perestroyka: the economy*. Washington, DC: Brookings Institution.

Heybey, B., & Murrell, P. (1999). The relationship between economic growth and the speed of liberalization during transition. *Journal of Policy Reform*, 3(2), 121–37.

Heyman, D., & Leijonhufvud, A. (1995). *High inflation*. Oxford: Oxford University Press.

Hicks, J. (1969). *A theory of economic history*. Oxford: Clarendon Press.

Higgins, B. (1968). *Economic development*. New York: Norton.

Hillman, A. L. (1991). *Markets and politicians: politicized economic choice*. Dordrecht: Kluwer Academic.

Hindus, M. G. (1988). *Red bread: collectivization in a Russian village*. Bloomington: Indiana University Press.

Hinrichs, K., Roche, W., & Sirianni, C. (1991). *Working time in transition: the political economy of working hours in industrial nations*. Philadelphia: Temple University Press.

Hirschman, A. (1985). Reflections on the Latin American experience. In L. Lindberg & C. Maier (Eds.), *The politics of inflation and economic stagnation: theoretical approaches and international studies* (pp. 53–7). Washington, DC: Brookings.

Hoch, S. L. (1991). The banking crisis, peasant reform, and economic development in Russia, 1857–1861. *American Historical Review*, **96**(3), 795–820.

Hoch, S. L. (2004). Did Russia's emancipated serfs really pay too much for too little land? Statistical anomalies and long-tailed distributions. *Slavic Review*, **63**(2), 247–74.

Hoch, S. L. (1998). Famine, disease, and mortality patterns in the parish of Borshevka, Russia, 1830–1912. *Population Studies [London]*, **52**(3), 357–68.

Hoch, S. L. (1999). Tall tales: anthropometric measures of well-being in Imperial Russia and the Soviet Union, 1821–1960. *Slavic Review*, **58**(1), 61–70.

Hoch, S. L. (1994). On good numbers and bad; Malthus, population trends and peasant standard of living in late Imperial Russia. *Slavic Review*, **53**(1), 41–75.

Hoch, S. L. (1986). *Serfdom and social control in Russia: Petrovskoe, a village in Tambov*. Chicago: University of Chicago Press.

Hodgson, G. M. (1988). *Economics and institutions* Cambridge: Polity Press.

Hodson, R., & Kaufman, R. L. (1982). Economic dualism: a critical review. *American Sociological Review*, **47**(6), 727–39.

Hoekman, B., & Djankov, S. (1997). Determinants of the export structure of East European countries. *World Bank. Economic Review*.

Hoff, K. (1993). Land taxes, output taxes, and sharecropping: was Henry George right? In K. Hoff, B. Avishay, & J. E. Stiglitz (Eds.), *The economics of rural organization: theory, practice, and policy* (pp. 332–51). Oxford: Oxford University Press.

Hoff, K., Braverman, A., & Stiglitz, J. E. (1993). *The economics of rural organization: theory, practice, and policy*. Oxford: Oxford University Press.

Hoffmann, D. L. (1994). Land, freedom and discontent: Russian peasants of the central industrial region prior to collectivisation. *Europe-Asia Studies*, **46**(4), 637–48.

Hoffman, D. L. (1998). The 'peasantisation' of the Soviet working class. In J. Pallot (Ed.), *Transforming peasants: society, state and the peasantry, 1861–1930: selected papers from the Fifth World Congress of Central and East European Studies* (pp. 113–29). Basingstoke; New York: Macmillan; St. Martin's Press.

Hoffman, D. L., & Graziosi, A. (1995). Peasant metropolis: social identities in Moscow, 1929–1941. *Slavic Review*, **54**(4), 1090–92.

Hoffman, D. L., Kotsonis, Y., & Perrie, M. (2001). Russian modernity: politics, knowledge, practices. *Europe-Asia Studies*, **53**(5), 795–96.

Hoffman, P. T. (1991). Land rents and agricultural productivity – the Paris basin, 1450–1789. *Journal of Economic History*, **51**(4), 771.

Holquist, P., & Lih, L. T. (2004). Making war, forging revolution: Russia's continuum of crisis, 1914–1921. *Slavic Review*, **63**(2), 408–09.

Holzmann, R., Gács, J., Winckler, G., Ludwig-Boltzmann-Institut für Analysen der Wirtschaftspolitik. International Institute for Applied Systems Analysis & Universität des Saarlandes. Europa-Institut. (1995). *Output decline in Eastern Europe: unavoidable, external influence or homemade?* Dordrecht; Boston: Kluwer Academic Publishers.

Hosking, G. (1997). *Russia: People and Empire*. Cambridge, MA: Harvard University Press.

Hosking, G. A. (1973). *The Russian constitutional experiment; government and Duma*, 1907–1914. Cambridge: Cambridge University Press.

Hough, J. F. (1997). *Democratization and revolution in the USSR*, 1985–1991. Washington, DC: Brookings Institution.

Hough, J. F. (1988). *Opening up the Soviet economy*. Washington, DC: Brookings Institution.

Hough, J. F. (1980). *Soviet leadership in transition*. Washington, DC: Brookings Institution.

Hough, J. F. (1969). *The Soviet prefects; the local party organs in industrial decision-making*. Cambridge, MA: Harvard University Press.

Hounshell, D. A. (2000). The medium is the message, or how context matters: the Rand Corporation builds on economics of innovation, 1946–1962. In A. Hughes & T. Hughes (Eds.), *System, experts and computers*. Cambridge, MA: MIT Press.

Howes, S. (1993). Why not to aggregate up: the influence of aggregation on the ordering of distributions. London: Suntory-Toyota International Centre for Economics and Related Disciplines, London School of Economics.

Hueckel, G. (1981). Agriculture during industrialization. In R. Floud & D. McCloskey (Eds.), *The economic history of Britain since 1700* (pp. 182–203). Cambridge; New York: Cambridge University Press.

Huffman, W., & Evenson, R. E. (1989). Supply and demand functions for multiproduct U.S. cash grain farms: biases caused by research and other policies. *American Journal of Agricultural Economics*, **71**(3), 761–73.

Huffman, W. E., & Evenson, R. E. (1993). *Science for agriculture: a long-term perspective*. Ames: Iowa State University Press.

Hughes, J. (1996). *Stalinism in a Russian province: a study of collectivization and dekulakization in Siberia*. New York: St. Martin's Press in association with the Centre for Russian and East European Studies, University of Birmingham.

Hunter, H., Kaple, D. A. (1983). *The Soviet railroad situation*. Washington, DC: Wharton Econometric Forecasting Associates.

Hunter, H., & Szyrmer, J. (1992). *Faulty foundations: Soviet economic policies, 1928–1940*. Princeton, NJ: Princeton University Press.

Hunter, H., & Szyrmer, J. (1992). *Soviet economic policies, 1928–1940*. Princeton, NJ: Princeton University Press.

Hunya, G. (1993). *Economic transformation in East-Central Europe and in the newly independent states*. Boulder, CO: Westview Press.

Hutton, S., & Redmond, G. (2000). *Poverty in transition economies*. London; New York: Routledge.

Iakobson, L. I. (2000). *Gosudarstvennyi sektor ekonomiki, ekonomicheskaia teoriia i politika*. Moscow: TACIS.

Ianin, V. L. (1977). *Sel'skoe khoziaistvo i krest'ianstvo SSSR v sovremennoi sovetskoi istoriografii: materialy XVI sessii Simpoziuma po izucheniiu problem agrarnoi istorii, Kishinev, 1976*. Kishinev: Izd-vo Shtiintsa.

Ianson, I. E. (1879). *Ocherk pravitel'stveynnykh mer po pereseleniiu krest'ian posle izdaniia polozheniia 19-go fevralia 1861 goda*. St. Petersburg.

Ianson, I. E. (1881). *Opyt statisticheskogo issledovaniia o krest'ianskikh nadelakh i platezhakh*. St. Petersburg.

Ianzhul, I. I. (1884). *Fabrichnyi byt moskovskoi gubernii*. St. Petersburg.

Iastrebova, O. K. (2002). Credit, finance and investment in agriculture. *Factor markets in Russia's agri-food sector: frameworks of further analysis* (pp. 108–34). Moscow: IRIS, USAID.

Iatsunskii, V. (1973). *Sotsial'no-ekonomicheskaia istoriia Rossii XVIII–XIX vv. Izbrannye trudy*. Moscow: Nauka.

Ibragimova, D. K. (1997). *NEP i perestroika: massovoe soznanie sel'skogo naseleniia v usloviiakh perekhoda k rynku*. Moscow: Pamiatniki istoricheskoi mysli.

Ickes, B. (2001). Dimensions of transition. In B. Granville & P. Oppenheimer (Eds.), *Russia's post communist economy*. Oxford: Oxford University Press.

Ignatovich, I. (1902). *Pomeshchichi krest'iane nakanune osvobozhdeniia*.St. Petersburg: izd-vo L. F. Panteleeva.

Ignatovich, I. (1911). Krest'ianskie volneniia. In A. K. Dzhivelegov, S. P. Mel'gunov, & V. I. Picheta (Eds.), *Velikaia Reforma, Russkoe obshchestvo i krestianskii vopros v proshlom i nastoiashchem*. Moscow.

Iguiniz, J. (1987). Peru: agriculture, crisis and macroeconomic policy. *Cepal Review*, 0(33), 157–70.

Il'in, V. V., Panarin, A. S., & Akhiezer, A. S. (1996). *Reformy i kontrreformy v Rossii: Tsikly modernizatsionnogo protsessa*. Moscow: Izd-vo Moskovskogo universiteta.

Illarionov, A., Layard, R., & Orszag, P. (1997). The conditions of life. In A. Åslund (Ed.), *Russia's economic transformation in the 1990s* (pp. 137–58). London: Pinter.

Immergut, E. M., & Jochem, S. (2006). The political frame for negotiated capitalism: electoral reform and the politics of crisis in Japan and Sweden. *Governance*, 19(1), 99–134.

Inglot, T. (1995). The politics of social policy reform in post-communist Poland: government responses to the social insurance crisis during 1989–1993. *Communist and Post-Communist Studies*, 28(3), 361–73.

Institute for the Economy in Transition. (2002). *Problemy agroprodovol'stvenogo sektora*. Moscow: Institute of the Economy in Transition.

Institute for the Economy in Transition (2003). *Russian economy, update September 2003*. Moscow: Institute for the Economy in Transition.

Ioffe, G., & Nefedova, T. (1997). *Continuity and change in rural Russia: a geographical perspective*. Boulder, CO: Westview Press.

Ioffe, G., & Nefedova, T. (2000). Areas of crisis in Russian agriculture: a geographic perspective. *Post Soviet Geography and Economics*, 41(4), 288–305.

Ioffe, G., & Nefedova, T. (2001). Transformation of the Russian food system at close range: a case study of two oblasts. *Post Soviet Geography and Economics*, 42(5), 329–61.

IRIS. (1999). *Reorganizatsiia sel'skokhoziastvennykh predpriatii: ikh effektivnost' i ustoichivoe razvitie*. Moscow; Golitzino: IRIS; USAID.

IRIS. (2001). Factor markets in Russia's agri-food sector: frameworks of further analysis. Golitzino II: IRIS, USAID.

Isupov, A. A. (1980). *Naselenie SSSR–po dannym Vsesoiuznoi perepisi naseleniia 1979 goda*. Moscow: Izd-vo polit. lit-ry.

Ivankina, E., Rtishchev, I., Serova, E., Khramova, I., Karlova, N., Tikhonova, T. (2000). *Nekotorye aktual'nye voprosy agrarnoi politiki Rossii*. Moscow: Institut ekonomiki perekhodnogo perioda.

Ivanov, L. (1977). *Novye vremena – Novye zaboty: Ocherki*. Moscow: Sov. pisatel'.

Ivanov, P. I. (1846). *Opyt istoricheskago izsliedovaniia o mezhevanii zemel' v Rossii*. Moscow: Tip. S. Selivanovskago.

Ivantsov, D. N. (1915). *K kritike russkoi urozhainoi statistiki: opyt analiza nekotorykh offitsial'nykh i zemskikh tekushchikh dannykh*. Petrograd: Tip. V. F. Kirshbauma.

Jansson, H., & Sandberg, S. (2008). Internationalization of small and medium sized enterprises in the Baltic Sea region. *Journal of International Management*, 14(1), 65–77.

Jasny, N. (1949). *The socialized agricultulre of the USSR: plans and performance*. Stanford, CA: Stanford University Press.

Jasny, N. (1957). *The Soviet 1956 statistical handbook: a commentary*. East Lansing: Michigan State University Press.

Jasny, N. (1966). *Khrushchev's crop policy*. Glasgow: George Outram & Co. Ltd.

Jazbec, B. (2000). Structural reforms and real exchange rates in transition economies. *Economic and Business Review*, 2(3), 265–81.

Jeffries, I. (1996). *Problems of economic and political transformation in the Balkans*. New York: Pinter.

Jeffries, I. (1993). *Socialist economies and the transition to the market: a guide*. London; New York: Routledge.

Jensen, M. C., & Meckling, W. H. (1979). Rights and production functions: an application to labor-managed firms and codetermination. *Journal of Business*, 52(4), 469–506.

Johanson, M. (2008). Institutions, exchange and trust: a study of the Russian transition to a market economy. *Journal of International Management*, **14**(1), 46–64.

Johnson, D. (1963). *Agricultural production*. In A. Bergson & S. Kuznets (Eds.), *Economic trends in the Soviet Union* (p. 24). Cambridge, MA: Harvard University Press.

Johnson, D. (1948). Allocation of agricultural income. *Journal of Farm Economics*, 30(4), 724–49.

Johnson, D. G., & Brooks, K. M. (1983). *Prospects for Soviet agriculture in the 1980s*. Bloomington: Indiana University Press.

Johnson, D., & Kahan, A. (1959). Soviet agriculture: structure and growth. In A. Bergson & S. Kuznets (Eds.), *Joint Economic Committee of the United States Congress* (pp. 201–38). Washington, DC: Joint Economic Committee.

Johnson, P. A., & Takeyama, L. N. (2001). Initial conditions and economic growth in the US states. *European Economic Review*, **45**(4–6), 917–27.

Johnson, R. N., & Libecap, G. D. (2002). Contracting problems and regulation: the case of the fishery. In L. G. Anderson (Ed.), *Collected essays. Fisheries economics: Volume 1*. International Library of Environmental Economics and Policy. Burlington, VT: Aldershot.

Johnson, S. (1994). Production efficiency and agricultural reform in Ukraine. *American Agricultural Economics Association and the Association for Comparative Economic Studies*. Boston, MA.

Johnson, S., Kaufmann, D., & Shleifer, A. (1998). The unofficial economy in transition. *Brookings Papers on Economic Activity*, **1997**(2), 159–239.

Johnson, S., & Temin, P. (1993). The macroeconomics of NEP. *Economic History Review*, **46**(4), 750–67.

Johnston, B. F., & Clark, W. C. (1982). *Redesigning rural development: a strategic perspective*. Baltimore; London: Johns Hopkins University Press.

Johnston, B. F., & Cownie, J. (1969). The seed fertilizer revolution and labour force absorption. *American Economic Review*, **59**(4), 569–82.

Johnston, B., & Mellor, J. W. (1961). The role of agriculture in economic development. *American Economic Review*, **51**(September), 566–93.

Joint Research Group (1998). *The problem of capital flight from Russia*. Moscow: Institute of Economics, and The Center for the Study of International Economic Relations, University of Western Ontario, Canada.

Jones, D. (1997). The nature and performance of small firms in Bulgaria. In H. Brezinski & M. Fritsch (Eds.), *The emergence and evolution of markets* (pp. 131–50). Cheltenham: Edward Elgar.

Jones, D. C., & Miller, J. B. (1997). *The Bulgarian economy: lessons from reform during early transition*. Aldershot; Brookfield, VT: Ashgate.

Jones, D. W. (1975). Migration and urban unemployment in dualistic economic development. Chicago: Department of Geography, University of Chicago.

Jones, R. E. (1991). Ukrainian grain and the Russian market in the late eighteenth and early nineteenth centuries. In I. S. Koropeckyj (Ed.), *Ukrainian economic history:*

interpretive essays (pp. 210–27). Cambridge, MA: Harvard Ukrainian Research Institute.

Jones, S. (1997). Privatization of Cereals Marketing in the Former Centrally Planned Economies: A Review of Issues. In L. D. Smith & N. Spooner (Eds.), *Cereals Sector Reform in the Former Soviet Union and Central and Eastern Europe* (pp. 67–92). Wallingford: CAB International.

Joravsky, D. (1970). *The Lysenko affair*. Cambridge, MA: Harvard University Press.

Jorgenson, D. W., & Gollop, F. M. (1992). Productivity growth in U.S. agriculture – a posterior perspective. *American Journal of Agricultural Economics*, 74(3), 745.

Jorgenson, D. W., Gollop, F. M., & Fraumeni, B. M. (1987). *Productivity and U.S. economic growth*. Cambridge, MA: Harvard University Press.

Josling, T. (1974). Agricultural policies in developed countries: a review. *Journal of Agricultural Economics*, 25(1), 229–65.

Kabuzan, V. M. (1963). *Narodonaselenie Rossii v vosemnadtsati-pervoi polovine deviatnadtsatogo v*. Moscow: Nauka.

Kabuzan, V. M. (1971). *Izmeneniia v razmeshchenii naseleniia Rossii*. Moscow: Nauka.

Kabuzan, V. M. (1976). *Zaselenie Novorossii: (Ekaterinoslavskoi i Khersonskoi gubernii): v XVIII-pervoi polovine XIX veka (1719–1858 gg.)*. Moscow: Nauka.

Kabuzan, V. M. (1992). *Narody Rossii v pervoi polovine XIX v; chislennost' i etnicheskii sostav*. Moscow: Nauka.

Kabuzan, V. M. (1995). *Russkie v mire: Dinamika chislennosti naseleniia 1719–1989, Formirovanie etnicheskikh i politicheskikh granits russkogo naroda*. St Petersburg: Blits.

Kafengauz, L. B. (1910). *Razvitie russkogo sel'skokhoziastvennogo mashinostroeniia*. Kharkov.

Kafengauz, L. B. (1910). *Sindikaty v russkoi zhelieznoi promyshlennosti. K voprosu o kontsentratsii proizvodstva v Rossii*. Moscow: Tip. T-va I. D. Sytina.

Kafengauz, L. B., & Figurovskaia, N. K. (1994). *Evoliutsiia promyshlennogo proizvodstva Rossii, poslednaia tret' XIX v.-30-e gody XX v*. Moscow: Epifanii.

Kafengauz, L. B., Kondakov, V. A., Khanykin, V. A., Bukshpan, I. A. M., & Solonevich, I. (1994). *Evoliutsiia ekonomicheskoi zhizni rossiiskogo obshchestva: sotsial'nye utopii i deistvitel'nost'*. Tiumen: Sovmest. ros.-*likhtenshtein*. predpriiatie "Likht".

Kagan, F. W. (1999). *The military reforms of Nicholas I: the origins of the modern Russian army*. Basingstoke; New York: Macmillan: St. Martin's Press.

Kahan, A. (1963). Soviet statistics of agricultural output. In R. D. Laird (Ed.), *Soviet agricultural and peasant affairs* (pp. 143–60). Lawrence, KS: University of Kansas Press.

Kahan, A. (1967). Government policies and the industrialization of Russia. *Journal of Economic History*, 27(4), 460–77.

Kahan, A. (1973). Notes on serfdom in Western and Eastern Europe. *Journal of Economic History*, 33(1), 86–99.

Kahan, A. (1989). *Russian economic history: the nineteenth century*. Chicago: The University of Chicago Press.

Kahan, A., & Hellie, R. (1985). *The plow, the hammer, and the knout: an economic history of eighteenth-century Russia*. Chicago: University of Chicago Press.

Kakhk, I., & Uibu, K. (1980). *O sotsial'noi strukture i mobil'nosti estonskogo krest'ianstva v pervoi polovine XIX veka*. Tallin: Eesti raamat.

Kalantaridis, C., & Labrianidis, L. (2004). Rural entrepreneurs in Russia and the Ukraine: origins, motivations, and institutional change. *Journal of Economic Issues*, 38(3), 659–82.

Kaldor, N. (1975). What is wrong with economic theory? *Quarterly Journal of Economics*, 89(3), 347–57.

Kaldor, N. (1977). Equilibrium theory and growth theory. In M. Baskin (Ed.), *Economics and human welfare; essays in honour of Tibor Scitovsky*. New York: Academic Press.

Kalugina, Z. I. (2000). Survival strategies of enterprises and families in the contemporary Russian countryside. In L. A. Norsworthy (Ed.), *Russian views of the transition in the rural sector: structures, policy outcomes, and adaptive responses*. Washington, DC; The World Bank.

Kaneda, H. (1969). Economic implications of the 'Green Revolution' and the strategy of agricultural development in West Pakistan. *Pakistan Development Review*, 9(2), 111–43.

Kang, S. J. (2002). Relative backwardness and technology catching up with scale effects. *Journal of Evolutionary Economics*, 12(4), 425–41.

Kantor, S. E. (1998). *Politics and property rights: the closing of the open range in the postbellum South*. Chicago: University of Chicago Press.

Kaplan, H. H. (1995). *Russian overseas commerce with Great Britain during the reign of Catherine II*. Philadelphia: American Philosophical Society.

Kaplan, H. H., Roosevelt, P. R., & Kraa, D. (1981). *Russia's impact on the Industrial Revolution in Great Britain during the second half of the eighteenth century*. Wiesbaden: Harrassowitz.

Karamazova, M. (2002). Treteiski sudy v agrarnoi sfere: praktika i perspektivy. *Agrarnaia Reforma: Ekonomika. i Pravo*, 3(21, May–June), 23.

Karamzin, N. M., & Pipes, R. (1959). *Karamzin's memoir on ancient and modern Russia*. Cambridge: Harvard University Press.

Karcz, J. F. (1965). The new Soviet agricultural program. *Soviet Studies*, 7(2), 129–161.

Karcz, J. F. (1966). Seven years on the farm: retrospect and prospects. *Soviet economic prospects for the seventies* (pp. 383–451). Washington, DC: Congress of the United states, Joint Economic Committee.

Karcz, J. (1967). Thoughts on the grain problem. *Soviet Studies*, 18(4), 399–434.

Karcz, J. F. (1968). Soviet agriculture: a balance sheet. In V. G. Treml (Ed.), *The development of the Soviet economy: plan and performance* (pp. 108–46). Washington, DC: Frederick A. Praeger.

Karcz, J. F. (1979). *The economics of communist agriculture: selected papers*. Bloomington, IN: International Development Institute.

Karhunen, P., Lofgren, J., & Kosonen, R. (2008). Revisiting the relationship between ownership and control in international business operations: lessons from transition economies. *Journal of International Management*, 14(1), 78–88.

Karlova, N., Tikhonova, T., Serova, E., Khramova, I., & Shik, O. (2002). *The agrifood sector*. Moscow: Institute for the Economy in Transition.

Karnaukhova, E. S. (1951). *Razmeshchenie sel'skogo khoziaistva Rossii, 1861–1914 gg* Moscow: Nauka.

Karpov, N. (1925). *Agrarnaia politika Stolypina*. Leningrad: Rabochee izd-vo "Priboi".

Karshenas, M. (1995). *Industrialization and agricultural surplus: a comparative study of economic development in Asia*. Oxford: Oxford University Press.

Kashchenko, S. G. (1995). *Reforma 19 Fevralia 1861 g. na severo-zapade Rossii*. Moscow: Mosgorarkhiv.

Katsenelenbaum, Z. S. (1923). Sel'skokhoziastvennyi kredit v Rossii. *Sotsialistichekoe khoziastvo* (6–8).

Katz, A. (1972). *The politics of economic reform in the Soviet Union*. New York; Washington: Praeger Publishers.

Kaufman, A. A. (1918). *Agrarnyi vopros v Rossii*, Moscow.

Kaufman, A. A. (2000 [1915]). Voprosy ekonomiki i statistiki krest'ianskogo khoziastva. In Kravchenko, A. I. (ed.) *Antologiia sotsial'ko-ekonomicheskoi mysli v Rossii dorevoliutsionnoi period*. St Petersburg: RKhGI.

Kaufmann, D., Kraay, A., & Zoido-Lobatón, P. (1999). Aggregating governance indicators. Washington, DC: World Bank.

Kaufmann, D., Kraay, A., & Zoido-Lobaton, P. (2000). Governance matters from measurement to action. *Finance and Development*, 37(2), 10–13.

Kaufman, R. R. (1972). *The politics of land reform in Chile*, 1950–1970: *public policy, political institutions, and social change*. Cambridge, MA: Harvard University Press.

Kavelin, S. P. (1914). *Mezhevanie i zzemleustroitstvo, Teoreticheskoe i prakticheskoe rukovodstva*. Moscow.

Kayden, E. M., & Antsyferov, A. N. (1929). *The coöperative movement in Russia during the war. consumers' coöperation*. New Haven; London: Yale University Press; H. Milford Oxford University Press for the Carnegie Endowment for International Peace: Division of Economics and History.

Kazantseva, N. D., Pavlov, I. V., & Ruskol, A. A. (1955). *Kolkhoznoe pravo*. Moscow: Gosudarstvennoe izd- vo iuridicheskoi literatury.

Kazi, S. (1984). Intersectoral tax burdens in Pakistan: a critical review of existing evidence and some new estimates. *Pakistan Development Review*, 23(4).

Kelly, W. J. (1976). Railroad development and market integration in tsarist Russia: evidence on oil products and grain. *Journal of Economic History*, **36**(4), 908–16.

Kemme, D. M. (1991). *Economic transition in Eastern Europe and the Soviet Union: issues and strategies*. New York; Boulder, CO: Institute for East-West Security Studies, distributed by Westview Press.

Kemme, D. M. (2003). Russian financial transition: the development of institutions and markets for growth. In J. P. Hardt (Ed.), *Russia's uncertain economic future* (pp. 183–211). Armonk, NY; London: Sharpe.

Kendrick, J. W. (1973). *Postwar productivity trends in the United States*, 1948–1969. New York: National Bureau of Economic Research, distributed by Columbia University Press.

Kerans, D. (2001). *Mind and labor on the farm in black-earth Russia*, 1861–1914. Budapest; New York: Central European University Press.

Khalilzadeh-Shirazi, J., & Shah, A. (1991). *Tax policy in developing countries*. Washington, DC: The World Bank.

Khanin, I. (1991). *Razvitie ekonomicheskogo rosta SSSR*. Novosibirsk: RAN.

Khlystun, V. (1999). Status and prospects of creating a favourable investment climate in the agroindustrial complex of Russia. *Agricultural finance and credit infrastructure in transition economies*. Proceedings of OECD Expert Meeting, Moscow, February 1999 (pp. 83–8). Paris: OECD.

Khodarkovsky, M., & LeDonne, J. P. (2002). Russia's steppe frontier: the making of a colonial empire, 1500–1800. *Cahiers du monde russe*, 43(4), 763–65.

Khriashcheva, A. I. (1921). *Krest'ianstvo v voine i revoliutsii: statistiko-ekonomicheskie ocherki*. Moscow: VSNKh.

Khromov, P. A. (1950). *Ekonomicheskoe razvitie Rossii v XIX–XX vekakh*. Moscow: Gospolitizdat.

Khromov, P. A. (1967). *Ekonomicheskoe razvitie Rossii: ocherki ekonomiki Rossii s drevneishikh vremen do Velikoi Oktiabr'skoi revoliutsii*. Moscow: Nauka.

Kiani, A. (2008). TFP and MIRR in the Agricultural Crop Sub-Sector of Sindh. *European Journal of Social Sciences*, 7, pp. 43–57.

Kieniewicz, S. (1969). *The emancipation of the Polish peasantry*. Chicago: University of Chicago Press.

Kim, B. K. (2003). The politics of chaebol reform, 1980–1997. In S. Haggard, W. Lim, & E. Kim (Eds.), *Reforming the chaebol: economic crisis and corporate restructuring in Korea* (pp. 53–78). Cambridge, MA; New York; Melbourne: Cambridge University Press.

Kim, B., & Pirttila, J. (2006). Political constraints and economic reform: empirical evidence from the post-communist transition in the 1990s. *Journal of Comparative Economics*, 34(3), 446–66.

Kim, Y. C. (1995). *The Southeast Asian economic miracle*. New Brunswick, NJ: Transaction Publishers.

Kingston-Mann, E., & Mixter, T. (1990). *Peasant economy, culture, and politics of European Russia*, 1800–1921. Princeton, NJ: Princeton University Press.

Kir'ianov, I. I., & Volin, M. S. (1989). *Rabochii klass Rossii ot zarozhdeniia do nachala XX v*. Moscow: Nauka.

Kirkow, P. (1998). *Russia's provinces: authoritarian transformation versus local autonomy?* London; New York: Macmillan; St. Martin's Press.

Kiselev, S. V. (2002). The macroeconomic and structural shifts in a context of the rural labor market development. *Factor markets in Russsia's agri-food sector frameworks of further analysis* (pp. 178–95). Moscow: IRIS, for USAID.

Kitanina, T. M. (1978). *Khlebnaia torgovlia Rossii v 1875–1914 gg (Ocherki prav-itel'snvennoi politiki)*. Leningrad: Nauka.

Klipper, M. Z. (1998). The governance of privatized firms: authority, responsibility and disclosure. *Economics of Transition*, 6(1), 101–11.

Klochek, V., Alexeyev, A., & Tretyukhin, N. (1982). *Soviet foreign trade: today and tomorrow*. Moscow: Progress Publishers.

Knell, M. (1996). *Economics of transition: structural adjustments and growth prospects in Eastern Europe*. Cheltenham; Brookfield, VT: Elgar.

Knell, M. (1996). Structural adjustments and growth: is Eastern Europe catching up? In M. Knell (Ed.), *Economics of transition: structural adjustments and growth prospects in Eastern Europe* (pp. 1–24). Cheltenham: Elgar.

Kochin, M. (1996). Decollectivization of agriculture and the planned economy. *American Journal of Political Science*, 40(3), 717–39.
Koenker, D. (1981). *Moscow workers and the 1917 Revolution*. Princeton, NJ: Princeton University Press.
Koenker, D., & Rosenberg, W. G. (1989). *Strikes and revolution in Russia, 1917*. Princeton, NJ: Princeton University Press.
Kokhn, M. P. (1926). *Russkie indeksy tsen*. Moscow-Leningrad: Ekonomicheskaia zhizn'.
Kolchin, P. (1987). *Unfree labor: American slavery and Russian serfdom*. Cambridge, MA: Belknap Press of Harvard University Press.
Kolodezhnyi, V. N. (2002). Evoliutsiia zemel'noi politiki sovetskoi vlasti. In D. F. Aiatskov (Ed.), *Sobstvennost' na zemliu v Rossii: Istoriia i sovremennost'* (pp. 348–399). Moscow: ROSSPEN.
Komitet Rossiiskoi Federatsii po zemel'nym resursam i zemleustroitstvu (1995). *Gosudarstvennyi (natsional'nyi) doklad o sostoianii i ispol'zovanii zemel' rossiiskoi federatsii za 1974*. Moscow: Komitet Rossiiskoi Federatsii po zemel'nym resursam i zemleustroistvu.
Komitet Verkhovnogo Soveta RF po zakonodatel'stvu (1993). *Sbornik normativnykh aktov o regulirovanii grazhdanskikh pravootnoshenii v Rossiiskoi Federatsii*. Moscow: Respublika.
Komov, N. V. (1993). Zemel'nyie otnosheniia i zemel'naia reforma v Rossii. *Zemlia Rossii*, 1, 1–7.
Koopman, R. B. (1989). *Efficiency and growth in agriculture: a comparative study of the Soviet Union, United States, Canada, and Finland*. Agricultural and Trade Analysis Division, Economic Research Service, USDA.
Kopsidis, M. (2000). Disintegration of Russian grain markets in transition: political and economic dimensions. *Post-Communist Economies*, 12(1), 47–60.
Korelin, A. P. (1988). *Sel'skkokhozaistvennyi kredit v Rossii v konntse XIX-nachale XX v*. Moscow: Nauka.
Korelin, A. P. (2002). Stolypinskaia agrarnaia ora v aspekte zemel'noi sobstvennosti. In D. F. Aiatsko (Ed.), *Sobstvennost' na zemliu v Rossii: istoriia i sovremennost'*. (pp. 240–96). Moscow: ROSSPEN.
Kornai, J. (1980). *The economics of shortage*. New York: North Holland.
Kornai, J. (1993). Transformational recession: a general phenomenon explained through the example of Hungary's development. *Economie Appliqué*, 46(2), 181–227.
Kornai, J. (1997). The citizen and the state: reform of the welfare system. *Struggle and hope: essays on stabilization and reform in a post-socialist economy* (pp. 239–54). Cheltenham: Edward Elgar.
Kornai, J., Maskin, E., & Roland, G. (2003). Understanding the soft budget constraint. *Journal of Economic Literature*, 41(4), 1095–1136.
Korostelina, K. (2008). Identity, autonomy and conflict in republics of Russia and Ukraine. *Communist and Post-Communist Studies*, 41(1), 79–91.
Kotsonis, Y. (1998). How peasants became backward: agrarian policy and cooperatives in Russia, 1905–1914. In J. Pallot (Ed.), *Transforming peasants: society, state and the peasantry, 1861–1930: selected papers from the Fifth World Congress of Central and East European Studies* (pp. 15–36). Basingstoke; New York: Macmillan; St. Martin's Press.

Kovács, J. (1995). *Technological lag and intellectual background: problems of transition in East Central Europe*. Aldershot, Hants; Brookfield, VT: Dartmouth Publishing Company.

Koval'chenko, I. D. (1959). *Krest'iane i krepostnoe khoziaiistvo Riazanskoi i Tambovskoi gubernii v pervoi polovine XIX veka; k istorii krizisa feodal'no-krepostnicheskoi sistemy khoziaistva*. Moscow: Izd-vo Moskovskogo universiteta.

Koval'chenko, I. D. (1979). *Massovye istochniki po sotsial'no-ekonomicheskoi istorii Rossii perioda kapitalizma*. Moscow: Nauka.

Koval'chenko, I. D. (1967). *Russkoe krepostnoe krest'yanstvo v pervoi polovine XIX v*. Moscow: Izd-vo Moskovskogo universiteta.

Koval'chenko, I. D., & Milov, L. V. (1974). *Vserossiiskii agrarnyi rynok XVIII – nachalo XX veka*. Moscow: Nauka.

Koval'chenko, I. D., Moiseenko, T. L., & Selunskaia, N. B. (1988). *Sotsial'no-ekonomicheskii stroi krest'ianskogo khoziaistva evropeiskoi Rossii v epokhu kapitalizma: istochniki i metody issledovaniia*. Moscow: Izd-vo Moskovskogo universiteta.

Koval'chenko, I. D., Selunskaia, N. B., & Litvakov, B. M. (1982). *Sotsial'no-ekonomicheskii stroi pomeshchichego khoziaistva Evropeiskoi Rossii v epokhu kapitalizma: istochniki i metody izucheniia*. Moscow: Nauka.

Koval'chenko, I. D., & Tishkov, V. A. (1991). *Agrarnaia evoliutsiia Rossii i SShA v XIX-nachale XX veka: materialy sovetsko-amerikanskikh simpoziumov*. Moscow: Nauka.

Kozlova, E. N. (1993). Razvitiia kooperatsii v Rossii i ee rol' v obnovlenii strany (1906–1917 gg). In N. K. Figurovskaia (Ed.), *Kooperatsiia, stranitsy istorii* (pp. 27–47). Moscow: International Fund for the History of Science.

Kramer, M. (1996). *Travels with a hungry bear: a journey to the Russian heartland*. Boston: Houghton Mifflin.

Kravchenko, A. I. (2000). *Antologiia sotsial'no-ekonomicheskoi mysli v Rossii: dorevoliutstionnyi period*. St. Petersburg: Russkii Khristianskii Gumanitarnyi Institut.

Kravis, I. B., Heston, A. W., Summers, R. (1978). *International comparisons of real product and purchasing power*. Baltimore, MD: Published for the World Bank, Johns Hopkins University Press.

Kravis, I. B., Heston, A. W., Summers, R. (1982). *World product and income: international comparisons of real gross product*. Baltimore, MD: Published for the World Bank, Johns Hopkins University Press.

Krueger, A. (1993). Virtuous and vicious circles in economic development. *American Economic Review*, 83(May), 351–55.

Krueger, A. O., Schiff, M., & Valdes, A. (1988). Measuring the Impact of Sector-Specific and Economy-Wide Policies on Agricultural Incentives in LDCs. *World Bank Economic Review*, 2(3), 255–271.

Krueger, G., & Ciolko, M. (1998). A note on initial conditions and liberalization during transition. *Journal of Comparative Economics*, 26(4), 718–34.

Krugman, P. (1992). *Geography and trade*. Cambridge, MA: MIT Press.

Krusekopf, C. C. (2000). Land-tenure institutions and agricultural productivity in post-reform China. Seattle: University of Washington.

Kruze, E. E. (1976). *Polozhenie rabochego klassa Rossii v 1900–1914 gg*. Leningrad: Akademiia Nauk.

Kuhn, T. S. (1962). *The structure of scientific revolutions*. Chicago: University of Chicago Press.

Kurer, O. (1996). The political foundations of economic development policies. *Journal of Development Studies*, 32(5), 645–68.

Kurer, O. (1997). *The political foundations of development policies*. London: University Press of America.

Kurer, O. (2005). Corruption: an alternative approach to its definition and measurement. *Political Studies*, 53(1), 222–39.

Kurer, O. (2006). The Papua New Guinean malaise: from redistributive politics to a failing state. *Pacific Economic Bulletin*, 21(1), 84–99.

Kuromiya, H. (1990). *Stalin's Industrial Revolution: politics and workers, 1928–1932*. Cambridge; New York: Cambridge University Press.

Kuromiya, H. (1998). *Freedom and terror in the Donbas: a Ukrainian-Russian borderland, 1870s–1990s*. Cambridge; New York: Cambridge University Press.

Kushnirsky, F. I. (2001). A modification of the production function for transition economies reflecting the role of institutional factors. *Comparative Economic Studies*, 43(1), 1–30.

Kussmaul, A. (1990). *A general view of the rural economy of England, 1538–1840*. Cambridge: Cambridge University Press.

Kuzio, T. (1998). *Contemporary Ukraine: dynamics of post-Soviet transformation*. Armonk, NY: M. E. Sharpe.

Kuznetsov, Y. (1997). Learning in networks: enterprise behaviour in the former Soviet Union and contemporary Russia. In J. Nelson, C. Tilly, & L. Walker (Eds.), *Transforming post-communist political economies*. Washington, DC: National Academy Press.

Kuznetsov, Y. (1997). Learning to learn: emerging patterns of enterprise behavior in the Russian defense sector, 1992–1995. In J. B. Sedaitis (Ed.), *Commercializing high technology: East and West* (pp. 181–204). Lanham, MD: Rowman & Littlefield.

Kwack, S.-Y. (1990). The economic development of the Republic of Korea, 1965–1981. In L. J. Lau (Ed.), *Models of development: a comparative study of economic growth in South Korea and Taiwan* (pp. 65–125). San Francisco: ICS Press.

Kydd, J. & Bird, K. (1997). Reforming the Cereals Sector in Transition Economies: An Overview of Issues. In L. D. Smith and N. Spooner (Eds.), *Cereals Sector Reform in the Former Soviet Union and Central and Eastern Europe* (pp. 9–37). Wallingford, UK: CAB International.

Labán, R., & Sturzenegger, F. (1998). Fiscal conservatism as a response to the debt crisis. In F. Sturzenegger & M. Tommasi (Eds.), *The political economy of delayed reform* (pp. 105–26). Cambridge, MA: MIT Press.

Ladman, J. R., & Tinnermeier, R. L. (1983). The political economy of agricultural credit: the case of Bolivia. In J. D. V. Pischke, D. W. Adams, & G. Donald (Eds.), *Rural financial markets in developing countries* (pp. 337–45). Baltimore; London: The Johns Hopkins University Press.

Laeven, L., Klingebiel, D., & Kroszner, R. (2002). *Financial crises, financial dependence and industry growth*. Washington, DC: World Bank.

LaFont, S. (1998). *Women in transition: voices from Lithuania*. Albany: State University of New York Press.

Laird, R. D. (1963). The politics of Soviet agriculture. In R. D. Laird (Ed.), *Soviet agricultural and peasant affairs*. Lawrence, KS: University of Kansas Press.
Laird, R. D. (1963). *Soviet agricultural and peasant affairs*. Lawrence, KS: University of Kansas Press.
Laird, R. D., & Laird, B. A. (1978). *The Soviet farm manager as an entrepreneur*. Washington, DC: The Wilson Center Kennan Institute for Advanced Russian Studies.
Lak, S. S. (1896). *Russkii rubl'*. Odessa: Iuzhno-Russk. O-va Pechatnogo Dela.
Lane, D., & Cameron, R. (1999). *The transition from communism to capitalism: ruling elites from Gorbachev to Yeltsin*. New York: St. Martin's Press.
Lane, T., Ghosh, A., Hamann, J., Phillips, S., Schulze-Ghattas, M., & Tsikata, T. (1999). *IMF-supported programs in Indonesia, Korea, and Thailand: a preliminary assessment*. Washington, DC: IMF.
Lankes, H.-P., & Venables, T. (1996). Foreign direct investment in economic transition: the changing pattern of investment. *Economics of Transition*, 4(2), 331–48.
Lapidus, G. W. (1999). Asymmetrical federalism and state breakdown in Russia. *Post Soviet Affairs*, 15(1), 74–82.
Leathers, H. (2002). Comments on paper by Eu. Serova, N. Karlova and V. Petrichenko. *Factor markets in Russsia's agri-food sector frameworks of further analysis* (pp. 172–74). Moscow: IRIS, for USAID.
Ledeneva, A. V. (1998). *Russia's economy of favours: blat, networking and informal exchange*. Cambridge: Cambridge University Press.
LeDonne, J. P. (1984). *Ruling Russia: politics and administration in the Age of Absolutism*, 1762–1796. Princeton, NJ: Princeton University Press.
LeDonne, J. P. (2004). *The grand strategy of the Russian empire*, 1650–1831. Oxford; New York: Oxford University Press.
LeDonne, J. P., & Sunderland, W. (2000). The Russian empire and the world, 1700–1917: the geopolitics of expansion and containment. *Journal of World History*, 2(2), 390–91.
Ledyaev, V. (2008). Domination, power and authority in Russia: basic characteristics and forms. *Journal of Communist Studies and Transition Politics*, 24(1), 17–36.
Lee, C. H. (2005). The political economy of institutional reform in Korea. *Journal of the Asia Pacific Economy*, 10(3), 257–77.
Lee, K., & Lim, C. (2001). Technological regimes, catching-up and leapfrogging: findings from the Korean industries. *Research Policy*, 30(3), 459–83.
Leff, N. (1979). Entrepreneurship and economic development: the problem revisited. *Journal of Economic Literature*, 17(1), 46–64.
Lenin, V. I. (1931). *Agrarnaia programma russkoi sotsial-demokratii*. Moscow: Gos. Sotsial'no-Ekonomicheskoe Izd-vo.
Lenin, V. I. (1974). *The development of capitalism in Russia*. Moscow: Progress Publishers.
Lenin, V. I. (1970). *Podgotovitel'nye materialy k knige* "Razvitie kapitalizma v Rossii." Moscow: Politizdat.
Lenin, V. I. (1947, 1952). *Razvitie kapitalizma v Rossii; protsess obrazovaniia vnutrennego rynka dlia krupnoi promyshlennosti*. Moscow: Gos. izd-vo polit. lit'ry.

Leonard, C.S. (forthcoming). Agricultural Productivity in Russia, 1861–1913: From Inertia to Ferment In M. Olsson and P. Svensson (Eds), *Agricultural Production and Productivity in Europe*. Turnhout, Belgium: Brepols.

Leonard, C. S. (2002). *Microeconomic change in Central and East Europe*. Basingstoke: Palgrave Macmillan.

Leonard, C. S. (1999). The political economy of delayed tax reform in transition Russia. St. Petersburg: St Petersburg University, School of Management.

Leonard, C. S. (1989). Postscript. In G. Grantham & C. Leonard (Eds.), *Agrarian organization in the century of industrialization: Europe, Russia, and North America* (p. 2 v.). Greenwich, CT: JAI Press.

Leonard, C. S. (2000). Rational resistance to land privatization: the response of rural producers to agrarian reforms in pre- and post-Soviet Russia. *Post Soviet Geography and Economics*, 41(December), 605–29.

Leonard, C. S. (1993). *Reform and regicide: the reign of Peter III of Russia*. Bloomington: Indiana University Press.

Leonard, C. S. (1998). Rural poverty in transition countries. *Poverty in transition*. New York: United Nations Development Program.

Leonard, C. S. (1990). The Russian peasant commune under serfdom. In R. P. Bartlett (Ed.), *Land commune and peasant community in Russia: communal forms in imperial and early Soviet society* (pp. 121–42). New York: St. Martin's Press.

Leonard, C. S. (2002). Transition paths. In C. Leonard (Ed.), *Microeconomic change in Central and East Europe* (pp. xi–xix). Basingstoke: Palgrave Macmillan.

Leonard, C. S. (2007). WTO accession, institutions, and Russian agriculture. In S. Sutyrin (Ed.), *Development of international trading system: prospects for emerging markets*. St. Petersburg: St. Petersburg University.

Leonard, C., & Ljungberg, J. Population and living standards in Europe 1870–1914. In S. Broadberry & K. O'Rourke (Eds.), *Economic history of modern Europe* (Ch. 5). Cambridge: Cambridge University Press.

Leonard, C. S., & Serova, E. (2001). The reform of Russian agriculture, 1990–1998. In B. Granville & P. Oppenheimer (Eds.), *Russia's post-communist economy* (367–98). Oxford: Oxford University Press.

Leontovitsch, V. (1957). *Geschichte des Liberalismus in Russland*. Frankfurt am Main: V. Klostermann.

Lerman, Z. (2003). Agricultural output and productivity in the former Soviet republics. *Economic Development and Cultural Change*, 51(4), 999–1018.

Lerman, Z. (2001). Agriculture in transition economies: from common heritage to divergence. *Agricultural Economics*, 26(2), 95–114.

Lermon, Z. (2001). A decade of land reform and farm restructuring: what Russia can learn from the world experience. *Quarterly Journal of International Agriculture*, 40(1.Special Issue), 5–28.

Lerman, Z. (1998). Does land reform matter? Some experiences from the former Soviet Union. *European Review of Agricultural Economics*, 25(3), 307–30.

Lerman, Z. (2000). From common heritage to divergence: why the transition countries are drifting apart by measures of agricultural performance. *American Journal of Agricultural Economics*, 82(5), 1140–48.

Lerman, Z. (2002). The impact of land reform on the rural population. In D. J. O'Brien & S. K. Wegren (Eds.), *Rural reform in post-Soviet Russia* (pp. 42–67). Washington, DC: Woodrow Wilson Center Press.

Lerman, Z. (1999). Land reform and farm restructuring: what has been accomplished to date? *American Economic Review*, **89**(2), 271–75.

Lerman, Z. (2002). Privatization of land in Russia. *Economic Systems*, **26**(2), 149–51.

Lerman, Z. (Ed. (2007). *Russia's Agricultural In Transition: Factor Markets and Constraints on Growth*. Lanham, Md: Lexington Books.

Lerman, Z. (2000). Status of land reform and farm restructuring in Central and Eastern Europe: a regional overview. In C. Czaki & Z. Lerman (Eds.), *Structural change in the farming sectors in Central and Eastern Europe: lessons for EU accession* (pp. 3–21): Second World Bank/FAO Workshop, June 27–29, 1999.

Lerman, Z., & Brooks, K. M. (1994). Land reform and farm restructuring in Russia. *World Bank. Discussion papers, No. 233*. Washington, DC: World Bank.

Lerman, Z., Csáki, C., & Feder, G. (2002). *Land policies and evolving farm structures in transition countries*. Washington, DC: World Bank, Development Research Group Rural Development.

Lerman, Z., Csáki, C., & Feder, G. (2004). *Agriculture in transition: land policies and evolving farm structures in post-Soviet countries*. Lanham, MD: Lexington Books.

Lerman, Z., & Schreinemachers, P. (2005). Individual farming as a labour sink: evidence from Poland and Russia. *Comparative Economic Studies*, **47**(4), 675–95.

Levine, H. S. (1987). Anatomy of Gorbachev's economic reform: comment. *Soviet Economy*, 3(3), 242–45.

Levine, H. S. (1992). Soviet economic reform: the transition problem. In W. S. Kern (Ed.), *From socialism to a market economy* (pp. 85–97). Kalamazoo, MI: University Press.

Levine, W. E. (2002). *Tropics, germs, and crops: how endowments influence economic development*. Washington, DC: Center for Global Development.

Levinthal, D. A. (1998). The slow pace of rapid technological change: gradualism and punctuation in technological change. *Industrial and Corp Change*, 7(2), 217–47.

Lévy-Leboyer, M., & Bourguignon, F. (1985). *L'économie française au XIXe siècle: analyse macro-économique*. Paris: Economica.

Lewellen, T. C. (1978). *Peasants in transition: the changing economy of the Peruvian Aymara: a general systems approach*. Boulder, CO: Westview Press.

Lewin, M. (1965).. The immediate background of Soviet collectivisation. *Soviet Studies*, 17(2), 162–97.

Lewin, M. (1984). Rural society in twentieth century Russia: an introduction. *Social History*, **9**, 171–80.

Lewin, M. (1985). *The making of the Soviet system: essays in the social history of interwar Russia*. New York: Pantheon.

Lewis, W. A. (1954). Economic development with unlimited supplies of labour. *Manchester School of Economics and Social Studies*, **20**(May), 139–92.

Lewis, W. A. (1955). *Theory of economic growth*. London: Allen and Unwin.

Li, W. (1999). A tale of two reforms. *Rand Journal of Economics*, 30(1), 1–21.
Liashchenko, P. I. (1970). *History of the national economy of Russia, to the 1917 Revolution*. New York: Octagon Books.
Liashchenko, P. I. (1956). *Istoriia narodnogo khoziastvo SSSR. Sotsializm*: Moscow.
Liashchenko, P. I. (1925). *Ocherki agrarnoi evolìutsii Rossii*: Moscow.
Liashchenko, P. I. (1927). *Russkoe zernovoe khoziastvo*.
Libecap, G. D. (1989). Distributional issues in contracting for property rights. *Journal of Institutional and Theoretical Economics*, 145(1), 6–24.
Libecap, G. D. (1993). Entrepreneurship, property rights and economic development. In G. D. Libecap (Ed.), *New learning on entrepreneurship. Advances in the study of entrepreneurship, innovation, and economic growth. Greenwich, Conn.* (pp. 67–83). Greenwich, CT; London: JAI Press.
Libecap, G. D. (1986). Property rights in economic history: implications for research. *Explorations in Economic History*, 23(3), 227–52.
Libecap, G. D., & Johnson, R. N. (1979). Property rights, nineteenth-century federal timber policy, and the conservation movement. *Journal of Economic History*, 39(1), 129–42.
Liefert, W. M. (2001). Agricultural reform: major commodity restructuring but little institutional change. In J. P. Hardt (Ed.), *Russia's uncertain economic future* (pp. 253–82). Washington, DC: Joint Economic Committee, Congress of the United States.
Liefert, W. M. (2005). The allocative efficiency of material input use in Russian agriculture. *Comparative Economic Studies*, 47(1), 214–23.
Liefert, W. M. (1997). Comparative advantage and government budget effects: an application to the grain trade of the former USSR. *American Journal of Agricultural Economics*, 79(3), 715–25.
Liefert, W. M. (2002). Comparative (dis?)advantage in Russian agriculture. *American Journal of Agricultural Economics*, 84(3), 762–67.
Liefert, W. M. (1997). Grain sector reform and food security in the countries of the FSU. In L. D. Smith & N. Spooner (Eds.), *Cereals sector reform in the former Soviet Union and Central and Eastern Europe* (pp. 93–107). Walingford, Oxon: CAB International.
Liefert, W. M. (2008). Measuring the Success of Agricultural Transition: An Application to Russia. In " in *Agricultural Economics and Transition: What Was Expected, What We Observed, the Lessons Learned*, C. Csaki, and C. Forgacs (Eds.). Halle, Germany: IAMO, 44–54.
Liefert, W. M. (1990). The Soviet gain from trade with the West in fuel, grain, and machinery. *Weltwirtschaftliches Archiv*, 126(1), 78–96.
Liefert, W. M., Gardner, B., & Serova, E. (2003). Allocative efficiency in Russian agriculture: the case of fertilizer and grain. *American Journal of Agricultural Economics*, 85(5), 1228–33.
Liefert, W. M., Liefert, O. & Serova, E. (2009). Russia's Transition to Major Player in World Agricultural Markets. *Choices*, 24(2), 1.
Liefert, W., Lerman, Z., Gardner, B. & Serova, E. (2005). Agricultural Labor in Russia: Efficiency and Profitability. *Discussion Paper*. Jerusalem: Center for Agricultural Economic Research, Department of Agricultural Economics and Managment, Hebrew University.

Liefert, W. M. et al. (1996). Producer subsidy equivalents for Russian agriculture: estimation and interpretation. *American Journal of Agricultural Economics*, 78(3), 792–98.

Liefert, W. & Swinnen, J. (2002). Changes in Agricultural Markets in Transition Economies. in Economic Research Service, U. (ed.) *Agricultural Economic Report*. Washington, D.C.: USDA.

Lih, L. T. (1990). *Bread and authority in Russia*, 1914–1921. Berkeley: University of California Press.

Lin, J. Y. (1988). The household responsibility system in China's agricultural reform – a theoretical and empirical study. *Economic Development and Cultural Change*, 36(3), S199–S224.

Lin, J. Y., Yao, X., & Wen, G. J. (1990). China's agricultural development: recent experience and policy issues. In C. K. Eicher & J. M. Staatz (Eds.), *Agricultural development in the third world* (pp. 480–502). Baltimore; London: The Johns Hopkins University Press.

Lincoln, W. B. (1990). *The great reforms: autocracy, bureaucracy, and the politics of change in Imperial Russia*. DeKalb: Northern Illinois University Press.

Lincoln, W. B. (1982). *In the vanguard of reform: Russia's enlightened bureaucrats*, 1825–1861. DeKalb: University of Northern Illinois Press.

Lindert, P. (1991). Historical patterns of agricultural policy. In C. P. Timmer (Ed.), *Agriculture and the state: growth, employment, and poverty in developing countries* (pp. 29–83). Ithaca, NY: Cornell University Press.

Linz, J. J., & Stepan, A. C. (1996). *Problems of democratic transition and consolidation: southern Europe, South America, and post-communist Europe*. Baltimore, MD: Johns Hopkins University Press.

Lipski, S. (2002). O gosudarstvennom regulirovanii pereraspredeleniia zemel' sel'skokhoziastvennogo naznacheniia. *Agrarnaia Reforma: Ekonomika. i Pravo*, 3(21, May–June), 15–16.

Litoshenko, L. N. (1925). *Natsional'nyi dokhod SSSR*. Moscow: Finansovoe Izd-vo NKF SSSR.

Litoshenko, L. N. (2001). *Sotsializatsiia zemli v Rossii*. Novosibirsk: Sibirskii khronograf.

Lituev, V. N. (1997). *Zemel'naia sobstvennost' kak dvorianskaia monopolia v kapitalisticheskoi Rossii: teoreticheskie voprosy, informatsionnaia baza dannykh, upravlenie zemel'nym rynkom*. Moscow: Sobranie.

Litvack, J. I. (1996). Regional demands and fiscal federalism. In C. Wallich (Ed.), *Russia and the challenge of fiscal federalism* (pp. 218–40). Aldershot: Avebury.

Litvak, B. G. (1972). *Russkaia derevnia v reforme 1861 goda: Chernozemnyi tsentr*. Moscow: Nauka.

Liu, S., Carter, M. R., & Yao, Y. (1998). Dimensions and diversity of property rights in rural China: dilemmas on the road to further reform. *World Development*, 26(10), 1789–1806.

Loganov, G. (1906). *Statistika zemlevladeniia evropeiskoi Rossii po uezdam*. St. Petersburg: Tipografiia Ministerstva Vnutrennikh Del.

Lonkila, M., & Gladarev, B. (2008). Social networks and cellphone use in Russia: local consequences of global communication technology. *New Media and Society*, 10(2), 273–93.

Luchinskaia, A. V. (1913). Arest zarabotnoi platy rabochago za nedobory po otstovskoi zemle. *Trudy Iuridicheskkago Obshchestva 1912*, **6**, 354–68.

Lueck, D. (1993). Contracting into the commons. In T. L. Anderson & R. T. Simmons (Eds.), *The political economy of customs and culture: informal solutions to the commons problem* (pp. 43–60). Lanham, MD: Rowman & Littlefield.

Lukauskas, A. J. (1997). *Regulating finance: the political economy of Spanish financial policy from Franco to democracy*. Ann Arbor: University of Michigan Press.

Luong, P. J., & Weinthal, E. (2004). Contra coercion: Russian tax reform, exogenous shocks, and negotiated institutional change. *American Political Science Review*, **98**(1), 139–52.

Luttrell, C. B. (1980). The Russian grain embargo: dubious success. *Federal Reserve Bank of St. Louis Review*, **62**(7), 2–8.

Lybecker, K. (1999). *Product piracy: the sale of counterfeit pharmaceuticals in developing countries*. Berkeley: University of California Press.

Macey, D. A. J. (1990). Gorbachev and Stolypin: Soviet agrarian reform in historical perspective. In W. Moskoff (Ed.), *Agricultural reform in the Gorbachev era* (pp. 3–18). Armonk, NY: M. E. Sharpe.

Macey, D. A. J. (1987). *Government and peasant in Russia, 1861–1906: the prehistory of the Stolypin reforms*. DeKalb: Northern Illinois University Press.

Macey, D. A. J. (1998). 'A wager on history': the Stolypin agrarian reforms as process. In J. Pallot (Ed.), *Transforming peasants: society, state and the peasantry, 1861–1930* (pp. 149–73). Houndmills; Basingstoke; Hampshire: Macmillan.

Macey, D. A. J., Pyle, W., & Wegren, S. K. (2004). *Building market institutions in post-communist agriculture: land, credit, and assistance*. Lanham, MD: Lexington Books.

Macours, K., & Swinnen, J. F. M. (2000). A comparison of agrarian transition in Russia, China, and Eastern Europe. In P. Wehrheim, K. Frohbert, E. Servoa, & J. von Braun (Eds.), *Russia's agro-food sector: towards truly functioning markets* (pp. 9–35). Boston; Dordrecht; London: Kluwer Academic Publishers.

Macours, K., & Swinnen, J. (2000). Impact of initial conditions and reform policies on agricultural performance in Central and Eastern Europe, the former Soviet Union, and East Asia. *American Journal of Agricultural Economics*, **82**(5), 1149–55.

Macours, K., & Swinnen, J. F. (2002). Patterns of agrarian transition. *Economic Development and Cultural Change*, **50**(2), 365–94.

Maddala, G. (1979). A note on the form of the production function and productivity. In assembly of behavioral and social sciences (U.S.) panel to review productivity statistics (Ed.), *Measurement and interpretation of productivity* (pp. 309–17). Washington, DC: National Academy of Sciences.

Maddison, A. (1969). *Economic growth in Japan and the USSR*. London: Allen & Unwin.

Maddison, A. (1995). *Monitoring the world economy*, 1820–1992. Paris: Development Centre of the Organisation for Economic Co-operation and Development.

Maddison, A. (2006). *The world economy. Volume 1: a millennial perspective. Volume 2: historical statistics*. Paris; Washington, DC: Organisation for Economic Co-operation and Development.

Magagna, V. (1991). *Communities of grain: rural rebellion in comparative perspective*. Ithaca: Cornell University Press.

Magnin, E. (2002). Path-dependence and initial conditions in the transition process: the cases of Hungary and Romania. *East West Journal of Economics and Business*, 5(1–2), 67–87.

Male, D. (1971). *Russian peasant organisation before collectivisation; a study of commune and gathering* 1925–1930. Cambridge: Cambridge University Press.

Malerba, F. (1992). Learning by firms and incremental technical change. *Economic Journal*, 102(413), 845–59.

Malia, M. E. (1961). *Alexander Herzen and the birth of Russian socialism*, 1812–1855. Cambridge, MA: Harvard University Press.

Malleret, T. (1992). *Conversion of the defense industry in the former Soviet Union*. New York: Institute for East-West Security Studies.

Manellia, A. I. (2000). *O finansovom sostoianii sel'skogo khoziastva Rossiiskoi Federatsii*. Moscow: Center for Economic Conjuncture of the Government of the Russian Federation.

Marer, P., Zecchini, S. (1991). *The transition to a market economy*. Paris: Organisation for Economic Co-operation and Development.

Marnie, S. (1992). *The Soviet labour market in transition*. Florence: European University Institute.

Masal'skii, V. (1899). *Sel'skokhoziastvennye opytnye uchrezhdeniia v Rossii*. St. Petersburg.

Maskin, E., & Xu, C. (2001). Soft budget constraint theories: from centralization to the market. *Economics of Transition/European Bank for Reconstruction and Development*, 9(1), 1–27.

Mathijs, E. (1997). Process and politics of agrarian reform in Hungary. In J. F. M. Swinnen (Ed.), *Political economy of agrarian reform in Central and Eastern Europe* (pp. 237–68). Aldershot, Hants; Brookfield, VT: Ashgate.

Mathijs, E. (1997). An historical overview of Central and Eastern European land reform. In J. F. M. Swinnen (Ed.), *Political economy of agrarian reform in Central and Eastern Europe* (pp. 33–54). Aldershot, Hants; Brookfield, VT: Ashgate.

Matiukhin, V., & Bezrukov, V. (2001). *Ekonomicheskoe i finansovoe sostoianie sel'skhokhoziastvennykh tovaroproizvoditelei (po rezul'tatam provedennogo v ianvarie 2001 g. vyborochnogo eksPress.-oprosa)*. Moscow: Federal Presidential Agency for Government Communications and Information of the Russian Federatioin and the Center for Economic Conjuncture of the Government of the Russian Federation.

Matthews, M. (1993). *The passport society: controlling movement in Russia and the USSR*. Boulder, CO: Westview Press.

Maynard, J. (1962). *The Russian peasant and other studies*. New York: Collier Books.

McAuley, A. (1977). *Soviet anti-poverty policy* 1955–1975. Madison: University of Wisconsin Institute for Research on Poverty.

McAuley, A. (1979). *Economic welfare in the Soviet Union: poverty, living standards, and inequality*. Madison; London: University of Wisconsin Press; Allen & Unwin.

McAuley, M. (1984). *Bureaucracy and revolution: the lesson from Leningrad, 1917–1927*. Colchester: University of Essex Press.
McAuley, A. (1994). Poverty and anti-poverty policy in a quasi-developed society: the case of Uzbekistan. *Communist Economies and Economic Transformation*, 6(2), 187–201.
McCaffray, S. P., & Gregory, P. R. (1997). The politics of industrialization in tsarist Russia: the association of southern coal and steel producers, 1874–1914. *American Historical Review*, 102(5), 1531–32.
McCargo, D. (2005). Network monarchy and legitimacy crises in Thailand. *Pacific Review*, 18(4), 499–519.
McCauley, M. (1976). *Khrushchev and the development of Soviet agriculture: the virgin land*. London: Macmillan [for] the School of Slavonic and East European Studies.
McCauley, M. (1995). *The Khrushchev era*: 1953–1964. London; New York: Longman.
McCloskey, D. (1976). English open fields as behavior towards risk. In P. Uselding (Ed.), *Research in economic history* (pp. 124–70). Greenwich, CT: JAI Press.
McFaul, M. (1999). The political economy of social policy reform in Russia: ideas, institutions, and interests. In L. Cook, M. A. Orenstein, & M. Rueschemeyer (Eds.), *Left parties and social policy in postcommunist Europe* (pp. 207–34). Boulder, CO; Oxford: Westview Press.
McFaul, M. (1999). Institutional design, uncertainty, and path dependency during transitions: cases from Russia. *Constitutional Political Economy*, 10(1), 27–52.
McFaul, M. (2000). *Russia's unfinished revolution: political change from Gorbachev to Putin*. Ithaca, NY: Cornell University Press.
McFaul, M. (2000). State power, institutional change, and the politics of privatization in Russia. In V. Wright & L. Perotti (Eds.), *Privatization and public policy* (pp. 199–232). Cheltenham; Northampton, MA: Elgar, distributed by American International Distribution Corporation.
McGuire, M. C., & Olson Jr., M. (1996). The economics of autocracy and majority rule: the invisible hand and the use of force. *Journal of Economic Literature*, 34(1), 72–96.
McKay, J. P. (1974). Foreign enterprise in Russian and Soviet industry: a long term perspective. *Business History Review*, 48(3), 336–56.
McKay, J. P. (1970). *Pioneers for profit: foreign entrepreneurship and Russian industrialization* 1885–1913. Chicago: University of Chicago Press.
McKinnon, R. I. (1991). *The order of economic liberalization: financial control in the transition to a market economy*. Baltimore, MD: Johns Hopkins University Press.
Meliukhina, O. (1994). *Russian agriculture and agrarian policy*. Moscow: Gaidar Institute for the Economy in Transition.
Meliukhina, O. (1995). Regionalizatsiia agrarnoi i prodovol'zstvennoi politiki Rossii v 1992–1994 godakh. *Predprinimatel'stvo v Rossii*(3–4), 26–9.
Meliukhina, O., & Serova, E. (1996). Otsenka urovnia gosudarstvennoi podderzhki sel'skogo khoziastva: primenimost' standartnykh metodov v perekhodnoi ekonomike. *Voprosy Ekonomiki* (7), 101–11.

Mellor, J. (1984). Agriculture on the road to industrialization. In C. K. Eicher & J. M. Staatz (Eds.), *Agricultural development in the third world* (pp. 70–88). Baltimore, MD: The Johns Hopkins Press.

Melton, E. (1987). Proto-industrialization, serf agriculture and agrarian structure: two estates in nineteenth-century Russia. *Past and Present*, 115, 69–106.

Mendel, A. P. (1961). *Dilemmas of progress in tsarist Russia: legal Marxism and legal populism*. Cambridge, MA: Harvard University Press.

Mendel, A. P. (1965). Peasant and worker on the eve of the First World War (in discussion). *Slavic Review*, 24(1), 23–33.

Menger, C. (1963). *Problems of economics and sociology*. Urbana: University of Illinois Press.

Merl, S. (1981). *Der Agrarmarkt und die neue ekonomische Politik: die Anfange staatlicher Lenkung der Landwirtschaft in der Sowjetunion*, 1925–1928. Munchen; Wien: Oldenbourg.

Merl, S. (1988). Did the kolkhoz system really fulfill the initial aims of the party in the 1930s? In J. C. Brada & K. E. Wadekin (Eds.), *Socialist agriculture in transition: organizational response to failing performance* (pp. 77–97). Boulder, CO: Westview Special Studies on the Soviet Union and Eastern Europe series.

Merl, S. (1990). The role of agriculture in Soviet industrialization. In K. E. Wadekin (Ed.), *Communist agriculture: farming in the Soviet Union and Eastern Europe* (pp. 3–22). London; New York: Routledge.

Mesiatsev, P. A. (1922). *Zemel'naia i selsko-khoziaistvennaia politika v Rossii*. Moscow: Novaia derevnia.

Mespoulet, M. (1999). Zemstvo statisticians: the making of a new intellectual profession in Russia in the prerevolutionary era (1880–1917). The case of Saratov. *Cahiers du Monde Russe*, 40(4), 573–624.

Metzer, J. (1984). Railroads and the efficiency of internal markets: some conceptual and practical considerations. *Economic Development and Cultural Change* 33(1): 61–70.

Metzer, J. (1977). *Some economic aspects of railroad development in Tsarist Russia*. New York: Arno Press.

Meyer, J. R. (1973). Notes on serfdom in Western and Eastern Europe: discussion. *Journal of Economic History*, 33(1), 100–05.

Midelfart Knarvik, K. H., & Tvedt, J. (1999). The choice of trade regime: delayed reform under productivity fluctuations and cost of structural change. *Journal of Policy Reform*, 3(1), 67–80.

Migdal, J. S. (1975). *Peasants, politics, and revolution; Pressures toward political and social change in the third world*. Princeton, NJ: Princeton University Press.

Migulin, P. P. (1899). *Russkii gosudarstvennyi kredit v Rossii, 1769–1899*. Kharkov. Vol 1.

Mikhailovskii, V. G. (1921). Tezisy doklada 'Urozhai v Rossii, 1801–1914 gg.' *Biulleten' Tsemtral'nogo Statisticheskogo Upravleniia*, 50.

Milanovic (1998). *Explaining the increase in inequality during the transition*. Washington, DC: World Bank.

Milanovic, B. (1998). *Income, inequality, and poverty during the transition from planned to market economy*. Washington, DC: World Bank.

Milanovic, B., & Jovanovic, B. (1999). *Change in the perception of the poverty line during the times of depression: Russia, 1993–1996*. Washington, DC: World Bank.

Milgrom, P. R., North, D., & Weingast, B. R. (1990). The role of institutions in the revival of trade: the medieval law merchant, private judges, and the champagne fairs. *Economic and Politics*, I, 1–23.

Milgrom, P., & Roberts, J. (1992). *Economics, organisations and management*. Englewood Cliffs, NJ: Prentice Hall.

Millar, J. R. (1971). The agricultural surplus hypothesis: a reply to Alec Nove. *Soviet Studies*, 23(2), 302–06.

Millar, J. R. (1974). Mass collectivization and the contribution of Soviet agriculture to the First Five-Year Plan: a review article. *Slavic Review*, 33, 750–60.

Millar, J. R. (1990). Post-Stalin agriculture: performance and prospects. In S. J. Linz (Ed.), *The Soviet economic experiment*. Urbana: University of Illinois Press.

Millar, J. R. (1970). A reformulation of A. V. Chayanov's theory of the peasant economy. *Economic Development and Cultural Change*, 18(2), 219–29.

Millar, J. R. (1990). *The Soviet economic experiment*. Urbana: University of Illinois Press.

Millar, J. R. (1987). *Soviet interview project*, 1979–1983. Ann Arbor, MI: Inter-university Consortium for Political and Social Research.

Millar, J. R. (1970). Soviet rapid development and the agricultural surplus hypothesis. *Soviet Studies*, 22(1), 77–93.

Millar, J. R. (1971). *The Soviet rural community; a symposium*. Urbana: University of Illinois Press.

Millar, J. R., & Guntzel, C. A. (1970). The economics and politics of mass collectivization reconsidered: a review article. *Explorations in Economic History*, 8(1), 103–16.

Millar, J. R., & Linz, S. J. (1990). *The Soviet economic experiment*. Urbana: University of Illinois Press.

Miller, M. S. (1926). *The economic development of Russia*, 1905–1914: *with special reference to trade, industry, and finance*. London: P. S. King & Son.

Millward, R. (1982). An economic analysis of the organization of serfdom in Eastern Europe. *Journal of Economic History*, 42(3), 513–48.

Milov, L. V. (1999). *Agrarnye tekhnologii v Rossii IX–XX vv; materialy XXV sessiia Simpoziuma po agrarnoi istorii Vostochnoi Evropy*. Arzamas: Arzamasskii gos. pedagogicheskii in-t.

Milov, L. V. (1965). *Issledovanie ob "ekonomicheskikh primechaniakh" k general'nomu mezhevaniiu: k istorii russkogo krest'ianstva i sel'skogo khoziaistva vtoroi poloviny XVIII v*. Moscow: Izd-vo Moskovskogo universiteta.

Milov, L. V. (1998). *Velikorusskii pakhar' i osobennosti rossiiskogo istoricheskogo protsesa*. Moscow: ROSSPEN.

Milov, L. V. (2000). *Zazhitochnoe krest'ianstvo Rossii v istoricheskoi retrospektive: zemlevladenie, zemlepol'zovanie, proizvodstvo, mentalitet, XXVII sessiia simpoziuma po agrarnoi istorii Vostochnoi Evropy: tezisy dokladov i soobshchenii Vologda, 12–16 sentiabria 2000 g*. Moscow: Institut rossiiskoi istorii RAN.

Milov, L. V. (2002). *Zemlevladenie i zemlepol'zovanie v Rossii: sotsial'no-pravovye aspekty; XXVIII sessiia Simpoziuma po agrarnoi istorii Vostochnoi Evropy; tezisy dokladov i soobshchenii. Kaluga, 24–28 sentiabria 2002 g.* Moscow: Institut rossiiskoi istorii RAN.

Ministry of Agriculture and State Domains (1902). *Svod statisticheskikh svedenii po sel'skomu khoziastvu Rossii k kontsu XIX veka.* St. Petersburg: Tipografiia V. F. Kirshbaum, Ministry of Finance.

Ministry of Internal Affairs (1872). *Statisticheskii Vremennik Rossiiskoi Imperii.* St. Petersburg: Tsentral'nyi Statisticheskii Komitet.

Mironov, B. N. (2010). Blagosostoianie naseleniia i revoliutsiia v imperskoi Rossii XVIII-nachalo XX veka. Moscow: Novyi khronograf.

Mironov, B. N. (1992). Consequences of the price revolution in eighteenth-century Russia. *Economic History Review*, **45**(3), 457–78.

Mironov, B. N. (1995). Diet, health, and stature of the Russian population from the mid-nineteenth to the beginning of the twentieth century. In J. Komlos (Ed.), *The biological standard of living on three continents* (pp. 59–79). Boulder, CO; Oxford: Westview Press.

Mironov, B. N. (1991). The effect of education on economic growth – the case of Russia in the 19th and 20th centuries. *Revista de Historia Economica*, **9**(1), 165.

Mironov, B. N. (1991). *Istoriia v tsifrakh: matematika v istoricheskikh issledovaniiakh.* Leningrad: Nauka.

Mironov, B. N. (1985). *Khlebnye tseny v Rossii za dva stoletiia, XVIII–XIX vv.* Leningrad: Nauka.

Mironov, B. N. (1999). New approaches to old problems: the well-being of the population of Russia from 1821 to 1910 as measured by physical stature. *Slavic Review*, 58(1), 1–26.

Mironov, B. N. (1990). The Russian peasant commune after the reforms of the 1860s. In B. Eklof & S. Frank (Eds.), *The world of the Russian peasant: post emancipation culture and society.* Boston: Unwin Hyman.

Mironov, B. N. (1990). *Russkii gorod v 1740–1860-e gody: demograficheskoe, sotsial'noe i ekonomicheskoe razvitie.* Leningrad: Nauka.

Mironov, B. N. (1999, 2003). *Sotsial'naia istoriia Rossii perioda imperii–XVIII-nachalo XX v; genezis lichnosti, demokraticheskoi semi, grazhdanskogo obshchestva i pravovogo gosudarstva.* St. Petersburg: D. Bulanin, translated, Ed. Ben Eklof (1999). *A social history of Imperial Russia*, 1700–1917 (Boulder, CO: Westview Press).

Mironov, B. N. (1999). Tall requirements and 'small' reality. *Slavic Review*, 58(1), 80–90.

Mironov, B. N. (1981). *Vnutrennii rynok Rossii: vo vtoroi polovine XVIII-pervoi polovine XIX v.* Leningrad: Nauka.

Mironov, B. N. (2010). Wages and prices in imperial Russia, 1703–1913. *Russian Review*, **69**(1), 47–72.

Mironov, B. & A'hearn, B. (2008). Russian living standards under the tsars: anthropometric evidence from the Volga. *Journal of Economic History*, **68**, 900–929.

Mokyr, J. (1990). Punctuated equilibria and technological progress. *The American Economic Review*, 80(2), 350–54.

Monov, A. I., Averin, I. G., Pogozhev, V. P., & Florent'ev, L. (1978). *Sel'skoe khoziaistvo Nechernozemnoi zony RSFSR.* Moscow: Kolos.

Moon, D. (2001a). *The abolition of serfdom in Russia, 1762–1907*. Harlow: Longman.
Moon, D. (1996). Estimating the peasant population of late Imperial Russia from the 1897 census: a research note. *Europe-Asia Studies*, 48(1), 141–53.
Moon, D. (2001b). The Inventory Reform and Peasant Unrest in Right-Bank Ukraine in 1847–48. *Slavonic and East European review*, 79, 653–697.
Moon, D. (1997). Peasant migration and the settlement of Russia's frontiers, 1550–1897. *Historical Journal*, 40(4), 859–94.
Moon, D. (1992). Russian peasant volunteers at the beginning of the Crimean War. *Slavic Review*, 51(4), 691.
Moon, D. (1992). *Russian peasants and tsarist legislation on the eve of reform: interaction between peasants and officialdom, 1825–1855*. Basingstoke: Macmillan, in association with the Centre for Russian and East European Studies, University of Birmingham.
Moon, D. (1999). *The Russian peasantry 1600–1930: the world the peasants made*. London: Longman.
Moon, D., Serra, G., & West, J. P. (1993). Citizens' contacts with bureaucratic and legislative officials. *Political Research Quarterly*, 46(4), 931–41.
Moore, M. (1988). Economic growth and the rise of civil society: agriculture in Taiwan and South Korea. In G. White (Ed.), *Developmental states in East Asia* (pp. 113–52). New York: St. Martin's Press.
Moorsteen, R., & Powell, R. P. (1966). *The Soviet capital stock, 1928–1962*. Homewood, IL: Richard D. Irwin, Inc.
Morachevskii, V. V. (1910). *Sel'skokhoziastvennyi kredit v Rossii*. St. Petersburg.
Morris, M. W. (1994). *Stalin's famine and Roosevelt's recognition of Russia*. Lanham, MD: University Press of America.
Moskoff, W. (1990). *Perestroika in the countryside: agricultural reform in the Gorbachev era*. Armonk, NY; London: M. E. Sharpe.
Mosse, W. E. (1992). *Alexander II and the modernization of Russia*. London; New York: I. B. Tauris & Co., distributed by St. Martin's Press.
Mosse, W., & Thompstone, S. (1998). An economic history of Russia, 1856–1914. *Russian Review*, 57(2), 298–99.
Moutos, T. (1998). Trade in quality goods, trading regimes and unemployment in transition economies. *Economics of Transition*, 6(2), 397–408.
Mozolin, V. P. (1992). *Pravo sobstvennosti v Rossiiskoi Federatsii v period perekhoda k rynochnoi ekonomiki*. Moscow: Institute Gosudarstva i prava RAN.
Mukhin, V. F. (1888). *Obychnyi poriadok nasledovaniya u krest'ian*. St. Petersburg.
Murphy, K. M., Shleifer, A., & Vishny, R. W. (1992). The transition to a market economy – pitfalls of partial reform. *Quarterly Journal of Economics*, 107(3), 889–906.
Murphy, S. (2006). Concentrated market power and agricultural trade. *Ecofair Trade Dialogue Discussion Papers*. Wuppertal: Wuppertal Institute for Climate, Environment and Energy.
Murrell, P. (1992). *An antidote to shock therapy: an evolutionary approach to the East European transition*. Washington, DC: The Woodrow Wilson Centre.
Murrell, P. (1995). The transition according to Cambridge, Mass. *Journal of Economic Literature*, 33(March).

Nafziger, S. (2008). Democracy Under the Tsars? The Case of the Zemstvo. *Department of Economics, Williams College, working paper* 2008–24; http://EconPapers.repec.org/RePEc:wil:wileco:2008–24.

Nafziger, S. & Tracy Dennison (2007). Micro-Perspectives on 19th-century Russian Living Standards. Department of Economics Working Papers 2007–7, Department of Economics, Williams College.

Nagy, P. M., & Ofer, G. (2002). The meltdown of the Russian state. *European Journal of Political Economy*, 18(3), 611–13.

National Bureau of Economic Research (1960). *Trends in the American economy in the nineteenth century*. Princeton, NJ: Princeton University Press.

Naumov, V. P., & Kosakovskii, A. A. (1997). *Kronshtadt, 1921*. Moscow: Mezhdunarodnyi fond "Demokratiia."

Nee, V., & Seldon, M. (1989). Peasant entrepreneurship and the politics of regulation in China. In V. Canee & D. Stark (Eds.), *China and Eastern Europe: remaking the economic institutions of socialism* (pp. 169–207). Stanford, CA: Stanford University Press.

Nefedova, T. G., Polian, P. M., Trevish, A. I., & Semenov-Tian-Shanskaia, V. P. (2001). *Gorod i derevnëìa v Evropeiskoi Rossii: sto let peremen: pamiati Veniamina Petrovicha Semenova-Tian-Shanskogo*. Moscow: OGI.

Nelson, J. (1990). *Economic crisis and policy choice: the politics of adjustment in the third world*. Princeton, NJ: Princeton University Press.

Nelson, R. (1993). *National innovation systems: a comparative analysis*. New York: Oxford University Press.

Nelson, R. R., & Winter, S. G. (1982). *An evolutionary theory of economic change*. Cambridge, MA: The Belknap Press of Harvard University.

Neuhold, H., Havlik, P., & Suppan, A. (1995). *Political and economic transformation in East Central Europe*. Boulder, CO: Westview Press.

Nguyen, D. (1979). On agricultural productivity differences among countries. *American Journal of Agricultural Economics* (August), 566–70.

Neupokoev, V. I. (1987). Gosudarstvennie povinnosti krest'ian Evropeiskoi Rossii v kontse XVIII nachale XIX vv. Moscow: Academy of Sciences.

Nickolsky, S. (1998). The treadmill of socialist reforms and the failures of post-communist 'revolutions' in Russian agriculture: is there an alternative? In I. Szelényi (Ed.), *Privatizing the land: rural political economy in post-communist societies* (pp. 191–212). London: Routledge.

Nifontov, A. S. (1974). *Zernovoi priozvodstvo Rossii vo vtoroi polovine XIX veka*. Moscow: Nauka.

Nikonov, A. A. (1995). *Spiral' mnogovekovoi dramy: agrarnaia Nauka. i politika Rossii (XVIII–XX vv.)*. Moscow: Entsiklopediia rossiiskikh dereven'.

Nimitz, N. (1967). Farm employment in the Soviet Union, 1928–1963. In J. F. Karcz (Ed.), *Soviet and East European agriculture* (pp. 175–205). Berkeley and Los Angeles: University of California Press.

Nolan, P. (1988). *The political economy of collective farms: an analysis of China's post-Mao rural reforms*. Cambridge: Polity Press.

Nolan, P. (1995). *China's rise, Russia's fall: politics, economics and planning in the transition from Stalinism*. New York: St. Martin's Press.

Norgaard, O. (2000). *Economic institutions and democratic reform: a comparative analysis of post-communist countries*. Cheltenham: Elgar.

Norsworthy, L. A., & Paluba, O. (2000). Impact of transition: approaches and findings. In L. A. Norsworthy (Ed.), *Russian views of the transition in the rural sector: structures, policy outcomes, and adaptive responses* (pp. 1–15). Washington, DC: The World Bank.

North, D. C., & Thomas, R. P. (1970). An economic theory of the growth of the Western world. *Economic History Review, Second Series*, 23(1), 1–17.

North, D. C., & Weingast, B. R. (1989). Constitutions and commitment: the evolution of institutions governing public choice in seventeenth-century England. *Journal of Economic History*, **49**(4), 803–32.

Nove, A. (1992). *An economic history of the USSR*, 1917–1991. London: Penguin Books.

Nove, A. (1996). Economics of transition: some gaps and illusions. In M. Knell (Ed.), *Economics of transition: structural adjustments and growth prospects in Eastern Europe* (pp. 49–69). Cheltenham: Elgar.

Nove, A. (1992). Some thoughts on the end of NEP. In L. Edmondson & P. Waldron (Eds.), *Economy and society in Russia and the Soviet Union*, 1860–1930: *essays for Olga Crisp* (pp. 234–43). London: Macmillan Press, in association with the School of Slavonic and East European Studies, University of London.

Nove, A. (1988). *Stalinism and After: The Road to Gorbachev*. London: Routledge.

Nureev, R. M., & Runov, A. B. (2002). Nazad k chastnoi sobstvennosti ili vpered k chastnoi sobstvennosti? *Obshchestvennye nauki i sovremennost'*, (5), 7–21.

Nuti, M. (1991). Stabilization and reform sequencing in the reform of Central and Eastern Europe. In S. Commander (Ed.), *Managing inflation in socialist economies in transition* (pp. 155–74). Washington, DC: EDI, World Bank.

Nuti, D. M., & Portes, R. (1993). Central Europe: the way forward. In R. Portes (Ed.), *Economic transformation in Central Europe: a progress report*. London; Luxembourg: Centre for Economic Policy Research.

Nutter, G. (1959). The structure and growth of Soviet industry: a comparison with the United States. *Joint Economic Committee of the Congress of the United States*, pp. 95–117. Washington, DC: Joint Economic Committee.

Nutter, G. (1962). *Growth of industrial production in the Soviet Union*. Princeton, NJ: Princeton University Press.

Nye, J. S., Donahue, J. D., & Sanchez, O. (2002). Governance in a globalizing world. *Latin American Politics and Society*, **44**(2), 165–69.

Oates, W. (1999). An essay on fiscal federalism. *Journal of Economic Literature*, 37(September), 1120–48.

O'Brien, D. J. (1996). *Social capital and adaptation to social change in Russian villages*. Glasgow: Centre for the Study of Public Policy University of Strathclyde.

O'Brien, D. J., Patsiorkovskii, V. V., & Dershem, L. D. (2000). *Household capital and the agrarian problem in Russia*. Aldershot: Ashgate

O'Brien, D. J., & Wegren, S. K. (2002). *Rural reform in post-Soviet Russia*. Washington, DC; London: Woodrow Wilson Center Press; The Johns Hopkins University Press.

O'Brien, P. & De La Escosura, L. (2002). Agricultural productivity and European industrialization. *Economic History Review*, 45(summer), 514–36.
Obruchev, N. N. (1871). *Voenno-statisticheskii sbornik*. St. Petersburg: Voennaia Tipografiia.
Obukhov, V. M. (1927). Dvizhenie urozhaev zernovykh kul'tur v Evropeiskoi Rossii v period 1883–1915 g.g. In V. G. Groman (Ed.), *Vlianie neurozhaev na narodnoe khoziastvo Rossii* (pp. 1–159). Moscow: Rossiiskaia assotsiatsiia nauchno-issledovatel'skikh institutov obshchestvennykh nauk.
Obukhov, V. M., & Strumilin, S. G. (1949). *Urozhainost' i meteorologicheskie faktory statisticheskie issledovaniia*. Moscow: Gosplanizdat.
O'Connor, G. C. (2006). Open, radical innovation: toward an integrated model in large established firms. In H. W. Chesbrough, W. Vanhaverbeke, & J. West (Eds.), *Open innovation: researching a new paradigm* (pp. 62–81). Oxford: Oxford University Press.
OECD (1999). *Agricultural finance and credit infrastructure in transition economies*. Paris: Organisation for Economic Co-operation and Development.
OECD (2000). *Agricultural policies in emerging and transition economies*. Paris: Organisation for Economic Co-operation and Development.
OECD (2007). *Agricultural policies in non-OECD countries: monitoring and evaluation 2007*. Paris: Organisation for Economic Co-operation and Development.
OECD (1997, 2000, 2002). *Agricultural policies in transition economies: trends in policies and support*. Paris: Organisation for Economic Co-operation and Development.
OECD. (1993, 1995). *Agricultural policies, markets and trade in the Central and Eastern European countries, selected new independent states, Mongolia and China, monitoring and outlook*. Paris: Organisation for Economic Co-operation and Development.
OECD (1994). *Agriculture and the environment in the transition to a market economy*. Paris; Washington, DC: Organisation for Economic Co-operation and Development.
OECD (1999). *Agriculture at a glance in emerging and transition economies*. Paris: Organisation for Economic Co-operation and Development.
OECD (1996). *The changing social benefits in Russian enterprises*. Paris: Organisation for Economic Co-operation and Development.
OECD (1995, 2002). *OECD economic surveys: the Russian Federation*. Paris: Organisation for Economic Co-operation and Development.
OECD (1994, 1998). *Review of agricultural policies*. Paris; Washington, DC: Organisation for Economic Co-operation and Development.
OECD (1995). *Technological change and structural adjustment in OECD agriculture*. Paris: Organisation for Economic Co-operation and Development.
OECD (2004). *Russian Federation: progress and reform challenges*. Paris: Organisation for Economic Co-operation and Development.
Ofer, G. (1987). Soviet economic growth: 1928–1985. *Journal of Economic Literature*, 25, 1767–1833.
Oganovskii, N. P. (1917). *Individualizatsiya zemlevladeniya v Rossii i eya posledstviya*. Moscow: Tip. T-va "Zadruga."

Oganovskii, N. P., & Kondrat'ev, N. D. (1923). *Sel'skoe khoziaistvo Rossii v XX veke: sbornik statistiko-ekonomicheskikh svedenii za 1901–1922 g.g.* Moscow: Novaia Derevnia.

Ognivtsev, S. B., Arsen'kina, L. F., Gal'minas, F. A., Briunina, R. F., Rybakova, R. A., & Shapiro, V. I. (2002). Dinamika razvitiia zhivotnovodcheskogo podkompleksa APK v RF za 1990–2001 gg. *Vlast', biznes i krest'ianstvo: mekhanizmy effektivnogo vzaimodeistviia: Nikonovskie chteniia–2002* (pp. 97–99). Moscow: Rossiiskaia Akademiia Selskokhoziastvennykh Nauk, Vserossiiskii Institut agrarnykh problem i informatiki, Fond Podderzhki Agrarnoi Reformy i Sel'skoto Razvitiia.

O'Grada, C. (1994). British agriculture, 1860–1914. *The economic history of Britain since 1700*. Cambridge: Cambridge University Press.

Okun', S. B. (1957). *Ocherki istorii SSSR; vtoraia chetvert' XIX veka*. Leningrad.

Olmstead, A. L., & Rhode, P. W. (2007). *Conceptual issues for the comparative study of agricultural development*. Working paper, SSRN, http://ssrn.com/abstract=945353.

Olmstead, A. L., & Rhode, P. W. (1993). Induced innovation in American agriculture: a reconsideration. *Journal of Political Economy*, 101(1), 100–18.

Olmstead, A. L., & Rhode, P. W. (2001). Reshaping the landscape: the impact and diffusion of the tractor in American agriculture, 1910–1960. *Journal of Economic History*, 61(3), 663–98.

Olmstead, A. L., & Rhode, P. W. (2002). The red queen and the hard reds: productivity growth in American wheat, 1800–1940. Cambridge, MA: NBER.

Olson, M. (1993). Dictatorship, democracy, and development. *American Political Science Review*, 87(3), 567–76.

Olson, M. (1963). *The economics of the wartime shortage, a history of British food supplies in the Napoleonic War and in World Wars I and II*. Durham, NC: Duke University Press.

Olson, M. (1992). The hidden path to a successful economy. In C. Clague & G. C. Rausser (Eds.), *The emergence of market economies in Eastern Europe* (pp. 55–76). Oxford: Blackwell.

Olson, M. (1965, 2000). *The logic of collective action: public goods and the theory of groups*. Cambridge, MA: Harvard University Press.

Olson, M. (2000). *Power and prosperity: outgrowing communist and capitalist dictatorships*. New York: Basic Books.

Olson, M. (1982). *The rise and decline of nations: economic growth, stagflation, and social rigidities*. New Haven, CT; London: Yale University Press.

Oman, C. P., & Wignaraja, G. (1991). *The postwar evolution of development thinking*. London: Macmillan in association with the OECD Development Centre.

Omel'chenko, O. A. (1993). "Zakonnaia monarkhiia." *Ekateriny Vtoroi: prosveshchennyi absoliutizm v Rossii*. Moscow: O. A. Omel'chenko.

Oppenheimer, J., Swistak, P., Wallis, J. J., Ostrom, E., Wallerstein, M., Moene, K. O., Lohmann, S., Green, D. P., Smith, J. K., Alt, J. E., Lassen, D. D., & Olson, M. (2003). On the shoulders of giants: essays in honour of Mancur Olson. *Journal of Theoretical Politics*, 15(3), 235–365.

O'Relley, Z. E. (1986). Changing status of collectivized and private agriculture under central planning: to increase output, state socialist Hungary combines private with state enterprises. *American Journal of Economics and Sociology*, **45**, 9–16.

O'Rourke, K. (1997). The European Grain Invasion, 1870–1913. *Journal of Economic History*, 57(4), 775–801.

Orlovsky, D. (1976). Recent studies on the Russian bureaucracy. *Russian Review*, 35(448–67).

Orlovsky, D. (1981). *The limits of reform: the ministry of internal affairs in Imperial Russia*, 1802–1881. Cambridge, MA: Harvard University Press.

Osborne, S. (2002). Comments on paper by Eu. Serova, N. Karlova and V. Petrichenko. *Factor markets in Russia's agri-food sector: frameworks of further analysis* (pp. 175–77). Moscow: IRIS, USAID.

Osborne, S., & Trueblood, M. (2002). An examination of economic efficiency of Russian crop production in the reform period. In ERS (Ed.), *Economic research service, USDA*. Washington, DC: Department of State.

Ostrom, E. (1990). *Governing the commons: the evolution of institutions for collective action*. Political Economy of Institutions and Decisions series. Cambridge; New York; Melbourne: Cambridge University Press.

Ostrom, E., Gardner, R., & Walker, J. (1994). *Rules, games, and common-pool resources*. Ann Arbor: University of Michigan Press.

Ostrom, E., & Schlager, E. (1996). The formation of property rights. In S. Hanna, C. Folke, & K. G. Maler (Eds.), *Ecological, economic, cultural, and political principles of institutions for the environment* (pp. 127–56). Washington, DC: Island Press

Otsuka, K., Cordova, V., & David, C.-C. (1992). Green revolution, land reform, and household income distribution in the Philippines. *Economic Development and Cultural Change*, 40(4), 719–41.

Owen, T. C. (1981). *Capitalism and politics in Russia: a social history of the Moscow merchants*, 1855–1905. Cambridge; New York: Cambridge University Press.

Owen, T. C. (1991). *The corporation under Russian law*, 1800–1917: *a study in tsarist economic policy*. Cambridge; New York: Cambridge University Press.

Owen, T. (1983). Entrepreneurship and the structure of enterprise in Russia, 1800–1880. In G. Guroff & F. V. Carstenson (Eds.), *Entrepreneurship in Imperial Russia and the Soviet Union* (pp. 59–83). Princeton, NJ: Princeton University Press.

Owen, T. C. (1991). The population ecology of corporations in the Russian empire, 1700–1914. *Slavic Review*, 50(4), 807.

Owen, T. C. (1990). *Ruscorp: a database of corporations in the Russian Empire*, 1700–1914. Ann Arbor, MI: Inter-university Consortium for Political and Social Research.

Owen, T. C. (1995). *Russian corporate capitalism from Peter the Great to perestroika*. New York: Oxford University Press.

Owen, T. C., & Rieber, A. J. (2007). Dilemmas of Russian capitalism: Fedor Chizhov and corporate enterprise in the railroad age. *Journal of Modern History*, **79**(1), 223–24.

Painter, M. (2005). The politics of state sector reforms in Vietnam: contested agendas and uncertain trajectories. *Journal of Development Studies*, **41**(2), 261–83.

Pallot, J. (1998). *Land reform in Russia, 1906–1917: peasant responses to Stolypin's project of rural transformation*. Oxford; New York: Clarendon Press; Oxford University Press.

Pallot, J. (2007). Measuring social and economic change in rural Russia: surveys from 1991 to 2003. *Russian Review*, **66**(3), 544–45.

Pallot, J. (1982). *Social change and peasant land-holding in pre-revolutionary Russia*. Oxford: School of Geography, University of Oxford.

Pallot, J. (1998). *Transforming peasants: society, state and the peasantry, 1861–1930: selected papers from the Fifth World Congress of Central and East European Studies*. Basingstoke; New York: Macmillan; St. Martin's Press.

Pallot, J., & Nefedova, T. G. (2007). *Russia's unknown agriculture: household production in post-socialist Russia*. Oxford: Oxford University Press.

Pallot, J., & Shaw, D. J. B. (1990). *Landscape and settlement in Romanov Russia, 1613–1917*. Oxford; New York: Clarendon Press; Oxford University Press.

Pannell, C. W., & Schmidt, P. (2006). Structural change and regional disparities in Xinjiang, China. *Eurasian Geography and Economics*, **47**(3) 329–352.

Pardo, I. (2004). *Between morality and the law: corruption, anthropology and comparative society*. Aldershot, Hampshire; Burlington, VT: Ashgate.

Parker, W. (1975). *Introduction*. In W. Parker & E. J. Jones (Eds.), *European peasants and their markets* (pp. 3–22). Princeton, NJ: Princeton University Press.

Paskhaver, I. S. (1968). *Sel'skoe khoziaistvo SSSR v pokazatel'iakh statistiki*. Moscow: Statistika.

Patenaude, B. M. (1995). Peasants into Russians: the utopian essence of war communism. *Russian Review*, **54**(4), 552–70.

Patenaude, B. M. (2002). *The big show in Bololand: the American relief expedition to Soviet Russia in the famine of 1921*. Stanford, CA: Stanford University Press.

Patenaude, B. M., & Cockfield, J. H. (2004). The big show in Bololand: the American relief expedition to Soviet Russia in the famine of 1921. *Slavic Review*, **63**(1), 193–94.

Patterson, O. (1969). *The sociology of slavery; an analysis of the origins, development, and structure of Negro slave society in Jamaica*. Rutherford, NJ: Fairleigh Dickinson University Press.

Patterson, O. (1982). *Slavery and social death: a comparative study*. Cambridge, MA: Harvard University Press.

Pavlovskii, G. A. (1968). *Agricultural Russia on the eve of the revolution*. New York: H. Fertig.

Penson Jr., J. B. (1991). Macroeconomic policy research: discussion. *American Journal of Agricultural Economics*, 73(5), 1364–66.

Perotta, L. (1998). *The higher up don't want to and the lower down cannot: analysis of focus groups village community*. Kiev: CPER.

Petrikov, A. (2002). Aktual'nye problemy ekonomicheskoi i sotsial'noi politiki v agrarnoi sfere. *Agrarnaia Reforma: Ekonomika i Pravo*, **6**(24, Nov–Dec), 1–4.

Pick, D. H., Arnade, C., & Vasavada, U. (1995). Technology gaps and trade in agriculture. *Weltwirtschaftliches Archiv*, 131(3), 509–25.

Pintner, W. M. (1959). Inflation in Russia during the Crimean War period. *American Slavic and East European Review*, **18**(1), 81–7.

Pintner, W. (1967). *Russian economic policy under Nicholas I*. Ithaca, NY: Cornell University Press.

Pintner, W. M. (1978). *Russia as a great power, 1709–1856: reflections on the problem of relative backwardness, with special reference to the Russian Army and Russian society*. Washington, DC: Kennan Institute for Advanced Russian Studies.

Pintner, W. M. (1984). The burden of defence in Imperial Russia, 1725–1914. *The Russian Review*, 43, 231–59.

Pintner, W. M., Rowney, D. K., & Bennett, H. A. (1980). *Russian officialdom: the bureaucratization of Russian society from the seventeenth to the twentieth century*. London: Macmillan.

Pipes, R. (1992). *Russia under the old regime*. New York: Collier Books.

Pipes, R. (1997). *The formation of the Soviet Union: communism and nationalism, 1917–1923: with a new preface*. Cambridge, MA: Harvard University Press.

Pipes, R. (1999). *Property and freedom*. New York: Alfred A. Knopf.

Pirttila, J. (2001). Fiscal policy and structural reforms in transition economies: an empirical analysis. *Economics of Transition*, 9(1), 29–52.

Pirumova, N. M. (1977). *Zemskoe liberal'noe dvizhenie: sotsial'nie korni i evoliutsiia do nachala XX veka*. Moscow: Nauka.

Pisano, J. A. (2002). Reorganisation and its discontents: a case study in Voronexzh oblast'. In D. J. O'Brien & S. K. Wegren (Eds.), *Rural reform in post-Soviet Russia* (pp. 298–324). Washington, DC: Woodrow Wilson Center Press.

Pischke, J. D. V., Adams, D. W., & Donald, G. (1983). Changing perceptions of rural financial markets. In J. D. V. Pischke, D. W. Adams, & G. Donald (Eds.), *Rural financial markets in developing countries* (pp. 1–14). Baltimore, MD; London: The Johns Hopkins University Press.

Pitzer, J. S., & Baukol, A. P. (1991). Recent GNP and productivity trends. *Soviet Economy*, 7(1), 46–82.

Ploss, S. I. (1965). *Conflict and decision-making in Soviet Russia; a case study of agricultural policy, 1953–1963*. Princeton, NJ: Princeton University Press.

Podkolzin, B. I. (1993). Kooperativnyk kredit v Rossii: konteptual'nye istoki (rubezh 60–70kh godov XIX veka). In N. K. Figurovskaia (Ed.), *Kooperatsiia. Stranitsy istorii* (pp. 131–55). Moscow: International Fund for the History of Science.

Pogrebinskii, A. P. (1954). *Ocherki istorii finansov dorevoliutsionnoi Rossii (XIX-XX vv.)*. Moscow: Gosfinizdat.

Poirson, H. (2001). The impact of intersectoral labour reallocation on economic growth. *Journal of African Economies*, 10(1), 37–63.

Polishchuk, L. (1997). Missed markets: implications for economic behavior and institutional change. In J. Nelson, C. Tilly, & L. Walker (Eds.), *Transforming post-communist political economies* (pp. 80–101). Washington, DC: National Academy Press.

Polopolus, L. C., & Emerson, R. D. (1991). Entrepreneurship, sanctions, and labor contracting. *Southern Journal of Agricultural Economics*, 23(1), 57–68.

Polunov, A., Owen, T. C., & Zakharova, L. (2005). *Russia in the nineteenth century: autocracy, reform, and social change, 1814–1914*. Armonk, NY: M. E. Sharpe.

Pomfret, R. W. T. (1996). *Asian economies in transition: reforming centrally planned economies*. Cheltenham; Brookfield, VT: E. Elgar.

Popkin, S. L. (1979). *The rational peasant: the political economy of rural society in Vietnam*. Berkeley; London: University of California Press.

Popov, V. (2001). Reform strategies and economic performance of Russia's regions. *World Development*, **29**(5), 865–86.

Popovsky, M. (1984). *The Vavilov affair*. Hamden, CT: Archon Books.

Portes, R. (1993). *Economic transformation in Central Europe: a progress report*. London; Luxembourg: Centre for Economic Policy Research; Office for Official Publications of the European Communities.

Portes, R. (1994). Transformation traps. *Economic Journal*, **104**(426), 1178–89.

Poshkus, B. (1997). Inner reserves of the Russian AIC. *AIC: Economics, Management*, 3, 11–19.

Postel-Vinay, G. (1994). The dis-integration of traditional labour markets in France: from agriculture and industry to agriculture or industry. In G. Grantham & M. MacKinnon (Eds.), *Labour market evolution: the economic history of market integration, wage flexibility and the employment relation*. London; New York: Routledge.

Pounds, N. J. G., & Spulber, N. (1957). *Resources and planning in Eastern Europe*. Bloomington: Indiana University Press.

Poznanski, K. (1995). *The evolutionary transition to capitalism*. Boulder, CO: Westview Press.

Praust, R. E. (1999). Semeinye khoiastva i tenevaia ekonomika. agrarnogo sektora Rossii. *Reorganizatsii sel'skokhoziastvennykh predpriiiatii: ikh effektivnost' i uctoichivoe razvitie* (pp. 54–73). Moscow: Institut ekonomiki perekhodnogo perioda.

Preobrazhensky, E. A. (1922). *From New Economic Policy to socialism: a glance into the future of Russia and Europe*. London: Plough Press.

Prokopovich, S. N. (1918). *Opyt ischisleniia narodnago dokhoda 50 gub. Evropeiskoi Rossii v*. Moscow: Soviet Vserossiiskikh kooperativnykh s'iezdov.

Prokopovich, S. N. (1923). *Ocherki khozìaistva sovetskoi Rossii*. Berlin: Obelisk.

Prokopovich, S. N. (1952). *Narodnoe khoziaistvo SSSR*. New York: Izd-vo im. Chekhova.

Proskuriakova, N. A. (2002). *Zemel'nye banki Rossiiskoi imperii*. Moscow: ROSSPEN.

Prosterman, R., G. Mitchell and B. Rorem (1997). Prospects for Family Farming in Russia. *Europe Asia Studies*, **49**(8) 1383–1407.

Pryor, F. L. (1992). *The red and the green. The rise and fall of collectivized agriculture*. Princeton, NJ: Princeton University Press.

Przeworski, A. (1995). *Sustainable democracy*. Cambridge; New York: Cambridge University Press.

Rabinowitch, A. (1968). *Prelude to revolution; the Petrograd Bolsheviks and the July 1917 uprising*. Bloomington: Indiana University Press.

Rabinowitch, A. (1976). *The Bolsheviks come to power: the Revolution of 1917 in Petrograd*. New York: Norton.

Radosevic, S. (1996). Prospects of building science and technology capabilities in Central and Eastern Europe. In M. Knell (Ed.), *Economics of transition: structural adjustments and growth prospects in Eastern Europe* (pp. 185–209). Cheltenham: Edward Elgar.

Raeff, M. (1971). *Imperial Russia 1682–1825: the coming of age of modern Russia.* New York: Knopf.
Raeff, M. (1983). *The well-ordered police state: social and institutional change through law in the Germanies and Russia, 1600–1800.* New Haven, CT: Yale University Press.
Ramamurti, R. (1999). Why haven't developing countries privatized deeper and faster? *World Development*, 27(1), 137–55.
Ranis, G., & Fei, J. (1966). Agrarianism, dualism and economic development. In I. Adelman & E. Thorbecke (Eds.), *Theory and design of economic development.* Baltimore, MD: The Johns Hopkins University Press.
Rapaczynski, A. (1996). The roles of the state and the market in establishing property rights. *Journal of Economic Perspectives*, 10(2), 87–103.
Rashin, A. G. (1940). *Formirovanie promyshlennogo proletariata v Rossii.* Moscow: Gosudarstvennoe sotsial'no-ekonomicheskoe izd-vo.
Rashin, A. G. (1956). *Naselenie Rossii za 100 let* (1811–1913), *Statisticheskii ocherki.* Moscow: Gosudarstvennoe statisticheskoe izd-vo.
Rasizade, A. (2008). Putin's mission in the Russian Thermidor. *Communist and Post-Communist Studies*, 41(1), 1–25.
Rastianikov, V. G., & Deriugina, I. V. (2005). *Ekonomicheskii rost v agrarnom sektore Rossii: Problemy XX veka.* Moscow: Statistika Rossii.
Rauch, J. E., & Evans, P. B. (2000). Bureaucratic structures and bureaucratic performance in less developed countries. *Journal of Public Economics*, 75, 49–71.
Rauner, I. L. (1981). *Klimat i urozhainost' zernovykh kul'tur.* Moscow: Nauka.
Raup, P. M. (1972). Some consequences of data deficiencies in Soviet agriculture. In V. Treml & J. P. Hardt (Eds.), *Soviet economic statistics* (pp. 263–84). Durham, NC: Duke University Press.
Ravallion, M. (1992). *Poverty comparisons: A guide to concepts and methods.* Washington, DC: The World Bank.
Ravallion, M., & Chen, S. (1996). *What can new survey data tell us about recent changes in distribution and poverty?* Washington, DC: The World Bank.
Reardon, T. et al. (1997). Promoting sustainable intensification and productivity growth in Sahel agriculture after macroeconomic policy reform. *Food Policy*, 22(4), 317–27.
RECEP (2000). *Russian economic trends.* Moscow.
Rein, M., Friedman, B. L., & Wörgötter, A. (1997). *Enterprise and social benefits after communism.* Cambridge: Cambridge University Press.
Rein, M., Friedman, B. L., & Wörgötter, A. (1997). *Introduction.* In M. Rein, B. L. Friedman, & A. Wörgötter (Eds.), *Enterprise and social benefits after communism* (pp. 1–22). Cambridge: Cambridge University Press.
Remington, T. F. (1999). *Politics in Russia.* New York: Longman.
Remnek, R. B. (1977). *Social scientists and policy making in the USSR.* New York: Praeger.
Rieber, A. J. (1971). Alexander II: a revisionist view. *Journal of Modern History*, 43(1), 42–58.
Rieber, A. J. (1988). Landed property, state authority, and civil war. *Slavic Review*, 47(1), 29–38.

Rieber, A. J. (1982). *Merchants and entrepreneurs in Imperial Russia*. Chapel Hill, NC: University of North Carolina Press.
Rieber, A. J. (1966). *The politics of autocracy; letters of Alexander II to Prince A. I. Bariatinskii*, 1857–1864. Paris: Mouton.
Rimashevskaya, N., & Voitenkova, G. (2000). Impoverishment and social exclusion in Russia. In S. Hutton & G. Redmond (Eds.), *Poverty in transition economies* (pp. 35–51). London; New York: Routledge.
Risnes, B., & Skyner, L. (2001). *Nµringsvirksomhet i Russland: rettslige rammebetingelser*. Oslo: Norsk utenrikspolitisk institute.
Robbins, R. G. Jr (1975). *Famine in Russia, 1891–1892; the imperial government responds to a crisis*. New York: Columbia University Press.
Robinson, G. T. (1932). *Rural Russia under the old régime; a history of the landlord-peasant world and a prologue to the peasant revolution of 1917*. London; New York: Longmans, Green and Company.
Rodionova, G. (2002). Reorganizatsiia sel'skokhoziastvennykh predpriatii i sel'skoe soobshchestvo. *Agrarnaia Reforma: Ekonomika i Pravo*, **2**(20, March–April), 12–14.
Rodrik, D. (1996). Understanding economic policy reform. *Journal of Economic Literature*, **34**, 9–41.
Rogalina, N. L. (2002). Agrarnye reformy v Rossii 10–20-kh godov (istoriko-sravnitel'nyi analiz). In G. N. Sevost'ianov (Ed.), *Rossiia v XX veke: Reformy i revoliutsii* (pp. 543–63). Moscow: Nauka.
Rogers, E. M. (1962). *Diffusion of innovations*. New York: Free Press of Glencoe.
Roland, G. (2000). *Transition and economics: politics, markets, and firms*. Cambridge, MA: MIT Press.
Romanelli, E., & Tushman, M. (1994). Organizational transformations as punctuated equilibrium: an empirical test. *Academy of Management Journal*, **37**, 1141–66.
Roosa, R. A., & Owen, T. C. (1997). *Russian industrialists in an era of revolution: the Association of Industry and Trade*, 1906–1917. Armonk, NY: M. E. Sharpe.
Rose, R., Mishler, W., & Munro, N. (2008). Time matters: adapting to transformation. *Journal of Communist Studies and Transition Politics*, **24**(1), 90–114.
Rosenkopf, L., & Tushman, M. L. (1998). The coevolution of community networks and technology: lessons from the flight simulation industry. *Industrial and Corporate Change*, 7: 311–346
Rosenstein-Rodan, P. N. (1943). Problems of industrialisation in eastern and south-Eastern Europe. *Economic Journal*, **53**, 202–11.
Rosenzweig, M. (1988). Risk, implicit contracts and the family in rural areas of low-income countries. *Economic Journal*, **98**(393), 1148–70.
Roskomstat (1993). *Proizvodstvo zerna v Rossiiskoi Federatsii*. Moscow: Goskomstat Rossi.skoi Federatsii.
Rosovsky, H. (1954). The serf entrepreneur in Russia. *Explorations in Entrepreneurial History* (May), 207–33.
Rosovsky, H. (1959). Japanese capital formation: the role of the public sector. *Journal of Economic History*, **19**(September), 350–73.
Ross, C. (2004). *Russian politics under Putin*. Manchester; New York: Manchester University Press, distributed exclusively in the United States by Palgrave.

Ross, C. (2008). The tortuous path of local government reform in the Russian Federation. In *Local government in Central and Eastern Europe: the rebirth of local democracy*. London: Routledge.

Rossia. Ministerstvo zemledeliia. Otdel sel'skoi ekonomiki i selkhokhoziastvennoi statistiki (1881–1919). *God v sel'skokhoziastvennom otnoshenii po otvetam, poluchennym ot khoziaev*. St. Petersburg.

Roth, A. (1996). Comment [on a paper by Amos Tversky]. In K. Arrow, E. Colombatto, M. Perlman, & C. Schmidt (Eds.), *The rational foundations of economic behavior: proceedings of the IEA Conference held in Turin, Italy* (pp. 198–202). London: Macmillan Press, Ltd.

Roth, A. (1996). Adaptive behaviour and strategic rationality: evidence from the laboratory and the field. In K. Arrow, E. Colombatto, M. Perlman, & C. Schmidt (Eds.), *The rational foundations of economic behavior: proceedings of the IEA Conference held in Turin, Italy* (pp. 255–73). London: Macmillan Press, Ltd.

Rozelle, S. (1994). Decision-making in China's rural economy: the linkages between village leaders and farm households. *China Quarterly*, 0(137), 99–124.

Rozelle, S. (1996). Gradual reform and institutional development: the keys to success of China's agricultural reforms. In J. McMillan & B. Naughton (Eds.), *Reforming Asian socialism: the growth of market institutions* (pp. 197–220). Ann Arbor: University of Michigan Press.

Rozelle, S., & Li, G. (1998). Village leaders and land-rights formation in China. *American Economic Review*, **88**(2), 433–38.

Rozelle, S., & Swinnen, J. F. (2004). Success and failure of reform: insights from the transition of agriculture. *Journal of Economic Literature*, **42**(2), 404–56.

Rozelle, S. et al. (1997). Liberalization and rural market integration in China. *American Journal of Agricultural Economics*, **79**(2), 635–42.

Rosenberg, W. G. (1993). Review: Understanding Peasant Russia. A Review Article. *Comparative Studies in Society and History*, 35(4), 840–849.

RSFSR (1957). *Narodnoe Khoziastvo RSFSR, Statisticheskii sbornik*. Moscow: Gosudarstvennoe statisticheskoe izd-vo.

RSFSR (1983). *RSFSR v tsifrakh v 1982 godu: kratkii statisticheskii sbornik*. Moscow: Finansy i statistika.

RSFSR (1957). *RSFSR za sorok let*. Moscow: Gosudarstvennoe statisticheskoe izd-vo.

Rubenking, E. M. (1976). *The Soviet tractor industry: progress and problems*. Washington, DC: Joint Economic Committee.

Rubinshtein, N. L. (1957). *Selskoe khoziaistvo Rossii vo vtoroi polovine XVIII v; istoriko-ekonomicheskii ocherk*. Moscow: Gos. izd-vo polit. lit-ry.

Russia (1922). *Voenno-konskaia perepis' 1922*. Moscow.

Russia (1956). *Narodnoe khoziaistvo SSSR; statisticheski sbornik*. Moscow: Tsentral'noe statisticheskoe upravlenie.

Russia. Ministerstvo sel'skogo khoziaistva (1965–1987). *Sel'skoe khoziaistvo Rossii*. Moscow: Ministerstvo sel'skogo khoziastva.

Russian S. F. S. R. (1957). *National economy of the U.S. S.R; statistical returns*. Moscow: Foreign Language Pub. House.

Russian S. F. S. R. (1920). *Pogubernskie itogi 10% vyborochnoi sel'sko-khoziaistvennoi perepisi krest'ianskikh khoziaistv 1919 goda*. Moscow: Tsentral'noe statisticheskoe upravlenie.

Russian S. F. S. R. (1966). *RSFSR v tsifrakh*. Moscow: "Statistika."

Rutherford, B. (2004). "Settlers" and Zimbabwe: politics, memory, and the anthropology of commercial farms during a time of crisis. *Identities*, 11(4), 543–62.

Rutherford, T. F., Tarr, D. G. (2006). *Regional impacts of Russia's accession to the World Trade Organization*. Washington, DC: World Bank. Development Research Group Trade Team.

Rutherford, T. F., Tarr, D. G., & Shepotylo, O. (2005). *The impact on Russia of WTO accession and the DOHA agenda: the importance of liberalization of barriers against foreign direct investment in services for growth and poverty reduction*. Washington, DC: World Bank. Development Research Group Trade Team.

Ruttan, V. W. (1984). Integrated rural development programs: a historical perspective. *World Development*, 12(4).

Ruttan, V. W. (1984). Models of agricultural development. In C. K. Eicher & J. M. Staatz (Eds.), *Agricultural development in the third world* (pp. 89–98). Baltimore, MD: The Johns Hopkins Press.

Ruttan, V.-W. (2001). *Technology, growth, and development: an induced innovation perspective*. New York; Oxford: Oxford University Press.

Ruttan, V., & Hayami, Y. (1984). Induced innovation model of agricultural development. In C. K. Eicher & J. M. Staatz (Eds.), *Agricultural development in the third world* (pp. 97–114). Baltimore, MD: The Johns Hopkins Press.

Ruttan, V. W., & Stout, T. T. (1974). Regional differences in factor shares in American agriculture. *Journal of Farm Economics*, 42(1), 52–68.

Ryan, B., & Gross, N. (1950). The diffusion of hybrid seed corn in two Iowa communities. *Rural Sociology*, 8, 15–24.

Ryavec, K. W. (2003). *Russian bureaucracy: power and pathology*. Lanham, MD: Rowman & Littlefield.

Rykachev, A. (1911). Tseny na khleb i na trud v S. Petersburge za 58 let. *Vestnik finansov, promyshlennosti i torgovli*, 31.

Rylko, D. N. (2002). New agricultural operators, input markets and vertical sector coordination. *Factor markets in Russia's agri-food sector: frameworks of further analysis* (pp. 50–74). Moscow: IRIS, USAID.

Ryndziunski, P. G. (1983). *Krest'iane i gorod v kapitalisticheskoi Rossii vtoroi poloviny XIX veka: vzaimootnoshenie goroda i derevni v soëtsial'no-ekonomicheskom stroe Rossii*. Moscow: Nauka.

Ryndziunski, P. G. (1966). *Krest'ianskaia promyshlennost' v poreformennoi Rossii (60–80-e gody XIX v.)*. Moscow: Nauka.

Ryndziunski, P. G. (1978). *Utverzhdenie kapitalizma v Rossii 1850–1880 gg*. Moscow: Nauka.

Sabherwal, R., Hirschheim, R., & Goles, T. (2001). The dynamics of alignment: insights from a punctuated equilibrium model. *Organization Science*, 12(2), 179–97.

Sachs, J. (1997). Why Russia has failed to stabilize. In A. Åslund (Ed.), *Russia's economic transformation in the 1990s* (pp. 127–36). London: Pinter.

Sachs, J. D., & Woo, W. T. (1994). Structural factors in the economic reforms of China, Eastern Europe and the former Soviet Union. *Economic Policy*, 9, 101–45.

Safronov, S. G. (1977). Vopros o sobstvennosti na zemliu v sibirskoi istoricheskoi literatury. *Krest'ianskaia obchina v Sibiri XVII-nachala XX v* (pp. 266–86). Novosibirsk: Nauka.

Sah, R., & Stiglitz, J. (1992). *Peasants versus city-dwellers: taxation and the burden of economic development*. Oxford: Oxford University Press.

Sahn, D., Dorosh, P., & Younger, S. (1997). *Structural adjustment reconsidered: economic policy and poverty in Africa*. Cambridge, MA: Cambridge University Press.

Saith, A. (1985). *The agrarian question in socialist transitions*. London; Totowa, NJ: F. Cass.

Sakwa, R. (2007). *Putin: Russia's choice*. Abingdon; New York: Routledge.

Sanchez, O. (2005). Some thoughts on the political economy of Latin America. *Governance*, 18(2), 313–23.

Saunders, D. (1992). *Russia in the age of reaction and reform* 1801–1881. London; New York: Longman.

Schaber, G. (1993). Developing comparative databases. *Sharing data through the information cooperative: Second CIESIN Users Workshop*. Atlanta, GA: CEPS/INSTEAD.

Schlager, E., & Ostrom, E. (1993). Property-rights regimes and coastal fisheries: an empirical analysis. In T. L. Anderson & R. T. Simmons (Eds.), *The political economy of customs and culture: informal solutions to the commons problem* (pp. 13–42). Lanham, MD: Rowman & Littlefield.

Schlager, E., & Ostrom, E. (1992). Property-rights regimes and natural resources: a conceptual analysis. *Land Economics*, 68(3), 249–62.

Schleifer, A., & Vasiliev, D. (1996). Management ownership and Russian privatization. In R. Frydman, C. W. Gray, & A. Rapaczynski (Eds.), *Corporate governance in Central Europe and Russia, insiders and the state* (pp. 62–77). Budapest; London; New York: Central European University Press.

Schneider, F., & Enste, D. (2000). Shadow economies around the world: size, causes and consequences. Washington, DC: IMF.

Schönfeld, R. (1993). *Transforming economic systems in East Central Europe*. München: Südosteuropa-Gesellschaft.

Schoonover, D. (1979). Soviet agricultural policies. *Joint Economic Committee. Congress of the United States* (pp. 87–115). Washington, DC: U.S. Government.

Schoors, K. (2001). The credit squeeze during Russia's early transition: a bank-based view. *Economics of Transition/European Bank for Reconstruction and Development*, 9(1), 205–28.

Schoors, K. (2003). The fate of Russia's former state banks: chronicle of a restructuring postponed and a crisis foretold. *Europe-Asia Studies*, 55(1), 75–100.

Schreyer, P. (2001). *Measuring productivity: measurement of aggregate and industry-level productivity growth*. Paris; Washington, DC: Organisation for Economic Co-operation and Development.

Schroeder, G. E. (1991). Anatomy of Gorbachev's economic reform. In E. A. Hewett & V. H. Winston (Eds.), *Milestones in glasnost and perestroyka: the economy* (pp. 204–24). Washington, DC: The Brookings Institution.
Schroeder, G. E. (1991). Gorbachev: "radically" implementing Brezhnev's reforms. In E. A. Hewett & V. H. Winston (Eds.), *Milestones in glasnost and perestroyka: the economy* (pp. 36–46). Washington, DC: The Brookings Institution.
Schroeder, G. E. (1988). Gorbachev's economic reforms. In R. D. Liebowitz (Ed.), *Gorbachev's new thinking: prospects for joint ventures* (pp. 53–68). Cambridge, MA: Harvard University Press.
Schroeder, G. (1973). Recent developments in Soviet planning and incentives. *Joint Economic Committee. Congress of the United States* (pp. 11–38). Washington, DC: Joint Economic Committee.
Schroeder, G. (1979). The Soviet economy on a treadmill of 'reforms.' In Joint Economic Committee (Ed.), *Joint Economic Committee, Congress of the United States* (pp. 312–66). Washington, DC: Joint Economic Committee.
Schultz, T. W. (1945). *Agriculture in an unstable economy*. New York: McGraw-Hill Book Co.
Schultz, T. (1964). *Transforming traditional agriculture*. New Haven, CT: Yale University Press.
Schultz, T. W. (1945). *Food for the world*. Chicago: University of Chicago Press.
Schulze, E. (1999). Privatization of agricultural enterprises in Central and Eastern European countries. In K. Frohbert & P. Weingarten (Eds.), *Studies on the agricultural and food sector in Central and Eastern Europe;* 2 (pp. 159–73). Kiel: Wissenschaftsverlag Vauk.
Schwartzman, D. (1976). *Innovation in the pharmaceutical industry*. Baltimore, MD: Johns Hopkins University Press.
Schwarz, M., Lazear, E., & Rosen, S. (2002). Russia in transition. *Harvard Institute of Economic Research working papers*. Harvard University Institute of Economic Research.
Scott, D. (1957). *Russian political institutions*. New York: Rinehart & Company.
Scott, J. C. (1976). *The moral economy of the peasant*. New Haven, CT: Yale University Press.
Scott, J. C. (1985). *Weapons of the weak: everyday forms of peasant resistance*. New Haven; London: Yale University Press.
Sdobnov, S. I. (1976). *Sel'skoe khoziaistvo v desiatoi ptatiletke*. Moscow: Nauka.
Sedaitis, J. B. (1997). Commercializing state-owned R & D: a Russia-United States comparison. *Commercializing high technology: East and West* (pp. 145–66). Lanham: Rowman & Littlefield.
Sedik, D. J. (1991). *The formation and demise of market socialism under the Soviet New Economic Policy*, 1921–29. Ph.D. dissertation, University of California.
Sedik, D. (1993). A note on Soviet per capita meat consumption. *Comparative Economic Studies*, 15(3), 39–48.
Sedik, D. (1994). Systemic differences and stabilization policies in Germany and the USSR, 1923–28. In A. Aganbegyan, O. Bogomolov, & M. Kaser (Eds.), *Economics in a changing world, proceedings of the Tenth World Congress of the International Economic Association, Moscow* (pp. 187–200). London: St Martin's Press, in association with the International Economic Association.

Sedik, D., Foster, C., & Liefert, W. (1996). Economic reforms and agriculture in the Russian Federation, 1992–95. *Communist Economies and Economic Transformation*, 8(2), 133–48.

Sedik, D., Trueblood, M., & Arnade, C. (1999). Corporate farm performance in Russia, 1991–1995: an efficiency analysis. *Journal of Comparative Economics*, 27(3), 514–33.

Semevskii, V. I. (1903). *Krest'iane v tsarstvovanie Imperatritsy Ekateriny II*. St. Petersburg: Tip. M. M. Stasyulevicha.

Semevskii, V. I. (1888). *Krestianskii vopros v Rossii v XVIII i pervoi polovinii XIX veka*. St. Petersburg: Obshchestvennaia pol'za.

Semevskii, V. I., Iakovlev, V. A., & Shchegolev, P. E. (1905). *Obshchestvennyia dvizheniia v Rossii v pervuiu polovinu XIX veka*. St. Petersburg: M. V. Pirozhkov.

Sen, A. (1973). *On economic inequality*. Oxford: Oxford University Press.

Sen, A. (1983). Poor, relatively speaking. *Oxford Economic Papers*, 35, 153–69.

Sen, A. K. (1981). *Poverty and famines: an essay on entitlement and deprivation*. Oxford: Oxford University Press.

Seniavskii, A. S. (2006). *NEP: ekonomicheskie, politicheskie, i sotsial'nokulturnye aspekty*. Moscow: ROSSPEN.

Serova, E. (1999). *Agrarnaia ekonomika*. Moscow: Gosudarstvennyi universitet. Vysshaia shkola ekonomiki.

Serova, E. (1996). *Disparitet tsen v Agropromyshlennom Komplekse v perekhodnykh usloviiakh*. Moscow: Institute for the Economy in Transition.

Serova, E. (1997). *Institutsionnal'nye reformy v agropromyshlennom komplekse*. Moscow: Institute for the Economy in Transition.

Serova, E. (2000). Reform and economic behaviour in Russian agriculture. In L. A. Norsworthy (Ed.), *Russian views of the transition in the rural sector: structures, policy outcomes, and adaptive responses* (pp. 102–17). Washington, DC: World Bank.

Serova, E. (2000). Russia's agro-food sector: state of the art. In P. Wehrheim, K. Frohbert, E. Servoa, & J. von Braun (Eds.), *Russia's agro-food sector: towards truly functioning markets* (pp. 81–106). Boston; Dordrecht; London: Kluwer Academic Publishers.

Serova, E. (2000). Vlianie privatizatsii i reorganizatsii kolkozov i sovkhozov na rossiiskoe sel'skoe khozaistvo. *Reorganizatsiia se'skokhoziastvennykh predpriatii: ikh effektivnost' i ustoichivoe razvitie* (pp. 4–35). Moscow: Analiticheskii Tsentr Agroprodovol'stvennoi Ekonomiki.

Serova, E., Karlova, N., & Petrichenko, V. (2002). Russia: the market of purchased inputs for agriculture. *Factor markets in Russia's agri-food sector: frameworks of further analysis* (pp. 135–71). Moscow: IRIS, USAID.

Serova, E. V., & Shick, O. V. (2006). National project 'development of the agrifood sector.' *Analytical center reports*. Moscow: Analytical Center, Agrifood Economics, Institute for the Economy in Transition.

Serova, E. V., & Shick, O. V. (2006). National project 'development of the agrifood sector': Implementation progress and prospects. *Analytical center reports*. Moscow: Analytical Center, Agrifood Economics, Institute for the Economy in Transition.

Severin, B. (1987). Solving the Soviet livestock feed dilemma: key to meeting food program targets. *Gorbachev's economic plans* (pp. 45–59). Washington, DC: U.S. Congress, Joint Economic Committee.

Shagaida, N. (1999). "Privatizatsiia zemli i reorganizatsiia sel'skokhoziastvenykh predpriatii": neformal'nai istoriia. Programma "Privatizatsiia zemli i reorganizatsiia sel'skokhoziastvenykh predpriatii": *Podvedenie itogov* (pp. 22–30). Moscow: RosAgroFond.

Shagaida, N. (2002). The land market. *Factor markets in Russia's agri-food sector: frameworks of further analysis* (pp. 81–107). Moscow: IRIS, USAID.

Shagaida, N. (2005). Agricultural land market in Russia: living with constraints. *Comparative Economic Studies*, **47**(1), 127–40.

Shah, A. (1994). *The reform of intergovernmental fiscal relations in developing and emerging market economies*. Washington, DC: The World Bank.

Shah, A., & Whalley, J. (1991). The redistributive impact of taxation in developing countries. In J. Khalilzadeh-Shirazi & A. Shah (Eds.), *Tax policy in developing countries* (pp. 166–87). Washington, DC: The World Bank.

Shambayati, H. (1994). The rentier state, interest groups, and the paradox of autonomy: state and business in Turkey and Iran. *Comparative Politics*, **26**(3), 307–32.

Shane, M. D., & Liefert, W. M. (2000). The international financial crisis: macroeconomic linkages to agriculture. *American Journal of Agricultural Economics*, **82**(3), 682–87.

Shanin, T. (1972). *The awkward class; political sociology of peasantry in a developing society: Russia 1910–1925*. Oxford: Clarendon Press.

Shanin, T. (1987). *Peasants and peasant societies: selected readings*. Oxford: Basil Blackwell.

Shanin, T. (1986). *Russia, 1905–07: revolution as a moment of truth*. London: Macmillan.

Shanin, T. (1985). *Russia as a 'developing society.'* Basingstoke: Macmillan.

Shapiro, J. C. (1990). Unemployment before 1917: what do we know? In R. W. Davies (Ed.), *From tsarism to the New Economic Policy: continuity and change in the economy of the USSR* (pp. 66–78). Ithaca, NY: Cornell University Press.

Shapiro, J. (1996). Russian unemployment and the excess wages tax. *Communist Economies and Economic Transformation*, **8**(1), 5–27.

Sharma, S. (1997). Major issues in restructuring and transition in Eastern Europe. In S. Sharma (Ed.), *Restructuring Eastern Europe: the microeconomics of the transition process* (pp. 1–13). Cheltenham: Edward Elgar.

Shcherbina, F. A. (1900). *Krest'ianskie byudzheti*. St. Petersburg: Imperatorskoe vol'noe ekonomicheskoe obshchestvo.

Sheng, A. (1996). Financial liberalization and reform, crisis, and recovery in the Chilean economy 1974–87. In A. Sheng (Ed.), *Lessons from the 1980s* (pp. 147–59). Washington, DC: World Bank.

Shepelev, E. F. (1998). Russian law and land privatisation. In P. Koslowski (Ed.), *Theory and ethics of the economic order* (pp. 184–97). The social market economy: studies in economic ethics and philosophy. Heidelberg; New York: Springer.

Shik, O. (2002). Obzor biudzhetnoi poderzhki APK v Rossii v 1994–2002 gg. In *Problemy agroprodovol'stvenogo sektora* (pp. 5–43). Moscow: Institute of the Economy in Transition.

Shin, J. S. (1996). *The economics of the latecomers: catching-up, technological transfer and institutions in Germany, Japan and South Korea*. London; New York: Routledge.

Shishkin, V. I., & Krasil'nikov, S. A. (1985). *Sotsialisticheskoe stroitel'stvo v sibirskoi derevne, noiabr 1919-mart 1921 g.* Novosibirsk: Nauka.

Shlapentokh, D. (2008). Islam and orthodox Russia: from Eurasianism to Islamism. *Communist and Post-Communist Studies*, 41(1), 27–46.

Shleifer, A., & Treisman, D. (2000). *Without a map: political tactics and economic reform in Russia*. Cambridge, MA: MIT Press.

Shleifer, A., & Vasilliev, D. (1996). Management ownership and Russian privatization. In R. Frydman, C. W. Gray, & A. Rapaczynski (Eds.), *Corporate governance in Central Europe and Russia, insiders and the state* (pp. 62–77). Budapest; London; New York: Central European University Press.

Shonholtz, R., & Shapiro, I. (1997). *Strengthening transitional democracies through conflict resolution*. Thousand Oaks, CA: Sage.

Shue, V. (1980). *Peasant China in transition: the dynamics of development toward socialism*, 1949–1956. Berkeley: University of California Press.

Shvanebakh, P. K. (1903). *Nashe podatnoe delo*. St. Petersburg: Tiografiia M. M. Stasiulevicha.

Sidel'nikov, S. M. (1973). *Agrarnaia reforma Stolypina*: Moscow: Izd-vo Moskovskogo Universiteta.

Siegelbaum, L. (1980). The Odessa grain trade: a case study in urban growth and development in tsarist Russia. *Journal of European Economic History*, 9(1), 113–51.

Silk, L. S., & Silk, M. (1996). *Making capitalism work*. New York: New York University Press.

Silvestri, A. (1993). The contrast between modernization and tradition: land ownership during the last decades of the tsarist empire. *Review of Central and East European Law*, No. 1, 1–19.

Simanjuntak, D. S. (2000). The Indonesian economy in 1999: another year of delayed reform. In C. Manning & P. van Diermen (Eds.), *Social aspects of reform and crisis* (pp. 58–76). Singapore Institute of Southeast Asian Studies, distributed by St. Martin's Press.

Simms, J. Y. (1977). The crisis in Russian agriculture at the end of the nineteenth century: a different view. *Slavic Review*, 36(4), 377–98.

Simonova, M. S. (1953). *Stolypinskaia agrarnaia reforma v guberniiakh tsentral'no-chernozemnoi zony (Voronezhskaia, Kurskaia, Orlovskaia, Tambovskaia)*. Moscow: Nauka.

Simonova, M. S., & Anfimov, A. M. (1987). *Krizis agrarnoi politiki tsarizma nakanune pervoi rossiiskoi revoliutsii*. Moscow: Nauka.

Sinel'nikov, S. (1995). *Biudzhetnyi krizis v Rossii*: 1985–1995 *gody*. Moscow: Evrazia.

Singh, K. (1999). *Rural development: principles, policies and management*. New Delhi; Thousand Oaks, CA; London: Sage Publications.

Sivkov, K. V. (1951). *Ocherki po istorii krepostnogo khoziastva i krest'ianskogo dvizheniia v Rossii v pervoi polovine XIX veka; po materialam arkhiva stepnykh votchin Iusupovykh*. Moscow: Nauka.
Skilling, H. G., & Griffiths, F. (1971). *Interest groups in Soviet politics*. Princeton, NJ: Princeton University Press.
Skinner, J. (1991). Prospects for agricultural land and financial institutions. In J. Khalilzadeh-Shirazi & A. Shah (Eds.), *Tax policy in developing countries* (pp. 139–53). Washington, DC: The World Bank.
Skinner, J. (1993). If agricultural land taxation is so efficient, why is it so rarely used? In K. Hoff, B. Avishay, & J. E. Stiglitz (Eds.), *The economics of rural organization: theory, practice, and policy* (pp. 352–73). Oxford: Oxford University Press.
Skocpol, T. (1985). Bringing the state back in: strategies of analysis in current research. In P. B. Evans, D. Rueschemeyer, & T. Skocpol (Eds.), *Bringing the state back in* (pp. 3–37). Cambridge; New York; Sydney: Cambridge University Press.
Skyner, L. (2003). *Land ownership in Russia: before and after communism*. New York; London: Routledge.
Skyner, L. (2001). Political conflict and legal uncertainty: the privatisation of land ownership in Russia. *Europe-Asia Studies*, 53(7), 981–1000.
Skyner, L. (2003). Property as rhetoric: land ownership and private law in pre-Soviet and post-Soviet Russia. *Europe-Asia Studies*, 55(6), 889–906.
Skyner, L. (2005). Rehousing and refinancing Russia: creating access to affordable mortgaging. *Europe-Asia Studies*, 57(4), 561–81.
Slay, B. (1994). *The Polish economy: crisis, reform, and transition*. Princeton, NJ: Princeton University Press.
Smetanin, N. E., Tikhonov, V. A., Lemeshev, M. I., & Belov, M. I. (1980). *Narodnokhoziyastvenyi agropomyshlennyi komplekc. Teoriia i praktika*. Moscow: Ekonomika.
Smith, J. E. (1990). *Patenting the sun: polio and the Salk vaccine*. New York: William Morrow and Company.
Smith, L. D., & Spooner, N. (1997). *Cereals sector reform in the former Soviet Union and Central and Eastern Europe*. Walingford: CAB International.
Smykov, I. I. (1978). *Zemledel'cheskoe proizvodstvo srednego povolzh'ia v poreformennoe vremia (60–90-e gody XIX v.)*. Minsk: Nauka i Tekhnika.
Snell, W. M., & Infanger, C. L. (1991). Analyzing extension's role in macroeconomic policy education. *American Journal of Agricultural Economics*, 73(5), 1355–63.
Sobolev, O. (2002). O problermakh funktsionnirovaniia zernovogo rykna Rossiiskoi Federatsii. *Agrarnaia Reforma: Ekonomika i Pravo*, 2(26, March–April), 12–13.
Soifer, V. (1993). *Vlast' i Nauka. Istoriia razgroma genetiki v SSSR*. Moscow: Lazur'.
Sokoloff, K.-L., & Engerman, S.-L. (2000). Institutions, factor endowments, and paths of development in the new world. *Journal of Economic Perspectives*, 14(3), 217–32.
Sokolov, A. K. (2001). *NEP v kontekste istoricheskogo razvitliia Rossii XX veka*. Moscow: Institut rossiiskoi istorii RAN.
Solimano, A. (1991). *On economic transformation in East-Central Europe: a historical and international perspective*. Washington, DC: The World Bank.

Solimano, A., Sunkel, O., & Bléjer, M. I. (1994). *Rebuilding capitalism: alternative roads after socialism and dirigisme*. Ann Arbor: University of Michigan Press.

Solomon, P. (2008). Law in public administration: how Russia differs. *Journal of Communist Studies and Transition Politics*, 24(1), 115–35.

Solov'eva, A. M. (1975). *Zheleznodorozhnyi transport Rossii vo vtoroi polovine deviatnadtsatogo v.* Moscow: Nauka.

Solov'eva, A. M., & Bovykin, V. I. (1990). *Promyshlennaia revoliutsiia v Rossii v XIX v.* Moscow: Nauka.

Solow, R. (1985). Economic history and economics. *American Economic Review*, 75(May), 328–31.

Somit, A., & Peterson, S. A. (1992). *The dynamics of evolution: the punctuated equilibrium debate in the natural and social sciences*. Ithaca; London: Cornell University Press.

Somogyi, L. (1993). *The political economy of the transition process in Eastern Europe: proceeding of the 13th Arne Ryde Symposium, Rungsted Kyst, 11–12 June 1992*. Aldershot; Brookfield, VT: E. Elgar.

Soviet Union. Tsentral'noe statisticheskoe upravlenie (1925). *Materialy po tekhushchei sel'skokhoziaistvennoi statistike*. Moscow: Izdanie Tsentral'noe statisticheskoe upravlenie, SSSR i RSFSR.

Soviet Union. Tsentral'noe statisticheskoe upravlenie (1927). *Ten years of Soviet power in figures, 1917–1927*. Moscow: Central Statistical Board.

Soviet Union. Ministerstvo sel'skogo khoziaistva i zagotovok (1953). *Sel'skoe khoziaistvo*. Moscow: [s.n.].

Soviet Union. Tsentral'noe statisticheskoe upravlenie (1956). *The national economy of the USSR; a statistical compilation*. Moscow: Foreign Languages Publishing House.

Soviet Union. Tsentral'noe statisticheskoe upravlenie (1958). *Forty years of Soviet power in facts and figures*. Moscow: Foreign Languages Pub. House.

Soviet Union. Tsentral'noe statisticheskoe upravlenie (1960). *Sel'skoe khoziaistvo SSSR*. Moscow: Tsentral'noe statisticheskoe upravlenie.

Soviet Union. Tsentral'noe statisticheskoe upravlenie (1971). *Sel'skoe khoziaistvo SSSR: statisticheskii sbornik*. Moscow: Statistika.

Soviet Union. Tsentral'noe statisticheskoe upravlenie (1991). *Narodnoe khoziaistvo SSSR*. Moscow: Gos. statisticheskoe izd-vo.

Spechler, M. C. (1980). The regional concentration of industry in Imperial Russia 1854–1917. *Journal of European Economic History* (Fall), 401–19.

Spoor, M. (2002). Policy regimes and the performance of the agricultural sector in Latin America and the Caribbean. *Journal of Agrarian Change*, 2(3), 381–400.

Spoor, M. E. (2003). *Transition, institutions, and the rural sector*. Lanham, MD; Oxford: Lexington Books.

Spulber, N. (1964). *Foundations of Soviet strategy for economic growth; selected Soviet essays, 1924–1930*. Bloomington: Indiana University Press.

Spulber, N. (1997). *Redefining the state: privatization and welfare reform in industrial and transitional economies*. Cambridge; New York: Cambridge University Press.

Spulber, N. (1991). *Restructuring the Soviet economy: in search of the market*. Ann Arbor: University of Michigan Press.

Spulber, N. (2003). *Russia's economic transitions: from late tsarism to the new millennium*. Cambridge; New York; Melbourne: Cambridge University Press.

Spulber, N. (1969, 1962). *The Soviet economy: structure, principles, problems*. New York: Norton.

Squire, L. (1993). Fighting poverty. *American Economic Review*, 83(May), 377–82.

SSSR (1959). *Zhivotnovodstvo SSSR, Statisticheskii sbornik*. Moscow: Gosudarstvennoe statisticheskoe izdatel'stvo.

Stahl, S. (1997). Transition problems in the Russian agriculture sector: a historical-institutional perspective. In A. Amin & J. Hausner (Eds.), *Beyond market and hierarchy: interactive governance and social complexity*. Cheltenham; Williston, VT: American International Distribution Corporation.

Stahl, S. (1998). Independent family farms versus hierarchical forms of organisation: spontaneous emergence of property rights structures in Russian agriculture. In P. Koslowski (Ed.), *Theory and ethics of the economic order* (pp. 158–183). The social market economy: studies in economic ethics and philosophy. Heidelberg; New York: Springer.

Stallings, B. B. (1990). Politics and economic crisis: a comparative study of Chile, Peru, and Colombia. In J. M. Nelson (Ed.), *The politics of adjustment in the third world* (pp. 113–67). Economic crisis and policy choice: Princeton, NJ: Princeton University Press.

Stark, D. (1996). Networks of assets, chains of debt: recombinant property in Hungary. In R. Frydman, C. W. Gray, & A. Rapaczynski (Eds.), *Corporate governance in Central Europe and Russia: insiders and the state* (pp. 109–50). Budapest; London; New York: Central European University Press.

Starr, S. F. (1972). *Decentralization and self-government in Russia*, 1830–1870. Princeton, NJ: Princeton University Press.

Staub, W. J., & Blase, M. G. (1974). Induced technological change in developing agricultures: implications for income distribution and agricultural development. *Journal of Developing Areas*, 8(4), 581–96.

Stepashin, S., & Gerashchenko, V. (1999). *Statement of the government of the Russian Federation and Central Bank of Russia on economic policies*. Moscow: Ministry of Finance.

Stern, N. (1997). The transition in Eastern Europe and the former Soviet Union: some strategic lessons from the experience of 25 countries over six years. In S. Zeccini (Ed.), *Lessons from the economic transition: Central and Eastern Europe in the 1990s* (pp. 35–58). Dordrecht; Boston: Kluwer Academic Publishers.

Stern, N. H., & Stiglitz, J. (1997). *A framework for a development strategy in a market economy: objectives, scope, institutions and instruments*. London: European Bank for Reconstruction and Development.

Stiglitz, J. E. (1993). *Financial systems for Eastern Europe's emerging democracies*. San Francisco: ICS Press.

Strauss, E. (1961). *The ruling servants; bureaucracy in Russia, France–and Britain?* New York: Praeger.

Strumilin, S. G. (1926). *Naemnyi trud v sel'skom khoziastve: statistiko-ekonomicheskii sbornik*. Moscow: Voprosy truda.

Strumilin, S. G. (1958). *Statistiko-ekonomicheskie ocherki*. Moscow: Gosstatizdat.

Strumilin, S. G. (1960). *Ocherki ekonomicheskoi istorii Rossii*. Moscow: Sotsial'no-ekonomicheskaia istoriia.

Strumilin, S. G. (1963–1965). *Izbrannye proizvedeniia*. Moscow: Nauka.

Stuart, G. (1972). *The collective farm in Soviet agriculture*. Lexington, MA: D.C. Heath.

Stuart, R. C., & Panayotopoulos, C. M. (1999). Decline and recovery in transition economies: the impact of initial conditions. *Post Soviet Geography and Economics*, 40(4), 267–80.

Sturzenegger, F., & Tommasi, M. (1998). The political economy of reform. Cambridge, MA: Harvard University Press.

Sturzenegger, F., & Tommasi, M. (1998). *Introduction*. In F. Sturzenegger & M. Tommasi (Eds.), *The political economy of reform* (pp. 1–33). Cambridge, MA: Harvard University Press.

Surin, M. N. (1915). *Dvizhenie sel'khoziastvennoi zarabotnoi platy v Moskovskoi gubernii za 30 let* (1884–1913 gg). Moscow: S. P. Iakovleva.

Sussman, N., & Yafeh, Y. (2000). Institutions, reforms, and country risk: lessons from Japanese government debt in the Meiji era. *Journal of Economic History*, 60(2), 442–67.

Sussman, N., & Yafeh, Y. (2002). *Constitutions and commitment: evidence on the relation between institutions and the cost of capital*. Hebrew University of Jerusalem.

Sutela, P. (1991). *Economic thought and economic reform in the Soviet Union*. Cambridge; New York; Melbourne: Cambridge University Press.

Sutela, P. (1996). Fiscal federalism in Russia. In B. Dallag & L. Mittone (Eds.), *Economic institutions, markets and competition: centralization and decentralization in the transformation of economic systems*. Cheltenham; Brookfield, VT: Edward Elgar, distributed by Ashgate.

Sutela, P. (2003). *The Russian market economy*. Helsinki: Kikimora.

Sutherland, D., Bradshaw, M., & Hanson, P. (2000). *Regional dynamics of economic restructuring across Russia*. Cheltenham; Northampton, MA: E. Elgar.

Suzuki, T. (1995). Modernization and village commune in Russia: intellectuals' discussion on the eve of the emancipation of serfs in 1861. *Waseda Economic Papers* (34), 41–50.

Suzuki, T. (1999). Administrative reform and the politics of budgetary retrenchment in Japan. *Social Science Japan Journal*, 2(2), 195–213.

Svavitskaia, Z. M., & Svavitskii, N. A. (1926). *Zemskie podvornye perepisi* 1880–1913, *pouezdnye itogi*. Moscow: Tsentral'noe Statisticheskoe Upravlenie.

Swaan, W. (1997). Knowledge, transaction costs and the creation of markets in post-socialist economies. In H. Brezinski & M. Fritsch (Eds.), *The emergence and evolution of markets* (pp. 115–32). Cheltenham: Elgar.

Swann, J. P. (1988). *Academic scientists and the pharmaceutical industry: cooperative research in twentieth century America*. Baltimore, MD: Johns Hopkins University Press.

Swinnen, J. (2005). Agricultural transformation: lessons from experience. *Agrekon*, 44(1), 17–36.

Swinnen, J. F. M. (1997). The choice of privatization and decollectivization policies in Central and Eastern European agriculture: observations and political economy hypothesis. In J. F. M. Swinnen (Ed.), *Political economy of agrarian reform in Central and Eastern Europe* (pp. 363–98). Aldershot; Brookfield, VT: Ashgate.

Swinnen, J. F. M. (1997). *Political economy of agrarian reform in Central and Eastern Europe* (pp. xix, 398). Aldershot; Brookfield, VT: Ashgate.

Swinnen, J. F. (2002). Political reforms, rural crises, and land tenure in Western Europe. *Food Policy*, 27(4), 371–94.

Swinnen, J., & Heinegg, A. (2002). On the political economy of land reforms in the former Soviet Union. *Journal of International Development*, 14(7), 1019–32.

Swinnen, J., & Rozelle, S. (2006). *From Marx and Mao to the Market: The Economics and Politics of Agricultural Transition*. Oxford: Oxford University Press.

Sylla, R. (1992). The role of banks. In R. Sylla & G. Toniolo (Eds.), *Patterns of European industrialization* (pp. 45–63). London; New York: Routledge.

Symons, L., & White, C. (1975). *Russian transport: an historical and geographical survey*. London: G. Bell & Sons.

Syrquin, M. (1986). Productivity growth and factor reallocation. In H. Chenery, S. Robinson, & M. Syrquin (Eds.), *Industrialisation and growth: a comparative study* (pp. 229–62). Oxford: Oxford University Press for the World Bank.

Szapáry, G., & Jakabv, Z. (1998). Exchange rate policy in transition economies: the case of Hungary. *Journal of Comparative Economics*, **26**, 691–717.

Székely, I. P., & Newbery, D. M. G. (1993). *Hungary: an economy in transition*. Cambridge: Cambridge University Press.

Szelényi, I. (1998). *Privatizing the land; rural political economy in post-communist societies*. London; New York: Routledge.

Taniuchi, Y. (1968). *The village gathering in Russia in the mid-1920s*. Birmingham: University of Birmingham Press.

Tanzi, V. (1999). The changing role of the state in the economy: an historical perspective. In K. Fukusaku, J. de Mello, & R. Luiz (Eds.), *Fiscal decentralisation in emerging economies: governance issues* (pp. 17–36). Paris: OECD.

Tanzi, V. (1993). Financial markets and public finance in the transformation process. In V. Tanzi (Ed.), *Transition to market: studies in fiscal reform* (pp. 1–30). Washington, DC: IMF.

Tanzi, V. (1993). *Transition to market: studies in fiscal reform*. Washington, DC: IMF.

Tarnovskii, K. N. (1969). Problemy agrarnoi istorii Rossii perioda imperializma v sovetskoi istoriografii (konets 1930-pervaia polovina 1950-khy godov). *Istoricheskie Zapiski*, 83, 201–22.

Tarrant, J. R. (1980). *Food policies*. New York: John Wiley & Sons.

Teliak, L. V. (1995). *Stolypinskaia agrarnaia reforma: istoriografiia* (1906–1917 *gg.*): *uchebnoe posobie po spetskursu*. Samara: (Izd-vo SamGPI).

Telytsin, V. L. (2002). "Litsom k derevne" i litso derevni. In S. A. Pavliuchenkov (Ed.), *Rossiia nepovskaia* (pp. 208–29). Moscow: Novyi khronograf.

Telytsin, V. L. (2002b). Reanimatsiia voennogo kommunzma v derevne. In S. A. Pavliuchenkov (Ed.), *Rossiia nepovskaia* (pp. 419–40). Moscow: Novyi khronograf.

Ter-Minassian, T. (2001). Fiscal Affairs Department introduces policy development and research initiatives. *IMF Survey*, 30(13), 213–17.

Thatcher, I. D., & Johnson, R. E. (2006). Late Imperial Russia: problems and prospects. *Europe-Asia Studies*, 58(3), 480–82.

Thirsk, W. (1991). Lessons from tax reform: an overview. In J. Khalilzadeh-Shirazi & A. Shah (Eds.), *Tax policy in developing countries* (pp. 57–71). Washington, DC: The World Bank.

Thirtle, C. & Bottomley, P. (1989). The Rate of Return to Public Sector Agricultural R&D in the UK, 1965–80. *Applied Economics*, **21**, pp. 1063–86.

Thomas, V., & Wang, Y. (1997). East Asian lessons from economic reforms. In W. T. Woo, S. Parker, & J. D. Sachs (Eds.), *Economies in transition: comparing Asia and Eastern Europe* (pp. 217–42). Cambridge, MA: The MIT Press.

Thompstone, S. (2004). The Russian technical society and British textile machinery imports. In D. Farnie & D. Jeremy (Ed.), *The fibre that changed the world: the cotton industry in international perspective, 1600–1990s*. Oxford: University of Oxford Press.

Thompstone, S. (1998). Tsarist Russia's investment in transport. *The Journal of Transport History* (March).

Thornton, J. (1997). Restructuring production without market infrastructure. In J. Nelson, C. Tilly, & L. Walker (Eds.), *Transforming post-communist political economies* (pp. 133–55). Washington, DC: National Academy Press.

Tikhomirov, M. N., & Milov, L. V. (1961). *Zakon sudny i liudem: kratkoi redaktsii*. Moscow: Nauka.

Tikhonov, B. V. (1978). *Pereselenie v Rossii vo vtoroi polovine XIX v; po materialam perepisi 1897g. i pasportnoi statistiki*. Moscow: Nauka.

Tillack, P., & Schulze, E. (2000). Decollectivization and restructuring of farms. In J. Braun, K. Frohbert, E. Serova, & P. Wehrheim (Eds.), *Russia's agro-food sector: towards truly functioning markets* (pp. 447–70). Boston; Dordrecht; London: Kluwer Academic Publishers.

Timmer, C. P. (1991). *Agriculture and the state: growth, employment, and poverty in developing countries*. Ithaca, NY: Cornell University Press.

Timmer, C. P. (1991). The role of the state in agricultural development. In C. P. Timmer (Ed.), *Agriculture and the state: growth, employment, and poverty in developing countries* (pp. 1–28). Ithaca, NY: Cornell University Press.

Tishev, V. A. (2000). O sostoianii i osobennostiakh denezhnogo obrashcheniia Rossii v kontse XIX – nachale XX veka. *Ekonomicheskaia istoriia Rossii XIX–XX vv; Sovremennyi vzgliad* (pp. 53–61). Moscow: ROSSPEN.

Tiukavkin, V. G. (2001). *Velikorusskoe krest'ianstvo i Stolypinskaia agrarnaia reforma*. Moscow: Nauka.

Tiurina, E. A., & Danilov, V. P. (1991). *Kooperativno-kolkhoznoe stroitel'stvo v SSSR, 1923–1927: dokumenty i materialy*. Moscow: Nauka.

Tiwari, D. N. (1995). Measurement of sustainability indicators and implications for macroeconomic policy modelling in developing countries. *Economie Appliquee*, 48(2), 181–214.

Todaro, M. P. (1969). A model of labor migration and urban unemployment in less developed countries. *American Economic Review*, **59**(March), 138–48.

Todaro, M. P. (1976). *Internal migration in developing countries: a review of theory, evidence, methodology and research priorities*. Geneva: International Labour Office of the U.N.

Tokmakoff, G. (1981). P. A. Stolypin and the third Duma: an appraisal of the three major issues (pp. xi, 246). Washington, DC: University Press of America.

Tommasi, M., & Velasco, A. (1996). Where are we in the political economy of reform. *Journal of Policy Reform*, 1, 187–238.

Tompson, W. J. (1997). *Khrushchev: a political life*. Basingstoke: Macmillan.

Tompson, W. J. (2003). *The Soviet Union under Brezhnev*. Harlow: Longman.

Toporowski, J. (1997). Financial fragility in the banking system of transitional economies in Eastern Europe. In S. Sharma (Ed.), *Restructuring Eastern Europe: the microeconomics of the transition process* (pp. 128–38). Cheltenham: Edward Elgar.

Torke, H.-J. (1974). *Die Staatsbedingte Gesellschaft im Moskauer Reich: Zar und Zemlja in der altrussischen Herrschaftsordnung*, 1613–1689. Leiden: Brill.

Török, Á. (1998). Corporate governance in the transition – the case of Hungary: do new structures help create efficient ownership control? In L. Halpern & C. Wyplosz (Eds.), *Hungary: towards a market economy* (pp. 159–91). Cambridge: Cambridge University Press.

Toumanoff, P. (1984). Some effects of land tenure reforms on Russian agricultural productivity, 1901–1913. *Economic Development and Cultural Change*, 34(4), 861–72.

Towne, M. W., & Rasmussen, W. D. (1960). Farm gross product and gross investment in the nineteenth century. In W. Parker (Ed.), *Trends in the American economy in the nineteenth century* (pp. 255–312). Princeton, NJ: Princeton University Press.

Townsend, R. M. (1995). Consumption insurance: an evaluation of risk-bearing systems in low-income economies. *Journal of Economic Perspectives*, 9(Summer), 83–102.

Townsend, R. F., & Thirtle, C. (1998). The effects of macroeconomic policy on South African agriculture: implications for exports, prices and farm incomes. *Journal of International Development*, 10(1), 117–28.

Townsend, R., & Thirtle, C. (2000). The effects of macroeconomic policies on agricultural prices, net farm incomes and exports: a vector autoregression approach. In C. Thirtle, J. van-Zyl, & N. Vink (Eds.), *South African agriculture at the crossroads: the effects of macroeconomic policy on South African agriculture, implications for exports, prices and farm incomes* (pp. 276–96). New York; London: St. Martin's Press; Macmillan Press.

Tracy, M. (1992). *Food and agriculture in a market economy: an introduction to theory, practice and policy*. New York: Agricultural Policy Studies.

Treml, V. G. (1982). Subsidies in Soviet agriculture: record and prospects, Soviet economy in the 1980s: problems and prospects. In *Congress of the United States, Joint Economic Committee* (pp. 171–86). Washington, DC: Joint Economic Committee.

Trethewey, R. (1974). The establishment of serfdom in Eastern Europe and Russia. *American Economist*, 18(1), 36–41.

Troinitskii, N. (1905). *Obshchii svod po Imperii rezul'tatov razrabotki dannykh pervoi Vseobshchei perepisi naseleniya, proizvedennoi 28 ianvaria 1897 goda*. St. Petersburg: Tsentral'nyi statisticheskii komitet.

Troinitskii, N. A. (1905). *Pervaia vseobshchaia perepis' Rossiiskoi Imperii, 1897g.* St. Petersburg: Tsentral'nyi statisticheskii komitet.

Troinitskii, A. G. (1982). *The serf population in Russia according to the 10th national census: a statistical study*. Newtonville, MA: Oriental Research Partners.

Troitskii, S. M. (1974). *Russkii absolutizm i dvorianstvo v XVIII v; formirovanie biurokratii*. Moscow: Nauka.

Trueblood, M. A., & Arnade, C. A. (2001). Crop yield convergence: how Russia's yield performance has compared to global yield leaders. *Comparative Economic Studies*, 43(2), 59–81.

Trueblood, M., & Osborne, S. (2002). Agricultural productivity and efficiency in Russia and Ukraine: building on a decade of reform. Washington, DC: ERS USDA.

Trueblood, M. A., & Ruttan, V. W. (1995). A comparison of multifactor productivity calculations of the U.S. agricultural sector. *Journal of Productivity Analysis*, 6(4), 321–31.

Tsentr ekonomicheskoi kon'iunktury (1997). *Razvitie rynka zerna v Rossii (Tendentsii proizvodstva zerna v Rossiiskoi Federatsii za 1970–1996 gody)*. Moscow: Center for Economic Conjuncture, Government of the Russian Federation.

Tsentr ekonomicheskoi kon'iunktury (1997). *Sel'skokhoziastvennoe proizvodstva Rossii: dinamika i effektivnost' (1970–1996 gody)*. Moscow: Center for Economic Conjuncture, Government of the Russian Federation.

Tsentral'noe statisticheskoe upravlenie (1919). *Itogi [vtoroi] Vserossiiskoi sel'skokhoziistvennoi. perepisi*. Moscow.

Tsentral'noe statisticheskoe upravlenie SSSR (1940). *Narodnoe khoziastvo SSSR: statisticheskii ezhegodnik*. Moscow: Financy i statistika.

Tsentral'noe statisticheskoe upravlenie (1963). *Osnovy kolkhoznogo prava*. Moscow: Tsentral'noe statisticheskoe upravlenie pri Sovete Ministrov RSFSR.

Tsentral'noe statisticheskoe upravlenie (1977). *Narodnoe khoziastvo RSFSR za 60 let, Statisticheskii ezhegodnik*. Moscow: Statistika.

Tucker, R. C. (1973). *Stalin as revolutionary*, 1879–1929; *a study in history and personality*. New York: Norton.

Tugan-Baranovskii, M. I. (1922). *Russkaia fabrika v proshlom i nastoiashchem: istoricheskoe razvitie russkoi fabriki v XIX v*. Moscow: Moskovskii rabochii.

Tugan-Baranovskii, M. I. (1970). *The Russian factory in the 19th century*. Homewood, IL: Published for the American Economic Association by R. D. Irwin.

Turnock, D. (1997). *The East European economy in context*. London; New York: Routledge.

Turubiner, A. M. (1958). *Pravo gosudarstvennoi sobstvennosti na zemliu v Sovietskom Soiuze*. Moscow.

Tushman, M., & Anderson, P. (2004). *Managing strategic innovation and change: a collection of readings*. New York: Oxford University Press.

Tushman, M. L., Nelson, R. R., Henderson, R. M., Clark, K. B., Barnett, W. P., Barley, S. R., Burkhardt, M. E., Brass, D. J., Cohen, W. M., Levinthal, D. A., Pisano, G. P., Schoonhoven, C. B., Eisenhardt, K. M., & Lyman, K. (1990). Technology, organisations and innovation. *Administrative Science Quarterly*, 35(1), 1–207.

Tushman, M. L., & Romanelli, E. (1985). Organizational evolution: a metamorphosis model of convergence and reorientation. In L. L. Cummings & B. M. Staw (Eds.), *Research in organizational behavior: an annual series of analytical essays and critical reviews* (pp. 171–222). Greenwich.

Umali Deininger, D., & Maguire, C. E. (1995). *Agriculture in liberalizing economies: changing roles for governments: proceedings of the Fourteenth Agricultural Sector Symposium*. Washington, DC: The World Bank.

United Nations (1999). The Least Developed Countries 1999 Report. New York; Geneva: United Nations Conference on Trade and Development.

United Nations Industrial Development Organisation (1995, 1997). *Industrial Development Global Report*. Oxford: Oxford University Press.

U.S. Congress. House Committee on Agriculture. Subcommittee on Foreign Agriculture and Hunger (1993). *Current agricultural situation in Russia: hearings before the Subcommittee on Foreign Agriculture and Hunger of the Committee on Agriculture, House of Representatives, One Hundred Third Congress, first session, March 30, 31, and April 1, 1993*. Washington, DC: U.S. GPO.

U.S. Congress. House Committee on Agriculture. Subcommittee on Livestock and Grains, & U.S. Congress. House Committee on Agriculture. Subcommittee on Departmental Operations (1972). *Sale of feed grains to Russia. Hearing before the Subcommittee on Livestock and Grains and the Subcommittee on Department Operations of the Committee on Agriculture, House of Representatives, Ninety-second Congress, first session. December 8, 1971*. Washington, DC: U.S. GPO.

United States Department of Agriculture (2007). Agricultural productivity in the U.S.: data documentation and methods: USDA, ERS.

United States Department of Agriculture, E. R. S. (1966). The USSR and Eastern Europe agricultural situation, review of 1965 and outlook for 1966. In H. E. Walters (Ed.), *The USSR and Eastern Europe agricultural situation*. Washington, DC: USDA.

United States Department of Agriculture. Economics Statistics and Cooperatives Service (1980). *Agricultural situation, USSR; review and outlook*. Washington, DC: Department of Agriculture Economics Statistics and Cooperatives Service.

Upchurch, M. L. (1961). Implications of economies of scale to national agricultural adjustments. *Journal of Farm Economics*, 43(5), 1239–46.

Utterback, J. M. (1994). *Mastering the dynamics of innovation: how companies can seize opportunities in the face of technological change*. Boston: Harvard Business School Press.

Uvarovsky, V. & Voigt, P. (2000). Russia's agriculture: eight years in transition – convergence or divergence of regional efficiency. *Discussion Papers*. Halle, Germany: Institute of Agricultural Development in Central and Eastern Europe.

Uzun, V. V. (1999). Privatizatsiia zemli i reorganizatsiia sel'skokhoziastvennykh predpriatii: idei, mekhanizmy, rezul'taty, problemy. *Reorganizatsiia sel'skokhoziastvennykh predpriatii: ikh effektivnost' i ustoichivoe razvitie* (pp. 36–53). Moscow; Golitzino: IRIS, USAID.

Uzun, V. V. (2002). Organizational types of the agricultural production in Russia. *Factor markets in Russia's agri-food sector: frameworks of further analysis* (pp. 16–44). Moscow: IRIS, USAID.

Vainshtein, A. L. (1960). *Narodnoe bogatstvo i narodnokhoziastvennoe nakoplenie predrevoliutsionnoi Rossii*. Moscow: Gosstatizdat.

Vainshtein, A. L. (1967). *Statistika narodnogo bogatstva*. Moscow: Nauka.

Vainshtein, A. L. (1969). *Narodnyi dokhod Rossii i SSSR: istoriia metodologiia ischisleniia, dinamika*. Moscow: Nauka.

Van Atta, D. (1994). Agrarian reform in post-Soviet Russia. *Post Soviet Affairs*, 10(2), 159–90.

Van Atta, D., & Macey, D. A. J. (1993). *The "farmer threat": the political economy of agrarian reform in post-Soviet Russia*. Boulder, CO: Westview Press.

Van Der Meer, C. L. J. (1989). Agricultural growth in the EC and the effect of the CAP. Proceedings of the twentieth international conference of agricultural economists held at Buenos Aires 24–31 August 1988. *Agriculture and governments in an interdependent world* (pp. 140–52). Hanover, NH: Dartmouth.

Van Zanden, J. L. (1991). The first green revolution: the growth of production and productivity in European agriculture, 1870–1914. *Economic History Review*, **44**, 215–39.

Varlamov, A., & Gal'chenko, S. (2002). Razvitie zemel'nykh otnoshenii v Rossii. *Agrarnaia Reforma: Ekonomika i Pravo*, 3(21, May–June), 17–22.

Varzar, V. E., & Kafengauz, L. B. (1929). *Svod statisticheskikh dannykh o fabrichno-zavodskoi promyshlennosti s 1887 po 1926 goda [microform]*. Moscow: Gos. izd-vo.

Vasiliev, S. A. (1997). Economic reform in Russia. In A. Åslund (Ed.), *Russia's transformatioin in the 1990s* (pp. 25–40). London; Washington, DC: Pinter.

Veblen, T. (1915). *Imperial Germany and the Industrial Revolution*. London: Routledge. Thoemmes Press.

Velasco, A. (1998). The common property approach to the political economy of fiscal policy. In F. Sturzenegger & M. Tommasi (Eds.), *The political economy of reform* (pp. 165–84). Cambridge, MA: Harvard University Press.

Venturi, F. (1983). *Roots of revolution: a history of the populist and socialist movements in nineteenth-century Russia*. Chicago; London: University of Chicago Press.

Vil'son, I. (1857). Atlas économique et statistique de la Russie d'Europe. 3e édition. St. Petersburg.

Vil'son, I. I. (1878). *Agriculture et économie rurale en Russie*. St. Pétersburg: Impr. Trenké & Fusnot.

Vil'son, I. (1869). *Ob'iasneniìa k khoziastvenno-statisticheskomu atlasu Evropeiskoi Rossii*. St. Petersburg: V tip. V. Bezobrazova.

Vil'son, I. I. (1878). *Vykupnye za zemli platezhi krest'ìan-sobstvennikov*. Moscow.

Viner, V. V. (1922). Sel'skokhoziastvennoe optynoe delo. *Novaia derevnia*.

Vinogradov, V. A. (2000). *Ekonomicheskaia istoriia Rossii XIX–XX vv; sovremennyi vzgliad*. Moscow: ROSSPEN.

Viola, L. (1987). *The best sons of the fatherland: workers in the vanguard of Soviet collectivization*. New York; Oxford: Oxford University Press.

Viola, L. (2002). *Contending with Stalinism: Soviet power & popular resistance in the 1930s*. Ithaca, N.Y; London: Cornell University Press.

Viola, L. (1996). *Peasant rebels under Stalin: collectivization and the culture of peasant resistance*. New York: Oxford University Press.

Vlasova, I. V., Gromyko, M. M., & Listova, T. A. (1989). *Russkie: semeinyi i obshchestvennyi byt*. Moscow: Nauka.

Voigt, P., & Hockman, H. (2008). Russia's transition process in the light of a rising economy: economic trajectories in Russia's industry and agriculture. *The European Journal of Comparative Economics*, 5(2), 179–95.

Voigt, P., & Uvarovsky, V. (2001). Developments in productivity and efficiency in Russia's agriculture: the transition period. *Quarterly Journal of International Agriculture*, 40(1), 45–66.

Volin, L. (1960). Agricultural policy of the Soviet Union. *Congress of the United States, Joint Economic Committee* (pp. 285–318). Washington, DC: Joint Economic Committee.

Volin, L. (1970). *A century of Russian agriculture-from Alexander II to Khrushchev*. Cambridge, MA: Harvard University Press.

Volin, L. (1955). The Malenkov-Khrushchev New Economic Policy. *Journal of Political Economy*, 62(3), pp. 187–209.

Volkov, S. (2002). Zemleustroitel'noe obespechenie oborota zemel' sel'skokhoziastvenogo naznacheniia. *Agrarnaia Reforma: Ekonomika. i Pravo*, 3(21, May–June), 7–10.

von Braun, J., Qaim, M., & Seeth, H. T. (2000). Poverty, subsistence production, and consumption of food in Russia: policy implications. In P. Wehrheim, K. Frohbert, E. Serova, & J. von Braun (Eds.), *Russia's agro-food sector: towards truly functioning markets* (pp. 301–22). Boston; Dordrecht; London: Kluwer Academic Publishers.

Von Hirschhausen, C. (1998). Industrial restructuring in Ukraine seven years after independence: from socialism to a planning economy? *Communist Economies & Economic Transformation*, 10(4), 451–65.

Von Laue, T. (1953). The high cost and gamble of the Witte system: a chapter in the industrialisation of Russia. *Journal of Economic History*, 13(4), 425–48.

Von Laue, T. (1960). The state and the economy. In C. Black (Ed.), *The transformation of Russian society* (pp. 209–35). Cambridge, MA: Harvard University Press.

Von Laue, T. H. (1963). *Sergei Witte and the industrialization of Russia*. New York: Columbia University Press.

Voznesenskii, N. A. (1979). *Izbrannye proizvedeniia*, 1931–1947. Moscow: Politizdat.

Vranken, L., & Swinnen, J. (2006). Land rental markets in transition: theory and evidence from Hungary. *World Development*, 34(3), 481–500.

Vronskii, O. G. (1999). *Gosudartvennaia vlast' Rossiiskoi imperii i problemy formirovaniia osnov perspektivnogo agrarnogo kursa na rubezhe XIX–XX vv*. Moscow.

Vronskii, O. G. (2000). *Gosudarstvennaia vlast' Rossii i krest'ianskaia obshchina v gody "velikikh potriasenii"* (1905–1917). Tula.

Vucinich, A. (1960). The state and the local community. In C. Black (Ed.), *The transformation of Russian society* (pp. 191–209). Cambridge, MA: Harvard University Press.

Vygodskii, S. L. (1931). *Sel'skkokhoziastvennyi kredit v dorevoliutsionnoi Rossii*. Moscow.

Vyltsan, M. A. (2000). Stalinskii produktoobmen i tovarnoe proizvodstvo 'osobogo roda' v 1930-e gody. In V. A. Vinogradov (Ed.), *Ekonomicheskaia istoriia Rossii XIX–XX vv; sovremennyi vzgliad* (pp. 122–31). Moscow: ROSSPEN.

Wade, R. A. (2001). *The Bolshevik Revolution and Russian civil war*. Westport, CT: Greenwood Press.

Wade, R. A. (2003). *Revolutionary Russia: new approaches to the Russian Revolution of 1917*. London: Routledge.

Wädekin, K. E. (1985). *Agriculture in inter-system comparison: communist and non-communist cases*. Berlin: In Kommission bei Duncker & Humblot.

Wädekin, K.-E. (1967). Comment. In J. F. Karcz (Ed.), *Soviet and East European agriculture*. Berkeley; Los Angeles: University of California Press.

Wädekin, K.-E. (1973). *The private sector in Soviet agriculture*. Berkeley; Los Angeles: University of California Press.

Wädekin, K.-E. (1989). The re-emergence of the kolkhoz principle. *Soviet Studies*, 41(1), 20–38.

Wädekin, K.-E. (1982). Soviet agriculture's dependence on the West. *Foreign Affairs*, 60(4), 882–903.

Wagner, W. G. (1983). The Civil Cassation Department of the Senate as an Instrument of Progressive Russia: The Case of Property and Inheritance Law. *Slavic Review*, **42**(1), 36–49.

Wagner, W. G. (1994). *Marriage, Property, and Law in Late Imperial Russia*; New York, Oxford: Oxford University Press.

Walder, A. G. (1996). *China's transitional economy*. Oxford; New York: Oxford University Press.

Waldron, P. (1998). *Between two revolutions: Stolypin and the politics of renewal in Russia*. London: UCL.

Walicki, A.. (1987). *Legal philosophies of Russian liberalism*. Oxford: Clarendon Press.

Walle, S. V., Thijs, N., & Bouckaert, G. (2005). A tale of two charters: political crisis, political realignment and administrative reform in Belgium. *Public Management Review*, 7(3), 367–90.

Wallich, C. I. (1994). *Russia and the challenge of fiscal federalism*. Washington, DC: World Bank.

Wallich, C. (1996). *Russia and the challenge of fiscal federalism*. Aldershot: Avebury.

Warner, A. (1998). The emerging Russian banking system. *Economics of Transition*, 6(2), 333–48.

Wcislo, F. W. (1990). *Reforming rural Russia: state, local society and national politics*, 1855–1914. Princeton, NJ: Princeton University Press.

Wedel, N. R. (1998). *Collision and collusion: the strange case of Western aid to Eastern Europe* 1989–1998. New York: St. Martin's Press.

Wegge, S. A. (1998). Chain migration and information networks: evidence from nineteenth-century Hesse-Cassel. *The Journal of Economic History*, 58(4), 957–86.

Wegren, S. K. (1998). *Agriculture and the state in Soviet and post-Soviet Russia*. Pittsburgh, PA: University of Pittsburgh Press.

Wegren, S. K. (2002). *The land question in Ukraine and Russia*. Seattle, WA: Henry M. Jackson School of International Studies, University of Washington.

Wegren, S. K. (1998). *Land reform in the former Soviet Union and Eastern Europe*. London; New York: Routledge.

Wegren, S. K. (2005). *Moral economy reconsidered [electronic resource]: Russia's search for agrarian capitalism*. New York: Palgrave Macmillan.

Wegren, S. K. (2002). Rural land privatization in Russia. *Economic Systems*, **26**(2), 175–78.

Wegren, S. K. (2002). Rural orientations to land privatization in Russia. *Journal of International Development*, **14**(7), 1033–43.

Wegren, S. K. (2004). Russian peasant farms and household plots in 2003: a research note. *Eurasian Geography and Economics*, **45**(3), 230–39.

Wegren, S. K. (2003). Why rural Russians participate in the land market: socio-economic factors. *Post Communist Economies*, **15**(4), 483–501.

Wegren, S. K., & Durgin, F. A. (1997). The political economy of private farming in Russia. *Comparative Economic Studies*, **39**(3–4), 1–24.

Wegren, S. K., O'Brien, D. J., & Patsiorkovski, V. V. (2003). Why Russia's rural poor are poor. *Post Soviet Affairs*, **19**(3), 264–87.

Wehrheim, P. (2000). The role of the agro-food sector in the macroeconomy: general equilibrium effects. In P. Wehrheim, K. Frohbert, E. Serova, & J. von Braun (Eds.), *Russia's agro-food sector: towards truly functioning markets* (pp. 155–79). Boston; Dordrecht; London: Kluwer Academic Publishers.

Wehrheim, P., Frohbert, K., Serova, E., & von Braun, J. (2000). *Russia's agro-food sector: towards truly functioning markets*. Boston; Dordrecht; London: Kluwer Academic Publishers.

Wei, S. J. (1998). Gradualism versus big-bang: speed and sustainability of reforms. In F. Sturzenegger & M. Tommasi (Eds.), *The political economy of reform* (pp. 269–84). Cambridge, MA: Harvard University Press.

Weimer, D. L. E. (1997). *The political economy of property rights: institutional change and credibility in the reform of centrally planned economies*. Cambridge; New York; Melbourne: Cambridge University Press.

Weisdorf, J. L. (2006). From domestic manufacture to Industrial Revolution: long-run growth and agricultural development. *Oxford Economic Papers*, **58**(2), 264–87.

Weissman, N. B. (1981). *Reform in tsarist Russia: the state bureaucracy and local government*, 1900–1914. New Brunswick, NJ: Rutgers University Press.

Weitzman, M. L. (1983). Some macroeconomic implications of alternative compensation systems. *Economic Journal*, **93**(372), 763–83.

Weitzmann, M. (1970). Soviet postwar economic growth and capital-labor substitution. *American Economic Review*, **60**(4), 676–92.

West, J. L., Petrov, I. U. A., Clowes, E. W., & Owen, T. C. (1998). *Merchant Moscow: images of Russia's vanished bourgeoisie*. Princeton, NJ: Princeton University Press.

Whatley, W., & Wright, G. (1994). Race, human capital, and labour markets in American history. In G. Grantham & M. MacKinnon (Eds.), *The economic history of market integration, wage flexibility and the employment relation* (pp. 270–91). London; New York: Routledge.

Wheatcroft, S. G. (1990). *Agriculture*. In R. W. Davies (Ed.), *From tsarism to the New Economic Policy: continuity and change in the economy of the USSR* (pp. 79–103). Ithaca, NY: Cornell University Press.

Wheatcroft, S. G. (1991). Crises and the condition of the peasantry in late Imperial Russia. In E. Kingston-Mann & T. Mixter (Eds.), *Peasant economy, culture, and politics of European Russia*, 1800–1921 (pp. 128–72). Princeton, NJ: Princeton University Press.

Wheatcroft, S. G. (1992). The 1891–92 famine in Russia: towards a more detailed analysis of its scale and demographic significance. In L. Edmondson & P. Waldron (Eds.), *Economy and society in Russia and the Soviet Union*, 1860–1930: *essays for Olga Crisp* (pp. 44–64). London: London Macmillan Press, in association with the School of Slavonic and East European Studies, University of London.

Wheatcroft, S. G. (1993). Famine and food consumption records in early Soviet history, 1917–25. In C. Geissler & D. J. Oddy (Eds.), *Pinter* (pp. 151–74). Leicester; New York: Leicester University Press; St. Martin's Press.

Wheatcroft, S. G., & Davies, R. W. (1985). *Materials for a balance of the Soviet national economy*, 1928–1930. Cambridge; New York: Cambridge University Press.

Wheatcroft, S. G., & Davies, R. W. (1994). *Agriculture*. In R. W. Davies, M. Harrison, & S. G. Wheatcroft (Eds.), *The economic transformation of the Soviet Union*, 1913–1945 (pp. 106–30). Cambridge; New York: Cambridge University Press.

Wheatcroft, S. G., & Davies, R. W. (1994). The crooked mirror of Soviet economic statistics. In R. W. Davies, M. Harrison, & S. G. Wheatcroft (Eds.), *The economic transformation of the Soviet Union*, 1913–1945 (pp. 24–37). Cambridge; New York: Cambridge University Press.

Wheatcroft, S. G., Davies, R. W., & Cooper, J. M. (1986). Soviet industrialization reconsidered: some preliminary conclusions about economic development between 1926 and 1941. *Economic History Review, Second Series*, 39(2), 264–94.

Whelan, H. W. (1982). *Alexander III & the State Council: bureaucracy & counter-reform in late Imperial Russia*. New Brunswick, NJ: Rutgers University Press.

Whisenhunt, W. B. (2001). *In search of legality: Mikhail M. Speranskii and the codification of Russian law*. Boulder, CO; New York: East European Monographs, distributed by Columbia University Press.

White, C. (1975). The impact of Russian railway construction on the market for grain in the 1860s and 1870s. In L. Symons & C. White (Eds.), *Russian transport: an historical and geographical survey* (pp. 1–45). London: G. Bell & Sons.

White, S., Pravda, A., & Gitelman, Z. Y. (1997). *Developments in Russian politics*. Durham, NC: Duke University Press.

Whitefield, S. (1993). *Industrial power and the Soviet state*. Oxford; New York: Clarendon Press; Oxford University Press.

Whitehouse, F. D., & Havelka, J. F. (1971). Comparison of farm output in the US, 1950–1971. In J. E. C. Congress of the United States (Ed.), *Soviet economic prospects for the seventies* (pp. 340–74). Washington, DC: U.S. Government Printing Service.

Wibbels, E. (2000). Federalism and the politics of macroeconomic policy and performance. *American Journal of Political Science*, 44(4), 687–702.

Willett, J. W. (1962). The recent record in agricultural production. *Dimensions of Soviet economic power*. Washington, DC: Joint Economic Committee, U.S. Congress.

Williams, C. (1996). Economic reform and political change in Russia, 1991–1996. In C. Williams, V. Chuprov, & V. Staroverov (Eds.), *Russian society in transition* (pp. 37–54). Aldershot: Dartmouth Publishing Company.

Williams, S. F. (2006). Liberal Reform in an Illiberal Regime: The Creation of Private Property in Russia, 1906–1915. Stanford: Hoover Institution Press.

Williamson, J. (1991). *The economic opening of Eastern Europe*. Washington, DC: Institute for International Economics.

Williamson, J. (1994). *The political economy of economic reform*. Washington, DC: Institute for International Economics.

Williamson, J., & Sanchez, O. (2005). The political economy of policy reform. *Governance*, 18(2), 323–24.

Williamson, J. G. (1965). Regional inequality and the process of national development: a description of the pattern. *Economic Development and Cultural Change*, 13, 3–45.

Williamson, O. E. (1985). *The economic institutions of capitalism: firms, markets, relational contracting*. New York: The Free Press.

Williamson, O. E. (1989). *Transaction cost economics*. In R. Schmalensee & R. Willig (Eds.), *Handbook of industrial organization* (pp. 135–82). Amsterdam: North Holland.

Winiecki, J. (1986). Are Soviet-type economies entering an era of long-term decline? *Soviet Studies*, 38(3), 325–48.

Winiecki, J. (1993). "Heterodox" *stabilization in Eastern Europe*. London: EBRD.

Winiecki, J., Kondratowicz, A., & Adam Smith Research Centre. (1993). *The macroeconomics of transition: developments in East Central Europe*. London; New York: Routledge.

Wirtschafter, E. (2008). *Russia's age of serfdom 1649–1861*. Malden, MA: Blackwell.

Witt, U. (1993). *Evolutionary economics*. Aldershot: Elgar.

Witte, S. I. (2003). Rasskazy i stenograficheskoi zapisi. *Vospominaniia*. St. Petersburg: Institut Istorii RAN. Vol 1, books 1–2.

Wolf, E. R. (1969). *Peasant wars of the twentieth century*. New York: Harper & Row.

Wollin, A. (1999). Punctuated-equilibrium: reconciling theory of revolutionary and incremental change. *Systems Research and Behavioral Science*, 16(4), 359–68.

Wong, L.-F., & Ruttan, V. W. (1988). Sources of differences in agricultural productivity growth among socialist countries. In A. Dogramaci & R. Färe (Eds.), *Applications of modern production theory: efficiency and productivity* (pp. 103–30). Boston; Dordrecht; Lancaster: Kluwer Academic Publishers.

Woo, W. T. (1997). Improving the performance of enterprises in transition economies. In S. Parker, W. T. Woo, & J. D. Sachs (Eds.), *Economies in transition: comparing Asia and Europe* (pp. 299–323). Cambridge, MA: The MIT Press.

World Bank (1986). Agricultural policies in industrial countries. *World development report 1986* (pp. 110–32). Oxford: Oxford University Press.

World Bank (1991). *Czechoslovakia: transition to a market economy*. Washington, DC: The World Bank.

World Bank (1996). *Fiscal management in Russia*. Washington, DC: The World Bank.

World Bank (1992). *Food and agricultural policy reforms in the former USSR: an agenda for transition*. Washington, DC: The World Bank, Studies of Economies in Transformation.

World Bank (1996). *From plan to market*. Oxford: Oxford University Press.

World Bank (1993). *Statistical handbook 1993: states of the former USSR*. Washington, DC: The World Bank.

World Bank (2000). *World development indicators*. Washington, DC: The World Bank.

Worobec, C. (1991). *Peasant Russia: family and community in the post-emancipation period*. Princeton, NJ: Princeton University Press.

Wortman, R. (1969). Judicial personnel and the court reform of 1864. *Canadian Slavic Studies*, 3(2), 224–34.

Wortman, R. (1976). *The development of a Russian legal consciousness*. Chicago; London: University of Chicago Press.

Wortman, R. (1995). *Scenarios of power: myth and ceremony in Russian monarchy*. Princeton, NJ: Princeton University Press.

Wortman, R., & Harriman, I. (2000). *Scenarios of power: myth and ceremony in Russian monarchy*. Princeton, NJ: Princeton University Press.

Wright, G. (1999). Can a nation learn? American technology as a network phenomenon. In N. Lamoreaux, D. Raff, & P. Temin (Eds.), *Learning by doing in markets, firms, and countries* (pp. 295–326). Chicago; London: University of Chicago Press, for NBER.

Wright, G. (1999). The civil rights revolution as economic history. *Journal of Economic History*, 59(2), 267–89.

Wright, G. (1992). The economics and politics of slavery and freedom in the U.S. South. In F. McGlynn & S. Drescher (Eds.), *The meaning of freedom: economics, politics, and culture after slavery* (pp. 85–111). Pittsburgh; London: University of Pittsburgh Press.

Wright, G. (1986). *Old South, New South: revolutions in the southern economy since the Civil War*. New York: Basic Books.

Wright, G. (1997). Towards a more historical approach to technological change. *Economic Journal*, 107(444), 1560–66.

Wright, G., & Kunreuther, H. (1975). Cotton, corn and risk in the nineteenth century. *Journal of Economic History*, 35(3), 526–51.

Wunner, N. (1998). Trade liberalization and political support in transition economies. *Economics of Transition*, 6(2), 409–26.

Wyplosz, C. (2000). Ten years of transformation: macroeconomic lessons. *CEPR Discussion Papers: 2254 (2000)*: C.E.P.R.

Xu, L. C., & Alcazar, L. (1999). Institutions, politics, and contracts: the attempt to privatize the water and sanitation utility of Lima, Peru. *World Bank. Policy Research Working Paper Series*: World Bank.

Yanbykh, R. (2000). Credit markets in rural Russia. In P. Wehrheim, K. Frohbert, E. Serova, & J. von Braun (Eds.), *Russia's agro-food sector: towards truly functioning markets* (pp. 409–28). Boston; Dordrecht; London: Kluwer Academic Publishers.

Yanbykh, R. (2000). Driving forces in Russian agrarian policy in the 1990s. In L. A. Norsworthy (Ed.), *Russian views of the transition in the rural sector: structures,*

policy outcomes, and adaptive responses (pp. 42–56). Washington, DC: The World Bank.
Yaney, G. L. (1973). *The systematization of Russian government: social evolution in the domestic administration of Imperial Russia, 1711–1905*. Urbana; London: University of Illinois Press.
Yaney, G. L. (1978). *The Imperial Russian government and the Stolypin land reform*. Ann Arbor; London: University Microfilms.
Yaney, G. L. (1982). *The urge to mobilize: agrarian reform in Russia, 1861–1930*. Urbana: University of Illinois Press.
Yang, C. K. (1959). *A Chinese village in early communist transition*. Cambridge, MA: Technology Press. Massachusetts Institute of Technology, distributed by Harvard University Press.
Yang, D. T., & An, M. Y. (2002). Human capital, entrepreneurship, and farm household earnings. *Journal of Development Economics*, **68**(1), 65–88.
Yee, J., Hauver, J. H., & Ball, V. E. (1993). Fixed factor models of agricultural productivity growth. *Applied Economics*, **25**, 1187–96.
Yeltsin, B. (2000). *Midnight Diaries*. London: Weidenfield & Nicolson.
Yergin, D. (1991). *The prize: the epic quest for oil, money, and power*. New York: Simon and Schuster.
Yergin, D., & Stanislaw, J. (1998). *The commanding heights: the battle between government and the marketplace that is remaking the modern world*. New York: Simon & Schuster.
Young, J., & Wilson, G. (2007). The view from below: local government and Putin's reforms. *Europe-Asia Studies*, **59**, 1071–88.
Zagashvili, V. (1998). Nalogovaia reforma i nalogovaia politika v Rossii. *Novoe pokolenie*, 3(2), 1–16.
Zaika, S. B. (2002). Agrarnyi Lobbizm i konkurentosposobost' sel'skogo khoziaistva, *Vlast', biznes i krest'ianstvo: mekhanizmy effektivnogo vzaimodeistviia: Nikonovskie chteniia–2002* (pp. 407–08). Moscow: Rossiiskaia Akademiia Selskokhoziastvennykh Nauk, Vserossiiskii Institut agrarnykh problem i informatiki, Fond Podderzhki Agrarnoi Reformy i Sel'skoto Razvitiia.
Zaionchkovskii, P. A. (1958). *Provedenie v zhizn' krest'ianskoi reformy 1861 g.* Moscow: Sotsial'no-ekonomicheskoi literaturoi.
Zaionchkovskii, P. A. (1954). *Otmena krepostnogo prava v Rossii*. Moscow: Politicheskaia literature.
Zaionchkovskii, P. A., & Wobst, S. (1978). *The abolition of serfdom in Russia*. Gulf Breeze, FL: Academic International Press.
Zaitseva, L. I. (1993). *Agrarnaia reforma P.A. Stolypina: v dokumentakh i publikatsiiakh kontsa XIX-nachala XX veka*. Moscow: Institut ekonomiki RAN.
Zak, A. N. (1911). *Krest'ianskii pozemel'nyi bank*, 1883–1910 gg. St. Petersburg.
Zakharova, L. G. (1973). Perepiska Ministra Vnutrennykh Del P. A. Valueva i gosudarstvennogo sekretaria S. N. Urusova v 1866 g. *Istoriia SSSR*(2).
Zakharova, L. G. (1984). *Samoderzhavie i otmena krepostnogo prava v Rossii, 1856–1861*. Moscow: Izd-vo Moskovskogo universiteta.
Zakharova, L. (1994). Autocracy and the reforms of 1861–1874 in Russia. In B. Eklof, J. Bushnell, & L. Zakharova (Eds.), *Russia's great reforms*, 1855–1881 (pp. 19–39). Bloomington: Indiana University Press.

Zakharova, L. G., Eklof, B., & Bushnell, J. (1992). *Velikie reformy v Rossii: 1856–1874*. Moscow: Izd-vo Moskovskogo universiteta.

Zakharova, L. G., Topchii, A. T., & Gorlanova, L. R. (1993). *Otmena krepostnogo prava v Rossii: ukazatel' literatury, 1856–1989 gg*. Tomsk: Izd-vo Tomskogo universiteta.

Zaslavskaia, T. I. (1966). *Raspredelenie po trudu v kolkhozakh*. Moscow: Ekonomika.

Zelenin, I. E. (2000). Agrarnaia politika i sel'skoe khoziastvo v SSSR posle 'Revoliutsii sverkhu' (1930-e gody). In V. A. Vinogradov (Ed.), *Ekonomicheskaia istoriia Rossii XIX–XX vv; sovremennyi vzgliad* (pp. 105–21). Moscow: ROSSPEN.

Zenkovskii, A. V. (1986). *Stolypin: Russia's last great reformer*. Princeton, NJ: Kingston Press.

Zhang, B. (1997). Total factor productivity of grain production in the former Soviet Union. *Journal of Comparative Economics*, **24**, 202–09.

Zhdanova, M. (1984). *RSFSR v tsifrakh v 1983 godu: kratkii statisticheskii sbornik*. Moscow: "Finansy i statistika."

Zhdanova, M. (1988). *Sel'skoe khoziaistvo SSSR: statisticheskii sbornik*. Moscow: Finansy i statistika.

Zhiromskaia, V. B. (2000). Naselenie Rossii v XX veke, 1900–1939 gg. In I. A. Poliakov (Ed.), *Naselenie Rossii v XX veke*. Moscow: Rossiiskaia politicheskaia entsiklopedia (ROSSPEN).

Zohoori, N., Mroz, B., Popkin, B., Glinskaya, E., Lokshin, M., Mancini, D., Kozyreva, P., Kosolapov, M., & Swafford, M. (1998). Monitoring the economic transition in the Russian Federation and its implications for the demographic crisis–the Russian longitudinal monitoring survey. *World Development*, **26**(11), 1977–93.

Zyrianov, P. N. (2002). Pozemel'nye otnosheniia v russkoi krest'ianskoi obschine vo vtoroi polovine XIX-nachale XX veka. In D. F. Aiatsko (Ed.), *Sobstvennost' na zemliu v Rossii: istoriia i sovremennost'* (pp. 153–95). Moscow: ROSSPEN.

Index